LUTHER'S WORKS

LUTHER'S WORKS

VOLUME 27

**LECTURES ON GALATIANS
1535
Chapters 5—6**

**LECTURES ON GALATIANS
1519
Chapters 1—6**

JAROSLAV PELIKAN
Editor

WALTER A. HANSEN
Associate Editor

CONCORDIA PUBLISHING HOUSE · SAINT LOUIS

Copyright 1964 by
CONCORDIA PUBLISHING HOUSE
Saint Louis, Missouri

Library of Congress Catalog Card No. 55-9898

MANUFACTURED IN THE UNITED STATES OF AMERICA

Contents

General Introduction	xii
Introduction to Volume 27	ix

Lectures on Galatians – 1535

CHAPTER FIVE	3
CHAPTER SIX	106
LUTHER'S PREFACE OF 1535	145

Lectures on Galatians – 1519

DEDICATION	153
THE SUBJECT	161
CHAPTER ONE	163
CHAPTER TWO	199
CHAPTER THREE	243
CHAPTER FOUR	283
CHAPTER FIVE	325
CHAPTER SIX	381
Indexes	411

General Introduction

THE first editions of Luther's collected works appeared in the sixteenth century, and so did the first efforts to make him "speak English." In America serious attempts in these directions were made for the first time in the nineteenth century. The Saint Louis edition of Luther was the first endeavor on American soil to publish a collected edition of his works, and the Henkel Press in Newmarket, Virginia, was the first to publish some of Luther's writings in an English translation. During the first decade of the twentieth century, J. N. Lenker produced translations of Luther's sermons and commentaries in thirteen volumes. A few years later the first of the six volumes in the Philadelphia (or Holman) edition of the *Works of Martin Luther* appeared. Miscellaneous other works were published at one time or another. But a growing recognition of the need for more of Luther's works in English has resulted in this American edition of Luther's works.

The edition is intended primarily for the reader whose knowledge of late medieval Latin and sixteenth-century German is too small to permit him to work with Luther in the original languages. Those who can, will continue to read Luther in his original words as these have been assembled in the monumental Weimar edition (*D. Martin Luthers Werke. Kritische Gesamtausgabe;* Weimar, 1883 ff.). Its texts and helps have formed a basis for this edition, though in certain places we have felt constrained to depart from its readings and findings. We have tried throughout to translate Luther as he thought translating should be done. That is, we have striven for faithfulness on the basis of the best lexicographical materials available. But where literal accuracy and clarity have conflicted, it is clarity that we have preferred, so that sometimes paraphrase seemed more faithful than literal fidelity. We have proceeded in a similar way in the matter of Bible versions, translating Luther's translations. Where this could be done by the use of an existing English version — King James, Douay, or Revised Standard — we have done so. Where it could not, we have supplied our own. To indicate this in each specific instance would have been pedantic; to adopt a uniform procedure would have been artificial — especially in view of Luther's own inconsistency in this regard. In each volume the translator will be responsible primarily for matters of text and language, while the responsibility of the editor will extend principally to the historical and theological matters reflected in the introductions and notes.

Although the edition as planned will include fifty-five volumes, Luther's writings are not being translated in their entirety. Nor should they be. As he was the first to insist, much of what he wrote and said was not that important. Thus the edition is a selection of works that have proved their importance for the faith, life, and history of the Christian Church. The first thirty volumes contain Luther's expositions of various Biblical books, while the remaining volumes include what are usually called his "Reformation writings" and other occasional pieces. The final volume of the set will be an index volume; in addition to an index of quotations, proper names, and topics, and a list of corrections and changes, it will contain a glossary of many of the technical terms that recur in Luther's works and that cannot be defined each time they appear. Obviously Luther cannot be forced into any neat set of rubrics. He can provide his reader with bits of autobiography or with political observations as he expounds a psalm, and he can speak tenderly about the meaning of the faith in the midst of polemics against his opponents. It is the hope of publishers, editors, and translators that through this edition the message of Luther's faith will speak more clearly to the modern church.

J. P.
H. L.

Introduction to Volume 27

THE term "Luther's *Galatians*" could conceivably be taken to refer to any one of five (or even six) commentaries on the Epistle to the Galatians by Martin Luther. Most often it is the *Galatians* published in 1535 that is referred to by this title. The first four chapters of that exposition have been published as Volume 26 of *Luther's Works*, together with our historical introduction to the entire commentary. Here in Volume 27 we are presenting the fifth and sixth chapters of the *Galatians* of 1535 (Weimar, XL-2, 1—184; St. Louis, IX, 600—771), as well as Luther's preface to the printed version of his lectures (Weimar, XL-1, 33—37; St. Louis, IX, 8—15), written in 1538. Underlying this commentary are notes from Luther's actual lectures in 1531; these notes, which have been preserved and are printed in the Weimar edition, could also be called "Luther's *Galatians*," as could perhaps the revised edition of the printed commentary, published in 1538, which has served as the basis for all previous translations into English.

But in addition to these two (or three) expositions, there are three interrelated commentaries on Galatians that date back to the beginnings of Luther's Reformation. The earliest of these three versions is a student notebook on Luther's lectures of 1516—17, first published in this century by Hans von Schubert and then revised for the Weimar edition by Karl Meissinger (Weimar, LVII). Using those lectures as a basis, but significantly revising and expanding some of his earlier judgments, Luther prepared a printed version of his exposition (Weimar, II, 445—618; St. Louis, VIII, 1352—1661) and published it in 1519. Four years later, in 1523, he published a revised and abbreviated version of the commentary, omitting most of the proper names and many of the *obiter dicta* that had appeared in the edition of 1519; the Weimar editors have documented these deviations in footnotes to the text of the 1519 *Galatians*.

Thus Luther's several commentaries on the Epistle to the Galatians provide unmatched source material for research into his intellectual and religious development for two decades or more; they are also extremely useful for a study of the methods of his editors. For the purposes of our edition, however, the versions of 1519 and 1535 seemed the most appropriate. As usual, Luther's letters provide the most extensive and reliable information about the progress of his exegetical works. On October 26, 1516, he wrote to Johann Lang, complaining of the burden of his duties and adding: "You write that yesterday you began [lecturing on] Book II of the *Sentences* [of Peter Lombard]. But tomorrow I shall begin the Epistle to the Galatians, although I am afraid that the presence of the plague may not permit it to continue once I have begun it." From the notebook of Luther's student we learn that his last lecture on Galatians was delivered on March 13, 1517.

Two years later Luther was engaged in preparing the lectures for publication. Still complaining about too much work, he wrote to Spalatin on Invocavit Sunday (March 13), 1519: "I am now giving birth to Paul's Epistle to the Galatians." On September 3, 1519, he was able to inform Lang: "I am told that the Epistle to the Galatians has been completed today." He dispatched a copy of the book to Spalatin on St. Maurice's Day (September 22), 1519; and on October 3 he wrote to Johann Staupitz: "Reverend Father, I am sending you two copies of my foolish Galatians. I am not as pleased with it as I was at first, and I see that it could have been expounded more completely and clearly. But who can do everything at once? In fact, who can manage to do very much continually? Nevertheless, I am confident that Paul is made clearer here than he has been before in [the commentaries of] others, even though it is not yet satisfactory to my taste."

Our edition of the *Galatians* of 1519 has attempted to identify the hundreds of citations from the Bible, the classics, the church fathers, and the medieval doctors with which the commentary is filled; as could be expected, quotations from Jerome and Augustine are the most frequent, but the extent of Luther's dependence on Erasmus is also evident. Even more interesting is Luther's effort, with the help of Erasmus and of Melanchthon, to go beyond the Vulgate to an understanding of the Greek text. In later years Luther reflected on the differences between his first and second sets of lectures on Galatians and tended to disparage his earlier work. Our edition will make it possible for the reader restricted to English to study those differences for himself and thus to examine at first hand the engagement with Sacred Scripture out of which Luther's reformatory work and thought emerged. J. P.

LECTURES ON GALATIANS
1535

Chapters 5–6

Translated by
JAROSLAV PELIKAN

CHAPTER FIVE

As he approaches the end of the epistle, Paul argues vigorously and passionately in defense of the doctrine of faith and of Christian liberty against the false apostles, who are its enemies and destroyers. He aims and hurls veritable thunderbolts of words at them to lay them low. At the same time he urges the Galatians to avoid their wicked doctrine as though it were some sort of plague. In the course of his urging he threatens, promises, and tries every device to keep them in the freedom achieved for them by Christ. Therefore he says:

1. *For freedom Christ has set us free; stand fast therefore.*

That is: "Be firm!" Thus Peter says (1 Peter 5:8-9): "Be sober, be watchful. Your adversary the devil prowls around like a roaring lion, seeking someone to devour. Resist him, firm in your faith." "Do not be smug," he says, "but be firm. Do not lie down or sleep, but stand." It is as though he were saying: "Vigilance and steadiness are necessary if you are to keep the freedom for which Christ has set us free. Those who are smug and sleepy are not able to keep it." For Satan violently hates the light of the Gospel, that is, the teaching about grace, freedom, comfort, and life. Therefore as soon as he sees it arise, he immediately strives to obliterate it with all his winds and storms. For this reason Paul urges godly persons not to be drowsy and smug in their behavior but to stand bravely in the battle against Satan, lest he take away the freedom achieved for them by Christ.

Every word is emphatic. "Stand fast," he says, "in freedom." In what freedom? Not in the freedom for which the Roman emperor has set us free but in the freedom for which Christ has set us free. The Roman emperor gave — indeed, was forced to give — the Roman pontiff a free city and other lands, as well as certain immunities, privileges, and concessions.[1] This, too, is freedom; but it is a political

[1] The Donation of Constantine, which purported to be a deed of gift from Constantine to the pope, had been exposed as a forgery by Lorenzo Valla in 1440.

freedom, according to which the Roman pontiff with all his clergy is free of all public burdens. In addition, there is the freedom of the flesh, which is chiefly prevalent in the world. Those who have this obey neither God nor the laws but do what they please. This is the freedom which the rabble pursues today; so do the fanatical spirits, who want to be free in their opinions and actions, in order that they may teach and do with impunity what they imagine to be right. This is a demonic freedom, by which the devil sets the wicked free to sin against God and men. We are not dealing with this here although it is the most widespread and is the only goal and objective of the entire world. Nor are we dealing with political freedom. No, we are dealing with another kind, which the devil hates and attacks most bitterly.

This is the freedom with which Christ has set us free, not from some human slavery or tyrannical authority but from the eternal wrath of God. Where? In the conscience. This is where our freedom comes to a halt; it goes no further. For Christ has set us free, not for a political freedom or a freedom of the flesh but for a theological or spiritual freedom, that is, to make our conscience free and joyful, unafraid of the wrath to come (Matt. 3:7). This is the most genuine freedom; it is immeasurable. When the other kinds of freedom — political freedom and the freedom of the flesh — are compared with the greatness and the glory of this kind of freedom, they hardly amount to one little drop. For who can express what a great gift it is for someone to be able to declare for certain that God neither is nor ever will be wrathful but will forever be a gracious and merciful Father for the sake of Christ? It is surely a great and incomprehensible freedom to have this Supreme Majesty kindly disposed toward us, protecting and helping us, and finally even setting us free physically in such a way that our body, which is sown in perishability, in dishonor, and in weakness, is raised in imperishability, in honor, and in power (1 Cor. 15:42-43). Therefore the freedom by which we are free of the wrath of God forever is greater than heaven and earth and all creation.

From this there follows the other freedom, by which we are made safe and free through Christ from the Law, from sin, death, the power of the devil, hell, etc. For just as the wrath of God cannot terrify us — since Christ has set us free from it — so the Law, sin, etc., cannot accuse and condemn us. Even though the Law denounces us and sin terrifies us, they still cannot plunge us into despair. For faith, which is the victor over the world (1 John 5:4), quickly declares: "Those things have nothing to do with me, for Christ has set me free from them." So it is that death, which is the most powerful and horrible thing in the world, lies conquered in our conscience through this freedom of the Spirit. Therefore the greatness of Christian freedom should be carefully measured and pondered. The words "freedom from the wrath of God, from the Law, sin, death, etc.," are easy to say; but to feel the greatness of this freedom and to apply its results to oneself in a struggle, in the agony of conscience, and in practice — this is more difficult than anyone can say.

Therefore one's spirit must be trained, so that when it becomes conscious of the accusation of the Law, the terrors of sin, the horror of death, and the wrath of God, it will banish these sorrowful scenes from its sight and will replace them with the freedom of Christ, the forgiveness of sins, righteousness, life, and the eternal mercy of God. Although the consciousness of these opponents may be powerful, one must be sure that it will not last long. As the prophet says (Is. 54:8), "In overflowing wrath for a moment I hid My face from you, but with everlasting love I will have compassion on you." But this is extremely difficult to bring about. Therefore the freedom that Christ has achieved for us is easier to talk about than it is to believe. If it could be grasped in its certainty by a firm faith, no fury or terror of the world, the Law, sin, death, the devil, etc., could be too great for it to swallow them up as quickly as the ocean swallows a spark. Once and for all this freedom of Christ certainly swallows up and abolishes a whole heap of evils — the Law, sin, death, the wrath of God, finally the serpent himself with his head (Gen. 3:15); and in their place it establishes righteousness, peace, life, etc. But blessed is the man who understands and believes this.

Therefore let us learn to place a high value on this freedom of ours; not the emperor, not an angel from heaven, but Christ, the Son of God, through whom all things were created in heaven and earth, obtained it for us by His death, to set us free, not from some physical and temporary slavery but from the spiritual and eternal slavery of those most cruel and invincible tyrants, the Law, sin, death, the devil, etc., and to reconcile us to God the Father. Now that these enemies have been defeated and now that we have been reconciled to God through the death of His Son, it is certain that we are righteous in the sight of God and that all our actions are pleasing to Him; and if there is any sin left in us, this is not imputed to us but is forgiven for the sake of Christ. Paul is speaking very precisely when he says that we should stand in the freedom for which Christ has set us free. Therefore this freedom is granted to us, not on account of the Law or our righteousness but freely, on account of Christ. Paul testifies to this and demonstrates it at length throughout this epistle; and Christ says in John 8:36: "If the Son makes you free, you will be free indeed." He alone is thrust into the middle between us and the evils that oppress us. He conquers and abolishes them, so that they cannot harm us any longer. In fact, in place of sin and death He grants us righteousness and eternal life, and He changes slavery and the terrors of the Law into the freedom of conscience and the comfort of the Gospel, which says (Matt. 9:2): "Take heart, My son; your sins are forgiven." Therefore he who believes in Christ has this freedom.

Reason does not see how great a matter this is; but when it is seen in the Spirit, it is enormous and infinite. No one can realize with language or thought what a great gift it is to have — instead of the Law, sin, death, and a wrathful God — the forgiveness of sins, righteousness, eternal life, and a God who is permanently gracious and kind. The papists and all self-righteous people boast that they also have the forgiveness of sins, righteousness, etc.; they also lay claim to freedom. But all these things are worthless and uncertain. In temptation they vanish instantly, because they depend on human works and satisfactions, not on the Word of God and on Christ. Therefore it is impossible for any self-righteous people to know what freedom from sin, etc., really is. By contrast, our freedom has as its foundation Christ, who is the eternal High Priest, who is at the right hand of God and intercedes for us. Therefore the freedom, forgiveness of sins, righteousness, and life that we have through Him are sure, firm, and eternal, provided that we believe this. If we cling firmly to Christ by faith and stand firm in the freedom with which He has made us free, we shall have those inestimable gifts. But if we become smug and drowsy, we shall lose them. It is not in vain that Paul commands us to be vigilant and to stand, because he knows that the devil is busily engaged in trying to rob us of this freedom that cost Christ so much, and to tie us up again in the yoke of slavery through his agents. Thus there follows:

And do not submit again to a yoke of slavery.

Paul has been speaking very seriously about grace and Christian freedom, and has urged the Galatians in many words to continue in these. He commands them to stand, because it is very easy to lose all this either by carelessness and smugness or by a relapse from grace and faith into the Law and works. But because to reason this does not seem to be dangerous, since reason vastly prefers the righteousness of the Law to the righteousness of faith, therefore he denounces the Law of God with great indignation; contemptuously and scornfully he calls it a "yoke," in fact, a "yoke of slavery." That is how Peter spoke in Acts 15:10: "Why do you make trial of God by imposing a yoke?" In this way Paul turns the tables completely. For the false apostles minimized the importance of the promise and magnified the Law and its works in the following way: "If you want to be set free from sin and death, and to obtain righteousness and life, keep the Law; be circumcised; observe days, months, seasons, and years; perform sacrifices. Then this obedience to the Law will justify and save you." Paul says the exact opposite. "Those who teach the Law in this way," he says, "do not set consciences free; they ensnare them. They ensnare them in a yoke, indeed in a yoke of slavery."

Therefore Paul speaks with complete contempt and in an exceedingly reproachful manner about the Law when he calls it a snare of the harshest slavery and of a servile yoke. He does not do this without reason. The wicked notion that the Law justifies clings to the reason very stubbornly, and the whole human race is finally so entangled and conquered by it that it can be rescued only with the utmost difficulty. Here Paul seems to be comparing those who seek righteousness through the Law to oxen that have been subjected to a yoke. Just as oxen that bear the yoke with great effort get nothing out of it but their food and are slaughtered when they are no longer fit to bear the yoke, so those who seek righteousness in the Law are captive and are oppressed with a yoke of slavery, that is, with the Law; and when finally, after great effort and sorrow, they have worn themselves out with the works of the Law, all the reward they get is that they are miserable slaves forever. Slaves of what? Of sin, death, the wrath of God, the devil, the flesh, the world, and all creatures. Therefore no slavery is greater or severer than the slavery of the Law. Hence it is not without reason that Paul calls it "a yoke of slavery"; for, as we have often said earlier, the Law only demonstrates and increases sin, accuses, terrifies, condemns, works wrath, and finally brings consciences to the point of despair — which is the most wretched and the harshest slavery (Romans 3, 4, 7).

This is why Paul uses such passionate words. He would dearly love to stir and persuade them not to let themselves be influenced by the false apostles and not to let these men ensnare them once more in the yoke of slavery. It is as though he were saying: "The issue here is no trifle or mere nothing; it is an issue between either endless, eternal freedom or slavery." For just as the freedom from the wrath of God and from every evil is not political freedom or a freedom of the flesh but an eternal freedom, so the slavery of sin, death, and the devil, which oppresses those who seek to be justified and saved through the Law, is not a physical slavery, which lasts for a while, but a perpetual slavery. For self-righteous people of this kind, who take everything very seriously — and they are the ones whom Paul is discussing — are never serene and peaceful. In this life they are always in doubt about the will of God and are afraid of death and of the wrath and judgment of God; and after this life they will suffer eternal destruction as punishment for their unbelief.

Therefore the workers of the Law are very rightly called "martyrs of the devil," if I may use the common expression. They earn hell by greater toil and trouble than that by which the martyrs of Christ earn heaven.[2] They are worn down by a double contrition: while they are in this life, performing many great works, they torture themselves miserably without reason; and when they die, they receive eternal damnation and punishment as their reward. Thus they are most miserable martyrs both in the present life and in the future life, and their slavery is eternal. It is not so with believers, who have troubles only in the present life. Therefore we must stand fast in the freedom Christ has acquired for us by His death, and we must be diligently on our guard not to be ensnared once more in a yoke of slavery. This is what is happening today to the fanatical spirits: falling away from faith and freedom, they have a self-imposed temporal slavery in this life, and in the life to come they will be oppressed by an eternal slavery. The papists do not listen to the Gospel; they persecute it. But even though these men use the freedom of the Gospel — for many of them are Epicureans — they are really slaves of the devil,

---

[2] On the "martyrs of the devil" cf. also *Luther's Works*, 13, p. 123.

who holds them captive at his pleasure. Therefore the eternal slavery of hell awaits them. So much for Paul's vigorous and serious exhortation, which is surpassed by the one that follows.

2. *Now I, Paul, say to you that if you receive circumcision, Christ will be of no advantage to you.*

Paul is profoundly moved, and in great zeal and fervor of the Spirit he speaks sheer thunderbolts against the Law and against circumcision. In his anger over the great wickedness of it all, the Holy Spirit wrests such passionate words out of him, as though he were saying: "Behold, I, Paul, etc. I, I say, who know that I have the Gospel, not from men but through the revelation of Jesus Christ; I, who know for certain that I have a divine commandment and authority to teach and define doctrine — I announce to you a judgment that is indeed new but is sure and true, namely, that if you receive circumcision, Christ will simply be of no advantage to you." This is a very harsh judgment when Paul says that receiving circumcision is the same as making Christ null and void — not indeed simply in Himself but for the Galatians, who were deceived by the tricks of the false apostles into believing that in addition to faith in Christ circumcision was necessary for believers, and that without it they could not obtain salvation.

This teaching is the touchstone by which we can judge most surely and freely about all doctrines, works, forms of worship, and ceremonies of all men. Whoever (whether he be a papist, a Jew, a Turk, or a sectarian) teaches that anything beyond the Gospel of Christ is necessary to attain salvation; whoever establishes any work or form of worship; whoever observes any rule, tradition, or ceremony with the opinion that thereby he will obtain the forgiveness of sins, righteousness, and eternal life — will hear the judgment of the Holy Spirit pronounced against him here by the apostle: that Christ is of no advantage to him at all. And since Paul had the courage to pronounce this judgment against the Law and against circumcision, which had been established by God — something that is truly remarkable — what would he not have had the courage to say against the chaff of human traditions?

Therefore this passage is a terrible thunderbolt against the entire kingdom of the pope. To speak only of the best among them, all the priests, monks, and hermits did not trust in Christ, whom they most slanderously and blasphemously regarded as an angry judge, accuser, and condemner; they trusted in their own works, righteousnesses, vows, and merits. Hence they hear their judgment in this passage, namely, that Christ is of no use to them. For if they are able to abolish sins and to merit the forgiveness of sins and eternal life by their own righteousness and ascetic life, what good does it do them that Christ was born, suffered, shed His blood, was raised, conquered sin, death, and the devil, when they themselves can overcome these monsters by their own powers? It is indescribable what great wickedness it is to make Christ useless. Therefore Paul pronounces these words out of great indignation of mind and the stirring of the Spirit: "If you receive circumcision, Christ will be of no advantage to you; that is, no benefit at all will come to you out of all His blessings, but He has done all this in vain so far as you are concerned."

This makes it abundantly clear that there is nothing more wicked under the sun than doctrines of human traditions and works; for with one blow they abolish and overthrow the truth of the Gospel, faith, the true worship of God, and Christ Himself, in whom the Father has established all things. Col. 2:3 states: "In Christ are hid all the treasures of wisdom and knowledge"; and in the ninth verse we read: "In Him the whole fullness of Deity dwells bodily." Therefore anyone who is a founder or a worshiper of the doctrine of works suppresses the Gospel, nullifies the death and victory of Christ, obscures His sacraments and abolishes their proper use, and is a denier, an enemy, and a blasphemer of God and of all His promises and blessings. Anyone who is not frightened away from human traditions and from trust in his own righteousness and works and who is not aroused to yearn for freedom in Christ by the fact that Paul calls the Law of God "a yoke of slavery" is harder than a rock or a bar of iron.

Therefore the statement is very clear: If anyone receives circumcision, that is, trusts in his circumcision, Christ will be of no advantage to him; that is, He will have been born and have suffered to no avail. For, as I said earlier, Paul is not discussing the actual deed in and of itself, which has nothing wrong in it if there is no trust in it or presumption of righteousness; but he is discussing how the deed is used, namely, the trust and the righteousness that are attached to the deed. We must understand Paul in accordance with the subject matter under discussion or the argument in process, which is that men are not justified by the Law, by works, or by circumcision. He is not saying that works in and of themselves are nothing, but that trust in works and righteousness on the basis of works causes Christ to be of no advantage. Therefore anyone who receives circumcision with the idea that it is necessary for justification will receive no benefit from Christ.

Let us remember this well in our personal temptations, when the devil accuses and terrifies our conscience to bring it to the point of despair. He is the father of lies (John 8:44) and the enemy of Christian freedom. At every moment, therefore, he troubles us with false terrors, so that when this freedom has been lost, the conscience is in continual fear and feels guilt and anxiety. When that "great dragon, the ancient serpent, the devil, the deceiver of the whole world, who accuses our brethren day and night before God" (Rev. 12:9-10) — when, I say, he comes to you and accuses you not only of failing to do anything good but of transgressing against the Law of God, then you must say: "You are troubling me with the memory of past sins; in addition, you are telling me that I have not done anything good. This does not concern me. For if I either trusted in my performance of good works or lost my trust because I failed to perform them, in either case Christ would be of no avail to me. Therefore whether you base your objections to me on my sins or on my good works, I do not care; for I put both of them out of sight and depend only on the freedom for which Christ has set me free. Therefore I shall not render Him useless to me, which is what would happen if I either presumed that I shall attain grace and eternal life because of my good works or despaired of my salvation on account of my sins."

Let us learn, therefore, to distinguish Christ as completely as possible from all works, whether good or evil; from all laws, whether divine or human; and from all distressed consciences. For Christ does not pertain to any of these. He does indeed pertain to sad consciences, not to trouble them even more but to raise them up again and to comfort them when they have been troubled. Therefore if Christ appears in the guise of a wrathful judge or lawgiver who demands an accounting of how we have spent our lives, we should know for certain that this is not really Christ but the devil. For Scripture portrays Christ as our Propitiator, Mediator, and Comforter. This is what He always is and remains; He cannot be untrue to His very nature. Therefore when the devil assumes the guise of Christ and argues with us this way: "At the urging of My Word you were obliged to do this, and you failed to do so; and you were obliged to avoid that, and you failed to do so. Therefore you should know that I shall exact punishment from you," this should not bother us at all; but we should immediately think: "Christ does not speak this way to despairing consciences. He does not add affliction to those who are afflicted. 'A bruised reed He will not break, and a dimly burning wick He will not quench' (Is. 42:3). To those who are rough He speaks roughly, but those who are in terror He invites most sweetly: 'Come to Me, all who labor and are heavy laden' (Matt. 11:28); 'I came not to call the righteous, but sinners' (Matt. 9:13); 'Take heart, My son; your sins are forgiven' (Matt. 9:2); 'Be of good cheer, I have overcome the world' (John 16:33); 'The Son of man came to seek and to save the lost' (Luke 19:10)." Therefore we should be on our guard, lest the amazing skill and infinite wiles of Satan deceive us into mistaking the accuser and condemner for the Comforter and Savior, and thus losing the true Christ behind the mask of the false Christ, that is, of the devil, and making Him of no advantage to us. So much for personal temptations and for the proper way of dealing with them.

3. *I testify again to every man who receives circumcision that he is bound to keep the whole Law.*

The first disadvantage is great enough, when Paul says that Christ is of no advantage to those who receive circumcision. This next one is no smaller, when he says that those who receive circumcision are bound to keep the whole Law. He is so serious in speaking these words that he confirms them with an oath. "I testify," that is, I swear by all that is holy. These words can be explained in two ways, negatively and positively. Negatively they mean:

"I testify to every man who receives circumcision that he is a debtor to the observance of the whole Law; that is, even in the very act of circumcision he does not receive circumcision, and even in the fulfilling of the Law he does not fulfill it but transgresses it." This seems to me to be the simple and true meaning of Paul in this passage. Later on (6:13) he explains himself when he says: "Even those who receive circumcision do not themselves keep the Law," as he did earlier (3:10), when he said: "All who rely on works of the Law are under a curse." It is as though he were saying: "Even if you receive circumcision, this does not mean that you are righteous and free from the Law; but by this very act you have become more bound and enslaved by the Law. By the very act of trying to satisfy the Law and to be set free from it you have involved yourselves all the more completely in its yoke, so that it has all the more right to accuse and condemn you. That is a crab's way of making progress, like washing away dirt with dirt!"

What I am saying here on the basis of the words of Paul I learned from my own experience in the monastery about myself and about others. I saw many who tried with great effort and the best of intentions [3] to do everything possible to appease their conscience. They wore hair shirts; they fasted; they prayed; they tormented and wore out their bodies with various exercises so severely that if they had been made of iron, they would have been crushed. And yet the more they labored, the greater their terrors became. Especially when the hour of death was imminent, they became so fearful that I have seen many murderers facing execution die more confidently than these men who had lived such saintly lives.[4]

Thus it is certainly true that those who keep the Law do not keep it. The more men try to satisfy the Law, the more they transgress it. The more someone tries to bring peace to his conscience through his own righteousness, the more disquieted he makes it. When I was a monk, I made a great effort to live according to the requirements of the monastic rule. I made a practice of confessing and reciting all my sins, but always with prior contrition; I went to confession frequently, and I performed the assigned penances faithfully. Nevertheless, my conscience could never achieve certainty but was always in doubt and said: "You have not done this correctly. You were not contrite enough. You omitted this in your confession." Therefore the longer I tried to heal my uncertain, weak, and troubled conscience with human traditions, the more uncertain, weak, and troubled I continually made it. In this way, by observing human traditions, I transgressed them even more; and by following the righteousness of the monastic order, I was never able to reach it. For, as Paul says, it is impossible for the conscience to find peace through the works of the Law, much less through human traditions, without the promise and the Gospel about Christ.

Therefore those who wish to be justified and made alive by the Law fall further short of righteousness and life than do tax collectors,

[3] We have translated *optima conscientia* as "with the best of intentions."

[4] See Luther's similar comments, *Luther's Works*, 22, p. 360.

sinners, and harlots. These latter cannot rest on confidence in their own works, which are such that they cannot trust that they will obtain grace and the forgiveness of sins on their account. For if the righteousness and the works done according to the Law do not justify, much less do sins committed against the Law justify. Therefore such people are more fortunate than the self-righteous in this respect; for they lack trust in their own works, which, even if it does not completely destroy faith in Christ, nevertheless hinders it very greatly. On the other hand, the self-righteous, who refrain from sins outwardly and seem to live blameless and religious lives, cannot avoid a presumption of confidence and righteousness, which cannot coexist with faith in Christ. Therefore they are less fortunate than tax collectors and harlots, who do not offer their good works to a wrathful God in exchange for eternal life, as the self-righteous do, since they have none to offer, but beg that their sins be forgiven them for the sake of Christ.

Therefore anyone who keeps the Law with the idea that he wants to be justified through it is obligated to keep the whole Law; that is, he has not kept even one letter of the Law. The Law was not even given with the purpose that it should justify, but that it should disclose sin, frighten, accuse, and condemn. Therefore the more someone endeavors to have regard for his conscience with the Law or works, the more uncertain and disturbed he makes it. Ask all the monks who labor earnestly to gain peace of conscience with their traditions whether they can declare with certainty that their way of life pleases God and that they are in a state of grace before God on account of it. If they are willing to admit the truth, they will reply: "I do indeed live a blameless life, and I observe the rule of my monastic order diligently. But I cannot declare for sure whether or not this obedience of mine is pleasing to God."

In *The Lives of the Fathers* there is a narrative about Arsenius. I referred to it earlier.[5] Although Arsenius had lived for a long time in the greatest sanctity and self-denial, he still began to fear and grieve deeply when he sensed that death was not far off. When he was asked why he feared death although he had spent his entire life in saintliness and had served God continually, he replied that he had indeed lived blamelessly according to the judgment of men, but

---

[5] On Arsenius see the remarks earlier in this commentary, *Luther's Works*, 26, p. 149, note 70.

that the judgments of God were different from those of men. With his saintliness and asceticism this man attained nothing except a fear and a horror of death. If he was saved, it was necessary that he lose all his own righteousness and trust only in the mercy of God, saying: "I believe in Jesus Christ, the Son of God, our Lord, who suffered, was crucified, and died for my sins."

Another interpretation is an affirmative one, namely, that he who receives circumcision is also obligated to keep the whole Law. For he who accepts Moses in one point is obliged to accept him in all points. He who observes one part of the Law as a matter of necessity must observe all the other parts of it. Nor does it help if you want to say that circumcision is necessary, but that the remaining laws of Moses are not. The same principle by which you are obliged to receive circumcision obliges you to accept the whole Law. Now to observe the whole Law is tantamount to pointing out in fact that the Christ has not yet come. If this is true, then all the Jewish ceremonies and laws about foods, places, and seasons must be observed; and we must still look for the Christ, who is to make the kingdom and priesthood of the Jews obsolete and is to establish a new kingdom throughout the world. But all Scripture testifies, and the facts themselves show, that Christ has already come, has redeemed the human race by His death, has abrogated the Law and has fulfilled what all the prophets predicted about Him. Therefore He abolished the Law and granted grace and truth (John 1:17). Accordingly, the Law does not justify; neither do its works. It is faith in the Christ who has already come that justifies.

Today there are those who, like the false apostles at that time, have wanted to bind us to certain laws of Moses that pleased them. This is completely intolerable. For if we permit Moses to rule over us in one respect, we are forced to endure his whole regime. Therefore we do not allow ourselves to be oppressed by any law of Moses at all. We grant, of course, that we should read and listen to Moses as one who predicted Christ and witnessed to Him, also that we should look to him for examples of outstanding laws and moral precepts; but we do not grant him any authority over our conscience.

Let him remain where he lies dead and buried, and "no man knows the place of his burial" (Deut. 34:6).[6]

The first interpretation, the negative one, seems to me to be more

[6] On Deut. 34:6 cf. *Luther's Works*, 26, p. 151.

spiritual and more apt. Both of them, however, are good, and both condemn the righteousness of the Law. The first says that we are so far from being justified by the Law that the more we try to fulfill the Law, the more we transgress it; the second says that anyone who wants to keep part of the Law is obligated to keep the whole Law. In either case Christ is of no advantage to those who want to be justified by the Law. From this it follows that by all this Paul means that the Law is the denial of Christ. It is remarkable that Paul has the courage to declare that the Law of Moses, given to the people of Israel by God, is the denial of Christ. Then why did God give the Law? Before the coming of Christ, when His coming in the flesh was still something to be expected, it was necessary. "The Law was our custodian until Christ came" (Gal. 3:24). But now that Christ has appeared, "we are no longer under a custodian" (Gal. 3:25). We have said enough about this issue earlier, at the end of the third chapter.[7] Therefore anyone who teaches the Law teaches the denial of Christ and of all His benefits, makes God a liar, yes, makes the Law itself a liar; for it is a witness to the promises about Christ, and it prophesied that Christ would be the King, not of the Law but of grace.

4. *You are severed from Christ, you who would be justified by the Law; you have fallen away from grace.*

Here Paul expounds himself by showing that he is not speaking simply about the Law or about the act of circumcision but about the confidence or presumption of justification through it, as though he were saying: "I do not condemn circumcision or the Law as such. I am permitted to eat, drink, and associate with Jews in accordance with the Law; I am permitted to circumcise Timothy,[8] etc. What I do condemn is the desire to be justified through the Law, as though Christ had not yet come or as though, while present, He were not able to justify by Himself. This is being severed from Christ. Therefore he says: "You are severed"; that is, "You are Pharaohs, namely, free of Christ.[9] Christ has stopped being and working in you. You have no more of the knowledge, the Spirit, the attitude, the favor,

[7] See Luther's exegesis of Gal. 3:25, *Luther's Works*, 26, 345 ff.

[8] Cf. *Luther's Works*, 26, p. 61, note 39.

[9] On this interpretation of the meaning of "Pharaoh" cf. Luther's comments in his sermon on Ex. 12:29 (W, XVI, 651—652), where he refers to this passage.

the freedom, the life, and the working of Christ. You are utterly separated from Him, so that He has no more dealings with you or you with Him."

It must be noted and pointed out carefully that Paul declares the desire to be justified through the Law to be nothing else than being separated from Christ and being made completely useless by Him.[10] What can be said against the Law that is more powerful, or what can be set in opposition to this thunderbolt? Therefore it is impossible for Christ and the Law to dwell in the heart at the same time. Either the Law or Christ has to yield. But if you are of the opinion that Christ and trust in the Law can dwell together in the heart, then you should know for sure that not Christ but the devil is dwelling in your heart under the mask of Christ, and that he is the one who is accusing you, terrifying you, and demanding the Law and your works as the condition of righteousness. For, as I said a little earlier, the genuine Christ does not chide you for your sins; nor does He command you to trust in your good works. And genuine knowledge of Christ, or faith, does not discuss whether you have done good works to obtain righteousness or evil works to obtain damnation; but it simply declares: "If you have done good works, you are not justified on their account; and if you have done evil works, you are not damned on their account." I am not taking any of their glory away from good works; nor am I praising evil works. But I am saying that in the issue of justification I must see how I am to keep Christ, lest He become useless to me if I wish to be justified by the Law. For Christ alone justifies me, in opposition to my evil works and without my good works. If I feel this way about Christ, I grasp the genuine Christ; but if I think that He demands the Law and works of me as a condition for righteousness, then He has become of no advantage to me, and I am severed from Him.

These declarations and threats against the righteousness of the Law and against self-righteousness are terrifying; at the same time they are very sure principles, which reinforce the doctrine of justification. Therefore this is the final conclusion: You must give up either Christ or the righteousness of the Law. If you keep Christ, you are righteous in the sight of God. If you keep the Law, Christ is of no avail to you; then you are obligated to keep the whole Law,

[10] In later editions this apparent mistake is rectified, and the text is changed to read "and for Him to become utterly useless to us."

and you have your sentence (Deut. 27:26): "Cursed be he who does not, etc." We speak about human traditions just as we did about the Law: Either the pope and his religious must give up everything in which they have trusted until now, or Christ will be of no avail to them. From this it is easy to judge how dangerous and corrosive the papal doctrine has been, for it has led us a very long way from Christ and has made us completely of no avail to Him.[11] In Jer. 23:26-27 God complains: "The prophets prophesy lies and prophesy the deceit of their own heart, with the purpose of making My people forget My name." Therefore just as the false prophets lost the true interpretation of the Law and of the doctrine about the Seed of Abraham, who was to bless all the nations, and just as they preached their own dreams, so that the people forgot their God, so the papists have obscured and oppressed the Gospel of Christ, so that it fell into disuse, and have set forth only the doctrine of works, with which they have led the whole world very far away from Christ. He who considers these things seriously cannot help being horrified.

You have fallen away from grace.

That is: "You are no longer in the realm of grace." For just as someone on a ship is drowned regardless of the part of the ship from which he falls into the sea, so someone who falls away from grace cannot help perishing. The desire to be justified by the Law, therefore, is shipwreck; it is exposure to the surest peril of eternal death. What can be more insane and wicked than to want to lose the grace and favor of God and to retain the Law of Moses, whose retention makes it necessary for you to accumulate wrath and every other evil for yourself? Now if those who seek to be justified on the basis of the Moral Law fall away from grace, where, I ask, will those fall who, in their self-righteousness, seek to be justified on the basis of their traditions and vows? To the lowest depths of hell! No, they are carried to heaven; for that is what they themselves have taught: "Those who have lived in accordance with the rule of Francis, etc., the peace and mercy of God is upon them; he who has observed chastity, obedience, etc., will have eternal life." You must put these empty and wicked trifles behind you and pay attention to what Paul teaches here and to what Christ says (John 3:36): "He who believes in the Son of God has eternal life; he who does not believe in the

---

[11] On the clarification of this in later editions cf. note 10 above.

Son shall not see life, but the wrath of God rests upon him"; and again (John 3:18): "He who does not believe is condemned already."

Besides, the doctrine of the papists about human traditions, works, vows, merits, etc., was so widespread in the world that it was regarded as the best and the surest. By means of it the devil established and most strongly reinforced his kingdom. Therefore it is no wonder that today, when it is being attacked by us and scattered "like chaff before the wind" (Ps. 1:4), Satan is raging so ferociously, filling everything with turmoil and scandals, and stirring up the whole world against us. Therefore someone may say that it would have been better to be silent, and that then none of these evils would have arisen. We ought to set greater store by the favor of God, whose glory we proclaim, than by the rage of the world, which persecutes us. For what are the pope and the whole world in comparison with God, whom we surely should praise and to whom we should give preference over all creatures? In addition, the wicked increase the uproar and the scandals which Satan arouses in order to crush or at least to distort our teaching. We, on the other hand, emphasize the comfort and the inestimable fruit of this doctrine; this we vastly prefer to all those turmoils, sects, and scandals. We, of course, are small and weak; and we are carrying a heavenly treasure in earthen vessels (2 Cor. 4:7). But though the vessels may be weak, the treasure is infinite and incomprehensible.

These words, "You have fallen away from grace," should not [12] be looked at in a cool and careless way; for they are very emphatic. Whoever falls away from grace simply loses the propitiation, forgiveness of sins, righteousness, freedom, life, etc., which Christ earned for us by His death and resurrection; and in place of these he acquires the wrath and judgment of God, sin, death, slavery to the devil, and eternal damnation. This passage is a powerful support and reinforcement for our doctrine of faith or the doctrine of justification; and it gives us marvelous comfort against the ragings of the papists, who persecute and condemn us as heretics because we teach this doctrine. This passage really ought to strike terror into all the enemies of faith and grace, that is, all the partisans of works, to make them stop persecuting and blaspheming the Word of grace, life, and eternal salvation. But they are so calloused and obstinate that "seeing they do not see, and hearing" — this horrible sentence pronounced against

---

[12] The *Nun* of the Weimar text is plainly a typographical error for *Non*.

them by the apostle — "they do not hear" (Matt. 13:13). Therefore let us let them alone, for they are blind leaders of the blind (Matt. 15:14).

5. *For through the Spirit, by faith, we wait for the hope of righteousness.*

Paul concludes here with a beautiful exclamation,[13] saying: "You want to be justified by the Law, by circumcision and works. We do not do this, lest Christ become of no advantage to us, lest we be obligated to keep the whole Law, lest we be severed from Christ, and lest we fall away from grace. But through the Spirit, by faith, we wait for the hope of righteousness." The individual words should be weighed carefully, for they are very emphatic. He did not merely want to say, as he usually does otherwise, "We are justified by faith" or "through the Spirit by faith"; but he added: "We wait for the hope of righteousness," including hope at the same time, so that he might cover the whole content of faith. When he says "through the Spirit by faith," we must consider the antithesis expressed by the word "Spirit," as though he were saying: "We do not want to be justified by the flesh, but we do this in order to be justified by the Spirit. And when we say 'Spirit,' we do not mean a fanatic or an autodidact, as the sectarians boast of the Spirit;[14] but our Spirit is 'by faith.'" The Spirit and faith have been discussed at length earlier. But here he not only says: "We are justified through the Spirit by faith"; but he continues: "We wait for the hope of righteousness," which is a new addition.

In the usage of Scripture "hope" is taken in two senses: as the thing hoped for and as the feeling of hope. It is meant as the thing hoped for in Col. 1:5: "because of the hope laid up for you in heaven," that is, the thing hoped for. It is meant as the feeling of hope in Rom. 8:24-25: "Hope that is seen is not hope. For who hopes for what he sees? But if we hope for what we do not see, we wait for it with patience." Thus in this passage "hope" can be taken in both senses, and accordingly the passage can have two meanings. The first is: "Through the Spirit, by faith, we wait for the hope of our righteousness, that is, the hoped-for righteousness, which is surely to

---

[13] The term used here is *epiphonema*, on which see also *Luther's Works*, 26, p. 389, note 23.

[14] For Luther's criticism of autodidacts, apparently aimed at Zwingli, cf. also *Luther's Works*, 3, p. 5, and *Luther the Expositor*, p. 125.

be revealed in due time." The second meaning is: "Through the Spirit, by faith, we wait for righteousness with hope and longing; that is, we are justified, and still we are not yet justified, because our righteousness is still hanging in hope, as Rom. 8:24 says: 'In hope we were saved.' For as long as we live, sin still clings to our flesh; there remains a law in our flesh and members at war with the law of our mind and making us captive to the law of sin (Rom. 7:23). While these passions of the flesh are raging and we, by the Spirit, are struggling against them, the righteousness we hope for remains elsewhere.[15] We have indeed begun to be justified by faith, by which we have also received the first fruits of the Spirit; and the mortification of our flesh has begun. But we are not yet perfectly righteous. Our being justified perfectly still remains to be seen, and this is what we hope for. Thus our righteousness does not yet exist in fact, but it still exists in hope."

This is a very important and pleasant comfort with which to bring wonderful encouragement to minds afflicted and disturbed with a sense of sin and afraid of every flaming dart of the devil (Eph. 6:16). For, as we know from our own experience, in such a conflict of conscience the sense of sin, of the wrath of God, of death, of hell, and of every terror holds powerful sway. Then one must say to him who is distressed: "Brother, you want to have a conscious righteousness; that is, you want to be conscious of righteousness in the same way you are conscious of sin. This will not happen. But your righteousness must transcend your consciousness of sin and you must hope that you are righteous in the sight of God. That is, your righteousness is not visible, and it is not conscious; but it is hoped for as something to be revealed in due time. Therefore you must not judge on the basis of your consciousness of sin, which terrifies and troubles you, but on the basis of the promise and teaching of faith, by which Christ is promised to you as your perfect and eternal righteousness." Thus in the midst of fears and of a consciousness of sin my hope — that is, my feeling of hope — is aroused and strengthened by faith, so that it hopes that I am righteous; and hope — that is, the thing hoped for — hopes that what it does not yet see will be made perfect and will be revealed in due time.

Both interpretations are good; but the first, which sees it as the

[15] The Latin term is *manet ibi locus*, which might possibly mean also: "It remains a possibility."

feeling of hope, brings more abundant comfort. For my righteousness is not yet perfect or conscious. Yet I do not despair on that account; but faith shows me Christ, in whom I trust. When I have taken hold of Him by faith, I struggle against the fiery darts of the devil (Eph. 6:16); and through hope I am encouraged over against my consciousness of sin, since I conclude that perfect righteousness has been prepared for me in heaven. Thus both things are true: that I am righteous here with an incipient righteousness; and that in this hope I am strengthened against sin and look for the consummation of perfect righteousness in heaven. These things are correctly understood when they are put into practice.

Here the question arises what the difference is between faith and hope. The sophists have really sweat over this issue, but they could not show anything definite.[16] Even for us, who study Sacred Scripture very diligently and interpret it with a far greater spirit and understanding (without trying to boast), it is difficult to find any difference. For faith and hope have such a great affinity that the one cannot be separated from the other. And yet there is some difference between them, which is to be based on their differing functions [17] and aims.

Therefore faith and hope differ first in their subjects, because faith is in the intellect and hope is in the will; yet they cannot be separated in fact, just as the two cherubim of the mercy seat cannot be separated (Ex. 25:19). In the second place, they differ in their function; for faith commands and directs the intellect, though not apart from the will, and teaches what must be believed. Therefore faith is teaching or knowledge. Hope is exhortation, because it arouses the mind to be brave and resolute, so that it dares, endures, and lasts in the midst of evils and looks for better things. Furthermore, faith is a theologian and a judge, battling against errors and heresies, and judging spirits and doctrines. On the other hand, hope is a captain, battling against feelings such as tribulation, the cross, impatience, sadness, faintheartedness, despair, and blasphemy; and it battles with joy and courage, etc., in opposition to those great evils. Finally, they differ in their objects. As its object faith has truth, and it teaches us to cling to this surely and firmly; it looks to the word

---

[16] Cf. the discussion of Augustine, *Faith, Hope, and Charity [Enchiridion]*, II, 8.

[17] Thus we have read the word *contrariis* as an adjective in this context.

of the object, that is, to the promise. Hope has goodness as its object; and it looks to the object of the word, that is, to the thing promised or the things to be hoped for, which faith has ordered us to accept.

Therefore when I take hold of Christ as I have been taught by faith in the Word of God, and when I believe in Him with the full confidence of my heart — something that cannot happen without the will — then I am righteous through this knowledge. When I have been thus justified by faith or by this knowledge, then immediately the devil comes and exerts himself to extinguish my faith with his tricks, his lies, errors and heresies, violence, tyranny, and murder. Then my battling hope grasps what faith has commanded; it becomes vigorous and conquers the devil, who attacks faith. When he has been conquered, there follow peace and joy in the Holy Spirit. In fact, therefore, faith and hope are scarcely distinguishable; and yet there is some difference between them. To make this difference clearer, I shall explain the matter by means of an analogy.

In the political realm prudence and fortitude are different; for prudence is one thing, and fortitude is another. And yet they stick together so closely that they cannot be easily separated.[18] Now fortitude is a steadiness of mind, which does not despair in the midst of adversity but endures bravely and looks for better things. But unless fortitude is directed by prudence, it becomes rashness; on the other hand, unless fortitude is added to prudence, prudence is useless. Therefore just as in the political realm prudence is vain without fortitude, so in theology faith is nothing without hope, because hope endures and lasts in the midst of evils and conquers them. And, on the other hand, just as fortitude without prudence is rashness, so hope without faith is presumptuousness about the Spirit and a tempting of God; for since it lacks the knowledge of the truth or of Christ, which faith teaches, it is a blind and rash fortitude. First of all, therefore, the believer must have a correct understanding and an intellect informed by faith, by which the mind is governed amid afflictions, so that in the midst of evils it hopes for the best things that faith has commanded and taught.

Therefore faith is like dialectic, which conceives the idea of all the things that are to be believed; and hope is like rhetoric, which develops, urges, persuades, and exhorts to steadiness, so that faith does not collapse in temptation but keeps the Word and holds firmly

---

[18] Perhaps an allusion to Aristotle, *Nicomachean Ethics*, III, 6—9.

to it.[19] Now just as dialectic and rhetoric are distinct arts and yet bear such affinity to each other that neither can be separated from the other — because without dialectic the orator cannot teach anything that is sure, while without rhetoric a dialectician cannot move his hearers, but he who combines them both teaches and persuades — so faith and hope are distinct feelings; for faith is something other than hope, and hope is something other than faith, and yet, because of the great affinity between them, they cannot be separated. Therefore just as dialectic and rhetoric perform certain tasks for each other, so do faith and hope. Thus the distinction between faith and hope in theology is the same as that between intellect and will in philosophy, between prudence and fortitude in the political realm, between dialectic and rhetoric in public speaking.

In other words, faith is conceived by teaching, when the mind is instructed about what the truth is; hope is conceived by exhortation, because by exhortation hope is aroused in the midst of afflictions, comforting the man who has already been justified by faith, so that he does not surrender to evil but acts even more bravely.[20] But if the torch of faith did not illumine the will, hope could not persuade the will. Therefore we have faith, by which we are taught, by which we become wise, understand heavenly wisdom, take hold of Christ, and abide in His grace. Once we cling to Christ by faith and confess Him, immediately our enemies, the world, the flesh, and the devil, rise up against us, hating and persecuting us most bitterly in body and spirit. Believing this way, then, we are justified through the Spirit by faith, and we wait for the hope of our righteousness. We wait with patience, however; for what we feel and see is the exact opposite. The world and its ruler, the devil (John 16:11), accuse us of every sort of evil, outwardly and inwardly. In addition, sin still clings to us and continually saddens us. Yet in all this we neither faint nor falter; but we encourage our will bravely with faith, which illumines, instructs, and rules the will. And thus we remain constant and conquer all evils through Him who loved us (Rom. 8:37), until our righteousness, in which we now believe and hope, is revealed.

Thus we began by faith, we persevere by hope, and we shall have everything by that revelation. As long as we live meanwhile, because

---

[19] Cf. the explanation of this distinction in Aristotle, *Rhetoric*, I, 1.

[20] Vergil, *Aeneid*, VI, 96; cf. also *Luther's Works*, 1, p. 214, note 59, and the reference there to the researches of Peter Meinhold.

we do believe, we teach the Word and plant the knowledge of Christ in others. As we teach, we suffer persecution, in accordance with the saying (Ps. 116:10): "I have believed, therefore have I spoken; but I am greatly afflicted." But as we suffer, we are bravely encouraged by hope, and Scripture exhorts us with the sweet and very comforting promises which faith has taught us. And thus hope is born and grows in us, "that by steadfastness and by the encouragement of the Scriptures we might have hope" (Rom. 15:4).

And so it is not without reason when Paul — in Rom. 5:3-5, Rom. 8:17-25, and elsewhere — joins patience and tribulations to hope; for hope is aroused by them. By contrast, faith is prior to hope; for it is the beginning of life and begins before any tribulation, since it learns about Christ and grasps Him without having to bear a cross. Nevertheless, cross and conflict follow immediately upon the knowledge of Christ. When this happens, the mind should be encouraged to find the fortitude of the Spirit — since hope is nothing but theological fortitude, while faith is theological wisdom or prudence — which has its place in endurance, according to the statement (Rom. 15:4): "that by steadfastness, etc." So these three abide (1 Cor. 13:13): faith teaches the truth and defends it against errors and heresies; hope endures and conquers all evils, physical and spiritual; love does everything good, as follows in the text (Gal. 5:6). Thus a man is whole and perfect in this life, both inwardly and outwardly, until the revelation of the righteousness for which he looks, which will be consummated and eternal.

In addition, this passage contains very important instruction and comfort. The instruction is that we are not justified through works, ceremonies, sacrifices, and the whole system of worship in the Mosaic Law, much less through human works and traditions, but through Christ alone. Whatever there is in us beside Him — whether it be intellect or will, activity or passivity, etc. — is flesh, not Spirit. Therefore whatever the world has that is very good and holy apart from Christ is sin, error, and flesh. And so circumcision, the observance of the Law, as well as the works, religious observances, and vows of the monks and of all the self-righteous, are of the flesh. "But we," Paul says, "go far beyond all this to live in the Spirit, because through faith we hold to Christ, and in tribulation we wait by hope for that righteousness which we already possess by faith."

The comfort is this, that in your deep anxieties — in which your consciousness of sin, sadness, and despair is so great and strong that it penetrates and occupies all the corners of your heart — you do not follow your consciousness. For if you did, you would say: "I feel the violent terrors of the Law and the tyranny of sin, not only waging war against me again but completely conquering me. I do not feel any comfort or righteousness. Therefore I am not righteous but a sinner. And if I am a sinner, then I am sentenced to eternal death." But battle against this feeling, and say: "Even though I feel myself completely crushed and swallowed by sin and see God as a hostile and wrathful judge, yet in fact this is not true; it is only my feeling that thinks so. The Word of God, which I ought to follow in these anxieties rather than my own consciousness, teaches much differently, namely, that 'God is near to the brokenhearted, and saves the crushed in spirit' (Ps. 34:18), and that 'He does not despise a broken and contrite heart' (Ps. 51:17). And here Paul then teaches that through the Spirit, by faith, those who are justified do not yet feel the hope of righteousness but still wait for it."

When the Law accuses and sin terrifies you, and you do not feel anything except the wrath and judgment of God, do not despair on that account. But "take the armor of God, the shield of faith, the helmet of hope, and the sword of the Spirit" (Eph. 6:13, 16, 17); and find out by experience what a good and brave warrior you are. By faith take hold of Christ, the Lord of the Law and of sin and of everything that accompanies them. When you believe in Him, you are justified — something that your reason and the consciousness of your heart do not tell you amid your temptation, but only the Word of God. Then, in the conflicts and fears that continually return to plague you, you should patiently look with hope for the righteousness that you have only by faith, though only in an incipient and imperfect form, until it is revealed perfectly and eternally in due time. "But I am not conscious of having righteousness, or at least I am only dimly conscious of it!" You are not to be conscious of having righteousness; you are to believe it. And unless you believe that you are righteous, you insult and blaspheme Christ, who has cleansed you by the washing of water with the Word (Eph. 5:26) and who in His death on the cross condemned and killed sin and death, so that through Him you might obtain eternal righteousness and life. You cannot deny this, unless you want to be obviously wicked, blasphemous, and contemptuous of God, of all the divine promises, of

Christ, and of all His benefits. Then you cannot deny either that you are righteous.

Let us learn, therefore, that amid great and horrible terrors, when the conscience feels nothing but sin and supposes that God is wrathful and Christ is hostile, we must not consult the consciousness of our own heart. No, then we must consult the Word of God, which says that God is not wrathful, but that He has regard for those who are afflicted, are contrite in spirit, and tremble at His Word (Is. 66:2), and that Christ does not turn away from those who labor and are heavy-laden (Matt. 11:28) but revives them. Therefore this passage teaches clearly that the Law and works do not bring righteousness and comfort, but that this is achieved by the Spirit through faith in Christ; amid anxieties and tribulations He arouses hope, which endures and conquers evil. Very few people know how weak and feeble faith and hope are in cross and conflict; then faith and hope seem to be "a dimly burning wick" (Is. 42:3), which a strong wind is about to blow out. But those who in hope believe against hope (Rom. 4:18) amid these conflicts and fears; that is, those who fight against the consciousness of sin and of the wrath of God by faith in the promise of Christ, eventually experience that this poor little spark of faith (as it seems to reason, because it is hardly aware of it) will become like elemental fire,[21] which fills all heaven and swallows up all terrors and sins.

Truly devout people have nothing dearer and more precious in the whole world than this doctrine; for those who hold to this know what the whole world does not know, namely, that sin and death, as well as other calamities and evils, both physical and spiritual, work out for the good of the elect. They also know that God is present most closely when He seems to be farthest away, and that He is most merciful and most the Savior when He seems most to be wrathful and to punish and condemn. They know that they have eternal righteousness, for which they look in hope as an utterly certain possession, laid up in heaven, when they are most aware of the terrors of sin and death; and that they are the lords of everything when they seem to be the poorest of all, according to the words "as having nothing, and yet possessing everything" (2 Cor. 6:10). This is what Scripture calls gaining comfort through hope. But this art is not learned without frequent and great trials.

[21] Cf. Luther's discussion of the rainbow, *Luther's Works*, 2, 66.

6. *For in Christ Jesus neither circumcision nor uncircumcision is of any avail, but faith working through love.*

The sophists apply this passage in support of their doctrine that we are justified by love or by works. For they say that even when faith has been divinely infused — and I am not even speaking of faith that is merely acquired — it does not justify unless it has been formed by love. They call love "the grace that makes one acceptable," namely, that justifies, to use our term, or rather Paul's; and they say that love is acquired by our merit of congruity, etc. In fact, they even declare that an infused faith can coexist with mortal sin. In this manner they completely transfer justification from faith and attribute it solely to love as thus defined. And they claim that this is proved by St. Paul in this passage — "faith working through love" — as though Paul wanted to say: "You see, faith does not justify; in fact, it is nothing unless love the worker is added, which forms faith." [22]

But all these things are monstrosities thought up by idle men. Who could stand for the teaching that faith, the gift of God that is infused in the heart by the Holy Spirit, can coexist with mortal sin? If they were speaking about acquired or historical faith and about a natural opinion derived from history, they could be endured; indeed, they would be right if they were speaking about historical faith.[23] But to believe this way about infused faith is to admit openly that they understand nothing at all about faith. In addition, they read this passage from Paul through a colored glass, as the saying goes, and they distort the text to suit their own dreams. For Paul does not speak of "faith, which justifies through love," or of "faith, which makes acceptable through love." They themselves invent such a text and impose it upon this passage by violence. Much less does he say: "Love makes one acceptable." Paul does not speak this way, but he speaks of "faith working through love." He says that works are done on the basis of faith through love, not that a man is justified through love. And who is such an uneducated grammarian that he cannot understand from the force of the words that being justified is one thing and working is another? For Paul's words are clear and plain: "faith *working* [24] through love." Therefore it is an obvious trick when

---

[22] Cf. also *Luther's Works*, 24, p. 321.

[23] On *fides historica* see *Luther's Works*, 22, p. 153, note 120.

[24] We have used italics where the original has capitals.

they suppress the true and genuine meaning of Paul and interpret "working" to mean "justifying" and "works" to mean "righteousness," although even in moral philosophy they are forced to admit that works are not righteousness, but that works are done by righteousness.[25]

Furthermore, Paul does not make faith unformed here, as though it were a shapeless chaos without the power to be or to do anything; but he attributes the working itself to faith rather than to love. He does not suppose that it is some sort of shapeless and unformed quality; but he declares that it is an effective and active something, a kind of substance or, as they call it, a "substantial form."[26] He does not say: "Love is effective." No, he says: "Faith is effective." He does not say: "Love works." No, he says: "Faith works." He makes love the tool through which faith works. Now who does not know that a tool has its power, movement, and action, not from itself but from the artisan who works with it or uses it? For who would say that an axe gives the power and motion of cutting to a carpenter, or that a ship gives the power and motion of sailing to a sailor? Or, to cite an example used by Isaiah (10:15), who would say: "The saw wields the carpenter, and the staff lifts the hand"? It is no different when they say that love is the form of faith or that it grants power and movement to faith, that is, that it justifies. Since Paul does not even give love the credit for works, how would he give it credit for justification? Therefore it is certain that when this passage is distorted to refer to love rather than to faith, this is a great insult not only to Paul but to faith and love themselves.

But this is what happens to lazy readers and to those who superimpose their own ideas on the reading of Sacred Scripture. What they should do is to come to it empty, to derive their ideas from Sacred Scripture, then to pay careful attention to the words, to compare what precedes with what follows, and to make the effort of grasping the authentic meaning of a particular passage rather than attaching their own notions to words or phrases that they have torn out of context. For in this passage Paul is not dealing with the question of what faith is or of what avails in the sight of God; he is not discussing justification. He has already done that very thoroughly.

[25] Thus Aristotle says: "There is a difference between . . . the act of justice and what is just." *Nicomachean Ethics*, V, 7.

[26] The Latin terms are *efficax et operosa quidditas* and *forma substantialis*.

But in a brief summary [27] he draws a conclusion about the Christian life, saying: "In Christ Jesus neither circumcision nor uncircumcision is of any avail, but faith working through love," that is, a faith that is neither imaginary nor hypocritical but true and living. This is what arouses and motivates good works through love. This is the equivalent of saying: "He who wants to be a true Christian or to belong to the kingdom of Christ must be truly a believer. But he does not truly believe if works of love do not follow his faith." Thus he excludes hypocrites on both sides, on the right and on the left, from the kingdom of Christ. On the left he excludes the Jews and the work-righteous; for he says: "In Christ no circumcision, that is, no works or worship or kind of life are of any avail, but faith alone, without any trust in works." On the right he excludes the lazy, the idle, and the sluggish, because they say: "If faith without works justifies, then let us not do any works; but let us merely believe and do whatever we please!" "Not so, you wicked men," says Paul. "It is true that faith alone justifies, without works; but I am speaking about genuine faith, which, after it has justified, will not go to sleep but is active through love."

As I have said, therefore, Paul is describing the whole of the Christian life in this passage: inwardly it is faith toward God, and outwardly it is love or works toward one's neighbor. Thus a man is a Christian in a total sense: inwardly through faith in the sight of God, who does not need our works; outwardly in the sight of men, who do not derive any benefit from faith but do derive benefit from works or from our love. When one has heard or recognized this form of the Christian life, namely, as I have said, that it is faith and works, one has not yet said what faith is and what love is; for this is another matter for discussion. Earlier Paul has discussed faith, its internal nature, power, and function, and has taught that it is righteousness or rather justification in the sight of God. Here he connects it with love and works; that is, he speaks of its external function. Here he says that it is the impulse and motivation of good works or of love toward one's neighbor. Therefore no one with any sense can take this passage to refer to the business of justification in the sight of God; for it is speaking of the total life of Christians, and it is faulty dialectic or the fallacy of composition and division to attribute to one part what

[27] Here again Luther uses the term *epiphonema;* cf. p. 20, note 13.

is said of the whole.[28] Dialectic must avoid figures of speech like synecdoche or hyperbole, which rhetoric uses; for it is the discipline of teaching, defining, distinguishing, and comparing with as much precision as possible. What kind of dialectic would it be to argue: "Man is both soul and body, and he cannot exist without soul and body. Therefore the body has the power of understanding, and the soul does not understand alone"? It is the same kind of dialectic to argue: "The Christian life is faith and love, or faith working through love. Therefore love justifies, not faith alone."

But away with human opinions! From this passage we also learn how horrible the darkness is in those Egyptians (Ex. 10:21) who despise not only faith but also love in Christianity and who instead wear themselves out with self-chosen works, tonsures, special garb or food, and endless other masks and externals by which they want to give the impression of being Christians. But here stands Paul in supreme freedom and says in clear and explicit words: "That which makes a Christian is faith working through love." He does not say: "That which makes a Christian is a cowl or fasting or vestments or ceremonies." But it is true faith toward God, which loves and helps one's neighbor — regardless of whether the neighbor is a servant, a master, a king, a pope, a man, a woman, one who wears purple, one who wears rags, one who eats meat, or one who eats fish. Not one of these things, not one, makes a man a Christian; only faith and love do so. The rest are all lies and idolatry. And yet nothing is more contemptible than this very faith and love among those who claim to be the most Christian and to be actually a holier church than the holy church of God itself. On the other hand, they admire and boast of their masquerade and sham of self-chosen works, under which they nourish and conceal their horrible idolatry, wickedness, greed, filth, hatred, murder, and the whole kingdom of hell and the devil. So powerful is the might of hypocrisy and superstition in every age, from the beginning to the end of the world.

7. *You were running well; who hindered you from obeying the truth?*

These words are clear. Paul declares that he taught correctly before and is teaching correctly now; at the same time he suggests rather subtly that the Galatians had been running correctly before,

---

[28] A fallacy of composition is said to have been committed "when what is proposed, in a divided sense, is afterwards taken collectively." Charles P. Krauth, *A Vocabulary of the Philosophical Sciences* (New York, 1879), p. 191.

that is, had obeyed the truth and had believed and lived correctly, but that they were not doing so now, after they have been led astray by the false apostles. Moreover, he uses a new expression here when he calls the Christian life a "running." To the Hebrews running or walking means living or behaving.[29] Teachers and learners "run" when the former teach purely and the latter receive the Word with joy (Matt. 13:20) and when the fruits of the Spirit follow in both. This is what happened while Paul was present, as he testified in chapters three and four as well as here, when he says: "You were running well; that is, you were living a good life and pursuing the right course toward eternal life, which the Word promised you."

But the words "You were running well" contain comfort. For with these words Paul pays attention to the trial by which the devout are disciplined; to themselves their life seems dreary, closer to crawling than to running. But when there is sound teaching — which cannot be without results, since it brings the Holy Spirit and His gifts — the life of the devout is strenuous running, even though it may seem to be crawling. To us, of course, it seems that everything is moving ahead slowly and with great difficulty; but what seems slow to us is rapid in the sight of God, and what hardly crawls for us runs swiftly for Him. Likewise, what is sorrow, sin, and death in our eyes is joy, righteousness, and life in the eyes of God, for the sake of Christ, through whom we are made perfect. Christ is holy, righteous, happy, etc., and there is nothing that He lacks; thus there is nothing that believers in Him lack either. Therefore Christians are really runners; whatever they do runs along and moves forward successfully, being advanced by the Spirit of Christ, who has nothing to do with slow enterprises.

Those who fall away from grace and faith to the Law and works are hindered in this running. This is what happened to the Galatians; they were persuaded and led astray by the false apostles, whom Paul attacks obliquely with the words "Who hindered you from obeying the truth?" He spoke the same way earlier (3:1): "Who has bewitched you so that you do not obey the truth?" Paul indicates here incidentally that men are so violently crazed by false teaching that they accept lies and heresies as truth and as spiritual teaching, while they swear that the sound teaching which they had loved originally is in error, but that their error is sound teaching; this position they defend

[29] Cf. also Luther's comments, *Luther's Works*, 14, p. 288.

with all their might. Thus the Galatians, who were running along very well at first, were led by the false apostles into the opinion that they had been in error and were moving along very slowly when they had followed Paul as their teacher. But later, when they had been led astray by the false apostles and were forsaking the truth completely, they were so bewitched by these false arguments that they believed their whole life was moving along and running very successfully. Today the same thing is happening to those who have been deceived by the fanatical spirits. This is why I am often wont to say that a fall from sound doctrine is not human but demonic, from the very heights of heaven to the lowest depths of hell. Men who persevere in error are so far away from acknowledging their sin that they even defend it as the height of righteousness. Therefore it is impossible for them to be forgiven.

8. *This persuasion is not from Him who called you.*

This is outstanding comfort and instruction. In this way Paul teaches how those who have been led astray by wicked teachers are to be set free from their false persuasions. The false apostles were great men, much more impressive in their teaching and piety than Paul was. The Galatians were deceived by this false front and supposed that they were listening to Christ when they heard them; therefore they supposed that their own [30] persuasion came from Christ. In opposition to this, Paul indicates subtly and modestly that this persuasion and teaching had not come from Christ, who had called them in grace, but from the devil; and thus he set many of them free from this persuasion. Thus today we call many, who have been led astray by the sectarians, back from their error when we show them that the opinions of the sectarians are fanatical and wicked.

This comfort applies also to all who, in their affliction and temptation, develop a false idea of Christ. For the devil is a highly skilled persuader; he knows how to inflate a minute and almost ridiculous peccadillo until the one who has been tempted supposes it to be the most heinous offense, worthy of eternal punishment. Here the troubled mind should be encouraged in the manner in which Paul encouraged the Galatians, namely, by being told that this thought or persuasion does not come from Christ; for it conflicts with the Word of the Gospel, which portrays Christ, not as an accuser or a harsh task-

[30] We have read *ipsorum* for the *ipsorem* in the Weimar text.

master but as "gentle and lowly in heart" (Matt. 11:29), as a merciful Savior and Comforter.

But Satan has a thousand tricks [31] and turns this upside down by setting against it the Word and the example of Christ, as follows: "Of course, Christ is gentle, kind, etc., but only to those who are righteous and holy. By contrast, He threatens sinners with wrath and perdition (Luke 13:27-28) and declares that unbelievers are already condemned (John 3:18). In addition, Christ did many good works and endured many evils, and He commands us to imitate His example. But your life does not correspond to Christ's either in word or in deed, because you are a sinner and an unbeliever. In short, you have done nothing good. Therefore the statements that describe Christ as a Judge, etc., rather than the comforting ones about Christ the Savior, are those that pertain to you." When this happens, he who has been assailed should comfort himself this way:

"Scripture presents Christ in two ways. First, as a gift. If I take hold of Him this way, I shall lack nothing whatever. 'In Christ are hid all the treasures of wisdom and knowledge' (Col. 2:3). As great as He is, He has been made by God my wisdom, righteousness, sanctification, and redemption (1 Cor. 1:30). Therefore even if I have committed many great sins, nevertheless, if I believe in Him, they are all swallowed up by His righteousness. Secondly, Scripture presents Him as an example for us to imitate. But I will not let this Christ be presented to me as exemplar except at a time of rejoicing, when I am out of reach of temptations (when I can hardly attain a thousandth part of His example), so that I may have a mirror in which to contemplate how much I am still lacking, lest I become smug. But in a time of tribulation I will not listen to or accept Christ except as a gift, as Him who died for my sins, who has bestowed His righteousness on me, and who accomplished and fulfilled what is lacking in my life. For He 'is the end of the Law, that everyone who has faith may be justified' (Rom. 10:4)."

It is profitable to know this, not only that we may each have a sure remedy in a time of temptation — a remedy with which to throw off the poison of despair when Satan tries to infect us with it — but also that we may be able to resist the raging sectarians of our time. For the Anabaptists have nothing in their entire teaching more impressive than the way they emphasize the example of Christ and the bearing

---

[31] On the meaning of this term cf. also *Luther's Works*, 26, p. 196, note 15.

of the cross, especially because there are clear passages in which Christ urges His disciples to bear the cross. Therefore we must learn how to resist this Satan when he transforms himself into the appearance of an angel (2 Cor. 11:14), namely, by distinguishing when Christ is proclaimed as a gift and when as an example. Both forms of proclamation have their proper time; if this is not observed, the proclamation of salvation becomes a curse.

To those who are afraid and have already been terrified by the burden of their sins Christ the Savior and the gift should be announced, not Christ the example and the lawgiver. But to those who are smug and stubborn the example of Christ should be set forth, lest they use the Gospel as a pretext for the freedom of the flesh and thus become smug. Therefore let every Christian learn to be able to shake off the false idea of Christ that Satan urges upon him in his terror and affliction, and to say: "Satan, why are you debating with me now about deeds? I am already frightened and troubled enough because of my deeds and my sins. Indeed, since I am already troubled and burdened, let me hear, not you with your accusation and condemnation but Christ, the Savior of the human race, who says that He came into the world to save sinners (1 Tim. 1:15), to comfort the despairing, and to proclaim release to the captives (Luke 4:18). This is the real Christ in the most precise sense of the word, and no one else besides Him. I can find an example of a holy life in Abraham, Isaiah, John the Baptist, Paul, and other saints. But they cannot forgive my sins, deliver me from your power and from death, save me, and give me life. Only Christ is qualified to do these things, He whom God the Father has marked with His seal. Therefore I shall not listen to you as my teacher; but I shall listen to Christ, of whom the Father has said (Matt. 17:5): 'This is My beloved Son, with whom I am well pleased; listen to Him.' " Let us learn to encourage ourselves with faith this way amid the temptation and persuasion of false doctrine; otherwise the devil will either lead us astray through his agents or kill us with his flaming darts (Eph. 6:16).

9. *A little yeast leavens the whole lump.*

Jerome and those who have followed him accuse St. Paul of distorting many passages in Holy Scripture into an alien meaning. Therefore they say that in Paul there are contradictions that are not contradictions in their own doctrine.[32] But they accuse the apostle unjustly. For with accuracy and prudence he can make general statements particular, just as above (3:13) he made the general statement, "Cursed be everyone who hangs on a tree," particular by applying it very appropriately to Christ; or he makes particular statements general, as when he applies this particular statement, "A little yeast, etc.," generally by referring it both to doctrine — as in this passage, where he is dealing with justification — and to life or to evil morals, as in 1 Cor. 5:6.

The entire epistle gives ample evidence of how disappointed Paul was over the fall of the Galatians and of how often he pounded at them — now with reproof, now with appeals — about the very great and inestimable evils that would follow their fall unless they reconsidered. This care and admonition, so fatherly and truly apostolic, had no effect at all on some of them; for very many of them no longer acknowledged Paul as their teacher but vastly preferred the false apostles, from whom they imagined that they had derived true doctrine rather than from Paul. Finally the false apostles undoubtedly slandered Paul among the Galatians in this way: Paul, they said, was a stubborn and quarrelsome man, who was shattering the harmony among the churches on account of some trifle, for no other reason than because he alone wanted to be right and to be praised. With this false accusation they made Paul detestable in the eyes of many. Others, who had not yet fallen completely away from Paul's teaching, imagined that there was no harm in disagreeing a little with him on the doctrines of justification and faith. Accordingly, when they heard Paul placing such great emphasis on what seemed to them a matter of such minor importance, they were amazed and thought: "Granted that we have diverged somewhat from Paul's teaching and that there is some fault on our side, still it is a minor matter. Therefore he should overlook it or at least not place such great emphasis on it. Otherwise he could shatter the harmony among the churches with this unimportant issue."

Paul answers them with this excellent proverbial statement: "A little yeast leavens the whole lump." This is a caution which Paul emphasizes. We, too, should emphasize it in our time. For the sectarians who deny the bodily presence of Christ in the Lord's

---

[32] See Luther's attack on Jerome and Erasmus in *The Bondage of the Will* (W, XVIII, 723).

Supper accuse us today of being quarrelsome, harsh, and intractable, because, as they say, we shatter love and harmony among the churches on account of the single doctrine about the Sacrament. They say that we should not make so much of this little doctrine, which is not a sure thing anyway and was not specified in sufficient detail by the apostles, that solely on its account we refuse to pay attention to the sum total of Christian doctrine and to general harmony among all the churches. This is especially so because they agree with us on other articles of Christian doctrine.[33] With this very plausible argument they not only make us unpopular among their own followers; but they even subvert many good men, who suppose that we disagree with them because of sheer stubbornness or some other personal feeling. But these are tricks of the devil, by which he is trying to overthrow not only this article of faith but all Christian doctrine.

To this argument of theirs we reply with Paul: "A little yeast leavens the whole lump." In philosophy a tiny error in the beginning is very great at the end. Thus in theology a tiny error overthrows the whole teaching. Therefore doctrine and life should be distinguished as sharply as possible. Doctrine belongs to God, not to us; and we are called only as its ministers. Therefore we cannot give up or change even one dot of it (Matt. 5:18). Life belongs to us; therefore when it comes to this, there is nothing that the Sacramentarians can demand of us that we are not willing and obliged to undertake, condone, and tolerate, with the exception of doctrine and faith, about which we always say what Paul says: "A little yeast, etc." On this score we cannot yield even a hairbreadth. For doctrine is like a mathematical point. Therefore it cannot be divided; that is, it cannot stand either subtraction or addition. On the other hand, life is like a physical point. Therefore it can always be divided and can always yield something.[34]

The tiniest speck in the eye is harmful to the sight. Therefore the Germans say about remedies for the eyes: "Nothing is good for the eyes." And Christ says (Luke 11:34): "Your eye is the lamp of your body; when your eye is sound, your whole body is full of light." And again (v. 36): "If your body has no part dark, it will be wholly bright." By this allegory Christ indicates that the eye, that is, doctrine, must be completely pure, clear, and sincere, having no part dark

---

[33] Cf. also *This Is My Body, Luther's Works*, 37, pp. 27—28.

[34] On this distinction cf. *Luther's Works*, 13, p. 120, note 68.

and no dark spots. And James said very beautifully, not by his own spirit but undoubtedly on the basis of what he had heard from the fathers (James 2:10): "Whoever fails in one point has become guilty of all of the Law." Therefore doctrine must be one eternal and round golden circle, in which there is no crack; if even the tiniest crack appears, the circle is no longer perfect. What good does it do the Jews to believe that there is one God and that He is the Creator of all, to believe all the doctrines, and to accept all of Holy Scripture, when they deny Christ? "Therefore whoever fails in one point has become guilty of all of it."

Hence this passage must also be considered carefully in opposition to the argument by which they accuse us of offending against love and thus doing great harm to the churches. We are surely prepared to observe peace and love with all men, provided that they leave the doctrine of faith perfect and sound for us. If we cannot obtain this, it is useless for them to demand love from us. A curse on a love that is observed at the expense of the doctrine of faith, to which everything must yield — love, an apostle, an angel from heaven, etc.! Therefore when they minimize this issue in such a dishonest way, they give ample evidence of how highly they regard the majesty of the Word. If they believed that it is the Word of God, they would not play around with it this way. No, they would treat it with the utmost respect; they would put their faith in it without any disputing or doubting; and they would know that one Word of God is all and that all are one, that one doctrine is all doctrines and all are one, so that when one is lost all are eventually lost, because they belong together and are held together by a common bond.

Therefore let us leave the praise of harmony and of Christian love to them. We, on the other hand, praise faith and the majesty of the Word. Love can sometimes be neglected without danger, but the Word and faith cannot. It belongs to love to bear everything and to yield to everyone. On the other hand, it belongs to faith to bear nothing whatever and to yield to no one. Love yields freely, believes, condones, and tolerates everything. Therefore it is often deceived. Yet when it is deceived, it does not suffer any hardship that can really be called a hardship; that is, it does not lose Christ, and therefore it is not offended but keeps its constancy in doing good even toward those who are unthankful and unworthy. In the issue of salvation, on the other hand, when fanatics teach lies and errors under the guise of truth and make an impression on many, there love is certainly not to be exercised, and error is not to be approved. For what is lost here is not merely a good deed done for someone who is unthankful, but the Word, faith, Christ, and eternal life. Therefore if you deny God in one article of faith, you have denied Him in all; for God is not divided into many articles of faith, but He is everything in each article and He is one in all the articles of faith. Therefore when the Sacramentarians accuse us of neglecting love, we continually reply to them with this proverb of Paul's: "A little yeast, etc." And another proverb says: "A man's reputation, his faith, and his eye do not stand being played with." [35]

I have said this at some length to encourage our own people and to instruct others, who are perhaps offended by our firmness and who do not think that we have definite and serious reasons for this firmness. Therefore let us not be moved when they make such a boast of their zeal for love and harmony; for he who does not love God and His Word does not count for anything, regardless of what or how much else he may love. Accordingly, Paul warns both preachers and hearers with this statement not to think that the doctrine of faith is little or nothing and that we can play around with it as we please. It is a sunbeam coming down from heaven to illumine, brighten, and direct us. Just as the world with all its wisdom and power cannot bend the rays of the sun which are aimed directly from heaven to earth, so nothing can be taken away from or added to the doctrine of faith without overthrowing it all.

10. *I have confidence in you through the Lord.*

It is as though Paul were saying: "I have warned, encouraged, and rebuked you enough, if you will only listen. Yet I have confidence in you through the Lord." Here the question arises whether Paul did right in saying that he had confidence in the Galatians, especially since Sacred Scripture forbids confidence in men (Ps. 118:8). Both faith and love have confidence, but their objects are different. Faith has confidence in God; therefore it cannot be deceived. Love has confidence in men; therefore it is often deceived. The confidence that love has is so necessary for this present life that without it life on earth could not go on. If one man did not believe and trust another, what would our life on earth be? Christians are more ready to believe

[35] Cf. *Luther's Works*, 9, p. 89, note 19.

someone for the sake of love than are the sons of this world, for confidence toward men is a result of the Spirit or of Christian faith in the devout. Therefore Paul even has confidence in the Galatians who have fallen — but through the Lord, as though he were to say: "I have confidence in you to the extent that the Lord is in you and you are in Him, that is, to the extent that you remain in the truth. If you fall away from this through deception by the agents of Satan, I shall no longer have confidence in you." In this way it is permissible for the godly to believe, and have confidence in, men.

That you will take no other view than mine.

"Namely, no other view of doctrine and of faith than the one you have heard and learned from me; that is, I am confident that you will not accept another doctrine, one that differs from mine."

And he who is troubling you will bear his judgment, whoever he is.

With this sentence Paul acts as a judge seated in tribunal and condemns the false apostles; he gives them the exceedingly hateful name "troublers of the Galatians," even though the latter regarded them as very godly teachers who were far better than Paul. At the same time he wants to arouse the Galatians by means of this horrible sentence which he pronounces on the false apostles with such assurance, so that they will avoid them as the deadliest pestilence. It is as though he were to say: "Why do you listen to those pests, who do not teach you but only trouble you? The doctrine they give you is nothing but the troubling of the conscience. Therefore no matter how great they are, they will have their condemnation." From the words "whoever he is" it is evident enough that the false apostles were men who appeared to be very good and saintly; and perhaps there was among them some outstanding pupil of the apostles, a man of great prestige and authority. For Paul does not use such powerful and meaningful words without reason. He speaks the same way in the eighth verse of the first chapter: "Even if we, or an angel from heaven, should preach to you a gospel contrary to that which we preached to you, let him be accursed." And there is no doubt that they were deeply offended by this violent language of the apostle and thought to themselves: "Why does Paul sin against love? Why is he so stubborn about such a trifle? Why is he so precipitate in pronouncing a sentence of eternal condemnation on those who are just as much ministers of Christ as he is?" He does not hesitate on account of any of this, but with confidence and assurance he goes ahead to curse and condemn those who offend against the doctrine of faith, even though in their outward appearance they are saintly, learned, and highly esteemed men.

In a similar way we today regard those men as excommunicated and condemned who say that the doctrine of the sacrament of the body and blood of Christ is uncertain or who do violence to the words of Christ in the Lord's Supper. With the utmost rigor we demand that all the articles of Christian doctrine, both large and small — although we do not regard any of them as small — be kept pure and certain. This is supremely necessary. For this doctrine is our only light, which illumines and directs us and shows the way to heaven; if it is overthrown in one point, it must be overthrown completely. And when that happens, our love will not be of any use to us. We can be saved without love and concord with the Sacramentarians, but not without pure doctrine and faith. Otherwise we shall be happy to observe love and concord toward those who faithfully agree with us on all the articles of Christian doctrine. In fact, so far as we are concerned, we shall have peace with our enemies; and we shall pray for those who slander our doctrine and persecute us out of ignorance, but not with those who knowingly offend against one or more articles of Christian doctrine and against their conscience.

By his example Paul teaches us to be as firm as he is when he predicts with complete assurance that they will bear their judgment on account of a matter that seemed not only trivial but even wicked to the false apostles and their disciples; for both groups thought they were teaching in a proper and godly way. Therefore, as I often warn you, doctrine must be carefully distinguished from life. Doctrine is heaven; life is earth. In life there is sin, error, uncleanness, and misery, mixed, as the saying goes, "with vinegar." Here love should condone, tolerate, be deceived, trust, hope, and endure all things (1 Cor. 13:7); here the forgiveness of sins should have complete sway, provided that sin and error are not defended. But just as there is no error in doctrine, so there is no need for any forgiveness of sins. Therefore there is no comparison at all between doctrine and life. "One dot" of doctrine is worth more than "heaven and earth" (Matt. 5:18); therefore we do not permit the slightest offense against it. But we can be lenient toward errors of life. For we, too, err daily in our life and conduct; so do all the saints, as they earnestly confess in the Lord's Prayer and the Creed.[36] But by the grace of God our doctrine is pure; we have all the articles of faith solidly established in Sacred Scripture. The devil would dearly love to corrupt and overthrow these; that is why he attacks us so cleverly with this specious argument about not offending against love and the harmony among the churches.

11. *But if I, brethren, still preach circumcision, why am I still persecuted? In that case the stumbling block of the cross has been removed.*

Paul wants to try everything to call the Galatians back; therefore he now argues on the basis of his own example. He says: "I have brought upon myself the bitterest hatred and the persecution of the high priests, of the elders of the people, and of my entire nation, because I deny that circumcision brings righteousness. If I attributed righteousness to circumcision, the Jews would not only not lie in ambush for me but would even praise and love me extravagantly. But now, because I preach the Gospel of Christ and the righteousness of faith, together with the abrogation of the Law and of circumcision, I suffer persecution. On the other hand, in order not to have to bear the cross and the bitter hatred of the Jewish people, the false apostles preach circumcision; in this way they curry the favor of the Jews and keep them as their friends." Similarly he says in the sixth chapter (v. 12): "They would compel you to be circumcised, etc." In addition, they would like to bring it about that there be no dispute at all, but only peace and harmony, between Gentiles and Jews. But it is impossible for this to happen except at the cost of the doctrine of faith, which is the doctrine of the cross and is full of stumbling blocks.

Therefore when Paul says: "If I still preach circumcision, why am I still persecuted? In that case the stumbling block of the cross has been removed," he wants to show that it would be an absurdity and a disgrace if the stumbling block of the cross were to end. He speaks the same way in 1 Cor. 1:17: "Christ sent me to preach the Gospel, not with eloquent wisdom, lest the cross of Christ be emptied of its power." It is as though he were saying: "I would not be willing to remove the stumbling block and the cross of Christ." Here someone

---

[36] Cf. the fuller explanation of this on pp. 83 f.

may say: "Christians must be quite insane if they expose themselves to dangers voluntarily. For all they accomplish with their preaching is to gain for themselves the anger and hatred of the world and to create stumbling blocks. And that, as the saying goes, is laboring in vain and simply looking for trouble."[37] "This fact," says Paul, "does not offend or bother us at all; it only makes us courageous and optimistic about the success and growth of the church, which flourishes and grows under persecution." For Christ, the Head and the Bridegroom of the church, must "rule in the midst of His foes" (Ps. 110:2). On the other hand, when the cross and the raging of tyrants and heretics have been removed, and the stumbling blocks have come to an end, and when the devil "guards his own palace, and his goods are in peace" (Luke 11:21), this is a sure sign that the pure teaching of the Word has been taken away.

Bernard had this in mind when he said that the church is in the best position when it is under pressure on every side from the power and craft of Satan, and that it is in the worst position when it is most at peace. By a fine use of catachresis he cites this statement from the canticle of Hezekiah (Is. 38:17): "Lo, in peace was my greatest bitterness" and put it into the mouth of the church when it is living in security and peace.[38] Therefore Paul regards it as a sure sign that what is being preached is not the Gospel if the preaching goes on without its peace being disturbed. On the other hand, the world regards it as a sure sign that the Gospel is a heretical and seditious doctrine when it sees that the preaching of the Gospel is followed by great upheavals, disturbances, offenses, sects, etc. Thus God wears the mask of the devil, and the devil wears the mask of God; God wants to be recognized under the mask of the devil, and He wants the devil to be condemned under the mask of God.

The term "stumbling block of the cross" may be understood either actively or passively. The cross immediately follows the teaching of the Word, in accordance with the statement of Ps. 116:10: "I believed; therefore I have spoken. But I am greatly afflicted." Now the cross of Christians is ignominious and merciless persecution; therefore it is a great stumbling block. To begin with, they suffer as though they

---

[37] This was a common argument of the pagan critics of Christianity; cf. Arnobius, *Against the Pagans*, II, 76.

[38] On the meaning of "catachresis" cf. *Luther's Works*, 12, p. 346, note 16.

were the vilest scoundrels. The prophet Isaiah predicted this about Christ Himself (53:12): "He was numbered with the transgressors." In addition, the punishments of thieves and criminals are commuted, and people are touched by pity toward them, so that there is no stumbling block connected with the punishment. But because the world regards Christians as dangerous men, it believes that no punishment that can be inflicted on them is severe enough. Nor is it touched by any pity toward them, but it imposes the most shameful kind of death on them. By this means it seeks to gain a dual advantage: first, it offers service to God by killing them (John 16:2); and secondly, it hopes to reestablish public peace by getting rid of these nuisances. Thus the cross and death of the godly are filled with stumbling blocks. "Do not let that bother you," says Paul, "the inhuman treatment and the continuance of the cross and of the stumbling block, but rather let it encourage you; for as long as these things continue, the Christian cause is doing very well."

Christ also comforts His followers in this way in Matt. 5:11-12: "Blessed are you when men revile you and persecute you and utter all kinds of evil against you falsely on My account. Rejoice and be glad, for your reward is great in heaven; for so men persecuted the prophets who were before you." The church will not permit this joy to be taken away from it. Therefore I would not want the pope, the bishops, the princes, and the fanatical spirits to be in accord with us; for such accord would be a sure sign that we had lost the true doctrine. In short, the church must suffer persecution because it teaches the Gospel purely. The Gospel proclaims the mercy and the glory of God; it discloses the wickedness and the wiles of the devil, portraying him in his true colors and taking away his mask of divine majesty, by which he has made an impression on the whole world. That is, it shows that all the forms of worship, religious ways of life, and monastic orders invented by men, as well as the traditions about celibacy, special foods, etc., by which men think they can gain the forgiveness of sins and justification, are all ungodly things and "doctrines of demons" (1 Tim. 4:1). Thus there is nothing that vexes the devil more than the proclamation of the Gospel; for this takes away from him the mask of God and shows him up for what he is, not God but the devil. Therefore it is unavoidable that when the Gospel flourishes, the stumbling block of the cross will follow; otherwise it is sure that the devil has not really been attacked but has only been gently caressed. If he is really attacked, he does not remain quiet but begins to raise a terrible disturbance and to create havoc everywhere.

Therefore if Christians want to keep the Word, they must not be offended or frightened when they see the devil breaking his reins and running wild, or the whole world in tumult, or tyrants in a rage, or sects arising. But they should know for a certainty that these are signs, not of terror but of joy, as Christ interpreted them when He said (Matt. 5:12): "Rejoice and be glad." Therefore may the stumbling block of the cross never be taken away, which is what would happen if we were to preach what the ruler of this world (John 14:30) and his members would like to hear, namely, the righteousness of works; then we would have the devil friendly to us, the world on our side, and the pope and the princes kindly disposed toward us. But because we illumine the blessings and the glory of Christ, they persecute us and rob us of our goods and our very lives.

12. *I wish those who unsettle you would mutilate themselves!*

Is this proper for an apostle, not only to declare that the false apostles are troublemakers, to condemn them, and to hand them over to the devil but even to call evil down upon them and to wish that they would perish and be utterly destroyed — in other words, to curse them? It seems to me that Paul is making an allusion to circumcision, as though he were saying: "They are forcing you to be circumcised. I wish that they themselves would be mutilated from the very foundation and root!"

Here the question arises whether Christians are permitted to curse.[39] Yes, they are permitted to do so, but not always and not for just any reason. But when things come to the point where the Word is about to be cursed or its teaching — and, as a consequence, God Himself — blasphemed, then you must invert your sentence and say: "Blessed be the Word and God! And cursed be anything apart from the Word and from God, whether it be an apostle or an angel from heaven!" Thus Paul says earlier (1:8): "Even if we, or an angel from heaven, etc., let him be accursed." Here one can tell that "a little yeast" was so important to Paul that he even presumed to curse the false apostles, men who gave the appearance of great

---

[39] See the discussion of this in *Luther's Works*, 14, pp. 257—258.

authority. Therefore let us not underestimate the importance of the yeast of doctrine either. No matter how little it is, if it is despised, this causes the eventual loss of truth and salvation, and the denial of God. For when the Word is distorted and, as necessarily follows, when God is denied and blasphemed, there is no hope of salvation left. But if we are the ones who are slandered, cursed, and killed, there is still One who can revive us and set us free from the curse, from death, and from hell.

Therefore let us learn to praise and magnify the majesty and authority of the Word. For it is no trifle, as the fanatics of our day suppose; but one dot (Matt. 5:18) is greater than heaven and earth. Therefore we have no reason here to exercise love or Christian concord, but we simply employ the tribunal; that is, we condemn and curse all those who insult or injure the majesty of the divine Word in the slightest, because (5:9) "a little yeast leavens the whole lump." But if they let us have the Word sound and unimpaired, we are prepared not only to exercise charity and concord toward them but to offer ourselves as their slaves and to do anything for them. But if they refuse, let them perish and be banished to hell, and not only they themselves but the whole world with all its godly and ungodly inhabitants, just as long as God remains; for if He remains, life and salvation remain, and so do the truly godly.

Therefore Paul acts properly when he curses these troublemakers and pronounces the sentence that they are accursed along with everything they are or teach or do, and when he calls down upon them the evil that they may be cut off from this life, and especially from the church, that is, that God may not govern and prosper their teaching and all their actions. This curse proceeds from the Holy Spirit. Thus in Acts 8:20 Peter curses Simon: "Your silver perish with you!" The use of curses is frequent in Holy Scripture against those who disturb the Spirit this way, especially in the Psalms. Thus in Ps. 55:15: "Let death come upon them; let them go down to hell alive." And again (Ps. 9:17): "The wicked shall depart to hell."

Up to this point Paul has been reinforcing the doctrine of justification with powerful arguments. Now, in order not to skip anything, he has interspersed the discussion with rebukes, commendations, exhortations, and warnings. At the end he has added the example of himself, his own suffering of persecution on account of this doctrine. In this way he warned the faithful not to be offended or frightened but to rejoice and be glad if they see tumults, stumbling blocks, and sects arise during the age of the Gospel. For the more violently the world rages against the Gospel, the better the position of the Gospel is.

This should be a very pleasant comfort for us. For it is sure that the world hates and persecutes us for no other reason than that we present the truth of the Gospel. It does not accuse us of being thieves, adulterers, murderers, etc.; but what it despises in us is solely this, that we teach Christ faithfully and purely, and that we do not forsake the heritage of the truth. Therefore we should know for certain that our doctrine is holy and divine, because the world hates it so bitterly. Otherwise there is no doctrine too wicked, stupid, ridiculous, or dangerous for the world to accept it, embrace and defend it gladly, in fact, to treat it reverently, support it, fawn upon it, and convert everyone to it. The teaching of godliness, life, and salvation, together with its ministers, is the only one that it despises and treats in an utterly shameful way. This is evident proof that the world is angry with us only because of its hatred of the Word. Therefore when our opponents raise the objection against us that our doctrine produces nothing but war, sedition, stumbling blocks, sects, and endless other evils, let us reply: "Blessed be the day when it becomes possible to see all this! But the whole world is in an uproar. All right. If it were not in an uproar, and if the devil were not in such a rage and were not creating such havoc everywhere, we would not have the pure doctrine which such tumults and havoc inevitably follow. Therefore what you think of as evil we regard as the highest good."

Now there follow exhortations and commandments about good morals. For the apostle makes it a habit, after the teaching of faith and the instruction of consciences, to introduce some commandments about morals, by which he exhorts the believers to practice the duties of godliness toward one another. Even reason understands and imparts this part of his teaching to some extent, but it knows nothing at all about the teaching of faith. Therefore to avoid the impression that Christian teaching undermines good morals and conflicts with political order, the apostle also admonishes about good morals and about honest outward conduct, the observance of love and harmony, etc. Thus the world has no right to accuse Christians of undermining good morals or of disturbing public peace and respectability; for they teach morals and all the virtues better than any philosophers or teachers, because they add faith.

13. *For you were called to freedom, brethren; only do not use your freedom as an opportunity for the flesh, but through love be servants of one another.*

It is as though Paul were saying: "Now you have obtained freedom through Christ. That is, you are far above all laws, both in your own conscience and in the sight of God; you are blessed and saved; Christ is your life. Therefore even though the Law, sin, and death may frighten you, they can neither harm you nor cause you to despair. This is your brilliant and inestimable freedom. Now it is up to you to be diligently on your guard not to use your freedom as an opportunity for the flesh."

This evil is very widespread, and it is the worst of all the evils that Satan arouses against the teaching of faith: that in many people he soon transforms the freedom for which Christ has set us free into an opportunity for the flesh. Jude complains of this same thing in his epistle (ch. 4): "Admission has been secretly gained by some ungodly persons who pervert the grace of our God into licentiousness." For the flesh simply does not understand the teaching of grace, namely, that we are not justified by works but by faith alone, and that the Law has no jurisdiction over us. Therefore when it hears this teaching, it transforms it into licentiousness and immediately draws the inference: "If we are without the Law, then let us live as we please. Let us not do good, let us not give to the needy; much less do we have to endure anything evil. For there is no Law to compel or bind us."

Thus there is a danger on both sides, although the one is more tolerable than the other. If grace or faith is not preached, no one is saved; for faith alone justifies and saves. On the other hand, if faith is preached, as it must be preached, the majority of men understand the teaching about faith in a fleshly way and transform the freedom of the spirit into the freedom of the flesh. This can be discerned today in all classes of society, both high and low. They all boast of being evangelicals and boast of Christian freedom. Meanwhile, however, they give in to their desires and turn to greed, sexual desire, pride, envy, etc. No one performs his duty faithfully; no one serves another by love. This misbehavior often makes me so impatient that I would want such "swine that trample pearls underfoot" (Matt. 7:6) still to be under the tyranny of the pope. For it is impossible for this people of Gomorrah to be ruled by the Gospel of peace.

What is more, we ourselves, who teach the Word, do not perform our own duty with as much care and zeal here in the light of truth as we used to in the darkness of ignorance. The more certain we are about the freedom granted to us by Christ, the more unresponsive and slothful we are in presenting the Word, praying, doing good works, enduring evil, and the like. And if Satan were not troubling us inwardly with spiritual trials and outwardly with persecution by our enemies and with the contempt and ingratitude of our own followers, we would become utterly smug, lazy, and useless for anything good; thus in time we would lose the knowledge of Christ and faith in Him, would forsake the ministry of the Word, and would look for some more comfortable way of life, more suitable to our flesh. This is what many of our followers are beginning to do, motivated by the fact that those who labor in the Word not only do not get their support from this but are even treated shamefully by those whom their preaching of the Gospel has set free from the miserable slavery of the pope. Forsaking the poor and offensive figure of Christ, they involve themselves in the business of this present life; and they serve, not Christ but their own appetites (Rom. 16:18), with results that they will experience in due time.

We know that the devil lies in wait especially for us who have the Word — he already holds the others captive to his will — and that he is intent upon taking the freedom of the Spirit away from us or at least making us change it into license. Therefore we teach and exhort our followers with great care and diligence, on the basis of Paul's example, not to think that this freedom of the Spirit, achieved by the death of Christ, was given [40] to them as an opportunity for the flesh or, as Peter says, "to use as a pretext for evil" (1 Peter 2:16), but for them to be servants of one another through love.

As we have said, therefore, the apostle imposes an obligation on Christians through this law about mutual love in order to keep them from abusing their freedom. Therefore the godly should remember that for the sake of Christ they are free in their conscience before God from the curse of the Law, from sin, and from death, but that according to the body they are bound; here each must serve the other through love, in accordance with this commandment of Paul. Therefore let everyone strive to do his duty in his calling and to help his

[40] For the reading *donatum* in the Weimar text we have substituted *donatam*.

neighbor in whatever way he can. This is what Paul requires of us with the words "through love be servants of one another," which do not permit the saints to run free according to the flesh but subject them to an obligation.

Of course, it is impossible to teach or persuade unspiritual people of this teaching about the love to be mutually observed among us. Christians comply with it voluntarily. But when the others hear this freedom proclaimed, they immediately draw the inference: "If I am free, then I have the right to do whatever I please. This thing belongs to me; why should I not sell it for as much as I can? Again, if we do not obtain salvation on account of good works, why should we give anything to the poor?" In their great smugness such people shrug off this yoke and obligation of the flesh, and they transform the freedom of the Spirit into the license and lust of the flesh. Although they will not believe us but will make fun of us, we make this sure announcement to these smug despisers: If they use their bodies and their powers for their own lusts — as they are certainly doing when they refuse to help the poor and to share, but defraud their brethren in business and acquire things by fair means or foul — then they are not free, as they loudly claim to be, but have lost both Christ and freedom, and are slaves of the devil, so that now, under the title of "Christian freedom," their state is seven times as bad as it used to be under the tyranny of the pope (Matt. 12:43-45). For when the devil who has been cast out of them returns to them, he brings with him seven spirits more evil than himself. Therefore their last state becomes worse than the first.

We for our part have the divine command to preach the Gospel, which announces to all men, if only they believe, the free gift of freedom from the Law, from sin, from death, and from the wrath of God, for the sake of Christ. We have neither the intention nor the authority to conceal this freedom or to obscure and cancel it once it has been made public through the Gospel; for Christ has granted it to us and has achieved it by His death. Nor are we able to compel those swine, who are rushing headlong into the license of the flesh, to be servants of others with their bodies and their possessions. Therefore we do what we can. That is, we diligently admonish them that this is what they should do. If we do not accomplish anything with these warnings of ours, we commit the matter to God, to whom it belongs anyway. In His own time He will inflict just punishment on them. Meanwhile, however, we are comforted by the fact that our labor and our diligence are not in vain among the godly, many of whom have undoubtedly been rescued by our ministry from the slavery of the devil and have been transferred to the freedom of the Spirit. These few — who acknowledge the glory of this freedom, who at the same time are ready to be the servants of others through love, and who know that according to the flesh they are debtors to the brethren — give us a happiness that is greater than the sadness that can be caused by the infinite number of those who abuse this freedom.

Paul speaks in clear and precise terms when he says: "You were called to freedom." To prevent anyone from imagining that he means the freedom of the flesh, he explains himself and says what kind of freedom he has in mind: "Only do not use your freedom as an opportunity for the flesh, but through love be servants of one another." Therefore every Christian should know that in his conscience he has been established by Christ as a lord over the Law, sin, and death, and that they do not have jurisdiction over him. On the other hand, he should know also that this external obligation has been imposed on his body, that through love he should serve his neighbor. Those who understand Christian freedom differently are enjoying the advantages of the Gospel to their own destruction and are worse idolaters under the name "Christian" than they used to be under the pope. Now Paul shows beautifully on the basis of the Decalog what it means to be a servant through love.

14. *For the whole Law, etc.*

Once Paul has laid the foundation of Christian doctrine, he usually "builds on the foundation with gold, silver, and precious stones" (1 Cor. 3:12). Now, as he says to the Corinthians (1 Cor. 3:11), "no other foundation can anyone lay" than Jesus Christ or the righteousness of Christ. On this foundation he now builds good works, and truly good ones, all of which he includes in the brief commandment: "You shall love your neighbor, etc." It is as though he were saying: "When I say that through love you should be servants of one another, I mean what the Law says elsewhere (Lev. 19:18): 'You shall love your neighbor as yourself.'" This is the real way to interpret Scripture and the commandments of God. The notion that the sophists have about the word "love" is completely cold and vain. They say that "to love" means nothing else than to wish someone well, or that love is a quality inhering in the mind by which a person elicits the motivation in his heart or the action which they call "wishing well." [41] This is a completely bare, meager, and mathematical love, which does not become incarnate, so to speak, and does not go to work. By contrast, Paul says that love should be a servant, and that unless it is in the position of a servant, it is not love.

But while Paul is giving commands about love, he simultaneously reproaches the false teachers in passing. He aims his arrows at them in order to defend and support his doctrine of works against them, as though he were saying: "Up to this point, my dear Galatians, I have been teaching you about true spiritual life. Now I shall teach you about truly good works, to make you recognize that the silly and fanatical ceremonial works, which are all that the false apostles insist on, are far inferior to the true works of love." The wild insanity of all wicked teachers and fanatical spirits is such that they not only forsake the true foundation of pure and sound doctrine but never even attain to truly good works, because they cling to their superstitions. Therefore, as Paul says (1 Cor. 3:12), they merely "build on the foundation with wood, hay, and stubble." Thus the false apostles, who were such vigorous defenders of works, did not teach or insist that works of love were to be performed, that Christians were to love one another, and that they should be ready to lend their aid to their neighbors in any need, not only with their possessions but also with their whole body, that is, with their lips, hands, heart, and all their powers. All they insisted on was that circumcision be observed and that special days and months be observed, and they were unable to teach any other good works. For once Christ, the foundation, has been destroyed and the doctrine of faith has been obscured, it is impossible for any true use, practice, or idea of good works to continue. When a tree has been chopped down, its fruit must also perish.

The sectarians today have similar delusions about the doctrine of good works; therefore it is inevitable that they should teach fanatical and superstitious works. They have abandoned Christ, chopped down the tree, and subverted the foundation. Therefore they build on the sand (Matt. 7:26) and cannot build anything except wood, hay, and stubble (1 Cor. 3:12). They make a magnificent show of love, humility, and the like. But in fact, as John says (1 John 3:18), they do not

---

[41] See the representative discussion in Thomas Aquinas, *Summa Theologica*, II-II, Q. 25—26.

love in deed and in truth but in word and speech. They also make a pretense of great sanctity, and by this pretense of sanctity they impress people into supposing that their works are wonderful and are pleasing to God. But if you shine the light of the Word on them, you will discover that they are mere trifles having to do with silly and meaningless matters. All they deal with are special places, seasons, vestments, partiality among persons, etc. Therefore it is as necessary that faithful preachers urge good works as that they urge the doctrine of faith. For Satan is enraged by both and bitterly resists them. Nevertheless, faith must be implanted first; for without it one cannot understand what a good work is and what is pleasing to God.

Satan's hatred for truly good works is evident also from this: All men have a certain natural knowledge implanted in their minds (Rom. 2:14-15), by which they know naturally that one should do to others what he wants done to himself (Matt. 7:12). This principle and others like it, which we call the law of nature, are the foundation of human law and of all good works. Nevertheless, human reason is so corrupted and blinded by the malice of the devil that it does not understand this inborn knowledge; or, even if it has been admonished by the Word of God, it deliberately neglects and despises it. So great is the power of Satan! To this there is added another evil, namely, that the devil makes all the self-righteous and the heretics so insane that they overlook the doctrine of truly good works and, instead, insist on childish ceremonies or certain ostentatious works that they themselves have invented. A reason that is ignorant of faith will glorify these works and take great pleasure in them.

Thus under the papacy people used to perform those foolish and meaningless works, neither commanded nor demanded by God, with the utmost pleasure, diligence, and zeal, and at great cost. We recognize this same zeal for meaningless things in the sectarians of our day and in their disciples, especially in the Anabaptists. But in our churches, where the true doctrine of good works is set forth with great diligence, it is amazing how much sluggishness and lack of concern prevails. The more we exhort and arouse our people to do good works, to practice love toward one another, and to get rid of their concern for the stomach, the more lazy and listless they become for any practice of godliness. Therefore Satan violently hates and hinders the doctrine, not only about faith but also about good works;

in our midst he seeks to keep our people from learning it or, if they know it, from living up to it in their deeds; beyond our group the hypocrites and heretics neglect it completely, and in its place they teach foolish ceremonies or silly and fanatical works, by which unspiritual men are easily swayed. For the world is ruled, not by the Gospel and faith but by the Law and superstition.

Therefore the apostle admonishes Christians seriously, after they have heard and accepted the pure doctrine about faith, to practice genuine works as well. For in the justified there remain remnants of sin, which deter and dissuade them both from faith and from truly good works. In addition, the human reason and flesh, which resists the Spirit in the saints (in the wicked, of course, it has dominant control), is naturally afflicted with Pharisaic superstitions and, as Ps. 4:2 says, "loves vain words and seeks after lies"; that is, it would prefer to measure God by its own theories rather than by His Word and is far more ardent about doing works that it itself has chosen than about doing those that God commands. This is why faithful preachers must exert themselves as much in urging a love that is unfeigned or in urging truly good works as in teaching true faith. Therefore let no one think that he knows this commandment, "You shall love your neighbor," perfectly. It is very short, and so far as its words are concerned, it is very easy. But show me the preachers and hearers who truly practice and produce it in their teaching and living. I see both groups taking it easy! Thus the words "Through love be servants of one another" and "You shall love your neighbor as yourself" are eternal words, which no one can adequately ponder, teach, and practice. It is amazing that godly people have this trial: their conscience is immediately wounded if they omit some trifling thing that they should have done, but not if, as happens every day, they neglect Christian love and do not act toward their neighbor with a sincere and brotherly heart. They do not put as high an estimate on the commandment of love as they do on their own superstitions, from which they are never completely free in this life.

Therefore Paul is chiding the Galatians with the words "The whole Law is fulfilled in one word." It is as though he were saying: "You are fine people! You are immersed in your superstitions and ceremonies about special places, seasons, and foods, which are of no benefit either to you or to anyone else; meanwhile you neglect love, which is the only thing that has to be observed. How insane you are!"

Thus Jerome also says: "We punish our bodies with vigils, fasts, and labors; but we neglect love, which is the lord and master of all works." [42] This is especially evident in the monks. They rigidly observe their traditions about ceremonies, food, and clothing; if someone neglects anything here, be it ever so small, he commits a mortal sin. But they are not the least bit frightened by the fact that they not only neglect love but even hate one another bitterly.

With this commandment, therefore, Paul not only teaches good works but condemns fanatical and superstitious works. He not only "builds on the foundation with gold, silver, and precious stones" (1 Cor. 3:12), but he also destroys the wood and burns out the hay and stubble. It was indeed an act of generosity when God gave many ceremonies to the Jews. Thereby He wanted to indicate that the human mind, which was naturally superstitious, did not care about love at all but was fascinated by ceremonies and took pleasure in the righteousness of the flesh. Meanwhile, however, God testified by specific examples, even in the Old Testament, how important love always was to Him; for He wanted the Law and all its ceremonies always to yield to love. When David and his companions were hungry and did not have anything to eat, they ate the holy bread, which, according to the Law, not laymen but only priests were permitted to eat (1 Sam. 21:6). Similarly, the disciples violated the Sabbath by plucking ears of grain (Matt. 12:1). And according to the interpretation of the Jews, Christ Himself violated the Sabbath by healing the sick on the Sabbath (Luke 13:14). All this shows that love is much to be preferred to all laws and ceremonies, and that God does not require anything of us as much as love toward our neighbor. Christ testifies to this when He says (Matt. 22:39): "And a second is like it."

14. *For the whole Law is fulfilled in one word: You shall love your neighbor as yourself.*

It is as though Paul were saying: "Why are you burdening yourselves with the Law? Why do you so anxiously strain and vex yourselves with the ceremonial laws about foods, seasons, special places, etc., and with the proper way of eating, drinking, keeping festival, and performing sacrifices? Forget about this nonsense, and listen to what I am saying! The whole Law is completely summarized in this

---

[42] Jerome, *Commentarius in Epistolam S. Pauli ad Galatas, Patrologia, Series Latina,* XXVI, 437.

one word: 'You shall love your neighbor as yourself.' God certainly takes no pleasure in this observance of ceremonial laws; nor does He need it. But this is what He now requires of you: that you believe in Christ, whom He Himself has sent. Then you will be made perfect in Him and will have everything. Now if to faith, the worship that is most pleasing to God, you want to add laws, then you should know that in this very brief commandment, 'You shall love your neighbor as yourself,' all laws are included. Strive to observe this commandment; for if you observe it, you will fulfill all the laws."

Paul is an outstanding interpreter of the commandments of God. For he compresses all of Moses into a very brief summary and shows that in all his laws, which are almost endless, nothing is contained except this very brief word: "You shall love your neighbor as yourself." Reason, of course, is offended at this stinginess and paucity of words, when it is stated so briefly "Believe in Christ" and "You shall love your neighbor as yourself." Therefore it despises both the doctrine of faith and the doctrine of truly good works. To those who have faith, however, this stingy and paltry phrase "Believe in Christ" is the power of God (Rom. 1:16), by which they overcome sin, death, and the devil, and obtain salvation. So also serving another person through love seems to reason to mean performing unimportant works such as the following: teaching the erring; comforting the afflicted; encouraging the weak; helping the neighbor in whatever way one can; bearing with his rude manners and impoliteness; putting up with annoyances, labors, and the ingratitude and contempt of men in both church and state; obeying the magistrates; treating one's parents with respect; being patient in the home with a cranky wife and an unmanageable family, and the like. But believe me, these works are so outstanding and brilliant that the whole world cannot comprehend their usefulness and worth; indeed, it cannot estimate the value of even one tiny truly good work, because it does not measure works or anything else on the basis of the Word of God but on the basis of a reason that is wicked, blind, and foolish.

Therefore men are completely mistaken when they imagine that they really understand the commandment to love. They have it written in their hearts, of course, because by nature they judge that one should do to others what one wants done to oneself (Matt. 7:12). But it does not follow that they understand this. For if they did, they would demonstrate it in their actions and would prefer love to all other works. Nor would they exaggerate and inflate their own childish toys, that is, such nonsense and superstition as this: walking around with a sour face and a downcast head, living a celibate life, subsisting on bread and water, dwelling in the desert, wearing dirty clothes, and the like. These unnatural and superstitious works, which they decide upon without either the command or the approval of God, they regard as so brilliant and saintly as to surpass and obscure love, which is the sun that outshines all works. The blindness of human reason is so incomprehensible and infinite that it cannot form sound judgments even about life and works, much less about the doctrine of faith. Therefore we must battle unremittingly not only against the opinions of our own heart, on which by nature we would rather depend in the matter of salvation than on the Word of God, but also against the false front and saintly appearance of self-chosen works. Thus we shall learn to praise the works that each man performs in his calling — even though in external appearance they appear to be trivial and contemptible — provided that they have been commanded by God, and, on the other hand, to despise the works that reason decides upon without a commandment from God, regardless of how brilliant, important, great, or saintly they seem to be.

Elsewhere I have expounded this commandment carefully and at greater length; [43] therefore I am discussing it quite briefly here. It is a brief statement, expressed beautifully and forcefully: "You shall love your neighbor as yourself." No one can find a better, surer, or more available pattern than himself; nor can there be a nobler or more profound attitude of the mind than love; nor is there a more excellent object than one's neighbor. Therefore the pattern, the attitude, and the object are all superb. Thus if you want to know how the neighbor is to be loved and want to have an outstanding pattern of this, consider carefully how you love yourself. In need or in danger you would certainly want desperately to be loved and assisted with all the counsels, resources, and powers not only of all men but of all creation. And so you do not need any book to instruct and admonish you how you should love your neighbor, for you have the loveliest and best of books about all laws right in your own heart. You do not need any professor to tell you about this matter; merely consult your own heart, and it will give you abundant instruction

---

[43] One exposition of this commandment is in Luther's sermon on the Gospel for the Eighteenth Sunday After Trinity (W, X-1-II, 399—409).

that you should love your neighbor as you love yourself. What is more, love is the highest virtue. It is ready to be of service not only with its tongue, its hands, its money, and its abilities but with its body and its very life. It is neither called forth by anything that someone deserves nor deterred by what is undeserving and ungrateful. A mother cherishes and cares for her child simply because she loves him.

Finally, no creature toward which you should practice love is nobler than your neighbor. He is not a devil, not a lion or a bear or a wolf, not a stone or a log. He is a living creature very much like you. There is nothing living on earth that is more pleasant, more lovable, more helpful, kinder, more comforting, or more necessary. Besides, he is naturally suited for a civilized and social existence. Thus nothing could be regarded as worthier of love in the whole universe than our neighbor. But such is the amazing craft of the devil that he is able not only to remove this noble object of love from my mind with great skill but even to persuade my heart of the exactly opposite opinion, so that it regards the neighbor as worthy, not of love but of the bitterest hatred. He can accomplish this very easily, merely by suggesting to me: "Look, this man suffers from such and such a fault. He has chided you. He has done you damage." Immediately this most lovable of objects becomes vile, so that my neighbor no longer seems to be someone who should be loved but an enemy deserving of bitter hatred. In this way Satan can do an amazing job of making the attitude of love in our hearts cold and neglectful; in fact, he can extinguish it completely, so that we forget our love for our neighbor and yield only to our base desires. In addition, there are our superstition and negligence, as well as the offenses committed by our neighbors, which transform us completely from lovers into haters. Thus all that is left to us of this commandment are the naked and meaningless letters and syllables "You shall love your neighbor as yourself."

Thus we do not believe, much less observe, the meaning of this commandment. Now our neighbor is any human being, especially one who needs our help, as Christ interprets it in Luke 10:30-37. Even one who has done me some sort of injury or harm has not shed his humanity on that account or stopped being flesh and blood, a creature of God very much like me; in other words, he does not stop being my neighbor. Therefore as long as human nature remains in him, so long the commandment of love remains in force, requiring of me that I not despise my own flesh and not return evil for evil but overcome evil with good (Rom. 12:21). Otherwise love will never "bear, endure," etc. (1 Cor. 13:7). It does not amputate a diseased limb but cherishes it and takes care of it. "And those parts of the body which we think less honorable," Paul says (1 Cor. 12:23), "we invest with the greater honor." But many people are so unmindful of this commandment that even when they know someone who is endowed with many outstanding qualities and virtues, but can find even one little flaw or blemish in him, they will look only at this and will forget all his good qualities and assets. You will find many mockers so inhuman and spiteful that they do not refer to the objects of their malice by their proper names but describe them with some contemptuous nickname like "Cockeyed" or "Hooknose" or "Bigmouth." [44] In short, the world is the kingdom of the devil, which, in its supreme smugness, despises faith and love and all the words and deeds of God.

This is why Paul commends love to the Galatians and to all Christians, and exhorts them through love to be servants of one another. It is as though he were saying: "There is no need to burden you with circumcision and the ceremonies of Moses. But above all persevere in the doctrine of faith, which you have received from me. Afterwards, if you want to do good works, I will show you in one word the highest and greatest works, and the way to keep all the laws: Be devoted to one another through love. You will not lack for people to help, for the world is full of people who need the help of others." This is the perfect doctrine of both faith and love. It is also the shortest and the longest kind of theology — the shortest so far as words and sentences are concerned; but in practice and in fact it is wider, longer, deeper, and higher than the whole world.

15. *But if you bite and devour one another, take heed that you are not consumed by one another.*

With these words Paul testifies that there can be no peace or concord in the churches, either in thought or in life, if the foundation, that is, the doctrine of faith, is undermined by wicked teachers; but that immediately there will arise some dissension and notion or other over doctrine, faith, and works. Once the concord of the church has

[44] Terence, *Eunuchus*, III, 5, 53.

been violated, there is neither limit nor end to this evil. The authors of the schism disagree among themselves, with one demanding this work as necessary for righteousness and the other demanding another work. Everyone supports his own notion and superstition but rejects that of another. Here it is inevitable that parties and factions arise, which then bite and devour one another, that is, judge and condemn, until finally they are all consumed. In addition to Scripture, this is demonstrated by the example of all ages in history. When Africa had been overthrown by the Manicheans, the Donatists soon followed. They disagreed among themselves and were split into three sects.[45] In our own time the Sacramentarians were the first to defect from us; then the Anabaptists, none of whom are in agreement with one another. Thus a sect always produces other sects, and one condemns the others. According to the mathematicians, beyond the unit there is an infinite progression of numbers. Thus if the unity of the Spirit is injured and destroyed, it is impossible for concord to remain either in doctrine or in morals; but in both areas new errors will go on arising into infinity. We saw this very well under the papacy. Because the doctrine of faith lay neglected, it was impossible for the concord of the Spirit to remain. When this was removed by the doctrine of works, almost endless sects of monks arose. They rivaled one another in measuring their sanctity on the basis of the strictness of their orders and the difficulty of the superstitious works they themselves had thought up. On this basis they wanted to be regarded as saintlier than the others. In addition, monks not only of differing orders but even of the same order disagreed with one another. One Minorite would envy another, as one potter envies another.[46] Ultimately there were as many different opinions in any monastery as there were monks. Therefore they nourished rivalries, contention, quarrels, virulence, backbiting, and devouring back and forth in their midst so long that finally, in accordance with this saying of Paul's, they were consumed.

But those who accept the doctrine of faith and, in accordance with this commandment of Paul's, love one another do not criticize someone else's way of life and works; but each one approves the way of life of another and the duties which the other performs in

[45] Thus among the Donatists there arose the Rogatists, the Maximianists, and the Claudianists.

[46] The saying *Ut figulus figulo* sounds proverbial.

his vocation. No godly person believes that the position of a magistrate is better in the sight of God than that of a subject, for he knows that both are divine institutions and have a divine command behind them. He will not distinguish between the position or work of a father and that of a son, or between that of a teacher and that of a pupil, or between that of a master and that of a servant; but he will declare it as certain that both are pleasing to God if they are done in faith and in obedience to God. In the eyes of the world, of course, these ways of life and their positions are unequal; but this outward inequality does not in any way hinder the unity of spirit, in which they all think and believe the same thing about Christ, namely, that through Him alone we obtain the forgiveness of sins and righteousness. As for outward behavior and position in the world, one person does not judge another or criticize his works or praise his own, even if they are superior; but with one set of lips and one spirit they confess that they have one and the same Savior, Christ, before whom there is no partiality toward either persons or works (Rom. 2:11).

This is impossible for those who neglect the doctrine of faith and love and who teach superstitious works. A monk does not concede that the works which a layman performs in his calling are as good and acceptable to God as his own. A nun thinks much more highly of her own way of life and of her own works than she does of the way of life and works of a housewife who has a husband; for she believes that her own works merit grace and eternal life, but that the works of the other woman do not. And for this reason such men, in their wicked greed for gold,[47] battled furiously. They also persuaded the world that their station in life and their works were much greater and holier than the station and works of laymen. If they themselves did not accept and support this notion of the sanctity of their works to this very day, they would not have preserved their eminent position and their authority for very long. Therefore you will never persuade a monk or any other self-righteous person, whoever he may be, that the works of an ordinary Christian, done in faith and in obedience to God, are better and more acceptable to God than those superstitious and marvelous works of his, which he himself has invented. For once the foundation has been undermined, work-righteous people cannot help concluding that the true saints are they themselves, who perform such grand and brilliant works

---

[47] An allusion to Vergil, *Aeneid*, III, 56.

and who, as the Anabaptists imagine today, suffer need, hunger, cold, and tattered clothing, rather than those others who own property, etc. Therefore it is impossible for them to be at peace with those who do not agree with their opinions, but they will bite and devour them.

By contrast, Paul teaches that such occasions for discord are to be avoided; and he shows how they can be avoided. "The way to achieve concord," he says, "is this: Let each do his duty in that way of life into which God has called him. Let him not exalt himself above others or criticize the works of others while he praises his own as though they were better, but let them be servants of one another through love." This is the plain and simple doctrine of good works. Those who "have made shipwreck of their faith" (1 Tim. 1:19) and who have acquired fanatical opinions about faith and about life or works do not do this. They immediately come to disagreement among themselves about the doctrine of faith and of works, and they bite and devour one another; that is, they accuse and condemn, as Paul says about the Galatians here: "If you bite and devour one another." It is as though he were saying: "Do not accuse and condemn one another on account of circumcision or on account of the observance of holidays or of other ceremonies. Instead, act in such a way that you are servants of one another through love. Otherwise, if you persist in biting and devouring one another, take heed that you are not consumed, that is, that you do not perish altogether, even physically." This is what happens nearly always, especially to the originators of sects, as it happened to Arius and others, and to some in our own time.[48] For he who lays his foundation in the sand (Matt. 7:26) and who builds upon it with wood, hay, and stubble (1 Cor. 3:12) will inevitably be destroyed and consumed; for all these things are ready for the fire. It goes without saying that such biting and devouring are usually followed by the destruction not only of a single city but of entire regions and kingdoms. Now he interprets what it means to be a servant of one's neighbor through love.

It is difficult and dangerous to teach that we are justified by faith without works and yet to require works at the same time. Unless the ministers of Christ are faithful and prudent here and are "stewards of the mysteries of God" (1 Cor. 4:1), who rightly divide the Word

---

[48] This may be a covert attack on Zwingli, for Luther believed that a theology which had begun as a rejection of the doctrine of the real presence in the Lord's Supper had ended as a repudiation of the Gospel itself.

of truth (2 Tim. 2:15), they will immediately confuse faith and love at this point. Both topics, faith and works, must be carefully taught and emphasized, but in such a way that they both remain within their limits. Otherwise, if works alone are taught, as happened under the papacy, faith is lost. If faith alone is taught, unspiritual men will immediately suppose that works are not necessary.

Earlier the apostle began to exhort them to good works and to say that the whole Law is fulfilled in one word, namely, "You shall love your neighbor as yourself." Here the thought could occur to someone: "Throughout the epistle Paul is taking righteousness away from the Law. He says (2:16): 'A man is not justified by works of the Law.' And again (3:10): 'All who rely on works of the Law are under a curse.' But now, when he says that the whole Law is fulfilled in one word, he seems to have forgotten the cause he has set forth in this entire epistle and to maintain the exact opposite, namely, that those who do works of love fulfill the Law and are righteous." To this possible objection [49] he replies with the words:

16. *But I say, walk by the Spirit, and do not gratify the desires of the flesh.*

It is as though Paul were saying: "I have not forgotten my earlier discussion of faith. Nor am I retracting it now when I exhort you to mutual love and say that the whole Law is fulfilled in love. I am maintaining the very same thing that I did earlier. To make sure that you understand me properly, I add: 'Walk by the Spirit!'"

Although Paul spoke precisely and distinctly here, it did not do any good. For the sophists took the statement of Paul, "Love is the fulfilling of the Law" (Rom. 13:10), and by misinterpreting it they argued: "If love is the fulfilling of the Law, then love is righteousness. Therefore if we love, we are righteous." These fine fellows argue from the word to the deed, from doctrine or from the commandments to life, as follows: "The Law commands love. Therefore the work follows immediately." It is completely fallacious to argue from commandments and to draw conclusions about works.

Of course, we should keep the Law and be justified by keeping it; but sin gets in the way. The Law prescribes and commands that we love God with all our heart, etc., and our neighbor as ourselves (Matt. 22:37-39); but from this it does not follow: "This is written,

[49] On the meaning of *occupatio* cf. *Luther's Works*, 26, p. 424, note 49.

and therefore it is done; the Law commands love, and therefore we love." You cannot produce anyone on earth who loves God and his neighbor as the Law requires. In the life to come, when we shall be completely cleansed of all our faults and sins and shall be as pure as the sun, we shall love perfectly and shall be righteous through our perfect love. But in this present life such purity is hindered by our flesh, to which sin will cling as long as we live. And thus our corrupt love of ourselves is so powerful that it greatly surpasses our love of God and of our neighbor. Meanwhile, however, to make us righteous also in this present life, we have a Propitiator and a mercy seat, Christ (Rom. 3:25). If we believe in Him, sin is not imputed to us. Therefore faith is our righteousness in this present life. In the life to come, when we shall be thoroughly cleansed and shall be completely free of all sin and fleshly desire, we shall have no further need of faith and hope.

Therefore it is a great error to attribute justification to a love that does not exist or, if it does, is not great enough to placate God; for, as I have said, even the saints love in an imperfect and impure way in this present life, and nothing impure will enter the kingdom of God (Eph. 5:5). But meanwhile we are sustained by the trust that Christ, "who committed no sin and on whose lips no guile was found" (1 Peter 2:22), covers us with His righteousness. Shaded and protected by this covering, this heaven of the forgiveness of sins and this mercy seat, we begin to love and to keep the Law. As long as we live, we are not justified or accepted by God on account of this keeping of the Law. But "when Christ delivers the kingdom to God the Father after destroying every authority" (1 Cor. 15:24), and when "God is everything to everyone" (1 Cor. 15:28), then faith and hope will pass away, and love will be perfect and eternal (1 Cor. 13:8). The sophists do not understand this. Therefore when they hear that love is the summary of the Law, they immediately draw the inference: "Therefore love justifies." Or, on the other hand, when they read in Paul that faith justifies, they add: "that is, when it has been formed by love." But this is not what Paul means, as has been said at length above.[50]

If we were pure of all sin, and if we burned with a perfect love toward God and our neighbor, then we would certainly be righteous and holy through love, and there would be nothing more that God

---

[50] See p. 28, note 22.

could require of us. That does not happen in this present life but must be postponed until the life to come. We do indeed receive the gift and the first fruits of the Spirit here (Rom. 8:23), so that we do begin to love; but this is very feeble. If we loved God truly and perfectly, as the Law requires when it says (Deut. 6:5): "You shall love the Lord your God with all your heart, etc.," then poverty would be as pleasant for us as riches, sorrow the same as pleasure, death the same as life. Indeed, one who loved God truly and perfectly would not be able to live very long but would soon be devoured by his love. But human nature now is so submerged in sin that it cannot think or feel anything correct about God. It does not love God; it hates Him violently. Therefore, as John says (1 John 4:10), "not that we loved God but that He loved us and sent His Son to be the expiation for our sins." And above (2:20): "Christ loved me and gave Himself for me"; and in the fourth chapter (vv. 4-5): "God sent forth His Son, born under the Law, to redeem those, etc." When we have been redeemed and justified through this Son, we begin to love, as Paul says in Rom. 8:3-4, "What the Law could not do, in order that the just requirement of the Law might be fulfilled in us," that is, that it might begin to be fulfilled. Therefore what the sophists taught about the fulfillment of the Law is sheer imagination.

With the words "walk by the Spirit" Paul shows how he wants his earlier statements to be understood: "Through love be servants of one another" (5:13) and "Love is the fulfilling of the Law" (Rom. 13:10). It is as though he were saying: "When I command you to love one another, I am requiring of you that you walk by the Spirit. For I know that you will not fulfill the Law. Because sin clings to you as long as you live, it is impossible for you to fulfill the Law. But meanwhile take careful heed that you walk by the Spirit, that is, that by the Spirit you battle against the flesh and follow your spiritual desires." Thus he has not forgotten the matter of justification. For when he commands them to walk by the Spirit, he clearly denies that works justify. It is as though he were saying: "When I speak about the fulfilling of the Law, I do not intend to say that we are justified by the Law. But what I am saying is that there are two contrary guides in you, the Spirit and the flesh. God has stirred up a conflict and fight in your body. For the Spirit struggles against the flesh, and the flesh against the Spirit. All I am requiring of you now — and, for that matter, all that you are able to produce — is that you follow the guidance of the Spirit and resist the guidance of the flesh. Obey the former, and fight against the latter! Therefore when I teach the Law and urge you on to mutual love, do not suppose that I have retracted the doctrine of faith and am now attributing justification to the Law or to love. What I mean to say is that you should walk by the Spirit and not gratify the desires of the flesh."

Therefore Paul uses his words with precision and care, as though he were saying: "We have not yet attained the fulfillment of the Law. Consequently, we must walk and be exercised by the Spirit, so that we think, say, and do what is of the Spirit and resist what is of the flesh." This is why he adds: "And do not gratify the desires of the flesh." It is as though he were saying: "The desires of the flesh are not yet dead, but they always sprout up to talk back and fight back against the Spirit." No saint has a flesh so holy that when it is offended it would not rather bite and devour or at least subtract something from the commandment of love. Even at the first impact he cannot restrain himself from irritation with his neighbor, a desire for revenge, and hatred for him as though he were an enemy — or at least less love than he should have according to this commandment. This happens even to saints.

Therefore the apostle has established this as a rule for the saints: that they should be servants of one another through love, that they should bear one another's weaknesses and burdens (6:2), and that they should forgive one another's trespasses (Matt. 6:12-15). Without such ἐπιείκεια it is impossible for peace and concord to exist among Christians. It is unavoidable that you are offended frequently and that you offend in turn. You see much in me that offends you; and I, in turn, see much in you that I do not like. If one does not yield to the other through love on matters like this, there will be no end to the argument, discord, rivalry, and hostility. Therefore Paul wants us to walk by the Spirit, so that we do not gratify the desires of the flesh. It is as though he were saying: "Even though you are aroused to anger or envy against an offending brother or against someone who does something unkind to you, still resist and repress these feelings through the Spirit. Bear with his weakness, and love him, in accordance with the command: 'You shall love your neighbor as yourself.' For your brother does not stop being your neighbor simply because he lapses or because he offends you, but that is the very time when he needs your love for him the most.

The commandment 'You shall love your neighbor' makes the same requirement, namely, that you not submit to your flesh — which hates, bites, and devours when it is offended — but that you fight back at it by the Spirit and that through the Spirit you continue in your love for your neighbor, although you may find nothing in him that deserves your love."

The sophists interpret "the desires of the flesh" as sexual desire.[51] It is indeed true that every godly person, especially one who has not yet attained maturity or who lives a celibate life, is subject to sexual desire. So corrupt and unsound is our flesh that not even married people are free of sexual desire. Whoever examines his feelings carefully — and I am speaking now about devout married people of both sexes — will discover that he likes the form or the manner of some other woman more than he does his own. One grows tired of one's lawful wife and loves a woman who is forbidden to him. In everything it happens this way: What a man has, he despises; what he does not have, he loves.

> Of things most forbidden we always are fain:
> And things most denied we seek to obtain.[52]

Thus I do not deny that the desires of the flesh include sexual desire. Yet it includes not only sexual desire but also all the other evil emotions with which godly people are burdened, though some more violently than others, such as pride, hatred, greed, impatience, etc. In fact, a little later Paul enumerates among the works of the flesh not only these coarse vices but also idolatry, party spirit, and the like (5:20), which are emotions that have a better reputation. Thus it is clear that he is speaking about the whole desire of the flesh and the entire realm of sin, which struggles against the realm of the Spirit in the godly, who have received the first fruits of the Spirit (Rom. 8:23). And so he is speaking not only about sexual desire or pride but also about unbelief, distrust, despair, hatred, contempt for God, idolatry, heresy, etc.

It is as though Paul were saying: "I am writing that you should love one another. You do not do this, nor can you do it; for you have the flesh, corrupted as it is by evil desire, which not only arouses sin in you but is itself a sin. Otherwise, if you had perfect love, no sorrow or misfortune would be great enough to disturb it; for it would

---

[51] Cf. Luther's criticism, *Luther's Works*, 13, p. 95.

[52] We have taken over our version of this verse from the English translation of Luther's *Lectures on Galatians* done in the sixteenth century.

be spread throughout your body. No wife would be too ugly for her husband to love her intensely and to lose all interest in other women, even the most beautiful ones. This does not actually happen. Therefore it is impossible for you to be justified by love. Do not think, therefore, that I am retracting my doctrine about faith. Faith and hope must remain, so that we may be justified by the former and encouraged by the latter to persevere in adversity. Finally, we are servants of one another through love, because faith is not idle even though love is tiny and weak. Thus when I command you to walk by the Spirit, I make it abundantly clear that you are not justified by love.

"Moreover, when I say that you should walk by the Spirit and should not obey the flesh or gratify the desires of the flesh, I am not requiring of you that you strip off the flesh completely or kill it, but that you restrain it. God wants the world to endure until the Last Day. This cannot happen unless men are born and reared; and this, in turn, requires that the flesh continue, and consequently also that sin continue, since the flesh cannot be without sin. And so if we look at the flesh, we are sinners; if we look at the Spirit, we are righteous. We are partly sinners and partly righteous. Yet our righteousness is more abundant than our sin, because the holiness and the righteousness of Christ, our Propitiator, vastly surpasses the sin of the entire world. Consequently, the forgiveness of sins, which we have through Him, is so great, so abundant, and so infinite that it easily swallows up every sin, provided that we persevere in faith and hope toward Him."

It must be noted in addition that Paul is writing all this not only to hermits and monks, who lead a celibate life, but to all Christians. I say this to keep us from making the same mistake the papists make. They imagined that this commandment pertained only to the clergy. The apostle exhorts them to walk by the Spirit, that is, to tame and subdue their flesh with vigils, fasts, and labors, and thus to live chastely; and then he tells them not to gratify the desires of the flesh, that is, sexual desire. As though all the desires of the flesh were overcome when sexual desire has been repressed and tamed, even though they have not even been able to repress this by any discipline of the flesh! Not to mention anyone else, Jerome, who was a great champion and defender of chastity, frankly confesses this: "O how often," he says, "I imagined that I was in the midst of the pleasures of Rome when I was stationed in the desert, in that solitary wasteland which is so burned up by the heat of the sun that it provides a dreadful habitation for the monks!" And again: "I, who because of the fear of hell had condemned myself to such a hell and who had nothing but scorpions and wild animals for company, often thought that I was dancing in a chorus with girls. My face was pale from fasting, but my mind burned with passionate desires within my freezing body; and the fires of sex seethed, even though the flesh had already died in me as a man." [53] If Jerome, who subsisted on bread and water in the desert, felt such fires of passion, what do you suppose is felt by the clergy of our day, the worshipers of the god Belly, who stuff and stretch themselves with so many delicacies that it is amazing they do not burst? Thus these words are addressed neither to monks nor only to sinners in the world, but to the church catholic and to all the faithful. They are the ones whom Paul exhorts to walk by the Spirit in order not to gratify the desires of the flesh, that is, to restrain not only the coarse drives of the flesh, such as sexual desire, anger, impatience, etc., but also the "spiritual" ones, such as doubt, blasphemy, idolatry, contempt and hatred of God, etc.

Nor does Paul demand of the faithful that they completely destroy and kill their flesh, but that they control it in such a way that it will be subject to the Spirit. In Rom. 13:14 he commands us to make provision for the flesh.[54] For just as we should not be cruel to other people's bodies or trouble them with unjust requirements, so we should not do this to our own bodies either. According to Paul's command, therefore, we should make provision for our flesh, to enable it to bear the requirements of both the mind and the body; yet he wants us to make provision for it to meet its needs, not "to gratify its desires." Thus if your flesh becomes lascivious, repress it by the Spirit. If it persists, get married! "For it is better to marry than to be aflame with passion" (1 Cor. 7:9). When you do this, you walk by the Spirit; that is, you follow the Word and will of God. As I have said, this commandment about walking by the Spirit pertains not only to hermits and monks but to all the faithful, even if they are not aflame with passion. Thus a prince walks by the Spirit when he does his duty diligently, rules his subjects well, punishes

---

[53] See *Luther's Works*, 22, pp. 266—267.

[54] Apparently Luther is reading the prohibition in Rom. 13:14 as a parallel to Eph. 4:26.

the guilty, and defends the innocent. His flesh and the devil oppose him when he does this, and they urge him to start an unjust war or to yield to his own greedy desires. Unless he follows the Spirit as his guide and obeys the Word of God when it gives him correct and faithful warning about his duty, he will gratify the desires of the flesh.

17. *For the desires of the flesh are against the Spirit, and the desires of the Spirit are against the flesh; for these are opposed to each other, to prevent you from doing what you would.*

When Paul says that the desires of the flesh are against the Spirit, etc., he impresses upon us at the same time that we are to be conscious of the desires of the flesh — not only of sexual desire, that is, but of pride, anger, sadness, impatience, unbelief, etc. But he wants us to be conscious of them in such a way that we do not give in to them or gratify them, that is, that we do not say and do what our flesh impels us to do. Thus when it impels us to anger, we should, as Ps. 4:4 teaches, "be angry" in such a way that we "sin not." It is as though Paul wanted to say: "I know that your flesh impels you to anger, envy, doubt, unbelief, and the like. But resist it by the Spirit, so that you do not sin. But if you forsake the guidance of the Spirit and follow the flesh, you will gratify the desires of the flesh, and you will die" (Rom. 8:13). Thus this statement is to be understood as applying not only to sexual desire but to the whole realm of sin.

I take the words "to prevent you from doing what you would" in the sense of inability, so that it means "so that you are unable to do what you would." This passage shows clearly that Paul is writing this to the saints, that is, to the church which believes in Christ, which is baptized, justified, and regenerated, and which has the forgiveness of sins. Yet he also says that it has a flesh which battles against the Spirit. He speaks about himself the same way in Rom. 7:14: "I am carnal, sold under sin"; again (Rom. 7:23): "I see in my members another law at war with the law of my mind"; and again (Rom. 7:24): "Wretched man that I am!" Here not only the sophists but even some of the fathers exert themselves anxiously to make excuses for Paul; for they regard it as unworthy of a "chosen instrument" of Christ (Acts 9:15) to say that he was sinful.[55] We for our part give credence to Paul's words when he candidly confesses that

---

[55] Cf. Luther's gloss on Rom. 7:10, directed against Lyra and others (W, LVI, 68).

he is sold under sin, is a captive of sin, has a law at war with himself, and serves the law of sin with his flesh. Here they reply that the apostle is saying these things in the name of the wicked. But the wicked do not complain about their rebellion, conflict, and captivity to sin; for sin has powerful dominion over them. Therefore these complaints really belong to Paul and to all the saints. Thus it is not only unwise but even wicked when they make the excuse that Paul and other saints have no sin. For with this notion, which is derived from their ignorance of the doctrine of faith, they have deprived the church of great comfort, have done away with the forgiveness of sins, and have made Christ useless.

Hence Paul is not denying that he has flesh and the faults of the flesh when he says: "I see in my members another law." And so it is not incredible that at one time or another he experienced sexual desire. Yet it is my opinion that it was successfully checked by the many great trials of mind and body with which, as his epistles show, he was continually being disciplined and troubled. Or if in a gay and vigorous mood he became conscious of sexual desire, anger, or impatience, he resisted them by the Spirit and did not permit these feelings to control him. Therefore let us by no means permit such silly glosses to rob us of these extremely comforting passages, in which Paul describes the conflict going on between the flesh and the Spirit in his own body. The sophists and the monks have never experienced spiritual trial. The only battle they have ever carried on has been to repress and overcome sexual desire. This victory made them so proud — although in fact they never managed to control their desire — that they regarded themselves as far better and saintlier than married people. I am not even speaking about the horrible sins of every kind which they nurtured and strengthened by this false appearance: party spirit, pride, hatred, contempt for their neighbor, trust in their own righteousness, presumption, neglect of godliness and of the Word, unbelief, blasphemy, and the like. Against these sins they did not battle; in fact, they did not even think of them as sins. They supposed that righteousness lay only in the observance of their foolish and wicked vows, and that unrighteousness lay in the neglect of these.

But we declare it as a certainty that Christ is our principal, complete, and perfect righteousness.[56] If there is nothing on which we

---

[56] The Latin terms are *capitalis, rotundus,* and *perfectus.*

can depend, still, as Paul says (1 Cor. 13:13), "these three abide: faith, hope, love." Thus we must always believe and love, and we must always take hold of Christ as the Head and the Source of our righteousness. "He who believes in Him will not be put to shame" (Rom. 9:33). In addition, we should take pains to be righteous outwardly as well, that is, not to yield to our flesh, which is always suggesting something evil, but to resist it through the Spirit. We must not be broken up with impatience at the ingratitude and contempt of the rabble, who abuse Christian freedom; but by the Spirit we must overcome these and all other trials. To the extent that by the Spirit we struggle against the flesh, to that extent we are outwardly righteous, even though it is not this righteousness that makes us acceptable in the sight of God.

Therefore let no one despair when he feels his flesh begin another battle against the Spirit, or if he does not succeed immediately in forcing his flesh to be subject to the Spirit. I, too, wish that I had a firmer and more steadfast spirit, one that could not only despise the threats of tyrants, the heresies planted by the fanatical spirits, and other offenses and tumults which they stir up, but could quickly shake off the fears and sorrows of the mind and could even get rid of its fear of the sharpness of death to receive it as a most welcome guest instead. "But I see in my members another law at war with the law of my mind" (Rom. 7:23). Other men struggle with lesser trials, such as poverty, dishonor, impatience, and the like.

No one should be surprised or frightened when he feels this conflict of the flesh against the Spirit in his body, but he should fortify himself with these words of Paul: "The desires of the flesh are against the Spirit" and "These are opposed to each other, to prevent you from doing what you would." With these statements he is comforting those who are undergoing trials, as though he were saying: "It is impossible for you to follow the Spirit as your guide through everything without some awareness of hindrance by the flesh. Your flesh will be an obstacle, the sort of obstacle that will prevent you from doing what you would. Here it is sufficient if you resist the flesh and do not gratify its desires, that is, if you follow the Spirit rather than the flesh, which is easily disturbed by impatience, which seeks revenge, grumbles, hates, bites back, etc." When someone becomes aware of this battle of the flesh, he should not lose heart on this account; but by the Spirit he should fight back and say: "I am a sinner, and I am aware of my sin; for I have not yet put off my flesh, to which sin will cling as long as it lives. But I will obey the Spirit rather than the flesh. That is, by faith and hope I will take hold of Christ. I will fortify myself with His Word, and thus fortified I will refuse to gratify the desires of the flesh."

It is very useful to the faithful to know this doctrine of Paul well and to meditate on it, because it gives wonderful comfort to them in their trial. When I was a monk, I used to think that my salvation was undone when I felt any desires of the flesh, that is, any malice or sexual desire or anger or envy against any of my brothers. I tried many methods. I made confession every day, etc. But none of this did any good, because the desires of the flesh kept coming back. Therefore I could not find peace, but I was constantly crucified by thoughts such as these: "You have committed this or that sin; you are guilty of envy, impatience, etc. Therefore it was useless for you to enter this holy order, and all your good works are to no avail." If I had properly understood Paul's statements, "The desires of the flesh are against the Spirit" and "These are opposed to each other," I would not have tortured myself to such a point but would have thought to myself, as I do nowadays: "Martin, you will never be completely without sin, because you still have the flesh. Therefore you will always be aware of its conflict, according to the statement of Paul: 'The desires of the flesh are against the Spirit.' Do not despair, therefore, but fight back, and do not gratify the desires of the flesh. Then you will not be under the Law."

I remember that Staupitz used to say: "More than a thousand times I have vowed to God that I would improve, but I have never performed what I have vowed. Hereafter I shall not make such vows, because I know perfectly well that I shall not live up to them. Unless God is gracious and merciful to me for the sake of Christ and grants me a blessed final hour [57] when the time comes for me to depart this miserable life, I shall not be able to stand before Him with all my vows and good works." [58] This despair is not only truthful but is godly and holy. Whoever wants to be saved must make this confession with his mouth and with his heart. The saints do not rely on their own righteousness; they sing with David (Ps. 143:2): "Enter

---

[57] The word *horula* is a Latin version of Luther's familiar term for the hour of death, *stündlin*.

[58] This was a favorite anecdote of Luther's; cf. *Luther's Works*, 23, p. 271.

not into judgment with Thy servant, for no man living is justified before Thee"; and (Ps. 130:3): "If Thou, O Lord, shouldst mark iniquities, Lord, who could stand?" Therefore they gaze at Christ, their Propitiator, who gave His life for their sins. And if there is any remnant of sin in their flesh, they know that this is not imputed to them but is pardoned by forgiveness. Meanwhile they battle by the Spirit against the flesh. This does not mean that they do not feel its desires at all; it means that they do not gratify them. Even though they feel their flesh raging and rebelling against the Spirit and feel themselves falling into sins and living in them, they do not become downcast on that account or immediately suppose that their way of life, their social station, and the works they have done in accordance with their calling are displeasing to God. No, they fortify themselves with their faith.

Thus there is great comfort for the faithful in this teaching of Paul's, because they know that they have partly flesh and partly Spirit, but in such a way that the Spirit rules and the flesh is subordinate, that righteousness is supreme and sin is a servant. Otherwise someone who is not aware of this will be completely overwhelmed by a spirit of sadness and will despair. But for someone who knows this doctrine and uses it properly even evil will have to cooperate for good. For when his flesh impels him to sin, he is aroused and incited to seek forgiveness of sins through Christ and to embrace the righteousness of faith, which he would otherwise not have regarded as so important or yearned for with such intensity. And so it is very beneficial if we sometimes become aware of the evil of our nature and our flesh, because in this way we are aroused and stirred up to have faith and to call upon Christ. Through such an opportunity a Christian becomes a skillful artisan and a wonderful creator, who can make joy out of sadness, comfort out of terror, righteousness out of sin, and life out of death, when he restrains his flesh for this purpose, brings it into submission, and subjects it to the Spirit. Those who become aware of the desires of their flesh should not immediately despair of their salvation on that account. It is all right for them to be aware of it, provided that they do not assent to it; it is all right for anger or sexual desire to be aroused in them, provided that they do not capitulate to it; it is all right for sin to stir them up, provided that they do not gratify it. In fact, the godlier one is, the more aware he is of this conflict. This is the source of the complaint of the saints in the Psalms and throughout Scripture. The hermits, monks, sophists, and all the work-righteous know nothing whatever about this conflict.

Here someone may say that it is dangerous to teach that a person is not damned simply because he does not immediately overcome the passions of the flesh which he feels; for when this doctrine is broadcast among the rabble, they will become smug, inert, and lazy. This is what I meant when I said earlier that if we teach faith, carnal people will neglect works; but if we urge works, faith and the comfort of consciences will be lost. Here no one can be compelled, nor can any definite rule be prescribed. But let everyone examine himself carefully to see which passion of the flesh affects him most powerfully. When he discovers this, let him not be smug or flatter himself; but let him be on guard, and by the Spirit let him struggle against it, so that, if he cannot bridle it, he will at least not gratify it.

All the saints have had and experienced this struggle of the flesh with the Spirit. We, too, experience it. Whoever consults his own conscience, provided that he is not a hypocrite, will surely find that his own situation is just as Paul describes it here, namely, that the desires of the flesh are against the Spirit. Therefore every saint feels and confesses that his flesh resists the Spirit and that these two are opposed to each other, so that he cannot do what he would want to, even though he sweats and strains to do so. The flesh prevents us from keeping the commandments of God, from loving our neighbors as ourselves, and especially from loving God with all our heart, etc. Therefore it is impossible for us to be justified by works of the Law. The good will is present, as it should be — it is, of course, the Spirit Himself resisting the flesh — and it would rather do good, fulfill the Law, love God and the neighbor, etc. But the flesh does not obey this will but resists it. Yet God does not impute this sin, for He is gracious for the sake of Christ. It does not follow from this, however, that you should minimize sin or think of it as something trivial because God does not impute it. It is true that He does not impute it, but to whom and on what account? Not to the hardhearted and smug but to those who repent and who by faith take hold of Christ the Propitiator, on whose account sins are forgiven them and the remnants of sin are not imputed to them. Such people do not minimize sin; they emphasize it, because they know that it cannot be washed away by any satisfactions, works, or righteousness, but only by the death of Christ. Yet they do not despair because of its size but are persuaded that it is forgiven them on account of Christ.

I say this to keep anyone from supposing that once faith has been accepted, sin should not be emphasized. Sin is really sin, regardless of whether you commit it before or after you have come to know Christ. And God hates the sin; in fact, so far as the substance of the deed is concerned, every sin is mortal. It is not mortal for the believer; but this is on account of Christ the Propitiator, who expiated it by His death. As for the person who does not believe in Christ, not only are all his sins mortal, but even his good works are sins, in accordance with the statement (Rom. 14:23): "Whatever does not proceed from faith is sin." Therefore it is a pernicious error when the sophists distinguish among sins on the basis of the substance of the deed rather than on the basis of the persons.[59] A believer's sin is the same sin and sin just as great as that of the unbeliever. To the believer, however, it is forgiven and not imputed, while to the unbeliever it is retained and imputed. To the former it is venial; to the latter it is mortal. This is not because of a difference between the sins, as though the believer's sin were smaller and the unbeliever's larger, but because of a difference between the persons. For the believer knows that his sin is forgiven him on account of Christ, who has expiated it by His death. Even though he has sin and commits sin, he remains godly. On the other hand, when the unbeliever commits sin, he remains ungodly. This is the wisdom and the comfort of those who are truly godly, that even if they have sins and commit sins, they know that because of their faith in Christ these are not imputed to them.

From this it is evident who the true saints are. They are not stumps and stones, as the sophists and monks imagine. They are not people who remain unaffected by anything or who never experience the desires of the flesh. But, as Paul says, the desires of their flesh are against the Spirit. Therefore they have sin and are capable of committing sin. Ps. 32:5-6 testifies that saints confess their transgressions and pray for the forgiveness of the guilt of their sin; it says: "I said: 'I will confess my transgression to the Lord'; then Thou didst forgive the guilt of my sin. Therefore let everyone who is godly offer prayer to Thee." The entire church, which certainly is holy, prays

---

[59] This is the familiar distinction between sin *penes substantiam facti* and sin *penes personam*.

that its sins may be forgiven; and it believes in the forgiveness of sins.[60] In Ps. 143:2 David prays: "Enter not into judgment with Thy servant; for no man living is righteous before Thee"; and in Ps. 130:3-4: "If Thou, O Lord, shouldst mark iniquities, Lord, who could stand? But there is forgiveness with Thee." This is how the greatest saints speak and pray — David, Paul, etc. Therefore all saints speak and pray in the same spirit. The sophists do not read the Scriptures; or if they do read them, they read them with a veil before their eyes (2 Cor. 3:14). Therefore they are unable to come to a proper judgment about anything, neither about sin nor about holiness.

18. *But if you are led by the Spirit, you are not under the Law.*

Paul cannot forget about his doctrine of faith; but he keeps on repeating and emphasizing it, even when he is dealing with good works. Here someone may raise the objection: "How can it be that we are not under the Law? After all, Paul, you yourself teach that we have a flesh whose desires are against the Spirit, a flesh that opposes, vexes, and enslaves us. And we are really conscious of our sin; nor can we be set free in the sense in which we would most like to be free. This is surely what it means to be under the Law. Then why do you say, Paul, that we are not under the Law?" "Do not let this bother you," he says. "Only concentrate on this, that you be led by the Spirit, that is, that you obey the will which is opposed to the flesh and that you refuse to gratify the desires of the flesh; for this is what it means to be led and drawn by the Spirit. And then you will not be under the Law." Thus Paul speaks of himself in Rom. 7:25: "I serve the Law of God with my mind; that is, in the Spirit I am not guilty of any sin. But with my flesh I serve the law of sin." And so the godly are not under the Law, namely, by the Spirit; for the Law is unable to accuse them and to carry out its sentence of death against them, even though they are conscious of their sin and confess that they are sinners. Through Christ, "who was born under the Law to redeem those who were under the Law" (4:4-5), the Law has been deprived of its legal hold on them. In the godly, therefore, the Law does not dare accuse as sin that which truly is a sin against the Law.

Therefore the dominion of the Spirit is so powerful that the Law cannot accuse that which is truly sin. For Christ, our Righteousness,

---

[60] See p. 42, note 36; also pp. 83—85.

whom we grasp by faith, is beyond reproach; therefore He cannot be accused by the Law. As long as we cling to Him, we are led by the Spirit and are free from the Law. Thus even when the apostle is teaching good works, he does not forget about his discussion of justification but continually points out that it is impossible for us to be justified by works of the Law. The remnants of sin cling to our flesh, which, as long as it lives, does not stop having desires against the Spirit. Yet this does not endanger us at all; for we are free of the Law, provided that we walk by the Spirit.

With the words "If you are led by the Spirit, you are not under the Law" you can give powerful comfort to yourself and to others who are experiencing severe trials. It often happens that a man is so fiercely attacked by anger, hatred, impatience, sexual desire, mental depression, or some other desire of the flesh that he simply cannot get rid of it, no matter how much he wants to. What is he to do? Should he despair on this account? No, but he should say: "My flesh is battling and raging against the Spirit. Let it rage as long as it pleases! But you do not give in to it. Walk by the Spirit, and be led by Him, so that you do not gratify its desires. If you do this, you are free of the Law. Of course, it will accuse and frighten you; but it will do so in vain." In such a battle of the flesh against the Spirit, therefore, there is nothing better than to have the Word in view and to draw from it the comfort of the Spirit.

Nor should a person in the midst of trial be affected by the devil's great ability to exaggerate our sin, which causes one to think that he will completely collapse under attack, so that he is conscious of nothing except the wrath of God and despair. Here he must not at any cost follow his own consciousness; he must follow only the word of Paul: "If you are led by the Spirit, you are not under the Law." If he clings to this with firm faith, he will have a mighty defense with which he can quench all the flaming darts that the evil one aims at him (Eph. 6:16). No matter how much the flesh may seethe and rave, none of its agitation or fury can harm or condemn him; for as one who walks by the Spirit and who is led by Him, he refuses to give in to the flesh or to gratify its desires. When the flesh is agitated and raging, therefore, the only remedy is that we take "the sword of the Spirit, which is the Word of God" (Eph. 6:17), and do battle against it. Then we shall undoubtedly emerge as the victors, even though we may think the exact opposite during the battle. But if we lose sight of the Word, we have no aid or counsel left. I am saying this on the basis of my own experience. I have suffered many trials of all sorts, and the most severe ones at that. But as soon as I took hold of some statement of Scripture as my holy anchor, I found security, and my trials subsided; without the Word it would have been impossible for me to endure them even for a short time, much less to overcome them.

In this discussion of the conflict between the flesh and the Spirit, Paul teaches, in summary, that the reconciled or the saints cannot accomplish what the spirit wishes. For the spirit would want to be completely pure, but the flesh that is attached to it will not permit this. Yet they are saved; this happens through the forgiveness of sins, which is in Christ. Moreover, because they walk by the Spirit and are led by Him, they are not under the Law. That is, the Law cannot accuse and terrify them; and even if it tries to do so, it cannot bring them to the point of despair.

19. *Now the works of the flesh are plain.*

This passage is rather similar to the statement of Christ (Matt. 7:16-17): "You will know them by their fruits. Are grapes gathered from thorns, or figs from thistles? So every sound tree bears good fruit, but the bad tree bears evil fruit." Clearly Paul is teaching the same thing in the present passage as Christ in that passage, namely, that works and fruit are ample evidence whether trees are sound or bad, whether men follow the guidance of the flesh or that of the Spirit. It is as though he were saying: "To keep any of you from pleading that he did not understand my present discussion of the conflict between the flesh and the Spirit, I shall first place before your eyes the works of the flesh, most of which are recognized as such even by the wicked; then I shall discuss the fruit of the Spirit." Paul is doing this because there were many hypocrites among the Galatians, just as there are today among us. They pretended to be pious, made a boast of the Spirit, and, so far as the words were concerned, had an excellent knowledge of true doctrine; but at the same time they walked by the flesh, not by the Spirit, and they performed its works. Therefore Paul accused them publicly of not being the sort of people they pretended to be. And to keep them from shrugging off his warning, he pronounces a horrible sentence on them, namely, that they will not inherit the kingdom of God; this he does in the hope that the warning will make them mend their ways.

It is not surprising that every age has its peculiar temptations, even for the godly. Thus the young man is especially tried by sexual desire, the mature man by ambition and vainglory, the old man by avarice. As I said earlier, there has never been a saint whose flesh did not often incite him to impatience, anger, etc. Therefore Paul is speaking of saints when he says here that the desires of their flesh are against the Spirit. And so the desires and the conflicts of the flesh will not vanish; yet they will not vanquish [61] those who are aware of them. For this is how they should think about the matter: It is one thing to be aroused by the flesh and not to tolerate its desires any further but to walk and to withstand by the Spirit; it is quite another thing to give in to the flesh and to do its works with a smug air, to persist in them, and yet at the same time to put on a pretense of piety and to make a boast of the Spirit. He comforts the former group by saying that they are being led by the Spirit and are not under the Law; he threatens the latter group with eternal destruction.

Nevertheless, it sometimes happens that the saints may lapse and gratify the desires of their flesh. Thus David, in a great and horrible lapse, fell into adultery and was responsible for the murder of many when he had Uriah die in battle (2 Sam. 11). Thereby he gave his enemies an excuse to be boastful against the people of God, to worship their idol, and to blaspheme the God of Israel. Peter also lapsed horribly when he denied Christ. But no matter how great these sins were, they were not committed intentionally; they were committed because of weakness. In addition, when they had been admonished, these men did not persist stubbornly in their sins but returned to their senses. Later on (6:1) Paul commands that such men be received, instructed, and restored, saying: "If a man is overtaken, etc." Those who sin because of weakness, even if they do it often, will not be denied forgiveness, provided that they rise again and do not persist in their sins; for persistence in sin is the worst of all. If they do not return to their senses but stubbornly go on gratifying the desires of their flesh, this is the surest possible sign of dishonesty in their spirit.

Thus no one will ever be without desire as long as he lives in the flesh. Consequently, no one will ever be free of temptation either.

[61] With the play on the words "vanish" and "vanquish" we have sought to reproduce the play on the Latin words *abesse* and *obesse*.

Different people are tempted in different ways, according to the diversity in their makeup or attitude. One person is subject to graver feelings, such as mental depression, blasphemy, unbelief, or despair; another, to more obvious ones, such as sexual desire, anger, or hatred. But here Paul demands of us that we walk by the Spirit and resist the flesh. Anyone who yields to his flesh and persists in smugly gratifying its desires should know that he does not belong to Christ; though he may pride himself ever so much on the title "Christian," he is merely deceiving himself.

As I have already indicated briefly, this passage provides us with the greatest possible comfort when it tells us that it is impossible to live without any desires and temptations of the flesh, in fact, without sin. It admonishes us not to act like the men of whom Gerson writes, who labored to rid themselves of any awareness of temptation or sin, in other words, to become nothing but stones.[62] The sophists and monks had the notion about the saints that they were merely logs and blocks, utterly lacking in any feeling. Surely Mary felt a great sorrow in her mind when her Son was lost (Luke 2:48).[63] Throughout the Psalms David complains that he is being almost swallowed up by the great sorrow that came from the magnitude of his temptations and sins. Paul also complains that he feels "fighting without and fear within" (2 Cor. 7:5), and that with his flesh he serves the law of sin (Rom. 7:25). He says that he suffers "anxiety for all the churches" (2 Cor. 11:28), and that God had mercy on him by restoring Epaphroditus to life when he was near to death, lest he should have sorrow upon sorrow (Phil. 2:25-27). And so the saint as defined by the sophists resembles the wise man as defined by the Stoics, who invented a kind of wise man that has never existed in the universe. With this foolish and wicked notion, which was born of their ignorance of this Pauline doctrine, the sophists brought themselves and innumerable others to the brink of despair.

When I was a monk, I often had a heartfelt wish to see the life and conduct of at least one saintly man. But meanwhile I was imagining the sort of saint who lived in the desert and abstained from food and drink, subsisting on nothing but roots and cold water. I had derived this notion about unnatural saints from the books not

[62] On Gerson's view of temptation see also *Luther's Works*, 13, p. 113.

[63] The reference here appears to be to Luke 2:48, not to Luke 2:35, as the Weimar editors suggest.

only of the sophists but even of the fathers. For Jerome writes somewhere as follows: "I am not saying anything about food and drink, since it is a luxury even for those who are feeble to take a little cold water and to eat some cooked food." [64] But now that the light of truth is shining, we see with utter clarity that Christ and the apostles designate as saints, not those who lead a celibate life, who are abstemious, or who perform other works that give the appearance of brilliance or grandeur but those who, being called by the Gospel and baptized, believe that they have been sanctified and cleansed by the blood and death of Christ. Thus whenever Paul writes to Christians, he calls them saints, sons and heirs of God, etc. Therefore saints are all those who believe in Christ, whether men or women, whether slaves or free. And they are saints, on the basis, not of their own works but of the works of God, which they accept by faith, such as the Word, the sacraments, the suffering, death, resurrection, and victory of Christ, the sending of the Holy Spirit, etc. In other words, they are saints, not by active holiness but by passive holiness.

Such genuine saints include ministers of the Word, political magistrates, parents, children, masters, servants, etc., if they, first of all, declare that Christ is their wisdom, righteousness, sanctification, and redemption (1 Cor. 1:30), and if, in the second place, they all do their duty in their callings on the basis of the command of the Word of God, abstaining from the desires and vices of the flesh for the sake of Christ. They are not all of equal firmness of character, and many weaknesses and offenses are discernible in every one of them; it is also true that many of them fall into sin. But this does not hinder their holiness at all, so long as they sin out of weakness, not out of deliberate wickedness. For, as I have already said several times, the godly are conscious of the desires of the flesh; but they resist them and do not gratify them. When they fall into sin unexpectedly, they obtain forgiveness, if by faith they return to Christ, who does not want us to chase away the lost sheep but to look for it. On no account, therefore, am I to jump to the conclusion that those who are weak in faith or morals are unholy, when I see that they love and revere the Word, receive the Lord's Supper, etc.; for God has received them and regards them as righteous through the forgiveness of sins. It is before Him that they stand or fall (Rom. 14:4).

[64] Luther may be thinking of the argumentation in the second book of Jerome's treatise *Against Jovinian*.

This is how Paul speaks about the saints everywhere. And I am happy to give thanks to God for His superabundant gift, which I sought when I used to be a monk; for I have seen, not one saint but many, in fact, innumerable genuine saints, not the kind that the sophists portrayed but the kind that Christ and the apostles portray and describe,[65] the kind to which, by the grace of God, even I belong. For I have been baptized; and I believe that Christ, my Lord, has redeemed me from sin by His death and has granted me eternal righteousness and holiness. And let anyone be accursed who does not give Christ the honor of believing that he has been justified and sanctified by His death, the Word, the sacraments, etc.

When we have repudiated this foolish and wicked notion about the name "saints" — which we suppose applies only to the saints in heaven, and on earth to hermits and monks who perform some sort of spectacular work — let us now learn from the writings of the apostles that all believers in Christ are saints. The world admires the holiness of Benedict, Gregory, Bernard, Francis, and men like that, because it hears that they performed works that looked magnificent and unusual. Surely St. Ambrose, Augustine, and others were saints also. They did not live such an ascetic and horrible life as these others but remained in human society, eating ordinary food, drinking wine, and wearing fine, decent clothing. So far as the ordinary customs of life were concerned, there was almost no difference between them and other respectable men; and yet they deserve to be preeminent over the ones mentioned earlier. For without any superstition they taught the faith of Christ in its purity, battled against heretics, and purified the church of innumerable errors. Their company brought joy to many, and especially to the sorrowful and the distressed, whom they encouraged and comforted with the Word; for they did not withdraw from human society but carried out their responsibilities amid frequent disturbances. Those others, by contrast, not only taught many things that were contrary to the faith but were also the originators of many superstitions, errors, and ungodly forms of worship. Therefore unless they took hold of Christ in the hour of death and trusted solely in His death and victory, their ascetic life was of no use to them at all.

This makes it clear enough who the genuine saints are and what sort of life should be called saintly: not the life of those who hide

---

[65] For the obvious typographical error *descibunt* we have read *describunt*.

away in caves and crannies, torture their bodies by fasting, wear hair shirts, etc., with the idea that they will have some special reward in heaven, exceeding that of other Christians, but the life of those who have been baptized and who believe in Christ, etc. These latter do not manage all at once to divest themselves of the old Adam with all his activities; but throughout their life the desires of the flesh remain with them, although the awareness of these does not harm them as long as they do not permit them to dominate them but subject them to the Spirit. This doctrine brings comfort to godly minds, so that they do not despair when they feel the darts of the flesh, with which Satan attacks their spirit (Eph. 6:16). This is what many men did under the papacy; they thought that they were not supposed to feel any desires of the flesh at all. And yet neither Jerome nor Gregory nor Benedict nor Bernard nor any of the others whom the monks set forth to be imitated as examples of chastity and of all Christian virtues could get to the point of not feeling any desires of the flesh at all. Of course, they felt such desires, and powerfully too, as some of them frankly confess in more than one passage in their books.[66] Therefore God did not impute against them these minor misdemeanors, or even the dangerous errors that some of them brought into the church. Thus Gregory was the originator of Low Mass, the greatest abomination there has ever been in the church founded by Christ.[67] Others invented monasticism, wicked forms of worship, and self-chosen acts of religious devotion. Cyprian maintained that those who had been baptized by heretics were to be rebaptized.[68]

Therefore we correctly confess in the Creed that we *believe* a holy church. For it is invisible,[69] dwelling in the Spirit, in an "unapproachable" place (1 Tim. 6:16); therefore its holiness cannot be seen. God conceals and covers it with weaknesses, sins, errors, and various offenses and forms of the cross in such a way that it is not evident to the senses anywhere. Those who are ignorant of this are immediately offended when they see the weaknesses and sins of those who

---

[66] From the manuscript notes on Luther's lectures it is evident that he was thinking of Jerome here.

[67] Low Mass or *missa privata* does indeed date back to the early Middle Ages, but the role of Pope Gregory I in its development is not historically substantiated.

[68] Cf. Augustine's extensive discussion of Cyprian's views on rebaptism, *De baptismo*, II.

[69] Luther's more usual term for "invisible" is *abscondita*, "hidden."

have been baptized, have the Word, and believe; and they conclude that such people do not belong to the church. Meanwhile they imagine that the church consists of the hermits, monks, etc., who honor God only with their lips and who worship Him in vain, because they do not teach the Word of God but the doctrines and commandments of men (Matt. 15:8-9). Because these men perform superstitious and unnatural works, which reason praises and admires, they are regarded as saints and as the church. Anyone who thinks this way turns the article of the Creed, "I believe a holy church," upside down; he replaces "I believe" with "I see." Such forms of human righteousness and self-chosen holiness are actually a kind of spiritual sorcery, by which the eyes and minds of men are blinded and led away from the knowledge of true holiness.

But we teach that the church has no spot or wrinkle (Eph. 5:27) but is holy, though only through faith in Jesus Christ; in addition, it is holy in its life, in the sense that it refrains from the desires of the flesh and practices its spiritual gifts. But it is not yet holy in the sense of being delivered and rescued from all evil desires or of having purged out all wicked opinions and errors. For the church always confesses its sin and prays that its trespasses may be forgiven (Matt. 6:12); it also "believes in the forgiveness of sins." And so the saints sin, fall, and even err; but they do so through ignorance. For they do not want to deny Christ, to lose the Gospel, to cancel their Baptism, etc. This is why they have the forgiveness of sins; and if through ignorance they err in doctrine, this is forgiven, because at the end they acknowledge their error and depend solely on the truth and grace of God in Christ. This is what Jerome, Gregory, Bernard,[70] and others did. Therefore let Christians strive to avoid the works of the flesh; they cannot avoid its desires.

It is extremely beneficial to the faithful to be aware of the uncleanness of their flesh; for it will keep them from being puffed up by a vain and wicked notion about the righteousness of works, as though they were acceptable to God on its account. The monks were puffed up this way and thought that they were so holy on account of their holy way of life that they peddled their righteousness and holiness to others, even though meanwhile they were convicted

---

[70] In the lecture notes Luther refers explicitly to Bernard's refusal to trust in his own works, as expressed in his declaration, *Perdite vixi,* which Luther quotes in many of his works; cf. *Luther's Works,* 22, p. 52, note 42.

of their uncleanness by their own hearts. So dangerous a plague is it to trust in one's own righteousness and to dream that one is pure. But we are not in a position to trust in our own righteousness, for we are aware of the uncleanness of the flesh. This awareness humbles us, so that we hang our heads and cannot trust in our own good works; and it compels us to run to Christ the Propitiator, who does not have a corrupt or blemished flesh but has an altogether pure and holy flesh, which He gave for the life of the world. In Him we find a righteousness that is complete and perfect. Thus we abide in a humility that is not fictitious or monastic but authentic, because of the filth and the faults that cling to our flesh; if God wanted to judge severely, we would deserve eternal punishment on account of these. We are not proud in the sight of God, but we acknowledge our sins humbly and with a contrite heart; and we seek forgiveness, rely on the benefaction of Christ the Mediator, move into the presence of God, and pray that our sins be forgiven on His account. Therefore God stretches the immense heaven of grace over us and for the sake of Christ does not impute to us the remnants of sin that cling to our flesh.

I am saying this in order that you may avoid the wicked errors of the sophists about the holiness of life. Our minds were so obsessed by these errors that we were unable to get rid of them without great effort. Therefore be very careful to distinguish properly between true and hypocritical righteousness or holiness. Then you will be able to look at the kingdom of Christ with eyes other than those that reason uses, that is, with spiritual eyes; and you will be able to assert with certainty that a saint is one who has been baptized and who believes in Christ. Such a saint will also abstain from the desires of the flesh by means of the faith through which he is justified and through which his sins, past and present, are forgiven; but he is not completely cleansed of them. For the desires of the flesh [71] are still against the Spirit. This uncleanness remains in him to keep him humble, so that in his humility the grace and blessing of Christ taste sweet to him. Thus such uncleanness and such remnants of sin are not a hindrance but a great advantage to the godly. For the more aware they are of their weakness and sin, the more they take refuge in Christ, the mercy seat (Rom. 3:25). They plead for His assistance, that He may adorn them with His righteousness and make their faith increase by

---

[71] We have read *Caro* instead of *Carno*.

providing the Spirit, by whose guidance they will overcome the desires of the flesh and make them servants rather than masters. Thus a Christian struggles with sin continually, and yet in his struggle he does not surrender but obtains the victory. I have said this to make you understand, not on the basis of human imaginations but of the Word of God, who the genuine saints are. We see that Christian teaching is of the greatest possible help in encouraging consciences, and that it is the sort of teaching that does not deal with cowls, tonsures, rosaries, and similar useless matters but with the most difficult and most important issues, namely, how we are to overcome the flesh, sin, death, and the devil. Because this teaching is unknown to the self-righteous, it is impossible for them either to instruct one erring conscience or to bring comfort and peace to one conscience that is in the throes of terror and despair.

Immorality, impurity, licentiousness,

20. *idolatry, sorcery, etc.*

Paul does not enumerate all the works of the flesh, but he uses a certain number in place of the infinite number of such works. First he mentions several species of sexual desire. Now sexual desire is not the only work of the flesh, as the papists imagined; they are such chaste men that they classified marriage, of which God Himself is the Author, and which they themselves numbered among the sacraments, as a "work of the flesh." But, as we have said several times before, Paul enumerates idolatry, etc., among the works of the flesh also. Thus this passage makes it very clear what "flesh" means to Paul. Now whoever wants to know what these individual terms mean, let him read, if he wishes, the old commentary which we prepared in 1519; for there, as well as we could, we pointed out in sufficient detail the content and import of the individual terms in this entire catalog of the works of the flesh and fruits of the Spirit.[72] Our chief purpose this time has been to set forth the doctrine of justification as clearly as possible as we were expounding the Epistle to the Galatians.

Idolatry.

The highest forms of religion and holiness, and the most fervent forms of devotion of those who worship God without the Word and command of God, are idolatry. Thus under the papacy it was regarded

---

[72] See pp. 367 ff.

as an act of the greatest spirituality when the monks sat in their cells and meditated about God and His works, or when their fervent devotions so inflamed them as they genuflected, prayed, and contemplated heavenly things that they wept for sheer pleasure and joy. There was no thinking here about women or about any other creature, but only about the Creator and His marvelous works. And yet this action, which reason regards as eminently spiritual, is a "work of the flesh" according to Paul. Thus every such form of religion, which worships God without His Word and command, is idolatry. The more spiritual and holy it appears to be, the more dangerous and destructive it is; for it deflects men from faith in Christ and causes them to rely on their own powers, works, and righteousness. Such is the religion of the Anabaptists today, although day by day they are betraying that they are possessed by the devil and are seditious and bloodthirsty men.

Therefore fasting, wearing a hair shirt, holy activity, and the monastic rule and whole way of life of the Carthusians, the strictest of orders, are all works of the flesh; for they imagine that they are holy and will be saved, not through Christ, whom they fear as a stern judge, but through the observance of their monastic rule. They think about God, about Christ, and about things divine, not on the basis of the Word of God but on the basis of their own reason. On this basis they imagine that their monastic habit, their diet, and their whole conduct are holy and are pleasing to Christ; they hope not only to placate Him with the asceticism of their life but to obtain from Him a recompense for their good works and their righteousness. And so the thoughts that they imagine to be most spiritual are not only the most unspiritual but even the most wicked; for they exclude and despise the Word, faith, and Christ, and they seek to wash away their sins and to obtain grace and eternal life by trust in their own righteousness. Therefore all forms of worship and religion apart from Christ are the worship of idols. Only with Christ is the Father well pleased (Matt. 3:17; Matt. 17:5). Whoever listens to Him and does what He commands is beloved for the sake of the Beloved. But He commands us to believe His Word, to be baptized, etc., not to invent new forms of worship.

I have said earlier that the works of the flesh are plain; and surely adultery, fornication, and the like, are familiar to everyone. But idolatry is so impressive and spiritual that it is familiar to only a few, and only to those who believe in Christ. For when a Carthusian lives in chastity, fasts, prays, observes the canonical hours, sacrifices, etc., he not only does not believe that he is an idolater and is doing the work of the flesh, but he is firmly persuaded that he is being directed and guided by the Spirit; that he is walking by the Spirit; that he is thinking, speaking, and doing nothing but spiritual things; and that he is worshiping God in a manner that is very pleasing to Him. No one will be able to persuade the papists and their Antichrist today that Low Mass is the height of blasphemy and idolatry, the most horrible there has ever been in the church which the apostles founded. They are blind and obstinate; therefore they have a distorted judgment about God and about divine things, regarding idolatry as the ultimate in true worship and regarding faith as idolatry. But we who believe in Christ and have His mind "judge all things, but are ourselves to be judged by no one" (1 Cor. 2:15) truly and in the sight of God.

From all this it is clear that by "flesh" Paul means whatever there is in man, including all three powers of the soul, namely, the will that desires, the will that becomes angry, and the intellect.[73] The works of the will that desires are immorality, impurity, etc.; those of the will that becomes angry are quarrels, contentions, murder, etc.; those of the reason or the intellect are error, false forms of religion or worship, superstition, idolatry, heresy, that is, party spirit, etc. It is very important to know this well, because in the entire realm of the pope the word "flesh" was obscured so badly that "work of the flesh" meant only sexual intercourse or overt sexual desire. From this it followed necessarily that they could not understand Paul. But here we see clearly that among the works of the flesh Paul numbers idolatry and party spirit, which are the height of wisdom, religion, and holiness in man. Papal religion gave such an appearance of holiness that great men like Gregory, Bernard, and others were deceived by it for a while. In Colossians (2:18) Paul calls it "angelic worship." But regardless of how holy and spiritual it seems, it is nothing but the work of the flesh, an abomination and idolatry that is contrary to the Gospel, to faith, and to the true worship of God. Godly believers, who have spiritual eyes, see this; but self-righteous people think differently. Just as it is impossible to persuade a monk that his vows are works of the flesh, so a Turk is completely unwilling

---

[73] The more usual division was into the nutritive, the sensitive, the imaginative, and the appetitive.

to believe that his observance of the Koran, his ablutions, and the other ceremonies that he observes are works of the flesh. It is certainly important that idolatry is included among the works of the flesh.

Sorcery.

I have spoken about sorcery earlier (ch. 3).[74] This was a common sin in our own times before the revelation of the Gospel. When I was a boy, there were many witches who cast spells upon cattle and upon people, especially upon children. They also damaged the crops through storms and hail, which they caused by their sorcery.[75] Now that the Gospel has been revealed, such things are unheard of, because the Gospel drives the devil and all his illusions from their seat of power. But he still casts an even more horrible spell, namely, a spiritual one, upon men through his sorcery.

Among the works of the flesh Paul numbers sorcery, which, as everyone knows, is not a work caused by the desires of the flesh but is an abuse or imitation of idolatry. Witchcraft makes a pact with demons, while superstition or idolatry makes a pact with God, though with a false god rather than the true God. Thus idolatry is really spiritual sorcery. For just as witches cast spells upon cattle and people, so idolaters, that is, all self-righteous men, would like to cast a spell upon God, to make Him the way they imagine Him in their ideas; that is, they do not want Him to justify us by mere grace and faith in Christ but to regard their acts of worship and self-chosen works and to grant them righteousness and eternal life on account of these. But they are actually casting a spell upon themselves rather than upon God; for if they persist in this wicked notion of theirs about God, they will die in their idolatry and will be damned. Most of the works of the flesh are sufficiently well known not to require any explanation.

Party spirit.

By "party spirit" Paul is not referring only to the civil dissension that arises between citizens and magistrates when one does not respect the other and, in reliance on his power or on the support of the rabble, exalts himself above the other, looking down upon him and

---

[74] On sorcery see the discussion earlier in this commentary, *Luther's Works,* 26, pp. 189 ff.

[75] Cf. also *Luther's Works,* 24, pp. 74—75.

setting himself in public opposition to him. In such circumstances it is inevitable that public peace be violated and that party spirit, revolution, and the overthrow of governments should follow. What he is denouncing here is not chiefly the party spirit that arises in the household or in the state on account of physical or mundane matters; it is the kind that arises in the church on account of doctrine, faith, and works. Heresies have always existed in the church, as has been said earlier more than once; but the pope is the supreme heresiarch and the head of all heretics. He has covered the world with endless sects, as it was once covered by the Flood. No monk could agree with another, for they measured their sanctity by the strictness of their monastic rules. Thus a Carthusian claimed to be holier than a Franciscan, etc. In the papal church, therefore, there is no unity of the Spirit, no concord of minds. No, there is the height of discord. They do not have one and the same doctrine, faith, religion, worship, and mind; but they are all extremely diverse. Among Christians, however, all these things are one and the same and are shared by all: the Word, faith, worship, religion, the sacraments, Christ, God, the heart, the feelings, the soul, the will. And this spiritual concord is not harmed at all by differences in social status and outward conditions, as has been said several times earlier. Those who have this unity of the Spirit can also form a sure judgment about all the sects. Otherwise no one understands them. Thus no theologian under the papacy understood that in this passage Paul is condemning all the forms of worship and religion, the continence, and the apparently respectable behavior and holy life of all the papists and sectarians. They supposed that he was talking about overt idolatry and the heresies of the pagans, who openly blaspheme the name of Christ.

21. *Drunkenness, carousing.*

Paul is not saying that drinking and eating are works of the flesh; he is speaking of drunkenness and carousing, and nothing is more widespread in our lands today. Those who are addicted to such debauchery, which is more degraded than the behavior of animals, should know that they are not spiritual, regardless of their boasting, but that they are following the flesh and are performing its works. Such people heard the dreadful sentence pronounced upon them that they shall not inherit the kingdom of God. Thus Paul wants Christians to avoid drunkenness and intoxication and to live a sober and frugal life, lest a well-fed flesh provoke them into wantonness; for the flesh is usually powerfully stimulated after excessive drinking and gluttony. Yet it is not sufficient to restrain only the violent sexual appetite that accompanies intoxication; but even a sober flesh must be held in control, lest it gratify its desires. For it often happens that those who are the most sober are the most tempted. Thus Jerome writes about himself: "My lips," he says, "were pale with fasting, and my mind was inflamed with desires in the midst of my cold body. My flesh had already preceded me in death, but the fires of sexual desire were still fuming." [76] I, too, experienced this when I was a monk. Therefore merely abstaining from food does not extinguish the heat of sexual desire by itself; but the Spirit must be added, that is, meditation on the Word, faith, and prayer. Fasting does indeed overcome the coarser outbursts of sexual desire; but the desires of the flesh themselves are conquered, not by any abstinence from food and drink but by an earnest meditation on the Word and by the invocation of Christ.

And the like.

For it is impossible to enumerate all the works of the flesh.

I warn you, as I warned you before, that those who do such things shall not inherit the kingdom of God.

This is a very harsh but most necessary sentence against the false Christians and smug hypocrites, who boast about the Gospel, faith, and the Spirit but meanwhile go on smugly performing the works of the flesh. Especially the heretics, however, who are puffed up with their opinions about matters that they suppose to be very spiritual, are completely carnal men, possessed by the devil; therefore they gratify the desires of the flesh with all the powers of their soul. Hence it was necessary to the highest degree for such a dreadful and fearful sentence to be pronounced by the apostle against such men, with their smug disdain and stubborn hypocrisy. "Those who do such things," he says, "shall not inherit the kingdom of God." Perhaps this severe sentence would frighten some of them thoroughly, so that they would begin to battle against the works of the flesh by the Spirit and stop performing them.

[76] See p. 69, note 53 above.

22. *But the fruit of the Spirit is love, joy, peace, patience, kindness, goodness, faith,*

23. *gentleness, self-control.*

Paul does not say "works of the Spirit," as he had said "works of the flesh"; but he adorns these Christian virtues with a worthier title and calls them "fruit of the Spirit." For they bring very great benefits and fruit, because those who are equipped with them give glory to God and by these virtues invite others to the teaching and faith of Christ.

Love.

It would have sufficed to list only love, for this expands into all the fruit of the Spirit. Hence Paul attributes to it all the fruit that comes from the Spirit, when he says (1 Cor. 13:4): "Love is patient and kind, etc." Nevertheless, here he wanted to list it among the fruit of the Spirit and to put it in first place. Thus he wanted to exhort Christians that above all they should love one another, through love outdo one another in showing honor (Rom. 12:10), and each regard the other as more excellent than himself — all this on account of the indwelling of Christ and the Holy Spirit, and on account of the Word, Baptism, and the other divine gifts which Christians have.

Joy.

This is the voice of the Bridegroom and the bride; it means joyful thoughts about Christ, wholesome exhortations, happy songs, praise, and thanksgiving, with which godly people exhort, arouse, and refresh one another. Therefore God is repelled by sorrow of spirit; He hates sorrowful teaching and sorrowful thoughts and words, and He takes pleasure in happiness. For He came to refresh us, not to sadden us. Hence the prophets, apostles, and Christ Himself always urge, indeed command, that we rejoice and exult. Zech. 9:9: "Rejoice greatly, O daughter of Zion! Shout aloud, O daughter of Jerusalem! Lo, your King comes to you." And often in the Psalms (32:11): "Be glad in the Lord." Paul says (Phil. 4:4): "Rejoice in the Lord always." And Christ says (Luke 10:20): "Rejoice that your names are written in heaven." When this is a joy of the Spirit, not of the flesh, the heart rejoices inwardly through faith in Christ, because it knows for a certainty that He is our Savior and High Priest; and outwardly it demonstrates this joy in its words and actions. The faithful rejoice also when the Gospel is disseminated, and when many come to faith and thus the kingdom of Christ is increased.

Peace.

Peace with both God and man, so that Christians are peaceful and quiet. They are not quarrelsome and do not hate one another but bear one another's burdens (Gal. 6:2) with patience; for without patience peace cannot continue, and therefore Paul places it right after peace:

Μακροθυμία.

I think this means a persistent patience, by which someone not only bears adversity, insults, injury, etc., but even waits patiently for some improvement in those who have harmed him. When the devil cannot conquer the victims of his temptation by force, he conquers them by persistence. He knows that we are earthen vessels (2 Cor. 4:7), which cannot stand frequent and continuous blows or shocks. Thus he conquers many by his persistence. To conquer this persistence of his, in turn, there is need of endurance, which waits patiently both for the improvement of those who use force against us and for the end of the trials caused by the devil.

Χρηστότης.

This means a gentleness and sweetness in manner and in one's entire life. For Christians should not be harsh and morose; they should be gentle, humane, affable, courteous, people with whom others enjoy associating, people who overlook the mistakes of others or put the best construction on them, people who willingly yield to others, who bear with the recalcitrant, etc. Thus even the heathen have said: "You should know the manners of your friend, not hate them." [77] That is how Christ was, as can be seen throughout the Gospels. We read of St. Peter that he cried whenever he remembered the kindness Christ had manifested in His daily life.[78] This is a very great virtue, and one that is necessary in every area of life.

Goodness.

This means willingly helping others in their need, being generous, and lending to them.

---

[77] The proverb reads: *Mores amici noveris, non oderis.*

[78] On the source of this legend see also *Luther's Works*, 24, p. 147, note 83.

Faith.

When Paul lists "faith" here among the fruit of the Spirit, it is obvious that he means faithfulness or honesty, not faith in Christ. Hence he says in 1 Cor. 13:7 that "love believes all things." Anyone equipped with this faith is not a suspicious person; he is a sincere one, with a simple and honest heart. Even if he is taken in and experiences something different from what he believes, he is so mild that he gladly overlooks this. In short, he believes everyone; but he does not trust anyone. On the other hand, those who lack this virtue are suspicious persons, troublesome, bitter, and venomous. They believe no one except themselves, cannot bear with anything, will not yield to anyone, insult and distort whatever they see and hear, and segregate themselves from anyone who does not belong to their class. When this happens, it is impossible for love, friendship, concord, and peace to be preserved among men. But when these have been taken away, this present life becomes nothing but biting and devouring. Now love believes all things and so is often deceived. In this it does well; for it is better to be deceived with some degree of loss than for the general friendship and concord among men to perish. Faithfulness means, then, that one man keeps faith with another in the matters that pertain to this present life. For what would this present life of ours be if one person did not believe the other person?

Gentleness.

This is the virtue by which one is not easily provoked to anger. Innumerable occasions in this life provoke us to anger, but they are conquered by gentleness.

Self-control.

This refers to sobriety, temperance, or moderation in every walk of life. Paul contrasts it with the works of the flesh. Therefore he wants Christians to live a chaste and sober life; not to be adulterers, immoral or lustful persons; to marry if they cannot live chastely; not to be contentious; not to go to court, etc.; not to be drunken, not to be addicted to intoxication; but to abstain from all these things. All this is included in chastity or self-control. Jerome explains it exclusively as virginity, as though married people could not be chaste or as though the apostle had written this only to virgins.[79] In Titus 1:8 and 2:5 Paul definitely admonishes bishops and younger women, both of them married, to be chaste and pure.

Against such there is no law.

There is a Law, of course, but not against such. Thus Paul says elsewhere (1 Tim. 1:9): "The Law was not laid down for the just." For the just man lives as though he had need of no Law to admonish, urge, and constrain him; but spontaneously, without any legal constraint, he does more than the Law requires. And so the Law cannot accuse and condemn the just; nor can it disturb their consciences. It tries, of course; but when Christ has been grasped by faith, He dispels the Law with all its terrors and threats. Thus it is completely abrogated for them, first in the Spirit, but then also in works. It does not have the right to accuse them; for spontaneously they do what the Law requires, if not by means of perfectly holy works, then at least by means of the forgiveness of sins through faith. So a Christian fulfills the Law inwardly by faith — for Christ is the consummation of the Law for righteousness to everyone who has faith (Rom. 10:4) — and outwardly by works and by the forgiveness of sins. But those who perform the works of the flesh and gratify its desires are accused and condemned by the Law, both politically and theologically.

24. *And those who belong to Christ have crucified the flesh with its passions and sins.*

This whole discussion of works shows that true believers are not hypocrites. Therefore no one should deceive himself. Whoever belongs to Christ, says Paul, crucifies the flesh with all its diseases and faults. For because the saints have not yet completely shed their corrupt flesh, they are inclined toward sinning. They do not fear and love God enough, etc. They are aroused to anger, envy, impatience, sexual desire, and similar feelings; nevertheless, they do not carry out these feelings, because, as Paul says here, they crucify their flesh with its passions and faults. This takes place when they not only repress the wantonness of the flesh by fasting or other kinds of discipline, but when, as Paul said earlier (5:16), they walk by the Spirit; that is, when the threat that God will punish sin severely

---

[79] Jerome, *Commentarius in Epistolam S. Pauli ad Galatas, Patrologia, Series Latina,* XXVI, 449.

warns them and frightens them away from sinning; and when, instructed by the Word, by faith, and by prayer, they refuse to yield to the desires of the flesh. When they resist the flesh this way, they nail it to the cross with its passions and desires. Thus although the flesh is still alive and in motion, it cannot accomplish what it wishes, because it is fastened to the cross by its hands and feet. As long as they live in this world, therefore, the faithful crucify their flesh; that is, they are aware of its desires, but they do not yield to them. Dressed in the armor of God, with faith, hope, and the sword of the Spirit (Eph. 6:11-17), they fight back at the flesh; and with these nails they fasten it to the cross, so that against its will it is forced to be subject to the Spirit. Eventually, when they die, they will put it off completely; and in the resurrection they will have a flesh that is pure, without any passions or evil desires.[80]

25. *If we live by the Spirit, let us also walk by the Spirit.*

Earlier Paul had explicitly included party spirit and envy among the works of the flesh and had pronounced the sentence upon those who are envious and who are the originators of party spirit that "they shall not inherit the kingdom of God" (v. 21). Now, as though he had forgotten what he did a little earlier, he begins a new lecture of rebuke against those who provoke and envy one another. Why does he do this? Was it not enough to have done so once? Paul is doing this deliberately; for he wants to inveigh vigorously against the dreadful vice called κενοδοξία,[81] which created disturbances in all the churches of Galatia and which has always been dangerous and destructive in the Christian Church. Hence in writing to Titus (1:7) he says that one should not be appointed bishop if he is "arrogant," that is, if he takes pleasure in his own teaching and authority. For, as Augustine says very correctly, pride is the mother of all heresies;[82] indeed, as both sacred and profane history testifies, it is the source of all sin and ruin.

As you know, κενοδοξία is a widespread evil in every class of society and in every period of history, and it was vigorously attacked

[80] Although the original has the superscription Chapter Six here, we have followed the chapter divisions now in use.

[81] Actually the adjective κενόδοξος is used here; the noun appears only in Phil. 2:3.

[82] Cf., for example, Augustine, *Reply to Faustus the Manichean*, XXII, 22.

even by heathen poets and historians.⁸³ There is no district without someone or other who would like to appear wiser and greater than anyone else. Yet it is chiefly men of genius who suffer from this fault, men who contend about learning and wisdom. Here no one is willing to yield to the other, in accordance with the saying: "Anyone who would be willing to yield to the genius of another would not amount to anything." ⁸⁴ For it is pleasant to be pointed at and to have people say: "There he is!" Italy today is strongly infected with κενοδοξία, as Greece used to be. But in private persons, even in those who are in the government, this fault is not as pernicious as it is in those who are leaders in the church. Yet in the government, too, especially if it affects the leaders, it is the cause not only of disturbance and the overthrow of governments but even of the disturbance and collapse of kingdoms and empires. That is the testimony of both sacred and profane history.

But when this poison climbs up to the church or the spiritual realm, the damage it causes is inexpressible. For here the contention is not about learning, genius, beauty, wealth, kingdoms, empires, and the like; but the issue is between salvation and life or perdition and eternal death. Therefore Paul is very serious about warning those who are in the ministry of the Word about this fault. He says: "If we live by the Spirit, etc." It is as though he were saying: "If it is true that we live by the Spirit, then let us proceed in an orderly fashion and walk by the Spirit. For where the Spirit is present, He renews men and creates new attitudes in them. He changes men who are vainglorious, wrathful, and envious into men who are humble, gentle, and loving. Such men seek not their own glory but God's. They do not provoke and envy one another; they yield to one another and outdo one another in showing honor (Rom. 12:10). On the other hand, those who are greedy for glory, who provoke and envy one another, may indeed boast that they possess the Spirit and live by the Spirit. But they are deceiving themselves; for they obey the flesh and perform its works, and they have the judgment that they shall not obtain the kingdom of God."

Now just as there is nothing more dangerous in the church than this detestable vice, so there is nothing more common. For when

---

⁸³ See Luther's use of Terence's *Eunuchus* in support of this point (*Luther's Works*, 13, p. 182).

⁸⁴ The proverbial saying reads: *Qui volet ingenio cedere, nullus erit.*

God sends forth workers into His harvest, Satan immediately stirs up his servants too, who refuse to be regarded as inferior in any respect to those who are properly called. Here a controversy soon arises. The wicked refuse to yield to the godly even a hairbreadth; for they suppose themselves to be far superior to others in genius, in teaching, in godliness, and in the Spirit. Much less will the godly yield to the wicked, lest the doctrine of faith be endangered. In addition, the art and skill of the servants of Satan is such that among their followers they not only know how to simulate love, concord, humility, and other fruits of the Spirit; but they also praise one another, give preference to others over themselves, and say that others are better than they. Thus they want to appear to be anything but κενόδοξοι, and they swear that they have no other aim than the glory of God and the salvation of souls. Nevertheless, they are actually extremely eager for vainglory, doing everything to gain more respect and praise among men than others have. In short, they "imagine that godliness is a means of gain" (1 Tim. 6:5) and that the ministry of the Word was committed to them to make them famous. Therefore it is inevitable that they be the originators of dissensions and sects.

Because the κενοδοξία of the false apostles had been the reason why they had created disturbances in the churches of Galatia and had defected from Paul, he wanted to attack this fatal vice with a special lecture and discussion. In fact, this poison had provided Paul with the occasion for the composition of this entire epistle. If he had not composed it, all the labor he had expended in preaching the Gospel among the Galatians would have been expended in vain. For in his absence the false apostles had taken over in Galatia — men who gave the appearance of great authority and who, in addition to their pretense of seeking the glory of Christ and the salvation of the Galatians, had been associated with the apostles, whose footsteps they claimed to be following in their teaching. What is more, because Paul had not seen Christ in the flesh and had not been associated with the apostles, they looked down on him, repudiated his doctrine, and proclaimed their own doctrine as true and genuine. Thus they troubled the Galatians and aroused sects in their midst, so that they provoked and envied one another. This was the surest possible sign that neither the teachers nor the pupils were living and walking by the Spirit but were following the flesh and performing its works; that is, they had lost the true doctrine, faith, Christ, and all the gifts of the Spirit, and were worse than heathen.

Yet here Paul is not attacking only the false apostles who troubled the churches of his own time. But in the Spirit he foresees that there will be endless numbers of such men until the end of the world. Corrupted by this poisonous vice, they will break into the church without a call, boasting about the Spirit and about their heavenly doctrine and under this pretext overthrowing true faith and doctrine. We have seen some of these in our own time; without a call they thrust themselves into the kingdom of the Spirit, that is, into the ministry of the Word, and for a while they wanted to give the impression of teaching the same as we. With this pretense they acquired a good name and reputation as evangelical theologians who lived by the Spirit and who followed the principles of good order. But as soon as they had won over the minds of the crowd with their smooth talk, they took every opportunity to turn them away from the proper path. They began to teach something new, in the hope of becoming famous and of persuading the crowd that they had been the first to point out the errors in the church, to abolish and correct abuses, to overthrow the papacy, and to discover some outstanding new doctrine. Thus they hoped to lay claim to primacy among evangelical theologians. But because their glory was based not on God but on what men said, it could not be firm and stable; but, as Paul had prophesied, confusion arose, and "their end was destruction" (Phil. 3:19). "For the wicked will not stand in the judgment but are like chaff which the wind drives away" (Ps. 1:5, 4). The same judgment awaits all those who pursue their own aims rather than those of Christ Jesus in the preaching of the Gospel.

For the Gospel was not given that we might seek our own praise and glory through it or that the common people might acclaim us, its ministers, on account of it. But it was given that through it the blessing and glory of Christ might be illumined, that the Father might be glorified in His mercy, which He has shown us in Christ, His Son, whom He gave up for us and with whom He has given us all things (Rom. 8:32). Therefore the Gospel is the sort of teaching in which the last thing to look for is our own glory. It sets forth heavenly and eternal things which do not belong to us, which we have neither made nor earned, but which it offers to us in our unworthiness purely by the kindness of God. Then why should we lay claim to any glory on account of them? Therefore he who seeks his own glory in the Gospel speaks on his own authority. But he who speaks on his own authority is a liar, and there is unrighteousness in him; but He who seeks the glory of Him who sent Him tells the truth, and there is no unrighteousness in Him (John 7:18).

Therefore Paul is issuing a grave warning to all ministers of the Word when he says: "If we live by the Spirit, let us also walk by the Spirit." That is: Let us preserve order, namely, the doctrine of truth once handed down; and let us abide in brotherly love and in the concord of the Spirit. With simplicity of heart let us proclaim Christ and the glory of God, and let us ascribe to Him everything we receive. Let us not exalt ourselves over others, and let us not arouse sects. For this is not proceeding rightly; it is forsaking the principles of good order and replacing it with a new and perverse order.

From this it is evident that God had a good purpose in mind when He attached suffering to the teaching of the Gospel, and that He did so for a very necessary reason and for our own great benefit. For otherwise He would never have been able to repress and crush this beast called κενοδοξία. For if this teaching enjoyed only the admiration and praise of men, and if no persecution, suffering, or disgrace followed it, then certainly all who profess it would be infected by this poison and would perish. In this connection Jerome says somewhere that he has seen many who could endure all sorts of inconvenience in their bodies or in their finances, but no one who could despise praise of himself.[85] For it is impossible for a person not to be puffed up by a recital of praise for him. Even Paul, who had the Spirit of Christ, said that to keep him from being too elated by the abundance of revelations, a messenger of Satan was given him, to harass him (2 Cor. 12:7). Therefore Augustine says correctly: "If a minister of the Word receives praise, he is in danger; if a brother looks down on him and does not praise him, then the brother is in danger." [86] Whoever hears me preach the Word of God should give me honor for the sake of the Word. If he treats me with honor, he does well. But if I am proud on that account, I am in danger. On the other hand, if he looks down on me, I am out of danger; but he is not.

[85] See Jerome's criticism of certain monks, Letter CXXV, 16—17.

[86] On the love of praise cf. Augustine, *Confessions*, X, 37, 60—62; *City of God*, V, 13—14. From the manuscript of notes on Luther's lecture it is evident that here he was also thinking of St. Thomas.

Therefore we must use every means to see to it that we honor "what is good to us" (Rom. 14:16), that is, the ministry of the Word, the sacraments, etc., and that preachers and hearers hold one another in mutual esteem, in accordance with the commandment (Rom. 12:10): "Outdo one another in showing honor." But when this is done, the flesh is immediately tickled and becomes insolent. For there is no one even among the godly who would not rather be praised than insulted, unless someone is so firmly established in this regard that he remains unmoved by either criticism or praise, as that woman said of David in 2 Sam. 14:17: "My Lord the king is like the angel of God, for he remains unmoved by either blessing or cursing." Paul also says (2 Cor. 6:8): "In honor and dishonor, in ill repute and good repute." Men of this kind, who are neither elated by praise nor cast down by insults but simply strive to proclaim the glory of Christ and to seek the salvation of souls — men of this kind are following the principles of good order. But those who become proud when their praises are sung and who seek their own glory, not Christ's, as well as those who are moved by insult and slander to forsake the ministry of the Word — both of these have turned away from good order.

Therefore let everyone who boasts of the Spirit see to it that he remains in order. If you receive praise, you should know that Christ is being praised, not you; for the praise and glory belong to Him. The fact that you teach faithful doctrine and live a holy life is not your gift; it is God's. Therefore you do not receive the praise; God receives it in you. When you acknowledge this, you will remain in order. You will not be elated by praise — "For what have you that you did not receive?" (1 Cor. 4:7) — nor will you be moved by insult, slander, or persecution to desert your calling.

By a special grace, therefore, God has covered our glory today with slander, bitter hatred, persecution, and blasphemy from the whole world, as well as with contempt and ingratitude from our own followers among the peasants, the townspeople, and the nobles; because the hostility and persecution of these against the Gospel is secret and internal, it is more dangerous than that of the enemies who persecute it openly. God has done this to keep us from growing proud of our gifts. This millstone must be fastened round our neck to keep us from being infected by that poison of vainglory. There are, of course, some among our followers who honor us on account of the ministry of the Word; but where there is one who honors us,[87] there are a hundred who hate, despise, and persecute us. Therefore the slanders and persecutions of our opponents — as well as the great contempt, ingratitude, and secret bitter hatred of those in whose midst we live — are joyful sights which delight us so much that we easily forget vainglory.

Rejoicing in the Lord, who is our glory, we thus remain in order. In spiritual gifts we far surpass others; but because we acknowledge these as gifts of God, not our own, granted to us for building up the body of Christ (Eph. 4:12), we do not become proud on their account. For we know that more is required of him to whom much is given than of him to whom little is given (Luke 12:48). In addition, we know that "God shows no partiality" (Rom. 2:11). Therefore a faithful sexton is no less pleasing to God with his gift than is a preacher of the Word, for he serves God in the same faith and spirit. And so we should not honor the lowest Christians any less than they honor us. In this way we remain free of the poison of vainglory and walk by the Spirit.

But because the fanatical spirits seek their own glory, the favor and applause of men, peace with the world, and the serenity of the flesh rather than the glory of Christ and the salvation of souls — even though they continually swear that the latter is what they seek — they cannot restrain themselves but erupt in a proclamation of their own doctrine and labors and in insults and criticism of others; for their one aim is to acquire a better reputation and fame than others. "No one," they say, "ever knew this before I did. I was the first to see and teach this." Therefore they are all κενόδοξοι. That is, they do not make their boast in God but are glorious, brave, and daring when they receive applause from the crowd, whose favor they are very skillful in winning, because they can pretend anything by their words, actions, and writings. Without the applause of the crowd they are the most timid of men; for they hate the cross of Christ and persecution, and they run away from it. But when they have a cheering crowd, there is nothing so proud or courageous, no Hector or Achilles so brave and daring, as they.

The flesh is such a sly beast that it will not forsake good order, distort and corrupt true doctrine, or shatter the harmony of the church

---

[87] The question mark in the Weimar text after *reveretur* is clearly a mistake; it should be a comma.

for any other reason than for the sake of this accursed κενοδοξία. Therefore it is not without cause that Paul attacks it so sharply, both here and elsewhere. Thus in Gal. 4:17: "They make much of you, but for no good purpose; they want to shut you out, that you may make much of them." That is to say: "They want to put me into the shadow and to enhance themselves. They are not seeking the glory of Christ and your salvation but glory for themselves, disgrace for me, and slavery for you."

26. *Let us have no self-conceit,*

That is: "Let us not become vainglorious." As I have said, this means not glorying in God and in the truth but in lies and in the opinion, praise, and applause of the crowd. This is not a solid foundation for glory; it is a false one. Therefore it cannot endure for long. Whoever praises a man as a man, is lying; for there is nothing praiseworthy in him, but everything is damnable. So far as our own person is concerned, therefore, our glory is this: "All have sinned" (Rom. 3:23) and in the sight of God have been sentenced to eternal death. It is, however, another matter when our ministry receives praise. We should not only wish for this, but we should strive with all our might to make men praise it and revere it religiously; for this redounds to their salvation. Paul warns the Romans not to offend anyone, "so that what is good to you be not spoken of as evil" (Rom. 14:16); and elsewhere he says (2 Cor. 6:3): "so that no fault may be found with our ministry." Therefore when our ministry receives praise, we are not being praised in our own person; but, as the psalm says (105:3): "We are praised in God and in His holy name." [88]

no provoking of one another, no envy of one another.

Here Paul describes the effect of vainglory. A teacher of error or an originator of a new doctrine cannot help provoking others; and if they do not approve and accept his doctrine, he immediately begins to hate them bitterly. In our own time we have seen with what implacable hatred the fanatical spirits have been inflamed against us because we refused to yield to them and to approve their errors. We did not provoke them first, nor did we disseminate ungodly doctrine through the world; but we preserved good order, attacking abuses in the church and faithfully teaching the doctrine of justifica-

---

[88] It is not clear whether Luther is thinking of Ps. 105:3, of Ps. 89:17, or of both.

tion. Forsaking this, they taught many wicked doctrines in opposition to the Word of God, about the sacraments, about original sin, about the oral Word, etc.[89] In order not to lose the truth of the Gospel, we opposed them on these issues and condemned their wicked errors. They did not accept this; not only did they provoke us first through no fault of our own, but now they even envy us and hate us bitterly. They are motivated by nothing but vainglory, for they would like to put us into the shadow and to reign all by themselves. For they imagine that there is great glory in professing the Gospel, when in fact there is no greater disgrace in the eyes of the world.

[89] Cf. *Against the Heavenly Prophets, Luther's Works*, 40, 79—223.

CHAPTER SIX

1. *Brethren, if a man is overtaken in any trespass, you who are spiritual should restore him in a spirit of meekness.*

THIS is a second fine moral precept,[1] and one that is decidedly necessary for this age. For the Sacramentarians have seized upon this passage and draw from it the inference that in patience we should yield somewhat to our fallen brethren and should cover over their error through love, which "believes all things, hopes all things, endures all things" (1 Cor. 13:7).[2] Paul teaches here in explicit words that those who are spiritual should restore the erring in a spirit of meekness. They maintain that this issue is not important enough to warrant our breaking up Christian concord on account of this one doctrine, for the church has nothing more beautiful or more beneficial than concord. This is how they set forth the forgiveness of sins to us and accuse us of stubbornness because we refuse to yield a hairbreadth to them or to tolerate their error (though they do not want to admit publicly that this is what it is), much less to accuse and restore them in a spirit of gentleness. In this way these dear fellows embellish themselves and their cause, and create resentment against us among many people.

As Christ is my witness, nothing has grieved me so deeply for several years as this disagreement in doctrine. Even the Sacramentarians, if they are willing to admit the truth, know very well that I was not responsible for it. What I have believed and taught since the beginning of our cause about justification, about the sacraments, and about all the other articles of Christian doctrine I still believe and profess today, except with greater certainty; for it has deepened through study, practice, and experience, as well as through great and frequent temptations. Every day I pray Christ to keep me and

[1] From the lecture notes it seems that the first moral was the denunciation of vainglory.

[2] See p. 56, note 33.

strengthen me in this faith and confession to the day of His glorious coming. Amen. In addition, it is evident throughout Germany that at first the doctrine of the Gospel was not attacked by anyone except the papists. Among those who accepted it there was total agreement on all the articles of Christian doctrine. This agreement continued until the sectarians came forward with their new opinions, not only about the sacraments but about several other doctrines.[3] They were the first to disturb the churches and to break up their concord. Since that time more and more sects have inevitably arisen, and these were always followed by greater dissensions. Therefore they are doing us this enormous injury contrary to their own conscience and are arousing this unbearable resentment against us in the sight of the whole world beyond our deserts. It is very burdensome, especially in such an important matter, for an innocent man to endure the punishment that someone else has deserved.

But we could easily forget this injury and accept and restore them in a spirit of meekness if only they returned to the proper way and walked with us in an orderly manner; that is, if they believed and taught faithfully about the Lord's Supper and about the other articles of Christian doctrine, and if, in unanimous consensus with us, they proclaimed, not their own opinions but Christ, that the Son of God might be glorified through us and the Father through Him. But it is unbearable to us when they merely praise love and concord but minimize the issue of the Sacrament, as though it were a matter of little consequence what we believe about the Eucharist, which was instituted by Christ our Lord. We must proclaim concord in doctrine and faith as much as they proclaim concord in life. If they preserve this in its soundness together with us, we shall join them in praising the concord of love, which is to be subordinated to the concord of faith or of the Spirit. For if you lose this, you have lost Christ; and once you have lost Him, love will not do you any good. On the other hand, if you keep Christ and the unity of the Spirit, it does not matter if you dissent from those who corrupt the Word and who thus shatter the unity of the Spirit. I would rather that they depart from me and be my enemies, and the whole world along with them, than that I depart from Christ and have Him as an enemy; this is what would happen if I forsook His clear and simple Word and followed instead the vain notions by which they distort the words of Christ

---

[3] See p. 105, note 89.

to their own interpretation. A single Christ means more to me than an infinite number of concords in love.

As for those who love Christ and who faithfully teach and believe His Word, however, we are ready not only to preserve peace and concord with them but also to bear their sins and weaknesses, and to restore them when they fall, as Paul commands here, in a gentle spirit. That was how Paul bore with the weakness and the fall of the Galatians and of others misled by the false apostles, when they returned to their senses. Thus he received back into grace that Corinthian who had been guilty of incest (2 Cor. 2:7-8). Likewise, Onesimus, the runaway slave whose father he had become for the sake of Christ in his imprisonment in Rome (Philemon 10), was reconciled with his master by Paul. Therefore he carried out in practice what he teaches here and elsewhere about bearing with the weak and restoring the fallen, but toward those who were curable, that is, those who heartily acknowledged their sin, fall, and error and returned to their senses. By contrast, he dealt very severely with the false apostles, who obstinately defended their doctrine as right rather than wrong. "I wish," he said (5:12), "that those who unsettle you would mutilate themselves!" Again (5:10): "He who is troubling you will bear his judgment, whoever he is." And again (1:8): "Even if we, or an angel from heaven, etc., let him be accursed." Undoubtedly there were many who defended the false apostles against Paul, saying that they had the Spirit, were ministers of Christ, and preached the Gospel just as much as Paul; that although they did not agree with Paul on every point of doctrine, he should not pronounce such a horrible sentence upon them; and that all he would accomplish by his stubbornness would be to create a disturbance in the churches and to destroy their beautiful concord. Unmoved by these statements, he curses and condemns the false apostles with complete assurance, calling them disturbers of the churches and subverters of the Gospel of Christ. At the same time he praises his own doctrine so much that he wants everything to yield to it — concord in love, the apostles, an angel from heaven, or anything else.

Thus we do not permit this cause to be minimized either; for He whose cause it is, is great. Once He was small, when He lay in the manger; and yet even then He was so great that He was worshiped by angels and proclaimed as the Lord of all (Luke 2:11). Therefore we will not permit His Word to suffer injury in any doctrine. In the doctrines of the faith nothing should seem small or insignificant to us, as though we should or could surrender it. For the forgiveness of sins pertains to those who are weak in faith and morals, who acknowledge their sin and seek forgiveness, but not to the subverters of doctrine, who do not acknowledge their error and sin but defend them vigorously as though they were truth and righteousness. By this means they cause us to lose the forgiveness of sins, because they distort and deny the Word that proclaims and confers the forgiveness of sins. Therefore let them first come into accord with us in Christ; that is, let them acknowledge their sin and correct their error. Then if we are deficient in the spirit of meekness, they will have a right to accuse us.

Anyone who weighs the apostle's words carefully will see clearly that he is not speaking about heresies or about sins against doctrine but about much less important sins, into which a man falls, not on account of deliberate malice or on purpose but out of weakness. Hence he uses such kind and fatherly words, not calling it error or sin but "trespass." Then, to minimize and almost to excuse the sin and to remove the blame from the man, he adds: "If a man is overtaken," that is, if he is deceived by the devil or by the flesh. Even the word "man" serves to minimize the matter. It is as though he were saying: "What is more characteristic of a human being than to be able to fall, to be deceived, and to err?" Thus Moses says in Lev. 6:3: "Human beings make a habit of sinning." Therefore this is a statement filled with comfort, which once delivered me from death at the height of a struggle.[4] In this life the saints not only live in the flesh but even, by some urging or other from the devil, gratify the desires of the flesh; that is, they fall into impatience, envy, wrath, error, doubt, unbelief, etc. For Satan is continually attacking both the purity of doctrine, which he seeks to destroy by means of sects and discord, and the integrity of life, which he pollutes through our daily transgressions and offenses. For this reason Paul teaches us how to deal with those who have fallen this way, namely, that those who are strong should restore them in a gentle spirit.

It is of the greatest importance for those who are in charge of churches to know these things, so that when they try to cut everything to the quick, they do not forget this fatherly and motherly feel-

---

[4] There seems to be no other reference to this in Luther's writings, although there are many similar statements about other passages; cf., for example, *Luther's Works*, 14, p. 45, note 4.

ing which Paul requires here of those who carry on the cure of souls. He gave an illustration of this command of his in 2 Cor. 2:6-8, where he says: "For such an excommunicated person this punishment by the majority is enough; so you should rather turn to forgive and comfort him, or he may be overwhelmed by excessive sorrow." "So I beg you," he concludes, "to reaffirm your love for him." And so pastors should rebuke the lapsed sharply; but when they see them sorrowing, they should begin to cheer them up, to comfort them, and to make light of their sins as much as they can. Yet they should do all this in mercy, which they should set in opposition to the sins, so that the lapsed are not overwhelmed by excessive sorrow. The Holy Spirit is as generous and kind in bearing with sins and minimizing them as He is unyielding in maintaining and defending the doctrine of faith — provided that those who have committed the sins are sorry for them.

But here as everywhere else the "synagog" of the pope (Rev. 2:9) has taught and acted contrary to the precept and example of Paul. The Roman pontiff and the bishops have truly been tyrants and persecutors of consciences, for they continually burdened consciences with new traditions and condemned them by excommunication for the most trivial reasons. To make consciences obey their vain and wicked terrors more readily, they quoted these statements of Pope Gregory: "It is characteristic of good minds to fear guilt where there is no guilt"; and "Even our unjust statements should be feared." [5] With these statements, which the devil has dragged into the church, they established the practice of excommunication and the majesty of the papacy, of which the whole world is terrified. There is no need for such "goodness of mind," but it is enough to acknowledge guilt where it really exists. Who has given you the power, you Roman Satan, with your wicked statements to terrify and condemn minds that are already thoroughly terrified, when they should rather be cheered up, set free from their false terrors, and brought from lies to the truth? All this you omit; and in accordance with your title as "man of sin and son of perdition" (2 Thess. 2:3), you invent guilt where there is no guilt. Truly this is the craft and pretense of Antichrist, by which the pope has so firmly established the practice of excommunication and his own tyranny. No one could ignore his wicked statements without being regarded as intractable and alto-

---

[5] See also *Luther's Works*, 3, p. 349, note 29.

gether evil. Thus certain princes ignored them, but with an accusing conscience, because in that darkness they did not know that the pope's curses were meaningless.

Let those to whom the charge and care of consciences has been committed learn from this command of Paul how they are to deal with the lapsed. "Brethren," he says, "if a man is overtaken, do not embitter or sadden him even more; do not reject or condemn him. But correct, refresh, and renew him (for that is the import of the Greek word [6]); and by your meekness repair that about him which has perished through the devil's deception or through the weakness of his flesh. For the kingdom into which you have been called is not a kingdom of fear and of sadness; it is a kingdom of confidence and happiness. If you see some brother in terror because of a sin of which he has been guilty, run to him, and extend your hand to him in his fallen state. Comfort him with sweet words and embrace him in your motherly arms. The obdurate and stubborn, who fearlessly and smugly persist and continue in their sins, you should rebuke sharply. But those who are overtaken in a trespass and sorrow and grieve over their fall should be encouraged and instructed by you who are spiritual. And this should be done in a spirit of gentleness, not of zeal for righteousness [7] or cruelty, as some confessors did, who, when they should have refreshed thirsty hearts with some sweet comfort, gave them gall and vinegar to drink, just as the Jews did to Christ on the cross (Matt. 27:34).

On the basis of this we can well understand that the forgiveness of sins should not prevail in the area of doctrine, as the Sacramentarians maintain, but in the area of life and of our works. Here let no one condemn another. Let him not rebuke him furiously or harshly, as Ezekiel says of the shepherds of Israel that "with force and harshness they have ruled the flock of God" (Ezek. 34:4). But let one brother comfort another lapsed brother in a gentle spirit. And let the lapsed one, in turn, hear the word of him who is comforting him, and let him believe it. For God does not want to reject, but to "raise up all who are bowed down," as the psalm says (145:14); for He has paid a greater price for them than we have, namely, His

---

[6] Luther means the Greek word καταρτίζετε.

[7] The comma in the Weimar edition between *zeli* and *iusticiae* should be omitted, for Luther is using a phrase that occurs often in his writings: *zelus iusticiae*.

own life and blood. Therefore we, too, should come to their aid, heal and help them with the utmost gentleness. Thus we do not deny forgiveness to the Sacramentarians or other founders of wicked sects; but we sincerely forgive their insults and blasphemies against Christ, and we shall never again mention the injuries they have inflicted upon us, on the condition that they repent, forsake the wicked doctrine with which they have disturbed the churches of Christ, and walk in an orderly way together with us. But if they persist in their error and violate good order, it is useless for them to demand the forgiveness of sins from us.

Look to yourself, lest you, too, be tempted.

This is a rather serious warning. Its purpose is to put down the harshness and cruelty of those who do not cheer and restore the lapsed. "There is no sin," says Augustine, "that one man has committed that another man could not commit."[8] We are living on a slippery place; therefore if we become proud and forsake good order, it will be easier for us to fall than to stand. Therefore that man spoke rightly in *The Lives of the Fathers* when the report was brought to him that one of the brothers had fallen into fornication. "Yesterday it was he," he said, "and today it could be I."[9] Paul adds this serious warning to keep pastors from being harsh and unkind toward the fallen and to keep them from measuring their own holiness by comparison with the sins of others, as the Pharisee did (Luke 18:11). Instead, they should be moved by motherly feelings toward them and should think: "This man has fallen. It can happen that you, too, will fall, far more dangerously and disgracefully than he has." If those who are so ready to judge and condemn others took an accurate look at their own sins, they would discover that the sins of those who have fallen are "specks" and that their own are huge "logs" (Matt. 7:3).

"Therefore let any one who thinks that he stands take heed lest he fall" (1 Cor. 10:12). If David — such a holy man, filled with faith and with the Spirit of God, one who had received such outstanding promises and who had performed such great things for the Lord — fell so disgracefully and, though well along in years, was seized by

[8] Cf. *Luther's Works*, 9, pp. 260—261.

[9] This thought occurs often in the *Vitae patrum*, e. g., *Patrologia, Series Latina*, LXXVIII, 308—309, 963, 967.

youthful passion after the many different trials with which God had disciplined him, what right do we have to presume about our own constancy? By means of such examples God discloses our own weakness to us, so that we do not become puffed up but are properly fearful; He also discloses His judgment, namely, that there is nothing more intolerable to Him than pride, whether toward Him or toward the brethren. It is not in vain, therefore, that Paul says: "Look to yourself, lest you, too, be tempted." Those who have undergone temptations know how necessary this commandment is. But those who have not been tried by them do not understand Paul, and thus they are not moved by any mercy toward the fallen; this was evident in the papacy, where nothing but tyranny and cruelty prevailed.

2. *Bear one another's burdens, and so fulfill the Law of Christ.*

A very considerate commandment, to which Paul adds great praise as a kind of exclamation. The Law of Christ is the law of love. After redeeming and regenerating us and constituting us as His church, Christ did not give us any new law except the law of mutual love (John 13:34): "A new commandment I give to you, that you love one another, even as I have loved you"; and again (v. 35): "By this all men will know that you are My disciples." To love does not mean, as the sophists imagine, to wish someone else well,[10] but to bear someone else's burdens, that is, to bear what is burdensome to you and what you would rather not bear. Therefore a Christian must have broad shoulders and husky bones to carry the flesh, that is, the weakness, of the brethren; for Paul says that they have burdens and troubles. Love is sweet, kind, and patient — not in receiving but in performing; for it is obliged to overlook many things and to bear with them. In the church faithful pastors see many errors and sins which they are obliged to bear.[11] In the state the obedience of subjects never lives up to the laws of the magistrate; therefore if he does not know how to conceal things, the magistrate will not be fit to rule the commonwealth. In the family many things happen that displease the householder. But if we are able to bear and overlook our own faults and sins, which we commit in such great numbers every day,

[10] Cf. Thomas Aquinas, *Summa Theologica*, II-II, Q. 27, Art. 2.

[11] According to the lecture notes, Luther referred here to a saying of John Staupitz at the installation of a prior in Wittenberg: "The friars will not do what you want, but the very opposite."

let us bear those of others as well, in accordance with the statements: "Bear one another's burdens" and "You shall love your neighbor as yourself" (Lev. 19:18).

Since there are faults in every station of society and in all men, Paul sets forth the Law of Christ for Christians, by which he admonishes them to bear one another's burdens. Those who do not do this thereby give ample testimony that they do not understand even a dot (Matt. 5:18) of the Law of Christ, which is the law of love; as Paul says in 1 Cor. 13:7, it believes all things, hopes all things, and bears all the burdens of the brethren. Yet the fundamental principle is always preserved, according to which those who sin are not those who transgress the Law of Christ, namely, love, and who do injury to their neighbor, but those who do injury to Christ and to His kingdom, which He has established with His own blood. This kingdom is not preserved by the law of love but by the Word, by faith, by the Spirit. Hence this commandment that their burdens should be borne does not refer to those who deny Christ and who not only do not acknowledge their sin but defend it; nor to those who persist in their sins (who also partly deny Christ). Such people are to be avoided, lest we become partakers of their evil works. But those who believe and who gladly hear the Word, but who fall into sin against their will and, upon being admonished, not only listen but detest their sin and strive to correct their lives — these are "overtaken" and have the burdens that Paul commands us to bear. Here let us not be unkind and severe; but, following the example of Christ, who supports and bears such people, let us also support and bear them. If He does not punish them, even though He could do so with a perfect right, much less should we punish them.

3. *For if anyone thinks he is something, when he is nothing, he deceives himself.*

Here again Paul attacks the founders of sects and depicts them in their true colors, as men who are hard and merciless. They have only contempt for the weak and do not bear their burdens. Like sulky husbands or harsh schoolmasters, they insist that everything be just so. They do not like anything except what they themselves do. Finally, you will always have them as your bitter enemies unless you approve of all their sayings and doings and thoroughly accommodate yourself to their habits. Such men are completely proud, men who presume to arrogate everything to themselves. This is what Paul is saying here. They think they are something, that is, that they have the Spirit, that they understand all the mysteries of the Scriptures (1 Cor. 13:2), that they cannot err or fall, that they do not need any forgiveness of sins. Therefore Paul adds correctly that they are nothing, but that they deceive themselves with their foolish presumptions of holiness and wisdom. Thus they understand nothing either about Christ or about the Law of Christ; otherwise they would say: "Brother, you are having trouble with this fault; I am having trouble with another. God has forgiven me ten thousand talents. I shall forgive you ten denarii (Matt. 18:23-35)." But because they want to hold everything to the strictest requirement and refuse to endure and bear any of the burdens of the weak, men are offended by their harshness and begin to despise, to hate, and to run away from them. They do not seek counsel and comfort from them and do not care what or how they teach. But pastors actually should conduct themselves toward the people in their charge in such a way that they will respect and admire them, not for the sake of their own persons but for the sake of their ministry and of the Christian virtues, which should shine forth especially from them.

In this passage Paul has given a very beautiful description of such harsh and merciless saints when he says: "They think they are something"; that is, they are puffed up with their own foolish ideas and dreams, and have an exalted notion of their knowledge and sanctity; but in fact they are nothing and are merely deceiving themselves. It is an obvious deception when someone is persuaded that he is something but is nothing. Such men are described in Rev. 3:17 in these words: "You say, I am rich, I have prospered, and I need nothing; not knowing that you are wretched, pitiable, poor, blind, and naked."

4. *But let each one test his own work, and then his reason to boast will be in himself alone and not in his neighbor.*

Paul is continuing with his rebuke of the despicable men who are called "vainglorious." This desire for vainglory is an odious and accursed vice. It provides the occasion for all sorts of evil and creates disturbances in both the state and the individual conscience. And in spiritual matters it is a completely incurable evil. Although this passage can be understood as applying to the works of this life and behavior, yet chiefly the apostle is discussing the work of the ministry and attacking those κενόδοξοι who with their fanatical opinions disturb consciences that have been properly instructed.

It is characteristic of those who are infected with κενοδοξία that they do not care at all whether their "work," that is, their ministry, is pure or not; all they are interested in is acquiring the applause of the crowd. Thus when the false apostles saw that Paul had preached the Gospel to the Galatians purely and that they could not do any better, they began to slander what he had set forth so correctly and faithfully, and to elevate their doctrine above Paul's doctrine. In this way they curried the favor of the Galatians and made Paul repugnant to them. Thus those who are κενόδοξοι combine these three faults: first, they are exceedingly vainglorious; secondly, they are amazingly skillful at slandering the good things that others have said and done and thus at gaining the applause of the people for themselves; thirdly, when they have become celebrated among the people, albeit by the labor and risk of someone else, they become so brave and courageous that there is nothing they will not dare. Therefore they are destructive men, worthy of being completely accursed; and I hate them more than I do a dog or a snake.[12] "They look after their own interests, not those of Jesus Christ" (Phil. 2:21).

It is such men that Paul is attacking here. It is as though he were saying: "Such vainglorious spirits do their work, that is, preach the Gospel, with the purpose of gaining praise and applause among men; they want to be hailed by them as extraordinary and outstanding theologians, with whom Paul and others cannot even be compared. When they have obtained this reputation, they begin to slander the works, sayings, and deeds of others, and to praise their own grandly. In this cunning way they drive the crowd out of their minds. Because they have 'itching ears' (2 Tim. 4:3), the crowd not only takes pleasure in new doctrines; but, being sated and sick of the Word, they even enjoy watching their former teachers overshadowed and crowded out by new and supposedly glorious teachers." "This," he continues, "should not happen. Everyone should be faithful in his ministry, not looking out for his own glory or trusting in the fickle applause of the multitude but being concerned only that he do his job properly, that is, that he preach the Gospel purely. For if his work is done properly, he should know that he will not be lacking in glory before God and eventually also before other believers. When

---

[12] A reference to Horace, *Epistles*, I, 17, 30.

meanwhile he fails to gain any praise from the unthankful world, this should not bother him; for he knows that the purpose of his ministry is that Christ, not he, be glorified for it. Therefore armed 'with the weapons of righteousness for the right hand and for the left' (2 Cor. 6:7), let him say with a steady mind: 'I did not begin preaching the Gospel to make the world honor me. Therefore I shall not quit either on account of the dishonor with which it treats me.' Such a person teaches the Word and performs his ministry without any regard for persons, without any concern for praise, glory, fortitude, or wisdom. He does not depend on the praise of others but has it in himself."

Thus one who carries out his office correctly and faithfully does not care what the world says about him; he does not care whether it praises him or blames him. He has his boast within himself, which is the testimony of his conscience and a boasting in God. Therefore he can say with Paul (2 Cor. 1:12): "Our boast is this, the testimony of our conscience that we have behaved in the world with simplicity and godly sincerity, not by earthly wisdom but by the grace of God." Such a boast is pure and constant. For it does not depend on the judgment of others; it depends on one's own conscience. This is what gives us testimony that we have taught correctly, have administered the sacraments, and have done everything else correctly. Therefore it cannot be corrupted or abolished.

The other kind of boasting, which is what the κενόδοξοι have, is unsure and extremely hazardous; for they do not have it within themselves, but it depends on what the crowd thinks and says. Hence they cannot have the testimony of their own conscience that they have done everything with a simple and sincere mind solely to illumine the glory of God and to promote the salvation of souls. All they aim for is that on the basis of the work or labor of their preaching they themselves may become famous and glorious among men. Therefore they do indeed have a boast, a confidence, and a testimony — but only before men, not before themselves or before God. Believers do not want to have this kind of boast. If Paul had had praise and glory before men, not before himself, he would have been forced to despair when he saw many states, regions, and all Asia defecting from him (2 Tim. 1:15), and when he saw so many scandals and sects following upon his preaching. When Christ was alone, that is, when He was not only being hounded to death by the Jews but forsaken by His own disciples, He still was not alone; for the Father was with Him. Thus if our confidence and boasting today were dependent on the judgment and the favor of men, we would soon be forced to perish with sorrow of heart. For the papists, the fanatical spirits, and the entire world do not regard us as worthy of any praise or glory; in fact, they hate and persecute us ruthlessly, and they slander and strive to subvert our ministry and our teaching. Thus all we have before men is shame. But our joy and our boasting are in the Lord. Hence we are confident and happy as with the utmost faith and diligence we carry out the office into which God has placed us and which we know is pleasing to Him. When we do this, we do not care at all whether our work pleases or displeases the devil, or whether the world likes or dislikes us. For when we know that our work has been done properly, and when we have a good conscience in the sight of God, we go right ahead "in honor and dishonor, in ill repute and good repute" (2 Cor. 6:8). This is what Paul calls having one's boast within oneself.

Paul's warning against this most harmful vice is decidedly necessary. For the Gospel is the sort of teaching that both by its own nature and by the malice of Satan brings on the experience of the cross. Hence Paul calls it "the Word of the cross and of offense" (1 Cor. 1:18). It does not always have steadfast disciples. Today they join up and confess it; tomorrow they are offended by the cross, fall away, and deny it.[13] And so those who preach the Gospel to curry the applause and praise of men must perish and see their glory turned to shame as soon as the people stop applauding them. Let every preacher learn, therefore, to have his boast based, not on what others say but within himself. If there are some who praise him, as believers often do — Paul does say "in honor and dishonor" (2 Cor. 6:8) — let him accept this glory, but as an accident of his true glory; for he regards the testimony of his own conscience as the substance of his glory. Then he is "testing his own work"; that is, without any concern for his own glory he is bent only on carrying out his office in a fitting manner, that is, by preaching the Gospel purely and manifesting the proper use of the sacraments. When he tests his own work in this way, he will have his boast within himself, a boast that no one can take away from him. For it is planted, fixed, and established deep within his own heart, not in the mouths of others, whom

---

[13] From the lecture notes it is evident that Luther was thinking of Carlstadt.

Satan can easily deflect by turning their lips and tongue from blessing to the vilest of cursing.

"Therefore," says Paul, "if you yearn for glory, look for it in a skillful and solid fashion, not as it is located in the mouths of others but as it is in your own hearts. This is what happens when you carry out your office properly. In this way it will also follow that the glory you have within yourselves will then be followed by glory before others as well. But if your ground of boasting is in others, not in yourselves, the inner shame and confusion that you have within your own hearts will be followed by an outer confusion before others." We have seen this happening in our own time in the case of certain fanatical spirits.[14] They did not test their own work; that is, they were not concerned to teach the Gospel purely but used it to gain the applause of the crowd, in violation of the Second Commandment. Therefore their inner confusion was followed by an outer confusion, in accordance with the statement (Ex. 20:7): "The Lord will not hold him guiltless who takes His name in vain"; and (1 Sam. 2:30): "Those who despise Me shall be lightly esteemed." But if we seek first the glory of God through the ministry of the Word, our own glory will surely follow, according to the statement (1 Sam. 2:30): "Those who honor Me, I will honor." In short, let everyone "test," that is, be diligently concerned that his ministry be faithful; for this above all is required in ministers of the Word (1 Cor. 4:2). It is as though he were saying: "Let everyone strive to achieve this, that he preach the Word purely and faithfully; and let him consider nothing except the glory of God and the salvation of souls. Then his work will be good in a faithful and solid way, and in his conscience he will have his boast, the sort of boast that can say with confidence: 'This doctrine and my ministry are pleasing to God.' That is truly a great and excellent boast."

Now this statement can be applied fittingly to works performed by believers in any area of life. Thus someone who is a magistrate, a householder, a servant, a teacher, a pupil, etc., should remain in his calling and do his duty there, properly and faithfully, without concerning himself about what lies outside his own vocation. If he does this, he will have his boast within himself, so that he can say: "With my utmost faithfulness and diligence I have carried out the work of my calling as God has commanded me to; and therefore

---

[14] In the lecture notes Luther refers explicitly to Zwingli and Oecolampadius.

I know that this work, performed in faith and obedience to God, is pleasing to Him. If others slander it, that does not matter much." There are always those who despise and slander faithful teaching and living. But God has given a dire warning that He will destroy such slanderers. And so while such men search for vainglory, anxiously and long, and try to blacken the reputation of the true believers by their slanders, what Paul said will happen to them (Phil. 3:19): "They glory in their shame"; and elsewhere (2 Tim. 3:9): "Their folly will be known to all." Through whom? Through God, the righteous Judge, who will both expose their slanders and bring forth the right of the believers as the noonday (Ps. 37:6). The phrase "in himself alone," just to mention this in passing, must be interpreted in such a way that God is not excluded, namely, that everyone should know that his work, regardless of the station of life in which he is, is a divine work, because it is the work of a divine calling and has the command of God.

5. *For each man will have to bear his own load.*

This is a sort of reason in support of the previous statement about not depending on the judgments of others regarding oneself. It is as though Paul were saying: "It is the height of insanity to look for the ground of your boasting in others, not in yourself. For in your death struggle and at the Last Judgment it will not help you at all that others praised you. Others will not bear your load, but you will stand before the judgment seat of Christ (Rom. 14:10) and bear your own load alone. There your partisans will not be able to help you at all; for when we die, the voices of those who praise us will be stilled. 'On that day, when God judges the secrets of men' (Rom. 2:16), the testimony of your conscience will stand either for you or against you: against you if you have your boast in others; for you if you have it in yourself, that is, if your conscience bears testimony to you that you have carried out the ministry of the Word properly and faithfully, with a concern only for the glory of God and the salvation of souls, in other words, that you have done your duty rightly, in accordance with your calling." The words "Each man will have to bear his own judgment" are forceful enough to frighten us thoroughly, so that we do not yearn for vainglory.

It should also be noted that we are not dealing here with the doctrine of justification, where nothing matters except sheer grace and the forgiveness of sins, which are received by faith alone; there all works, even those that are the best and that have been done in accordance with a divine vocation, are in need of the forgiveness of sins, because we have not done them perfectly. But this is another issue. He is not treating the forgiveness of sins here, but he is comparing genuine and hypocritical works. Therefore what he says should be interpreted to mean that although the work or the ministry of a faithful pastor is not so perfect that he no longer needs the forgiveness of sins, nevertheless it is proper and perfect in itself as compared with the ministry of vainglorious men. Thus our ministry is proper and well established, because through it we seek the glory of God and the salvation of souls. The ministry of the fanatical spirits is not like this, for they seek their own glory. Although no work is able to grant the conscience peace before God, yet it is essential for us to be able to declare that we have performed our work in sincerity, in truth, and in a divine vocation; that is, that we have not corrupted the Word of God but have taught it purely. We have need of this testimony of our conscience that we have carried out our ministry well and have also lived a good life. Therefore we have a right to boast of our works to the extent that we know them to be commanded by God and pleasing in His sight. At the Last Judgment each man will have to bear his own load; therefore the praise of others will not do him any good there.

Thus far Paul has been attacking the poisonous vice of vainglory. No one is so strong that he does not need continual prayer to overcome this. For what believer does not enjoy being praised? The Holy Spirit alone is able to preserve us from being infected by this poison.

6. *Let him who is taught the Word share all good things with him who teaches.*

Here Paul is preaching to hearers that they should share all good things with their preachers. I often used to wonder why the apostle was so diligent in commanding the churches to provide for their preachers. For in the papacy I saw everyone contributing with great generosity for the construction of magnificent churches, for the increase in the income and the growth in the revenues of those who dealt with sacred things. Thus the social position and the wealth both of the bishops and of the other clergy increased so much that everywhere they had possession of the best and most fertile lands.

And so it seemed to me unnecessary for Paul to command this when the clergy were not only receiving donations of every good thing in abundance but were actually becoming very rich. Therefore I thought that people should be dissuaded from giving more rather than persuaded to give, for I saw that the excessive generosity of people was only increasing the greed of the clergy. But now we know the reason why formerly they had an abundance of every good thing, but now pastors and ministers of the Word suffer want.

Formerly, when wicked and false doctrine was taught, the pope became an emperor, and the cardinals and bishops became kings and princes of the world; so abundant was their prosperity, derived from the Patrimony of Peter [15] — who claimed not to have any silver or gold (Acts 3:6) — and from so-called "spiritual goods." But now that the Gospel has begun to be preached, those who confess it are about as rich as Christ and the apostles once were! We are finding out by experience how conscientiously people observe this commandment about providing for the preachers of the Word, which Paul so persistently urges and inculcates upon hearers both here and in other passages. We do not know of a single city today that provides for its preachers. They are not being provided for from any donations given to Christ, to whom no one gives anything. For when He was born, He used a manger instead of a cradle, because there was no room for Him in the inn (Luke 2:7). While He lived on earth, He had nowhere to lay His head (Matt. 8:20). At the end He was stripped of His clothing; and He died a miserable death on the cross, naked, hanging between two thieves (Matt. 27:28-38). No, our preachers are being provided for from donations given to the pope in exchange for the abominations of suppressing the Gospel, teaching human traditions, and establishing wicked forms of worship.[16]

When I read the exhortations in which Paul preaches to the churches either about providing for their own preachers or about contributing something for the alleviation of the poverty of the saints in Judea, I am deeply amazed, and I blush with shame that such a great apostle is compelled to use so many words in obtaining this favor from the churches. To the Corinthians he presents this matter

---

[15] The Patrimony of Peter refers to the estates belonging to the Church of Rome, but Luther (like his contemporaries) sometimes used the term to refer to all the States of the Church.

[16] This was true of Luther's Black Cloister itself.

for two entire chapters.¹⁷ I would not be willing to defame Wittenberg, which is nothing compared with Corinth, as he defamed Corinth when he begged for support for the poor with such anxiety and solicitude. But that is the fate of the Gospel. When it is preached, not only is no one willing to give anything for the support of its ministers and the maintenance of schools; but everyone begins to rob and steal and to take all sorts of advantage of everyone else. In short, men seem suddenly to have degenerated into wild beasts. On the other hand, when the doctrines of demons (1 Tim. 4:1) are proclaimed, men become truly lavish and spontaneously offer everything to their seducers. The prophets denounce the same sin in the Jews, that they contributed to the support of godly priests and Levites only with reluctance but were extremely generous to the wicked ones.¹⁸

Only now do we understand how necessary this commandment of Paul's about providing for the ministers of the churches really was. There is nothing that Satan can bear less than the light of the Gospel. When it shines, he becomes furious and tries with all his might to extinguish it. He attempts this in two ways: first, by the deceit of heretics and the might of tyrants; secondly, by poverty and famine. Because Satan has been unable thus far to suppress the Gospel in our territories through heretics and tyrants, he is now trying the second way; he is depriving the ministers of the Word of their livelihood, so that poverty and famine will force them to forsake their ministry, and the unfortunate people, deprived of the Word, will eventually degenerate into animals. To make this dreadful evil come more quickly, Satan is vigorously pressing it through wicked magistrates in the cities and nobles in the country, who are seizing and misappropriating the possessions of the churches, from which the ministers of the Gospel should get their living.¹⁹ "From the hire of a harlot," says the prophet Micah (1:7), "she gathered her possessions, and to the hire of a harlot they shall return." In addition, Satan leads even good men away from the Gospel by means of satiety. A constant and daily attention to the Word makes it cloying and contemptible to many, who then gradually become neglectful in the practice of all the duties of godliness. No one nowadays is bring-

---

17 It is not clear whether Luther means 1 Cor. 9 and 10 or 2 Cor. 8 and 9.

18 Luther may be thinking of passages like Joel 1:9-13.

19 See p. 126.

ing up his children in the knowledge of good literature, much less of sacred literature, but only in ways of making a living. All these are efforts by Satan for suppressing the Gospel in our territories, and that without the might of tyrants or the deceit of heretics.

Thus it is not useless for Paul to admonish the hearers of the Word to share all good things with those who teach. He says to the Corinthians (1 Cor. 9:11): "If we have sown spiritual good among you, is it too much if we reap your material benefits?" Therefore hearers should minister in their material needs to those from whom they have received spiritual benefits. But today the peasants, the townspeople, and the nobles only abuse our doctrine to get rich. Formerly, under the dominion of the pope, there was no one who did not pay something to the priests annually for so-called anniversary Masses,[20] vigils, etc. The mendicant friars had their share too. Trade with Rome[21] and the daily offerings also got something. Our people have been set free from these and endless other exactions by the Gospel. But they are so far from being grateful for this freedom that they have been changed from prodigal donors to thieves and robbers, who will not give even a pittance either for the Gospel or for its ministers or for the holy poor. This is the surest possible sign that they have already lost the Word and faith and have been excommunicated from our blessings, for it is impossible that true believers would permit their pastors to suffer need. But because they laugh and poke fun when their pastors suffer some sort of adversity, and because they deny them their support or do not give it as faithfully as they should, it is certain that they are worse than heathen. Soon they will learn by experience what calamities will follow this ingratitude, for they will lose both their material and their spiritual goods. It is inevitable that grave punishment should follow this sin. I am sure that the only reason why the churches in Galatia, Corinth, etc., were so confused by the false apostles was that they had neglected their faithful teachers. Finally it is the utmost justice that someone who refuses an obol to the God who offers every good thing and eternal life should end up giving a gold piece to the devil, who offers him every kind of calamity and eternal death. Whoever is not willing to serve God in a small way for his

---

[20] Anniversary Masses were those said for the departed at the anniversary of their death; at one time they were said daily for a year.

[21] Luther is referring especially to the indulgence traffic.

own great advantage, let him serve the devil in a big way to his own supreme loss. Only now that the Word is shining do we see what the devil and the world are.

When Paul says "all good things," this is not to be taken to mean that everyone should share all his possessions with his preacher. No, it means that he should provide for him liberally, giving him as much as is needed to support his life in comfort. The word κατηχούμενος is familiar to anyone who knows Greek.

7. *Do not be deceived; God is not mocked.*

The apostle is so serious in advocating this topic of support for preachers that he adds a threat to his denunciation and exhortation, saying: "God is not mocked." With this he hits the nail squarely on the head [22] so far as the morals of our own countrymen are concerned. In their utter smugness they look down on our ministry and regard it as some sort of joke or game. And so they try, especially the nobles, to make their pastors subject to them as though they were vile slaves. If we did not have a prince who is as pious and devoted to the truth as ours is,[23] they would have driven us out of this territory long since. When the pastors ask for their pay or complain that they are suffering need, they exclaim: "Priests are greedy! They want to have an abundance of every good thing. No one can satisfy their insatiable greed. If they were truly evangelical, they would have to give up all private property, follow the pauper Christ as paupers, and bear every indignity." Paul addresses a horrible threat here to fine fellows of this kind, who do this sort of thing and yet want to give the impression that they are not poking fun but are true evangelicals who worship God religiously. "Do not be deceived," he says, "God is not mocked." It is as though he were saying: "Surely you have not deceived God, but only yourselves. You will not mock God, but God will mock you" (Ps. 2:4). There is a well-known little verse that says: "You have not deceived me, your teacher, but yourself." [24] But the headstrong nobility and the peasant class remain completely unmoved by this dreadful threat. When the death struggle comes, however,

---

[22] We have used this as an approximate English equivalent for *acu tangere*, "to touch with a needle"; cf. Plautus, *Rudens*, V, 2, 19.

[23] When these lectures were delivered, Luther's prince was the Elector John; but by 1535, when they were printed, he had been replaced by John Frederick.

[24] *Disticha Catonis*, ed. by Marcus Boas (Amsterdam, 1952), Book III, Preface, p. 149; see also *Luther's Works*, 23, p. 362; note 43.

they will find out whether they have deceived themselves or us (though not really us but, as Paul says here, God Himself). Meanwhile, because they arrogantly despise our warnings, we are saying these things for our own comfort, so that we know that it is better to suffer injury than to commit it; for patience is always innocent. Besides, God will not permit us, His ministers, to perish of hunger; but when the rich suffer need and are hungry, He will feed us, and in the days of famine He will provide for us.

For whatever a man sows, that he will also reap.

All this pertains to the topic of support for ministers. I do not like to interpret such passages; for they seem to commend us, as in fact they do. In addition, it gives the appearance of greed if one emphasizes these things diligently to one's hearers. Nevertheless, people should be taught also about this matter, in order that they may know that they owe both respect and support to their preachers. Christ teaches the same thing in Luke 10:7: "Eating and drinking what they provide, for the laborer deserves his wages"; and Paul says elsewhere (1 Cor. 9:13-14): "Do you not know that those who are employed in the temple service get their food from the temple, and those who serve at the altar share in the sacrificial offerings? In the same way the Lord commanded that those who proclaim the Gospel should get their living by the Gospel." It is important for us who are in the ministry to know this, so that we do not have a bad conscience about accepting for our work wages that accrue to us from papal properties. Although these things were acquired by sheer fraud, nevertheless God despoils the Egyptians (Ex. 3:22), that is, the papists, of their possessions and transfers them to a good and pious use. This does not happen when the nobles seize them and expropriate them for their own misuse; it happens when those who proclaim the glory of God and faithfully instruct the youth derive their livelihood from them. It is impossible that one man should be devoted to household duties day and night for his support and at the same time pay attention to the study of Sacred Scripture, as the teaching ministry requires. Since God has commanded and instituted this, we should know that we may with a good conscience enjoy what is provided for the comfortable support of our lives from church properties to enable us to devote ourselves to our office. Therefore no one should give himself any scruples about this, as though it were not permissible to make use of these properties.

8. *For he who sows to the flesh will from the flesh reap corruption; but he who sows to the Spirit will from the Spirit reap eternal life.*

Now Paul adds a metaphor and an allegory. He applies the general statement about sowing to the particular case of providing for ministers, saying: "He who sows to the Spirit, that is, he who provides for preachers of the Word, performs a spiritual work and will reap eternal life." Now the question is whether we merit eternal life by good works, for that is what Paul seems to be asserting in this passage. Earlier (ch. 3) we discussed at sufficient length the passages that speak about works and rewards.[25] It is extremely necessary, following Paul's example, to exhort believers to do good works, that is, to exercise their faith through good works; for unless these works follow faith, this is the surest possible sign that the faith is not genuine. Therefore the apostle says: "He who sows to the flesh [some read: 'to his own flesh'],[26] that is, who does not share anything with the ministers of the Word but only feeds and takes care of himself, as the flesh wants him to, will from the flesh reap corruption, not only in the life to come but even in the present life. The possessions of the wicked will collapse, and eventually they themselves will perish miserably." The apostle was eager to exhort hearers to be generous and kind toward their preachers. It is a miserable business that the malice and ingratitude of men should be such that admonitions of this kind are necessary in the churches.

The Encratites abused this passage to support their fanatical opinion against marriage and interpreted it this way: "He who sows to the flesh will reap corruption; that is, he who marries will be damned. Therefore a wife is something damnable, and marriage is evil, because in it there is a sowing to the flesh." [27] Those foul beasts were so utterly devoid of judgment that they did not see what the apostle was talking about. I am warning you about this in order that you may see that the devil, through his agents, can easily divert simple hearts from the truth. He will soon have an infinite number of such agents. In fact, Germany already has many of them, because it persecutes and kills believers in some places and neglects them

[25] See the discussion earlier in this commentary, *Luther's Works*, 26, pp. 261 ff.

[26] Actually both the Greek and the Latin texts have "his own" here.

[27] On the Encratites cf. Irenaeus, *Adversus haereses*, I, 28; also *Luther's Works*, 24, p. 228.

in others. Let us arm ourselves against these errors and others like them, and let us learn to grasp the genuine meaning of Scripture. As any man equipped with plain common sense can see, Paul is not speaking about marriage; he is speaking about support for the ministers of the churches. And although this support is material, he still calls it "sowing to the Spirit." On the other hand, he calls scraping for money and looking out for oneself "sowing to the flesh." He pronounces the former blessed both in this life and in the life to come, but the latter he pronounces accursed both in this life and in the life to come.

9. *And let us not grow weary in well-doing; for in due season we shall reap, if we do not lose heart.*

As Paul is about to conclude the epistle, he passes from the particular to the general and exhorts us in general to all good works, as though he were saying: "Let us be liberal and kind, not only toward the ministers of the Word but toward all men; and let us not grow weary." For it is easy to do good once or twice, but to stay with it and not to be overcome by the ingratitude or malice of those you are helping — this is work and labor. Therefore he exhorts us not only to do good but also not to grow weary in doing good. To persuade us of this more easily, he adds: "For in due season we shall reap, if we do not lose heart." It is as though he were saying: "Watch and wait for the eternal harvest that is to come. Then no human ingratitude or malice will be able to dissuade you from well-doing. In the time of harvest you will receive the most abundant fruit from your sowing." With these sweet words he exhorts the faithful to do good works.

10. *So, then, as we have opportunity, let us do good to all men, and especially to those who are of the household of faith.*

This is the conclusion of Paul's exhortation about the liberal support of the ministers of the churches and about generous contributions to all who are in need. It is as though he were saying (John 9:4): "Let us do good while it is day; for when the night comes, we cannot work." When the light of truth is taken away, men do indeed perform many works; but it is all in vain, because those who walk in the darkness do not know where they are going. Therefore their whole life, work, suffering, and death are in vain.

With these words he obliquely stabs the Galatians, as though he were saying: "Unless you abide in the sound doctrine which you have received from me, it will not do you any good to perform many good works, to endure suffering, etc." Thus he said earlier (3:4): "You experienced so many things in vain." "The household of faith" is a new phrase to designate those who belong to our fellowship of faith; first among these are the ministers of the Word, and then other believers.

11. *See with what large letters I am writing to you with my own hand.*

Paul concludes the epistle with an exhortation to his readers and a sharp rebuke or invective against the false apostles.

Earlier he had cursed and anathematized them, but now he repeats this. Yet he accuses them seriously with other words, to deter the Galatians and call them back from the authority of the false apostles. "You have the sort of teachers," he says, "who (1) seek only their own glory, (2) run away from persecution, and (3) neither understand nor carry out in their own practice what they teach." If anyone, especially an apostle, recommended a preacher on the basis of these three virtues, such a preacher would deserve to be avoided by everyone. But not all the Galatians heeded this warning of Paul's. Paul is not slandering the false apostles when he inveighs against them so vehemently; he is judging them by his apostolic authority. Thus when we call the pope Antichrist and call the bishops and the fanatics [28] accursed, we are not insulting them; we are judging by divine authority that they are accursed, in accordance with the statement (1:8): "Even if we, or an angel from heaven, etc." For the former persecute the doctrine of Christ, and the latter subvert it.

"See," says Paul, "with what large letters I am writing to you with my own hand." He says this to persuade them and to show them his maternal feelings for them, as though he were saying: "Never have I written such an epistle with my own hand to any church as I have written to you." He dictated the others and merely signed his name, together with a final greeting, in his own hand, as is evident at the end of his epistles.[29] It seems to me that with

---

[28] From the lecture notes it is evident that Luther means Oecolampadius and Carlstadt.

[29] Luther is thinking of passages like 1 Cor. 16:21, Col. 4:18, and 2 Thess. 3:17.

these words he is referring to the length of the epistle; there are others who interpret them otherwise.[30] Now there follow an accusation and a condemnation.

12. *It is those who want to make a good showing in the flesh that would compel you to be circumcised, and only in order that they may not be persecuted for the cross of Christ.*

Paul uses the significant word εὐπροσωπῆσαι; in German we would say "to be well mannered," "to know how to make a good impression."[31] "Their primary virtue," he says, "is that they fawn upon dignitaries and prelates. To gain their favor and to preserve their own glory unharmed, they are compelling you to receive circumcision. For the leaders of the Jews stubbornly resist the Gospel and defend Moses. The false apostles are striving to accommodate themselves to the demand of these men that they live outwardly and regulate their lives as they require. To keep the favor of these men and to avoid the persecution of the cross, they teach that circumcision is necessary for salvation." This is how certain sycophants of the pope, the bishops, and the princes are today.[32] They cry out against us and viciously slander our writings, not from a devotion to the defense of the truth, which they attack and blaspheme in opposition to their own conscience, but merely to please their idols — the pope, the bishops, the kings and princes of this world — and to avoid suffering the persecution of the cross of Christ. If the Gospel provided them with the comforts of the flesh that they get from the wicked bishops and princes, and if wealth, pleasure, and peace and quiet for the flesh followed the confession of the Gospel, they would immediately come over to our side.

"Your teachers," says Paul, "are exceedingly vain men. They have no concern for the glory of Christ or for your salvation, but they are interested only in their own glory. In addition, because they are afraid of persecution, they proclaim the righteousness of the flesh; otherwise they would draw upon themselves the hate and persecution of men. Therefore even though you may listen to them intently and

---

[30] Jerome, *Commentarius in Epistolam S. Pauli ad Galatas, Patrologia, Series Latina,* XXVI, 463.

[31] The German words are *wol geberden, sich fein wissen zu stellen.*

[32] From the lecture notes it appears that Luther is thinking specifically of Crotus Rubianus; he accuses him of sycophancy also in a letter to Justus Menius, October 18, 1531 (W, *Briefe,* VI, 208).

for a long time, you will still be listening to men who worship their own bellies, seek their own glory, and flee the cross (Phil. 3:18-19)." The emphasis here is on the word "compel." For circumcision in itself is nothing; but to compel circumcision and to claim that righteousness and satisfaction lie in the observance of it, but that neglect of it is a sin — this is an insult to Christ. This matter has been discussed at sufficient length above.

13. *For even those who receive circumcision do not themselves keep the Law, but they desire to have you circumcised that they may glory in your flesh.*

Here Paul is a heretic; for he says that the false apostles and the whole Jewish nation, who were circumcised, did not keep the Law, in fact, that those who were circumcised did not fulfill the Law by fulfilling the Law. This is contrary to Moses, who says that to be circumcised is to observe the Law and not to be circumcised is to invalidate the covenant of God (Gen. 17:14). The Jews were circumcised for no other reason than to observe the Law, which commanded that every male be circumcised on the eighth day. All this has been treated at length earlier and does not have to be repeated here. It belongs to the description of the false apostles, to deter the Galatians from listening to them, as though he were saying: "See, I am showing you and describing for you what your teachers are like: first, that they are vainglorious men who seek only their own interests and care only for their bellies; secondly, that they are men who run away from persecution; and finally, that they teach nothing that is sure or true, but that everything they say or do is a sham. Therefore even though outwardly they observe the Law in their gestures and ceremonies, they do not really observe it by such observance." For the Law cannot be fulfilled without the Holy Spirit, and the Holy Spirit cannot be received without Christ. Unless He has been received, the human spirit remains unclean; that is, it despises God and seeks its own glory. Therefore whatever part of the Law it may perform is hypocritical and is a double sin. For an unclean heart does not keep the Law but only pretends outwardly to be keeping it; thus it is only confirmed even more deeply in its wickedness and hypocrisy.

This sentence, "Those who receive circumcision do not keep the Law," should be carefully noted; for it means that those who are circumcised are not really circumcised. It can be applied also to other works. Whoever does works, prays, or suffers apart from Christ, does his works, prays, and suffers in vain; for "whatever does not proceed from faith is sin" (Rom. 14:23). Therefore it does not do anyone any good to receive circumcision outwardly or to fast and pray, while inwardly he goes on despising grace, the forgiveness of sins, faith, Christ, etc., and remains arrogant in his self-confidence and presumption about his own righteousness, all of which are horrible sins against the First Table. These are then accompanied by sins against the Second Table, such as disobedience, sexual lust, rage, anger, hatred, etc. Thus he speaks accurately when he says: "Those who receive circumcision do not keep the Law but merely give the outward appearance of keeping it." For such pretense is a double wickedness in the sight of God.

"What are the false apostles doing when they want you to receive circumcision? They want you to receive circumcision, not that you may be justified, although this is their pretext, but that they may glory in your flesh. Now who does not have utter contempt for this poisonous vice of ambition or desire for glory which is being pursued at such peril to human souls?" "These are exceedingly vain men," he continues, "who serve their belly and fear persecution. Besides, and worst of all, they compel you to receive circumcision according to the Law in order that they may misuse your flesh for their own glory, to the eternal damnation of your souls. The advantage you receive from this is damnation in the sight of God. In the sight of the world, of course, it will enable the false apostles to boast that they are your teachers and you their disciples. Yet they teach you something that they themselves do not do." Thus he rebukes the false apostles quite sharply and harshly.

The words "that they may glory in your flesh" should be read with emphasis, as though he were saying: "They do not have the Word of the Spirit. Therefore it is impossible for you to receive the Spirit from their preaching. They are merely vexing your flesh and making you into unspiritual and self-righteous men who outwardly observe prescribed days, seasons, sacrifices, etc., according to the Law, but without the Spirit; for all these are purely material things, from which you derive nothing but useless labor and damnation. On the other hand, they derive from it an opportunity to boast that they are the teachers of the Galatians and have called them back from the doctrines of that heretic Paul to their mother, the synagog. (Thus the sycophants of the papists today boast that they are calling the victims of their subversion back to the bosom of the church.) But we do not glory in your flesh; we glory in your spirit, because you have received the Spirit through our preaching" (Gal. 3:2).

14. *But far be it from me to glory except in the cross of our Lord Jesus Christ.*

The apostle comes to the very point of indignation, and in his agitated state he erupts with the words: "But far be it from me, etc.," as though he were saying: "The carnal boasting of the false apostles is such a loathsome disease that I would like to see it buried in hell, for it has proved to be the destruction of many. Let those who wish, glory in the flesh; and let them perish with their accursed glory! The only glory I have left is this, that I glory in the cross of Christ." He speaks the same way in Rom. 5:3: "We rejoice in our sufferings"; and in 2 Cor. 12:9: "I will all the more gladly boast of my weaknesses." Here Paul shows what true Christian boasting is, namely, to boast, rejoice, and be proud in suffering, shame, weakness, etc. The world not only regards Christians as the most despicable of men; but with vehemence and what it regards as righteous zeal it hates, persecutes, condemns, and kills them as a dangerous menace to both the spiritual and the earthly realm, in other words, as heretics and revolutionaries. But because they are not suffering on account of murder, stealing, and other such crimes, but on account of Christ, whose blessings and glory they proclaim, they glory in their afflictions and in the cross of Christ. With the apostles they "rejoice that they are counted worthy to suffer dishonor for the name of Christ" (Acts 5:41). So today, when the pope and the whole world persecute us, cruelly damn and kill us, we should glory and exult in this; for we are not undergoing all this on account of our misdeeds as thieves, robbers, etc. (1 Peter 4:15), but on account of Christ, our Savior and Lord, whose Gospel we teach in its purity.

Our boasting increases and is confirmed by two facts: (1) that we are sure that we have the pure and divine doctrine, (2) that our cross or suffering is the suffering of Christ. When the world persecutes and slays us, therefore, we do not have any reason to complain and lament, but only to rejoice and exult. The world regards us as miserable and abominable; but Christ, who is greater than the world and for whose sake we are suffering, pronounces us blessed and commands us to rejoice. "Blessed are you," He says (Matt. 5:11-12), "when men revile you and persecute you and utter all kinds of evil against you falsely on *My* [33] account. Rejoice and be glad." Therefore our boasting is far different from that of the world, which does not glory in its affliction, shame, persecution, death, etc., but in its power, wealth, peace, honor, wisdom, and righteousness. But sorrow and confusion lie at the end of such glory and rejoicing.

"The cross of Christ" does not mean, of course, the wood that Christ carried on His shoulders and to which He then was nailed. No, it refers in general to all the afflictions of all the faithful, whose sufferings are the sufferings of Christ. 2 Cor. 1:5: "We share abundantly in Christ's sufferings"; and Col. 1:24: "I rejoice in my sufferings for your sake, and in my flesh I complete what is lacking in Christ's afflictions for the sake of His body, that is, the church." Therefore "the cross of Christ" refers in general to all the afflictions which the church suffers on Christ's account, as Christ Himself testifies when He says in Acts 9:4: "Saul, Saul, why do you persecute Me?" Saul had not done any violence to Christ, but only to His church. But whoever touches this, touches the apple of His eye (Zech. 2:8). The head is more sensitive and responsive in its feeling than the other parts of the body, as experience teaches. When the small toe or some other tiny part of the body is hurt, the face immediately shows that it feels this; the nose contracts, the eyes flash, etc. In the same way Christ, our Head, makes our afflictions His own, so that when we, who are His body, suffer, He is affected as though the evils were His own.

It is helpful to know this, so that we are not overly sad or even completely desperate when we see our enemies persecuting, excommunicating, and murdering us, or when we see the heretics hating us so bitterly. Then we should think that, following the example of Paul, we ought to glory greatly in the cross which we have received because of Christ, not because of our own sins. When we consider the sufferings we receive only so far as we ourselves are involved in them, they become not only troubling but intolerable. But when the second person pronoun "Thy" is added to them, so that we can say (2 Cor. 1:5): "We share abundantly in Thy sufferings, O Christ," and, as the psalm says (44:22), "For Thy sake we are slain all day

---

[33] We have used italics where the original has capital letters.

long," then our sufferings become not only easy but actually sweet, in accordance with the saying (Matt. 11:30): "My burden is light, and My yoke is easy."

Now it is evident that the only reason we must endure the hate and persecution of our opponents today is that we preach Christ purely. If we were to deny Him and to accept their wicked errors and godless forms of worship, they would not only stop hating and persecuting us but would even offer us honors, riches, etc. Because we suffer all this on Christ's account, we can most certainly glory with Paul in the cross of our Lord Jesus Christ, that is, not in power, the goodwill of men, riches, etc., but in trouble, weakness, sorrow, fightings of body and fears of spirit (2 Cor. 7:5), persecution, and every evil. Therefore we hope that it will soon happen that Christ will say to us what David said to Abiathar the priest (1 Sam. 22:22): "I have occasioned the death of all these persons." Or, as the prophet says (Is. 37:23): "You have not mocked the Children of Israel, but *Me*," as though He were saying: "Whoever does harm to you does harm to Me, for you would not have had to undergo this if you had not preached My Word and confessed Me." Thus John 15:19 says: "If you were of the world, the world would love its own; but because I chose you out of the world, therefore the world hates you." This has been discussed earlier.

Through whom the world has been crucified to me, and I to the world.

This is a characteristically Pauline expression, "the world has been crucified to me" (that is, I regard the world as condemned), and "I have been crucified to the world" (that is, the world regards me as condemned in turn). "Thus we crucify and condemn each other. I curse all the righteousness, the doctrine, and the works of the world as the venom of the devil. The world, in turn, curses my doctrine and my deeds and judges me to be a dangerous man, a heretic, a seditionist, etc." So today the world has been crucified to us, and we to the world. We curse and condemn the doctrine, the Masses, the religious orders, the vows, the worship, the works, the life, and all the abominations of the pope and of the heretics as the very filth of the devil. They, in turn, persecute and slay us as subverters of religion and disturbers of the public peace.

The monks imagined that the world was being crucified to them when they entered the monastery.³⁴ But it is not the world, but Christ, who is being crucified this way. In fact, the world is delivered from crucifixion and given a new lease on life by the presumption of saintliness and the trust in their own righteousness that characterizes those who entered the religious life. Therefore it is a clumsy distortion of this statement of the apostle to apply it to entry into the religious life. He is speaking about something far more difficult: that what Paul and any other saint or Christian regards as divine wisdom, righteousness, and power, is regarded and condemned by the world as the utmost foolishness, wickedness, and weakness; and, on the other hand, what the world regards as the ultimate in religion and the worship of God, the faithful know to be the worst possible blasphemy. Thus believers judge the world; and the world, in turn, judges believers. But the correct judgment is on the side of the believers, for "the spiritual man judges all things" (1 Cor. 2:15). Therefore the judgment of the world about religion or about righteousness in the sight of God conflicts with the judgment of believers as much as the devil conflicts with God. Now God is crucified to the devil, and the devil to God. That is, God condemns the doctrine and works of the devil, for, as John says (1 John 3:8), "the reason the Son of God appeared was to destroy the works of the devil"; and, on the other hand, the devil condemns and subverts the Word and the works of God; for "he is a murderer and the father of lies" (John 8:44). In the very same way, the world condemns the doctrine and life of believers, calling them vicious heretics and disturbers of the public peace. The believers, in turn, call the world "the son of the devil," who faithfully follows the footsteps of his father, that is, who is just as much a murderer and a liar as his father is. Now in Holy Scripture "world" means not only the obviously wicked and infamous but the best, the wisest, and the holiest of men. This is what Paul has in mind when he says: "through whom the world has been crucified to me, and I to the world."

At the same time Paul subtly attacks the false apostles, as though he were saying: "All glory apart from the cross of Christ I hate in the extreme and despise as an accursed thing. I regard it as not only dead but dead in the most wretched way, as someone sentenced to the cross dies a most wretched death. For the world with all its glory is crucified to me, and I to the world. Therefore let all those who

³⁴ See, for example, John of Damascus, *Barlaam and Joasaph*, XII, 108.

glory in your flesh, not in the cross of Christ, be accursed." With these words Paul testifies that he hates the world with the perfect hatred of the Holy Spirit, and that the world, in turn, hates him with the perfect hatred of the spirit of evil. It is as though he were saying: "It is impossible to conclude any peace between me and the world. Then what should I do? Shall I surrender and teach what the world wants me to teach? No. But with an undaunted spirit I shall attack it even more boldly, disdaining and crucifying it as completely as it disdains and crucifies me."

Finally Paul teaches here how to battle against Satan, who is continually attacking us with different physical troubles. Inwardly, too, he constantly strikes our heart with his flaming darts (Eph. 6:16), in the hope that by such persistence, if not in any other way, he can overthrow our faith and lead us away from the truth and from Christ. To battle against him, we must use the same method that we see St. Paul himself using when he proudly disdained the world. So we should disdain the devil, its chief, with all his powers, tricks, and infernal rage; and relying on Christ's protection, we should berate him this way: "Satan, the more you harm me and try to harm me, the more I will lord it over you and make fun of you. The more you frighten me and try to bring me to the point of despair, the more I shall trust and boast, in the very midst of your rage and malice, not in my own strength but in that of Christ, my Lord, whose power is made perfect in my weakness. Therefore when I am the weakest, then I am the strongest (2 Cor. 12:9-10)." But when Satan sees that his threats and terrors are having an effect, he is happy and terrifies those who are terror-stricken even more.

15. *For in Christ Jesus neither circumcision counts for anything, nor uncircumcision, but a new creation.*

It is amazing that Paul should say that in Christ Jesus neither circumcision nor uncircumcision counts for anything. He should rather have said: "Either circumcision or uncircumcision counts for something, since these two are contrary to each other." But now he denies that either one counts, as though he were saying: "We must go higher, for circumcision and uncircumcision are far too low to count for righteousness in the sight of God. They are, of course, contrary to each other; but that has nothing to do with Christian righteousness, which is not earthly but heavenly and therefore does not consist in physical things. And so whether you receive circumcision or do not receive it is all the same, for neither counts for anything in Christ Jesus."

The Jews were greatly offended when they heard that circumcision did not count for anything. They were perfectly ready to concede that uncircumcision did not count for anything, but to say the same about the Law and about circumcision was unbearable for them to hear. To defend the Law and circumcision they were ready to fight to the point of bloodshed. Today the papists are contending vigorously in defense of their traditions about eating meat, celibacy, feriae, etc.; and they curse and excommunicate us for teaching that in Christ Jesus these traditions do not count for anything. In the same way some of our followers, who are no less stupid than the papists, regard freedom from the traditions of the pope as something so necessary that they are afraid of committing sin if they do not violate or abolish all of them immediately.[35] But Paul says that what we have counting for our justification is something far more precious than the Law or circumcision, more precious than the observance or the violation of the papal traditions. In Christ Jesus, he says, neither circumcision nor uncircumcision, neither celibacy nor marriage, neither eating nor fasting, etc., counts for anything. Food does not commend us to God; we do not become better by abstaining from it or worse by eating it. These things are far too trivial. Indeed, the whole world with all its laws and its righteousness is far too insignificant to warrant their being dragged into the discussion of justification.

The reason and wisdom of the flesh does not understand this. It does not understand the things that pertain to the Spirit of God (1 Cor. 2:14), and therefore it maintains that righteousness is founded on something external. But we have been so well instructed on the basis of the Word of God that we declare with assurance that there is nothing under the sun that counts for our righteousness in the sight of God except Christ alone or, as he says here, "a new creation." Now political laws, human traditions, ecclesiastical ceremonies, and even the Law of Moses are matters located outside Christ; therefore they do not count for righteousness in the sight of God. It is, of course, permissible to use them as good and necessary things, but in their proper place and time. But if they are summoned into the discussion of justification, they do not count for anything at all but

[35] Cf. *Luther's Works*, 40, pp. 231—232.

get in the way; for "in Christ Jesus neither circumcision counts for anything, nor uncircumcision, but a new creation."

With the two terms "circumcision" and "uncircumcision" Paul excludes everything that belongs to the whole universe and denies that it counts for anything in Christ Jesus, that is, in the area of faith and salvation. By synecdoche he uses the part for the whole; that is, by "uncircumcision" he means all the Gentiles, and by "circumcision" he means all the Jews with all their powers and all their glory. It is as though he were saying: "Whatever the Gentiles can accomplish with all their wisdom, righteousness, laws, power, kingdoms, and empires counts for nothing in Christ Jesus. Likewise, whatever the Jews are and whatever they can do with Moses, with their Law, circumcision, worship, temple, kingdom, and priesthood does not count for anything either." In Christ Jesus or in the issue of justification, therefore, there is to be no dispute about the laws of either the Gentiles or the Jews, about whether the Ceremonial or the Moral Law justifies; but this negative statement is to be applied absolutely: "In Christ Jesus neither circumcision counts for anything, nor uncircumcision."

Does this mean that laws are evil? No. They are actually good and useful, but in their proper order and proper place, namely, in material and political matters, which cannot be administered without laws. In addition, we also observe certain ceremonies and laws in the churches, not because such observance counts for justification, but for the sake of good order, a good example, tranquillity, and harmony, in accordance with the statement (1 Cor. 14:40): "All things should be done decently and in order." But if laws are set forth and required as though their observance justified and their nonobservance damned, then they must be completely abrogated and repealed; otherwise Christ will lose His position and glory as the only One who justifies, sends the Spirit, etc. With these words Paul clearly affirms that neither circumcision counts for anything nor uncircumcision, but a new creation. But since in Christ neither the laws of the Gentiles nor those of the Jews count for anything, it was a completely ungodly action when the pope compelled us to attach our confidence to his laws.

A new creation, by which the image of God is renewed (Col. 3:10), does not happen by the sham or pretense of some sort of outward works, because in Christ Jesus neither circumcision nor uncircumcision counts; but it is "created after the likeness of God in righteousness and holiness" (Eph. 4:24). When works are performed, they do indeed give a new outward appearance, which captures the attention of the world and the flesh. But they do not produce a new creation, for the heart remains as wicked and as filled with contempt of God and unbelief as it was before. Thus a new creation is a work of the Holy Spirit, who implants a new intellect and will and confers the power to curb the flesh and to flee the righteousness and wisdom of the world. This is not a sham or merely a new outward appearance, but something really happens. A new attitude and a new judgment, namely, a spiritual one, actually come into being, and they now detest what they once admired. Our minds were once so captivated by the monastic life that we thought of it as the only way to salvation; now we think of it quite differently. What we used to adore, before this new creation, as the ultimate in holiness now makes us blush when we remember it.

Therefore a new creation is not a change in clothing or in outward manner, as the monks imagine, but a renewal of the mind by the Holy Spirit; this is then followed by an outward change in the flesh, in the parts of the body, and in the senses. For when the heart acquires new light, a new judgment, and new motivation through the Gospel, this also brings about a renewal of the senses. The ears long to hear the Word of God instead of listening any longer to human traditions and notions. The lips and the tongue do not boast of their own works, righteousness, and monastic rule; but joyfully they proclaim nothing but the mercy of God, disclosed in Christ. These changes are, so to speak, not verbal; they are real. They produce a new mind, a new will, new senses, and even new actions by the flesh, so that the eyes, the ears, the lips, and the tongue not only see, hear, and speak otherwise than they used to, but the mind itself evaluates things and acts upon them differently from the way it did before. Formerly it went about blindly in the errors and darkness of the pope, imagining that God is a peddler who sells His grace to us in exchange for our works and merits. Now that the light of the Gospel has risen, it knows that it acquires righteousness solely by faith in Christ. Therefore it now casts off its self-chosen works and performs instead the works of its calling and the works of love, which God has commanded. It praises God and proclaims Him, and it glories and exults solely in its trust in mercy through Christ. If it has to bear some sort of evil or danger, it accepts this willingly and joyfully, although the flesh goes on grumbling. This is what Paul calls "a new creation."

16. *Peace and mercy be upon all who walk by this rule.*

Paul has added this as a conclusion. This is the only true rule by which we should walk, namely, the new creation. The Franciscans wickedly distort this passage and apply it to their monastic rule.[36] On this basis these blasphemous and sacrilegious men have proclaimed that their rule is far holier than others because it was established and confirmed by apostolic testimony and authority. Now certainly Paul is not speaking here about cowls, tonsures, cinctures, sandals, bellowing in church, and similar stupid trifles that belong to the life of the Minorites; he is speaking about a new creation, which is neither circumcision nor uncircumcision, but "a new nature, created after the likeness of God in true righteousness and holiness" (Eph. 4:24), which is inwardly righteous in the spirit and outwardly holy and pure in the flesh. The Franciscans and all the other monks do indeed have a righteousness and holiness; but this is hypocritical and ungodly, because they hope to be justified by the observance of their rule, not solely by faith in Christ. In addition, although they make an outward pretense of holiness and do restrain their eyes, hands, tongue, and other parts of their body, they still have an unclean heart, filled with the desires of the flesh, envy, anger, sexual lust, idolatry, contempt and hatred for God, blasphemy toward Christ, etc. They are violent enemies of the truth.

Therefore let the rule of Francis, of Dominic, and of all the others be accursed: first, because by them the blessings and the glory of Christ have been obscured and overthrown, and the Gospel of grace and life has been totally crushed; secondly, because they have filled the world with endless idolatry, false worship, wicked religion, self-chosen works, and the like. But let only this rule, about which Paul is speaking here, be blessed. By it we live in faith in Christ and are made a new creation, that is, truly righteous and holy through the Holy Spirit, not through sham or pretense. Upon those who walk by this rule there comes peace (that is, the favor of God, the forgiveness of sins, and serenity of conscience) and mercy (that is, help

---

[36] The original *Rule* of Francis was prepared at Rivo Torto in 1210, but it is no longer in existence. The so-called *Regula prima* or "*Rule* of 1221" had been greatly expanded by Luther's time.

in affliction and forgiveness for the remnants of sin still in the flesh). In fact, even if those who walk by this rule are overtaken in a fault or in some sort of lapse, still, because they are children of grace and peace, they obtain mercy, so that their sin and lapse is not imputed against them.

Upon the Israel of God.

Here Paul attacks the false apostles and the Jews, who boasted about their fathers, their election, the Law, etc. (Rom. 9:4-5). It is as though he were saying: "The Israel of God are not the physical descendants of Abraham, Isaac, and Israel but those who, with Abraham the believer (3:9), believe in the promises of God now disclosed in Christ, whether they are Jews or Gentiles." This argument has been treated at length earlier, in the third chapter.[37]

17. *Henceforth let no man trouble me.*

Paul concludes the epistle with some irritation and indignation, as though he were saying: "I have preached the Gospel faithfully as I received it by revelation from Christ Himself. Whoever does not want to follow it may follow anything he wishes, provided that he does not bother me anymore. In brief, this is what I have to say: that Christ, whom I have proclaimed, is the only High Priest and Savior of the world. Therefore let the world either walk according to this rule, about which I have been speaking here and throughout this epistle, or let it perish forever."

For I bear on my body the marks of the Lord Jesus.

Just as the Minorites claim that the earlier sentence, "all who walk by this rule," was spoken about their rule, so they imagine that this one must apply to the stigmata of their Francis.[38] I think that what they say about this matter is a pure fiction and a joke. But even if Francis did bear stigmata on his body, as he is portrayed, they were not printed on him on account of Christ. He printed them on himself by some sort of foolish devotion or, more likely, vainglory, by which he was able to flatter himself into believing that he was so dear to Christ that He had even printed His wounds on his body.

---

[37] See the earlier discussion in *Luther's Works*, 26, pp. 244—248.

[38] The stigmata of Francis were believed to have been supernaturally impressed on his body on September 17, 1224.

Paul's real meaning in this passage is this: "The marks printed on my body show clearly whose servant I am. If I sought to please men, if I insisted on circumcision and the observance of the Law as something necessary for salvation, or if I gloried in your flesh after the fashion of the false apostles, there would be no need for me to bear these marks on my body. But because I am a servant of Jesus Christ and walk by the true rule, that is, because I preach and confess publicly that no one, without exception, can obtain grace, righteousness, and salvation apart from Christ, therefore I must also bear the insignia of Christ, my Lord. These are not stigmata that I have invited upon myself; they are marks that were inflicted on me against my will by the world and by Satan, on account of Jesus, whom I affirm to be the Christ."

Therefore these marks are the troubles or sufferings of the body, as well as the arrows of the devil and the mental fears that Paul mentions throughout his epistles and Luke in the Book of Acts. 1 Cor. 4:9: "I think that God has exhibited us apostles as last of all, like men sentenced to death; because we have become a spectacle to the world, to angels and to men." And again (1 Cor. 4:11-13): "To the present hour we hunger and thirst, we are ill-clad and buffeted and homeless, and we labor, working with our own hands. We are reviled, persecuted, and slandered. We have become the refuse of the world, the offscouring of all things." In 2 Cor. 4:4-5 he says: "Through great endurance, in afflictions, hardships, calamities, beatings, imprisonments, tumults, labors, watching, hunger." And in chapter 11:23-26: [39] "With very great labors, many imprisonments, with countless beatings, and often near death. Five times I have received at the hands of the Jews the forty lashes less one. Three times I have been beaten with rods; once I was stoned. Three times I have been shipwrecked; a night and a day I have been adrift at sea; on frequent journeys, in danger from rivers, danger from robbers, danger from my own people, danger from Gentiles, danger in the city, danger in the wilderness, danger at sea, danger from false brethren."

These are the true stigmata, that is, imprinted marks, about which the apostle is speaking here; we, too, by the grace of God, bear them on our body today on account of Christ. For the world persecutes and slays us; false brethren hate us bitterly; and Satan terrifies us

---

[39] Here the original has "chapters 11 and 12."

inwardly in our hearts with his flaming darts (Eph. 6:16) — all this for no other reason than that we teach that Christ is our righteousness and life. We do not choose these stigmata because of some sweet devotion, nor do we enjoy suffering. But because the world and Satan inflict them on us against our will, on account of Christ, we are compelled to endure them. In the Spirit, who is always wholesome and who glories and rejoices, we glory with Paul that we bear them on our body; for they are a seal and a sure evidence of true doctrine and faith. Paul has said all this with a certain amount of indignation.

18. *The grace of our Lord Jesus Christ be with your spirit, brethren. Amen.*

This is Paul's final farewell. He ends the epistle with the same words with which he began it, as though he were saying: "I have proclaimed Christ to you purely. I have begged you and scolded you. I have not omitted anything that I thought you needed. There is nothing further that I can do for you except to pray from my heart that our Lord Jesus Christ may add His blessing and His increase to my labor, and may rule you by His Spirit forever. Amen."

So far the exposition of the epistle of St. Paul to the Galatians. May the Lord Jesus Christ, our Justifier and Savior, who has granted me the grace and ability to expound this epistle and has granted you the grace and ability to hear it, preserve and confirm both you and me. From the heart I pray that we may grow more and more in the knowledge of grace and of faith in Him, so that we may be blameless and beyond reproach until the day of our redemption. To Him, with the Father and the Holy Spirit, be praise and glory forever and ever. Amen. Amen.

Luke 2:14: "Glory to God in the highest, and on earth peace, good will to men."

Is. 40:9 (1 Peter 1:25): "The Word of the Lord abides forever."

LUTHER'S PREFACE OF 1535

I MYSELF can hardly believe that when I delivered these public lectures on St. Paul's Epistle to the Galatians, I was as wordy as this book shows that I was. Nevertheless, I recognize that all the thoughts which I find set down in this book with such diligence by my brethren are really mine, so that I am compelled to admit that all of them, or at least most of them, were spoken by me in my public presentation. For in my heart there rules this one doctrine, namely, faith in Christ. From it, through it, and to it all my theological thought flows and returns, day and night; yet I am aware that all I have grasped of this wisdom in its height, width, and depth are a few poor and insignificant firstfruits and fragments.

Therefore I am ashamed to have my poor and feeble comments on this great apostle and chosen instrument of God (Acts 9:15) published. But I am forced to be ashamed of this very shame and to become shameless and bold by the infinite and horrible desecration and abomination that have always raged in the church of God and do not stop raging today against that single solid rock which we call the doctrine of justification, namely, that we are redeemed from sin, death, and the devil and endowed with eternal life, not through ourselves and certainly not through our works, which are even less than we are ourselves, but through the help of Another, the only Son of God, Jesus Christ.

Satan attacked this rock in Paradise when he persuaded our first parents to forsake their faith in the God who had given them life and who promised enduring life, and to try to become like God by means of their own wisdom and virtue (Gen. 3:5). In a further attack upon it that liar and murderer (John 8:44), who will always be completely consistent, soon set brother to kill brother, and this for no other reason than that by faith his godly brother had offered to God a more acceptable sacrifice (Heb. 11:4), while he, the wicked brother, who offered his works without faith, was not pleasing to God. Later there followed a continuous and unbearable persecution of this faith by Satan through the sons of Cain, until God was compelled to cleanse the world once and for all through the Flood and thus to preserve Noah, the herald of faith and righteousness (2 Peter 2:5). Yet Satan still kept his own line of descent through Ham, the third son of Noah. But who could recite it all? For thereafter the whole world went mad in opposition to this faith, inventing endless idols and religions, by which, as Paul says (Acts 14:16), everyone went his own way, in the hope of placating a god or a goddess or gods or goddesses by his own works, in other words, of redeeming himself from evil and sin by means of his own work, without the help of Christ. The acts and books of all the heathen provide plenty of evidence for all this.

But the heathen are nothing in comparison with Israel, the people or synagog of God, who not only were endowed beyond all others with the sure promises given to the fathers and then with the Law handed down by God through angels (Gal. 3:19) but were continually being reassured by the presence of the sayings, miracles, and deeds of the prophets. And yet Satan, that is, the insane idea of self-righteousness, made such headway among them that they killed all the prophets and finally even their promised Messiah, the very Son of God Himself, and all for the same reason, namely, because they all taught that men are pleasing to God by the grace of God, not by our own righteousness. From the beginning this has been the fundamental principle of the devil and of the world: "We do not want to seem to be doing evil, but whatever we do must be approved by God and agreed to by all His prophets. If they do not do this, they must die! Down with Abel, long live Cain! That must be our law." And so it is.

But in the church of the Gentiles something happened and is still happening that is so serious as to make the madness of the synagog seem like child's play. For the latter, as Paul says, did not recognize their Christ, and therefore they crucified the Lord of glory (1 Cor. 2:8). But the church of the Gentiles accepted Christ and confessed Him as the Son of God, who has become our righteousness, as it sings, announces, and teaches publicly. Yet while this confession stands, the very people who claim to be the church are killing, persecuting, and raging against those who believe, do, and teach nothing except that Christ is precisely what the others are forced to confess about Him with their hypocritical words and actions. For if those who hold sway today in the name of Christ could hold on to their dominion without the name of Christ, they would disclose openly what they really think of Him in their hearts. For their real opinion of Him is far lower than that of the Jews, who at least think that He is *thola*, that is, a thief who deserved to be crucified.[1] But people nowadays think of Him as a fable, resembling the mythical deities among the heathen; this can be seen in Rome at the curia of the pope, and almost everywhere in Italy.[2]

Thus because Christ is a laughingstock among His own Christians (for that is still what they want to be called), because Cain goes on killing Abel without interruption, and because the abomination of Satan now has its greatest dominion ever — therefore it is necessary to set forth this doctrine as diligently as possible and to put ourselves in opposition to Satan, regardless of whether we are inarticulate or eloquent, learned or ignorant. For if every human being were to keep silent, it would be necessary for this rock to be acclaimed by the rocks and stones themselves (Luke 19:40).

Therefore I, too, am willing to do my duty and to permit this extremely wordy commentary to be released. Thus I want to arouse my brethren to resist the wiles and the malice of Satan. In these most recent and final hours of history he has been provoked into such a rage against the knowledge of Christ in its revived form that men who previously seemed to be possessed by demons and to be insane now seem to have become demons themselves, possessed by even more horrible demons and by an insanity that goes even beyond the demonic. This is caused by the awesome realization which this enemy of truth and life has that the horrible day of his destruction is near and imminent — a day that is for us the delightful day of our redemption, because it spells the end of his tyranny. Thus it is understandable that with all his members and his powers under threat, he becomes agitated, as a thief or an adulterer does when he is caught in the act by the rising sun.

For without even mentioning the abominations of the pope for now, who has ever heard before of the rise of so many monstrosities as we are witnessing during these days among the Anabaptists alone? Satan is stirring up his followers with such agitation everywhere that he seems about to breathe the final gasp of his dominion. It almost

[1] On the meaning of this term cf. *Luther's Works*, 14, p. 269, note 25.
[2] Cf. p. 384, note 5, on Italy.

seems as though through them he were bent not only on suddenly overthrowing the world with sedition but also on devouring all of Christ and the church through innumerable sects. He does not fume and rage this way against the lives and opinions of other men. Think of adulterers, thieves, murderers, perjurers, or of ungodly, sacrilegious, and unbelieving men. In fact, he grants them peace in his own house, sweetly caressing them and treating them very indulgently. So in the early days of the church he not only left all the idolatries and religions of the whole world quiet and undisturbed but even supported them magnificently; only the church and the religion of Christ were the object of his universal attack. Later on he granted peace to all the heretics; only the Catholic doctrine did he trouble. So today his only concern is the one that is always characteristic of him, namely, to persecute our Christ, who is our righteousness, without any works of ours; for thus it is written of him (Gen. 3:15): "You shall bruise His heel."

But it is not so much in opposition to them as for the benefit of our own people that these reflections of ours about this epistle of St. Paul are being published. Let these readers either thank me in the Lord for my diligence or forgive me for my weakness and boldness. Actually, I would not want this book to win the approval of the wicked but only to irritate them, along with their god. For it is addressed, at the cost of great effort, only to those to whom Paul wrote this epistle, namely, to those who are troubled, afflicted, vexed, and tempted, to those who are miserable Galatians in faith; for they are the only ones who understand it. Let anyone who is not this way listen to the papists, the monks, the Anabaptists, and the many other teachers of infinite wisdom and self-invented religion; and let him vigorously reject our position, without bothering to understand it.

The papists and the Anabaptists are harmoniously agreed today on this one proposition, over against the church of God, despite their verbal pretenses: namely, that a work of God is dependent on the worthiness of man. For this is what the Anabaptists teach: "Baptism is nothing unless a person is a believer." On the basis of this principle, as it is called, it necessarily follows that none of the works of God are anything if a man is not good. Now Baptism is a work of God, but an evil man can make it not a work of God.

From this it follows further: Marriage and the position of a magistrate or a servant are all works of God; but because men are evil, therefore these are not works of God. Ungodly men have the sun, moon, earth, water, air, and everything that has been subjected to man. But because they are ungodly rather than godly, the sun is not the sun; and the moon, the earth, water, and air are not what they are. The Anabaptists themselves had bodies and souls before their rebaptism; but because they were not godly, they did not have genuine bodies and souls. Similarly, they admit that their parents were not truly married, because they had not been rebaptized; therefore all the Anabaptists are illegitimate children, and all their parents were adulterers and fornicators. Nevertheless, they inherit the possessions of their parents, even though they admit that they are illegitimate and disinherited.

Who does not see here that the Anabaptists are not men possessed but are themselves demons possessed by even worse demons? Thus also the papists do not stop urging works and the worthiness of persons even today in opposition to grace, giving powerful help, at least in words, to their brethren, the Anabaptists. These wolves are joined at the tail, even though they have different heads.[3] They pretend to be fierce enemies publicly; but inwardly they actually believe, teach, and defend the same doctrine, in opposition to Christ, the only Savior, who is our only righteousness. Therefore let everyone who can, cling to this doctrine. And let the others, who make shipwreck (1 Tim. 1:19), be borne where the sea and the winds want to bear them, until they return to the ship or swim to shore. But I shall speak of the Anabaptists elsewhere if Christ the Lord permits. Amen.

[3] Apparently an allusion to the story of Samson (Judges 15:4).

LECTURES ON GALATIANS 1519

Chapters 1–6

Translated by
RICHARD JUNGKUNTZ

DEDICATION

To the most distinguished gentlemen, doctors of pure and true theology, Messrs. Peter Lupinus of Radheim, custodian, and Andreas Bodenstein of Carlstadt, archdeacon, canons of All Saints at Wittenberg, ordinaries, etc., his teachers to be esteemed in Christ, Brother Martin Luther, the Augustinian, offers greetings.

IN these days, most distinguished sirs, I have babbled forth some trifling observations about indulgences, matters surely of no consequence about matters — as it seemed to me — of no consequence but, as I have now learned by experience, matters of the greatest consequence about matters of the greatest consequence. For in my remarkable stupidity and very serious blundering I was measuring sins and errors by the standard of God's commandments and the most holy Gospel of Christ. Those friends of mine, however, in keeping with their reputation for wisdom, do not measure any kind of work whatever by any standard but the power of the pope and the privileges of the Roman Church. It is because of this that we had such a difference of opinion and that I aroused such uproar against myself on the part of those superlative Christians and supremely religious professors of sacred theology. And what I have always feared has happened to me. Some have one opinion about me, some have another opinion. To some I have seemed impious; to others, biting; to others, vainglorious; to others, something else, which is the common lot of those who build in public, as the common saying goes, and write for public consumption. I find almost as many teachers as readers, and free of charge at that. Under their wholesome guidance and leadership I have had to learn — if I was not to be obstinate and to become a heretic — that no one can commit a more serious offense than the person who has doubts about the opinions of men or opposes them because of a desire to debate, even though in the meantime he has denied Christ and faith in Christ, that is, has indulged in some childish sport. On this subject, when I was at Augsburg, I had a very fatherly and kindly schoolmaster, as you know.¹ And because of the most illustrious direction of these most illustrious men it has come about that this new and admirable freedom of Christians, according to which everything else goes unpunished and only one law is left against which it is possible for sin to be committed today, holds sway. This is the power of the pope and the privileges of the Roman Church. Hence to wink at and consent to all the swamps of shame and corruption which, starting from Rome under the innocent and sacred name of the pope and the Roman Church, overflow the whole earth without ceasing — this is something holy. To have praised and honored them as though they were the highest virtues — this is piety. To have murmured against them — this is sacrilege. So great is the wrath of the fury of the Lord Almighty, and so great the deserts of our impious thanklessness, that for so long a time we have had to endure the tyranny of hell, in which, as we groan in vain with many a groan, we see that the holy and awesome name of Christ, in which we have been justified, sanctified, and glorified, is given as a pretext for such foul, such filthy, such fearful enormities of greed, tyranny, lust, and godlessness; that it is being forced into the service of vices; and — what is the worst evil of all — that the name of Christ is being blotted out by means of the name of Christ; that the church is being laid waste by means of the name of the church; and, in general, that we are being mocked, deceived, and brought to ruin by those things through which we should have been brought to salvation. Consequently, while those men busy themselves with those very great things, while they bite, while they cut themselves with knives for their Baal (1 Kings 18:28), while they sacrifice to their god from Lindus,² and while they vaunt the *extravagantes* ³ with their explanations, those most faithful witnesses to Rome's erudition, I have decided to turn to the least important things, that is, to the Divine Scriptures, and among these to those which come from the author of least consequence (as, in fact, his own name attests),⁴ the apostle

¹ Luther is referring to Cardinal Cajetan, before whom he had appeared in Augsburg, October 12, 1518.

² The allusion is to the strange rite at Lindus on Rhodes, where Hercules was worshiped with formal and ceremonial cursing.

³ The *extravagantes* were the papal decretals outside the compilation of Gratian.

⁴ A play on the Latin word *paulus*, which means "little."

Paul. So far was he from being the greatest of the apostles or the supreme pontiff that he even declares that he is the least of the apostles and not worthy to be called an apostle (1 Cor. 15:9) — so far is he from boasting that he is the saintliest. In fact, he sprang from the tribe of Benjamin (Rom. 11:1), who is called by Joseph the least of his brothers (Gen. 42:34). And in order that nothing might fail to be very small, he determines not to know anything but Jesus Christ, yet not even Him except as crucified (1 Cor. 2:2), that is, as the least and last of all, since he was by no means unaware that to deal with those greatest and most important of all matters, namely, with the power of the Roman Church and its decrees, was not permissible for him, a most inept and unlearned apostle, but that only the thrice greatest theologians were permitted to do this. I am hopeful, however, that this effort of mine will be more successful, because it has to do with those matters that are a mere nothing, namely, with the power of Christ, by which He is powerful in us even against the gates of hell (Matt. 16:18), and about the privileges of the heavenly church, which knows neither supremely great Rome nor most holy Jerusalem nor any place and does not seek Christ here or there but worships the Father in spirit and in truth (John 4:23). For why should such great men be moved or excited by these trifles, since they lie outside their competence? Therefore I now come before the public the more safely because I avoid those things by which they are excited and deal with petty items that suit my littleness. As for the rest, if anything is left of that ancient tragedy that arose concerning great things, I leave it to them — both because I am only one person and small and weak, but especially because they are standing idle all the day (Matt. 20:6), whereas I am very busy. For it is not necessary for both sides of a cause to torment themselves. There is trouble enough if one side is grieved and distressed.

Furthermore, most noble sirs, to speak seriously to you, I have this respect for the Roman pontiff and his decrees that there is no one superior to him; and I except no one but this vicar's Prince, Jesus Christ, our Lord and Lord of all. I give His Word such preference over the words of His vicar that I have no hesitation at all in passing judgment according to it on all the words and deeds of His vicar. For I want him to be subject to this unbreakable rule of the apostle (1 Thess. 5:21): "Test everything, hold fast what is good." From this yoke, I say, I will not let anyone shake his neck free, no matter whether he goes by the name of mother or schoolmistress of the churches;[5] and so much the more because in our age we have seen that some councils are repudiated and others again are confirmed,[6] that theology is dealt with by mere opinions, that the meaning of the laws depends on one man's arbitrary decision, and that everything is thrown into such confusion that almost nothing certain is left for us. But that even many decretals are inconsistent with the sense of the Gospel is clearer than light, so that actual necessity itself compels us to flee for refuge to the most solid rock of Divine Scripture and not to believe rashly any, whoever they may be, who speak, decide, or act contrary to its authority. Nor do I think that one needs to fear what Cardinal Cajetan and Sylvester Prierias,[7] who quibble that even in matters of faith the mere word of a man is sufficient, fawningly say to the contrary. St. Augustine teaches that no one should be believed, no matter how greatly he may excel in sanctity and learning (even the highest degree of sanctity, I believe), unless he convinces you by Holy Writ or acceptable reasoning, lest we be tricked if we play some other game.[8] But these good counselors in Christ want to drive us into this illusion by force. So many times did St. Peter fall; and on one occasion, even after receiving the Spirit, he erred with most serious peril to souls.[9] And we elevate to the perfection of the apostles men who crawl along far below the lofty plane of the apostles, as if Christ lied when He promised that He would be with us to the end of the world (Matt. 28:20). To such an extent do we look for other Christs, on whose nod of assent and dissent the church should depend. It is sufficient for the Roman pontiff to be the supreme pontiff. It would be most impious to attribute to him in addition virtue and wisdom equal to the virtue and wisdom of Christ, as some have the audacity to do. Yet, to confess it frankly, I myself scarcely know what or where the Roman Church is, since those loathsome babblers play in such a way with, joke with, and confuse the names of the Roman Church. Sylvester carves it into

---

[5] A combination of two titles for the church, *mater* and *magistra*.

[6] Luther seems to be referring to changing attitudes toward the reform councils of the preceding century.

[7] On Cajetan cf. p. 154, note 1; on Prierias, cf. p. 157, note 10.

[8] See also Luther's *Ad dialogum Silvestri Prieriatis de potestate papae responsio* (W, I, 647).

[9] Matt. 27:69-75; Acts 10; Gal. 2:11-14.

three churches: the pope, the cardinals, and the people. Since this distinction is official and adequate, and the members do not agree, he causes the pope and the cardinals to be regarded as being outside the church among the pagans, as persons who are not in the church according to its essence. Or he will place three Christs at the head of those three churches. In fact, on the strength of so great an authority Christ will not belong to the church, since He is not the church according to its power, according to its representation, or according to its essence.[10] Cardinal Cajetan peddles himself everywhere in Germany as the Roman Church, since he is learned enough to invent apostolic *brevia* [11] under its name. The Roman Church is that fine copyist who, when he was going to publish that very beautiful explanation in which Cajetan glories so fittingly — although in his formulary he found neither Scripture passages nor any reasons, but only that it had been the custom and the tradition from time immemorial — right faithfully smeared these very things on his parchment. Everywhere these impious scoundrels sell themselves as the Roman Church, just as it suits each one, as merely with the lead and wax of the Roman Curia they dupe and drain all Germany. What are they doing with such caricatures of the holy names "pope" and "Roman Church" except that they take us Germans to be mere blockheads, dunces, simpletons, and, as they say, barbarians and beasts,[12] while they even ridicule the incredible patience with which we endure the way they dupe and swindle us? Therefore in such a great muddle of facts and words I return from this great forest of Sylvesters [13] to the city of Augsburg, and meanwhile I shall follow the judgment whereby the princes of Germany at their most recent assembly [14] distinguished in a proper, holy, and majestic way between the Roman Church and the Roman Curia. For how could they have rejected the levies of 10, 5, and 2 percent (that is, the marrow and the sudden

---

10 Cf. Sylvester Prierias, *In praesumptuosas Martini Lutheri conclusiones de potestate papae dialogus* (St. Louis, XVIII, 314).

11 A reference to the charge that Cajetan himself was the author of the *Brevia apostolica*, which bore the name of Pope Leo X; cf. *Luther's Works,* 31, pp. 286 ff.

12 This seems to be a reminiscence of Luther's journey to Rome of 1510—11; see also p. 384, note 5.

13 A pun on the Latin word *silva.*

14 Luther is referring to the *Gravamina* of the German nation presented at Augsburg the previous year.

devastation once for all of Germany in its entirety) which they knew had been sanctioned in that most sacred (if I may say so) Roman council and had been demanded by such great emissaries of the apostolic see unless finally, though at a late hour, they had become wise and had realized that this was not a decree of the Roman Church but an invention of the Roman Curia? They saw, of course (wonderful to say, and what no Sylvesters and no Cajetans can believe), that the council and the pope had erred and can err,[15] and that the name "Roman Church" is one thing, while what is carried on in the name of the Roman Church is something else; that it is one thing to be an emissary of the Roman Curia and something else to be an emissary of the Roman Church; that the latter brings the Gospel, but the former looks for money. Where do those barbarians and beasts get such ability to judge, except that God, finally grown weary of the blasphemies against Him and of the mockery and abuse of His name and that of the holy Roman Church, wanted to warn the Roman lords to put aside jest and sport and hereafter to have serious concern for the affairs of the church before they draw blood by wringing Germany's nose too hard (Prov. 30:33)? Therefore, I, too, following the very beautiful example of these lay theologians, make a very long, wide, and deep distinction between the Roman Church and the Roman Curia. The former I know to be the utterly pure bridal bed of Christ, the mother of the churches, the mistress of the world (but in the spirit, that is, mistress over the sins, not over the affairs of the world), the bride of Christ, the daughter of God, the terror of hell, the victory over the flesh; and — what shall I say? — all things are hers, according to Paul in 1 Cor. 3:22 f. She, however, is Christ's, and Christ is God's. The Curia, on the other hand, is known by its fruits (Matt. 7:20). Not that it should be considered important that our possessions and rights are torn away, since it is settled in heaven that in this life Christians suffer oppression, Nimrods, and mighty hunters (Gen. 10:8-9). Nor will the church be freed from this condition except by death; it is a palm tree, and the more powerfully it is oppressed, the higher it rises in Kedesh. But it is a misery beyond all tears that these things are done by brothers and fathers to brothers and sons (as the Lord says in the prophet [Jer. 19:9] that the children are devoured by their parents), something that would scarcely be

---

[15] Cf. Luther's statements at the Leipzig Debate of July, 1519, *Luther's Works*, 31, p. 322.

done by a Turk; or if it were done, at least the holy name of Christ would not be used as a cloak for such foul abominations, which is the most intolerable affront of all to Christ and the church. By all means let property and life go to ruin. But why should we allow the eternal name of the Lord to be so foully besmirched? In no way, therefore, may one resist the Roman Church; but for kings, princes, and whoever could do so to resist the Roman Curia would be a matter of far greater piety than to resist the Turks themselves. Perhaps these things are being expressed too wordily and too freely. But for the sake of those who, along with these mockers, make an endless mockery of Christ, I have been compelled to explain myself, in order that they may know that they are mistaken when they cry that I, who love not only the Roman Church but the whole church of Christ with the purest love, am hostile to the Roman Church. Then, too, I am certain that one day I must die and at the coming of our Lord Jesus Christ must render an account of the truth — whether I have kept it silent or have spoken it — and in general of the talent entrusted to me, lest I be declared guilty of having hidden it (Matt. 25:26-30). Let those who want to rage do so by all means. Only let me not be found guilty of impious silence. I am conscious of being a debtor to the Word, no matter how unworthy I am. It has never been possible to discuss the Word of God without incurring danger of bloodshed; but just as the Word died for us, so it requires, in turn, that we die for it when we confess it. The servant is not greater than his master. "If they persecuted Me," says Christ (John 15:20), "they will also persecute you; if they have kept My Word, they will also keep yours."

But I return to my own case; and I refer to you, most noble sirs, or (to use Paul's expression) confer with you on this study of mine of Paul's epistle. A slight thing it is indeed. It is not so much a commentary as a testimony of my faith in Christ, lest perhaps I have run in vain and have not adequately grasped Paul's meaning (Gal. 2:2). For here, because it is God's affair and surely of the utmost importance, I am eager to be instructed by any child. I, too, would certainly have preferred to wait for the commentaries promised long ago by Erasmus, a man preeminent in theology and impervious to envy.[16] But since he is postponing this (God grant it may not be for

---

[16] For our identification of Luther's references to Erasmus we have consulted two works of the Dutch humanist: his *Annotationes* to the Greek New Testament with Latin translation and his *Paraphrasis*. These are contained, respectively, in Vol. VI and Vol. VII of the Hildesheim edition of his *Opera*.

long), the situation which you see forces me to come before the public. I know, of course, that I am a child and unlearned, but in spite of this (so bold I may be) I am devoted to Christian piety and instruction; and in this respect I am more learned than those who have made nothing but a mockery and laughingstock of God's commandments with their impious parading of human laws. I have had only one aim in view. May I bring it about that through my effort those who have heard me interpreting the letters of the apostle may find Paul clearer and may happily surpass me. But even if I have not achieved this, well, I shall still have wasted this labor gladly; it remains an attempt by which I have wanted to kindle the interest of others in Paul's theology; and this no good man will charge against me as a fault. Farewell.

THE SUBJECT OF PAUL'S EPISTLE TO THE GALATIANS

ALTHOUGH the Galatians had first been taught a sound faith by the apostle, that is, taught to trust in Jesus Christ alone, not in their own righteousnesses or in those of the Law, later on they were again turned away by the false apostles and led to trust in works of legalistic righteousness; for they were very easily deceived by the fact that the name and the example of the great and true apostles were falsely appealed to as commending this. For in the whole life of mortal men there is nothing more deceptive than superstition, that is, than the false and calamitous imitation of the saints. When you look at their works alone and not at their heart as well, it is easy for you to become an ape and a leviathan, that is, to add something and thereby to turn the true religion into superstition or impiety.[17] For — to demonstrate this with the example at hand — the apostles were preserving some ceremonial laws throughout the churches of Judea, just as Jerome testifies that Philo wrote regarding Mark.[18] But those foolish people, not knowing for what reason the apostles did this, soon added on their own the idea that the things they had seen practiced by such great apostles were necessary for salvation, and that no account had to be taken of the one man Paul, who had neither seen or heard Christ on earth.

But, as Peter had explained very clearly in Acts 15:7-11, the apostles observed these practices, not as being necessary but as being permissible and as doing no harm to those who place their trust for salvation, not in these things themselves but in Jesus Christ. For to those who believe in Christ whatever things are either enjoined or forbidden in the way of external ceremonies and bodily righteousnesses are all pure, adiaphora, and are permissible, except insofar

---

[17] The source of this etymology appears to be Jerome, *Liber interpretationis hebraicorum nominum, Corpus Christianorum, Series Latina,* LXXII, 133.

[18] Jerome, *De viris illustribus,* 8, 10.

as the believers are willing to subject themselves to these things of their own accord or for the sake of love. Paul toils with such great ardor to recall the Galatians to this understanding that he takes absolutely no account of Peter and of all the apostles so far as their person, condition (that is, rank), and what people call "position" are concerned. Finally he glories with a kind of very holy pride that he received nothing from them but was rather commended by them. He makes no concession whatever to the opinion of the apostles by which, as he saw, slander of the evangelical truth was being occasioned among the more ignorant; and he considers it far better that he himself and the apostles themselves be without glory than that the Gospel of Christ be nullified.

CHAPTER ONE

1. *Paul an apostle*

Now that the whole Christian world knows Greek, and the *Annotations* of that most eminent theologian Erasmus are in everyone's hands and are diligently used, there is no need to point out what the word "apostle" means in Greek — except to those for whom I am writing, not Erasmus.[1] For the word "apostle" has the same meaning as "one who has been sent." And, as St. Jerome teaches, the Hebrews have a word which they pronounce "Sila," that is, a person to whom, from the act of sending, the name "Sent" is applied.[2] Thus in John 9:7: "Go, wash in the pool of Siloam (which means Sent)." And Isaiah, in his eighth chapter (v. 6), is not unaware of this hidden meaning when he says: "This people have refused the waters of Shiloah that flow gently." So, too, in Gen. 49:10: "Until Shiloh comes," which Jerome has translated with "the one who is to be sent." On the basis of this passage Paul, writing to the Hebrews (3:1), seems to call Christ an Apostle, that is, a Silas. And in Acts (15:22) Luke mentions a certain Silas.

A more important consideration, however, is the fact that "apostle" is a modest name but at the same time a marvelously awesome and venerable one, a name which expresses equally both remarkable lowliness and loftiness. The lowliness lies in the fact that he is sent, thus bearing witness to his office, his role as servant, his obedience. Furthermore, no one should be impressed by the name as being a title of honor, rely on it, or boast of it. No, by the name of the office he should be drawn at once to Him who does the sending, to Him who authorizes it. From Him one then gains a conception of the majesty and loftiness of him who has been sent and is a servant, in order that

---

[1] Erasmus, *Annotationes ad locum, Opera,* VI, 801.

[2] Jerome, *Commentarius in Epistolam S. Pauli ad Galatas, Patrologia, Series Latina,* XXVI, 355; henceforth this will be cited as *Commentarius,* followed by an Arabic numeral referring to the column in Vol. XXVI of the Latin *Patrologia.*

he may be received with reverence, not as in our age, when the terms "apostleship," "episcopate," and all the rest have begun to be words expressive, not of an office but of prestige and authority. These men Christ calls by the apposite name in John 10:8 — not "those who have been sent" but "those who come." And interpreting Himself, He calls them "thieves and robbers," since they do not bring the Word of Him who sends them to feed the sheep with it but carry off their own gain and thereby slaughter the sheep. "All who came," He says — that is, were not sent — "are thieves and robbers." And, as the apostle says in Rom. 10:15: "How will they preach unless they are sent?" Would that the shepherds and leaders of the Christian people in our day properly weighed these teachings! For who can preach unless he is an apostle? But who is an apostle except one who brings the Word of God? And who can bring the Word of God except one who has listened to God? But the man who brings his own dogmas or those that rest on human laws and decrees, or those of the philosopher — can he be called an apostle? Indeed, he is one who comes as a thief, a robber, and a destroyer and slayer of souls. The blind man washes in Siloam and receives his sight (John 9:7), and the waters of Siloam are healthful; they are not the strong, proud waters of the king of the Assyrians (Is. 8:7). He, namely, God, sent His Word, and in that way He healed them (Ps. 107:20). A man *comes*, and his own word comes with him; and he causes the woman with an issue of blood to become worse. To put it clearly, this means that as often as the Word of God is preached, it renders consciences joyful, expansive, and untroubled toward God, because it is a Word of grace and forgiveness, a kind and sweet Word. As often as the word of man is preached, it renders the conscience sad, cramped, and full of fear in itself, because it is a word of the Law, of wrath and sin; it shows what a person has failed to do and how deeply he is in debt.

Therefore the church, since its beginning, has never been less happy than it is now; and daily it becomes unhappier, because it is harassed by so many decrees, laws, and statutes, and by almost countless torments, and is far more cruelly weakened than it was by the torturers at the time of the martyrs.[3] And so far are the prelates from being touched by this destruction of souls, so far from being "grieved

---

[3] It is not clear whether Luther means that the decline of the church set in with the pontificate of Innocent III (d. 1216) or earlier; on this problem see also *Luther's Works*, 21, p. 59, note 20.

over the ruin of Joseph" (Amos 6:6), that they even add pain to the pain of our wounds, as though they were offering a service to God (John 16:2).

— *not from men nor through man, but through Jesus Christ and God the Father, who raised Him from the dead —*

2. *and all the brethren who are with me.*

At the very outset Paul strikes an indirect blow at the false apostles of the Galatians; he implies that they had been sent, not by Jesus Christ but either by themselves or by other apostles, whose teaching, however, they were misrepresenting.

This is by all means a point to be noted, that Christ wanted no one to be made an apostle by men or by the will of men but as the result of a call from Him alone. For this reason the apostles did not dare elect Matthias; they gained his appointment from heaven in answer to their prayer (Acts 1:24-26). And it was from heaven that God called Paul himself and made him an apostle (Acts 9:4 ff.), in particular through the voice of the Holy Spirit (Acts 13:2). "Set apart for Me," He says, "Paul and Barnabas for the work to which I have called them." Thus Paul boasts in Rom. 1:1 f. that he was set apart for the Gospel of God, inasmuch as he himself, together with Barnabas, was set apart for the uncircumcised and the Gentiles, while the rest of the apostles were sent to those who were circumcised (Gal. 2:7, 9).

Note also that Paul makes the name "apostle" so emphatically expressive of an office and of dignity that he uses it as a participle and says "an apostle, not from men," which means "sent, not from men" — unless his speech here smacks of a Hebraism, as in Ps. 45:8: "Your robes are all fragrant with myrrh and aloes and cassia." All these facts aim to make you see with what care Christ has established and fortified His church, lest anyone rashly presume to teach without being sent by Him or by those whom He has sent. For just as the Word of God is the church's first and greatest benefit, so, on the other hand, there is no greater harm by which the church is destroyed than the word of man and the traditions of this world. God alone is true, and every man a liar (Ps. 116:11). Finally, just as David once left behind all the means with which Solomon was to build the temple (1 Chron. 22:14), so Christ has left behind the Gospel and other writings, in order that the church might be built by means of them, not by human decrees. How wretchedly this has now been neglected, indeed perverted, for more than 300 years is clear enough from the condition of all things in the church today.

St. Jerome concludes from this passage that there are four kinds of apostles.[4] First, those who are such, not by men or through man but through Jesus Christ and God the Father, as were formerly the prophets and all the apostles. Secondly, those who are such by God's doing indeed but through man, as were the apostles' disciples and those who lawfully succeed the apostles till the end of the world, as do bishops and priests. But this class cannot exist without the first, from which it has its origin. Thirdly, those who are such by a man's doing or that of men and not of God, as when someone is ordained as a result of favoritism and the efforts of men. Thus we now see very many being elected to the office of priest, not by the decision of God but by the favor of the rabble for a price. That is the statement of Jerome. If this evil was already growing strong in the time of Jerome, why be surprised if it reigns in triumph today? For to this class must belong all those who offer themselves for bishoprics and priesthoods before they are called, gluttonous and glory-hungry creatures that they are. For this reason we see well enough how much good the church gets out of them. The fourth kind consists of those who are called neither by God nor by men or through man but by themselves, as were the false prophets and the false apostles of whom Paul says: "Such men are false apostles, deceitful workmen, disguising themselves as apostles of Christ" (2 Cor. 11:13). And the Lord says in John 10:8: "All who came were thieves and robbers"; and Jeremiah says (23:21): "I did not send the prophets, yet they ran; I did not speak to them, yet they prophesied." One must beware of this evil most of all. For it was on this account that Christ did not allow the demons to speak, even though they were telling the truth, lest under the guise of truth a death-dealing lie find entrance, since he who speaks of his own accord cannot speak without lying, as Christ says in John 8:44. Accordingly, in order that the apostles might not speak on their own authority, He gave them His Spirit, of whom He says: "For it is not you who speak, but the Spirit of your Father speaking through you" (Matt. 10:20). And again: "I will give you a mouth and wisdom" (Luke 21:15).

Here (trifling though it is) I cannot pass over the foolish complaint made especially by many monks and priests — at that, it rep-

---

[4] Jerome, *Commentarius*, 336.

resents a sharp enough temptation — that they have a talent from the Lord and consequently are impelled to teach because the command of the Gospel makes it necessary for them to do so. Therefore if they do not teach, they believe in their utterly foolish conscience that they are hiding the talent which they have from their Lord and are liable to condemnation (Matt. 25:26-30). This the devil does, in order to make them unstable in the vocation to which they have been called. My dear brother, with a single word Christ sets you free from this complaint. Look at the Gospel, which says: "He called his servants and entrusted to them his property" (Matt. 25:14). "He called," it says; but who has called you? Wait for Him who calls. Meanwhile be untroubled. In fact, even if you were wiser than Solomon himself and Daniel, still, if you are not called, avoid spreading the Word more than you would shun hell itself. If God needs you, He will call you. If He does not call you, you will not burst with your wisdom. As a matter of fact, it is not true wisdom either; to you it only seems to be. And it is very foolish for you to imagine what fruit you are able to produce. Nobody produces fruit by means of the Word unless he is called to teach without wishing for it. For One is our Teacher, Jesus Christ (Matt. 23:10). He alone, through His called servants, teaches and produces fruit. But the man who teaches without being called does so to his own harm and that of his hearers, because Christ is not with him.

Accordingly, by saying that he was sent "not from men" the apostle contrasts himself with the false apostles; and by saying "not through man" he contrasts himself with the believers themselves, who had been sent by the apostles. Such, therefore, is the introduction he employs against three classes of apostles. And Jerome bears witness that from among the Jews certain ones who believed in Christ proceeded to Galatia and taught that Peter, James, and John were observing the Law, as will be seen later.[5]

But it seems pointless to insert here a reference to Christ's resurrection. The apostle, however, has the habit of gladly mentioning the resurrection of Christ, especially against those who trust in their own righteousness. Thus he also mentions it at greater length in the salutation of his Epistle to the Romans (Rom. 1:4), because here, too, he is arguing vigorously against work-righteousness. For those who maintain that righteousness comes by works deny Christ's resurrec-

[5] See pp. 301 ff.

tion and even ridicule it. In Rom. 4:25 Paul says: "Christ was put to death for our trespasses and raised for our justification." Consequently, he who presumes that he is righteous in any other way than by believing in Christ rejects Christ and considers Christ's Passion and resurrection useless. On the other hand, he who believes in Christ, who died — he himself at the same time dies to sin together with Christ; and he who believes in the resurrected and living Christ — he himself, by the same faith, also rises and lives in Christ, and Christ lives in him (Gal. 2:20). Therefore the resurrection of Christ is our righteousness and our life, not only by way of an example but also by virtue of its power. Apart from Christ's resurrection no one can rise, no matter how many good works he does. On the other hand, through His resurrection anyone at all rises, no matter how much evil he has done, as this is treated at greater length in Romans. Perhaps another reason for Paul's practice of mentioning the resurrection in his salutations is this, that the Holy Spirit was given through the resurrection of Christ and by this Spirit the apostleship and other gifts were distributed (1 Cor. 12:4 ff.). In this way, therefore, Paul declares that he is an apostle by divine authority through the Spirit of the resurrection of Jesus Christ.

"And all the brethren who are with me." "All the brethren," says Paul. With these words he seems to be attacking the same false apostles, who, as Jerome remarks, were saying that Paul himself, when he was in other circles, also gave to his teaching a flavor different from that of what he had taught the Galatians.[6] A further reason is that for setting people straight it helps very much to have the opinion and consensus of many persons regarding the same matter.

To the churches of Galatia:

In other epistles Paul writes to the church of a single city; here he is writing to the churches of many cities and of a whole province. And particularly noteworthy is the observation which St. Jerome aptly makes at this point, namely, that these are called churches even though the apostle censures them for being corrupted with error.[7] From this fact, he says, one should learn that the term "church" can be used in two ways: both for one that has no spot or wrinkle and is truly the body of Christ (Eph. 5:17) and for one that is assembled in Christ's

---

[6] Jerome, *Commentarius*, 337.

[7] Jerome, *Commentarius*, 337.

name but is without complete and perfect virtues. In the same way the word "wise" is applied in two ways: not only to those who have this virtue in its fullness and perfection but also to those who are beginning to be wise and are in a position to advance in wisdom. Of those who are perfect it is said: "I send you wise men" (Matt. 23:34); of those who are beginning to be it is stated: "Reprove a wise man, and he will love you" (Prov. 9:8). In accordance with this meaning one should also understand the other virtues, namely, that the terms "brave," "prudent," "chaste," "just," and "temperate" are sometimes taken in their full sense and sometimes improperly. But one must by all means have this understanding about perfection. For in this life no one, not even an apostle, is so perfect that he should not become more so. In fact, as the wise man says: "When a man has finished, he is just beginning" (Ecclus. 18:7). Therefore you may speak of some persons as perfect for the purpose of comparing them with others. In other respects they themselves also begin every day and make progress.

Therefore St. Augustine gives a better explanation when he reserves the church without spot or wrinkle for the life to come — the church which no longer says: "Forgive us our debts."[8] Nevertheless, the opinion held by Jerome and Origen is right: that the words from the apostle's letter serve well to combat the heretics, who — in order to arrogate to themselves the name "church," as though they alone were saints — immediately find fault with a church by calling it a Babylon in which wicked persons are intermingled.[9] Indeed, if there are wicked persons in a church, surely one should hasten to it; and, in keeping with this example of Paul, one should shout, exhort, entreat, beg, and frighten, and should try everything to make them good. But one should not withdraw and cause a schism because of that sacrilegious fear of God (as they call it) and that impious zeal of conscience. What kind of love is it that has decided neither to endure the wicked nor to help them? It is madness clothing itself most improperly with the name of love. What answer will they give here? The apostle calls them churches that were afflicted, not with wayward conduct (for this alone offends the proud and makes them heretical) but with a false faith; and the entire substance on the basis of which they could be called churches was being destroyed.

[8] Augustine, *De correctione Donatistarum*, 9, 39.
[9] Jerome, *Commentarius*, 337.

3. *Grace be to you and peace from God the Father and our Lord Jesus Christ.*

The apostle distinguishes this grace and peace from that which the world is able to give to itself or a man can give to himself. For the grace of God the Father and of our Lord Jesus Christ takes away sins, since it is spiritual and hidden. Thus the peace of God brightens, calms, and gladdens a man's heart as he stands secretly in God's presence. And, as has been said elsewhere, grace takes away the guilt, and peace takes away the punishment, so that in this way righteousness and peace kiss each other (Ps. 85:10) and are in accord. But when this happens, one immediately loses the grace and peace of men, of the world, and of the flesh, that is, of oneself and of the devil. On the other hand, everyone else becomes angry and troubled. For he who is in God's grace does what is pleasing to God. Therefore he soon displeases the devil, the world, and his own flesh; and as long as he is righteous in the sight of God, he is a sinner to his flesh and to the world. Thus war breaks out — war on the outside but peace within — within, I say, not in a way that can be felt and pleasurably experienced with the senses, at least not always, but in an invisible way and through faith. For the peace of God passes all understanding (Phil. 4:7); that is, it cannot be comprehended except through faith. Thus, conversely, he who is in the grace of the world and in his own grace, and pleases himself — he immediately sins before God and incurs His wrath. "For whoever wishes to be a friend of this world," says James (4:4), "makes himself an enemy of God." Consequently, war soon follows in this case too — war on the inside with God and peace on the outside with the world, because "'There is no peace for the wicked,' says the Lord" (Is. 48:22). Nevertheless, Ps. 73:3 speaks of "seeing the peace of the sinners," and in Ps. 37:7 the sinner "prospers in his way." Therefore this war, too, is hidden and takes place imperceptibly, at least sometimes. Accordingly, these four pairs balance themselves in a kind of scale: the grace of God and the world's displeasure, the peace of God and the world's perturbation, the grace of the world and God's displeasure, the peace of the world and God's perturbation. Thus Christ says in John 16:33: "In the world you will have tribulation; but in Me you will have peace. But be of good cheer; I have overcome the world." And later in this chapter Paul writes: "If I were still pleasing men, I would not be a servant of Christ" (Gal. 1:10); that is, I would not be pleasing

Him. In this salutation, therefore, Paul has set down the substance of his teaching, namely, that no one can be righteous except through the grace of God, and by no means through works; and that a troubled conscience is not set at rest except through the peace of God, and therefore not through the works of any virtue or satisfaction.

But why was it not enough for the apostle to say "from God our Father" without adding "and our Lord Jesus Christ"? He makes this addition in order to point out the difference between the kingdom of grace and the kingdom of glory. The kingdom of grace is a kingdom of faith, in which Christ reigns as a man placed over all things by God the Father in accordance with Ps. 8:6-7. In this kingdom He receives gifts from God for men, as Ps. 68:18 states; and this holds true until the Last Judgment. For then, as the apostle teaches in 1 Cor. 15:24-28, He will turn the kingdom over to God His Father, and God will be all in all when He will have destroyed every authority and power. This is the kingdom of glory, in which God Himself will reign through Himself, no longer through His humanity for the purpose of stirring up faith. It is not that the two kingdoms are different from each other, but they are ruled over in different ways — now in faith and "dimly" (1 Cor. 13:12) through the humanity of Christ, then visibly and in the revelation of Christ's divine nature. For this reason the apostles usually call Christ the Lord; but they call the Father God, even though Christ and the Father are the same God. As I have said, however, they do this because of the difference in the kingdom, which consists of us, who are cleansed in faith but whose salvation will be in plain view.

4. *Who gave Himself for our sins to deliver us from the present evil age, according to the will of our God and Father;*

5. *to whom be the glory forever and ever. Amen.*

Every one of these words has a specific meaning and is also emphatic. With them Paul now asserts positively that the Law and man's will amount to nothing at all unless one believes that Christ was delivered for our sins.

Paul says: "Who gave" as a free gift to those who did not merit it; he does not say: "He bestowed" as a reward to those who were worthy. Thus he says in Rom. 5:10: "While we were enemies, we were reconciled to God by the death of His Son." But He did not give gold or silver. Nor did He give a man or all the angels. No, he gave "Himself," than whom there is nothing greater.[10] Nor does He have anything greater. He gave, I say, so inestimable a price "for our sins," for something so despicable and so utterly deserving of hatred. Oh, the grace and the love of God toward us! With what choice and well-suited words Paul commends the mercy of God the Father and renders it surpassingly sweet to us! Where now are those who boast proudly of free will? Where is the learning of moral philosophy? Where is the virtue of laws, sacred as well as secular, if our sins are so great that they could not be taken away except by paying a price so great? What are we doing when we try to make ourselves righteous by our own will and by laws and teachings except that we cover our sins with a false appearance of righteousness or virtue and make incurable hypocrites? What does virtue profit if sins remain? Therefore we must despair of all these things; and where faith in Christ is not taught, we should consider every virtue to be nothing else than a veil of iniquity and a covering for every kind of filth, just as Christ describes the Pharisees (Matt. 23:25-27). Accordingly, the virtues of the heathen are nothing but frauds,[11] unless you maintain that it was useless for Christ to have been delivered for our sins, that He wanted to pay such a great price in vain for what we were able to achieve by our own strength.

But do not pass over this pronoun "our" with contempt. For it will profit you nothing to believe that Christ was delivered for the sins of other saints and to doubt that He was delivered for your sins. For both the ungodly and the demons believe this (James 2:19). No, you must take for granted in steadfast confidence that He was delivered for your sins too, and that you are one of those for whose sins He was delivered. This faith justifies you; it will cause Christ to dwell, live, and reign in you. This faith is the testimony which the Holy Spirit bears to our spirit: that we are the sons of God (Rom. 8:16). Therefore if you take notice, you will easily realize that this feeling is not in you because of your own strength. Consequently, it must be acquired through a spirit that is humble and despairs of itself.

Therefore the statements that man is uncertain as to whether he is in the state of salvation or not are fables of the celebrated scho-

---

[10] The phrase *quo maius nihil est neque habet* is an echo of Anselm.

[11] See, for example, Augustine, *City of God*, II, 19.

lastics.[12] Beware of ever being uncertain that so far as you yourself are concerned, you are lost. You must be sure of this. Moreover, you must strive to be certain and firm in faith in Christ, who was delivered for your sins. If this faith is in you, how can it happen that you are unaware of it, since St. Augustine asserts that it is most assuredly seen by him who has it?[13]

Now look! Paul does not say "for your sins"; he says "for our sins." For he was certain. Thus he also says "to deliver us," not "to deliver you." Thus with the thunderbolt of the Word he again crushes confidence in the will and in the works of the Law and our own righteousness. It is not those things, he says, that save us; it is Christ, who was delivered — if only you believe that you are saved. But this is a spiritual, not a bodily, deliverance. It takes place when the soul dies to the world and is crucified to it, that is, to the lusts that are present in the flesh of all men. Paul explains this at greater length in Titus 2:12, where he says: "Denying ungodliness and worldly lusts, let us live soberly, righteously, and godly in this world." In this passage he has expressed both ideas, namely, life in this world (he implies that the world is not evil) and worldly lusts, because in this world evil lusts abound. It is for this reason that in this passage he adds "from the present evil age." Otherwise, if by "evil age" he wanted the actual passage of time to be understood, he would teach that all who believe in Christ should be taken from this life right now. Thus in 1 Cor. 5:10, where he explains that this is not what he wanted, he says that "then you would need to go out of the world." By this he means: "It was not my wish that you should flee from life, but that you should flee from the vices and lusts that are in the world," as is also stated in 2 Peter 1:4: "Fleeing that corruption that is in the world because of lust." Moreover, this figurative way of speaking is aptly and amply explained by St. Jerome when he says: "Just as woodlands get a bad name when they are filled with brigandage, and just as we detest a sword by which human blood has been shed and a cup in which poison has been prepared — not because of a fault on the part of the cup and the sword but because those who have used them in an evil way deserve hatred — so the world, which is a period of time, is not good or evil per se but is called either good or evil according to those who are in it."[14] Simi-

---

12 Cf. also *Luther's Works*, 21, p. 38, note 13.
13 See, for example, the passage cited in *Luther's Works*, 26, p. 377, note 16.
14 Jerome, *Commentarius*, 338.

larly, St. Augustine understands the evil world to be the evil people in the world.[15] But you must understand all this in such a way that you recognize yourself, too, as part of this evil (cf. Ps. 116:11). For every man is a liar, and there is not a righteous one on earth (cf. Rom. 3:10; Ps. 14:3), lest because of pride you be lifted up too much above the rest. Therefore since Christ rescues you from the world, He certainly rescues you from yourself as from the worst enemy of all, just as Paul says in Rom. 7:18: "Nothing good dwells with me, that is, in my flesh." By your own strength, therefore, you will not overcome the evil world and your own vices; your works are in vain unless Christ alone delivers you. So beware lest fastings, vigils, zealous efforts, temperance, sobriety, and other virtues make you an incorrigible hypocrite.

"According to His will." This means: The fact that we are rescued is not due to the progress of our own virtue; it is due to the merciful will of God (Rom. 9:16). As Ps. 51:18 says: "Do good, O Lord, to Zion in Thy good pleasure"; and Luke 2:14: "And on earth peace to men of good will" — not their good will but God's, since in Greek the word is εὐδοκία. For just as men are called men of mercy and vessels of mercy (Rom. 9:23) because they are accepted through the mercy of God, not because of their own merit, so they are called men of good will because they are saved by the good pleasure of God's will, not by their own strength. Therefore "the glory" remains "to God alone forever. Amen," as the apostle has said here. For if we are able to accomplish anything, certainly this must be credited, not to God's glory but to ours. But far be it from one who is dust and nothing to have praise and glory.

Note, therefore, with what force Paul hits the Galatians and their teachers in what is only the salutation, which, in view of the contents of this epistle, is a most appropriate introduction.

6. *I am astonished that you are so quickly deserting Him who called you in the grace of Christ and turning to a different gospel —*

7. *not that there is another gospel, but there are some who trouble you and want to pervert the Gospel of Christ.*

St. Jerome says there is a transposition of words here, and he adjusts it as follows: "I marvel that you are so quickly removed from

---

[15] Augustine, *Epistolae ad Galatas expositio, Patrologia, Series Latina*, XXXV, 2108.

Christ Jesus, who called you into grace." [16] The Greek text has "of God" instead of "of Christ"; and, as Erasmus points out, this can be rendered into Latin both with the genitive and with the ablative case. Erasmus also understands "which is not another" to mean "which is nothing or none." [17] Here, if I were permitted to offer a conjecture of my own, I would believe that the apostle means to say that there is no other gospel than that which he himself had preached. And the meaning would become clearer if the conjunction "unless" were changed to "but," so that then — if I may be so bold — this text would read: "I marvel that you are so quickly removed from God, who called you through grace, to another gospel, although there is no other gospel; but there are certain people who are disturbing you and want to pervert the Gospel of Christ." But it will not be an awkward reading either if one decides to keep the transposition of words and to read "from him who called you through God's grace or by God."

Paul's statement is a strong one, and yet it is very restrained. Although he shows later that he is completely on fire with indignation, here he says that he is astonished. In other words, he moves in a pleasant manner, not as he did in his initial onslaught. This is certainly a good example to all leaders in the church, especially to those who are quick to hurl thunderbolts even for something of no importance. Paul does not say that the Galatians are erring, that they are sinning; he says that by a greater evil they have been brought completely outside the Gospel and have been estranged from God. For it is more tolerable if a tree remains standing with several of its branches broken or after it has been injured by some other damage than if it is torn out of its place completely and removed to a spot where it must wither and become barren. Such a terrible thing it is to seek one's own righteousness and to trust in works of the Law and of the free will. For this means denying Christ, rejecting grace and truth, and, as Paul will teach later, making an idol out of oneself. This is what Job 31:27-28 speaks of: "If I have kissed my hand with my own mouth, which is an act of the greatest wickedness and a denial of the most high God." For to kiss the hand with one's own mouth is, as the saintly fathers understand it, to praise one's own works and to trust in one's own righteousness.[18] And the result of this wicked-

---

[16] Jerome, *Commentarius*, 343.

[17] Erasmus, *Annotationes ad locum*.

[18] Cf. for example, Augustine, *Annotationes in Job*, 31, *Patrologia, Series Latina*, XXXIV, 860.

ness is that we do not glory in God but in ourselves, and that we take God's glory away from Him. This sinful practice is attributed to the Baal-worshipers in 1 Kings 19:18 when it speaks of those "who have not bent their knees before Baal and every mouth that has not worshiped him by kissing his hand." And Is. 2:8 says: "They bow down to the work of their own hands, to what their fingers have made." On the other hand, in Ps. 2:12 there is the statement: "Kiss the Son" (which is how the Hebrew text reads, instead of "accept instruction"); [19] that is to say, believe in Christ with a pure faith, and worship Him. For faith is the debt that is owed to truth, and there is no truth except God alone. Hence faith is the kind of worship that is most genuine and is personal.

From this we understand St. Augustine's statement that evil is of two kinds: against faith and against good morals.[20] An evil that has to do with faith, even though accompanied by excellent moral behavior, produces heretical, haughty, and schismatic individuals whom Scripture properly calls ungodly, in Hebrew רְשָׁעִים. Evil ways make sinners without harming faith, at least the faith of others; that is, these sinners do not fight against faith, even though they know that they themselves do not have it and that they should have it. Hence they are easily curable. But an evil that has to do with faith soon finds fault with and persecutes the faith of others in order to establish its own faith.

St. Jerome notes that the verb "pervert," since it is a translation of the Greek μεταστρέψαι, means to set behind what is in front and to put in front what is behind. For it is a future infinitive.[21] And so Paul wants to say: "These people are trying to have the Gospel, which is a teaching of the Spirit and of grace, reduced to a letter that has long since been abandoned, even though the Gospel has brought it about that more and more progress is made into the spirit of liberty. This, I say, is what they want; but they will not be able to prevail."

Certainly today, too, the Gospel has been perverted in a great part of the church, since they are teaching the people nothing but

[19] Cf. *Luther's Works*, 12, pp. 82 ff.

[20] Augustine, *Epistolae ad Galatas expositio, Patrologia, Series Latina*, XXXV, 2116—2117.

[21] Jerome, *Commentarius*, 343. What Luther calls a "future infinitive" here is in fact an aorist.

the decrees of the popes and the traditions of men who turn their backs on the truth; or the Gospel is treated in such a way that it does not differ at all from laws and moral precepts. The knowledge of faith and of grace is despised even by the theologians themselves.

St. Jerome also thinks that the verb "you are deserting" is fittingly applied to the Galatians, because in Hebrew Galatia means "removal" [22] — as if the apostle had taken their own name as the occasion for this opening statement and were saying: "You really are Galatians and are quick to be removed; the fact is in keeping with your name" — namely, by way of an allusion to the Hebrew. And such allusions to foreign languages are not in poor taste if they occur in a suitable context. For instance, if you were to say concerning Rome: "You really are Rome" in Hebrew this means "proud and lofty." For what else does the apostle do in his Epistle to the Romans but smash their pride and arrogance, as though he were in very fact alluding to the name "Rome"? [23]

8. *But even if we, or an angel from heaven, should preach to you a gospel contrary to that which we preached to you, let him be accursed.*

9. *As we have said before, so now I say again: If anyone is preaching to you a gospel contrary to that which you received, let him be accursed.*

As Jerome attests, the Greek term ἀνάθεμα is properly a word of the Jews.[24] Among them it is called חָרְמָה. In Joshua 6:17 we read: "And let this city and all things that are in it be anathema." In Hebrew this is חֵרֶם; and it means "devastation," "destruction," "massacred." Then, since it is a word of malediction, it is taken in the sense of a curse, an execration, an imprecation. Thus Ps. 42:6 says: "Therefore I remember Thee from the land of Jordan and of Hermon [חֶרְמוֹנִים], from Mt. Mizar." Here the soul, distressed by its sins, is consoling itself with the memory of Christ, who was crucified and made anathema for it. For "the dew of Hermon," which is described in Ps. 133:3 as coming down on Mt. Zion, is also certainly

---

[22] Jerome, *Commentarius*, 344.

[23] This suggestion for the etymology of the name "Rome" appears in Jerome, *Liber interpretationis hebraicorum nominum*, *Corpus Christianorum, Series Latina*, LXXII, 159.

[24] Cf. Luther's letter to Johann Lang, February 19, 1518 (W, *Briefe*, I, 148).

an expression that refers to the crucified Son of God. People who speak Latin, however, would say "anathematized" or, if they are literal, "Let him be a thing anathematized." The Hebrews frequently use abstract expressions. But let the grammarians worry about whether the Greek term ἀνάθεμα, which signifies those things that are hung up and set apart in the temples, has the full force of the Hebrew word. For us it is enough that the apostle, aflame with zeal for the Gospel, should wish that he himself and the angels from heaven, to say nothing of the other apostles, would be ostracized, accursed, execrated, cut off, and disgraced rather than that the truth of the Gospel be endangered; and this he repeats twice. This is not because he believed that the angels from heaven, he himself, or the apostles would preach something else; it is because it was imperative that those who, under the pretext of the apostles' name and example, were teaching the Law should be crushed as with a violent attack and, as he writes to Titus (1:11), that their mouths be stopped and they be utterly and totally cut off. It is as if he were saying: "You boast to me of the name and authority of the apostles. Go beyond this, and imagine that both I and the angels from heaven were teaching or were able to teach something else. Even these I want to be anathema. How much less you should be frightened by those who lay claim to being apostles!"

Would that in our age, too, there were such trumpets of Christ to oppose the relentless and violent promoters of papal decrees and decretals! Under the name of the apostles Peter and Paul and of the Church of Rome these men are besetting us to such an extent that if we do not believe that everything stated, written, and even dreamed up in the papal decrees and decretals is necessary for salvation, they, with the most shameless effrontery, have the audacity to pronounce us heretics, even though no one is a heretic unless he sins against the Word of faith. Moreover, those words of men are so concerned with outward behavior and so devoid of faith that no greater benefit could be rendered to faith than if once for all they were thoroughly and totally done away with. What do you think Paul would have done if in our day he had seen that so many useless, yes, ruinous laws of men are raging throughout the whole world and utterly abolishing Christ — Paul, who flies into such a passion against the laws of God that were delivered through Moses and were doing away with Christ in only one place, namely, among the

Galatians? Therefore let us say confidently with Paul: "Damned and accursed be every doctrine from heaven, from earth, or from whatever source it is brought — every doctrine that teaches us to trust in works, righteousness, and merits other than those that belong to Jesus Christ." And by saying this we are not being insolent toward the popes and the successors of the apostles; we are being dutiful and truthful toward Christ. For one must prefer Him to them; and if they should refuse to allow this, we must shun them altogether as being anathema.

10. *For am I now persuading men, or God?*

Those who read the apostle only in Latin, or rather in a translation, understand the first part of this question as requiring an affirmative answer and the second part as requiring a negative reply. Consequently, since nobody persuades God, to whom all things are evident, the only conclusion then left is that he is persuading men. Moreover, in this passage the word "to persuade" has the connotation of "to bring to faith," as in the last chapter of Acts (28:23): "Trying to convince them about Jesus both from the Law of Moses and from the prophets." For no one can be driven to faith by force; one can only be drawn and brought to it, as John 6:44 says: "No one can come to Me unless My Father draws him." Yet in our day the Roman Curia forces Turks, yes, even Christians, to faith, that is, to a hatred of faith and to their own destruction. But even though Jerome, Augustine, and Ambrose understand the passage in this way, still the view of Erasmus is more satisfactory.[25] He explains this verse, which in Greek has the accusative case, as meaning: "Am I now recommending human ideas or divine?" That is: "The doctrine which I am teaching is not from men; it is from God," as Paul will presently explain at greater length when he says that his Gospel is neither according to man nor from man (Gal. 1:11-12). Moreover, this is a figure of speech that is not unusual even in Latin: "I read Vergil; I comment on Jerome"; and in 1 Cor. 1:23-24: "We preach Christ, the power of God." It is, therefore, a metonymy. What precedes squares well with this interpretation, as if Paul were saying: "Why should I not wish that those who teach other doctrines be anathema? I am

---

[25] Augustine, *Epistolae ad Galatas expositio, Patrologia, Series Latina,* XXXV, 2109; Jerome, *Commentarius,* 345; Ambrose (ascribed), *Commentaria in XII epistolas beati Pauli, Patrologia, Series Latina,* XVII, 361; Erasmus, *Annotationes ad locum.*

not teaching human doctrines, am I? Am I not rather teaching divine doctrines, before which all things heavenly and earthly should rightly be silent and give place? And that which opposes the divine doctrines deserves to be accursed." But a translation of our own can also be brought in here if the verb "to persuade" is taken intransitively. Just as Rom. 14:6 says: "He who eats, eats in honor of the Lord," so here the sense would be: "As to the fact that I persuade or am a persuader, I am not doing this for men or to confer glory or favor on men; it is God and His glory that I am serving by doing this." And this meaning fits in very well with what follows: "If I still were pleasing men, etc."; as if he were saying that by his persuading he had not been pleasing men but only God.

Furthermore, this adverb "now" refers to the entire time of Paul's apostleship, not to the time when this letter was written. For actually he is not teaching the grace of God anew in this epistle; he is recalling to that grace those who have fallen, and he is strengthening those who already know it. For this reason he will also speak allegorically later on (4:24-31), something that is not suitable for persons who have to be instructed and to whom "tongues are for a sign," as he says in 1 Cor. 14:22. Therefore the meaning is: "Let those who teach something else be accursed, because ever since I was converted from the traditions of laws, I no longer teach human doctrines; I teach doctrines that are divine." And observe carefully please that he has the courage to call the Law of Moses human doctrines, even though it was delivered through angels. More about this later.

Or am I trying to please men? If I were still pleasing men, I should not be a servant of Christ.

Paul says this because the false apostles were teaching righteousness based on the Law to escape suffering persecution at the hands of the Jews, who were raging against all men on behalf of the Law of Moses and in opposition to the Word of the cross, as he writes in 1 Thess. 2:14 f. He also speaks of this later on, in the sixth chapter: "It is those who want to make a good showing in the flesh that would compel you to be circumcised, and only in order that they may not be persecuted for the cross of Christ" (v. 12). Resolute, therefore, against this spirit of pusillanimity, Paul teaches that men must be despised out of love for Christ, and that no word should be omitted for the sake of pleasing them.

In this passage "men" is emphatic; it means "those who, according to their first birth from Adam, are merely men, apart from Christ and from faith in Him." For since these people are alienated from the truth, they are of necessity filled with lying and with hatred of the truth. Thus every man is a liar (cf. Ps. 116:11); and in 1 Cor. 3:4 we read: "Are you not men?" And according to Scriptural usage, it is almost a reproach to be called a man. For Scripture does not give man his name in a metaphysical sense, according to his essence (for in this sense the theologians see in man nothing but what is praiseworthy); but Scripture speaks theologically and names him as he is in the eyes of God.[26] The righteous, on the other hand, are usually not called men; they are called gods. Ps. 82:6: "I say: 'You are gods, sons of the Most High, all of you; nevertheless, you shall die like men.'" For this reason, as Ps. 53 truthfully says: "God will scatter the bones of those who please men; they are confounded, because God has rejected them." Why? Because, so long as they fear persecution, they deny God and His Word out of love for men. On the other hand, there is this statement: "The Lord guards all their bones" (cf. Ps. 34:21). Whose bones? Those of the righteous. Who are they? Those who are displeasing to men. They are honored, because God is their protector. And Luke 16:15 says: "What is exalted among men is an abomination in the sight of God." But since we, too, are men, it is necessary that we be displeasing also to ourselves, in keeping with the Word of Christ: "He who loves his life will lose it" (John 12:25).

Therefore let those people who have learned from the tree [27] of Porphyry and from the teachings of Aristotle and other philosophers how to praise, boast of, and love rational man and then to trust in their own precepts and to justify their own counsels — let them see how well their wisdom savors of the truth of God, which allots everything human to falsehood, vanity, and destruction. Therefore it teaches that it is to be lamented whenever it happens that we human beings are praised as possessing reason, because of our free will, and, in short, because of all our works, since Paul declares that it is impossible for one who pleases himself or men to be a servant of Christ, that is, of the truth.

[26] Cf. *Luther's Works*, 12, pp. 310—312.

[27] The "tree of Porphyry" was a tabular view of the categories of Aristotle, used for teaching and reference.

Moreover, here the word "please" has a spiritual meaning; that is, it signifies the desire to please, since, of course, it does not rest with us whom we please or displease, as the apostle himself makes sufficiently clear in this passage. Although he had first said: "Or am I trying to please?" he does not say next: "If I were still trying to please." No, he says: "If I were still pleasing." So also in 1 Cor. 10:33: "Please all men in all things, just as I please all men in everything." How do you please all men? Paul goes on: "Not seeking my own advantage, but that of many." Here it is. To please is to seek to please all men, even if perchance one pleases no one at all or very few. For so far as Christ and His Christians are concerned, it is a rule that in seeking to please and to do those things by which they should please they displease, in keeping with the passage: "In return for my love they were accusing me" (Ps. 109:4). And again: "They have hated me for no reason" (Ps. 69:4). Similarly (Ps. 120:7): "They were assailing me for no reason," that is, even though I gave them reason to love me. In keeping, therefore, with the example of Christ, all our benefits must be done away with, in order that we may seek to please all men and in no way seek how to please ourselves [28] but, as Paul says in Rom. 15:2: "Let each one please the other for his good, for his edification," not by any means to satisfy his own desires and foolish notions, etc.

11. *For I would have you know, brethren, that the Gospel which was preached by me is not man's gospel.*

12. *For I did not receive it from man, nor was I taught it, but it came through a revelation of Jesus Christ.*

Here Paul shows that he was right in anathematizing those teachers. In a lengthy discourse and with many proofs he shows that the things he has been teaching are divine, not human. "First of all," he says, "in order that you may know that my Gospel is divine, I did not receive it from man, nor was I taught it, but it came through a revelation of Jesus Christ." Here St. Jerome distinguishes in the following way between "to receive" and "to learn": A person "receives" when he is induced to believe in what is first made known to him; he "learns" when he begins to understand the meaning of the things that are

---

[28] We have followed the suggestion of the Weimar editors and have added the word "ourselves."

expressed figuratively in what he receives.[29] I understand it in this way: He who begins is "receiving"; he who makes progress in his knowledge of the Gospel is "learning." But what if the apostle should want the verb "to receive" to be connected with the phrase "from man," and the verb "to learn" to be construed alone? Then, of course, the sense would be: "Neither from man nor from the teaching of any man did I receive it, nor was it transmitted to me by anyone. But neither did I learn it from myself. I did not find it out by my own effort, nor did I seek it; I received it from God through Christ's revelation alone, and I learned it with Him as my Teacher," namely, on the road (as St. Jerome thinks), that is, when Paul heard the voice of Christ after he had set out for Damascus (Acts 9:4-6).

Here the same St. Jerome notes that Christ is being proclaimed by Paul as God, because the apostle says "not from man, but through Christ." Accordingly, Christ is more than a man. He also gives a very wholesome warning about how great a danger it is to speak in the church without the revelation of Christ, lest by a false interpretation a gospel of man be made out of the Gospel of Christ, which is what is now happening wherever they adulterate Scripture either by accepting human opinions or by devising comments based on their own teaching. Moreover, in this passage Paul takes the word "man" as referring not only to the wicked but also to the apostles themselves, since he will presently say that he was not instructed by them and that he did not confer with them soon after the revelation. This he does in order to reinforce what he has said above, namely, that even if the apostles or he himself were to teach something else (since they are human beings), nevertheless that which he had taught once for all must not be given up, since he had received this neither from the apostles nor from himself. Consequently, whatever else the false apostles were teaching, whether under the name of the apostles or even of Paul, must be considered anathema. For the only gospel — or rather delusion — they could have was one received from man. Paul, however, had the truth from Christ.

The Gospel and the Law, taken in their proper sense, differ in this way: The Law proclaims what must be done and left undone; or better, it proclaims what deeds have already been committed and omitted, and also that possible things are done and left undone

[29] Jerome, *Commentarius*, 347.

(hence the only thing it provides is the knowledge of sin); the Gospel, however, proclaims that sins have been remitted and that all things have been fulfilled and done. For the Law says: "Pay what you owe"; but the Gospel says: "Your sins or forgiven you." Thus in Rom. 3:20 we read: "Through the Law comes knowledge of sin"; and in the fourth chapter Paul says (v. 15): "The Law works wrath; for where there is no Law, there is no transgression." But concerning the Gospel Luke 24:46 f. says: "Thus it was necessary that Christ should suffer and rise again from the dead, and that repentance and remission of sins should be preached to all nations in His name." (Note especially in "His" name, not in "ours.") Here you see the preaching of the remission of sins through the name of Christ, that is, the Gospel. And in Rom. 10:15 we read: "How beautiful are the feet of those that preach the Gospel of peace, that bring the good news," that is, the remission of sins and grace, the fulfilling of the Law through Christ. Therefore he who has been justified through grace flees from the Law to the Gospel and says (Matt. 6:12): "Forgive us our debts."

But why does Christ give many rules and much instruction in the Gospel if it is the business of the Law to do this? Likewise, why do the apostles give many rules in spite of the fact that they are preachers of the Gospel? My answer is: Teachings of this sort, which are transmitted in addition to faith (for in the Gospel salvation and the remission of sins are made known to those who believe, as is stated in John 1:12: "To those who believed in His name, as many as received Him, He gave power to become children of God"), are either explanations of the Law whereby sin should be recognized more clearly, in order that the more surely sin is felt, the more ardently grace may be sought; or they are aids and observances by which the grace already received and the faith that has been bestowed may be guarded, nurtured, and perfected, just as happens when a sick person begins to receive care.

Therefore the voice of the Gospel is sweet, as the bride in the Song of Solomon declares: "Thy voice sounds in my ears, for it is sweet" (2:14); and again: "Thy love is better than wine and fragrant with the finest perfumes" (1:2-3). That is, the words of Christ with which He nourishes His believers are better than the words of the Law, because they breathe the perfume of grace by which the wounds of nature are healed through the remission of sins. Thus in Ps. 45:2:

"Grace is poured into Thy lips" — not knowledge, not understanding, which are also poured out on the lips of Moses, but grace; that is: "Thy words are full of grace and cheer to lost sinners, because they announce forgiveness and grace." It is also for this that the psalmist prays when he says (51:13): "I shall teach the wicked Thy ways, and the ungodly will be converted to Thee," as if he were saying: "Let me not, I pray, teach the ways of men and the doctrines of our own righteousness, since thereby they will not be converted to Thee but will be turned farther away from Thee. I pray Thee to open my lips, so that my mouth may rather make known Thy praise, that is, the grace by which Thou forgivest sins. For the result of this will be that man will praise, glorify, and love Thee when he realizes the goodness of Thy mercy and does not, in his self-righteousness, praise himself. For those who are righteous do not accept instruction, are not converted to Thee, do not praise Thee, but praise themselves. They are well; they need no physician (Matt. 9:12). Hence it is impossible for the praise of Thy grace to be made known to them." Of these people it is stated at once in the same psalm: "Deliver me from bloodguiltiness, O God, God of my salvation; and my tongue will sing aloud of Thy righteousness (v. 14), not of the righteousness of men but of Thy grace, by which Thou dost bestow righteousness on us, through which Thou art also the God of our salvation."

But it has been asked which Gospel Paul preached — Luke's, Matthew's, or somebody else's. On the basis of a statement somewhere in Eusebius or in Origen, St. Jerome thinks that Paul's Gospel was that of Luke.[30] As if there were not more gospels than those familiar four, since every apostle preached exactly what they all preached! For the Gospel is a good discourse, a message of peace about the Son of God, who became incarnate, suffered, and was raised again through the Holy Spirit for our salvation, as is described in Rom. 1:3-4 and as Zacharias says in Luke 1: "He has visited and redeemed His people" (v. 68); and later: "To give knowledge of salvation for the remission of sins through the tender mercy of our God" (vv. 77-78). Thus whenever the grace of God and the remission of sins effected through Jesus Christ are proclaimed, here the Gospel is really proclaimed. Accordingly, the epistles of Paul, Peter, and John are entirely and in fact gospels. And Paul did not preach Luke's gospel or anyone else's, since he says expressly that

---

[30] Jerome, *De viris illustribus*, 7.

the Gospel he preached was revealed to him, not by man or through man but by Jesus Christ alone, as he says later: ". . . to reveal His Son in me, in order that I might preach the Gospel concerning Him among the Gentiles." The Gospel, you see, is the teaching about God's Son, Jesus Christ.

13. *For you have heard of my former life in Judaism, how I persecuted the church of God violently and tried to destroy it;*

14. *and I advanced in Judaism beyond many of my own age among my people, so extremely zealous was I for the traditions of my fathers.*

According to the context, these statements must be understood as having been made by the apostle in order to strengthen the point he has already begun to make, namely, that his Gospel is not from man but that he is advocating things that are divine. I say this even though I know that St. Jerome looks at the matter in another way and abandons the line of thought. Therefore what the apostle means to say is: "I want you to be thoroughly aware that I was instructed neither by my forefathers nor by the apostles or any human beings but only by God — in order that this may give you the assurance that you have heard things that are divine, and in order that you may not be diverted on the strength of any names, whether my own or those of the apostles, to things that are human. Note that I am once more recounting, and reminding you of, my story. For you have heard, etc."

Moreover, Paul's words, as St. Jerome says, have a marvelous and beautiful exactness and emphasis.[31] "Life," he says, not "grace"; "former," not "just now"; "in Judaism," not "in faith in Christ"; not like the other persecutors but like a marauder and a brigand he was laying waste "the church of God" — not that he then believed it to be such, but he calls it by the name which he now knows. And again: "I advanced in Judaism," not "in the faith of Christianity"; "beyond many," not "beyond all" (in order to preserve his modesty); "beyond many of my own age," not "beyond those advanced in years"; "among my people," not "among the Gentiles"; for thus he is wont to call the Hebrew nation, as in 2 Cor. 11:26 ("danger from my own people, danger from Gentiles").

But I would not deny that while he is proving from his own

---

[31] Jerome, *Commentarius*, 348—349.

history that he has been teaching things that are divine, he incidentally also wishes to draw the Galatians back from the Law by means of his own example, in order that they may be admonished and aroused as they listen to him. If such a great zealot for the Law, who is far abler than those false apostles to boast of the Law and to find commendation in his own flesh (as he does in 2 Cor. 11 and Phil. 3), nevertheless regards all this as dung and has left it behind, how much more must we, who are in grace, refrain from reverting to the Law!

It should be noted that Jerome understands "the traditions of my fathers" to be the teachings of the Pharisees and the commandments of men.[32] But I am bold enough to think that Paul means the whole Law of Moses, and I shall point this out [33] on the basis of no other source than the apostle himself, who says in Phil. 3:4-7: "If anyone thinks he has reason for confidence in the flesh, I have more: circumcised on the eighth day, of the people of Israel, of the tribe of Benjamin, a Hebrew born of Hebrews; as to the Law, a Pharisee; as to zeal, a persecutor of the church of God; as to righteousness under the Law, blameless. But whatever gain I had, I counted as loss for the sake of Christ." You see that for the sake of Christ he counts as loss even circumcision and an unexceptionable righteousness of the Law. And later he says: "In order that I may be found in Him, not having a righteousness of my own, based on the Law, but that which is through faith in Jesus Christ" (v. 9).

Paul calls the Law the traditions of his fathers because he was instructed in that Law by men, his fathers and ancestors, and also because his fathers had received those traditions from Moses and passed them on to their sons, in keeping with the commandment of Ps. 78:5: "Which He commanded our fathers to teach to their children." For the apostle arranges everything polemically and sets it before the false apostles. It is his purpose to establish the fact that his Gospel is from God and in this way to compel the Galatians to remain steadfast in it. For this reason he also sets the traditions of his fathers — by way of disparaging them [34] — over against the Gospel, which he wants to be regarded as divine traditions.

[32] Jerome, *Commentarius*, 349.

[33] The Weimar text has *docebor*. This means "I shall be instructed"; or it could be a typographical error for *docebo*.

[34] On *tapinosis* cf. *Luther's Works*, 26, p. 362, note 5.

But to avoid causing anyone anxiety, let us treat this matter a little more extensively and in this way at the same time prepare the way for what must be said later on. The Law — not only the Ceremonial Law but also the Moral Law, indeed, even the most sacred Decalog, which contains God's eternal commandments — is the letter and a tradition of the letter, which, as St. Augustine amply demonstrates in his book *On the Spirit and the Letter*, neither gives life nor justifies but kills and causes sin to abound.[35] For no matter how much the Law is taught or observed, it does not purify the heart itself. But if the heart has not been purified, what else are good works, whether ceremonial or moral, but hypocrisy and the outward appearance of piety? Thus Christ says that the Pharisees look fine on the outside but are full of filth inside (Matt. 23:27). The result is that even though a person does not steal or commit adultery in the outward act, nevertheless he is either inwardly inclined toward those very deeds or abstains from them out of love for his own advantage or out of fear of punishment. And in this way he overcomes one sin by means of another, as St. Augustine says in his book *On Marriage and Concupiscence*.[36] For love of one's own advantage and fear of punishment are vices and a form of idolatry, inasmuch as love and fear are owed only to God. There is nothing, therefore, that sets one free from this impurity of the heart except faith, as is stated in Acts 15:9: "Purifying their hearts by faith," in order that in this way Paul's statement in Titus 1:15 may stand: "To the pure all things are pure, but to the corrupt and unbelieving nothing is pure." According to the same rule, he says in Rom. 2:21: "You who teach that one must not steal, do you steal?" St. Augustine's interpretation of this is "You steal" — not, of course, by the deed, which you teach must not be done, but in your guilty desire.

Therefore unless the doctrine of faith, by which the heart is purified and justified, is revealed, all instruction in all commandments is a matter of the letter and a tradition of the fathers. For the commandment teaches what must be done. Since this could not be done, the doctrine of faith (that is, the Gospel) teaches how it becomes possible. For this doctrine teaches one to flee for refuge to the grace of God and to implore God Himself as the Teacher and Doctor to write into our hearts with the finger of His Spirit His own

[35] Augustine, *On the Spirit and the Letter*, 14, 23.
[36] Augustine, *On Marriage and Concupiscence*, I, 4—5.

living, shining, and glowing letters, in order that we may be enlightened and inflamed by them and cry out: "Abba, Father!" (Gal. 4:6.) And this is not instruction of the fathers; it is divine instruction.

But pay attention, dear reader: If the apostle condemns his life in Judaism — the life that looked so fine — and the righteousness of the Law to such an extent that he regards them as dung and loss, what will those who praise human nature and laud moral works bring forward as an excuse? If this progress of the apostle was evil — which surely was approved by every rule of reason and even by the very Law of God, inasmuch as the "end" (as they call it)[37] of his life was zeal for God and for His Law — what will their actions be — their actions which they boast of with either another end or a similar end in mind? Surely they will be what Jeremiah said concerning prophets of this kind: "They have seen for you stupid visions and banishments; but they have not revealed your sins for you to provoke you to repentance" (Lam. 2:14). Therefore they take away from men the fear of God and teach them to be smug, as they prate that their moral deeds are good and that the works done in accordance with the rule of reason are not sins.

15. *But when He who had separated me from my mother's womb and had called me through His grace,*

16. *was pleased to reveal His Son to me, in order that I might preach Him among the Gentiles,*

It is one thing, therefore, to know the Law and to have excelled in its righteousness; it is another thing to know the Son of God. For the latter knowledge works salvation; the former works perdition. And note how thankfully and sincerely Paul acknowledges divine grace. He says: "The Son of God was revealed to me, not because I had progressed so far in the righteousness of the ancestral Law, not because of my own merit, but because it pleased God that it should happen this way, even though I had deserved by far the opposite. But the fact that it pleased Him without merits on my part proves that before I had been born, He set me apart for this destiny and in my mother's womb prepared me as such a one, and that He then called me through His grace, in order that from all this you might know that faith and the knowledge of Christ have come to me, not from the Law but from the grace of God, which

---

[37] The Latin word is *finis*.

predestined and called me. Consequently, it will not be possible for you to have salvation from the Law."

Others refer the verb "to separate" to what is stated in Acts 13:2: "Set apart for Me Paul and Barnabas for the work, etc." But this is a forced interpretation, since then they are compelled to understand "from my mother's womb" allegorically as the synagog. I pass over the scrupulous and risky way in which St. Jerome deals with this passage.[38] To me Paul seems to be speaking entirely of his predestination, but in brief and obscure fashion. In view of the power of comprehension the Galatians had, he considers it sufficient to have declared in simple terms that he has learned, taught, and preached Jesus Christ the Son of God, not of himself or of others but from the revelation given to him by the Father, in order that they may be sure that they have learned from Paul things that are divine. Now he continues; and he adds to his simple statement a historical account, to demonstrate that he has not been instructed by men and has not taught things that are human.

immediately I gave no assent to flesh and blood.

Here St. Jerome experiences a strange torture, and he himself tortures the text.[39] In the first place, to avoid the necessity of having the apostles called "flesh and blood" and of having to give in to Porphyry, who says reproachfully that Paul is presumptuous, Jerome understands "flesh and blood" to mean Jews and sinners, especially since Paul declares that afterwards he discussed his Gospel with the apostles, which here he denies. For the same word that is translated here with "gave assent" is translated later as "discussed." But let us dismiss these considerations. Whoever wishes may concern himself with them. Meanwhile I am more than satisfied with this, that Paul, who wants to show that he had taught the Galatians on the basis of revelation from God, did not first discuss his revelation with any human being but, after receiving the revelation, immediately preached Christ. As is written in Acts 9:19-20: "For several days he was with the disciples at Damascus. And in the synagogs immediately he proclaimed Jesus." "Immediately," that is to say, not first conferring with them. Hence one sees that Paul has omitted something. The complete context would be as follows: "Immediately I preached the

[38] Cf. Jerome, *Commentarius*, 349—350.

[39] Jerome, *Commentarius*, 351.

Son of God or proclaimed Him by means of the Gospel; I did not confer with men first." Thus the adverb "immediately" denies altogether that he had been instructed by men. On the contrary, it asserts that men were immediately instructed in Christ by him. For, as I have said, the apostle is speaking polemically. It is his purpose to prove that he has been teaching things that are divine. For once this has been proved as his chief argument, it will then be easy to demolish everything that has been transmitted to the Galatians in opposition to him. But as Jerome attests, "to confer," which in this passage is rendered by "gave assent," signifies something different from what it means among us, since, you see, we confer with a friend regarding the things we know and lay them on his heart and conscience, so to speak, to be either approved or disapproved after impartial deliberation. And even though the translator did not render this connotation of the word, still he did not depart altogether from the meaning. For he who confers with his friends in this way certainly has already given assent to them in his mind and offers himself to them as one who can be taught. But Paul did not want to be taught, nor did he ever intend to argue whether or not the things he had heard from God were correct. And very justly so. For it would have been wicked to try to strengthen the divine revelation — as if he were in doubt about it — with the counsel of men.

Accordingly, Porphyry, who makes a false statement about Paul and reproachfully calls him arrogant, accomplishes nothing. For it was not because of arrogance that Paul was unwilling to confer; it was for the sake of the glory that belongs to divine authority and to absolute truth that he did not want to do so. Nor could he have conferred without damage to his divine authority. But Porphyry is also mistaken in this, that he thinks Paul is speaking here of the apostles, when actually he is speaking of those who were in Damascus, whoever they were. For regarding the apostles he says at once: "Nor did I go up to those who were apostles before me" (Gal. 1:17). Therefore those whom he calls "flesh and blood" were others. And, as it seems to me, in a manner characteristic of him and of the Hebrews, he is making an allusion to the name "Damascus," which, according to its etymology, means "blood" and "sack"; [40] and in Scripture it is not unusual for this word to have the hidden

---

[40] Jerome, *Liber interpretationis hebraicorum nominum, Corpus Christianorum, Series Latina,* LXXII, 64, and passim.

meaning "flesh and blood," which means: "I did not confer with those who were at Damascus, who are flesh and blood." Still I would not deny that this same expression is used about the saints; nor would I hesitate to call the apostles themselves flesh and blood, even on the authority of Christ, who said to Peter: "Flesh and blood has not revealed this to you" (Matt. 16:17); that is: "You do not have this from yourself or from others." And in another place: "For it is not you who speak, but the Spirit of your Father" (Matt. 10:20). Here He indicates clearly that they are something different from the Spirit and the Spirit's revelation. Indeed, in themselves they are truly flesh and blood. Accordingly, this appropriate disparagement pleases me. By means of it he incurs the enmity of the false apostles by calling even God's saints flesh and blood in contrast with the majesty of the divine revelation. For if human words or examples, no matter how saintly, have begun to be boasted of in opposition to those that are divine, it is time for us confidently to regard whatever is not divine as flesh and blood, yes, as nothing.

17. *Neither did I go up to Jerusalem to the apostles who were my predecessors,*

"Not only did I not consult the people of Damascus, but I did not even consult the apostles who had been in the apostolate before me (for this is the meaning of 'my predecessors'). Yet it would have been necessary to do this if I had wanted to be taught through a man or by a man. Sufficient for me was the certain and infallible revelation of the Father."

Take note of Paul's indispensable pride or more correctly, of his fairness. He acknowledges that the other apostles were his predecessors; but he does not say that he is greater or, on the other hand, less important than they. For even though he declares that he is inferior to all and the least of the apostles so far as his person is concerned, yes, that he is not even worthy of being called an apostle (1 Cor. 15:9), nevertheless so highly does he esteem the office and the ministry (for this belongs to God, not to him) that he positively does not yield to anyone among the apostles. For no matter what the person of the apostles is, surely the office of all the apostles is identical and equal; they teach the same Christ, they have the same power, they are all sent in the same manner by the same One. Nevertheless, Paul says in 2 Cor. 11:5: "I think that I am not in the least inferior to these superlative apostles"; and in the twelfth chapter (v. 11): "For I am not at all inferior to these superlative apostles." How wonderfully he grants preference to them and makes himself their equal, humbly yielding to them in rank but confidently likening himself to them in his office and in power.

but I went away into Arabia; and again I returned to Damascus.

In Acts 9 Luke does not mention this withdrawal into Arabia but writes only that Paul came to Jerusalem after he had been let down over the wall. Hence St. Jerome searches for various explanations.[41] I follow the second one, namely, that, as Luke writes, Paul was in Damascus for several days after his baptism and during this time preached Christ in the synagog; that then, as Paul says here, he went away into Arabia and returned to Damascus, a fact which Luke has not mentioned; and that at this time those things occurred which Luke describes in detail, namely, that on account of a plot he was let down over the wall in a basket and came to Jerusalem. Thus St. Jerome troubles himself about why Paul recounts these things which Luke has not mentioned. In my boldness I think that Paul records this, as he records everything, in order to show that he did not come to the apostles or receive instruction from them but rather, relying on the divine revelation, first went away into Arabia to teach and then returned to Damascus and taught the same things — so certain, as is clear to see, was he of the revelation of Christ that had been given to him. For he would not be teaching these things in various places if he thought that they were of such a nature that they had to be discussed with the apostles or with men. But as to Jerome's opinion that Paul was in Arabia to no purpose, and as to his investigation of some things that are not explained — a man so great should have this privilege.

18. *Then after three years I went up to Jerusalem to see Peter, and remained with him fifteen days.*

Observe how careful Paul is to add "after three years" and not to say that he "heard" but that he "saw Peter." For his statement that he taught for three years in Damascus — evidently until he was forced to leave by way of the wall — is sure proof that he was not made a preacher of the Gospel by Peter but had already been one for a long

[41] Jerome, *Commentarius*, 352—353.

time when he came to Peter. It is his purpose to stop the mouths of the false apostles, who had asserted — perhaps by using as proof the fact that he came to Peter — that he was taught by Peter, through whose example they had stirred up the Galatians to observe the Law. But St. Jerome declared that he found a double meaning in this passage: one according to which it is asserted that Paul was taught by Peter, another according to which this is denied. In the *Letter to Paulinus,* however, Jerome inclines altogether toward the first meaning; he is of the opinion that the teacher of the Gentiles — to use his own words — was instructed in the mystery of the ogdoad and the hebdomad.[42] I mention this in order that the prudent reader may understand Jerome in this way and not arrive at a meaning contrary to the apostle Paul, who states all this with such thunderous emphasis that he proves with the strongest arguments that he had learned nothing from the apostles but had received everything from God alone (as has already been sufficiently stated). Although the fact that St. Jerome takes pleasure rather often in toying with the mystery of the fifteen days should not be treated with scorn, still it is altogether necessary to believe that the days have been mentioned in this passage by Paul not only because of his delight in the mystery but also because the historical fact required it — perhaps in order to show that he had been with Peter long enough if he had come for the purpose of teaching, or, to put it differently, that he had remained with him as a guest, not for the purpose of receiving instruction but merely in order to pay him a visit, since the receiving of instruction would have required a longer time.

19. *But I saw none of the other apostles except James, the Lord's brother.*

Paul does not want them to say: "If you did not receive instruction from Peter, at least you received it from the other apostles." But he did not see the other apostles, because (as Jerome says) they had been scattered all over the world for the preaching of the Gospel. But if this is true, what foundation is there for that fable about the separation of the apostles in which it is said that the apostles were separated in the thirteenth year after Christ's resurrection,[43] when in this passage Paul has found them scattered three or certainly four

[42] Jerome, *Commentarius,* 354; also *Epistles,* LIII, 2.
[43] Jerome, *Commentarius,* 356.

years after his conversion, while, on the other hand, it is clear that he was converted in the same year in which Stephen received the martyr's crown? But these questions I leave to others, who have leisure.

Take note of what Luke writes in Acts 9:26 ff., namely, that because the disciples were afraid of Paul, he was brought to the apostles by Barnabas, and that he went in and out with them. But here Paul admits that he saw none of the apostles except Peter and James. Accordingly, either Luke calls Peter and James "apostles" because they are more than one, or what St. Jerome says is true, namely, that the term "apostles," especially in the letters of Paul, includes many others, such as those who were ordained by the first apostles.

Concerning this James, whom the people commonly call James the Less, Eusebius says in the first chapter of the second book of his *Ecclesiastical History* that he was called the brother of the Lord because he was the son of Joseph, who was esteemed as if he were Christ's father. St. Jerome quotes this statement in his book *On Illustrious Men*, but he disagrees with it.[44] He says: "In the opinion of some, James was the son of Joseph by another wife; but in my opinion he was the son of Mary, the sister of the Lord's mother, of whom John makes mention in his Gospel." For John says (19:25): "Standing by the cross of Jesus were His mother and His mother's sister, Mary the wife of Cleophas, and Mary Magdalene." Likewise Mark 15:40: "Among whom were Mary Magdalene and Mary, the mother of James the Less and of Joses, and Salome." Matt. 27:56 agrees with this: "Among whom were Mary Magdalene and Mary, the mother of James and of Joses, and the mother of the sons of Zebedee." From these statements one gathers that James's Mary and Cleophas' Mary are the same person, namely, the sister of the Virgin Mary, that she is called Cleophas' Mary on account of her husband but James's Mary on account of her son, and that she is also the mother of Simon and Judas. For in the third book of his *Ecclesiastical History* Eusebius says that Cleophas was the brother of Joseph and that for this reason Simon was called the Lord's cousin.[45] Furthermore, Mark 6:3 seems to say this very plainly: "Is not this the carpenter, the son of Mary, the brother of James and Joses and Judas and Simon?" So those people are obviously in error who have invented a third Mary, whom

---

[44] Eusebius, *Ecclesiastical History*, II, 1, 2—4; Jerome, *De viris illustribus*, 2.
[45] Eusebius, *Ecclesiastical History*, III, 11, 2.

they call Salome's Mary. For Salome is a woman's name; and the one whom Mark calls Salome, Matthew calls the mother of the sons of Zebedee. But that there were only two Marys, namely, Mary Magdalene and James's Mary, is sufficiently proved by the fact that Matthew usually calls James's Mary "the other Mary" (28:1).

But let us put an end to this tedious business and take it that this James is called the Lord's brother — that is, a son of the Lord's foster father's brother or rather a son of His mother's sister — in order to distinguish him from the others who are called James. For all state that among Christ's disciples there were several named James. And though St. Jerome, in his book *Against Helvidius*, says with regard to this passage that James was called the Lord's brother on account of a similarity in virtue and wisdom rather than according to the flesh,[46] still the view which has been adduced above and is taken from the writings of distinguished men is more satisfactory.

20. *(In what I am writing to you, before God, I do not lie!)*

In a matter which, as it seems, is so unimportant the apostle swears an oath. Obviously he wants the Galatians to believe it to be true that he came to Jerusalem and that he saw no one of the apostles. He also wants them to believe the other things he has mentioned. Why is it necessary for him to swear an oath? He is troubled, and he feels that he is being hard pressed because of the reputation and the behavior of the apostles, on whom the false apostles were placing their reliance. Consequently, since he has nothing with which to confirm his story, he swears an oath in a holy and pious fashion, lest by the pretext and ostentatious display of apostolic and human authority the authority of the divine revelation by which he had taught the Galatians be diminished to the damage of their faith and of the Gospel. Moreover, he swears his oath not only in view of what he has said before but also in view of what remains to be said. For thus those who are disturbed beyond measure are wont to introduce an oath into what they are saying.

21. *Then I went into the regions of Syria and Cilicia.*

In Acts 9:29-30 Luke refers to this when he says that Paul spoke (in Jerusalem, of course) with the Gentiles "and disputed against

[46] Jerome, *De perpetua virginitate B. Mariae adversus Helvidium*, 15, *Patrologia, Series Latina*, XXIII, 209.

the Hellenists; but they were seeking to kill him. And when the brethren knew it, they brought him down to Caesarea and sent him off to Tarsus," which is in Cilicia.

Take note. Here you have what Paul did during the fifteen days he spent with Peter. He did not receive instruction, but he taught the Gentiles (for he was going to be, or already was, their apostle); and he disputed against the Hellenists, undoubtedly Jews, just as Stephen had done before him (Acts 7:1 ff.). Why, then, is it necessary for us to hear that he went to Syria and Cilicia? Obviously he is proving that he did not have the apostles as his teachers anywhere but was himself a teacher everywhere. He always has this fact in sight, and toward this he always bends the bow of his narrative, in order that he may finally strike most vigorously all those who were teaching and holding views in opposition to him because he taught things that were divine, not human, while they taught things that were human, not divine.

22. *And I was still not known by sight to the churches of Christ in Judea;*

23. *they only heard it said: He who once persecuted us is now preaching the faith he once tried to destroy.*

24. *And they glorified God because of me.*

Paul means, of course, not only that he was not instructed by Peter and the other apostles but also that he was not instructed by any others who were Christians in Judea and observed a mixture of the Law and faith. Indeed — and this is the best recommendation of Paul's teaching — although he himself had not been seen by them, still he had their testimony that he was preaching faith. For it is this faith alone that he is seeking to establish throughout the epistle. Now, therefore, he demonstrates on the authority of all the churches that he has been teaching rightly, because he was praised by those churches for preaching faith, and God was glorified. Although the false apostles were trying to drive the Galatians to the Law with the example of these churches, he clearly proves that they did not represent the example and authority of the churches of Judea truthfully to the Galatians. Those who previously grieved because Paul was attacking the faith are glorifying God because he is preaching faith. They are not complaining [47] about the Law. Why, then, are those teachers, under the false name of apostles, tempting the Galatians with a righteousness based on the Law? Therefore the fact remained that the churches of Judea kept the provisions of the Law, not because they were compelled to do so for the sake of salvation but out of unrestrained love, by rendering service to the weakness of others.

Would that in the church today our laws were taught and observed with similar understanding! Now, however, they rule in such a way that salvation is thought to rest in them and faith is almost blotted out. Paul gives faith completely free mastery over all human laws. We make human laws the tyrants over faith. Yet the lords and nobles do not care a hair about them; they devour the church in an enormous whirlpool of offenses and oppress only their subjects with so many unbearable burdens or in the most shameful manner sell anew the Christian liberty of these people — the liberty that is held captive by means of fetters of money — by granting pardon and indulgences.

[47] We have read *querentes* for *quaerentes*, which is the reading in the Weimar text.

CHAPTER TWO

1. *Then after fourteen years I went up again to Jerusalem with Barnabas, taking Titus along with me.*
2. *I went up by revelation; and I laid before them (but privately before those who were of repute) the Gospel which I preach among the Gentiles, lest somehow I should be running or had run in vain.*

AFTER proving sufficiently that he has become an apostle by divine revelation, not because of any man's teaching, Paul now proves that the revelation he had was sure and firm that he has not feared to have any men whatever, not even the apostles, as his judges, and also that he has not yielded to anyone's importunity.

First he says "after fourteen years." If to these you add the three years he mentioned above, you will find that he had already been preaching for seventeen or eighteen years before he wanted to have a discussion. Thus it seems impossible that what he had been preaching in so many places, to so many people, could have been recanted. It was not for his own sake, therefore, that he went up, as if he feared (as Jerome thinks)[1] that for seventeen years he had been preaching falsely. On the contrary, he went in order to show others that he had not been running in vain, since the rest of the apostles also approved his course. For if he had been in doubt as to whether he was teaching truth or falsehood, it would have been conspicuous and unheard-of rashness and godlessness on his part to postpone the necessary conference and to deceive so many people with uncertain teaching.

In the second place, he never would have "gone up" if he had not been admonished by a revelation of God, since he was not disturbed by the importunity of others — so far was he from entering a discussion because of a lack of confidence in the certainty of his doctrine. He had no need whatever of going up to Jerusalem for this reason.

Thirdly, he went to Jerusalem itself, where the leaders of the

[1] Jerome, *Commentarius*, 358.

synagog as well as of the church were to be found. He was ready to confer with them all, since he feared neither the multitude of the Jews nor the most zealous followers of the Law.

Fourthly, he did not go alone; he went "with Barnabas and Titus" (who were of different nationalities and thus very suitable witnesses) in order that no one might believe that he had acted in one way while present but acted otherwise when absent. For if he did too much for the Jews, Titus, who was a Gentile, would betray him; if, on the other hand, he did too much for the Gentiles, Barnabas, who was a Jew, would oppose him. Therefore take note of his confidence! — He took these two with him and had both of them as witnesses. In short, by presenting himself with both of them he intended to make it clear that he was at liberty to be a Gentile with Titus and a Jew with Barnabas. Thus he would prove the freedom of the Gospel in each case, namely, that it is permissible to be circumcised and yet that circumcision is not necessary, and that this is the way one should think of the entire Law.

Enough has been said above about the word "discussed" and "gave assent to." [2] Note also a figure of speech that is Hebraic in character or, to use a better description, is characteristic of Holy Scripture, namely, that "to run" signifies the office of teaching or proclaiming the Word of God — a figure taken from the sending and running of messengers. Thus I quoted above [3] from Jer. 23:21: "They ran, and I did not send them"; from Ps. 147:15: "His Word runs swiftly"; and from many similar passages in Holy Writ. This means that the heralds of God's Word must be ready and faithful messengers, so that they run rather than go. Thus Isaiah also says (52:7): "How beautiful are the feet of those who bring good tidings"; Ezekiel (1:6 ff.) describes his animals as having feet and running; Eph. 6:15 directs that our feet be shod with the equipment of the Gospel; and in Holy Writ the duties, the running, the sending, and all similar functions of the feet signify the ministry of God's Word. And the poets represent their Mercury in a way that is not much different.

Notice again that after fourteen years Paul finds the apostles in Jerusalem or — if he does not find them all — at least Peter, James, and John, and that he confers with them. The fable spread about a separation of the apostles — that they were separated in the thir-

[2] See p. 190.
[3] Cf. pp. 166 f.

teenth year — does not disturb me as much as it causes me to warn against our slipping easily into similar nonsense — which exists today in the greatest abundance — by disregarding very clear passages of Scripture and unwisely accepting any figment of superstition that is decked out with any label of piety.[4]

What *qui videbantur esse aliquid,* "those who were of repute," means is already known from the *Annotations* of Erasmus. In fact, St. Jerome has *qui videbantur,* that is, those who were of greater prestige and reputation. Hence *esse aliquid,* "to be something," is an addition.[5]

3. *But even Titus, who was with me, was not compelled to be circumcised, though he was a Greek.*

4. *But because of false brethren secretly brought in, who slipped in to spy out our freedom which we have in Christ Jesus, that they might bring us into bondage —*

5. *to them we did not yield submission even for a moment, that the truth of the Gospel might be preserved for you.*

St. Jerome points out that the Latin codices formerly contained the affirmative statement "to whom we yielded submission for a moment." [6] This reading he refutes both on the basis of the Greek and on the basis of the obvious sense of the preceding context, in which Paul denies that Titus was forced to be circumcised and shows rather that he had not yielded. Then Jerome busies himself with the conjunction "but" or "however" and says that it should be stricken, in order that the sequence may be: "But even Titus was not compelled to be circumcised because of false brethren secretly brought in." But if my guess has any merit, here Paul is using a transposition or — again in Hebraic fashion — an ellipsis, so that the conjunction "but" refers to the verb "we yielded" or another verb is understood along with it, namely, "We resisted, or put up a fight, and won out; and this we did, not out of hatred or contempt for the Law or the works of the Law but on account of false brethren who wanted to turn our freedom into slavery for us." Moreover, Paul often uses ellipses in

[4] Luther is referring to the legendary account of the composition of the Apostles' Creed; the legend dates back to about the fifth century.

[5] Erasmus, *Annotationes ad locum;* Jerome, *Commentarius,* 357.

[6] Jerome, *Commentarius,* 358—359; cf. Tertullian, *Adversus Marcionem,* V, 3, on this reading.

other passages because of the vehemence of his mood. Nor is this infrequent in the Old Testament, as, I believe, is sufficiently well known.

The statement "to these we did not yield submission even for a moment" could also have been expressed more clearly, namely, "to whom we did not yield for a time [so Jerome has it] [7] into subjection" or "that we might be subjected." This means: "We stood so firmly for evangelical freedom that they were unable to get even this from us that we yielded for a time and only for this occasion. As though we would later revert, after the purpose of the followers of the Law had been accomplished with this concession, since we are accustomed to do so many things with a view of time, place, and persons — things we are later free to disregard. But let this be done in those matters where divine truth and evangelical freedom do not come into danger. Where these are at stake, time, place, and person should not be considered." So much for points of grammar.

Otherwise the whole essence of this controversy has to do with the necessity or freedom of works of the Law, not with what works of the Law are. For the works of the Law and the Law itself were not put to death and done away with through Christ in the sense that one may not do them at all (as St. Jerome, instructed by his teacher Origen, contends in more than one passage)[8] but only in such a way that one believes salvation to be apart from them through Christ alone. He is the end of the Law, and the works of the Law were commanded with reference to His coming. For when Christ came, He did away with the works of the Law in this way that they can be looked upon as immaterial but no longer binding — as Paul will show later (Gal. 4:1 ff.) with the beautiful example of the heir who is a child. Therefore the other apostles, together with the Jews who were believers, did them. Paul and Barnabas, however, sometimes did them, and sometimes they did not do them — in order to show that these deeds were simply adiaphora and were in accord with the nature of the person who did them, as Paul says in 1 Cor. 9:20-21: "To the Jews I became as a Jew, in order to win Jews; to those under the Law I became as one under the Law, though not being myself under the Law. To those outside the Law I became as one outside the Law." How could he have unfolded the freedom of

[7] Jerome, *Commentarius*, 359.

[8] See p. 379, note 61.

the Gospel more clearly? "I came," he says, "to preach Christ to the Jews. But in order that they might listen to me it was necessary on their account for me not yet to use this freedom and show contempt for them together with their works. Therefore I did what they themselves were doing, until I could teach them that these things were not necessary but that faith in Christ was sufficient. In the same way I came to the Gentiles. At that time I did none of those things which I had done among the Jews; but until I could preach Christ to them, I ate and drank whatever they ate and drank. How would they have given me a hearing if I had immediately been disdainful of them in these neutral matters? If in other respects it is permitted, yes, even meritorious, to grieve, suffer, die, and toil for a brother and a neighbor, how much more it is permitted to do any works at all of the Law if brotherly love requires them! But you must know that these works should not be done under the compulsion of the Law — for that taskmaster was overcome by the Child who was given to us (Is. 9:6) — but that they should be done out of love, which serves freely and gladly. Therefore if your brother's need were to demand that you be circumcised, then you will be circumcised, not only without peril — because it is not done on account of the Law and its requirement — but even with a great deal of merit.

For this reason the apostle is careful not to say that he was unwilling or that it was not permitted; he says that he was not compelled to be circumcised. To be circumcised was not an evil thing; but now that Christ alone justifies us through grace, to be forced into circumcision as if this were necessary for your justification — this would be wicked and an insult to Christ's justifying grace. After Christ, therefore, the works of the Law are like riches, honor, power, civic righteousness, and any other temporal thing. If you have them, you are not on this account better in the sight of God; if you lack them, you are not on this account worse. But you would be very wicked if you were to assert that you must have them in order to please God.

Notice, therefore, the words of the apostle in which the essence of what he means is expressed. "Compelled," he says; likewise "freedom," "slavery," "subjection." With these words he sets forth plainly enough the fact that among them there were those who watched him closely because he sometimes observed the Law — in accordance with his liberty and freedom — and sometimes did the opposite — depending on whether he saw that it was serviceable for the gaining of souls and the preaching of the Gospel. And these people betrayed and reproached him because he did not observe the Law and did not circumcise the Gentiles. They wanted to put pressure on him. Here he calls this subjection and slavery. For the freedom of which he boasts that we have it in Christ consists in this, that we are not bound to a single outward work but are free with regard to anything you please, in regard to anyone you please, at any time, and in any manner, except where an offense is committed against brotherly love and peace, as Rom. 13:8 states: "Owe no one anything, except to love one another." Therefore a true Christian, as Paul says in the third chapter (v. 28), is neither free nor slave, neither Jew nor Gentile, neither male nor female, neither a cleric nor a layman, neither religious nor secular; he neither prays nor reads; he neither does nor leaves undone. On the contrary, he is entirely free with regard to everything. Depending on whether a thing has come to hand or has withdrawn, he does it or leaves it undone, as Samuel said to Saul (1 Sam. 10:6): "You shall be turned into another man" and (v. 7) "Do whatever your hand finds to do; the Lord is with you." But that one man takes a wife and another enters a monastery, that one man indentures himself to this work and another to that work — he does not do this under compulsion of the Law but subjects himself to servitude of his own accord. If he does this out of love, he is acting nobly; but if he does so because he is impelled by necessity or fear, he is acting in conformity with human nature, not as a Christian. Accordingly, the people of our day err most seriously, especially the clergy and the members of religious orders. On account of the pomp of external worship, on account of their rites and ceremonies — in which they have become entangled to the point of the hopeless destruction of their souls — they feel such disgust for others, who are not conspicuous by a similar outward show, that they quarrel endlessly and have the nerve to declare publicly that they are unwilling ever to agree or to make common cause with them.

Finally, in this passage "the truth of the Gospel" seems to be taken, not as the actual content of the Gospel but as the proper use of the Gospel, because the Gospel is always true, whereas its use is not seldom subverted by hypocrisy. For "the truth of the Gospel" means knowing that all things are permitted, that to the pure all things are pure (Titus 1:15), and that no work of the Law is necessary for salvation and righteousness, since the Law is dead and no longer compels; when one performs works of the Law, therefore, it is on account of love, not out of compliance with the Law.

6. And from those who were reputed to be something (what they were at any time makes no difference to me; God shows no partiality) —

It is only in this passage that Paul adds "to be something" to the verb "were reputed"; from here it has been taken by the scribes and added to the other two passages. There is again an ellipsis here: "From those, however, who were reputed to be something —" (supply "I received nothing"). Repeating this thought below, he says that "they contributed nothing to me" and uses the same word — *contulerunt* — as above.

St. Augustine refers the words "what they were at any time" to the unworthiness of the apostles, namely, that at one time they, too, were sinners.[9] But that this makes no difference to Paul, even though to those who were saying that he had been a persecutor and for this reason should not be compared to the rest he could have replied by saying that since God does not look upon a man's person, neither their apostleship nor his was worthless because of previous sins; for God calls all men to salvation in the same manner. But I like Saint Jerome's opinion. He refers the words to the worthiness of the apostles and thinks that they were spoken against the false apostles, who boasted of the honor the apostles had because they had kept company with Christ and had seen, heard, and learned everything in Christ's own presence.[10] For this reason, they said, people should prefer them to Paul and should observe the Law together with them. Paul, however, without finding any fault with the apostles and without admitting that these objections were true, opposes the false apostles with an answer that is excellent and salutary to the highest degree. He says that all this with which they are puffed up has nothing whatever to do with the matter. For a thing is not true or good because it is performed by someone who is great, saintly, or a person of some importance; it is true and good because it comes from God alone. For what did it profit the traitor Judas that he kept company with Christ and had all things in common with the apostles? Therefore those people boast in vain of the outward appearance and honor of the apostles in opposition to the Word of God, which He reveals and teaches without that person. If God disregarded the

---

[9] Augustine, *Epistolae ad Galatas expositio, Patrologia, Series Latina*, XXXV, 2112.

[10] Jerome, *Commentarius*, 360.

apostolic person in the case of Judas, certainly He did not regard it in the case of the others either.

And you must note that in this passage "person" is understood far differently from the way it is now used in the schools. For it does not signify a rational and indivisible substance,[11] as those people say; but it means an external quality of life, of activity, or of behavior, in view of which a man is able to judge, praise, censure, and name another human being and anything that is not spiritual, in accordance with the statement of 1 Sam. 16:7: "Man looks on the outward appearance, but the Lord looks on the heart," and in Ps. 7:9: "God, who triest hearts and reins." Therefore it is these evident things, whatever they may be, that you must understand by the terms "person," "face," "appearance," and personal attributes of this sort if you want to understand the Scriptures rightly when they speak about "regard for persons." Man always looks upon the persons, never at the heart. For this reason he always judges wrong. God never looks upon the persons; He always looks at the heart. For this reason He judges people rightly (cf. Ps. 96:10). Lastly, elsewhere the translator renders πρόσωπον with *facies*, "face" or "appearance"; but in Scripture *facies* properly signifies everything that is outwardly apparent. Thus in Mark 12:14: "For Thou regardest not the appearance of a man," and in 1 Sam. 16:7: "Do not look on his appearance." But since the word "person" has long since taken on another meaning, it would be a good thing if in the Bible *facies* were written everywhere in place of *persona*.[12]

You see, therefore, how very soundly Paul instructs us, lest we be deceived by a title, a name, a face, or a person and neglect his counsel. He says: "Test everything; hold fast what is good" (1 Thess. 5:21). What do you think he would say now if he heard that in the church everything is being taught without any testing by those who boast of the power, the saintliness, and the learning of the authorities they have? Boldly he asserts that the appearance of the apostles has nothing to do with the matter; yet the appearance of the apostles was saintliness, power, an intimate acquaintance with Christ, and things far greater than you would now find in any pope. But now the power

---

[11] The scholastic definition to which Luther refers is *rationalis individuaque substantia*.

[12] Luther is referring to the development of the term *persona* as a consequence of the Trinitarian and Christological controversies.

alone of the pope is sufficient; the saintliness alone of teachers has authority. Consequently, whatever has pleased their fancy is taught. But certainly the power of the pope — since it is the person, so to speak, of a man — is not regarded by God; neither is the notion that he is a saintly man or the reputation he has for wisdom. All these things relate to the person. For this reason they are not powerful enough to make it necessary for one to believe that all their opinions are true. But it is certain that the praising of their persons did not please the apostles themselves, since they knew that one should glory in the Lord (1 Cor. 1:31), not oneself or in one's apparent power or saintliness. And take note most carefully of this admonition given by Paul.

those, I say, who were of repute contributed nothing to me in discussion.

They did not again expound his Gospel for Paul and discuss it with him (for this is what the verb *conferre* means, as has already been stated). But neither was this necessary. It was enough that they gave their approval and — as follows — saw that the preaching of the Gospel to the uncircumcised had been entrusted to him. This he says in order to show that in the judgment of the apostles too — whom they were praising in opposition to Paul — he had already taught rightly and that the apostles stood with him against the false apostles, who boasted of persons. Therefore he now proceeds more extensively with this.

7. *But on the contrary, when they saw that I had been entrusted with the Gospel to the uncircumcised, just as Peter had been entrusted with the Gopsel to the circumcised*

8. *(for He who worked through Peter for the mission to the circumcised worked through me also for the Gentiles),*

9. *and when they perceived the grace that was given to me, James and Cephas and John, who were reputed to be pillars, gave to me and Barnabas the right hand of fellowship, that we should go to the Gentiles and they to the circumcised;*

10. *only they would have us remember the poor, which very thing I was eager to do.*

St. Jerome thinks that there has been a transposition and that one should take out what has been interpolated and read as follows: "But on the contrary, they gave to me and Barnabas the right hand of fellowship." [13] To me it seems that Paul, as was his custom, leaves out something from his discussion; for in the meantime he is swept along and digresses to other things. He even inserts a parenthesis. Thus he fails to get back to the discussion he has begun. Therefore I would supply a statement. Then Paul's words would read like this: "But they, on the contrary, saw and approved my position as I had stated it in the discussion; and when from this discussion they had seen, etc."

Behold, Paul's Gospel and Peter's are identical; the former is an apostle to the Gentiles, the latter is an apostle to the Jews. How, then, can the false apostles boast of Peter and the apostles over against Paul when these men teach the same thing? If Peter, James, and John had held opinions different from what Paul had taught the Galatians, they would certainly have rebuked him. Now, however, they not only commend him but also give him the right hand of fellowship. These struggles of the churches and the pontiffs for preeminence were not yet going on in the church. Peter, John, and James did not reject Paul and Barnabas as their unworthy associates and equals. But with the advance of time and the increase of vices, as Jerome says, fellowship gave way to power and preeminence.[14] The expression "the right hands of fellowship" also seems to have the character of a Hebraism and to be used instead of "the right hands that are allied" or given as a confirmation of fellowship — unless Paul prefers it to mean that they did not give their right hands for the sake of adoration, to be kissed as an avowal of reverence.

But note that in spite of this Paul pays heed to rank and to respect for station. He puts James ahead of Peter, because James was Bishop of Jerusalem, whereas the other apostles went forth and returned. For it is said that the apostles decided that in accordance with Christ's teaching (Matt. 23:11-12) Peter, James, and John should humble themselves, since they were ahead of the others and more prominent during Christ's lifetime.[15]

Paul does not say "who cooperated"; he says "who worked." Now what he means is the same as what he describes at length in 1 Cor. 12:4 ff., that "there are varieties of working, but the same God who

[13] Jerome, *Commentarius*, 360.

[14] Jerome, *Commentarius*, 362.

[15] Cf. Irenaeus, *Adversus haereses*, III, 12, 5, on the primacy of the church in Jerusalem.

works all in all." But on the authority of Erasmus the Greek word means more than the Latin *operari*, namely, "to show one's effective power"; hence Jerome, in his letter to Paulinus, speaks of a latent energy.[16] This is the grace of the Spirit, whereby He multiplies the various gifts and works in the apostles and operates powerfully in their hearers.

Observe the discriminating weigher of words: "Gospel for the uncircumcision, Gospel for the circumcision, apostolate for the circumcision, apostolate to the Gentiles." Paul mentions only the terms that refer to the office and the work. For he is unquestionably using the term "Gospel" in the sense of "the office of preaching the Gospel"; and he says "to the uncircumcision, to the Gentiles" because it was for the Gentiles that he was discharging this office. "Apostolate," however, expresses the office by the term itself. But in our own age they are merely names for rank. For it is a dreadful thing to contemplate how the Gospel is despised by those who sail under its banner if you consider what the Word of God is and at what cost its revelation to mankind was procured.

It was not enough to say "when they had seen that the Gospel was entrusted to me"; but he adds "when they had perceived the grace that was given me." They saw the ministry; they perceived the grace. What does he mean? Obviously the gift of wisdom because of which he was stronger in the Word than the rest; likewise the gift of power because of which he had done miracles among the Gentiles. It was from the Word and his work that the "grace" in him was perceived. Perhaps he thought it necessary to consider these two together, lest anyone who lacked the grace with which to fulfill a ministry of this kind assume the office of the Word. We see that the Gospel and the apostolic office are entrusted to many, but we do not perceive grace in these people; for they are unable to show this by word and deed.

"They were reputed to be pillars." Why, pray, does he not say: "They were pillars"? Does he envy them their honor? Far from it! But he is speaking of the fact as it is. For to be a pillar in the church is a matter of the person and is according to appearance, which God does not regard. For in the sight and opinion of men this is indeed necessary on account of those who are in subordinate positions; but it is not the fact itself, in which one must put trust. There must be

---

[16] Erasmus, *Annotationes ad locum;* cf. p. 308, note 35, on Jerome.

princes and kings, that is, those who, in the opinion of men, are reputed to be and are considered such. In other respects they are persons so far as the world and their outward life are concerned; within, where God sees, they are perhaps inferior to the lowest slaves. Thus the episcopacy, the priesthood, and every rank and station in the church are "persons"; they are not the eternally solid fact itself. Therefore Paul uses the verb "were reputed" most appropriately when speaking against the foolish people who look upon the persons in no other way than they look upon the true facts themselves. Hence the verb "were reputed" is not to be taken in the sense in which it is now used when we say of a thing that is false or apparent: "It seems to me." No, they simply "were reputed"; that is, they were held to be and accepted as pillars. And they were real pillars so far as that is possible in this life, in which all that is seen is the person and the outward appearance of things.

This, too, is an elliptical way of speaking: "that we to the Gentiles, but they to the circumcision." You must supply "should preach the Gospel" or "should be apostles." After all, one must become accustomed to this Pauline manner of speaking. But they did not divide their functions in such a way that Paul never taught a Jew and Peter never taught a Gentile; for the epistles of both men proved the contrary. Consequently, the adverb "only" cannot belong to the preceding statement. No, as Jerome thinks, the ministry was divided in such a way that to each people its own apostle was sent: to the Gentiles, one who was to teach the free faith without the burden of the Law; to the Jews, one who, for the sake of a faith that had to be gradually strengthened, was to bear with the Law implanted in them.[17]

"The poor," whom Paul calls "the poor among the saints" in Rom. 15:26, are those whom the Jews had robbed of their property because of Christ, as he writes to the Hebrews (11:36 ff), or those who had made their goods common property, as is written in Acts 4:32; perhaps also those who were suffering want at the time of the famine which Luke mentions in Acts (11:28) as having taken place under Claudius. But if you calculate the years, it is certain that those things which he tells about in this chapter took place under Claudius. Moreover, you notice that concern for the poor is the other work of the apostles. For Paul seems to have added this as an admonition, since

---

[17] Jerome, *Commentarius*, 361.

he knew what was going to happen: that the successors of the apostles would care for other things rather than for the poor.

One thing can justly be disturbing. Why does Paul put himself on a par with Peter in particular and make no mention of the other apostles? Indeed, he also assigns to Peter the apostolate to the circumcised, likewise without mentioning the others. Perhaps because — as Peter was the first among the apostles — it was he whom the false apostles praised most, to the detriment of the Gospel; or Paul again was warning of abominations that were to come.

11. *But when Cephas came to Antioch, I opposed him to his face, because he stood condemned.*

12. *For before certain men came from James, he ate with the Gentiles; but when they came, he drew back and separated himself, fearing the circumcision party.*

13. *And with him the rest of the Jews acted insincerely, so that even Barnabas was carried away by their insincerity.*

This is the Abel (cf. Judges 1:33) or great plain on which two most illustrious fathers, Jerome and Augustine, clashed fiercely.[18] Jerome relied for his basic argument on the fact that Paul acted in a similar way when he circumcised Timothy on account of the Jews who were in those regions (Acts 16:3) — certainly not because the Law required it, since in the fifteenth chapter (v. 28) the apostles had already resolved that the Gentiles should not be weighed down with the burdens of the Law. And Timothy's father had been a Gentile. What is more, in the same chapter Paul teaches that the dogmas and decrees of the apostles are to be kept; yet contrary to them he himself circumcises Timothy at that very time. Likewise he had his head shaved at Cenchreae and had taken a vow (Acts 18:18). And in Acts 21:23 ff. it is stated that he, together with four men who had taken a vow, entered the temple and purified himself while they were with him, and that an offering was made on his behalf. Likewise, according to his own testimony (1 Cor. 9:20), "To the Jews I became as a Jew."

Therefore St. Jerome says: "What emboldens Paul and gives him the right to dare censure in Peter, who was the apostle for the cir-

---

[18] On the controversy between Augustine and Jerome see the references given in *Luther's Works*, 26, p. 84, note 3.

cumcised, what he himself, the apostle of the Gentiles, is shown to have done?" Accordingly, Jerome thinks that Paul made use of a hypocritical reproof against Peter; he believes that because Peter had endangered grace by his hypocrisy, it was Paul's purpose to set him right by using what he (Jerome) calls an unusual manner of fighting, an unusual kind of hypocrisy, and an unusual way of arguing against him. The Greek text seems to favor this opinion; it reads "according to appearance," or "in appearance." For, as Erasmus says here, the preposition κατά with the accusative means "according to" or "for the sake of"; with the genitive, on the other hand, it means "against." But here it is κατὰ πρόσωπον, that is, "according to appearance," "in appearance," "apparently," "in the sight of others," namely, in pious hypocrisy thinking something else to himself. Another consideration is this, that in Greek it is not "he was blameworthy" but "he had been blamed," because he could have been blamed by the weak and ignorant even though he was not blameworthy.[19]

St. Augustine relies on the statement which Paul made above: "In what I am writing to you, before God, I do not lie" (1:20). For when Paul says that Peter was blameworthy and that he had opposed him openly and had reproved him — if these things did not take place in this way and without hypocrisy, Paul would not be speaking the truth now but would be telling at least an obliging lie. And in this way the authority of all Scripture will totter, if in a single passage one thing is said and another thing is meant.

For it must be either that Peter was really blameworthy and was really set right by Paul or that Paul lied when he set him right and reproved him. And even though St. Augustine's argument can be parried by means of the Greek text, which does not have "blameworthy" but "stood condemned" (as Jerome also notes), still it is true and certain that in view of Paul's action Peter was blameworthy, since Paul would not blame a person who was not worthy of blame. But let us look at the text, which will be the best judge in this matter.

In the first place, it is certain that Paul did not reprove Peter for having lived the way the Gentiles lived, as St. Jerome thinks. (For then he would really have been directing the same reproof against himself, and St. Jerome's opinion would stand on an altogether solid footing. Jerome thought that deeds done according to the Law are not permissible after Christ's Passion and bring on death. Here, you

[19] Erasmus, *Annotationes ad locum.*

see, the saintly man was in error. He had been misled by some of his forefathers.) But Paul reproved Peter because he acted in a hypocritical manner. It was Peter's hypocrisy, I say, that Paul did not stand for. He approves of what Peter had done by living as the Gentiles lived and again by living as the Jews lived. But he censures him for withdrawing and segregating himself from the foods of the Gentiles when the Jews came; for by this withdrawal Peter caused the Jews to believe that the ways of the Gentiles were forbidden and that the ways of the Jews were necessary, even though he knew that the ways of both were unrestricted and permissible. For this reason the text also points out that Peter was not unaware of the fact that these things were unrestricted, because Paul says that previously "he ate with the Gentiles" and that he feared those who had come from James. Accordingly, Peter did these things out of fear, not out of ignorance. For Paul does not say: "Why are you living like a Gentile?" Nor does he say: "Why are you reverting to Jewish practices?" (He was free to do both.) No, Paul says: "Why do you force the Gentiles to live like Jews?" This compulsion was reprehensible because of Peter's hypocrisy and his withdrawal, which led the Gentiles and the Jews to believe that Jewish ways were necessary and that Gentile ways were forbidden.

Thus Paul's complaint is not that the rest of the Jews concurred with respect to food, whether Gentile or Jewish (for they knew that this was permitted), but that they concurred in Peter's hypocrisy and in his forcing of Gentiles and Jews into Judaism as something that was necessary. Nor does he complain that Barnabas ate with them in Jewish or in Gentile fashion, but that he was misled into the same hypocrisy and concurred in forcing Gentiles and Jews into Judaism.

Therefore Paul is fighting against compulsion and on behalf of freedom. For faith in Christ is all that is necessary for our righteousness. Everything else is entirely without restriction and is no longer either commanded or forbidden. Consequently, if Peter had observed both customs in the proper spirit, as Paul boldly observed both customs, it would not have been necessary to censure him.

Accordingly, we say with regard to Jerome's opinion: "One must admit that in the Greek the word 'blamed' has reference to those who accused Peter before Paul because he had withdrawn from them and who induced Paul to resort to this censuring of Peter. Nevertheless, Peter was truly blameworthy."

Furthermore, let others reflect on whether Peter committed a mortal sin (as they call it) in this instance. This I know, that those who were being forced into Judaism by such hypocrisy would have perished had they not been brought back through Paul; for they began to look for justification in the works of the Law, not in faith in Christ. Consequently, Peter, together with the others, gave powerful offense — not in the matter of morals but in the matter of faith, involving eternal damnation. And Paul would not have opposed him so confidently either if there had been a slight and pardonable danger here. But failure to follow the truth of the Gospel is already the sin of unbelief.

I do not approve of that zeal for the saints which goes too far in excusing and extolling them, especially if it is in opposition to the meaning of Holy Scripture. It is better that Peter and Paul be thought of as having fallen into unbelief, yes, as being accursed, as Paul said above (1:8), than that one iota of the Gospel be lost.

Now as to the notion that the Greek κατὰ πρόσωπον, "to his face," serves to prove hypocrisy on Paul's part — this I do not endorse. Paul was not playing the hypocrite, but with all his heart he opposed Peter's harmful hypocrisy; and "to his face" means the same as "before all" or "in the open," as St. Ambrose also explains.[20] Thus later on Paul says: "I said to Cephas before them all" (2:14). For, as I have said above, in Scriptural usage *facies*, "face," means that which is in the open; it is the opposite of "hidden," so that in one case man sees and judges, but in the other case God sees and judges. With this word Paul does not, as foolish Porphyry charges, disclose his own impudence and arrogance. No, he discloses the urgency of the situation and the greatest modesty. For he did not reprove Peter until all the rest concurred; and then even Barnabas, his associate, had been misled. No one at all was now left to stand up for the truth of the Gospel, and what they had done was now becoming a warrant against evangelical freedom. It is because of his modesty that Paul did not reprove at once but first let them all be misled. The urgency, however, lay in this, that the Gospel was already being lost. On the other hand, if one stubbornly insists on the force of the Greek word, namely, that κατὰ πρόσωπον, "according to face," always means "according to appearance" — as in John 7:24: "Do not judge by appearances" — this still does not demand the conclusion that there was hypocrisy on Paul's part. On the contrary, the sense will be this: Paul was indeed in

---

[20] Ambrose (ascribed), *Commentaria in XII epistolas beati Pauli, Patrologia, Series Latina*, XVII, 369.

earnest when he opposed Peter and rebuked him verbally, but he did not do so from a malicious heart. It is in this way that Ecclus. 7:24 speaks: "Do you have daughters? Be concerned for their bodies, and do not show your face cheerful toward them." Thus parents are stern to their children "according to face," not from the heart, yet not hypocritically either. And every Christian should maintain cordial pleasantness and a feeling of unity when reproving a brother and disagreeing with him. But even of God Himself it is said (Lam. 3:33): "For He does not willingly afflict or grieve the sons of men." But who would say that God plays the hypocrite when He scourges men and rejects them? Thus Paul rebuked Peter with a real reproof. He was harsh toward Peter "to his face" but affectionate toward him in his heart. Therefore Peter's guilt was real and deserving to the highest degree of reproof, and in neither man was there any hypocrisy of the kind St. Jerome supposes. There was, however, that earlier hypocrisy by which Peter compelled the observance of Jewish and legalistic practices.

A question. Since Peter withdraw with pious thoughts, fearful of offending the weak, what would Paul do if in the same situation there were weak brethren on both sides, Gentiles as well as Jews? To whom would he yield? It is no great problem, you see, to concur with individuals separately. For if he were to eat with the Jews, he would offend the Gentiles, as Peter did; if he were to eat with the Gentiles, he would offend the Jews, as Peter feared in this case. In such an event the truth of the Gospel must be preserved and explained by stating the reason, as Paul does in this instance when he reproves Peter in the presence of all and asserts that it is permissible to live as the Gentiles do and as he did before, when he refused to let Titus, a Gentile, be circumcised and did not yield for even a moment. But if the weak Jews are unwilling to follow here, one must let them go. It is better for one group to be saved along with the truth of the Gospel than for both groups to be lost together with the Gospel.

But how I wish that this passage of the apostle's were very well known to all Christians, especially to the members of monastic orders, the clergy, and the many superstitious people who, because of papal laws or ordinances of their own, not infrequently subvert both evangelical faith and evangelical love! They do not even have judgment enough to lay aside their burdens when brotherly love demands it, unless the people again buy dispensations and special permissions with cash — although neither the popes nor the church can impose anything except to allow the free exercise of love and mutual beneficence. For even if the pope is able to grant some dispensation and there should be a reason for it — helpfulness, honor, or, what is most important, love — you now have need of no one's dispensation but your own. For no human law could go so far as to bind you in these cases by as much as a hair; but any law would always have these exceptions, whether it wants to or not. If, on the other hand, such reasons are not at hand and you follow only your own caprice, the pope's dispensation will surely be your ruination and destruction as well as his own. Alas, how many slaughterings of consciences this ignorance of God's Law and the laws of men has brought into the church!

I cannot omit mentioning a well-known story that is especially pertinent in this connection. In the first book of the *Tripartite History* it is said of St. Spiridon, Bishop of Cyprus, that he took in a stranger during Lent and, having nothing else to serve, set some pork before him, first, however, saying a prayer and asking God for permission. But when the guest had refused the pork and had declared that he was a Christian, Spiridon said: "All the more reason why you should not refuse; for to the pure all things are pure (Titus 1:15), as the divine Word has taught." [21] Not that I should want the precepts of our forefathers to be despised in any way; I want them to be correctly understood. For where necessity or love has indicated the contrary, there — especially if in addition there is the advice of a confessor or devout person — a precept of that kind should be broken in pious humility and reverence. Consequently, there is no need for those declarations of absolution and special permissions to be bought and sold. For if it is not permissible for you to break the laws for another reason, no dispensation, no declaration of absolution, and no special permission will of itself be sufficient for you. But if there is another reason, then you do not need those things, as I have said. In fact, I should urge the popes to take pity at last on the perils of the churches and finally to abolish those laws of theirs by which we see nothing but consciences being ensnared or money being fished out and, above all, faith in Christ being utterly stifled, that is, true Christians being wiped out and the church being filled with hypocrites and idols.

[21] On Spiridon (more precisely, Spyridon) cf. Sozomen, *Ecclesiastical History*, I, 11, whence the account came into the *Historia tripartita*.

14. *But when I saw that they were not straightforward about the truth of the Gospel, I said to Cephas before them all: If you, though a Jew, live like a Gentile and not like a Jew, how can you compel the Gentiles to live like Jews?*

Paul exposes Peter and uncovers the man's hypocrisy; for it is only this that he rebukes. Peter was pretending that he did not live like a Gentile, but that he lived like a Jew. But Paul says: "To be sure, you are living and you have lived like a Gentile, and now you are pretending something else. By this hypocrisy you are compelling the Gentiles to live, not like Gentiles but like Jews; and in this way you are driving them into the slavery of the Law." From this it becomes clear that Paul was not well enough understood by St. Jerome.[22] For Jerome has in mind the hypocrisy of which Peter was guilty by practicing Jewish customs on account of the Jews and keeping the law which he was not supposed to keep. But this is not the hypocrisy which Paul reproves or is concerned about. No, it is the hypocrisy of which Peter was guilty by separating himself from the foods of the Gentiles, as if he were not permitted to use them. For it was the latter hypocrisy that imperiled the Gospel, not the former.

There have been some who asserted that this was another Cephas, one of the seventy disciples, as is stated in Eusebius' *Ecclesiastical History*. But St. Jerome learnedly and vigorously tears this notion to pieces.[23] For with false zeal they wanted to protect Peter, even though Paul wrote these things to the Galatians for the purpose of stopping the mouths of those who were disparaging him because, as they said, his teaching was to be regarded below Peter's in importance. "On the contrary," he says, "my teaching does not come from men; it comes from God. Besides, not only was it approved by Peter and the apostles, but even Peter himself was set right by it." Now, therefore, they had nothing left to snarl at Paul, since even Peter fell into error with respect to the truth of the Gospel when he let his fear of the Jews induce him to deal unfairly with others by taking away from them the freedom he used to claim for himself. In this matter Paul unquestionably showed himself superior to Peter. But this superiority — as it is called — was no cause for pride, because it has to do with man's person, which God does not regard. Yet in time past it

[22] Jerome, *Commentarius*, 367.

[23] Eusebius, *Ecclesiastical History*, I, 12 (quoting Clement); Jerome, *Commentarius*, 365.

was man's person that caused the sees of Rome and Constantinople to contend in frightful dissension, as if it were the only thing necessary for the church, just as though the unity of the church rested on man's person and on superior power rather than on the faith, hope, and love that are in the Spirit.

Another thing that should not be overlooked — even though it is widely known — is the fact that the Hebrew — I should rather say Syriac — word *Cephe* is the same as the Greek πέτρος or πέτρα, the Latin *saxum* or *soliditas,* as the decretals taken from Leo and Ambrose also point out. Therefore the decretal of Nicholas — if the title is correct — is in error when it states that *Cephe* means "head." It makes this statement in order that in accordance with its well-known feeling of solicitude it may make Peter the head of the church in addition to Christ. The Greek word κεφαλή means "head"; the Syriac word *Cephe* does not have this meaning.[24]

15. *We ourselves, who are Jews by birth and not Gentile sinners,*

Paul compares the Jews and the Gentiles. "It is true," he says, "that we, who are Jews by nature, excel the Gentiles, who are sinners if they are compared with us, in the righteousness of the Law, since they have neither the Law nor the works of the Law. But this does not make us righteous before God. This righteousness of ours is external." In Rom. 1:18 ff. and 2:17 ff. Paul discusses this thought in detail. Here he declares first that the Gentiles were very great sinners; but in the second chapter he turns to the Jews and asserts that even though they are not such sinners as he had described the Gentiles to be, they are sinners nevertheless, because they have kept the Law outwardly but not inwardly, and while glorying in the Law have dishonored God by transgressing the Law.

16. *yet who know that a man is not justified by works of the Law but through faith in Jesus Christ, even we have believed in Christ Jesus, in order to be justified by faith in Christ, and not by works of the Law.*

"We are righteous," says Paul, "inasmuch as we are by nature Jews, not sinners, like the Gentiles; but it is a righteousness of the works of Law, and by this righteousness no one is justified before

---

[24] *Decretum Magistri Gratiani,* Part I, Dist. 22, c. 2 (Anacletus, not Nicholas), edited by Emil Friedberg (Leipzig, 1879), I, 73—74.

God. For this reason we, too, like the Gentiles, consider our own righteousness as dung and seek to be justified through faith in Christ — we who are now sinners along with the Gentiles and are justified along with the Gentiles, since God "made no distinction between us and them," as Peter says in Acts 15:9, "but cleansed their hearts by faith." But because this passage seems absurd to those who have not yet become accustomed to Paul's theology, and because even Saint Jerome wearies himself no end trying to understand this, we shall expand the comments we began to make above about the traditions of the fathers. Among the extant authors I fail to find anyone except Augustine alone who treats this thought in a satisfactory manner; and even he is not satisfactory everywhere. But where he opposes the Pelagians, the enemies of God's grace, he will make Paul easy and clear for you.[25]

Above all, therefore, it is necessary to know that there are two ways in which man is justified, and that these two ways are altogether contrary to each other.

In the first place, there is the external way, by works, on the basis of one's own strength. Of such a nature are human righteousnesses which are acquired by practice (as it is said) and by habit. This is the kind of righteousness Aristotle and other philosophers describe — the kind produced by laws of the state and of the church in ceremonies, the kind produced at the behest of reason and by prudence. For they think that one becomes righteous by doing righteous things, temperate by doing temperate things, and the like. This is the kind of righteousness the Law of Moses, even the Decalog itself, also brings about, namely, when one serves God out of fear of punishment or because of the promise of a reward, does not swear by God's name, honors one's parents, does not kill, does not steal, does not commit adultery, etc. This is a servile righteousness; it is mercenary, feigned, specious, external, temporal, worldly, human. It profits nothing for the glory to come but receives in this life its reward, glory, riches, honor, power, friendship, well-being, or at least peace and quiet, and fewer evils than do those who act otherwise. This is how Christ describes the Pharisees and how St. Augustine describes the Romans in the eighth chapter of the first book of *The City of God*.[26] Strangely

[25] Jerome, *Commentarius*, 368—369; Augustine, *On the Spirit and the Letter*, 57.

[26] Augustine, *City of God*, I, 8.

enough, this righteousness deceives even men who are wise and great, unless they have been well instructed in Holy Writ.

Jeremiah (2:13) calls this kind of righteousness "a broken cistern that holds no water"; yet, as he says in the same chapter (v. 23), it causes people to take for granted that they are without sin. It is completely like the actions which we see done by a monkey when it imitates human beings, or like those displayed by actors on stages and in plays. It is entirely characteristic of hypocrites and idols. Consequently, in the Scriptures it is called a lie and an iniquity. Hence the name *Bethaven*, "house of iniquity." [27] To their kind belong also those who deceive souls today, who in reliance on their free will make a good resolution (as they say) and, after eliciting from their natural powers the act of loving God above all things, at once take for granted in the most shameful manner that they have obtained the grace of God.[28] These are the people who strive to cure the woman with an issue of blood (that is, a guilty conscience) by means of works and, after exhausting her resources, make her worse (Mark 5:25-26).

In the second place, there is the inward way, on the basis of faith and of grace, when a man utterly despairs of his former righteousness, as though it were the uncleanness of a woman in menstruation, and casts himself down before God, sobs humbly, and, confessing that he is a sinner, says with the publican: "God, be merciful to me a sinner!" (Luke 18:13.) "This man," says Christ, "went down to his house justified" (v. 14). For this righteousness is nothing else than a calling upon the name of God. Now the name of God is mercy, truth, righteousness, strength, wisdom, and the accusation of one's own name. On the other hand, our name is sin, falsehood, vanity, and folly, as is written: "All men are liars" (Ps. 116:11) and "Every man walks in a vain show" (Ps. 39:6).

But calling upon the name of God, if it is in the heart and truly from the heart, shows that the heart and the name of the Lord are one and cling to each other. For this reason it is impossible for the heart not to share in the virtues in which the name of the Lord abounds. But it is through faith that the heart and the name of the Lord cling together (cf. Rom. 10:17). Faith, however, comes through the Word of Christ, by which the name of the Lord is preached, as

---

[27] Luther is thinking of passages like Joshua 7:2, Hos. 4:15, etc.
[28] Cf. *Luther's Works*, 12, p. 304, note 2.

is written: "I will tell of Thy name to my brethren" (Ps. 22:22), and again: "That men may declare in Zion the name of the Lord" (Ps. 102:21). Therefore just as the name of the Lord is pure, holy, righteous, true, good, etc., so, if it touches, or is touched by, the heart (which happens through faith), it makes the heart entirely like itself. Thus it comes about that for those who trust in the name of the Lord all sins are forgiven, and righteousness is imputed to them "for Thy name's sake, O Lord" (Ps. 25:11), because this name is good. This does not come about because of their own merit, since they have not deserved even to hear of it. But when the heart has thus been justified through the faith that is in His name, God gives them the power to become children of God (John 1:12) by immediately pouring into their hearts His Holy Spirit (Rom. 5:5), who fills them with His love and makes them peaceful, glad, active in all good works, victorious over all evils, contemptuous even of death and hell. Here all laws and all works of laws soon cease; all things are now free and permissible, and the Law is fulfilled through faith and love.

Behold, this is what Christ has gained for us, namely, that the name of the Lord (that is, the mercy and truth of God) is preached to us and that whoever believes in this name will be saved. Therefore if your conscience troubles you and you are a sinner and are seeking to become righteous, what will you do? Will you look around to see what works you may do or where you may go? No. On the contrary, see to it that you hear or recall the name of the Lord, that is, that God is righteous, good, and holy; and then cling to this, firmly believing that He is such a One for you. Now you are at once such a one, like Him. But you will never see the name of the Lord more clearly than you do in Christ. There you will see how good, pleasant, faithful, righteous, and true God is, since He did not spare His own Son (Rom. 8:32). Through Christ He will draw you to Himself. Without this righteousness it is impossible for the heart to be pure. That is why it is impossible for the righteousness of men to be true. For here the name of the Lord is used for the truth; there it is used for an empty show. For here man gives glory to God and confusion to himself; there he gives glory to himself and insult to God. This is the real cabala of the name of the Lord, not of the Tetragrammaton, about which the Jews speak in the most superstitious manner.[29] Faith in the name of the Lord, I say, is the understanding of the Law, the

[29] On interest in the cabala cf. *Luther's Works*, 26, p. 290, note 88.

end of the Law, and absolutely all in all. But God has placed this name of His on Christ, as He foretold through Moses.[30]

This is a righteousness that is bountiful, given without cost, firm, inward, eternal, true, heavenly, divine; it does not earn, receive, or seek anything in this life. Indeed, since it is directed toward Christ and His name, which is righteousness, the result is that the righteousness of Christ and of the Christian are one and the same, united with each other in an inexpressible way. For it flows and gushes forth from Christ, as He says in John 4:14: "The water that I shall give will become in him a spring of living water welling up to eternal life." Thus it comes about that just as all became sinners because of another's sin, so by Another's righteousness all become righteous, as Rom. 5:19 says: "As by one man's disobedience many were made sinners, so by the righteousness of one Man, Christ, many are made righteous." This is the mercy foretold by all the prophets; this is the blessing promised to Abraham and to his seed, as we shall see later.

Coming back now to the text, we see how right the apostle is when he says: "Knowing that a man is not justified on the basis of works of the Law but [as is obvious] only on the basis of faith in Jesus Christ, we too, believe in Christ Jesus, in order that we may be justified on the basis of faith in Jesus Christ, not on the basis of the works of the Law." In these words he describes both kinds of righteousness. He rejects the former and embraces the latter. May you do likewise, dearest brother. First hear that Jesus means "salvation" and that Christ means "the anointing of mercy"; then firmly believe this unheard-of salvation and mercy, and you will be justified. That is, believe that He will be your salvation and mercy, and beyond all doubt He will be. Therefore it is altogether godless and exceedingly heathenish to teach that remission of sins takes place through trifling little works of satisfaction and through compulsory acts of contrition, while — as the great mass of sententiarists [31] peddle their theology today — the doctrine of faith in Christ is completely neglected.

Nevertheless, it should be noted here that the apostle does not reject the works of the Law as Jerome also points out in this con-

---

[30] This is perhaps a reference to Ex. 23:20-22.

[31] The nickname *sententiastri* is a term of opprobrium for commentators on the *Sentences* of Peter Lombard.

nection.³² He rejects reliance on the works of the Law. That is, he does not deny that there are works, but he does deny that anyone can be justified through them. Therefore one must read the apostle's statement with emphasis and close attention when he says: "A man is not justified on the basis of the works of the Law"; as if he were saying: "I grant that works of the Law are done; but I say that a man is not justified because of them — except in his own sight and before men, and as a reward in this life. Let there be works of the Law, provided that one knows that in the sight of God they are sins and no longer true works of the Law." In this way he totally demolishes reliance on our own righteousness, because there is need of a far different righteousness — a righteousness beyond all works of the Law, namely, a righteousness of the works of God and His grace.

Furthermore, you must also observe that Paul speaks of "works of the Law" in general not merely of those that relate to the Ceremonial Law but certainly also of all the works of the Decalog. For these, too, when done apart from faith and the true righteousness of God, are not only insufficient; but in their outward appearance they even give hypocrites false confidence. Therefore he who wants to be saved must despair altogether of all strength, works, and laws.

Furthermore, you must note for yourself a manner of speaking that is characteristic of this apostle, namely, that he does not, as others are accustomed to do, call the works by which the Law itself is fulfilled "works of the Law." For the apostle's way of putting it accounts for the fact that very many fail to understand him. They cannot understand works of the Law as being anything but righteous and good, since the Law itself is good and righteous. Hence they are driven to understand the Law as meaning ceremonial requirements, because, as they say, these were evil and dead at that time. But they are mistaken. Just as the Ceremonial Law was good and holy at that time, so it is good and holy now; for it was instituted by God Himself.

The apostle consistently declares that the Law is fulfilled only through faith, not through works. Because the fulfilling of the Law is righteousness and this is surely a matter of faith, not of works, one cannot understand the works of the Law to mean those works by which the Law is satisfied. What then? The apostle's rule is this: It is not works that fulfill the Law, but the fulfillment of the Law

---

³² Jerome, *Commentarius*, 369.

produces works. One does not become righteous by doing righteous deeds. No, one does righteous deeds after becoming righteous. Righteousness and fulfillment of the Law come first, before the works are done, because the latter flow out of the former. That is why Paul calls them "works of the Law" in distinction from works of grace or works of God; for works of the Law are really the Law's, not ours, since they are done, not by the operation of our will but because the Law extorts them through threats or elicits them through promises. But whatever is not done freely of our own will but is done under the compulsion of another is no longer our work. No, it is the work of him who requires it. For works belong to him at whose command they are done. But they are done at the command of the Law, not at the pleasure of one's own will. It is clear enough that if a person were free to live without the Law, he would never do the works of the Law of his own accord. Hence the Law is called an enforcer when in Is. 9:4 it is spoken of as "the staff for his shoulder, the yoke of his burden, the rod of his oppressor, as on the day of Midian." For through the Child who was given to us (Is. 9:6) and in whom we believe we become free and take pleasure in the Law; and we no longer belong to the Law, but the Law belongs to us. And our works are not works of the Law; they are works of grace, from which there spring up freely and pleasantly those deeds which formerly the Law used to squeeze out with harshness and power.

You will understand this if you arrange works in four categories: (1) Works of sin, which are done under the domination of lust, with no resistance on the part of grace; (2) works of the Law, which are done when lust is held in check outwardly but glows all the more inwardly and hates the Law, that is, works that are good in appearance but evil in the heart; (3) works of grace, which are done when lust resists, but the spirit of grace is nevertheless victorious; (4) works of peace and perfect well-being, which are done with the fullest ease and pleasantness after lust has been extinguished — as will be the case in the life to come. Here there is only a beginning.

because by works of the Law shall no one be justified.

Paul draws the same conclusion in Rom. 3:9 ff. And there he proves it extensively on the basis of Ps. 14:3: "There is no one who is righteous, who does good." Therefore the works of the Law must be sins; otherwise they would certainly justify. Thus it is clear that

Christian righteousness and human righteousness are not only altogether different but are even opposed to each other, because the latter comes from works, while works come from the former. No wonder, therefore, that Paul's theology vanished entirely and could not be understood after Christians began to be instructed by men who declared falsely that Aristotle's ethics are entirely in accord with the doctrine of Christ and of Paul, by men who failed completely to understand either Aristotle or Christ. For our righteousness looks down from heaven and descends to us. But those godless men have presumed to ascend into heaven by means of their righteousness and from there to bring the truth which has arisen among us from the earth.

Therefore Paul stands resolute: "No flesh is justified on the basis of works of the Law," as Ps. 143:2 also says: "No man living will be justified before Thee." The only thing left is that the works of the Law are not works of righteousness — except of the righteousness that is of our own making.

17. *But if, in our endeavor to be justified in Christ, we ourselves were found to be sinners, is Christ, then, an agent of sin? Certainly not!*

This means: "We have already said that we trust in Christ in order that we may be justified by reason of faith in Christ. But if we are not justified in this way, indeed, if we are still found to be sinners and lacking justification — since you compel us to be justified on the basis of works of the Law — then justification by reason of faith is nothing, and by our faith in Him Christ has made us sinners who need the righteousness of the Law. But this is utterly absurd and means abolishing Christ completely, because in this way He would have rendered our sin something to be purged away by means of the Law, and the righteousness of the Law would now be better than that of Christ." For the apostle is arguing from what is impossible and absurd, as though he were saying: "If the Law is necessary for us who seek to be justified in Christ, then, although we have been justified through Christ, we shall still be found to be sinners and debtors to the Law. But if this is so, then Christ has not justified us but has only made us sinners, in order that we may be justified through the Law. This is impossible. Therefore this, too, is impossible, that the Law (I say) is necessary and that we are justified by the works of the Law. For when we have been justified in Christ, we are not found to be sinners. Then we are found to be righteous, because Christ is the agent, not of sin but of righteousness." This is the view of St. Jerome. St. Augustine's view is somewhat different and rather forced.[33]

To understand the apostle, however, you must note that in a veiled way he is comparing Moses with Christ. For this is Paul's way of speaking; he calls the Law the occasion for sin (cf. Rom. 7:11) and the power of sin (1 Cor. 15:56). For this reason he has the courage to call the ministry of the Law a dispensation of death and sin in 2 Cor. 3:7: "If the dispensation of death, carved in letters, etc." And in Rom. 7:9 ff. he tells how sin has killed through the Law. Hence he understands Moses, the agent of the Law, to be the agent of sin and death, because through the Law comes sin, and through sin comes death; for, he says in Rom. 4:15, "where there is no Law, there is no transgression." But Paul sets Christ, the Agent of righteousness who has fulfilled what Moses demanded through the Law, over against Moses. John 1:17 does not pass over this fact in complete silence. "The Law," says John, "was given through Moses; grace and truth came through Jesus Christ," as if he were saying: "The Law, not grace and truth, comes through Moses. Therefore it is rather sin and transgression that have been given through him." Accordingly, Christ is not a lawgiver; He is the Fulfiller of the Law. Every lawgiver is an agent of sin, because through the law he sets up the occasion for sin. For this reason God did not institute the old Law through Himself; He instituted it through angels. The new Law, however — that is to say, grace — He gave through Himself by sending the Holy Spirit from heaven.

But here again the misery of the church and of the Christians confronts me when I look at the forests, deserts, clouds, and oceans of Roman laws, the titles of which you would not be able to learn in your whole life. Here the apostle declares confidently that laws are dispensations of sins, whereas in spite of this our lawgivers boast that they confront sins and quarrels with heaps of laws. They fail to realize that experience itself, as it meets their eyes, proves this plan of theirs to be stupid.

Besides — to play with allegories on this occasion — I think that the ten plagues of Egypt were symbols not only of the Jewish

[33] Jerome, *Commentarius*, 369; Augustine, *Epistolae ad Galatas expositio, Patrologia, Series Latina*, XXXV, 2114.

Talmudic regulations [34] but also of those of the church. For because we read that the plagues were inflicted through the evil angels, it cannot be denied that they signify the doctrines and traditions of men; for "angel" certainly signifies a messenger of the Word and a teacher, as those angels of the Apocalypse (Rev. 16:1 ff.) also show with their plagues and vials. But the other plagues should perhaps be borne because of our sins. Our supplies of water are turned into blood; frogs — that is, glosses — disturb us with their incessant croaking; lice bite us and suck away all our substance; flies devour us as we toil and sweat; simple-hearted cattle are slaughtered; we are swollen up with blisters; we are taxed and smitten by a hailstorm of tyrannical violence; we are drained to the marrow by locusts. All this, I say, should perhaps be borne because of our sins. But the fact that the last evils are added, and we are blinded by a darkness that can be felt and finally, alas, are losing our birthright, the glory of righteousness and faith in Christ — this cannot be lamented enough. But since fatherly duty is asleep in the prelates, I at least am doing my brotherly duty by warning and begging that we, too, cry to the Lord, if perchance He may descend in mercy and deliver us from this iron furnace and this house of the harshest bondage.

I believe, however, that some are disturbed because the apostle says here that those who believe in Christ and are justified are not sinners, since no man is without sin, not even Paul himself, as he testifies of himself in Rom. 7:14 and 8:2. I answer: Everyone who believes in Christ is righteous, not yet fully in point of fact, but in hope. For he has begun to be justified and healed, like the man who was half-dead (Luke 10:30). Meanwhile, however, while he is being justified and healed, the sin that is left in his flesh is not imputed to him. This is because Christ, who is entirely without sin, has now become one with His Christian and intercedes for him with the Father. Thus after Paul has said that through the law of his members he was made captive to sin (Rom. 7:23), he declares: "There is no condemnation for those who are in Christ Jesus, who do not walk according to the flesh" (Rom. 8:1, 4). He does not say "no sin." On the contrary, much sin still remains; but it is not imputed for condemnation. It was with reference to this mystery, it seems, that

---

[34] The parallel between the ten plagues of Egypt and the Roman persecutions was a theme of Orosius, *Historiae adversus paganos*, VII, 27, *Corpus Scriptorum Ecclesiasticorum Latinorum*, V, 495—500; it appears also in Augustine, *City of God*, XVIII, 52.

Christ said: "It is finished" before He died on the cross (John 19:30). Therefore all such statements praising the righteous are to be understood in the same way, namely, that the righteous are not wholly perfect in themselves, but God accounts them righteous and forgives them because of their faith in His Son Jesus Christ, who is our Propitiation. These points St. Augustine discusses at length in his book *On Nature and Grace*.[35]

Those who ascribe to the baptized and the penitent only the weakness, the tinder,[36] and the sickness of nature err and deceive in a destructive manner, especially when they prate that what they should have said is not sin solely because of God's accounting and forgiving is not in itself sin.

18. *But if I build up again those things which I tore down, then I prove myself a transgressor.*

This means: "Through the preaching of faith I have taught that in Christ there is justification and that the Law has been fulfilled, and by doing so I have destroyed sins. If, on the other hand, I were now to teach that the Law must be observed and that it has not been fulfilled, what else would I be doing but again establishing sins and saying that they still have to be overcome by our works? In this way I would be doing nothing except to show that I did wrong either then or now. That is, I would be proving myself a transgressor. Indeed, I would be alienating myself from Christ, in whom I have been justified, and I would again be putting myself under the Law and under sins, just as I was before I had Christ."

Again the apostle is using his way of speaking. Consequently, the interpreters disagree. St. Jerome wants "torn down" and "built up again" to be understood as referring to the Law, that is, to the Ceremonial Law. Although this is a correct opinion, it is too narrow to fit other passages of Scripture in a satisfactory manner. St. Augustine says it is the works of the Law that are destroyed, rather the pride that glories in the works of the Law and relies on them. This view I do not condemn either.[37] But when comparing what the apostle says here with what he says in the preceding context and

---

[35] Augustine, *On Nature and Grace*, 69, 83, and passim.

[36] The Latin word is *fomes;* cf. *Luther's Works*, 13, p. 81, note 12.

[37] Augustine, *Epistolae ad Galatas expositio, Patrologia, Series Latina,* XXXV, 2115.

in other passages it seems to me that he is destroying sins — as I have said — not the Law, especially since in Rom. 3:31 he states that by faith he does not destroy the Law but rather establishes it. In Rom. 6:6, however, he destroys sins, "in order that the body of sin may be destroyed." For sins, which were there in abundance through the Law, are destroyed through faith; for sin is not destroyed unless the Law is fulfilled. But the Law is not fulfilled except through the righteousness of faith. So it comes about that through faith the Law is established and sins are destroyed — both at the same time. For since satisfaction is rendered to the Law through faith, sins cease, and the Law remains in power.

But to build up sins again means to preach the Law again and to think that it must be observed and fulfilled. Where the Law must be fulfilled, however, there righteousness has not yet been brought about; for not yet to have fulfilled the Law is sin. In this way the sins, concerning which it was taught that they were previously destroyed through faith, return. To build up sin, therefore, is the same as to weaken the Law, destroy it, and make it ineffectual. To destroy sin, however, is the same as to establish, build up, and fulfill the Law. Consequently, whoever teaches that the Law has been fulfilled and righteousness has been brought about is certainly destroying sins. But the one who does this is he who teaches that through faith in Jesus Christ men become righteous, that is, fulfillers of the Law. But he who says that the Law must be fulfilled and that righteousness has not been brought about is certainly once more establishing sins and restoring them to life. He is making people debtors to the Law and obliging them to observe it.

This, I say, is what I think the apostle means in this passage. He regularly teaches that the Law is destroyed through sin, as he says in Rom. 8:3: "What the Law, weakened by the flesh, could not do"; that is, it was not being fulfilled. For the flesh does not fulfill the Law. Therefore it weakens the Law. But the same figure of speech is found also in other passages of Scripture. Thus Jer. 35:16 says: "The sons of Jonadab have strengthened the commandment which their father gave them." Likewise (v. 14): "The words of Jonadab which he commanded proved to be strong." And Ps. 141:6 says: "They will hear my words, since they were powerful," that is, were made powerful, were strengthened and fulfilled. Again, as Ps. 18:36 says: "My footsteps were not weakened," that is, my ways were strengthened and fulfilled. But Ps. 11:3 says: "For they have destroyed what Thou broughtest to perfection," that is, they have broken Thy Law (as the Hebrew has it) to pieces.

But from the preceding it will be clear that this is also what was meant when the apostle said that those who have been justified in Christ are not found to be sinners. Accordingly, it is proved that for them sins have been destroyed. But if they were found to be sinners, the sins previously destroyed would now be restored. This would be blasphemy against Christ, who has destroyed sin and death for us if we believe in Him; and, as John says (1 John 3:9): "He who is born of God does not sin." I believe, however, that it is sufficiently evident that the apostle is not speaking only of ceremonial laws but certainly of the entire Law. For Christ would have contributed too little if He had destroyed only the sins against the Ceremonial Law. But since He has also destroyed the sins against the Decalog, it is now all the more evident that the ceremonial laws have been destroyed too, and that all laws have become free.

But again I am forced to admonish the reader who is accustomed to theology as it is commonly taught. Perhaps he will be confused when he hears that the Law has been fulfilled for all who believe in Christ. For he will say: "Why, then, is it taught that the Decalog and so many precepts of the Gospel and of the apostles must be fulfilled? And why are we daily exhorted to do the works they prescribe?" As has already been said, the answer is: How is it that those who have been justified in Christ are not sinners and are sinners nevertheless? For Scripture establishes both facts about the righteous man. John says in the first chapter of his canonical epistle:[38] "If we say we have no sin, we deceive ourselves, and the truth is not in us" (1 John 1:8). In the last chapter of the same epistle he says: "We know that everyone who is born of God does not sin, but God's generation (that is, the fact that he is born of God) preserves him, and the evil one will not touch him" (1 John 5:18). The same writer says in the third chapter (v. 9): "No one born of God commits sin, because His seed abides in him, and he is not able to sin." Behold, he is not able to sin, says John. Yet if he says he has no sin, he is lying. A similar contradiction may be seen in Job, whom God, who cannot lie, pronounces a righteous and innocent man in the first

---

[38] The reason for the designation "canonical" for 1 John is not clear; perhaps Luther means this as a synonym for "catholic epistle."

chapter (Job 1:8). Yet later on Job confesses in various passages that he is a sinner, especially in the ninth and seventh chapters: "Why dost Thou not take away my iniquity?" (9:20; 7:21.) But Job must be speaking the truth, because if he were lying in the presence of God, then God would not pronounce him righteous. Accordingly, Job is both righteous and a sinner.[39] Who will resolve these contradictory aspects? Or where are they in agreement? Obviously at the mercy seat, where the faces of the cherubim, which otherwise are opposed to one another, are in agreement. Therefore because righteousness and the fulfilling of the Law have been begun through faith, for this reason what is left of sin and falls short of fulfilling the Law is not imputed to them; for they believe in Christ. When faith has been born, you see, its task is to drive what is left of sin out of the flesh. It does so by means of various afflictions, hardships, and mortifications of the flesh, so that in this way the Law of God gives pleasure and is fulfilled not only in the spirit and in the heart but also in the flesh that still resists faith and the spirit which loves and fulfills the Law, as is beautifully described in Rom. 7:22 f. Therefore if you look at faith, the Law has been fulfilled, sins have been destroyed, and no Law is left. But if you look at the flesh, in which there is no good, you will be compelled to admit that those who are righteous in the spirit through faith are still sinners.

The apostle's whole concern, therefore, is that no one presume to bring righteousness into the heart through the works of the Law, as if the righteousness of faith, from which the works of the Law and its fulfillment flow into the flesh, did not already hold sway there. Take this comparison: Just as Christ, who is entirely without sin and the Head of the righteous, who owes no debt to the Law at all and needs no instruction as to what He should do, who already does all things even more abundantly than the Law directs, nevertheless governs and disciplines His body and flesh, the church, so as to make His righteousness flow into it, in order that even as He Himself is obedient to the Father in all things, so He may also render His body obedient, which as yet is not so obedient or without sin; in a similar way the spirit of the righteous man, although through faith it is now without sin and owes nothing to the Law, nevertheless still has a body

[39] The Latin is *simul iustus, simul peccator;* cf. *Luther's Works,* 26, p. 232, note 49.

unlike itself and rebellious, upon which it works and which it disciplines so as to render it, too, without sin, righteous, and holy like itself.

Therefore the Commandments are necessary only for sinners. On account of their flesh, however, the righteous, too, are sinners. But on account of the faith of the inner man, who, like God, persecutes, hates, and crucifies the sin in his flesh until in the life to come he is made perfect in both flesh and spirit and owes no debt to any law, this sinfulness is not imputed to them. From one point of view, therefore, the Law has been fulfilled, we owe the Law nothing, and sins have been destroyed. But those who seek righteousness through the works of the Law are themselves rebuilding even the sin of unbelief in opposition to faith, which is in the spirit. Indeed, through the works of the Law these most perverse of men extol the sin in the flesh — the sin which faith subdues all through life and which for this reason seems to be nonexistent — and it is on this that they establish as righteousness the fulfilling of the Law, not on faith. For they think that they are righteous if they have done the works of the Law, even though they have neither faith in Christ, which is the inner righteousness, nor purity of the flesh. But they pretend to have it. This means, however, that they are neither inwardly nor outwardly righteous but are deluding themselves and their fellowmen with mere appearance.

Consequently, the Commandments are necessary, not in order that we may be justified by doing the works they enjoin, but in order that as persons who are already righteous we may know how our spirit should crucify the flesh and direct us in the affairs of this life, lest the flesh become haughty, break its bridle, and shake off its rider, the spirit of faith. One must have a bridle for the horse, not for the rider.

19. *For I through the Law died to the Law, that I might live to God.*

This figurative way of speaking Paul develops more extensively in Rom. 7:2 ff., where he points out that a wife who survives is released from the law that had to do with her dead husband. All this will be gibberish to you unless you remove metaphysical deaths and changes from your mind. Just as death does away with death, sin does away with sin, captivity does away with captivity, freedom does away with freedom, slavery does away with slavery, life does away with life, good does away with good, evil does away with evil, curse does away with curse, light does away with light, darkness does away with darkness, day does away with day, night does away with night, so law does away with law. Of this there are many examples in Scripture, especially in Paul.

Obviously, then, Paul is referring to a twofold law. The one is the law of the spirit and of faith, by which one lives to God after sins have been overcome and the Law has been fulfilled, as has been sufficiently stated. The other is the law of the letter and of works, by which one lives to sin, since the Law has never been fulfilled but is hypocritically said to have been fulfilled. For through the Law a hatred of the Law is awakened, but through faith a love for the Law is infused. Consequently, the doer of the Law observes the Law with a hatred for the Law; that is, he disregards it most wickedly. Inwardly he desires one thing; outwardly he feigns something else. The spirit of faith, however, keeps the Law with love for the Law; that is, he fulfills the Law in the best way, even though by outwardly struggling with his sins he shows that he is a sinner. These two, therefore, are opposed to each other. Inwardly the man of the Law sins; outwardly he pretends righteousness. Inwardly the man of faith does what is good; outwardly he bears his sins and persecutes them.

Through the law of faith, therefore, Paul lives to God inwardly. At the same time he is dead to the Law. In the flesh, however, he does not yet live to God but is being made alive to God. He is not yet dead to the Law but is being put to death to the Law while striving to extend outwardly to the flesh the same purity of the heart that comes from faith. Because of this endeavor he deserves to be considered entirely alive to God and dead to the Law — according to the very same figurative way of speaking by which previously he was said to be a sinner and not a sinner, a fulfiller and not a fulfiller. For it is in the life to come that we live fully to God and are dead to the Law.

That in this passage living and dying are not taken in a physical or natural sense is shown by the very way in which the apostle uses the words. For he does not say simply that he has died; he says that he has died to the Law and is alive to God. But to live to the Law is to be under the Law and its dominion, as Rom. 7:1 states: "The Law is binding on a person only during his life." Just as a slave, according to the law of slavery and the law of nations, lives to his master as long as he is not set free, so we, while we are outside faith, serve the Law because we are under the sway of lust. We do the works of the Law under compulsion, and thereby we fail to fulfill the Law, which is fulfilled only through the love that comes from faith. But to die to the Law is to be made free from the Law. Just as any debtor, when he has died, is free from his creditor, so we, when through the grace of faith the old man begins to be put to death and sin, which abounded because of the Law, begins to be destroyed, die with this holy death; that is, we are made alive to righteousness — as Paul discusses in detail in Rom. 6 and 8 and with the same figurative way of speaking calls those who have died to sin alive to righteousness. Hence living to the Law means failing to fulfill the Law; dying to the Law means fulfilling the Law. The latter takes place through faith in Christ; the former takes place through the works of the Law. Thus in Rom. 3:28 Paul says: "For we hold that a man is justified by faith," which he also calls the law of faith. Likewise in Rom. 8:2: "The law of the Spirit of life (that is, of faith) has set me free from the law of death and sin," namely, from the Law which works and increases death and sin, as does every law, whether given by God or by man. Accordingly — as we began to do — we shall explain these two laws more clearly.

The law of the Spirit is one that is written with no letters at all, published in no words, thought of in no thoughts. On the contrary, it is the living will itself and the life of experience.[40] Furthermore, it is the very thing that is written in the hearts only by the finger of God. Rom. 5:5 states: "God's love has been poured into our hearts through the Holy Spirit." Jeremiah, too, speaks of this (31:33), as the apostle quotes him in Heb. 8:10 and 10:16: "I will put My laws into their minds and will write them on their hearts." This light of understanding in the mind, I say, and this flame in the heart is the law of faith, the new law, the law of Christ, the law of the Spirit, the law of grace. It justifies, fulfills everything, and crucifies the lusts of the flesh. Thus St. Augustine says beautifully on this passage: "In a sense the man who with a love of righteousness lives righteously lives the Law itself."[41] Take note of the words "with a love of righteousness." For this is something that is unknown to nature; it is acquired by faith. Thus 2 Cor. 3:3 states: "You are a letter from Christ delivered by us, written, not with ink but with the Spirit of the living God, not on tablets of stone but on tablets of human hearts."

[40] The Latin is *vita experimentalis;* cf., for example, Thomas Aquinas, *Summa Theologica;* II-II, Q. 172, Art. 1.

[41] Augustine, *Epistolae ad Galatas expositio, Patrologia, Series Latina,* XXXV, 2115.

The Law of the letter is everything that is written with letters, said with words, thought of in thoughts — whether it is tropological, allegorical, anagogical, or finally the doctrine of any mystery at all.[42] This is the Law of works, the old Law, the Law of Moses, the Law of the flesh, the Law of sin, the Law of wrath, the Law of death. It condemns everything, makes all men guilty, increases lusts, and slays; and the more spiritual it is, the more it does so — like the well-known Commandment "You shall not covet" (Ex. 20:17). For this Commandment makes more people guilty than the one that says: "You shall not kill" (Ex. 20:13) or the one that says: "Circumcise your foreskins" (Gen. 17:11) or prescribes similar ceremonies, because without the law of the Spirit a work is never performed well but is always feigned.

The logical conclusion is that the law of the Spirit is that which the Law of the letter requires. I mean the will. Ps. 1:1 says: "But his will (that is, his love) is in the Law of the Lord." Rom. 13:10 says: "Love is the fulfilling of the Law." And 1 Tim. 1:5 states that love is the end of the Law. To express it most plainly and simply, the Law of the letter and the law of the Spirit differ in the same way as the sign and the thing signified, as the word and the thing.[43] Hence when the thing has been obtained, the sign is no longer needed. Consequently, "the Law is not laid down for the just" (1 Tim. 1:9). But as long as we have only the sign, we are being taught to seek the thing itself.

Thus Moses and the prophets, and finally John the Baptist, direct us to Christ. The Law teaches what you owe and what you lack; Christ gives what you should do and have. Therefore those who use the Law otherwise than as a sign by which they are directed to Christ and by which they are to recognize their wretchedness and to seek grace misuse it in the worst way. They rely on their own strength; and as soon as they have heard the Law, they gird themselves to do the works it requires as they seek and presume to find in themselves the real substance of the Law, although they see that they have not found in themselves even the sign, that is, the Law itself.

Furthermore, it follows that every law of the letter is spiritual, just as it can be called spiritual, as Rom. 7:14 states: "We know that the Law is spiritual." And never do we read in Scripture that a law

[42] Cf. the medieval verse translated in *Luther's Works*, I, p. 87, note 10.

[43] Luther is employing the Augustinian distinction between *signum* and *signatum*.

which is written in letters is called carnal, although Origen, impelled by his own opinions, is frequently at great pains to make such a statement.[44] Paul, to be sure, has the expressions "law of the members" (Rom. 7:23) and "lust of the flesh." But this is not the letter; it is what is signified and forbidden by the letter of the Law. It is spiritual, therefore, because it requires the spirit of faith. That is, it is spiritual, not on account of the sign but on account of the thing, since no good work is done unless it is done out of a glad, willing, and joyful heart, that is, in the spirit of freedom. Otherwise — if a law which enjoins only spiritual works must be called spiritual — there will be no spiritual law except the one which, according to our theologians, gives commandments with regard to actions elicited from the heart; and even works of love will not be spiritual. To wash the feet of guests, to come to the aid of a person who is poor, to warn one who is in error, to pray for the sinner, to bear wrong — are these not activities of the body? Indeed, they are — no less than any ceremonial acts of both the Old and the New Testament. It is only the actual spirit of faith that makes a distinction among works. Otherwise there is no difference whatever among works — neither among those that can be done by the soul nor among those that can be done by the body. They are all carnal or according to the letter when they are done under the compulsion of the letter and apart from the law of the Spirit. When they are done because the law of the Spirit is present, then they are spiritual, as we shall see later.

And here, I believe, you see the source of my indignation against so many decrees, statutes, and decretals of the popes. Because of this tyranny the church now lies prostrate and is being laid waste day by day. For since love is growing cold and God is gradually taking away the law of the Spirit because of our sins, laws that cannot be fulfilled without that Spirit should have been done away with entirely. Instead, they are daily increased. This makes God very angry. The popes are imposing on people burdens that are unbearable — especially if you lack the money to buy release — burdens which they themselves would be unwilling or unable to move with even a finger. Meanwhile the feeding of the sheep with the Word of faith and of the Spirit is not even thought of by such watchful shepherds of Christ's sheep! What I bemoan is this, that through so many useless

---

[44] Luther is criticizing the common exegesis of 2 Cor. 3:6; e. g., in Augustine, *On Christian Doctrine*, III, 5; cf. *Luther's Works*, 2, p. 164, note 59.

and harmful laws nothing is being increased except endless offenses against God, since commandments must be fulfilled in the Spirit too. Yet we cannot have the Spirit from ourselves.

Meanwhile, however, I shall give my advice. In the first place, if you have the Spirit and can bear all those things willingly, then do so, just as if you, according to the will of God, were being oppressed under the Turk or some other tyrant. In fact, since the tyranny of laws oppresses consciences, it far exceeds the tyranny of the Turks, which oppresses only bodies or trifling things that have to do with the body — though even in this respect we do not find the Turks surpassing us, if you consider the robbery carried on in the matter of palliums and annates, and of other intolerable hucksterism connected with papal bulls. But if you are unwilling, go and buy with cash or favor — since it cannot be done any other way — the benefits that are owed to you free of charge, and shake your neck from this burden by means of special permissions. Here, however, I have in mind those injunctions the performance of which does not stand in the way of need or love. For such injunctions, as I have said before, should be confidently violated, even out of kindness, after consulting a good man. But here I am speaking of those things which you do unwillingly, even if need or love give no reason for not doing them. For in this case it is better for you to lose a little money than to torment your conscience with the noose of the laws. And do not fear that you are committing simony, since you are not making this purchase eagerly or willingly (for you would prefer that it be given you gratis) but are yielding against your will, as if there were importunate demands. If you are poor or are prevented because the place is far away, at least obey in public for the sake of avoiding offense. In private, however, when you are alone, consult a good man, and be certain that where your pastor has neglected to take care of you, Christ will deal all the more mildly with you, provided that you obey His commandments from the heart.

20. *I have been crucified with Christ; it is no longer I who live, but Christ who lives in me;*

Paul had said that he was dead to the Law; now he describes the manner of his death, which is the cross of Christ. What he says in Gal. 5:24 is pertinent here: "And those who belong to Christ have crucified the flesh with its lusts." And in 1 Peter 4:1 we read: "Since, therefore, Christ suffered in the flesh, arm yourselves with the same thought; for whoever has suffered in the flesh has ceased from sins"; and in the second chapter (v. 24) Peter says: "He Himself bore our sins in His body on the tree, that we might die to sin and live to righteousness." Accordingly, in the fourth chapter of the third book of his *On the Trinity* St. Augustine teaches that the suffering of Christ is both a sacrament and an example — a sacrament because it signifies the death of sin in us and grants it to those who believe, an example because it also behooves us to imitate Him in bodily suffering and dying.[45] The sacrament is what is stated in Rom. 4:25: "Who was put to death for our trespasses and raised for our justification." The example is what is stated in 1 Peter 2:21: "Christ suffered for us, leaving you an example, that you should follow in His steps." Paul treats of the sacrament very extensively in Rom. 6 and 8, in Col. 3, and in many other passages. Thus he says here, too, that he is crucified with Christ according to the sacrament, because he has put sin and lusts to death. What the apostle is saying is this: Those who seek to be justified through the works of the Law not only fail to crucify their flesh but even increase its lusts — so far are they from being able to be justified. For the Law is the strength of sin (1 Cor. 15:56) in that it stimulates lust and its contrary inclination even while forbidding it. But since faith in Christ loves the Law, which forbids lust, it now does the very thing the Law commands; it attacks and crucifies lust.

Therefore it is not the abolition of sin that comes through the Law; it is only the knowledge and the increase of sin, and by this one seeks in vain to be justified. Besides, the righteous man himself does not live; but Christ lives in him, because through faith Christ dwells in him and pours His grace into him, through which it comes about that a man is governed, not by his own spirit but by Christ's. For while we are driven by our own spirit, we follow our lusts and do not crucify them. Consequently, that we believe, that we are righteous, that we are dead to the Law, that we put our lusts to death — all this must be ascribed to Christ, not to us.

> *and the life I now live in the flesh I live by faith in the Son of God, who loved me and gave Himself for me.*

Erasmus comments very aptly. "And what I now live," that is, "the life I now live," as Paul also explains in Rom. 6:10; or "the time

---

[45] Augustine, *On the Trinity*, III, 4, 10.

that I live," as in 1 Peter 4:2: "So as to live for the rest of the time by the will of God." St. Jerome thinks that "to be in the flesh" means something else than "to live in the flesh," because elsewhere Paul has said (Rom. 8:9): "You are not in the flesh," and (v. 8): "Those who are in the flesh cannot please God." With regard to 2 Cor. 10:3 — "For though we walk in the flesh, still we do not make war according to the flesh" — I see this, that he always understands "walking according to the flesh" as something bad. But to the Philippians he writes (1:24) that it is "necessary to remain in the flesh." Therefore I do not know whether this distinction is constant.[46]

What the apostle means, however, is this: "I have said that it is no longer I who live, but that Christ lives in me. But — lest you think, or lest occasion seem to be given for future heretics to think, that the Christian life is outside the flesh, in the religion of the angels (cf. Col. 2:18),[47] in walking among wonders too high for oneself (cf. Ps. 131:1) — Christ lives in me in such a way that I still live my life in the flesh but do not live in the flesh in such a way that my life is of the flesh, in the flesh, or according to the flesh. No, then my life is in faith in the Son of God." It is true that the self-righteous, on the other hand, also live in the flesh — that is, they live in this present life — but they do not live this life in faith in Christ; they live it in the works of the Law. As a result, they live a life that is dead in sins. When Paul says that life in righteousness is a living life, he thereby ties the two kinds of life, physical and spiritual, together and says that physical life is truly life only then when one's life is lived in Christ and in the spirit of faith. For just as the Law puts its worshipers to death with a spiritual death by causing sin to grow strong and to increase, so it makes the life of the body dead, that is, sinful.

Where, then, are our neutralists,[48] who have invented a middle ground between sin and the righteousness of faith — namely, ethical goodness — although the apostle calls the very righteousness of the Law dead? But in the writings of the apostle only that is called dead which is already sin, as he says in 1 Cor. 15:56: "The sting of death

---

[46] Cf. Erasmus, *Paraphrasis, Opera*, VII, 951; Jerome, *Commentarius*, 371.

[47] The Weimar editors suggest that *in religione angelorum* be emended to *in regione angelorum;* but we have kept the reading as it stands, since it is clearly a quotation from Col. 2:18, which reads *in religione angelorum* in the Vulgate.

[48] Cf. p. 256, note 22.

is sin." And Rom. 5:12 speaks of "death through sin." Hence every dead work is "mortal" [49] and undeserving of merit. A work that is dead is at the same time a sin.

21. *I do not nullify the grace of God; for if justification were through the Law, then Christ died to no purpose.*

So great is the wrong of wanting to be justified through the Law by our own works and strength that the apostle calls this nullifying the grace of God. It is not only ingratitude, which in itself is very bad, but also contempt, since the grace of God should have been sought with the utmost zeal. But those people repudiate the grace that has been received free of cost. Certainly a severe rebuke.

This reasoning of the apostle is worthy of serious consideration. "If justification were through the Law, etc." Confidently he declares that either Christ died for nothing — which is the height of blasphemy against God — or that through the Law one has nothing but sin. For those men should be kept far away from Holy Writ who, with distinctions drawn from their own brains, bring into theology various kinds of righteousness and say that one is ethical, that another is the righteousness of faith, and speak of I know not what other kinds.[50] By all means let the state have its own righteousness, the philosophers their own, and everyone his own. But here one must take righteousness in the Scriptural sense; and the apostle says plainly that this righteousness does not exist except through faith in Jesus Christ and that all other works, even those of God's most holy Law, far from affording righteousness, are actually sins and make a man worse in the sight of God. Indeed, they are such great sins and so far away from righteousness that it was necessary for the Son of God to die in order that righteousness might be given to us. In theology, therefore, do not use the term "righteousness" for that which is outside faith in Christ. Moreover, if it is certain that it is not righteousness, it is equally certain that it is sin, and sin that is damnable.

Take note, therefore, of a new righteousness and a new definition of righteousness. For one usually says: "Righteousness is the virtue that renders to everyone his due." [51] Here it is stated that righteous-

---

[49] Cf. *Luther's Works*, 26, p. 121, note 37.

[50] For Luther's own version of "many kinds of righteousness" cf. the introductory remarks to his *Lectures* of 1531 (1535), *Luther's Works*, 26, p. 4.

[51] The definition comes from the first section of Book I of the *Institutes* of Justinian; cf. *Luther's Works*, 36, p. 357, note 17.

ness is faith in Jesus Christ or the virtue by which one believes in Jesus Christ, as in Rom. 10:10: "With the heart man believes unto righteousness"; that is, if anyone wants to be righteous, it is necessary for him to believe in Christ with his heart. And in the third chapter St. Jerome says: "Well put is that true statement of a wise man that the believer does not live as the result of righteousness but is righteous by faith." [52] A beautiful statement indeed!

It follows now that the man who is righteous through faith does not through himself give to anyone what is his; he does this through Another, namely, Jesus Christ, who alone is so righteous as to render to all what should be rendered them. As a matter of fact, they owe everything to Him. But he who believes in Christ and by the spirit of faith has become one with Him not only renders satisfaction now to all but also brings it about that they owe everything to him, since he has all things in common with Christ. His sins are no longer his; they are Christ's. But in Christ sins are unable to overcome righteousness. In fact, they themselves are overcome. Hence they are destroyed in him. Again, Christ's righteousness now belongs not only to Christ; it belongs to His Christian. Therefore the Christian cannot owe anything to anyone or be oppressed by his sins, since he is supported by such great righteousness.

This is that inestimable glory of the Christians; this is the indescribable regard of God's love for us — the regard whereby such great, such precious gifts have been given to us. And it is right for Paul to be so deeply concerned for these gifts, lest they be cast aside. Consequently, this righteousness is also called the righteousness that comes from God, as in 1 Cor. 1:30: "Whom God has made our wisdom, our righteousness and sanctification and redemption." Likewise Rom. 1:16 f.: "I am not ashamed of the Gospel; the righteousness of God is revealed in it through faith for faith, as it is written: 'The righteous man shall live by faith.'" And Rom. 10:3: "Being ignorant of the righteousness that comes from God, and seeking to establish their own, they did not submit to God's righteousness." This is the meaning of that statement in Ps. 31:1: "In Thy righteousness deliver me!" — not by any means in my righteousness, since it is from the Law and is sin. And again in Ps. 143:1: "Answer me in Thy righteousness." And in Ps. 72:1, 7: "Give the king Thy justice, O God, and Thy righteousness to the king's son. In his days will righteousness arise and

---

[52] Jerome, *Commentarius*, 376.

abundance of peace." And in Ps. 96:13: "He will judge the world with righteousness." But why multiply instances? In the Scriptures the righteousness of God is almost always taken in the sense of faith and grace, very rarely in the sense of the sternness with which He condemns the wicked and lets the righteous go free, as is the custom everywhere nowadays.

But if rendering of ourselves to everyone what is his must be called the righteousness of faith, then it is better to understand that we do this through a renunciation — as they call it — of all goods, as the Lord teaches in Luke 14:28 ff. in the parable of the man building a tower and of the one who was going to fight someone stronger than himself (vv. 31 ff.). For those who, in reliance on their own strength, seek to justify and save themselves through the works of the Law build a tower — after the example of those who began the Tower of Babel — and with their paltry supplies of works they go to meet Christ, who will be the all-powerful Judge. He counsels them to reckon up the costs first. They will find that they do not have the ability. Therefore let them give up all presumptuous claims to wisdom, virtue, and righteousness; and while He is still far away, let them ask for peace as they despair of themselves and in complete faith cast themselves on the mercy of the King who will come. For this is how Christ concluded that same parable: "So, therefore, whoever of you does not renounce all that he has cannot be My disciple" (Luke 14:33). This means that you will not be a Christian unless you cast away your own righteousnesses entirely and rely on faith alone.

CHAPTER THREE

1. *O foolish Galatians, who has bewitched you, that you should not obey the truth?*

Now Paul turns again to the Galatians. For Jerome thinks that up to this point he has been speaking against Peter.[1] But I do not know whether he said all this in the presence of Peter. I would suppose that he stopped talking with Peter at the place where he says: "Because by works of the Law shall no flesh be justified" (Gal. 2:16), since he is repeating what, as he writes shortly before this, he said to Peter: "Knowing that a man is not justified on the basis of works of the Law, etc." And I would suppose that from this point on he is again dealing with the Galatians and is overthrowing the works of the Law with the rest of his arguments. Nevertheless, let everyone have his own opinion about this.

Accordingly, Paul is glowing through and through with pious zeal. Although he has filled almost the whole epistle with proofs and refutations, yet now and then he mixes in an exhortation and a rebuke. Sometimes he also impresses the same things by way of repetition, as out of apostolic concern he tries everything. He calls them senseless, foolish, out of their minds. According to Jerome, he does so either because he is chiding them on account of a characteristic of their country, just as he brands the Cretans liars in his Epistle to Titus (1:12) and censures other nations for other vices, or because they had come from greater to lesser things and had begun to be children again, so to speak, by returning to the guardianship of the Law.[2] The latter seems to me the more probable, for in what follows he talks about rudiments, about a custodian, about an heir who is a youngster — obviously referring to their foolishness and childishness. The word "bewitched" also indicates this; for witchcraft is said to be harmful particularly to children and to those who have not reached the age of discretion, as Jerome also remarks.

[1] Jerome, *Commentarius*, 372.
[2] Jerome, *Commentarius*, 372.

But "to bewitch" means to do harm with an evil look, as Vergil says: "I do not know what eye is bewitching my tender lambs." [3] "God knows," says Jerome, "whether this is true or not, because it is possible that devils render a service to this sin." [4] This, I believe, is the ailment of little infants that our womenfolk commonly call *die elbe* or *das hertzgespan*, in which we see infants wasting away, growing thin, and being miserably tormented, sometimes wailing and crying incessantly.[5] The women, in turn, try to counter this ailment with I know not what charms and superstitions; for it is believed that such things are caused by those jealous and spiteful old hags if they envy some mother her beautiful baby. For this reason the Greek word, as Jerome attests, means not only to bewitch but also to envy.

Thus when the Galatians were like newborn infants in Christ and were growing auspiciously, they, too, were [6] harmed by the bewitching false apostles and were led back to the leanness, yes, the wretchedness of the Law. As a result, they were wasting away. And this is a very fine comparison; for just as an enchanter fastens baleful eyes on the infant until he does it harm, so a pernicious teacher fastens his evil eye, that is, his godless wisdom, on simple souls until he corrupts the true understanding in them. For in the Scriptures, as Luke 11:34 states, the eye signifies teaching and knowing, even the teacher himself, as in Job 29:15: "I was an eye for the blind," and in Matt. 18:9: "If your eye causes you to sin." These are the ones whom Scripture calls crafty men, mockers, and deceivers of souls. In Ps. 1:1 we read: "He does not sit in the seat of pestilence." The Hebrew text has "in the seat of the mockers." Prov. 3:32 states: "The perverse man is abomination to the Lord, but the upright are in His confidence."

But here the question arises whether in this passage one is to believe that the apostle is endorsing the notion that witchcraft amounts to something. St. Jerome thinks that he made use of a colloquialism and took an example from a notion of the common people, not because he knew that there was witchcraft.[7] In like manner some

[3] Vergil, *Eclogues*, III, 103.

[4] Jerome, *Commentarius*, 373.

[5] What Luther calls *hertzgespan* (or *Herzspann* in modern German) is cardialgia or heartburn.

[6] We have followed the Jena and St. Louis editors and have changed *sint* to *sunt*.

[7] Jerome, *Commentarius*, 372.

other things in Scripture — such as Arcturus, Orion, and the Pleiades in Job (38:31-32), and in Isaiah (13:21-22; 34:13) the ostriches, the onocentaurs, and the satyrs — seem to be taken from the fables of the heathen. As I have said, I believe that with God's permission those witches, with the aid of devils, are really able to harm little infants for the punishment of unbelievers and the testing of believers, since, as is evident from experience, they also work many other kinds of harm in the bodies of men as well as of cattle and everything. And I believe that the apostle was not unaware of this.

Before whose eyes Jesus Christ was publicly portrayed as crucified.

I see that this passage is treated in various ways. St. Jerome understands "publicly portrayed" to mean that the Galatians learned to know Christ crucified not only from the oral word of the apostles but also from the writings of the prophets, and thus that they knew Him as one who had been written about earlier than and before they knew Him as one who was spoken or preached about. And having been confirmed in their knowledge by this twofold instruction of the written word and the oral word, they should not have fallen away from Christ at all.[8] St. Ambrose, whom Lyra follows, thinks that because the Galatians put their trust in the works of the Law, Christ was publicly portrayed for them in the way that the jurists speak of "proscription"; that is, He was cast out, condemned, and exiled.[9] St. Augustine reads *praescriptus*, meaning "objected to"; and just as a possession is lost through an objection made by another person, so Christ has lost the Galatians, since the false apostles had objected to Him. None of these explanations appeals to me. Erasmus, not unlike Stapulensis, takes it to mean that Christ was described and portrayed for the Galatians in a picture, so to speak, in such a way that they had the clearest knowledge of Him, and yet, being bewitched and fooled, they do not recognize Him now.[10] For those who are under the spell of enchantments and illusions usually fail to discern what is perfectly plain to their eyes and see that which is nowhere at all. And the Greek word προεγράφη seems to lend support to this interpretation. It bothers me, however, that the expression "Christ is crucified in someone" is never used in a good sense in the Scriptures.

[8] Jerome, *Commentarius*, 373.

[9] Ambrose (ascribed), *Commentaria in XII epistolas beati Pauli, Patrologia, Series Latina*, XVII, 372.

[10] Cf. Erasmus, *Paraphrasis, Opera*, VII, 952.

For instance, Heb. 6:6 says: "Since they again crucify in themselves the Son of God." And above he does not say: "Christ was crucified in me." No, he says: "Christ lives in me" (Gal. 2:20). Here, however, he says that Christ is "crucified in you." He undoubtedly groans and is agitated as he makes the statement that Christ does not live in them but is dead; that is, that faith in Him has been blotted out through the righteousness of the Law.

Accordingly, if I were to venture a surmise of my own, I would say, in the first place, that I approve of the word *praescriptus*, whether it is understood of something written or of a picture, so that *praescriptus* means "placed before and shown to the eye." For Paul adds "before the eyes" in order to bring out this meaning. Secondly, if the conjunction "and" is deleted (as in the Greek), the text would stand as follows: "In whose eyes, or before whose eyes, Jesus Christ was presented, crucified among you." That is: "Behold, you yourselves see, and with the previously stated arguments I have brought it about that it is clearly pictured and written before your eyes that Jesus Christ has been crucified among you." That this is the sense will, I believe, not be denied if you consider what has gone before, yes, the line of thought of the whole epistle. For previously Paul had said: "I do not nullify the grace of God" (2:21) and "It is not I who live" (v. 20). Likewise: "If justification were on the basis of the Law, then Christ died to no purpose" (v. 21). All this leads to the conclusion that (just as among the Jews) Christ has been crucified among all those who put their trust, not in Him but in themselves and in the Law; for then the grace of God has been rejected, and Christ does not live in them. What, then, is left except that He has died and has been crucified among them? But in his fervor the apostle uses words that glow with much emphasis [11] and are impetuous, as it were. "Presented before your eyes," he declares, as if he were saying: "I do not know how I could show this more clearly." Then he mentions not only the name "Christ," but he mentions "Jesus Christ." He speaks both names with emphasis. Finally he adds the words "crucified among you." It would have been milder if this had not happened "among you who were so great"; and it would have been gentler if He had "died" or "suffered" or been "weak." But harshly he says "crucified among you," that is, treated by you in the most shameful manner.

[11] The technical term was *epitasis*.

What, pray, would he do if now, too, he saw that Christ is being crucified even more in the church by the laws of men? Surely he would say what he said with tears in his eyes in Acts 20:29: "After my departure fierce wolves will come in among you, not sparing the flock, etc."

2. *Let me ask you only this: Did you receive the Spirit by works of the Law or by hearing with faith?*

Note how effectively Paul deals with the subject on the basis of experience. For what excuse will they offer here? "Granted," he says, "that the rest of the arguments I have used are weak, what will you say here? Teach me only this. Come, let me be your pupil here. You who have busied yourselves with the works of the Law, tell me whether you ever received the Spirit before you came to faith by my proclamation of Christ?" Thus he confidently taunts them; and now, as they are bound, so to speak, with a chain that cannot be loosened, he says to them:

3. *Are you so foolish? Having begun with the Spirit, are you now ending with the flesh?*

It is clear, however, that this was written by the apostle for those who had come to faith out of Judaism and formerly had busied themselves with the works of the Law but then had received the Holy Spirit by a visible sign, as He used to be given at that time. Otherwise this passage would not bear hard enough upon them. Or at least he is writing for a mixed group of Gentiles and Jews, but for Gentiles who had previously been drawn under the Law by the Jews. Unless you were to say that the apostle is talking about the works of the Law into which they had fallen back from faith in Christ, which, in my opinion, is really more probable; for he was very sure that they had not received the Spirit from the false apostles as they had previously received it through Paul.

But I surely do not believe it when in this passage St. Jerome distinguishes the works of the Law from good works and thinks that Cornelius received the Spirit on the basis of works (Acts 10:44 ff.); [12] for it is clear that the Holy Spirit descended on them at Peter's preaching, that is, when they heard with faith, as he says here. Nor were Abraham, Moses, and the rest of the saints justified, as he tries

[12] Jerome, *Commentarius*, 374.

to maintain, on the basis of works of the natural law. No, they were justified on the basis of faith, as is written here and in Rom. 4:1 ff. The apostle is referring not only to the Ceremonial Law but to absolutely every law; for since it is faith alone that justifies and does good works, it follows that absolutely no works of any law whatever justify, and that the works of no law are good, but that only the works of faith are good. I have mentioned this however, to remind the reader of Jerome's writings of what Jerome himself claims both in his prolog and in his letter to St. Augustine, namely, that he wrote commentaries in which he was accustomed to adduce opinions of others but to let his readers have freedom of opinion.[13] For since not a few theologians and jurists fail to observe this, they sometimes follow monstrous opinions instead of the familiar doctrine of the church.

But the expression "by the hearing of faith" Erasmus, as always, explains beautifully to mean that which is audible, namely, as he says, the actual speaking that is heard.[14] Therefore "hearing of faith" means the same as the Word of faith that is heard. Acts 10:44: "While Peter was still saying this, the Holy Spirit fell on all who heard the Word." Likewise Is. 53:1: "Lord, who has believed what we have heard?" And Hab. 3:2: "O Lord, I heard the report of Thee, and I was afraid." Thus this is a frequent way of speaking in Scripture. Jer. 49:14 and Obad. 1:1 say: "We have heard tidings from the Lord."

Here, however, St. Jerome is again concerned with the question how the deaf become Christians,[15] especially since Rom. 10:14 says: "How are they to hear without a preacher? How are they to believe in Him of whom they have never heard?" And, as the apostle's step-by-step sequence puts it in that passage, first there is a sending, then preaching, then hearing, then believing, then an invoking, and thus the attaining of salvation. I shall add: How are infants saved, and how are they baptized, when they themselves do not hear? Jerome answers first that faith's coming from hearing can be taken as being partial or entire. But Paul overcomes this argument. "How," he says, "are they to believe in Him of whom they have never heard?" (Rom. 10:14.) Secondly, Jerome says that the deaf can learn the

[13] Jerome, *Commentarius*, 332—333.

[14] Cf. Erasmus, *Paraphrasis*, *Opera*, VII, 952.

[15] Jerome, *Commentarius*, 374—375.

Gospel from the attitude and the behavior of others. But where does this leave infants? Therefore I follow the opinion he mentions last, namely, that to the Word of God nothing is deaf and that it speaks to those ears of which it is said: "He who has ears to hear, let him hear" (Matt. 11:15). I like this answer very much, because the Word of God is not heard even among adults and those who hear unless the Spirit promotes growth inwardly. Accordingly, it is a Word of power and grace when it infuses the Spirit at the same time that it strikes the ears. But if it does not infuse the Spirit, then he who hears does not differ at all from one who is deaf. Consequently, when an infant is not confused by other things, it is easier for the very sound of the Word — the sound uttered through the ministry of the church — to be operative through the Spirit. Then there is greater susceptibility on the part of the child.

Most powerfully, therefore, Paul here strikes down the works of the Law, then also the dreams of our theologians who have invented the merit of congruity for obtaining grace.[16] But the apostle says: "Not by works but by the hearing of the Word." That is, if you endure the Word, then you may have rest from your works and may observe the Lord's Sabbath, in order that you may hear what the Lord your God says to you. Therefore be sure to mark this memorable lesson that Paul has given. If you want to obtain grace, then see to it that you hear the Word of God attentively or meditate on it diligently. The Word, I say, and only the Word, is the vehicle of God's grace. For what you call works of congruity either are evil or the grace that produces them must already have come. The verdict that the Spirit is received from the hearing of faith stands firm. All those who have received the Spirit have received it in this way. Therefore do not reject God's plan and fabricate your own way.

Note the words "ending with the flesh," that is, finishing, ceasing, defecting. From this passage it is clear that flesh is taken not only in the sense of sensuality or the lusts of the flesh but in the sense of everything that is outside grace and the Spirit of Christ. For it is certain that the Galatians are ending with the flesh, not because they were indulging in excesses and lusts or in carnality in some of their customs, but because they were abandoning faith and seeking the works of the Law and its righteousness. But the righteousness of the Law and its works are not just things of the senses, since to this there

---

[16] See the fuller discussion in *Luther's Works*, 26, 124 ff.

belong also the opinion and trust which are in the heart. Whatever, therefore, does not proceed from faith is flesh (Rom. 14:23). Heb. 9:10: "In various kinds of righteousness and washings of the flesh." Thus Gen. 6:3: "My Spirit shall not abide in man forever, for he is flesh." It does not say "for he *has* flesh"; the statement is "for he *is* flesh." And Rom. 7:18: "I know that nothing good dwells within me, that is, in my flesh." He himself, therefore, and his flesh are one and the same thing, as much as is descended from Adam. Thus again: "Flesh and blood will not possess the kingdom of God" (1 Cor. 15:50), and Matt. 16:17: "Flesh and blood has not revealed this to you." But 1 Cor. 3:3 also says: "You are still of the flesh, you are men," although their quarrel was only over the names of the apostles. Thus it comes about that every teaching and righteousness of all men, philosophers, orators, even pontiffs, is of the flesh, since they do not teach faith. And if you listen to the apostle here, you will realize that it is a serious misuse of words for those canonical regulations that are established with regard to ranks and riches to be called sacred canons.[17] On the other hand, nothing is so carnal and external that it does not become spiritual if it is done by the working of the Spirit of faith. The Galatians, therefore, are brought to an end in the flesh when they accept the attitude and opinion that come from any works of the Law whatever, especially when they have abandoned faith. But as to the fact that Origen and St. Jerome gather from the apostle's words that there is a threefold kind of man — the spiritual, the animal (which he understands to be neutral and intermediate), and the carnal — perhaps we shall see later what view to take.[18]

4. *Did you experience so many things in vain? — if it really is in vain.*

St. Jerome has various comments on this passage. Briefly, however, I follow just one opinion, namely, that when the Galatians were running well in faith in Christ, they had suffered many things, especially from the Jews, who never failed to persecute any Christian, as is clear from the Acts of the Apostles and many epistles of Paul. Yet they experienced these things in vain if by falling back into the Law they remained outside faith. Nevertheless, because he hopes that they will return, he says: "If it really is in vain"; as if he were saying: "If

[17] The "sacred canons" were the legislation dealing with ecclesiastical matters, including, as Luther notes here, questions of rights and privileges in the church.

[18] Cf. p. 363, note 42.

you return, you have not experienced in vain." For he argues from the loss they have experienced and from their vain toil in order to arouse them, because through the Law they have fallen away, not only from the righteousness of Christ but at the same time also from all His merits and rewards.

5. *Does He who supplies the Spirit to you and works miracles among you do so by works of the Law or by hearing with faith?*

You have to supply the words "supplies" and "works." But Paul is now repeating and driving home what he had already said above. For he inquires into their experience, and thereby he binds them very strongly. At the same time, however, it is his purpose to add and to append what follows. For earlier he had set before them only the fact that they had received the Spirit; but now he also adduces the fact that they had done mighty deeds, that is, miracles; and they could not deny that these had not been done previously on the strength of the works of the Law.

6. *Just as Abraham believed God, and it was reckoned to him as righteousness.*

Paul treats this example and argument extensively in Rom. 4:9, where he shows that Abraham had come to faith before circumcision and that this faith was reckoned to him as righteousness. It is probably true that this same passage had also been orally expounded by him among the Galatians and that now they are being reminded of it and recalled to their previous understanding of it.

7. *So you see that it is men of faith who are the sons of Abraham.*

"You see," therefore, from the Scripture passage just cited that Abraham's children are not those who come from his offspring or from circumcision. Rom. 4:11 states: "He received circumcision as a sign or seal of the righteousness which he had by faith while he was still uncircumcised. The purpose was to make him the father of all who believe without being circumcised, and who thus have righteousness reckoned to them." And Rom. 9:7-8 states: "And not all are children of Abraham because they are his descendants; but: Through Isaac shall your descendants be named. This means that it is not the children of the flesh who are the children of God, but the children of the promise are reckoned as descendants."

From this passage you see how intently and observantly Paul wants Scripture to be read. For who would have drawn these proofs from the text of Genesis: that Abraham believed before circumcision; that he obtained Isaac in no other way than through the promise; that this signifies that just as Isaac was received and called to be an offspring for him through the faith of Abraham, who believed God's promise, so no one else is Abraham's son or offspring except the one who is promised and received by faith; and that the proud boast of the Jews by which they glory in the flesh of their fathers had been shattered so long before this?

That figure of speech, "to be of faith," "to be of works," is now well enough known, I think. Those who believe "are of faith," and later, those who engage in works "are of the works of the Law." Of the same kind are the expressions "to be of the Law," "of circumcision," and similar ones in Paul.

But the apostle does not observe the rules of dialectical argumentation. For he says that the Spirit was supplied and mighty deeds were done as a result of the hearing of faith, and he proves this on the ground that this was the way in which Abraham's faith was reckoned as righteousness. Now is not the fact that faith is reckoned as righteousness a receiving of the Spirit? So either he proves nothing or the reception of the Spirit and the fact that faith is reckoned as righteousness will be the same thing. And this is true; it is introduced in order that the divine imputation may not be regarded as amounting to nothing outside God, as some think that the apostle's word "grace" means a favorable disposition rather than a gift.[19] For when God is favorable, and when He imputes, the Spirit is really received, both the gift and the grace. Otherwise grace was there from eternity and remains within God, if it signifies only a favorable disposition in the way that favor is understood among men. For just as God loves in very fact, not in word only, so, too, He is favorably disposed with the thing that is present, not only with the word.

Nor does it seem to be a logical argumentation when he says: "Abraham believed; therefore those who are of faith are the children of Abraham." According to the same dialectic, you could say: "Abraham had a son by his wife; or he ate; or he did something else. Therefore whoever does the same thing is a son of his." In the end

---

[19] See Luther's further development of this in his treatise *Against Latomus*, *Luther's Works*, 32, pp. 226—228.

the Jews will have their opinion confirmed, namely, that Abraham was circumcised, and therefore his children will be circumcised. The apostle, however, is thinking of Abraham when he got Isaac, who alone was promised to him as offspring on the strength of faith. For he was not commended for his faith when he begat Ishmael, but he was ordained as the father of faith and of many nations when he received his true son and legitimate offspring. Consequently, Isaac is not so much a son of the flesh as of faith. Abraham's flesh was unable to beget Isaac; his faith did so, albeit from his own flesh. Hence Isaac is not so much the son of Abraham as of one who believed God's promise. This is why so many words are used in Genesis to describe the promise of the offspring and Abraham's faith in this same promise, and to describe the naming, in Isaac, of the offspring that was promised and believed — in order to show that Abraham's children are not those who are born of the flesh but are those who are born of faith. Therefore what Paul had said rather briefly he now pursues more extensively: how the children of Abraham are those who are of faith, that is, because of the promise. And this did not happen with regard to Ishmael. For this reason Ishamael was not reckoned as offspring for Abraham.

8. *And the Scripture, foreseeing that God would justify the Gentiles by faith, preached the Gospel beforehand to Abraham, saying: In you shall all the nations be blessed.*

"Foreseeing," that is, seeing far in advance. "Scripture," that is, the Spirit in Scripture. If we take what is said here, "In you shall all the nations be blessed," as referring to what is written in Gen. 12:3, the apostle presents us with a difficulty — not only the one with which St. Jerome troubles himself, namely, that the apostles adduce the sense rather than the words;[20] but rather this difficulty, that at this time the promise of a son had not yet been made to Abraham and that he himself had not yet been commended for his faith. This happened in Gen. 15:4. Hence Jerome takes this as referring to Gen. 22:18, where after Abraham's trial, it is said: "And by your descendants shall all the nations of the earth be blessed because you have obeyed My voice." In the present passage, however, the apostle does not say, "in your offspring"; he says, "in you," as is stated in Gen. 12:3. Following Jerome, I, too, think that Paul omitted "in your offspring" out of a concern for brevity, since he intended to use both

[20] Jerome, *Commentarius*, 378.

expressions immediately after this. "Now to Abraham," he says, "the promises were made, and to his offspring." And so it is true that the promise was made both with reference to Abraham and with reference to his offspring. It makes no difference, however, which of the two statements he made here.

Since, then, it was to Abraham that these things were said, not to any kind of man or to one who was carnal, but to a man who already believed, was obedient, spiritual, and a completely different person — in short, to one who had the promise — it follows that Scripture wanted to teach us that there are no children of Abraham except those who are the children and the offspring of such a man, of this man Abraham — so much so that even those who were not of his flesh should become his children, namely, the Gentiles, as he says here, because God justifies the Gentiles through faith, as Scripture had foreseen and had declared to Abraham. Therefore we are blessed in Abraham. But in which Abraham? Surely in the Abraham who believed. But if we are outside Abraham, we are cursed instead, even if we are in the flesh of Abraham, because Scripture is not dealing with Abraham's flesh. Therefore those who believe God, as Abraham did, are in Abraham.

9. *So, then, those who are men of faith are blessed with Abraham, who had faith.*

Note the epithet applied to Abraham: "men of faith." They will be blessed together with Abraham, who believed, not together with the flesh that begets or does other things. For it is only to him as a believer that Scripture attributes children or offspring. Therefore those who are without faith do not bear the image and heritage of their father. Hence they are not really children either; they are bastards.

But some garrulous fellow will still object: "This kind of argumentation will not hold water either: Abraham believes; therefore those who believe are his children. For although Abraham gained a son and offspring through his faith, it does not follow from this that his children must believe. Otherwise everything Abraham gained by believing will have to believe or not belong to Abraham. But then it will be necessary for the land of Canaan to believe. It is enough, therefore, that Abraham believed and that he gained children; but it is not necessary that his children be believers on this account." The answer is: first, that the apostle thinks that for the Galatians, as rather unsophisticated people, it is enough if they know that they cannot be children of Abraham unless they are like him. The deeper explanation of this mystery, which he follows up in Rom. 9:6 ff.,[21] he purposely omits here. For in fact there are no children of Abraham except the children of the promise. Since, however, the divine promise and predestination cannot be false, it will turn out without difficulty and with unfailing logic that all who were promised are also believers, in order that in this way the faith of those who were promised may rest, not on the necessity of works nor on their faith but on the firmness of God's election. In this passage it was enough to commend the imitation of Abraham, not to drive home the sublimity of the promise and of predestination.

Accordingly, even though the aforementioned conclusion — "Abraham believes; therefore his children will believe" — does not hold water, unless you consider the children of the promise (who will be established neither in their own righteousness nor in that of Abraham, but in God's election, and who will not believe because they will be Abraham's children but will be Abraham's children because they will believe with the greatest certainty, since they will be granted to Abraham by God, who does not lie when He promises), still this conclusion does hold water: "Abraham believed; therefore his children should believe, if they want to be his children." This, I say, was enough for the foolish Galatians. Statements of a different kind had to be made to the wise Romans. And so Abraham's children are those who believe; others are not.

10. *For all who rely on works of the Law are under a curse; for it is written: Cursed be everyone who does not abide by all things written in the book of the Law, and do them.*

Paul had said that those who are of faith are blessed. Now with another argument and one taken from the opposite point of view he says that those who are of works are cursed. But note the apostle's strange syllogism. On the basis of Deut. 27:16 he states that those who do not do the things that are written in the book of the Law are cursed. From this negative statement he draws this positive conclusion: cursed are those who do the works of the Law. Does this not affirm what Moses denies? And to make the absurdity greater, Paul proves his affirmative conclusion through the negative statement of Moses.

[21] The original has "Rom. 10," but this is clearly a discussion of Rom. 9:6 ff.

A Festus Porcius would say: "Paul, you are mad; your great learning is turning you mad" (Acts 26:24). What, then, are we going to say? Are those blessed who do not do the works of the Law, even on the authority of so great an apostle? But Moses calls those cursed who do not do those works. Therefore it remains, as we have already said above, that all who are outside faith do indeed do the works of the Law; but they do not fulfill the Law. For the works of the Law are feigned works, as Paul also says below in chapter 6:13: "For even those who receive circumcision do not themselves keep the Law"; and in chapter 5:3: "I testify to every man who receives circumcision that he is bound to keep the whole Law."

Take note! If one receives circumcision, he is not fulfilling any of the whole Law; therefore he is not, even if he does any other work of the Law. The result is that with this word Moses has forced all men under the curse; and when he says: "Cursed be everyone, etc.," he means exactly what he would mean if he were to say: "No man will do these things that are written; therefore all will be cursed and in need of Christ as Redeemer." Hence so far as the apostle and the truth itself are concerned, it is firmly established that those who do the works of the Law do not fulfill the Law, and that when doing them they fail to do them, just as Christ said of such people that hearing they do not hear and seeing they do not see (Matt. 13:13). For to themselves they seem to be fulfilling the Law and to be doing the works of the Law. Instead, however, they are only pretending, since without grace they are able to cleanse neither the heart nor the body. For this reason nothing can be pure to the impure (Titus 1:15).

I think that by this time my neutralist opponents, who have devised certain works that are neutral — works that are good so far as morals are concerned — have been struck down sufficiently by this passage.[22] Here the apostle pronounces the works of the Law cursed — works of God's Law, I say, which surely were better than those dictated by nature, works, moreover, which will make smug persons of those who are snoring. But they say that the apostle is speaking of the ceremonial laws, which now bring death. On the contrary, the ceremonial laws neither are nor ever have been evil; but reliance on them is evil, as St. Augustine teaches.[23] Secondly, it is evident that

[22] See p. 239.

[23] Cf., for example, Augustine, *Contra duas epistolas Pelagianorum*, III, 10—11.

the apostle is speaking of all laws, because — not withstanding Jerome's objections — to Moses' words he has added "everyone" and "all" when he mentions "things written in the book of the Law." Most forceful, however, is the fact that presently he will say that Christ has redeemed us from the curse of the Law. But the Gentiles were never under the curse of the Ceremonial Law. Therefore all the redeemed were under the curse of the Law. For, as I have also said before, Christ would have achieved too little if He had freed us from circumcision, Sabbaths, clothing, foods, and washings, and not to a far greater extent from the more grievous sins against the Law — lust, greed, wrath, godlessness. Then He would really not have been a Savior of souls; He would have been a Savior of bodies, because all these things had to do with the body. Accordingly, the work of any law whatever is really sin and a curse if it is done outside faith, that is, outside purity of heart, innocence, and righteousness.

I want to leave it to the judgment of the reader whether it is the same thing or something different when Paul speaks of those "who rely on the works of the Law" and when Moses speaks of him "who does not remain" or, as the Hebrew has it, "does not confirm all things, etc., to do them." Perhaps it is one thing to do the works of the Law and another thing to do the things that are written, so that doing the things that are written is identical with fulfilling the Law and doing the works of the Law is identical with pretending fulfillment by means of certain outward works, as Christ says: "Why do you call Me 'Lord, Lord' and not do what I tell you?" (Luke 6:46.) And in Rom. 2:13 we read: "Not the hearers but the doers of the Law will be justified." For it is certain that the curse remains on both — on those who fail to do the works of the Law, as Moses says, and on those who rely on the works of the Law, as the apostle says. It is, therefore, altogether Paul's way of speaking, as I have said, that those who do the works of the Law are not doing the things that are written in the Law, in which faith is certainly written. Faith alone fulfills all the demands of the Law.

11. *Now it is evident that no man is justified before God by the Law, for the just shall live by faith.*

This is a general premise. Paul intends to explain the quotation from Moses. It is as if he were saying: "You hear from Moses that he who has not done the things that are written is cursed. In like manner, I have assumed that such people are those who rely on works." That both statements are true is proved by this, that before God no one will be justified in the Law. If he will not be justified before God, then he does not do the things that are written. But if this is the case, he is really cursed. For those who do the things that are written will be justified. But that those who busy themselves with the Law do not keep it is clearly proved by the statement that "the just shall live by faith" (Hab. 2:4). If Scripture is true here, as it must be, and the works of the Law, when they are without faith, are unquestionably dead, he who does them is unrighteous. If he is unrighteous, then he does not do the things that are written. Here I should also like the phrase "in the Law" to be understood as meaning "through the Law" or "by the Law," so that the sense is: Through the Law no one will be righteous before God. Thus the phrase at the same time includes the works of the Law.

12. *But the Law does not rest on faith.*

This is what I have said: that no one is justified by the Law, for the righteous man will be justified by faith alone. But the Law and faith are not the same thing. Neither the Law itself nor its works are from faith or with faith. Hence they are righteous before men; but they are not righteous before God, as the following statement shows.

For he who does them shall live by them.

This word from Lev. 18:5 he also quotes in Rom. 10:5. Now the apostle's meaning is this: The Law does not give life or justify before God; but he who does the things that belong to the Law will, as a human being, live by them, that is, he will evade the penalty of the Law and will gain the Law's reward; but he will not live in God or as a child of Abraham. Therefore ponder the force of these words. A man will live by the works of the Law even though he is dead before God. A man, I say, not a rightous man. And in those works, his own works, I say, he will live; that is, he will protect his life, lest he be killed by the judgment of the Law. The righteous man, however, will not live by those works; he will live by faith.

Therefore remember that in this passage you have learned from the apostle that the works of the Law are those by which we appear to be rightous before man and to be observers of the Law. But within, because faith is lacking, we are anything but righteous. Hence through the Law nothing is produced but a hypocrite and a tomb that is good to look at on the outside but is full of filth inside (Matt. 23:27). For the things that kept St. Jerome from understanding Paul in these and similar passages were his failure to recognize the works of the Law correctly and Origen's excessive allegorizing. For he says in this place that Moses and the prophets were under the works of the Law and under the curse, which is altogether false; for by faith they lived before God justified and sanctified even before the Law and the works of the Law were enjoined, of which he himself says that they were only ceremonial in nature. Nevertheless, later on, thanks to the power of the truth, he gets back on the road when he says that they were sinners according to the statement: "There is not a righteous man on earth who does good and never sins" (Eccl. 7:20), which surely must be understood of the Moral Law. Of the same sort is also the fact that he understands the words "the just lives by faith" in this way, that if faith has been added to a righteous man, then his righteousness will be a living one. Thus Jerome asserts that there are virtues without faith, but that they are deficient.[24] But let the prudent reader take these and other statements in such a way as to remember that these notions were brought in by St. Jerome from others. No one is righteous before faith. On the contrary, he is justified without charge, and he receives good instead of evil. For the apostle means to say that on the basis of the Law a man lives in the sight of his fellowman, but that the righteous man lives through faith in the sight of God, which means that faith is a man's righteousness, life, and salvation in the sight of God, and that righteousness does not come before faith, but that righteousness and life come through faith.

13. *Christ redeemed us from the curse of the Law, having become a curse for us — for it is written: Cursed be everyone who hangs on a tree —*

14. *that in Christ Jesus the blessing of Abraham might come upon the Gentiles, that we might receive the promise of the Spirit through faith.*

In the first place, I find fault with those who are not under the curse of the Law and who have no need of Christ as the Redeemer. They are those who assert that it is one thing to be against the Law and another thing to be against the intent of the Law. "He who acts contrary to the Law sins, but he who acts contrary to the Law's intent

---

[24] Jerome, *Commentarius*, 384.

does not sin but only comes short of what it good." [25] Who can endure this poison? But listen to the kind of proof they bring (but what they call "intent" is the fact that God requires the works of the Law to be done in love). If man, they say, were held to the intent of the Law, it would follow that he who exists outside grace would be sinning continually by not killing, not committing adultery, not stealing, etc. My answer is: He does not sin by not killing, etc.; but he sins inwardly by hating, lusting, secretly coveting, and when he is obviously angered. For this hidden uncleanness of the heart and of the flesh is not taken away except by faith through the grace of Christ. Therefore the intent of the Law is not this, that it be kept in grace, as though grace were a kind of requirement. But the Law aims to be kept. It cannot, however, be kept without grace. Therefore it compels one to seek grace. Accordingly, we are all under the curse of the Law, we who are without the grace of faith, as has already been stated enough. For since the just lives only by faith, the curse of the Law against those who do not believe is clear, lest we make Christ's work of redemption in vain or refer it only to ceremonial matters, from which even a human being could have redeemed us. Finally, then, the works of the Law could have been done with our own powers. It remains, therefore, that He has redeemed us from wrath, godlessness, lust, and the other evils planted in our heart and flesh through Adam and Eve, because of which we all were made unclean and were devoting ourselves to polluted righteousnesses. Thus we were fulfilling nothing of the Law. Therefore we were justly destined for a curse and for condemnation. So through the Law we have no aid. No, through it we have a disclosure and a reminder of our wickedness. But just as Paul tells the Corinthians that Christ was made sin for us in order that we might be the righteousness of God in Him (2 Cor. 5:21), so here he says that Christ was made a curse in order that in this same Christ the blessing of Abraham might come to the Gentiles. In an altogether similar way of speaking we may say: He died in order that we might be life in Him. He was brought to shame in order that we might be made an honor in Him. He became all things for us in order that we might become all things in Him. This means: If we believe in Him, we are already fulfilling the Law and are free from the curse of the

---

[25] This distinction is related to the question of keeping the Commandments *quoad substantiam facti;* cf. p. 404, note 36.

Law. For what we deserved — to be cursed and damned — He underwent and paid for us.

St. Jerome takes uncommonly great pains to keep from admitting that Christ was cursed by God.[26] First he considers the fact that the apostle does not reproduce the words of the Law as they are given in Deut. 21:23: "A hanged man is accursed by God." The apostle, however, following the Septuagint, says: "Cursed be everyone who hangs on a tree." He omits the little phrase "by God," which the Septuagint added. To put it briefly, even though the expressions "on a tree" and "everyone" are not found in the Hebrew text, nevertheless the preceding context compels one to understand Moses as speaking of anyone at all who is hanged on a tree. Consequently, the apostle has changed nothing that could be disturbing. Moreover, the fact that he omitted "by God" is not disturbing either. To the apostle it was certain that this would be understood as having been done by God. St. Augustine relates that certain ill-instructed persons wanted this to be understood of the traitor Judas, who hanged himself; Stapulensis has a different opinion.[27]

But the text of the apostle is clear. He says that Christ was made a curse, not because He had committed anything deserving of a curse, but because it is a general verdict of Scriptures that everyone who has hung on a tree has been cursed by God. Perhaps it was because it sounded dreadful for Christ to be called a curse that the apostle at once softened this statement by adducing the authority of Scripture. It means nothing, therefore, that St. Jerome does not want this word to be understood of Christ, since by adducing it as a general verdict the apostle wanted to prove that what he had said referred to Christ. For since Christ Himself says (Luke 22:37) on the basis of Is. 53:12 that He is to be "numbered with the transgressors," what is so monstrous about calling Him cursed together with those who are cursed? If He was numbered with the transgressors, certainly He must also be called what the transgressors are called and suffer what they suffer.

Man, however, is twofold. There is an inward man and an outward man. Thus there is also a twofold blessing and a twofold curse. The inner blessing is grace and righteousness in the Holy Spirit. This

---

[26] Jerome, *Commentarius*, 386—389.

[27] Augustine, *Epistolae ad Galatas expositio, Patrologia, Series Latina*, XXXV, 2119.

was specially promised to Abraham in Christ. The inner curse is sin and iniquity, as Ps. 119:21 states: "Cursed are those who turn aside from Thy commandments." And in Matt. 25:41 we read: "Depart, you cursed, etc." Jer. 48:10 says: "Cursed is he who does the work of the Lord with slackness"; and in Jer. 17:5 [28] we read: "Cursed is the man who trusts in man." The outward blessing consists in an abundance of bodily things. This was characteristic of the old Law. The curse is poverty, as Mal. 3:9 states: "And in your poverty you are cursed." Thus Christ cursed the fig tree, and it withered (Matt. 21:19). Thus Elisha cursed the children of Bethel (2 Kings 2:24). So let it be no cause for uneasiness that Christ, together with all His saints, is cursed with an outward curse and at the same time is blessed with the inward blessing, as Ps. 109:28 states: "Let them curse, but do Thou bless!" Thus, too, it is no ground for horror that Christ died, that He suffered, that He was crucified. No indeed. "Blessed are you," He says, "when men revile you" (Matt. 5:11).

But you will say: "You are not yet proving that He was cursed by God; for this is what bothered St. Jerome." My answer is: "The curses of men undoubtedly affect a person when God ordains it, as 2 Sam. 16:10 states: 'The Lord commanded him to curse David,' and in the same place: 'Let him alone, and let him curse; for the Lord has bidden him.' God did not command Shimei to curse, but when he was full of cursings, God — in order to use his wickedness for good — willed that he spew out his curses against David."

Moreover, as to St. Jerome's bold denial that anyone is ever found to be cursed by God in Scripture and that the name of God is never associated with a curse, I wonder how he understood this, that in Gen. 3:14 the serpent is cursed by God and that the earth is cursed in Adam's work (v. 17). But God also curses Cain in Gen. 4:11. In 2 Kings 2:24 Elisha cursed the children of Bethel in the name of the Lord. And in Hab. 3:14 we read: "Thou hast cursed with his shafts." And Mal. 2:2: "I will curse your blessings, and I will bless your cursings." Perhaps the saintly man was disturbed because in colloquial usage "curse" generally sounds as though it meant the destruction of all things, especially those that are spiritual and eternal. But it was certainly not in this way that Cain and the earth were cursed, for God says: "You are cursed from the ground." For perhaps St. Jerome

---

[28] Only the first of these two quotations from Jeremiah is identified in the original.

will understand the statement in Matt. 25:41 — "Depart, you cursed" — as meaning that a curse is being pronounced rather than that cursing is being done.

But back to the apostle. "That in Christ Jesus the blessing of Abraham might come upon the Gentiles"; that is to say, in order that the blessing promised to Abraham might be fulfilled, namely, that in faith he should be the father of many nations. This faith, I say, was promised in the blessing. Here again, therefore, he touches briefly and obscurely on the fact that the Gentiles will be children of Abraham, not because they will imitate him, but because they have received the promise; and that they will imitate him because they will be his children as a result of God's promise and its fulfillment, not as a result of the deeds and the imitating of the Gentiles. It is not the imitation that makes sons; it is sonship that makes imitators. But he adds "in Christ," lest he veer from his aim, because it was not on account of their own merits that the Gentiles became Abraham's children; they became God's children in no other way than through Christ, who merited this for them and was received by them through faith, as now follows: "That we might receive the promise of the Spirit" — that is, the promise that the Holy Spirit is to be given — "through faith"; for the Holy Spirit was promised to Abraham when the blessing of faith was promised to him. Because of Christ's merit faith is also given through the Holy Spirit in the Word and hearing of the Gospel.

15. *To give a human example, brethren: no one annuls even a man's will, or adds to it, once it has been ratified.*

The apostle cuts his thought short;[29] for one has to add: "So much less, then, should anyone spurn, or add to, the testament of God after it has been ratified."

Paul is giving "a human example" in order, as Jerome supposes, to persuade the unlearned Galatians of divine truths by means of a human analogy.[30] But in my judgment no one is so learned that he does not need analogies of this kind in learning to know Christ. On the contrary, this type of analogy was necessary to the highest degree. Otherwise it would be more difficult to understand than Rom. 4, where he treats the same thing without an example of this kind; and I have not yet seen anyone who could explain it adequately.

[29] Luther is referring to the grammatical phenomenon called "apocope."
[30] Jerome, *Commentarius*, 390.

Let us, therefore, set before our eyes both things: the analogy and the fact itself. Then we shall see with how strong an argument Paul again breaks down the righteousness of the Law. Now the conclusion he wants to draw is this: If righteousness can be acquired of ourselves through the Law and its works, the promise of a blessing made to Abraham is useless, because then we are able to become righteous without it through the Law; or it itself is surely not sufficient to justify if the righteousness of the Law has to be added to it; and thus the testament and promise of God is either superfluous, or it is deficient and requires the addition of something else. Both notions, however, are utterly detestable. Therefore the opposite is true, namely, that the righteousness of the Law is neither necessary nor sufficient. Take note! A very strong argument indeed!

So let us take a look. In every testament there is a testator. There is one for whom the testament is made; there is the testament itself; and there is the legacy that is being attested or bequeathed. This is the situation here. God is the Testator, for it is He Himself who promises and bequeaths. Abraham and his offspring are those for whom the testament is made as heirs of God, the Testator. The testament is the promise itself (Gen. 12:2 ff.[31] and 17:1 ff.). That which is bequeathed is the inheritance itself, that is, the grace and the righteousness of faith, namely, the blessing of the Gentiles in the offspring of Abraham. If, therefore, the grace of the promise and the righteousness of God, which has been tendered through Christ — and in this way God's testament has been ratified through His death, yes, executed and distributed — if this does not suffice unless you also have the righteousness of the Law, is God's testament, which has not only been declared but has also been ratified and fulfilled, not now rendered invalid, and is not something being added to it? But this should not be done even in the case of a man's testament. If grace is sufficient, however, and the testament of God is firm, it is clear that one should not seek the righteousness of the Law. The same thing is said in Rom. 4:14: "If it is the adherents of the Law who are to be the heirs, faith is null, and the promise is void" — because, as is evident, if the righteousness of the Law were enough, there would be no need of faith and of the grace promised to Abraham.

You see, therefore, how properly the apostle discusses Scripture. Consequently, those who think that he is speaking only of the Cere-

---

[31] The original has "Gen. 21," but Gen. 12:2 seems to be meant.

monial Law cannot understand him. For with the same argument he is drawing a conclusion against the righteousness of the Decalog. If we could become righteous by the works of the Decalog, faith and the blessing that was promised to Abraham and was to be spread among the Gentiles are useless; for then we are righteous without faith and without that blessing.

16. *Now the promises were made to Abraham and to his offspring.*

That is, the testament of God that was drawn up for Abraham. Here Paul calls it promises, but immediately after this he calls it a testament. Note, therefore, how he applies his analogy of a testament: "The promises," he says, "were spoken"; that is, the legacy, the testament. But what legacy? The blessing of the Gentiles in his offspring, that is, the grace of faith in Christ. Therefore he continues with the statement:

He does not say "in offsprings," as if in many; but as if in one, "in your Offspring," which is Christ.

The "as if" is a poor rendering. It would be better to say "as in many" and "as in one." This is clear from the force of the grammatical sense. Note how he teaches that the Offspring of Abraham means Christ, lest the Jews boast that they are the ones in whom the Gentiles are to be blessed — since they are so numerous that it can never be certain in whom the promise is satisfied — and lest the promise be imperiled again and God's testament collapse. Therefore it was necessary to name one offspring to whom this blessing should be given, not only for the sake of certainty but also for the sake of the unity of the one people of God, to prevent the rising of sects.

So you have the Testator, the testament, the substance of the testament, and those for whom it was made. Now it remains that it be ratified and that, after it has been ratified, it be revealed and distributed, that is, that the Gentiles receive this blessing in Christ.

17. *This is what I mean.*

That is: "Now I am saying what I had in mind; now I am explaining myself and making the application."

The testament that was ratified by God with reference to Christ.

That is, made valid through the death of Christ — made valid, moreover, "with reference to Christ," that is, in order that it may be distributed among the Gentiles as deposited in Christ. For through Christ the testament of God has been fulfilled with reference to Christ, for Christ did not die in order that grace of faith by which people should believe in someone else than Christ might be poured out. No, He died in order that they might believe in Him, Christ Himself.

The Law, which came four hundred and thirty years afterward, does not annul a covenant, so as to make the promise void.

In his ardor the apostle is speaking in a manner that is very dark and obscure. The testament of God, he says, which has been ratified with reference to Christ, should not be rendered void through the Law and its righteousness. It would, however, become void and would annul the promise altogether if its works were necessary for righteousness, as though the grace of the promise were not enough or were powerless to effect our righteousness.

Moreover, by adding the words "the Law, which came four hundred and thirty years afterward," he seems to be belittling the Law; as if he were saying: "If the promise had been given after the Law, it could seem to have been gained deservedly through the righteousness of the Law. Now, however, grace and righteousness are given so completely without the works of the Law that they were promised even many years before the Law, and much more before its righteousness, not because of anyone's merits, nor because of anyone's petitions, but solely because the mercy of God made the promise freely. How, then, will the Law annul this promise of grace and its fulfillment at this time? For it has performed no service at all either for the promise or for the fulfillment." And in Rom. 3:21 Paul says: "The righteousness of God has been manifested apart from the Law." Yes, according to Rom. 4:15, the Law has done the opposite, since, on the contrary, it works wrath and increases transgressions. Accordingly, far from depending on the Law and our works, righteousness should depend by all means on the utterly faithful promise of God, who does not lie, even if through the Law we become more wicked and more unworthy.

18. *For if the inheritance is by the Law, it is no longer by promise.*

This means that if the righteousness which was promised to Abraham in the blessing comes from the works of the Law and from us, the promise has been annulled and is superfluous. The same thing cannot come from us and from God; for He is truthful, but we are liars. With this statement Paul proves what he has already said, namely, that the promise is not annulled through the Law. Because, he says, if it comes from the Law, the promise is now annulled through the Law, just as he also says in Rom. 4:14: "If the inheritance is by the Law, the promise has been abolished." Above I have sufficiently commended the apostle's way of speaking, which considers the Law, the works of the Law, and the righteousness of the Law identical, because righteousness of this kind comes about solely because the Law requires it, not because of our volition. Our theologians speak of this as "of ourselves" or "of our own powers" or "out of purely natural strength." [32] For this reason they are unable to understand Paul, who seems to be making an accusation against the Law.

But God gave it to Abraham by a promise.

God did not give it through the Law; He granted it through His free promise, when the Law did not yet exist. Much less did He fulfill the promise by the coming of the Law. Thus here you have the whole argument of the apostle.

Now we must consider Paul's statement that the Law was given four hundred and thirty years later. For these years are computed from the time of Abraham's departure from his own land, when he first received the promise (Gen. 12:3), up to the departure of the Children of Israel, as follows: At the age of seventy-five Abraham emigrated from his own land (Gen. 12:4). But when he was a hundred years old, he begot Isaac (Gen. 21:5). Thus you have twenty-five years. When Isaac was sixty years of age, he begot Jacob and Esau (Gen. 25:26). Mark down sixty years. Jacob was ninety when he begot Joseph, as is gathered from many chapters of Genesis. Mark down ninety years. Joseph lived a hundred and ten years (Gen. 50:26). After him the slavery in Egypt lasted sixty-five years, as Jo. Annius says on the basis of Philo.[33] Then Moses was born. When he was eighty years old, the Children of Israel departed. Thus from Abraham's seventy-fifth year to Moses' eightieth year there are four hundred and thirty years. Let others concern themselves as to whether

---

[32] Cf. Thomas Aquinas, *Summa Theologica*, I—II, Q. 109, Art. 4, for the use of this terminology in high scholasticism.

[33] The reference to *Io. Annius ex Philone* seems to mean Annius of Viterbo (1432—1502), who edited Pseudo-Philo, *Breviarium de temporibus*, which Luther was to use in the preparation of his *Chronolgy* (cf. W, LIII, 9).

this reckoning is correct. I agree with St. Jerome, who says: "This matter has been investigated by many, and I do not know whether the answer has been found." [34] For I believe that the apostle said this, not on the basis of a computation but on the basis of Ex. 12:40, where it is stated: "The time that the people of Israel dwelt in Egypt was four hundred and thirty years." Stephen does the same thing when in Acts 7:6 he recounts the history on the basis of Gen. 15:13, where God foretells to Abraham that his offspring will be in slavery for four hundred years. But by putting both passages together Paul counts four hundred and thirty years.

Note in addition that the apostle calls the promises of God a testament. The same term is used in other passages of Scripture. In this way it was indicated darkly that God would die and that thus in God's promise, as in a formally announced testament, God's incarnation and suffering were to be understood. For, as Heb. 9:17 states, "A testament is ratified only at death." Hence God's testament was not to be ratified unless God died. In the same place (Heb. 9:15) it is stated of Christ: "Therefore He is the Mediator of a new testament, in order that they may receive the promise, since a death has occurred." And this is the day of Christ which Abraham recognized and rejoiced in when God gave His promise (John 8:56). Hence one can at the same time harmonize with this what Jerome mentions, namely, that in the Hebrew one finds "covenant" rather than "testament." [35] He who stays alive makes a covenant; he who is about to die makes a testament. Thus Jesus Christ, the immortal God, made a covenant. At the same time He made a testament, because He was going to become mortal. Just as He is both God and man, so He made both a covenant and a testament.

19. *Why, then, the Law?*

Because Paul has said that one does not have righteousness through the Law and has established this with very strong arguments, he sees that there is every right to object to his statement by asking what function the Law then serves, since every law seems to be laid down for the sake of righteousness and good morals. And you see well enough that he is speaking about every law, even that of the Decalog,

[34] Jerome, *Commentarius*, 390.
[35] Jerome, *Commentarius*, 390.

as in the fourth and fifth chapters of Romans. His answer, however, is this:

It was added because of transgressions, till the offspring should come to whom the promise had been made; and it was ordained by angels through an intermediary.

20. *Now an intermediary implies more than one; but God is one.*

Who would ever have expected such an answer, one that is certainly opposed to all who are wont to speak intelligently about the usefulness of the Law? He says that the Law was laid down or added and attached in order that transgressions might abound, in the same sense as he says in Rom. 5:20: "The Law came in to increase the trespass."

St. Jerome understands this passage in a negative sense and takes it to mean that through the Law transgressions are to be held in check.[36] But his view is contradicted by the following facts:

First, in that case it should rather have been said that the Law was given for the sake of justification; for a law is given for the sake of being kept.

Secondly, for the apostle this is a familiar way of speaking. "The Law is the power of sin" (1 Cor. 15:56), the opportunity for sin (Rom. 7:11), the Law of death (Rom. 7:10), the Law of wrath. Thus in Rom. 4:15 we read: "The Law brings wrath; but where there is no Law, there is no transgression." Thus it is certain that where there is no transgression, there is no remission; where there is no remission, there is no salvation. Accordingly, just as remission is there for the sake of salvation, so transgression is there for the sake of remission, and so the Law is there for the sake of transgression. The Law sets up sin, sin sets up remission, remission sets up salvation. All this is so because without the Law sin is dead and is not recognized (Rom. 5 and 7). Sin was in the world, but until Moses it was not imputed. The meaning, then, is this: The Law was laid down for the sake of transgression, in order that transgression might be and abound, and in order that thus man, having been brought to knowledge of himself through the Law, might seek the hand of a merciful God. Without the Law he is ignorant of his sin and considers himself sound.

[36] Jerome, *Commentarius*, 390—391.

In the third place, the clause that follows — "till the offspring should come" — does not agree with Jerome's view. For it is absurd that transgression be held in check until Christ should come, as if then it should not be held in check, whereas the apostle wanted to say the opposite, namely, that not only was sin not held in check by the Law, but that it was even increased, until Christ came and put an end to sin by fulfilling the Law and giving grace, as Gabriel says in Dan. 9:24: "In order that sin may have an end and everlasting righteousness be brought in," as if he were saying: "Sin had its beginning in Adam, was even increased through the Law, but will have an end through Christ alone, who brings everlasting righteousness after sin is dead, as we read in Ps. 111:3 and Ps. 112:3: 'His righteousness endures forever.'"

In the fourth place, Jerome's view does not agree with Paul's question (v. 21): "Is the Law, then, against the promises of God?" This would not be brought forward if the apostle wanted it to be understood that the Law was given for the sake of holding transgression in check, because in that case it would be for the promises, not against the promises. But now, because it increases sin and provokes wrath, it is evident that it does not induce God to fulfill His promises, but, on the contrary, that it irritates and hinders Him. With this view the context agrees beautifully. Otherwise you would have to invent as many opinions as there are syntactical constructions.

In the fifth place, as to Paul's phrase, "through an intermediary," it is my opinion that he says this because the Law was not put in our hands for us to fulfill, but that it was put in the hands of the Christ who was to come for Him to fulfill. Accordingly, it was laid down, not in order to effect justification but rather to accuse sinners and to require the hand of an intermediary. For man's pride had to be opposed, lest he believe that God's Son was made man because of his merits and thus become ungrateful for such great mercy. But now, having fallen into guilt because of the Law, we love God. The greater our unworthiness is, the greater is the love He has shown. For we can have knowledge through the Law, but Christ alone fulfills and achieves it.

"Till the offspring should come to whom the promise had been made," that is, in whom the blessing, the righteousness, and the fulfilling of the Law were to be given, and the transgressions which existed through the Law were no longer to be held in check but were to be blotted out. This is brought about through faith in Christ.

What follows now I do not find explained in the writings of any theologian. Jerome, Augustine, and Ambrose pass over it and say nothing except that Christ is the Mediator between God and men. They do not point out what connection the words have with one another or how they should be understood. Furthermore, the more recent commentators even devise unrelated things here. For this reason I submit to the pious reader the reflections I myself am able to offer.

"Ordained," says Paul, "by angels through an intermediary." And Blessed Stephen, too, says in Acts 7:53: "You who received the Law as delivered by angels and did not keep it." And in Heb. 2:2 we read: "For if the message declared by angels was valid." Therefore it is clear that the apostle means that the Law is a letter and for this reason is nothing else than the strength of sin, and, as he says in 2 Cor. 3:6: "The letter kills, but the Spirit gives life." It is indeed a great thing that it was ordained by angels; but this has no bearing on righteousness, since the angels are unable either to fulfill it for us or to give that by which it may be fulfilled. They have transmitted it to us in accordance with God's arrangement. This is the only thing they can do. But since it was transmitted according to God's arrangement, surely one must understand at the same time that it was to be fulfilled in its entirety. For the angels were not the authors of the Law; they were its servants, through whom, according to the arrangement, it was to come to us. That arrangement, then, is to be broken; and now it is not an angel who is to be the mediator between God and man. No, He Himself, who ordains by angels and has us at a distance from Himself — He Himself, I say, is to come and teach us the Law, He whose words will be Spirit and words of life (John 6:63). For it profits nothing for Him to send any messengers if He Himself does not come. The Law may have been ordained by angels, but it was not put in the hand of angels. No, it was put in the hand of a Mediator who should absolve and justify those who are accused through the Law. For I understand this expression "in the hand of a Mediator" to mean that He, as the One who alone is not subject to the Law, has the Law that was ordained through angels in His own power, so that He Himself is under no obligation to anyone and may set free from it anyone He wishes. On the other hand, the Law holds us in its hand and under its subjection through sin. With all this he wants to say that it is impossible for us to be saved through ourselves, but that it is easy through the hand of another, namely, a mediator. But if someone thinks that it should be understood as "ordained through angels in the hand, that is to say, in the power and on the authority of a mediator," I have no objection, provided that no one thinks that by "mediator" one must simply understand "Moses," who is the mediator of the Old Testament, just as the Epistle to the Hebrews (8:6) calls Christ the Mediator of a new and better testament.

As to the statement, "Now an intermediary implies more than one," from the term "intermediary" he now draws the conclusion that we are such sinners that the works of the Law cannot be sufficient. If, says he, you are righteous by the Law, then you do not need an intermediary; but neither does God, since He Himself is One and in complete agreement with Himself. It is between two parties, therefore, that a mediator is sought, namely, between God and man; as if he were saying: "It would be the most impious thanklessness if you reject your Mediator and send him back to God, who is One; but you are rejecting Him if you are able to be justified on the basis of the Law. Thus the result will be that He cannot be a Mediator for you, since you do not want one, or for God, since He does not need one. Now, therefore, the Law will also be in your hand and not ordained by angels so as to be fulfilled through a mediator; but it is fulfilled entirely by yourselves." If anything still lies hidden more deeply, let others look for it; I reef my sails.

21. *Is the Law, then, against the promises of God? Certainly not.*

After answering one question in this way he has raised another question for himself. For if the Law increases transgressions, it now seems to render ineffectual the goodness of Him who gives the promise. This would be true if the promise of the blessing rested on the Law or on our righteousnesses in the Law. Now, however, it rests solely on the truthfulness of Him who gives the promise. For this reason the Law is not against the promises of God. Indeed, it is for the promises of God. How? Because while the Law reveals sin and proves that no one can be justified through it — indeed, that sin is even increased through it — it compels that the fulfillment of the promise be sought, prayed for, and awaited all the more as much more necessary than when there was no Law. Therefore it is so far from being against the promises that it commends them vigorously and makes them most desirable to those whom it has humbled by the knowledge of their sins.

For if a law had been given which could make alive, then righteousness would indeed be by the Law.

This means that the Law is not against the promises, because it was given to cause death and to increase sin, namely, in order that through the Law a man might recognize how sorely he needs the grace of the promise, since through a law that is good, righteous, and holy he is only made worse. In this way he will not become smug in his reliance on the Law and in the trust he puts in its works but, apart from the Law, will seek something far different and better, namely, the promise. For if the Law could have given life, we would be righteous. Now, however, it kills instead and increases sin. But by this very fact it works for the promises as it compels them to be desired more urgently and utterly destroys all righteousness of works. For if it did not destroy, the grace of the promise would not be sought, would be received without gratitude, yes, would be repudiated, as happens in the case of those who do not rightly understand the Law. But it would not destroy unless it not only failed to justify or to make alive but also became the occasion for more sins and caused more deaths. For lust is always stimulated and becomes greater when it is forbidden. Therefore even though the Law seems to be against the promises as it increases sin among those who do not recognize sin through the Law, still this is not the fault of the Law, because when it is not rightly understood, it is not even a law. But the Law is rightly understood when sin is recognized through it. Where it is understood, however, and sin is recognized, there it certainly works for the promises, because it even causes the grace of the promise to be sighed for and shows at the same time how grace is not owed to a man for any merit of his. Therefore through an understanding of the Law the completely pure condescension of Him who gives the promise and the completely sincere thankfulness for the condescension that has been displayed stand sure and are confirmed.

22. *But the Scripture consigned all things to sin, that what was promised to faith in Jesus Christ might be given to those who believe.*

With this statement Paul gives an answer to both points: that the Law was laid down for the purpose of increasing transgression but, on the other hand, was not against the promises of God when it increased transgressions. "God," he says, "has consigned all things to sin through the Scripture"; that is, through the Law and the letter He has shown that we were sinners and powerless with regard to righteousness or the fulfillment of the Law, in order that in this way, by making sin manifest through the Law and by convincing men of their inability to fulfill the Law, He might make them humble and compel them to despair of themselves and to run trembling to the mercy of God that is freely offered in Christ, and in order that thus the promise made to Abraham might be "given," as he says here — given, I say, not paid, but given to those who are not worthy of it, and who through the Law have merited by far the opposite. This means that on the basis of faith in Christ grace and the blessing of justification would be given to all who believe in Him.

The same thing is stated in Rom. 11:32: "God has consigned all men to sin, that He may have mercy on all," and "that every mouth may be stopped, and the whole world may be held accountable to God. For no human being will be justified in His sight by works of the Law." (Rom. 3:19-20.) How did God consign them? Through the Scriptures, through the Law, through the letter, namely, as Paul has confidently explained above about the works of the Law, because Moses had written: "Cursed is everyone who does not abide by all things" (v. 10). This is what he says in Rom. 3:9, where he argues with confidence that Jews and Greeks are all under the power of sin; and in conformity with Ps. 14:3 he firmly pronounces the same judgment on all. "None is righteous," he says, "no one understands. All have turned aside, together they have gone wrong." (Rom. 3:10-12.) This is what he has the courage to say in Rom. 2:21, namely, to assert the guilt of the Jews, who relied on the fair appearance of their works, whereas he has no regard at all for this appearance. "You are doing the same things," he says, "that you condemn. You who teach that one should not steal are stealing, namely, by your covetousness." So certain was he, as it is also certain in very fact, that all things that are done outside grace are sins and hypocrisy pure and simple. Thus St. Augustine, too, in the ninth chapter of his book *On the Spirit and the Letter*, where he treats of the statement in the last chapter of Proverbs (31:26), "Law and kindness are on her tongue," makes the most excellent remark: "Therefore it is written of wisdom that she bears law and kindness on her tongue for this reason — law, in order that she may render the proud guilty; kindness, in order that she may justify the humbled." [37]

---

[37] Augustine, *On the Spirit and the Letter*, 9, 19.

Therefore the proposition "Every man is a liar" (cf. Ps. 116:11) stands firm, and the proposition "No man living is righteous before Thee" (Ps. 143:2) stands firm, in order that at the same time the glory of God, the praise of His grace, and the splendor of His mercy may stand firm. "To us," we read in Dan. 9:7, "belongs confusion, but to our God righteousness." You see, then, what it means to be justified through faith in Christ. It means that after learning to know your iniquity and weakness through the Law you despair of yourself, of your own strength, of your knowledge, of the Law, of works, in short, of everything, and that with trembling and confidence you humbly implore the right hand of Christ alone, namely, the hand of the Mediator, and firmly believe that you obtain grace, as Paul says in Rom. 10:13 on the basis of Joel 2:32: "Everyone who calls upon the name of the Lord will be saved." And at the same time you see that the whole human race, no matter with how much wisdom and righteousness it may shine before men, is nothing but an accursed mass of perdition.[38] This can also be learned from the Word of promise: "In your seed shall all nations be blessed" (Gen. 22:18). What else does it mean that all nations are to be blessed than that all nations were cursed? Thus the fact that they are to be blessed, to be saved, and to have everything the word "blessing" signifies has no other meaning than that they are sinful, lost, and doomed to everything the word "curse" signifies. Accordingly, the Law was given in order to increase sin. But the intent was not only that sin be increased, but that proud man should recognize this very thing and be terrified through the Law, and that after being driven into despair of himself he should thirst for mercy. Thus we read in Ps. 42:1: "As a hart longs for flowing streams, so longs my soul for Thee, O God." Likewise: "My tears have been my food day and night, while men say to me continually: 'Where is your God?'" (Ps. 42:3.) Hence all the crying, sobbing, and yearning of the fathers and the prophets, the anxious expectation of Christ, and the exceedingly important question concerning the burden of the Law.

Accordingly, the Law is good, righteous, and holy; but it does not justify. It shows me what I am, since through it I am provoked and hate righteousness more than before. It causes me to love lust more than before, since it was only out of terror at the threats of the Law

---

[38] For the term *massa perditionis* see, for example, Augustine, *On the Grace of Christ and on Original Sin*, II, 29, 34.

that I was held back from an evil deed, though never from evil lust. And, to put the matter before you by way of a comparison, water is good; but when poured over lime it sets the lime on fire. Is it the fault of the water that the lime becomes hot? Indeed, the lime, which was thought to be cold, is convicted by the water of what it has inside. Thus the Law incites lusts and hatreds, and exposes them; but it does not cure them. But if you pour oil over the lime, it does not become hot; then its hidden heat is extinguished. Thus when grace has been poured into our hearts through the Holy Spirit, it extinguishes hatred and lust.

I have used very many words to say these things because this fact cannot be driven home to our age sufficiently, so strong has the tyranny of the Law's righteousnesses again become. But observe this: If the most holy Law of God was not able to justify us but made us even more sinful, what will those oceans of our laws, traditions, and ceremonies in the church accomplish, especially when they are being kept with this notion, that men think they are justifying themselves thereby, and when they do not allow one to know what Christ is or why one should believe in Him? For they do not use those laws in order to learn to know sin through them or in order to exercise their faith in Christ by love freely given. But they trust that by having kept these laws they are righteous, and they believe that they need nothing else at all; or if they implore the grace of Christ, they implore it for the purpose of being able to do works of this kind, not in order to become free from the inner corruption and uncleanness of the flesh. Therefore, as I have often said, the church must perish utterly because of so many foolish and calamitous laws if God does not provide a remedy for us.

23. *Now before faith came, we were confined under the Law, kept under restraint until faith should be revealed.*

For all who are under the Law before being justified by faith the Law itself, he says, is a prison, as it were, in which they are confined and kept, because by the power and terror of the Law they are restrained from sinning freely. Besides, lust is unwilling and reluctant. For lust rages and hates the Law, its prison, but is nevertheless compelled to refrain from works of sin. Those, however, who have learned to know this wretchedness are truly humbled, sigh for grace, and are unable to trust in the righteousness of the Law, since they realize that through the Law they become opposed to the Law and inclined toward sin; for they would prefer that the Law did not exist, in order that they might be permitted to satisfy their lusts with impunity. But to have this preference is to hate the Law; to hate the Law is to hate truth, righteousness, and holiness. This is then not only sin but also a love of sin, not only not being righteous but also a hatred of righteousness. This is really what it means that sin is increased through the Law. For this reason St. Augustine says on this passage that the fact that through the Law they have been found to be transgressors of the Law itself has not served to destroy the Law for those who have come to faith but has been helpful to them, because through the knowledge of their greater illness it has brought about a stronger desire and a more ardent love for a physician.[39] For he to whom most is forgiven loves most (Luke 7:47). And this is also said in Rom. 5:20: "Where sin increased, grace abounded all the more." Therefore the Law was laid down not only to reveal and increase sin (otherwise it would have been better if it had been postponed till the Last Judgment, lest we be consumed by a double grief), but in order to humble us through the revelation of our sin and to drive us to Christ.

The clause "before faith came" is to be understood not only of the faith which was revealed after Christ but of all faith of all the righteous. For the same faith also came long ago to the fathers, because the Law of God, when first revealed to them, also compelled them to seek grace. Although at that time faith was not proclaimed in this way throughout the world, nevertheless it was proclaimed privately in the households of the fathers. And be careful not to arrange the words "confined in that faith" as if he wanted it understood that they were confined in faith as in a prison, since this is what he affirms concerning the Law. But we were confined in the prison of the Law; and this was until faith, that is, until the faith that was to come, or in order that we might desire to be set free through faith, just as he speaks above of "the testament of God ratified with regard to Christ," that is, in order to be ratified in the Christ who was to come; and, as he says presently, "the Law was our custodian until Christ came," that is, until Christ.

24. *So that the Law was our custodian until Christ came, that we might be justified by faith.*

[39] Augustine, *Epistolae ad Galatas expositio, Patrologia, Series Latina,* XXXV, 2124.

25. But now that faith has come, we are no longer under a custodian.

This is certainly a beautiful comparison. The term παιδαγωγός is derived from a word meaning "boy" and one meaning "to lead," because he is to lead and train boys. Paul says that just as a custodian is assigned to young boys to bridle their sportive youthfulness, so the Law was given to us to hold sins in check. But just as boys are held in check solely by fear of discipline, generally hate the custodian and prefer to be free, and do everything only when forced or when enticed by blandishments but never for love of the thing itself or of their own free will, so those who are under the Law are restrained from the works of sin by fear of the threats of the Law. They hate the Law and prefer to have their desires unrestricted. Moreover, they do everything under compulsion because of their fear of punishment or when they are enticed by love of a temporal promise. But they never do so out of a spontaneous and free desire. Then, when the boys attain to their inheritance, they realize how useful the custodian has been. Now they begin to esteem and praise the custodian's service and to condemn themselves for not having obeyed readily and willingly. Now, on the other hand, without a custodian and of their own accord, they gladly do the things they used to do unwillingly and with reluctance when they were under the custodian. Thus when we have acquired faith, which is our true inheritance promised to Abraham and to his offspring, we realize how holy and beneficial the Law is but how foul our desire is; and we love the Law, praise it, and commend it exceedingly, while, on the other hand, the more pleasing the Law itself grows, the more we condemn and blame our lusts. Now we do cheerfully and readily what the beneficial Law extorted from us outwardly by force and terror when we were ignorant yet was unable to extort inwardly. This is what Paul means when he says that now, after faith has come, we are not under a custodian. But the custodian has become our friend and is honored by us more than he is feared.

Secondly, take care, as I have said, not to read the text in this way: "The Law was our custodian *in* Christ," as if the Law were a custodian for us who are now alive in Christ, as our translation [40] reads and seems to mean; for this completely destroys the apostle's meaning. On the contrary, just as boys are under a custodian until they acquire

---

[40] The Latin to which Luther is referring reads: *Itaque lex paedagogus noster fuit in Christo.*

their inheritance — that is, to be trained by him for the purpose of attaining the inheritance — so the Law is our custodian *to* Christ, that is, in order that after being driven and trained by the Law we may be made ready to seek and sigh for Christ, for faith, and for the inheritance. For the Law, as I have said, prepares for grace in that it reveals and increases sin; it humbles the proud, so that they long for Christ's help. And the apostle supports this meaning with the clause that follows, "until Christ came," I say, namely, "that we might be justified by faith" — we who were made sinners through the Law. Thus we read in Ps. 69:16: "For Thy steadfast love is good, O Lord." Why? Because Thy Law, O Lord, is bitter. Accordingly, a boy will not remain under a custodian but will be instructed, so that receiving his inheritance may be sweeter for him. Thus the Law renders the grace of God sweeter and commends it. Accordingly, Paul sets forth the aim of the Law uncommonly well. He says that it is not our righteousness and our fulfilling of the Law but our sighing to Christ, in order that its fulfillment may be sought through faith in Him. But those who are self-righteous regard the laws themselves and their works as the aim of their laws. Nor do they prescribe them with a view to Christ; they do so with a view to works alone. As a result, they will perish forever, together with the Jews, whom they imitate. They understand neither the Law nor its works.

26. *For in Christ Jesus you are all sons of God, through faith.*

Because faith is the very blessing, the very inheritance promised to Abraham in his offspring, namely, Christ, for this reason he who has faith in Christ has the inheritance of God. If he has the inheritance, he is no longer under a custodian but is free, both lord and heir. But the inheritance is given to none except the sons. It follows, then, that one who believes in Christ is a son of God, as we read in John 1:12: "To those who believed in His name He gave power to become children of God."

27. *For as many of you as were baptized into Christ have put on Christ.*

Paul declares that they are sons of God through faith in Christ. "Baptism," he says, "brings it about that you put on Christ. But to put on Christ is to put on righteousness, truth, and every grace, and the fulfillment of the whole Law. Therefore through Christ you have the blessing and inheritance of Abraham. But if you have put on Christ, and if Christ is the Son of God, then you, too, by that same garment, are the sons of God." Now this is a figure of speech which the apostle also uses in Rom. 13:14, where he says: "But put on the Lord Jesus Christ," and in Eph. 4:24: "Put on the new man, created after the likeness of God in true righteousness and holiness" — true, he says, because the Law by itself puts on a holiness and righteousness of pretense.

28. *There is neither Jew nor Greek, there is neither slave nor free, there is neither male nor female.*

"You are righteous," says Paul, "not because you are a Jew and an observer of the Law, but because by believing in Christ you have put on Christ. Why, then, are you being dragged to Judaism by the false apostles? Just as in Christ there is no status for Jewish observance, so there is no other status either. It is characteristic of human and legalistic kinds of righteousness to be divided into sects, and for distinctions to be made according to works. Some profess, advocate, and pursue this; others, that. In Christ, however, all things are common to all; all things are one thing, and one thing is all things. Thus Paul says later, in chapter 5:6: "For in Christ Jesus neither circumcision nor uncircumcision is of any avail, but faith and the new creature." For this reason the Christian or believer is a man without a name, without outward appearance, without a distinguishing mark, without status. Ps. 133:1 says: "Behold, how good and pleasant it is when brothers dwell in unity!" Where there is unity, there is neither outward appearance nor a distinguishing mark. Nor is there a name. Thus the renowned martyr Attalus, on being asked concerning the name of his God, answered very well: "Those who are many are differentiated by names; he who is one does not need a name."[41] And for this reason Scripture calls the church concealed and hidden;[42] and one observes very well that as often as the righteous are described, they are described without any term for sect or status, as in Ps. 1:6: "For the Lord knows the way of the righteous." (He does not say "of the Jews, of men, of the aged, of children.") And in Ps. 15:1 we read: "O Lord, who shall sojourn in Thy tent?" He answers (v. 2): "He who walks blamelessly." (He does not say "the

[41] The story of Attalus is told in Eusebius, *Ecclesiastical History*, V, 1, 52.

[42] Cf. Luther's comments of the following year in his treatise against Alveld (W, VI, 294—296).

Jew, or one of this or that profession.") And in Ps. 111:1 it says: "In the company of the upright, in the congregation." (He does not say "of priests, of monks, of bishops.") One must pronounce the same judgment concerning every other status, because God does not regard the person (Acts 10:34). Therefore there is neither rich nor poor, neither handsome nor ugly, neither citizen nor farmer, neither Benedictine nor Carthusian, neither Minorite nor Augustinian. All these things are of such a nature that they do not make a Christian if they are present or an unbeliever if they are lacking; but they are certainly undertaken and done for the purpose of training and improving a Christian.

Hence St. Augustine says on this passage that in this mortal life a distinction of Jews and Gentiles, or of station or sex, remains on account of the body but is removed in the spirit through the unity of faith, because in regard to this unity not only the apostles but also the Lord Himself have handed down most salutary doctrines.[43] For Christ commands to give to Caesar the things that are Caesar's; the apostles command slaves to obey their masters, wives to be subject to their husbands, but all to obey the magistrates. Tribute to whom tribute is due, honor to whom honor is due. But all these things pertain to the person. This alone is required, that we render to such persons service that is not contrary to the unity of faith but is in accordance with the unity of faith, in order that the dissimilarity in outward station may not be stronger than the similarity in inward faith, as alas, we now see infinite varieties of strife and contention among what are called orders, ranks, religions, churches, crafts, nations, countries, families, friendships, and alliances, so that on this evidence itself it has been proved that faith has almost been extinguished in the church and that only masks remain, and, as Isaiah says of Babylon, satyrs, screech owls, and ostriches hold their mad revels there (Is. 13:21 f.).

For you are all one in Christ Jesus.

That is, you are one in faith in Christ; and if, according to the necessity of the body and of this life, there must be a division into distinct persons, just as there are many members, still you are one body under one Head.

[43] Augustine, *Epistolae ad Galatas expositio, Patrologia, Series Latina,* XXXV, 2125.

29. *And if you are Christ's, then you are Abraham's offspring, heirs according to promise.*

Because Paul has said that we have put on Christ and have been made one in Christ, therefore the same thing that has been said of Christ will be understood as said of us for Christ's sake. For Christ cannot be separated from us, and we cannot be separated from Him, since we are one with Him and in Him, just as the members are one in the head and with one head. Therefore just as God's promise can be understood of no one else than Christ, so, since we are nothing else than Christ, it must be understood of us too. Accordingly, we are truly Abraham's offspring and heirs, not according to the flesh but according to the promise, because we are those of whom mention is made in the promise, the nations, I mean, that are to be blessed in the offspring of Abraham. Thus in Rom. 9:8 the children of the promise are counted in the offspring. These are the children of God, not those who are children of the flesh.

CHAPTER FOUR

1. *I mean that the heir, as long as he is a child, is no better than a slave, though he is the owner of all the estate;*

2. *but he is under guardians and trustees until the date set by the father.*

THE apostle attacks the righteousness and works of the Law with still another battering ram, as he now draws a third analogy from the ways of men, one related to his earlier analogy of the custodian, dealing as it does with the same boy. But that analogy of the testament also pertains to a boy or at least an heir — so resourceful is the apostle in making clear the promise of God. In the first place, the boy who is an heir is no different from the slaves; he has no more authority over his father's property than a slave has. Secondly, he is nevertheless the lord of everything in hope and by the father's appointment. Thirdly, he is under tutors and administrators until the time previously fixed by the father. Whether the apostle is following the Roman laws or others here makes no difference; for, as Jerome says, the legal limit of an heir's minority under Roman laws is twenty-five years.[1] We shall use this example as far as is appropriate.

3. *So with us; when we were children, we were slaves to the elements of this world.*

Paul matches the details point for point. We are the boy who is an heir. The tutors are the elements of the world. We were no different from slaves, for we were in servitude. Nevertheless, we were lords of all, because, of course, the heavenly Father has predestined this. More than enough has been said about the heirs and the inheritance: that the heirs are the offspring of Abraham, that is, Christ and the Christian; that the inheritance, however, is grace and the blessing of the Christian faith among the Gentiles. But the servitude of the heirs has been spoken of previously with other words; for slaves are those

---

[1] Jerome, *Commentarius*, 396.

who do not serve for the inheritance that belongs to the head of the house but serve for reward or even do their tasks because they are compelled by the fear of punishment. For this reason, as Christ says, the slave does not remain in the house forever. The son, however, does remain in the house forever (John 8:35). This was beautifully pictured in Gen. 21:14, when Ishmael, the son of the slave woman, was cast out after the necessities of life had been given to him. And in Gen. 25:5 f. we read: "Abraham gave all he had to Isaac. But to the sons of his concubines Abraham gave gifts and sent them away from his son Isaac." Thus we, too, when we are without grace and in the Law, do the works of the Law like slaves, that is, either compelled by the fear of penalties or enticed by temporal reward. Nevertheless, we are instructed by all this in such a way that we sigh for the inheritance, that is, for faith and grace, by which we, snatched out of this state of slavery, may fulfill the Law in the freedom of the Spirit. Then we no longer fear punishment or desire a reward; that is, we are no longer slaves. In the meantime we are lords of all, since God predestined and prepared this inheritance for us and, through the slavish fear of punishment and the love of the things that are in the Law, instructs us in such a way that we long for that inheritance and do not remain in slavery with the Jews and hypocrites. We shall achieve this if we realize that through the fear of punishment and love of a reward it is not the love for the Law but rather a hatred of it that is increased in us; for, as I have said, we would prefer that there be no Law. Thus the Law certainly drives us to the inheritance through which we are made lords of everything, that is, possessors of the blessing in Christ through faith.

Various ideas have been held about the "elements of the world," the "guardians," and the "administrators." Briefly, here the elements are not to be taken in the philosophical sense as referring to fire, air, water, and earth; but, according to the apostle's characteristic way of speaking and in the grammatical sense, they are to be taken as referring to the very letters of the Law, the letters of which the Law consists, as also in 2 Cor. 3:6 and elsewhere (Rom. 2:27, 29) Paul calls the Law "the letter," so that "elements" in the plural are what is written, or the written Law. Nor is there need for any other proof than the authority of the apostle himself, who says: "We were under the elements of the world" and follows immediately (v. 5) with the words "to redeem those who were under the Law," in order to show that by Law and elements he understands the same thing. In other respects, those who are redeemed in the time of fulfillment are also under the natural elements. And later he says: "How can you turn back again to the weak and beggarly elements of this world, whose slaves you want to be once more?" And by way of explaining himself he follows with the words "You observe days and years." To observe days and years, therefore, means to turn back to the elements, that is, to the letter of the Law.

But neither does reason allow one to understand "elements" as idols or the elements of nature, as some have thought,[2] because nowhere does one read that the Jews ever worshiped the elements; because then Paul should rather have said: "We were under the power of idols or of darkness," as he does in the Epistle to the Romans and elsewhere;[3] and because he is saying in the broadest possible terms that without faith in Christ all men, as many as there are, have been slaves to the elements. If this is not understood of the Law, it is not understood at all; for, as Paul said above, the Law consigned all things to sin (Gal. 3:22), especially since here he does nothing else but compare the Law and grace, in order to exalt the latter and to bring down the former, but most of all because this is a manner of speaking that is usual for the apostle, as in Col. 2:8: "See to it that no one makes a prey of you by philosophy and empty deceit, according to human tradition, according to the elements of the world, and not according to Christ." For St. Jerome is not to be believed either when he mentions extraneous matters and holds that the elements in that passage are not the same as those mentioned in this epistle.[4] For they surely are the same. Jerome, you see, calls elements the writings and doctrines of the world, that is, of men, or rather the regulations concerning the affairs of the world. A little later in the same epistle (Col. 2:20) Paul says: "If with Christ you died to the elements of the world, why do you live as if you still belonged to the world?" That this is the apostle's meaning is proved at once by what follows, where Paul teaches about Jewish superstitions, as he does here too. But he uses the same manner of speaking in Heb. 5:12. "You need," he says, "to be taught what are the elementary principles of the words of God."

[2] Cf. Augustine, *Epistolae ad Galatas expositio, Patrologia, Series Latina,* XXXV, 2128—2129.
[3] Luther is thinking of Rom. 2:22, perhaps of Rom. 11:7 ff.
[4] Jerome, *Commentarius,* 397.

But Paul calls the Law "the elements of the world." He uses both words by way of tapinosis,[5] that is, by way of disparagement and degradation, in order to diminish the glory and reputation of the Law's righteousness and of its works. It is as if he were saying: "What do we have from the Law but letters, and letters devoid of the Spirit at that, so that they give no means by which they may be fulfilled? Nor are we able to fulfill them." Furthermore, he says "of the world" because they have to do with those things that are in the world, such as external works, just as what is known about God is spoken of as the knowledge of God. For the Law did not lead anyone to the Spirit but was observed solely in the flesh, while on the inside lust was rebellious and hated the Law.

Consider now how it is possible for the apostle to be understood by those who call tonsures, vestments, places, seasons, churches, altars, ornaments, and all that ceremonial pomp spiritual things. Indeed, they are forced to deny that these are worldly things, unless they, too, wish to be called worldly themselves, a notion from which they shrink most vigorously. But in denying that these things are worldly they at the same time shut themselves off from understanding the apostle, since he includes all these things in the term "world," as with contempt he calls the decrees and doctrines that have been established in these external matters "elements of the world." Yes, he includes even the outward works of the Decalog. Therefore in our age spiritual things are riches, tyranny, arrogance, liberty, or — on the highest level — prayers uttered without understanding and vestments and places appointed by the doctrines of men. But works of mercy and all other works and places of men are physical, even though they are holy to the highest degree when they arise from a spirit filled with faith.

But let us return to the apostle. The elements of which he speaks are guardians and administrators, just as the Law is a custodian, because, since the letter of the Law compels the unwilling to do its works for fear of punishment, it compels them at the same time to acknowledge this reluctance and to run to Christ, who gives the spirit of freedom. Therefore the Law does not destroy. No, it renders a most useful service, provided that you understand that through it, as through a loyal administrator, you are brought, yes, driven, to Christ and to your inheritance. But if you do not understand it in

---

[5] The figure here is *tapinosis;* cf. *Luther's Works,* 26, p. 362, note 5.

this way, it will be a taskmaster and an adversary for you, and will hand you over to torturers. It will be your judge and persecutor, because it will never leave your conscience at rest, inasmuch as you can never find in yourself and in your works the means by which it may be fulfilled and satisfied. But that is how those understand it who do not let themselves be directed by it to Christ but undertake to fulfill it by their own powers.

4. *But when the time had fully come, God sent forth His Son, born of woman, born under the Law,*

5. *to redeem those who were under the Law, so that we might receive adoption as sons.*

"When the time had fully come" is the expression Paul uses here for what he had spoken of above as the time previously fixed by the Father. For in this way God had fixed beforehand the time when the blessing promised to Abraham should be fulfilled in Christ, his Offspring. Not that the saintly fathers did not in the meantime obtain the same blessing, but that it was to be revealed throughout the world in Christ, and that He Himself, in whom both they and we are blessed, was to be manifested. And this he calls the fullness of time, that is, the fulfillment of the time previously fixed. Others call the fullness of time the time of fullness, that is, of grace. St. Jerome cites some commentator or other who says in self-contradiction: "If it was necessary for Him to be made under the Law, in order to redeem those that were under the Law, then it would also have been necessary for Him to be made without the Law, in order to redeem those — namely, the Gentiles — who were without the Law. Or if this was not necessary, then the former is also superfluous." [6] That commentator understands the apostle as speaking only of the Ceremonial Law, whereas the apostle is speaking about the whole Law. Christ, you see, did not redeem us from ceremonies only. No, He redeemed us from lusts or from the Law that forbids lust. For He was Himself under obligation to no one, yet He made Himself a debtor by living as if He were a sinner.

Hence the apostle's way of speaking has to be observed. For being under the Law does not mean that one lives contemporaneously with the Law and under its decree (in this sense neither Job nor Naaman the Syrian was under the Law; nor was the woman of

[6] Jerome, *Commentarius*, 398.

Zarephath in Sidon [Luke 4:26]); but it means to be under obligation to the Law, that you do not have the means of fulfilling it, and that you are deserving of all the penalties laid down by the Law. But although Christ was not and could not be under the Law, yet He was made sin and a sinner under the Law, not by doing things contrary to the Law, as we do, but by innocently assuming on our behalf the penalties for sin that were decreed by the Law. Hence all nations were under the Law, at least under the law of nature and of the Decalog. Therefore Christ was not made under the Law in the same way we are under the Law, just as He was not a curse and sin in the same way we are. He was subjected only according to the body, but we are subjected according to both body and spirit; and, as St. Augustine says in the third chapter of the fourth book of his *On the Trinity:* "With His singleness He harmonizes with our twofoldness and fills out a beautiful octave." [7]

Does not the expression "made of woman" seem to be almost an insult to Christ's virgin mother? For with the same verb Paul could have said: "Made of a virgin." St. Jerome thinks it was stated this way on account of Manichaeus, who says that Christ was born *through* a woman, not *of* a woman, and who asserts without proof that Christ's flesh was imaginary, not genuine.[8] For it can also be said that the apostle is paying honor to God's condescension, which came down so far that He was willing to be born not only of human nature but even of the weaker sex, and that for this reason the word for the sex was more suitable than the term for her state. At the same time it can be said that Paul is making the point that Adam was not made of woman and that Eve was made of man, not of woman, so that just as a woman made of man was the cause of sin and perdition, so a man made of woman would become the cause of righteousness and salvation.[9] The opposite sexes produce opposite results, and this could not be noted without the word for the sex. Yet in this passage Paul does not leave the virginity of Mary unimplied; for since all others come from man and woman, but He alone comes from woman — in this way he gives ample praise to the miracle, namely, that the mother is a virgin woman and that He is the Son of a virgin. Finally, because Christ had to be a natural

---

[7] Augustine, *On the Trinity,* IV, 3, 5—6.

[8] Jerome refers here not to the Manichaeans but to Marcion: *Commentarius,* 398.

[9] This is a summary of the argument of Anselm, *Cur deus homo,* II, 8.

human being and a son, it was necessary for Him to be born. For a birth to take place, however, there is also need of the female sex, because as a human being He would not be a son unless He had been born of a woman, just as Adam, as a human being, was not a son and Eve, as a human being, was not a daughter.

"Adoption as sons" is expressed more fittingly in the Greek word υἱοθεσία, which comes from "to place" and "son," just as the Latin word *legispositio* is made up in the same way from "to place" and "law." But this υἱοθεσία takes place, as Paul taught above, through faith in Christ, which, as God promised Abraham, would be in Him (that is, in Christ). For to believe in Christ is to put Him on, to become one with Him. But Christ is the Son. Therefore all who believe in Him are sons together with Him.

For the sake of those who are not yet sufficiently instructed in Christ I repeat what I have said rather often above, namely, that these expressions "to redeem," "that we might receive adoption," "you are sons," "He has sent the Spirit," "He is a son and heir, not a slave," and similar expressions are not to be understood as having been fulfilled in us, but that Christ has fulfilled this in order that it may also be fulfilled in us; for they have all been begun in such a way that from day to day they are achieved more and more. For this reason it is also called the Passover of the Lord, that is, a passing through (Ex. 12:11-12), and we are called Galileans, that is, wanderers, because we are continually going forth from Egypt through the desert, that is, through the way of cross and suffering to the Land of Promise.[10] We have been redeemed, and we are being redeemed continually. We have received adoption and are still receiving it. We have been made sons of God, and we are and shall be sons. The Spirit has been sent, is being sent, and will be sent. We learn, and we shall learn.

And so you must not imagine that the Christian's life is a standing still and a state of rest. No, it is a passing over and a progress from vices to virtue, from clarity to clarity, from virtue to virtue. And those who have not been en route you should not consider Christians either. On the contrary, you must regard them as a people of inactivity and peace, upon whom the prophet calls down their enemies.[11] Therefore do not believe those deceitful theologians who say to you:

[10] See p. 177, note 22.
[11] The reference to a "prophet" is not clear, but Luther may be thinking of a passage like Jer. 8:11.

"If you have only one, even the first, level of love, you have enough for salvation" — as with their stupid fancies they invent a love that is idle in the heart like wine in a barrel.[12] Love is not idle, but it continually crucifies the flesh and is unable to rest content at its own level; it expands itself to purge a man throughout his being. But in the time of temptation and of death these people, with their single level, will have neither the first nor the second level.

6. *And because you are sons, God has sent the Spirit of His Son into your hearts, crying: Abba! Father!*

St. Jerome has "our hearts." So does the Greek. Thus this indeed corresponds to Rom. 8:15: "You have received the spirit of sonship, in which we cry: 'Abba! Father!'" Paul does not say "in which you cry," even though he spoke to them in the second person. So he does here too. "Abba! Father!" — why did He say the same thing twice when there is no apparent grammatical reason? I like the popular explanation of the mystery, namely, that the same spirit of faith belongs to Jews and Gentiles, two peoples belonging to one God, just as the apostle says in Rom. 1:16 and 2:10: "To the Jew first and also to the Greek." [13]

Note that because the apostle has spoken about the sons of God, for this reason he calls the Holy Spirit the Spirit of the Son of God, in order to show that the same Spirit who is in Christ, the Son of God, has been sent to believers. Moreover, he plainly designates the Holy Trinity as one God. For since the Son is true God, He lives in God's Spirit, in whom without a doubt the Father also lives; and Him whom in another passage (Rom. 8:9) Paul calls the Spirit of God he here calls the Spirit of the Son. So we, too, have our being in God, move and live in Him (Acts 17:28). We have our being because of the Father, who is the "Substance" of the Godhead.[14] We are moved by the image of the Son, who, moved by a divine and eternal motion, so to speak, is born of the Father. We live according to the Spirit, in whom the Father and the Son rest and live, as it were. But these matters are too sublime to belong here.

The thing to which more attention must be given is this: the apostle testifies that the Spirit of sonship is also given at once to

---

[12] See the discussion of the levels of charity in Peter Lombard, *Sententiae*, III, 29, *Patrologia, Series Latina*, CXCII, 816—818.

[13] Jerome, *Commentarius*, 399.

[14] On "substance" in the Godhead cf. Augustine, *On the Trinity*, VII, 5, 10.

those who believe. "Because you are sons," he says, (through faith, of course, as has already been frequently stated) "God has sent the Spirit of His Son into our hearts." With this statement an answer is easily given to the question raised by those who ask how one can teach that man is justified and saved by faith alone. There is no cause for you to be disturbed. If faith is genuine and you are really a son, the Spirit will not be lacking. But if the Spirit is present, He will pour forth love and will release that whole symphony of virtues which in 1 Cor. 13:4 Paul attributes to love. "Love is patient and kind, etc." Consequently, when he speaks of justifying faith, he speaks of the faith that works through love, as he says elsewhere (Gal. 5:6). For it is faith that gains the giving of the Spirit, as he said above (Gal. 3:2): "Did you receive the Spirit by works of the Law or by hearing with faith?" On the other hand, the faith which causes the demons to shudder (James 2:19) and the ungodly to do miracles is not genuine faith, since they are not yet sons or heirs of the blessing.

7. *So you are no longer a slave but a son, and if a son, then an heir through God.*

St. Jerome reads "through Christ," and this is also the reading in Greek; for Paul adds this in order that no one may hope for this inheritance through the Law or from any other source than through Christ, because the blessing is promised and presented in the Offspring of Abraham, which is Christ. The same thing is stated in Rom. 8:17: "And if children, then heirs, heirs of God and fellow heirs with Christ."

Enough has been said about what "slave" and "slavery" mean, namely, one who keeps the Law and does not keep it. He keeps it with works, either from fear of punishment or because of a desire for advantage. He does not keep it willingly, because he would prefer that there were no Law. Inwardly, therefore, he now hates the righteousness of the Law which he feigns outwardly before men. The son, however, with the help of grace, keeps the Law freely, would not wish that there were no Law but rather rejoices that the Law exists. The former has only his hand in the Law of the Lord; the latter has his will in the Law of the Lord.

8. *Formerly, when you did not know God, you were in bondage to beings that by nature are no gods.*

Paul indicates plainly that the term "god" is used in a twofold sense: of Him who is God by nature, that is, the true, one, living, and eternal God; and of many others, who are false and dead gods, that is, human beings, beasts, and birds, as we read in Rom. 1:23: "And exchanged the glory of the immortal God for images resembling mortal man or birds or animals or reptiles." These, then, are gods, not by nature but in the opinion and mistaken notion of men who, contrary to the Second Commandment, take the name and glory of the true God in vain and have assigned it to them, just as now, too, the name of the Lord renders service to countless superstitions. For since His name is holy and terrible and men are most powerfully swayed by the terror it inspires, it cannot be used as a pretext for any iniquities and deceptions whatever except with most harmful consequences. By nature there is implanted in man a veneration for the divine name, but it is very difficult to know it when it is called upon in truth. This lack of knowledge, you see, draws people away from the true God in a most insidious fashion; and by it, says Paul, the Galatians, too, had at one time been deceived together with the rest of the Gentiles.

More recent teachers distinguish ignorance that is invincible, ignorance that is gross, and ignorance that is affected. Ignorance that is invincible, they say, excuses one from all sin; ignorance that is gross excuses one partially but not entirely; ignorance that is affected, however, accuses one all the more.[15] These distinctions seem to me to have been fabricated in order to do injury to God's grace and to inflate free will, then also to make men smug in their state of perdition. For so long as a man does what is within his power, he is smug, because invincible ignorance does no harm. In short, ignorance is, on the one hand, said to be invincible with reference to us and our powers. In that case it is certain that there is no such thing as ignorance that can be overcome, at least in those matters that pertain to God. In John 3:27 we read: "No one can receive anything except what is given him from heaven." And John 6:44 says: "No one can come to Me unless the Father draws him." For of ourselves we are capable of no good at all; we are capable only of erring, of increasing our ignorance, and of sinning. Consequently, he who tries by his own powers to escape from any ignorance whatever is blinding himself with a twofold sin and ignorance. First, because he is ignorant; secondly, because he does not know that he is ignorant and presumes to drive out ignorance by means of ignorance and to accomplish the

[15] See theses 35 and 36 of Luther's *Disputation Against Scholastic Theology*, *Luther's Works*, 31, p. 11.

work that belongs to God alone. Thus while he strives for improvement through himself, he goes from sin to godlessness, and what he should have sought from God he falsely claims to have found in himself. Christ alone, not our reason, is the Light and Life of all men. On the other hand, ignorance is said to be invincible with reference to God's grace toward us. In that case there is no such thing as invincible ignorance, because all things are possible to him who believes.

Therefore men should not be taught to have no fear of invincible ignorance, lest they trust in themselves and their own resources and give up their fear of God. On the contrary, whether they have done what is in their power or not, they should despair of themselves and put their trust in God alone, fear His judgment even in their good works, and hope in His mercy even in their evil works, in order that they may never do anything to make them smug and never commit any sin in which they despair. Thus there is always an invincible ignorance. Nevertheless, by the very fact that they fear and hope, they are entirely without ignorance. Accordingly, invincible ignorance affords no excuse; but confession and mournful recognition of invincible ignorance does afford an excuse, or rather obtains grace.

9. *But now that you have come to know God, or rather to be known by God, how can you turn back again to the weak and beggarly elements, whose slaves you want to be once more?*

I do not know whether the apostle is employing an argument based on their ingratitude or one that proceeds from the lesser to the greater. Let us test both. From the lesser to the greater: "If at that time, when you, ignorant of God, were serving false gods, you did not turn to the weak elements, why do you turn to them now, when you have learned to know God? At that time you seemed more in need of them, because Judaism far surpassed heathenism. But now, when you have become incomparably superior to Judaism, you surely have no need whatever of those elements." The argument based on ingratitude would be as follows: "You recall with what foul idolatry you served the unclean gods and that now, by God's mercy, you have been called to the worship of the true God — are you, then, not ashamed of such ingratitude, namely, that you are again departing from God, who called you from such great evils to such great benefits?" Or perhaps Paul, as he is wont to do, has combined the two arguments.

St. Augustine thinks that the statement "rather to be known by God" was made as if to give an explanation to the weak, because the uneducated could understand the knowledge of God by which he says they had come to know Him to have been a knowledge from face to face, and thus they could fail to understand the apostle. For this reason, thinks St. Augustine, he has explained himself by saying that they have come to be known rather than have learned to know.[16] Nonetheless, beneath this simple statement there lies concealed the lofty meaning that it is our function passively to receive God and His working within us, just as we see that a workman's tool is acted upon rather than that it does the acting. This he also says in Is. 12:26: "O Lord, Thou hast wrought for us all our works." Thus our knowing is a being known by God, who has also worked this very knowing within us. (For Paul is speaking of faith.) Therefore God has known us first. This is a very apt way of speaking for him to use against those who have now begun to rely on their own righteousness, as if they wanted to get ahead of God with their works and to prepare for God a righteousness that should be accepted by Him. This madness is characteristic of all who try to find their righteousness in laws and ceremonies. With the same statement, however, he touches at the same time on predestination in a hidden way, just as previously, in another place, he merely hints at it and then passes it by.[17] For it is not because they know that they are known; but, on the contrary, because they have been known, therefore they know. Consequently, all goodness and all glory for goodness belong not to him who wills or runs but to God, who is merciful (Rom. 9:16). One must maintain the same thing about faith and about the Spirit.

Note the weight of his words and the striking tapinosis. "To the elements," that is, to the letter and the symbols that stand for real things, since they themselves thought they had turned to the real thing itself. Then "weak," because the Law was certainly unable to help them to righteousness. Indeed, it rather increased their sin. And "beggarly," empty, because the Law is not only unable to carry you forward any farther but is unable even to preserve and sustain you in the state in which you are. On the contrary, it is necessary that you become worse through it. But the grace of faith in Christ is able

---

[16] Augustine, *Epistolae ad Galatas expositio, Patrologia, Series Latina*, XXXV, 2130—2131.

[17] Cf. p. 283.

not only to preserve you but also to carry you forward to perfection. It was stated above what the "elemental spirits" are and why. You see, then, how contemptuously he speaks of the Law in opposition to the boastful false apostles.

At this point St. Jerome asks whether Moses and the prophets knew God and thus did not observe the Law or whether they observed the Law and thus did not know God.[18] For the apostle sets these two things in opposition to each other, and it is dangerous to make either assertion about the prophets. But the apostle solves this difficulty with one word when he says: "You want to be their slaves once more." To observe the things of the Law is not evil, but to be in servitude to the things of the Law is evil. Now a man is in servitude if — as has already been stated often — he does these things because he is compelled by fear of threats, as if they were necessary for gaining righteousness. If done freely, however, they are no obstacle. Thus the prophets observed them, not with a view to obtaining righteousness but in order to practice love for God and for their neighbor. They themselves were justified on the basis of faith.

10. *You observe days and months and seasons and years!*

St. Augustine wavers in his exposition of this passage.[19] Yet he explains it in the light of the religious ceremonies of the Gentiles rather than in the light of those of the Jews. For he says that it is a very common error of the Gentiles that, as they conduct their affairs or look ahead to the outcomes of life and of their business concerns, they observe the days, months, seasons, and years designated by the astrologers and the Chaldeans. It is in this sense that the Decrees cite the apostle throughout, in line with their practice, according to which they are accustomed to cite also many other statements on the ground that they were spoken by the saintly fathers; but they fail to indicate why they were spoken.[20] Yet St. Augustine says at once that this must also be understood of the Jews.

St. Jerome understands the passage simply and correctly as referring only to the Jews.[21] "Days," he says, as Sabbaths and new

---

[18] Jerome, *Commentarius*, 401—402.

[19] Augustine, *Epistolae ad Galatas expositio, Patrologia, Series Latina*, XXXV, 2129.

[20] Thus Luther could say that "the pope in his canon law has put God to school." *Luther's Works*, 45, p. 144.

[21] Jerome, *Commentarius*, 403—404.

moons; "months," however, as the first and seventh month; "seasons," as those in which they came to Jerusalem three times each year; "years," however, as the seventh, the year of release, and the fiftieth, which they called the year of jubilee.

Jerome also asks whether we, too, are in the clutches of the same fault, because we observe the fourth day of the week (Wednesday), the day of the preparation (Friday), the Lord's Day, the forty-day fast season (Lent), Easter and Pentecost, and various seasons appointed in honor of the martyrs and differing from land to land. In answer he says, in the first place, that we do not observe the days of the Jews but observe other days. Secondly, that the days have been appointed, not to give greater distinction to the day on which we assemble but in order that faith in Christ may not be diminished by a disorderly assembly of the people. Thirdly, as he tries to give a sharper answer, he asserts that all days are equal, that the day of the resurrection is always holy, that it is always permissible to fast, always permissible to eat the Lord's body, always permissible to pray. For this reason fasts and assemblies are on days appointed by prudent men for the sake of those who have more time for the world than for God, etc. This is true, for Is. 66:23 predicted that it would be so. "There will be Sabbath upon Sabbath and month upon month." In fact, every day is a feast day in the new Law, except in this respect, that by order of the church a day is appointed for hearing God's Word, for receiving the Sacrament, and for joining in common prayers. But now our feast days have gone off into far greater superstitions than those of the Jews, to the point that people now think they do God a service if they multiply these days, not for the sake of praying, not for the sake of hearing God's Word, and not for the sake of receiving the Sacrament but merely for the sake of celebrating holidays. And as a matter of fact, they celebrate holidays with greater perfection than the Jews do; for the latter at least read Moses and the prophets, while we serve neither God nor man but take a complete vacation from absolutely everything, except that we serve the belly, idleness, and other excesses.

But even so the bishops do not have enough compassion on the people to abolish some of the feast days and decrease their number, perhaps because they fear the authority of the Roman pontiff, who decrees these things. As if this itself were not a godless thought, namely, that the Roman pontiff intended or was able to establish or to tolerate those days which, with so many monstrous deeds, worship the devil — to the utter disgrace of the Christian name and to the blaspheming of the Divine Majesty. Or if they think that the pope intends or is willing to tolerate these things, it is most godless to have obeyed and not to have totally and boldly shattered and nullified a man-made decree that tends toward such an affront to the Creator. No bishop or pastor is excused if he sees that in his church the feast days are spent in drunken brawls, games, licentiousness, murders, laziness, idle tales, and spectacles (as nearly all are spent, except for a few especially important ones), and then does not abolish them. He is not excused, I say, on the ground that this is not permissible without the authority of the pope; for even if an angel from heaven had so decreed, we still owe more to God's glory and honor. Whatever is decreed or whatever is tolerated by anyone to God's detriment must be boldly done away with, unless someone would prefer to make himself guilty of every evil by permitting such deeds. The commandment of the Roman Church is not binding if it cannot be kept to the honor and glory of God. But if it cannot be kept in this way, then I declare now that those who force us to respect this kind of commandment are godless, just as we are mocked by those utterly godless people who place the fear of man ahead of the fear of God and, under the title of pope and St. Peter, crown, yes, even worship, the devil in the church of Christ.

We are thinking of war against the Turks;[22] but in regard to this matter and other needs of the church that are far worse than the tyranny of the Turks we are unconcerned and sleep on both ears, as though it would not be better if the Turk came as a scourge of God indeed and cured our evils even by bodily death than if the people degenerated into worse Turks because of such license on their part and such laziness on the part of the pastors of the church. The Turk, of course, will kill our bodies and rob us of our land; but we are killing souls and depriving them of heaven — at least if the decree of the most recent council is true, namely, that souls are immortal, especially the souls of Christians.[23]

[22] Defense against the Turks had been the chief issue at the Diet of Augsburg the previous year.

[23] A reference to the bull *Apostolici regiminis*, promulgated at the eighth session of the Fifth Lateran Council (December 19, 1513), which was the first official definition of the immortality of the human soul; the appropriate decree is reprinted in Henry Denzinger, *The Sources of Catholic Dogma [Enchiridion Symbolorum]*, edited by Karl Rahner and translated by Roy J. Deferrari (Saint Louis, 1957), pp. 237—238 (No. 738).

Let us return to the apostle. Circumcision as well as feast days contributed nothing at all to righteousness. Nor did other things which he recounts in greater detail in Col. 2:16. Accordingly, they were not to be observed as necessary, certainly no more than our feast days confer righteousness on us when we observe them or any other burdensome traditions. But our righteousness comes from faith in Christ, which is not produced by ceremonies but freely makes use of ceremonies out of love for God and one's neighbor, unless the multiplication of feast days affords you this gain that thereby you, resting from the works of your hands, decrease your resources and thus come little by little to poverty, in keeping with the well-known Gospel passage: "Blessed are the poor" (Matt. 5:3). Consequently, feast days are of value, not for the worship of God but for bringing on poverty or for nullifying that most wholesome precept which God laid upon man of old: "In the sweat of your face you shall eat bread" (Gen. 3:19). But of this and other matters elsewhere. The church of Christ is in a sorry state with heaven and earth enraged over our sins.

11. *I fear you that I have labored over you in vain.*

St. Jerome thinks that "I fear you" is said instead of "I fear concerning you." [24] To me, too, the statement seems to smack of an ellipsis, as though the apostle wanted to terrify them with their danger and to say: "I fear that you are going to perish eternally and that thus I have done all my work among you in vain." But he changes his words, suppresses them as being harsh, and pleads only his own loss. For it is in keeping with the apostle's gentleness not to attack harshly those whom he wanted to regain, since indeed — as is characteristic of human feelings, especially when caught in a wrong — they are drawn and influenced more by gentleness than they are forced by threats and terror. And a powerful impression is made if you make the misfortunes of others your own and lament over those misfortunes, so that finally you arouse these people at least to join you in bewailing their misfortunes. Therefore Paul would be saying: "O Galatians, even if your misfortune does not disturb you very much, at least feel sorry for me; sympathize with me, since I fear that in your midst I have lost, not property, not reputation, not honor, not merely a word or a work but my full endeavor. It would have been

---

[24] Jerome, *Commentarius*, 405.

milder if I had merely said: 'Now I have worked, prayed, suffered many things, have been in many dangers for you' — as he recounts at length in his Epistle to the Corinthians (2 Cor. 11:23 ff.) — 'and all this I have now spent in vain.'" These words breathe Paul's own tears.

12. *Become as I am, for I also have become as you are.*

Here, too, obscurity produces a variety of interpretations. Saint Jerome adduces two.[25] The first is: "Be like me"; that is "Be strong and manly in faith in Christ, just as I now am" — in order that this may be an exhortation to greater perfection. "Because I also have become as you are"; that is to say: "I became so then, namely, when I first gave you the milk of the Gospel; for I made myself a child and weak for you by concealing the greater perfection. And I gave you the more elementary doctrines of faith and showed myself the kind of teacher you, in your weakness, would be able to understand. Accordingly, at that time I was like you. Pay me back, therefore, and be like me, that is, strong enough to understand me as I transmit more difficult things." The other interpretation is: "I, too, was once involved in ceremonies, just as you are now; but I considered them as dung, that I might gain Christ. You must do the same thing and be as I am now."

St. Augustine says that Paul means: "Be as I am. I despise the things of the Law, Jew though I am, because I also am as you are; that is, I am human, just as you are. If I, who am human like you, am at liberty to disregard the elements, you, too, will be at liberty to do so." [26]

It can also be thought of in this way: Because Paul had rebuked them harshly, now, to keep them from being provoked and feeling hurt, he anticipates them and demands that they show themsleves to him as he shows himself to them. Therefore the meaning would be: "I, at any rate, have not felt hurt by you; you have not provoked me. So do not feel hurt and provoked by me, but let us both bewail our common trouble. My trouble is that you are falling away. Consequently, I have not been hurt by you; I have been hurt by the trouble I now have. Therefore do not be hurt by my reproof. On the contrary, be hurt by your own trouble." What follows in the

---

[25] Jerome, *Commentarius*, 405.

[26] Augustine, *Epistolae ad Galatas expositio, Patrologia, Series Latina*, XXXV, 2131.

text seems to support this meaning. "You have not hurt me at all," he says. Not much different from this is the meaning one gets by connecting it with the preceding words as follows: "Since I am affected by this trouble of yours in no other way than if it were my own, in such a way that I am now truly made weak together with the weak, weep with those who weep (Rom. 12:15), and have become all things to all men (1 Cor. 9:22), I beg you again to become like me in my fear that I have labored in vain, and to fear with him who fears, to grieve with him who grieves that his labor is lost. Thus if you are not moved by your own trouble, you will be moved by mine and in this way may also come to bewail your own trouble." For thus, when our sins did not torment us, Christ also, as St. Bernard testifies, grieved and suffered for us, in order that by His grief on account of our sins He might the more strongly move us to mourn, just as He said to the women who were following Him: "Do not weep for Me, but weep for yourselves" (Luke 23:28).[27] In these matters I leave to the reader his free judgment.

12. *Brethren, I entreat you, you did me no wrong.*

St. Jerome connects this with the previous thought and reads it as follows: "Brethren, I entreat you, be as I am, because I am as you are. You have done me no wrong."[28] But since the apostle usually begins a new thought when he says: "Brethren, I entreat you," I do not know whether this order is to be maintained. What if by way of ellipsis he wanted to say the following or something like it: "I entreat you, forgive me; I have been harsh, but out of necessity. Bear with my zeal a little"? St. Jerome understands it as follows: "Since you did me no wrong before now, when I, who became weak, transmitted to you, who were children and weak, things that were weak — why am I being wronged by you now as I stir you up to greater things?" And this thought Paul supports from what follows, where he says that he had preached to them in weakness and nevertheless had been received as an angel of God, etc. It is certain, therefore, that with this text the apostle, because of his fatherly concern, is moderating and softening the harshness of his whole previous discourse. He had censured them for being foolish,

---

[27] Cf., for example, Bernard of Clairvaux, *Sermones de diversis*, XXXIV, 2, *Patrologia, Series Latina*, CLXXXIII, 631.

[28] Jerome, *Commentarius*, 406.

for having turned away quickly, for having reverted to the elements of the world, for ending with the flesh, for being bewitched. He had said that Christ was crucified among them, that grace was despised, that the testament of God was nullified, that they were changed from children to slaves, and now, to sum it up, that he had done everything in vain and had expended all his labor in vain. In this way he had indicated that almost everything about them was in a very bad and desperate state, and all this with vehemence and a most fervent zeal for guarding the grace of God. For this reason he now tempers and softens his reproach with the oil of gentleness. He demands that they be patient and concede something to the zeal for God with which he is zealous for them, just as he himself has been patient, conceding many things to them, also this present trouble. "I entreat you, dearest brethren," he says. "I have not said these things out of hatred for you; I am telling you the truth. But do not on this account consider me your enemy." For what he says below is sufficient evidence that he feared they had been offended too much: "Have I, then, become your enemy by speaking the truth?" (Gal. 4:16.) And again: "I could wish to be present with you now and to change my tone" (v. 20), as if he were saying: "I fear that what I have written may be too offensive," as we shall see. And in order to be most effective in trying to persuade them that he had not spoken these things in a bitter spirit or out of hatred, he begins to commend them most profusely: "I am not unfriendly to you, brethren; you have never wronged me at all. On the contrary, so far were you from wronging me that you gave me an exceptional welcome as an angel of God."

13. *You know it was because of weakness of the flesh that I preached the Gospel to you at first;*

14. *and though my condition was a trial to you, you did not scorn or despise me but received me as an angel of God, as Christ Jesus.*

"Weakness of the flesh." St. Jerome refers this to the Galatians as to people who were still too weak and carnal for Paul to be able to preach spiritual things to them.[29] This does not please me. On the contrary, it is a Pauline way of speaking, by which he expresses the lowliness of his condition; for weakness is the incapacity because of which the apostles — being paupers, despised, subject also to various persecutions, and, as he says to the Corinthians, "last of all" (1 Cor.

[29] Jerome, *Commentarius*, 407.

4:9) according to the flesh and in the sight of men — were regarded as altogether powerless and as nothing at all. Nevertheless, under this weakness they performed valorous deeds and were more powerful in word and in work than the whole world. Therefore the genitive "of the flesh" should not be taken as referring to the apostle or to the Galatians; it should be taken in an absolute sense and, just as it is put here by the apostle, should be contrasted with the spirit, as in Rom. 1:3-4: "Who was descended from David according to the flesh and designated Son of God in power according to the spirit of holiness." And in 1 Peter 3:18: "Being put to death in the flesh but made alive in the spirit." Thus here, too, "weakness of the flesh," that is, incapacity, is that which is according to the flesh, if you do not see the strength that is in the spirit.

But that "weakness" does signify what I have said is clear from Paul's Second Epistle to the Corinthians, where, recounting all the things he had done and suffered (11:18 ff.; 12:1 ff.), he says: "I will all the more gladly boast of my weakness, that the power of Christ may rest upon me," and "power is made perfect in weakness" (12:9), and "when I am weak, then I am strong" (v. 10). Therefore it is extraordinary praise for the Galatians that they were not offended by those stumbling blocks on account of which the whole world was offended and laughed at the apostles, both because of the weakness of the flesh and because of the folly of the cross, by which they taught that there is a future life and that all the things of this life, because of which men glory in their own strength, must be despised. Indeed, the Galatians had received Paul as an angel, as Christ Himself, undoubtedly with the greatest reverence and humility. But St. Jerome interprets the trial of the Galatians in several ways. In my opinion, however, his last explanation is the correct one. He says: "The abuses, the persecutions, and the like, which they saw he had endured and was enduring for the Word of Christ — especially from the Jews and also from the Gentiles — in his flesh, that is, in the sight of men (for in the spirit God was always triumphing in him through Christ, as he says elsewhere [2 Cor. 2:14]) — these things they did not spurn or despise, even though they were tempted by them in the strongest possible way to abandon the Word of faith for fear of such things." For today, too, this temptation quickly overthrows many who think of those who have suffered and have been afflicted for the sake of God's truth. At that time the Galatians were not at all disturbed by this, as they saw that the apostle was afflicted in every way. Paul is praising what is truly a kind of apostolic virtue on the part of those who overcame this temptation and received the apostle as though he were Christ. Do you not think that they did this at the risk of their lives and of everything they had? Did they not on Paul's account draw down upon themselves the violence and wrath of all Paul's enemies? They could not receive Paul without offending Paul's persecutors. Indeed, they provoked these persecutors all the more, because they not only received Paul but received him as an angel, as Christ, that is, with the greatest reverence — Paul, whom his adversaries treated with the greatest abuse and were seeking to kill as the worst of all.

On the basis of this passage St. Jerome admonishes the bishops. "Let them learn from the apostle," he says, "that the erring, foolish Galatians are called brothers; let them learn the soothing words of him who, after upbraiding them, says: 'I entreat you.' His entreaty is this, that they be imitators of him, just as he himself is of Christ. These facts knock down the haughtiness of the bishops, who, as though stationed on some lofty watchtower, scarcely condescend to look at mortals and to address their fellow servants."

I have quoted these words because in our age it is a miracle, yes, more than godlessness, even to mention the faults of the bishops. Jerome would have said something else if he had seen how for the most part the bishops of our age surpass kings and princes in their splendor, while, on the other hand, they fail to match even uneducated persons and women in Christian life or in knowledge. But the apostle, well aware of what he wrote to Timothy — "Reprove, entreat, rebuke, be urgent in season and out of season with all patience, etc." (2 Tim. 4:2) — teaches the same thing in this epistle by his example. He does not excommunicate, does not shout: "To the fire!" He does not pronounce them heretics offhand, does not lay upon them one burden after the other. No, he displays the fire of his love and the flames of his heart, because he has been eager to kill men's faults and errors, not men. He does not know the thunderbolts of a broad sentence; he knows only the thunderbolt of God's Word and the thunder of the Gospel, by which alone sinners are killed and made alive.

15. *Where, then, is your blessedness?*

[Paul asks this question] either because at one time he had called them blessed in view of the steadfastness of their great faith, or because those can be called truly blessed who are the kind of people he has praised the Galatians for being — unless someone thinks that the modesty of the apostle is indicated here, as though he wanted to say: "Where is now that reverence of yours for me, that concern and adoration, so to speak?" but modestly wanted to refer to their blessedness rather than to his own honor, in keeping with the example of Christ, whose custom it was to ascribe His miracles to the faith of those for whom they were done.[30] Or, if a simple meaning is wanted, he declares that their faith in Christ, in which they used to find their blessedness, is not what it used to be, and rebukes them on this account.

For I bear you witness that, if possible, you would have plucked out your eyes and given them to me.

St. Jerome thinks this is a hyperbole.[31] But I do not think it is necessarily a hyperbole, because from what was said before it is evident that they had even risked their lives for the apostle's sake. So it is not surprising that — if it could have been done, that is, if he himself were to permit it, and if it had to be done this way (otherwise why was it impossible, if they wanted to do so?) — they were even going to pluck out their eyes. But by speaking of their eyes in a hidden sense he may be alluding to a secret reprimand, namely, that those who at that time were very glad to surrender their eyes, that is, their understanding, to the apostle, in order to be taught the faith that makes the wise foolish and causes those who see not to see — that they have now allowed themselves to be offended by their own eyes, which the Lord commanded to be torn out and cast from us (Matt. 5:29).

See what it means for a shepherd to neglect Christ's sheep. Such love, such faith, such sincere religious devotion on the part of the Galatians the false apostles so quickly subverted in the short time during which the apostle was absent. What would the devil do where there is no shepherd, or if there is one who never tends or feeds Christ's sheep? Will it be possible for them to be protected by the mere title, name, or authority of the shepherd? For if these things are uninjured, the church is thought to be uninjured.

[30] Luther is thinking of passages like Mark 5:34 and Mark 10:52.
[31] Jerome, *Commentarius*, 408.

16. *Have I, then, become your enemy by telling you the truth?*

Jerome correctly explains this as referring to the truth which he is speaking to them in this epistle rather than to the truth in which he first instructed them.[32] For, as I have said, the apostle's concern is this: that the Galatians may not take too indignantly the things he had said against them thus far. Some of these things were rather harsh. Nevertheless, they were true. For this reason he anticipates them and says: "You do not accept my words, because they are harsh. But look rather at how true they are. Granted that I upbraided you rather harshly. Do you for this reason consider me an enemy and not rather a friend, because I speak the truth to you, harsh though it has to be?"

What a beautiful example of teaching the truth! For you have to inflict the wound in such a way that you also know how to alleviate and heal it. You have to be severe in such a way as not to forget kindness. Thus God, too, puts lightning into the rain and breaks up gloomy clouds and a dark sky into fruitful showers. And so the proverb has it that the storm in which lightning is mingled with rain is harmless, whereas the one that is dry and unaccompanied by rain is formidable and harmful. For the Word of God, too, should not always be angry or threaten forever.

17. *They are not zealous for you in a good way, but they want to shut you out in order that you may be zealous for them.*

He is meeting the excuse which he sees they can plead by saying: "As to the fact that we obeyed those teachers, we did it because they seemed to be seeking our welfare with devout zeal and (as people now say) with a good intention, especially since no one should be his own master; and, as is stated in Deut. 12:8: 'What seems right to us should not be done.'" Paul answers: "I know they have zeal, but not a zeal that is good or enlightened" (Rom. 10:2).

Here one must know that the verb "to be zealous," although it is often identical in meaning with "to imitate," is taken by the apostle in its customary usage, "to be jealous with love" or "to contend and strive out of love for someone." Furthermore — to treat the matter more fully in line with our opinion — loving occurs in two ways: in a good way and in an evil way. So does being zealous. For sometimes we love, but not in a good way. Thus sometimes we are zealous,

---

[32] Jerome, *Commentarius*, 409.

but not in a good way. But just as love means loving what is good, and hatred means hating what is evil, so zeal or jealousy combines both characteristics and, properly speaking, means hating what is evil in the thing that is loved; and the more fervently you love, the more ardently you will hate and look askance at evil in the person who is loved. Consequently, I usually understand zeal to mean love roused to anger, or envy rising from love. Thus the apostle says in 2 Cor. 11:2: "I feel a divine jealousy for you." And one cannot even imagine that he is speaking about imitation here, because he continues with the statement: "I betrothed you to one husband. But I am afraid that your thoughts will be led astray" (vv. 2-3). It is as if he were saying: "I love pure faith in such a way that I cannot help fearing and hating whatever would corrupt you," thus clearly explaining what it means to be zealous with a zeal that is of God. In fact, with this very expression he indicates that twofold zeal. "A divine zeal," namely, one that is according to God, is a hatred of what is evil in the thing that is loved, according to the truth, or a love of what is good and hatred of what is evil in the thing that is loved, according to the truth. A zeal that is of men is a hatred of what is evil in the thing that is loved, or a love of what is good and hatred of what is evil in the thing that is loved, but according to outward appearance and erroneously. Such is the zeal of the false apostles, of which he says: "They are zealous for you, but not in a good way"; that is, they seek your good and abhor your evil, but in an evil way, because they were seeking to establish the evil of righteousness through the Law among the Galatians, as if it were a good thing. This is that stupid zeal with which the Jews, too, as Paul writes to the Romans, are zealous for God, that is, for the things that belong to God. For "to be zealous" cannot be taken in the present passage as meaning "to imitate," because the false apostles certainly did not imitate the Galatians. On the contrary, he says: "But they want to shut you out," namely, from Christ and from trust in Him, to imprison you in a trust in the Law, "in order that you may be zealous for them." In this place the word can be used in the sense of "to imitate," although it is not inconsistent with the previous meaning if you understand him to be saying that the false apostles wanted to be loved by the Galatians, wanted to be courted with pious devotion, and wanted the Galatians to become zealous for them as pupils often are for their teachers, to love what came from them, and to hold in hatred what was opposed to them. And it would not have been inappropriate for him to say: "They want to shut us out." But to avoid even the appearance of arrogance, he says: "They want to shut you out, so that with you shut out they may at the same time shut us out also."

18. *But be zealous always for what is good, and not only when I am present with you.*

Paul is refuting the other part of their excuse, for the first part was that the false apostles were seeking the Galatians' welfare with devout zeal. This the apostle denies. "They are not zealous for you," he says, "in a good way. They seek not what is yours but what is their own, in order that they may boast of you." As he says later (Gal. 6:13), the other excuse is that one must be obedient and not trust oneself. To this he answers: "It is indeed good to be zealous and to imitate others, but do this always in a good thing, never in an evil one, and not only when I am present but even when I am absent, lest you seem to be doing it for my sake and not for the sake of the thing itself."

For this reason I am surprised that the translator and St. Jerome have passed over this text in such a way, although it is quite obscure if you say: "Be zealous for what is good in a good thing." What does it mean to be zealous for what is good in that which is good? On the basis of the Greek, therefore, Erasmus and Stapulensis properly rendered it in this way: "It is always good to be zealous in a good thing" or "Zeal in a good matter is always good." [33] For it is the infinitive "to be zealous," not the imperative "be zealous," unless some smart-aleck tamperer has done violence both to the translator and to Jerome. What the apostle means is this: "Test everything; hold fast what is good" (1 Thess. 5:21). We see that this rule was given by him to all his churches. Yet for many centuries it was entirely obliterated.

19. *My little children, with whom I am again in travail until Christ be formed in you!*

Look at the marvelous love of the apostle and how with his whole being he is nothing else but what the Galatians are! To such an extent does he take everything into himself, utterly forgetful of his own person. How he suffers in them, how he toils, how he seethes, how solicitous he is, not for any of his own concerns but for those of the

---

[33] Jerome, *Commentarius*, 409; cf. also Erasmus, *Paraphrasis, Opera*, VII, 958.

Galatians! What an apostolic model for the Christian pastor! True love does not seek its own advantage (1 Cor. 13:5). "My dearest little children, my motherly heart is tormented. I was your father. I became your mother. I am carrying you in my womb. I am forming and shaping you. I should like to give birth to you and bring you forth into life if somehow I could." St. Jerome praises this sentiment at great length; for this indeed is what it means to seek souls, not money.[34]

Note Paul's careful choice of words. He does not say: "Until I form Christ in you" but "until He be formed," as he ascribes more to the grace of God than to his own works. Like a mother, he carries them in a womb as undeveloped seed until the Spirit lends His aid and forms them into Christ. A preacher can be anxious over how he may give birth to Christians, but he is unable to form them. He is no more able to do so than a natural mother forms the fetus. She only carries what is to be formed and to be born. Neither did he say "until you are formed into Christ." No, his words are "until Christ be formed in you," because the Christian's life is not his own; it is Christ's, who lives in him, as he said above in the second chapter: "It is no longer I who live, but Christ who lives in me" (Gal. 2:20). It is necessary that we be destroyed and rendered formless, in order that Christ may be formed and be alone in us.

20. *I could wish to be present with you now and to change my tone.*

To Jerome this seems to say that Divine Scripture indeed edifies when it is read but is much more profitable if it is turned from letters into voice, as he also writes to Paulinus about the efficacy of the living voice.[35] This, however, is not the only meaning the apostle intends. But he says: "I could wish to be present with you now for this reason, that I could change my tone," not with a musical change but with a theological one; that is, because an epistle in its written form offends if it scolds too much; but if it is too complaisant, it does not have enough effect among the foolish. In so serious a matter what is written is dead; it gives only as much as it has. But if he were present, he could adjust his speech according to the different kinds of hearers he would have — could scold these, mollify those; plead with these, rebuke those; and change to whatever sentiment would be

[34] Jerome, *Commentarius*, 411—412.
[35] Jerome, *Commentarius*, 413; also Epistle LIII, 2.

appropriate at the time. For it is clear that the apostle is concerned lest in his previous remarks he may have inclined too far in the direction of scolding, and here, with his praising and flattering, too far toward commendation, being afraid in a most pious way of erring in both directions, either of hurting too much or of hitting less strongly than necessary. Consequently, he is in suspense between the two possibilities and is perplexed; he does not know what to do and is at a loss as to whether he should scold or commend. This meaning is borne out by the word that follows.

For I am perplexed about you.

This means, as Erasmus has very fittingly rendered it, "I am undecided, I am disturbed, and I have no plan whatever with regard to what I should do with you." St. Jerome has also said a great deal when commenting on this sentence.[36] Finally he states reluctantly, almost carelessly, and, while discussing other matters: "'I am perplexed about you,' says Paul, 'and in my uncertainty I am drawn this way and that, and, not knowing what to do, I am drawn in opposite directions. I am distressed and torn to pieces; for I do not know what words to utter first, etc.'" Such are Jerome's expressions as they are scattered here and there.

21. *Tell me, you who desire to be under the Law, have you not read the Law?*

Jerome and the Greek text read: "Have you not heard the Law?" Jerome takes pains to show that in this passage the Law means Genesis, the book from which the apostle takes what he is saying.[37] But since in Hebrew the five books of Moses are called the Torah, that is, the Law, it is not unfitting for the apostle to use the name "the Law" for the Book of Genesis, in which, if nothing else, at least circumcision, the principal and foremost law of all for the Jews, is certainly enjoined.

22. *For it is written that Abraham had two sons, one by a slave and one by a free woman.*

23. *But the son of the slave was born according to the flesh, the son of the free woman through promise.*

[36] Erasmus, *Annotationes ad locum;* Jerome, *Commentarius,* 413—414.

[37] Jerome, *Commentarius,* 414.

24. *Now this is an allegory.*

Not that these statements are to be understood allegorically in Genesis, but the apostle is indicating that what was said there in a literal sense is said by him by way of allegory.

The question arises in what way Ishmael was not also born through promise, since in Gen. 16 so many things are promised by the angel of the Lord to his mother concerning him before he was born.[38] Again, in the seventeenth chapter, many more things are promised to Abraham by God Himself concerning him, now that he had been born. St. Jerome brings up many points and leaves the matter unsettled. It is clear, however, that Ishmael was conceived, not because of the promise of God but because of the command of Sarah, and because of the natural vigor in the young woman Hagar. But Isaac was conceived by a sterile and aged mother through the supernatural strength of Him who gave the promise. For what the angel said to Hagar — "Behold, you are with child and shall bear a son" (Gen. 16:11) — is certainly not the statement of one who is promising that a conception is to take place; it is the statement of one who is predicting what will happen with regard to him who has already been conceived, or even of one who is giving a command. Accordingly, Isaac is the son of the promise — born, however, of the flesh but not conceived by the power of the flesh or according to the flesh.

These women are two covenants. One is from Mt. Sinai, bearing children for slavery; she is Hagar.

Because the Galatians were believers, they could be instructed with allegorical teachings. Otherwise, as Paul says in 1 Cor. 14:22: "Tongues are a sign for unbelievers." But to unbelievers nothing can be proved by allegorical statements, as St. Augustine also points out in his letter to Vincentius.[39] Or at least the case is this, that out of fatherly concern the apostle intentionally pictures his subject by means of comparisons and allegories for the Galatians, as for people who are rather weak, in order to fit the words to their power of comprehension. For people who are not very well instructed are fascinated (and with pleasure at that) by comparisons, parables, and allegories. For this reason Christ, too, as Matthew says (13:13), teaches by means of parables in the Gospel, so that everyone can

---

[38] Jerome, *Commentarius*, 414—415.

[39] Augustine, Epistle XCIII, 2, 6.

understand Him. So let us see how Paul makes use of this allegorical teaching to oppose the righteousness of the Law.

"These," he says, "are two covenants." That is, the two women, Sarah and Hagar, were a figurative example of the two covenants under one and the same Abraham, who represents the heavenly Father.

But — something I had almost passed by — there are some points that must also be noted about the mystical and allegorical interpretations, since this subject matter requires it and so does our time. There are usually held to be four senses of Scripture. They are called the literal sense, the tropological, the allegorical, and the anagogical, so that Jerusalem, according to the literal sense, is the capital city of Judea; tropologically, a pure conscience or faith; allegorically, the church of Christ; and anagogically, the heavenly fatherland.[40] Thus in this passage Isaac and Ishmael are, in the literal sense, the two sons of Abraham; allegorically, the two covenants, or the synagog and the church, the Law and grace; tropologically, the flesh and the spirit, or virtue and vice, grace and sin; anagogically, glory and punishment, heaven and hell, yes, according to others, the angels and the demons, the blessed and the damned.

This kind of game may, of course, be permitted to those who want it, provided they do not accustom themselves to the rashness of some, who tear the Scriptures to pieces as they please and make them uncertain. On the contrary, these interpretations add extra ornamentation, so to speak, to the main and legitimate sense, so that a topic may be more richly adorned by them, or — in keeping with Paul's example — so that those who are not well instructed may be nurtured in gentler fashion with milky teaching, as it were. But these interpretations should not be brought forward with a view to establishing a doctrine of faith. For that four-horse team (even though I do not disapprove of it) is not sufficiently supported by the authority of Scripture, by the custom of the fathers, or by grammatical principles. It is clear, in the first place, that the apostle makes no distinction in this passage between the allegorical and the anagogical sense. Indeed, what they call an anagogical sense he himself calls an allegory when he interprets Sarah as the heavenly Jerusalem which is above, our mother, that is, their anagogical Jerusalem. Furthermore, the holy fathers deal with allegory in a grammatical way along with the

---

[40] Cf. p. 235, note 42.

other figures of speech in Holy Writ, as St. Augustine teaches abundantly in his book *On Christian Doctrine*.⁴¹ Besides, "anagoge" denotes the general nature of what is said rather than a particular figure; that is, there is said to be an anagoge whenever, in a hidden way and separately, something else can be understood than what the words sound like. For this reason it is also translated with "transference" [*reductio*], which is also the meaning of "allegory," namely, "saying what belongs to something else." This means, as St. Jerome says, that it presents one thing in words, but that in meaning it signifies something else.⁴² Tropology, it is agreed, is a discussion of moral behavior; but there is nothing to prevent this from sometimes being an allegory, namely, when something else, which signifies good or bad moral behavior, is being said. On the part of the fathers, then, these terms seem to have been used freely because by a certain apprehensiveness they were forced into the confinement of this fourfold distinction, just as many people thoughtlessly make many other distinctions between matters that are identical in fact and in word.

There is greater need to call attention to the fact — which has been stated earlier — that in Origen and Jerome the spiritual sense seems to be the one which the apostle here calls allegory. For they take the outward form and historical account to be the "letter." But the mystical and allegorical interpretation they call "spiritual." And they call that man "spiritual" who understands everything in a lofty sense, and, as they say, allows nothing of the Jewish tradition. It is according to this principle that Origen and Jerome proceed in nearly all their writings. And, to put it boldly, it is not seldom that they slip into difficulties from which they cannot extricate themselves. But for me St. Augustine proceeds more expeditiously. For — to pass over the fact that the mystical sense is either allegorical or anagogical, or, in general, one that in secret holds something else than is shown openly, and that opposed to this there is the historical or formal sense — nevertheless, these two words, "letter" and "spirit," as also the "literal" and the "spiritual" understanding, have to be separated and kept in their own proper meaning. For the letter, as Augustine says with beautiful brevity on Ps. 71, is the Law without grace.⁴³

⁴¹ Augustine, *On Christian Doctrine*, III, 29, 40.

⁴² Jerome, *Commentarius*, 416.

⁴³ Augustine, *Enarrationes in Psalmos*, LXX, 19, *Corpus Christianorum, Series Latina*, XXXIX, 957.

But if this is true, then every law is "letter," whether it is allegorical or tropological. Finally, as we have said above, so is whatever can be written, said, or thought apart from grace. But grace alone is the "spirit" itself. Hence spiritual understanding does not mean what is mystical or anagogical (in which the ungodly also excel); but in the strict sense it means life itself and the Law as it is put into actual practice, since it has been written in the soul by the finger of God through grace. In short, it means that complete fulfillment which the Law commands and requires. For in Rom. 7:7 Paul calls even the Decalog a spiritual law, even though "You shall not covet" is still a "letter." But if by spiritual understanding is meant this, that it signifies the spirit which the Law requires in order to be fulfilled, then there is no law that is not spiritual. Moreover, only then is it a "letter" when the grace to fulfill it is not there. In that case it is a "letter" for me, not for itself, especially if it is understood in the sense that grace is not necessary.

We conclude, therefore, that in itself the Law is always spiritual; that is, it signifies the spirit which is its fulfillment. For others, however, though never for itself, it is a "letter." For when I say: "You shall not kill," you hear the sound of the "letter." But what does it signify? Surely this, that you should not be angry; that is, the very essence, which is gentleness and kindness toward one's neighbor. This, however, is love and the spirit by which the Law is fulfilled. From the fact that it signifies the thing that is truest and solely spiritual the Law is also called spiritual, because it always has this significance. But because it does not give us what it signifies, and is unable to give it, for us it is called a "letter," no matter how spiritual it itself is. Since no work is done well without love, however, it is clear that every law that commands a good work signifies and requires a good work, that is, a work of love, and that on this account it is spiritual. Hence we rightly call the spiritual understanding of the Law the understanding by which one knows that the Law requires the spirit, and which convinces us that we are carnal. But we rightly call that the literal understanding by which one thinks, yes, mistakenly believes, that the Law can be fulfilled by our own works and strength without the spirit of grace. For this reason the "letter" kills (2 Cor. 3:6), because it is never rightly understood so long as it is understood without grace, just as it is never rightly kept so long as it is kept without grace. In both cases it is death and wrath. These thoughts have been taken from St. Augustine's book against the Pelagians.[44]

To return to the apostle. "One is from Mt. Sinai, bearing children for slavery." Enough has been said on what that slavery of the Law is into which we are delivered when we receive the Law without grace. For then we keep it either out of fear of threatened evil or out of hope of gain, that is, hypocritically. In both cases we act like slaves, not like free men. But he calls it a "covenant." Hence to understand this one must also see here the sign of the testament. First there is the testament itself, which was the naming of the Land of Promise, as is written in Ex. 3:8. The testator was an angel in the Person of God. The legacy that was bequeathed was the land of Canaan itself. The people for whom the testament was being made were the Children of Israel, as Exodus describes all these details. But this testament was confirmed by the death of an animal and by its blood, with which they were sprinkled, as one reads in Ex. 24:8, because a sacrifice of the flesh was appropriate for a fleshly promise, a fleshly testament, and fleshly heirs. "She is Hagar," he says; that is, this testament of slavery that gives birth to slaves is an allegorical Hagar, the slave woman.

25. *For Sinai is a mountain in Arabia which is connected with that which now is Jerusalem and is in slavery with her children.*

In the first place, Paul makes the strange statement that Mt. Sinai is connected with Jerusalem, the city of Judea, although he says that the former is in Arabia. St. Jerome reads "which is coterminous" and says by way of explanation "which has the same boundary" — perhaps because Sinai is correctly said to border on Jerusalem, not because the mountain touches the city, but because Judea, where Jerusalem is situated virtually in the center, and the Arabian Desert, in which Mt. Sinai is located, have the same boundary.[45] For to the east Judea has Arabia Petraea, and next to this, toward the south, it touches the Arabian Desert, so that in this way, because of the contiguity of the whole, a part may be said to border on a part and to be connected. Stapulensis, exploring the force of the Greek word, says it must be understood to mean that Sinai is a connected mountain range; that is, it goes on and, by a kind of extension, touches or, to use a geo-

---

[44] Augustine, *On the Spirit and the Letter*, 14, 24.
[45] Jerome, *Commentarius*, 417.

graphical term, reaches all the way to, Jerusalem.[46] Certainly this can only be understood in the sense that Mt. Sinai is connected by means of its own land mass to the land mass of Jerusalem, just as Wittenberg is connected with Leipzig — the former in Saxony, the latter in Meissen. Likewise, Erasmus, that excellent man, adds that in Greek it reads as follows: "For Hagar is Mt. Sinai in Arabia, etc.," and that here "Hagar" is used in the neuter gender, so that the reference is to the mountain, which in Greek is neuter, although presently it is used in the feminine gender, where he says: "She is Hagar." Thus the sequence is: "She is Hagar. For here Hagar is Mt. Sinai in Arabia." And he says that in the comments of the Greek scholiasts it is pointed out that in Arabic Sinai is called Hagar.[47] And perhaps the apostle's very context has this meaning when he says: "Hagar is Mt. Sinai in Arabia," namely, "In Arabia, Hagar is and is called what we call Sinai" or "The Arabs give Mt. Sinai the name Hagar in their language" — in order that in this way he may give the reason for what he had said, namely, that one testament is from Mt. Sinai and that therefore this one is Hagar, because by a play on the Arabic word Mt. Sinai is called Hagar. Under God's governance, therefore, Hagar was in this way prepared as a figure of Mt. Sinai, which bears children into slavery through the Law. We said above, however, that the apostle does not shrink from playing on words in another language, because by a word play on their name in Hebrew he designated the Galatians, too, as "transferred," just as here he describes the slave woman Hagar by a word play in Arabic.[48] Moreover, Solomon, in his Song of Songs (4:8), calls Mt. Amana by the name Senir, and Hermon and Lebanon according to a variety of languages — as is written in Deut. 3:9: "To Mt. Hermon (the Sidonians call Hermon Sirion, while the Amorites call it Senir)" — as he derives an allusion and an allegory from a foreign language for the praise of his bride. Therefore since Paul said earlier that he was going to speak by way of allegory, it was fitting that by a kind of word play he should combine the name of the slave woman Hagar with Mt. Sinai when he began to treat of the Hagar testament — and this because of the advantage of their common name. Nor should any other reason be de-

[46] Jacque Lefèvre d'Étaples, *S. Pauli Epistolae xiv. ex vulgata editione, adjecta intelligentia ex Graeco cum commentariis* (1512).

[47] Cf. Erasmus, *Paraphrasis, Opera,* VII, 959.

[48] See p. 177, note 22.

manded of the apostle here, since he is allegorizing for the sake of the weak.

But what bearing does Paul's statement that Mt. Sinai is connected with Jerusalem have on the subject matter? Was it not enough that the one testament was of Sinai and of Hagar, the slave woman? There is nothing I have to say, since all the other commentators pass this by. Consequently, I have to divine the meaning. Apparently, he means this: that since one allegory gives birth to another, as happens in allegorizing, when he passes from Hagar, the slave woman, to Mt. Sinai because of their similarity in name, at the same time he incidentally passes in allegorical fashion from the earthly to the heavenly Jerusalem, being prompted by the same evidence, that is, a name, since what is translated as "vision of peace" [Jerusalem] is also called, and more correctly so, Sinai, that is, "trial." But before he applies the name Jerusalem in a transferred sense to the heavenly city, he is content with having merely compared the two and weaves in many allegories. Otherwise he would have said clearly: "For Jerusalem is the city in heaven that bears children into freedom." For with this statement he would have removed a very obscure anacoluthon. Therefore, says Paul, since the heavenly Jerusalem is separated by such a great distance from this earthly one, it makes no difference that the latter is not Sinai but is in Judea, which borders on Arabia. It is the same as if it were Sinai itself, on which it borders. It corresponds to that mountain because of their common border and also because they both participate in giving birth to the Law, since at no point is it adjacent to that heavenly city and does not belong to it either, but is related rather to Sinai-Hagar, to which it is adjacent.

Here I am making no mention of many marvelous methods of allegorizing which the apostle hints at here, lest I add greater darkness to what is already obscure. Therefore the words "Jerusalem which is now" must be referred to the future Jerusalem, just as Hagar referred to another Hagar. Consequently, the sense is: "Jerusalem which belongs to this life and which, both in fact and in symbolic meaning, is adjacent to Mt. Sinai." Furthermore, the reason for adding "and is in slavery with her children" is that he may make an exception of those who were in Jerusalem but belonged to the Jerusalem above. "I call that city Jerusalem," he says, "which now is and in the future will not be, and not in its entirety but so far as it is in slavery with its children, that is, those in it who are in slavery to the Law and are adjacent to its border. What it means to be in slavery to the Law has been stated sufficiently and to the point of tediousness.

Observe, too, the Hebraic way of speaking. They are called Jerusalem's children. Because the city is a mother, those who live in it are called children, as in Ps. 147:12-13: "Praise the Lord, O Jerusalem! He blesses your sons within you." Such expressions, however, are common and occur frequently in the prophets.

Now the allegorical interpretation of the names, according to Jerome.[49] Sarah means "princess" or "lady." For this reason Sarah's sons, the sons of a lady, the sons of a princess, are rightly called the sons of a free woman, while, on the other hand, the sons of the handmaid are sons of a slave woman and of slavery. For the apostle also comes near to expressing Sarah's name when he calls her "free." In Scripture, you see, princes are also called נְדִבוֹת, that is, free and willing. Hagar, on the other hand, means "journey abroad" or "foreigner," "resident," "sojourn"; and this is rightly contrasted with the citizens and members of God's household (Eph. 2:19). "You are not foreigners and guests," he says. It is as if he were saying: "You do not belong to Hagar; you belong to Sarah. You are not foreigners; you are sons of the free woman and lady." "The slave does not continue in the house forever; the son continues forever" (John 8:35). Now the righteousness of the Law is temporary; but the righteousness of Christ continues forever, because the one serves for pay in this life, while the other is a freely granted inheritance of the life to come. "Arabia" is the sunset or the evening, which verges toward the night, whereas in many passages the church and the Gospel are called the dawn and the morning.[50] Thus the Law and the synagog finally fade away, but grace reigns and takes its ease in the noonday of eternity. What if the apostle is also designating Arabia as a desert? For "Arabia" has this significance too. In fact, in Holy Writ, Arabia is nearly always understood to refer to the Arabian Desert. For Arabia Felix is called by the name Saba, as well as by the names of other parts of it; Arabia Petraea is called Cedar, Amon, Moab, and by many names. Arabia, therefore, seems to be so called because it is a wasteland, in order to signify the sterile and barren synagog, or the righteousness of the Law in the sight of God. While the church,

---

[49] Jerome, *Commentarius*, 417.

[50] Luther may be thinking of passages like Is. 58:8; cf. also *Luther's Works*, 13, pp. 297—303.

on the other hand, is fruitful in God's sight, even though it is a desert in the sight of men. According to St. Jerome, "Sinai" means "trial," that is, the unrest and the disturbance of peace that we have from the Law. For "through the Law comes knowledge of sin" (Rom. 3:20) and for this reason also the disturbing of one's conscience. "Jerusalem" means "vision of peace," namely, tranquillity of conscience; for through the Gospel we see in the church the remission of sins, which is peace of heart. "Ishmael" means "hearing of God" or "one who hears God," namely, the people who, coming before Christ, heard that He would come after them but did not see Him face to face and clearly. They heard the prophets and read Moses. Yet they did not know Christ as One who was present. They always had Him at their back; they always heard and never saw Him. This is the condition of everyone who wants to be justified on the basis of the Law. He hears of the righteousness of the Law and does not see that righteousness is in Christ. He looks at some things and hears other things; he looks at those things that are in front of him and at his own powers, not at the virtues of Christ. Nevertheless, he always hears himself being driven to righteousness through the Law, but he never comes to it. "Isaac" means laughter; for this is characteristic of grace, which, with its oil, makes glad the face of man (Ps. 104:15). Opposed to this is weeping. This is characteristic of guilt, which comes from the Law. Therefore each name, when compared with its opposites, shows in a beautiful way the difference between Law and Gospel, sin and grace, the synagog and the church, the flesh and the spirit, the old and the new.

26. *But the Jerusalem above is free, and she is the mother of us all.*

Paul would be saying: "The other testament is from the Jerusalem which is above." Meanwhile, however, by giving his attention to the other Jerusalem, he has changed the construction and has resorted to an anacoluthon. But he makes up for this with other words, because the other testament actually began in Jerusalem when the Holy Spirit was sent from heaven to Mt. Zion, as Is. 2:3 says: "For out of Zion shall go forth the Law, and the Word of the Lord from Jerusalem." And in Ps. 110:2 we read: "The Lord sends forth from Zion your mighty scepter." But because Jerusalem was indeed the earthly inheritance promised at Sinai by the earlier testament, whereas another inheritance is promised us in heaven — for this reason we also have another Jerusalem which is not adjacent to Mt. Sinai and is not close to or related, so to speak, to the slavery of the Law. But there is also this difference: The Law of the letter was given from Mt. Sinai to those to whom temporal blessings were promised; but the Law of the Spirit was given, not from Jerusalem but rather from heaven on the day of Pentecost. And to this Law heavenly blessings were promised. Consequently, just as Jerusalem is the mother and capital city of all those who, under the Sinaitic Law, are her children and her citizens, so the Jerusalem above is the mother of all those who are her children and her citizens under the Law of heavenly grace. For these taste the things that are above, not the things that are on the earth (Matt. 16:23), because they have the Spirit as a pledge and token of the promise, and as the first fruits of the future inheritance of the eternal city and the new Jerusalem.

27. *For it is written: Rejoice, O barren one that dost not bear; break forth and shout, thou who art not in travail; for the desolate hath more children than she who hath a husband.*

These words are written in Is. 54:1, and a strange antithesis and contradiction gives them the nature of a paradox. The barren and widowed rejoices in her many children, while, on the other hand, the one who is married and fertile is without children. Who will be able to understand this? Paul is being allegorical and is talking spiritually by taking a parable from physical generation, in which children are begotten by the man's insemination of the woman. That allegorical man who speaks of women as both married and widowed, as both barren and fruitful, is the Law. This, as St. Augustine says,[51] is expressed more aptly in the Greek, where the Law is called νόμος, in the masculine gender; just as it is also θάνατος of which the apostle likewise speaks in the masculine gender as the "last enemy" (1 Cor. 15:26). The Law, I say, the man of the synagog, or of any people whatever that is situated outside the grace of God, does indeed, though to his own grief, beget many children; but they are all sinners, because in their reliance on the wisdom of the Law and on righteousness by the works of the Law they glory in the Law, on the grounds that they have become such people as they are on the basis of the Law, and that in the whole outward appearance of their life

---

[51] Augustine, *Enarrationes in Psalmos*, LIX, 10, *Corpus Christianorum, Series Latina*, XXXIX, 762.

they have become similar to their parent, that is, the Law. And yet inwardly, in spirit, they differ far from the pattern of the Law, since in fact by the Law sin rather increases, as I have said. The Law discloses sin but does not take it away, a point which Paul treats at greater length in Rom. 7:5: "While we were living in the flesh, our sinful passions, aroused by the Law, were at work in our members to bear fruit for death."

And so that allegorical man inseminates his wife; that is, he teaches the synagog things that are good. But the synagog, forsaken by the spirit of grace, gives birth only to sinners, who pretend to fulfill the Law but, on the other hand, are aroused all the more against the Law, just as in the desert the Jews were against Moses, who was a type of the Law and of this man. From this man the church or any people at all is released through grace, by which it dies to the Law in such a way that it no longer needs the Law with its urging and demanding but of its own accord and freely does everything that belongs to the Law as if there were no Law, because "the Law is not laid down for the just" (1 Tim. 1:9). Thus it comes about that she who was subject to the Law, like a wife fruitful with sinful offspring, is now widowed, without the Law, and forsaken and barren, but with a good and fortunate widowhood and barrenness; for thereby she becomes the wife of another man, namely, of grace, or of Christ. For grace takes the place of the Law, and Christ takes the place of Moses. Endowed by this husband with another kind of fruitfulness, she speaks the well-known word of Is. 49:21-22: "Who has borne me these? I was bereaved and barren, exiled and put away, but who has brought up these? Behold, I was left alone; whence, then, have these come? Thus says the Lord God: 'Behold, I will lift up My hand to the nations and raise My signal to the peoples; and they shall bring your sons in their bosom, and your daughters shall be carried on their shoulders.'" These things are said because the church's children are instructed, not by the teaching of the letter but by the touch of the Spirit of God, as John 6:45 states: "They shall all be taught by God." For where the Spirit does not touch, there indeed the Law does the teaching; and people in great numbers bring forth issue, but only sinners, as I have said. And it is only the work of man that is carried on there. They produce the kind of people they themselves are, but neither kind is good. The good are produced without the Law, solely by the grace of the Spirit.

One must, however, be familiar with this allegorical way of speaking on Paul's part, lest the strange and unusual nature of his meaning becloud his words for us. For St. Augustine also points out in an excellent way that the intercourse of Lot's daughters with their father betokens what takes place here. Lot himself is the νόμος, namely, the Law, whom his daughters make drunk; that is, they misuse the Law. Nor do the synagogs of the nations understand it correctly. They make it drunk with the wine of their own understanding as they force the Law to be and to seem what it is not. Thereupon they are made pregnant by the Law which has been made drunk in this way. They are taught, they conceive, they assent, and they give birth to Moabites and Ammonites, that is, to men who are superstitious and without the grace of the Spirit, arrogant over the works of the Law — men who in all eternity do not enter the church of God. Hence Moab is rightly translated with "from the father," and Ammon is translated with "people of mourning," because this is the one boast of the self-righteous and the hypocrites: that they come from the Law, that they live according to the Law, that they appropriate the Scriptures to themselves alone, as though they were the legitimate children of the Law. For this reason Jerome says that Moab is very haughty.[52] Meanwhile, however, they do not notice how restless their conscience is and that they are a people of mourning, since without the grace that makes the heart sure they cannot be at rest in the works of the Law as they bear the burden and heat of the day in vain (Matt. 20:12). The elder daughter is more shameless; she boasts of having a son from her father. "Moab," she says, "from my father." This is sensuality and the flesh, in which the self-righteous boast that they are of the Law. For in the sight of man the works of the Law and the doers of the Law glitter. The younger daughter, however, does not boast; she calls her son an unhappy people. This is conscience, which has no rest from the Law and its works. On the contrary, it has unrest and disturbance. Enough of this.

Therefore the apostle is saying that our mother has many children, even though she is forsaken, barren, widowed, without a husband, without the Law, without children who have been taught and prepared on the basis of the Law. For this very reason she should rejoice and break forth, and shout for joy that she is barren in this

---

[52] Jerome, *Liber interpretationis hebraicorum nominum, Corpus Christianorum, Series Latina,* LXXII, 69.

way and neither gives birth nor endures travail, while in the meantime the children of the Law are decreasing and the children of grace are being multiplied. This matter is typified very beautifully by what is written about Hannah and Peninnah in 1 Sam. 1:4-5, especially if the song of Hannah is added. Therefore it could seem that Isaiah drew his prophecy, which the apostle cites here, from this passage, with the same Spirit attending and enlightening him. "Until she who was barren gave birth to very many," sings Hannah, "and she who had many children became weak, because no man is made strong in his own strength" (1 Sam. 2:5, 9).

28. *Now we, brethren, like Isaac, are children of promise.*

Paul is applying the allegory. "We, like Isaac"; that is, we are children of the free woman and lady, just as Isaac was. And just as he, through the flesh, was a son, not of the flesh but of the promise, so we are too, because we were promised to Abraham in his offspring, as has been said at greater length above. The Jews, however, are like Ishmael, that is, children of the slave woman, not of the promise but of the flesh. So are all who trust in being justified on the basis of the Law and its works.

29. *But as at that time he who was born according to the flesh persecuted him who was born according to the Spirit, so it is now.*

Gen. 21 does not describe what that persecution was with which Ishmael persecuted Isaac, but one can learn what it was from the words of Sarah. When she saw the son of Hagar, the Egyptian woman, playing with her son Isaac, she said to Abraham: "Cast out this slave woman with her son, for the son of this slave woman shall not be heir with my son Isaac" (v. 10). It is as if she were saying: "I see that he wants to rely on the fact that he is an heir. He despises my son and forgets that he is the son of a slave woman." Moreover, it appears that this "playing" was of such a nature that Ishmael, puffed up by his primogeniture, vaunted it as he ridiculed and insulted Isaac, just as if Ishmael were Abraham's first son. But Sarah, seeing this, maintained the opposite: "The son of a slave woman, I say, will not be the heir." She called Ishmael a slave woman's son by way of derogation. And the Hebrew text supports this meaning. There we have: "And when Sarah saw the son of Hagar, the Egyptian woman — the son whom she had borne to Abraham — laughing and playing" (for "with her son" is added in our Latin version of the text).

It is as if she were saying: "Hagar bore Ishmael to Abraham. This is why Ishmael was puffed up. This is why he was laughing and exulting in front of Isaac. On this account he, smug concerning the inheritance, was scorning Isaac, the true heir."

The symbolic meaning of the figure as Paul employs it is in harmony with this. For "so it is now," he says, "with Israel, who declare in their snobbery that they alone are the offspring of Abraham, that they alone are the heirs of the promise." But no one persecuted the true children of Abraham more cruelly than those very people, as we read in the Acts of the Apostles. For they are "Ishmael." They hear in the prophets that God will come after them; but when He is set before them, they do not recognize Him. In this they reflect the name, the sentiments, and the character of Ishmael, their father.

Finally, the word "playing" is the same as that from which the name Isaac is formed. This name is translated with "laughter" or "rejoicing," to signify perhaps that Ishmael was a facetious person and that with a sharp taunt he had given the name Isaac a turn which derided him who bore it, as if he considered him a truly laughable heir and a man of no account at all. For it is not for nothing that Scripture makes use of the word "playing" or "laughing" in this way and recounts that so saintly a woman was disturbed by it. The apostle, however, refers to this in order to strengthen the Galatians, lest they stop being men of Isaac's type on account of the persecution of those Ishmaelites, because it has to happen that way. But the result will be that the latter will be cast out, as now follows.

30. *But what does Scripture say? Cast out the slave and her son, for the son of the slave shall not inherit with the son of the free woman.*

Scripture speaks emphatically and says what is altogether contrary to the presumption of the slave woman and her son. "She is a slave woman," it says, "and presumes to be a lady. He is a slave woman's son; he laughs at the son of the lady and mocks him with ironic gibes. But God forbid! Let them rather be cast out." From this one understands again that the slave woman Hagar agreed to this or at least allowed her son Ishmael to laugh at Isaac, since she was hoping for the same thing her son was hoping for, namely, that she would become the lady of the house. Nor does Scripture say: "Cast out *your* son"; it says: "Cast out *her* son," asserting that Ishmael was the son of the slave woman, not the son of Abraham. "So it will be now too," says Paul. "The sons of the flesh are not heirs; the sons of the promise are. Accordingly, if you do not want to be cast out with the son of the slave woman, continue steadfastly as sons of the free woman. Scripture will not lie. Even against Abraham's will, yet on the authority of God, it declares that the son of the slave woman must be cast out."

31. *So, brethren, we are not children of the slave but of the free woman.*

Paul makes the application of the story and of the allegory and summarizes with a brief conclusion, which now is amply understood from what has already been said. For to be a son of the slave woman means to be a slave to the Law, to be under obligation to the Law, to be obliged to keep the Law, to be a sinner, a son of wrath (Eph. 2:3), a son of death, alienated from Christ, cut off from grace, with no share in the future inheritance, devoid of the blessing of the promise, a son of the flesh, a hypocrite, a hired servant, to live in the spirit of slavery, in fear, and whatever else he has mentioned here and elsewhere. For the names of this evil are infinite. And though our Latin translator has added the words "with which freedom Christ has set us free" to the end of this chapter,[53] let us nevertheless, together with the Greek text, treat this as the beginning of the fifth chapter.

[53] The Latin reads: *Itaque, fratres, non sumus ancillae filii, sed liberae: qua libertate Christus nos liberavit.*

CHAPTER FIVE

1. *For freedom Christ has set us free; stand fast, therefore, and do not submit again to a yoke of slavery.*

I AM driving home *ad nauseam* the fact that this is the freedom and the slavery of which Paul speaks in Rom. 6:20, 22: "When you were slaves of sin, you were free in regard to righteousness. But now that you have been set free from sin, you have become slaves of God." But let us set this up in a diagram:

Freedom from righteousness ⎫ ⎧ Service of sin
Service of righteousness ⎭ ⎩ Freedom from sin

For he who is free from sin has become a slave of righteousness; but he who is the slave of sin is free from righteousness, and vice versa.

I repeat all this because I know that on account of the multitude of grasshoppers and locusts the fruits of our land have reached the point that this slavery and freedom are generally not understood, so fixed and deeply rooted has the human falsehood about free will become in those who oppose and deny both. What is more, those whom the apostle was forced to oppose in the same sixth chapter of Romans also have a fleshly idea of freedom, as if in Christ it were permissible for anything at all to be done, whereas this freedom is such that because of it we do of our own accord and gladly, without regard for penalties or rewards, the things that are stated in the Law. But it is slavery when we do these things out of slavish fear or childish desire. Therefore it profits nothing. Neither is there any difference between a slave of sin and a slave of the Law, because he who is a slave of the Law is always a sinner. He never fulfills the Law except to put works on display, and a temporal reward is given to him just as it is given to children of slave women and concubines. But the inheritance goes to the son of the free woman. "Christ," he says, "has made us free with this freedom." It is a spiritual freedom, one to be preserved in the spirit. It is not that heathen kind, which even the pagan

Persius knew was not enough.[1] It is freedom from the Law, but in a way contrary to what usually takes place among men. For it is human freedom when laws are changed without effecting any change in men, but it is Christian freedom when men are changed without changing the Law. Consequently, the same Law that was formerly hateful to the free will now becomes delightful, since love is poured into our hearts through the Holy Spirit (Rom. 5:5). In this freedom, he teaches us, we must stand strongly and steadfastly, because Christ, who fulfills the Law and overcomes sin for us, sends the spirit of love into the hearts of those who believe in Him. This makes them righteous and lovers of the Law, not because of their own works but freely because it is freely bestowed by Christ. If you move away from this, you are both ungrateful to Christ and proud of yourself, since you want to justify and free yourself from the Law without Christ.

Note the stress of his words: "Not again," "not in slavery," "not to a yoke of slavery," "do not submit." Or, as it is expressed more meaningfully in Greek, μὴ ἐνέχεσθε, almost as he said above, namely, as if confined in prison. This means: "Lest you be confined, held in possession — as Erasmus says [2] — ensnared, entangled, under the most grievous and unbearable weight of the Law, in which, however, it is impossible to exist except as slaves and sinners. It is a lesser thing to be held fast; but to be held fast in slavery, that is hard, and it is hardest under the yoke of slavery, especially after receiving freedom.

"Stand fast," says Paul as he assumes greater things about them than he finds, namely, that they had not yet fallen; otherwise he would have said: "Arise." Now he says more courteously: "Stand fast," in order to teach at the same time that nobody should immediately reproach with no hope of recovering. No, one should reproach with strong reason for good hope — which the fulminators of our age fail to do; for them it is enough to have given vent to a terrible lust for power of their own.

2. *Now, I, Paul, say to you that if you receive circumcision, Christ will be of no advantage to you.*

After the apostle has torn to pieces the righteousness of the Law with many very strong arguments and has given an abundant account concerning faith in Christ, he now, no less vigorously, exhorts, terri-

---

[1] Aulus Persius Flaccus, *Satires*, V, sets forth the Stoic paradox that except for Stoic philosophers all men are slaves.

[2] Erasmus, *Annotationes ad locum*.

fies, threatens, and promises. He waters what he had already planted. And with manifestly apostolic warmth and zeal he tries and tempers everything, so that it is most pleasing to see such a reflection of apostolic concern. In the first place, he frightens with the thought that Christ is of no advantage if they receive circumcision; and he says: "I, Paul, announce this to you." He repeats his name to give weight to its authority. Here again I, too, repeat that it is not a bad thing to receive circumcision; but to look for righteousness in circumcision — for it was for this purpose that they were being circumcised — is godlessness. And it is easier to recognize a false reliance on righteousness in ceremonial works than it is in the moral works of the Decalog, for righteousness must not be sought through these works either; it must be sought through faith in Christ. I am mentioning this lest someone get the notion from what I am saying that the apostle is opposing only the ceremonial features of the Law. On the contrary, he has taken up the most manifest work of the Law, while at the same time he has in mind all the works of the Law.

Rom. 2:25 seems to contradict this. "Circumcision indeed is of value," says Paul, "if you obey the Law." How, says Jerome, is circumcision of value if you keep the Law, when Christ is of no advantage to those who have received circumcision?[3] Here the same saintly man brings together many considerations. Briefly, however, it is impossible for the Law to be fulfilled without Christ, as has already been said rather often. For the apostle holds this as a firm supposition, and he has sufficiently proved it. But those who keep the Law, that is, those who possess Christ, the Fulfiller of the Law, through faith are free to receive circumcision or not to receive circumcision. For them all things are profitable; all things work together for good (Rom. 8:28). But those who receive circumcision in slavish fashion and out of fear of the Law, because thereby they want to render satisfaction to the Law and to be justified by a necessary righteousness, are surely casting Christ and the grace of God aside, since they presume to fulfill the Law in another way than through Christ. Thus for these Christ is of no advantage because of circumcision, while because of Christ circumcision does no harm to the former.

With the same stupidity, yes, godlessness, those people perish who, either because of the trembling of their conscience or because of the peril of threatening death — when they finally realize one day that

---

[3] Jerome, *Commentarius*, 421—422.

their life is thoroughly bad as they see how far removed they are from the Law of God — either despair or with equal godlessness plunge ahead and want to render satisfaction for their sins and to start keeping the Law for the sake of soothing their conscience, since they think that they will be good if they fulfill what the Law prescribes. Furthermore, they do not understand "fulfilling" to be purely and simply "believing" (in Christ, the Fulfiller of the Law). On the contrary, they understand it to be satisfaction rendered to the Law by the performance of many works.

We learn these godless kinds of righteousness from the decrees of men and from the monstrous theology which has Aristotle as its head and Christ as its feet, since these decrees and these kinds of righteousness alone hold sway. For this is how they vaunt their petty works of satisfaction; and it is amazing what value they place on these with their traffic in indulgences, as if it were not enough to believe in Christ, in whom our righteousness, redemption, satisfaction, life, and glory are by faith alone (1 Cor. 1:30).

Therefore when, under the guidance of the Law, you have come to the knowledge of your sins, beware lest before all else you presume henceforth to satisfy the Law as one who intends to live a better life. But despair altogether of your past and future life, and trust boldly in Christ. Moreover, as one who believes, is justified in this way, and fulfills the Law, pray to Christ that sin may be destroyed also in your flesh and that the Law may be fulfilled there too, just as it has already been fulfilled in your heart through faith. Not until then will you be doing good works according to the Law.

Therefore I like the practice that nothing but the crucified Christ is impressed on those who are about to die, and that they are exhorted to faith and hope.[4] Here at least — no matter to what extent the deceivers of souls may have deluded our whole life — free will collapses, good works collapse, the righteousness of the Law collapses. Only faith and the invoking of God's completely pure mercy remain, so that I have often had the notion that there are either more or better Christians in death than in life. For the freer confidence is from one's own works, and the more exclusively it is directed toward Christ alone, so much better is the Christian it makes; and the good works of one's whole life should be directed toward this faith. But now we are being thrust upon our own merits by the fogs, clouds, and whirl-

---

[4] Cf. *Luther's Works*, 23, p. 360, note 40.

winds of human traditions and laws, and of ignorant interpreters of Scripture and preachers as well. By our own powers we strive to render satisfaction for our sins; and we do not direct our works toward purging the vices of the flesh and destroying the body of sin, but — as though we were already only pure and holy — we pile up like grain in a barn things with which to make God our debtor and to give them a seat, I do not know how high, in heaven. Blind! Blind! Blind! To all such people Christ is of no advantage. They strive to justify themselves by another plan.

It follows, moreover, that this expression, "you receive circumcision," expresses not so much the outward work as the inner longing for the work. For the apostle is speaking in spirit of the conscience within. The external work is immaterial. The whole difference, however, lies in the opinion, the intent, the conscience, the purpose, the motive, etc. Hence if the works of the Law are done out of a feeling that they are necessary and out of confidence that righteousness is gained by them, one turns aside in the counsel of the ungodly and stands in the way of sinners (cf. Ps. 1:1); and he who teaches this is sitting in the seat of pestilence. But if they are done in devout love, in trust, and in freedom, they are the merits of the righteousness that has already been gained through faith. Now they are done in devout love when they are done with a view to the need or the will of another person. For then they are not works of the Law; then they are works of love. Nor are they done on account of the Law, which commands; they are done on account of the brother, who wants or needs them, just as the apostle himself did them.

Let this axiom stand firm for you in the case of all works of any laws whatever. For if a priest or monk has done his ceremonial works, even his works of chastity and poverty, in such a way that he wants to be justified and good through them, he is godless and is denying Christ since one who has already been justified by faith should employ these works for purging his flesh and his old nature, in order that his faith in Christ may increase and hold sway alone in him, and in order that thus the kingdom of God may come. Hence he will do those works gladly, not to merit much but to be purified. Ah, how great a disease there now is in those droves of men who are monks and priests with the greatest weariness and for the sake of this life only, who fail to see by even a hairbreadth what they are, what they are doing, or what they are seeking!

Forgive me, dear reader, for using so many words. This Midian has come upon the church in such great numbers that there is need of six hundred Gideons, let alone three hundred trumpets and pitchers, for them to be driven away (Judg. 7:16). The strong waters of the Assyrians have come up to the neck of Judah, and the stretching out of his wings has filled the breath of your land, O Emmanuel, because we have refused the waters of Shiloah that flow gently (cf. Is. 8:6 ff.). And so with our keys that bind (Matt. 16:19) we have gained nothing but innumerable snares for souls.

3. *I testify again to every man who receives circumcision that he is bound to keep the whole Law.*

The first evil that should frighten you is the fact that Christ is of no advantage to you. This means nothing else than that the Law has not been fulfilled by you. Hence the second evil is the fact that the weight of the Law still rests on you and that you are bound to keep the whole Law. Most certainly both are exceedingly great misfortunes, namely, to be without so great a good that is in Christ and to be oppressed by so great an evil that comes from the Law.

But, I ask you, Paul, with what kind of logic will this sort of reasoning stand up, or even proceed? "You receive circumcision; therefore you are bound to keep the whole Law." Does not the man who receives circumcision keep at least the law of circumcision? Jer. 9:26 answers: "All these nations are uncircumcised; for all the house of Israel is uncircumcised in heart." Besides, the apostle is speaking on the basis of his supposition that there is no true work of any law unless it is done out of faith that makes the heart pure. Hence neither circumcision nor anything else whatever renders satisfaction to the Law, except outwardly and hypocritically. For only that work is good which proceeds from a good and pure heart. A good heart, however, is born only out of grace. Grace does not come from works; it comes from faith in Christ. Thus Abraham's circumcision would have amounted to nothing at all had he not first believed. After he had been accounted righteous on the basis of this faith, he did a good work by receiving circumcision. This is what Rom. 2:25 says: "If you break the Law, your circumcision becomes uncircumcision." What else does this mean than "He who is circumcised is uncircumcised, and he who keeps the Law fails to keep the Law"? For he does not keep it according to the more important and better part of himself, namely, his heart; he keeps it merely according to the flesh. Thus James says (2:10): "He who fails in one point has become guilty of all of it." For he who by faith fulfills one point fulfills them all, since faith is the fulfillment of all laws for the sake of Christ, the Fulfiller. But if you are without faith in one point, then you have it in none. Therefore he is right when he says that he who receives circumcision without faith, without the inward circumcision, does not receive circumcision. On the contrary, he performs no work of any law but is still under obligation to the whole Law.

It is St. Jerome's understanding that if they receive circumcision, it is also necessary for them to keep all the rest of the Law, as if the Galatians had kept only circumcision.[5] This notion does not please me, because the pseudapostles had imposed the whole Law of Moses upon the Galatians, as he said above: "You observe days and months and years and seasons!" (Gal. 4:10.) So what he wants is rather to show that through their observance of the Law by far the opposite had turned out to be the result for them, namely, no observance at all, in fact, an actual and greater transgression.

4. *You are severed from Christ, you who would be justified by the Law; you have fallen away from grace.*

Look! As I have said, it is not the work of circumcision that is condemned by the apostle; it is the trust in righteousness. "Who would be justified," says Paul, "by the Law." It is a sin of godlessness to want to be justified by the works of the Law. The works of the Law can be done properly by those who are righteous, but no godless person can be justified by them. Indeed, even the righteous man, if he presumes to be justified by those works, loses the righteousness he has and falls from the grace by which he had been justified, since he has been removed from a good land to one that is barren. Here again Paul seems to allude in hidden fashion to the Galatians' name — which signifies "a removal" — because they had fallen from grace into the Law.[6] You see, therefore, how consistently the apostle maintains that we are justified by faith alone, and that works are not the primary factors for acquiring righteousness but are the functions of a righteousness already obtained and the aids for increasing it.

[5] Jerome, *Commentarius*, 423.
[6] Cf. p. 177, note 22.

St. Jerome criticizes the Latin translator for using the expression "You have emptied yourselves," because, as he says, the meaning is rather "You have ceased from the work of Christ." [7] But I am uncommonly pleased with the emphasis this expression has. Paul wants to say: "You are idle, empty, devoid of Christ's work; and the work of Christ is not in you." Since indeed, as was said above, it is not the Christian who lives, speaks, works, and suffers; it is Christ who does all this in him. All his works are works of Christ, so inestimable is the grace of faith. Therefore he who is removed to the Law now lives in himself; he busies himself with his own work, his own life, his own word; that is, he sins and does not fulfill the Law. He has no interest in Christ; Christ does not dwell in him or make use of him. He observes an utterly wicked and miserable Sabbath, a rest from the works of the Lord, when, on the contrary, he should be observing a Sabbath from his own works and should be unoccupied and disengaged, in order that the Lord's work might be done in him, which as St. Augustine teaches, was formerly prefigured by the Sabbath.[8] Therefore he who believes in Christ empties himself and becomes disengaged from his own works, in order that Christ may live and work in him. But he who seeks to be justified by the Law empties himself of Christ and becomes disengaged from the works of God, in order that he may live and work in himself, that is, in order that he may perish and be destroyed.

5. *For through the spirit, by faith, we wait for the hope of righteousness.*

"Through the spirit, by faith" seems to be the Hebrew way of saying: "We, by the spirit that is from faith" or "Because we believe." Accordingly, we are waiting for the hope of righteousness, not in a fleshly way but in a spiritual way. But those who do not believe are devoid of the spirit. For this reason they wait for the hope of a righteousness of their own, in a fleshly way on the basis of works. Faith makes men spiritual; works make them fleshly. I have also said previously that without grace man can perform the Law only out of fear of punishment or hope of a promised reward. But in either case the action is fleshly and mercenary. For this reason it is not through

[7] Jerome, *Commentarius*, 424.

[8] Augustine, *Enarrationes in Psalmos*, XXXVII, 2, *Corpus Christianorum, Series Latina*, XXXVIII, 383.

the spirit that hope is waited for in that case, but it is by the flesh that something is striven for in order that they may enjoy it. For they do good, not out of love for righteousness but because they want the benefit of a reward.

What does Paul mean when he says that "we wait for the hope of righteousness"? Who waits for a hope? Some take "hope" to mean the thing hoped for, just as in the third book of *Sentences* it is stated that in Athanasius faith is taken to mean that which is believed or the words that express one's faith: "This is the catholic faith." [9] But I do not like to hear faith and hope understood in this way; for just as it is correct to say, "I live a life," so, without being absurd, it seems that one could say, "I hope a hope." Meanwhile, however, I shall not dispute the matter. Let everyone adopt whatever view he can or wishes. I know that it is a common figure of speech in Scripture to ascribe to faith and hope that which is attained by faith and hope; for in this way men are called gods (Ps. 82:6), are called truthful, righteous, holy — attributes which belong to God alone. They are people of this kind because they partake of and cling to God. Thus hope is called hoping or the thing hoped for because it is closely connected with things that are to come. For it does not cling to these things because of a purely arbitrary decision to misuse the word, as those whom I mentioned before think — just as those whom I spoke of before imagine that some are righteous of themselves, without clinging to the divine righteousness. No; for faith could not have a more valid reason for clinging to these things, since it clings to and agrees with the divine righteousness and truth. This is a matter of grace, not of nature.

6. *For in Christ Jesus neither circumcision nor uncircumcision is of any avail, but faith working through love.*

Here it is proved with the greatest clearness that circumcision is permitted. St. Jerome and his followers assail this with such an uproar because if circumcision is not permitted, then uncircumcision will be necessary.[10] But "uncircumcision," Paul says, "is of no avail." Therefore it is not necessary. Again, uncircumcision is also permitted, because if it is not permitted, then circumcision is necessary. But "circumcision is of no avail." Therefore it is not necessary. What,

[9] Peter Lombard, *Sententiae*, III, 23, 3, *Patrologia, Series Latina*, CXCII, 805.
[10] Jerome, *Commentarius*, 425—426.

then, is left, except what St. Augustine rightly says at this point, namely, that it is not true that Christ was of no advantage to Timothy because Paul circumcised him when he was already a Christian.[11] For Paul did this on account of the offense that others would take. He was by no means a hypocrite when he did so. No, he believed that it makes no difference whether one is circumcised or not circumcised. He enunciates this principle in 1 Cor. 7:19, where he says: "Neither circumcision counts for anything nor uncircumcision." For circumcision does no harm to him who does not believe that salvation depends on it.

In order to establish this principle of indifference, Paul has very prudently stated both cases; for if he had said: "Circumcision is of no advantage," then uncircumcision would seem necessary. On the other hand, if he had said: "Uncircumcision is of no avail," then circumcision would seem necessary. But now only one's opinion, one's trust, and one's conscience make a distinction between circumcision and uncircumcision, both of which are permitted, neither good nor evil, and matters of indifference, just as all other works of the Law are. Thus in 1 Cor. 7:18-19 he says: "Was anyone at the time of his call already circumcised? Let him not seek to remove the marks of circumcision. Was anyone at the time of his call uncircumcised? Let him not seek circumcision. For neither circumcision counts for anything nor uncircumcision, but keeping the commandments of God."

What is this? Do not those who receive circumcision keep God's commandment? Did He not give this commandment through Moses and Abraham? I have said above that those who are circumcised in the flesh without the circumcision of the heart are uncircumcised in the sight of God, although it is true that the Jews of necessity had to keep the ceremonial requirements of the Law until Christ came. For the promise to Abraham and the Law of Moses were in force until Christ came, as Moses clearly says in Deut. 18:15 that they should listen to the Prophet whom God was going to raise up, just as they listened to Moses himself. Accordingly, Moses did not want to be listened to after the coming of this Prophet, who is Christ, as the apostle Peter, in Acts 3:23, cites this same passage against the Jews. And when God gave Abraham the commandment of circumcision, He surely wanted this to remain in force only until the appearance

---

[11] Augustine, *Epistolae ad Galatas expositio, Patrologia, Series Latina*, XXXV, 2135—2136.

of the promised blessing. For with the coming of the Offspring with regard to whom the promise was made certainly the promise and the covenant of the promise, together with its seal, were simultaneously brought to an end. After the coming of Christ, therefore, circumcision is nothing. Nevertheless, it is a matter of indifference and permissible, just as is everything else concerning days, food, clothing, places, sacrifices, etc., even though they were of no value, even before the coming of Christ, if they were done without the inward righteousness, as Isaiah says (1:11): "What to Me is the multitude of your sacrifices?" And Micah asks (6:6): "What worthy offering shall I make to the Lord?" Thus in Heb. 9:10 it is stated that all these things were imposed until the time of reformation. But even the works of the Decalog were outside grace and must be brought to an end, in order that its works that are true in the spirit may take their place.

I have said these things to prevent anyone from thinking that I am asserting that even before Christ circumcision was a matter of indifference and neither good nor evil or that uncircumcision was permitted to the Jews; for Job and many others in the Orient — Naaman the Syrian; the son of the woman of Zarephath; King Nebuchadnezzar, after he had been converted — were righteous and yet uncircumcised, because they were not bound by the Law of Moses. Only the Jews, who had received circumcision, were bound.

When Paul speaks of "faith working through love," this is a clarification of his remarks that sheds light on them and gives understanding to the immature, in order that we may understand what kind of faith he is talking about so often, namely, one that is genuine and sincere, and, as he writes to Timothy (1 Tim. 1:5), is "from a good conscience and sincere faith." But the faith which our theologians call "acquired" is feigned. So is the faith which, even though it is "infused," is without love.[12]

Nor am I dealing here with the frivolous questions and the disgusting opinions with which they determine that "acquired" faith is a prerequisite for "infused" faith, as if the Holy Spirit were in need of us and we were not rather in need of Him in everything. For they dream that if a boy who has just been baptized were brought up among Turks and unbelievers without a Christian teacher, he would not be able to know the things a Christian must know. But this is nonsense, as if they did not experience before their eyes every day

---

[12] Cf. *Luther's Works*, 24, p. 321.

of what little advantage Christian teaching is to those who are not inwardly drawn by God, and, on the other hand, what great things are being done by those who are not outwardly taught as many great things as the theologians teach and are taught. It is something living, yes, life and reality, if the Spirit does the teaching. He knows, He speaks, He works all things in all. He whom God teaches is certainly no different from him whom God creates anew. For who teaches the unformed offspring of a man how to live, to see, to think, to speak, and to work, and the whole world to flourish in all its works? The aforementioned fabrications are ridiculous and give rise to utterly foolish thoughts about God. Therefore he who hears the Word of Christ sincerely and clings to Him in faith is at once also clothed with the Spirit of love, as Paul said above: "Did you receive the Spirit by works of the Law, or by hearing with faith?" (Gal. 3:2.) For if you hear Christ sincerely, it is impossible for you not to love Him forthwith, since He has done and borne so much for you. If you are able to love the person who gives you a present of twenty florins or honors you with some service, how will you fail to love Him who gives up, not gold but His very self for you, receives so many wounds for you, sweats blood and sheds it, dies and endures the uttermost? But if you do not love him, it is certain that you do not listen to these things sincerely and do not truly believe that they were done for you. For the Spirit brings it about that you do this. The other kind of faith, however, which does miracles, is a free gift of God bestowed on the ungrateful, who perform their works for their own glory. Of these Paul says in 1 Cor. 13:2: "If I have all faith, etc." Very judiciously, therefore, and very significantly he speaks of "faith working through love." That is, as Erasmus shows from the Greek,[13] a faith which is powerfully active, not one that snores once it has been "acquired" or one that is strong through miracles but one that is powerfully active through love. Just as he said earlier: "He who worked through Peter worked for me also for the Gentiles." For the word expresses energy.

7. *You were running well.*

It is a figure of speech in Scripture for the words "to go," "to walk," "to advance," "way," "road," "step," "footprints," and the like, to be taken in the sense of the way one lives or even in the sense of be-

---

[13] Cf. Erasmus, *Paraphrasis, Opera,* VII, 962.

lieving and of loving. For, as Augustine says, God is not approached locally; He is approached by one's disposition and by love, which means walking with the feet of one's heart and mind.[14] Hence Paul also says that our "citizenship is in heaven" (Phil. 3:20) when we occupy ourselves with the things that are above, where Christ is. Although these expressions are very common and frequent in Scripture, nevertheless there is need to call attention to them, because the error is now very general and prevalent everywhere by which, in the name of religion but contrary to religion, they keep running to Rome, Jerusalem, St. James's,[15] and a thousand other places, as if the kingdom of God were not within them instead (Luke 17:21). The grandiose and shameless displays of indulgences give no sluggish support to this ungodliness. Deluded by them, and because it does not know how to distinguish, the ignorant rabble far prefers this running hither and thither to the exercises of love by which alone one runs to God and which they could practice abundantly in their own localities. But greed strikes the shepherds blind and keeps them from opposing this widespread error.

But the apostle does not say: "You were walking"; he says: "You were running." By doing so he commends them exceedingly and flatters them in a fatherly manner. For "running" is characteristic of those who are perfect, as we read in Ps. 19:6: "And like a strong man runs its course with joy." And in 1 Cor. 9:24: "So run that you may obtain it." On the other hand, of those that are perfect and obstinate in evil Prov. 1:16 says: "For their feet run to evil, and they make haste to shed blood." And the same thing is repeated in Is. 59:7. Therefore to run in Christ means to hasten, to be aglow, to be perfect in faith and in love for Christ.

Who hindered you from obeying the truth?

"Who hindered you in your good race, and hindered you to such an extent that you did not believe the truth?" It is as if he were saying: "No one's cunning, no one's authority, no one's personal status or outward appearance, however great, should have moved you. Those who are snoring and hardly able to creep in Christ, that is, those who are rather weak, someone may be able to deceive, to

---

[14] For example, Augustine, *Confessions*, V, 2.

[15] A reference to Santiago de Compostela; cf. *Luther's Works*, 22, p. 250, note 36.

hinder, to seduce. But those who were running, who were aglow, and assuredly those who welcomed me as if they were welcoming Christ, who plucked out their eyes, who endured all dangers of property and life for my sake — who would not marvel at this, that they should so swiftly not only be hindered but even be carried away to the point that they do not believe the truth? You are Galatians indeed and too easily carried away, since you have been cast down so quickly from such a great height of perfection into such a great depth of contrary superstition." At the same time remember what human nature and free will are like if God withdraws His hand; then remember what people will do when they lack the good services of shepherds, since the Galatians, who were so great in Christ, fell away so quickly and so grievously when Paul was absent.

Away now with those who want to be shepherds of many places, yes, shepherds of many shepherds; and let them glory in their own power, though meanwhile they fail to provide pasture even for themselves! In fact, so thoroughly corrupt are men's attitudes today that they take what Christ said to Peter — "Feed My sheep" (John 21:17) — and interpret it to mean: "Be a superior over My sheep, and lord it over them." This is all it means today to feed Christ's sheep, even if they have not seen a syllable of the Gospel, which alone is the pasture of the sheep. Then these same people interpret the statement, "You are Peter, and on this rock I will build My church" (Matt. 16:18), to mean: "On the rock, that is, on the power of the church," whereas Christ meant this spiritually, to signify the solidity of faith. Out of faith in Christ, which is entirely spiritual, they are making for us a completely earthly kind of power. Consequently, there is no need for us to ask: "Who hindered you from obeying the truth?" No, we should ask: "Why does no one hinder you from obeying the falsehoods in which you are running in the worst possible way?" For what else should we do when the shepherds are on the lookout, not for a place to which we may run but for how extensively they themselves may rule?

You will have agreed with no one.

Jerome thinks that this little section should be entirely rejected because it is not found in any of the Greek books or in any writings of those who have commented on the apostle.[16] For this reason we, too, shall disregard it.

[16] Jerome, *Commentarius*, 429.

8. *This persuasion is not from Him who called you.*

St. Jerome reads "your persuasion" and has a great deal to say about free will. This discussion must be taken with caution, especially since he quotes the opinions of others, that is, records their interpretations. I like the thought of Erasmus, who says that the Greek text does not have "your" or "is" or "this," and that it is a reply to the question preceding it, as follows: "Who hindered you from obeying the truth; certainly nothing but a persuasion that does not come from God, who called you." [17]

But "persuasion" can be taken either as active or as passive, except that it is a severer rebuke and squares more with the preceding question if it is taken as passive. Then the sense is: "You were hindered because you were too quickly persuaded. You are Galatians; you are quickly carried away from Him who calls you," as Paul said above (Gal. 1:6). People so perfect should not have been so quickly persuaded, no matter how much the persuaders were urging them. Note again that Paul prefers to call faith a persuasion, because it is something that cannot be demonstrated unless you believe the one who is persuading you; for faith does not tolerate the quarrels of the sophists.

9. *A little yeast leavens the whole lump.*

These words are poorly translated in our editions, which have "A little leaven spoils the whole dough." The translator has given his own interpretation rather than the words of the apostle. But St. Jerome translates these words as follows: "A little leaven ferments the whole mixture." [18] Paul has the same thought, even the same words, in 1 Cor. 5:6: "Do you not know that a little leaven ferments the whole lump of dough?" It seems to be a familiar proverb of the apostle and certainly a very fine and emphatic one.

But in 1 Cor. 5:7-8 the apostle indicates plainly that there are two kinds of leaven when he says: "Cleanse out the old leaven," and again: "Not with the old leaven." Therefore there is also a new leaven. The old leaven is a pernicious teacher, a pernicious doctrine, a pernicious example. In the passage before us the apostle is speaking of the first and second items; in 1 Cor. 5:6 f. he is speaking of the third, where he orders that the fornicator be removed from their

---

[17] Jerome, *Commentarius*, 429; cf. Erasmus, *Paraphrasis*, *Opera*, 962.

[18] Jerome, *Commentarius*, 429.

midst like old leaven. "In order," he says, "that you may be fresh dough." Similarly in Matt. 16:6 and Luke 12:1: "Beware of the leaven of the Pharisees, which is hypocrisy," which the evangelists themselves later explain as referring to the teaching of the Pharisees. "Dough" or "mixture" is the people, a disciple, or the pious teaching of pure faith. But just as the leaven resembles the mixture, so perverse doctrine always takes on the appearance of truth and is not discerned except by the taste, that is, by the discerning of the spirit. The "new leaven" is Christ, the Word of Christ, and the work of Christ and of every Christian, that is, teacher, doctrine, and example. The "dough," however, is the people, the wisdom of the flesh, the old nature, the life of the world, etc.

For this reason Matt. 13:33 says: "The kingdom of heaven is like leaven which a woman took and hid in three measures of meal, till it was all leavened." The "woman," namely, the church, or the wisdom of God, "takes the leaven," that is, the Word of the Gospel, "and hides it," because the Word of faith thrives within the conscience, not in the outward works of the Law, as we read in Ps. 119:11: "I have laid up Thy Word in my heart." For faith justifies spiritually in the sight of God. "In three measures of meal" means in the definite number and measured sum of His elect. For according to Jerome,[19] *satum* is related to a Hebrew word for a kind of measurement customary in the province of Palestine. It has a capacity of a peck and a half. And it is just about this much that women usually take for meal that is to be leavened. So whatever symbolic interpretation anyone may have for the three "measures" must be allowed, provided that one understands it as a definite number and a measured sum of people, whether by election on the part of the Holy Trinity or otherwise. "Till it was all leavened"; that is, as I said above, the faith by which we are spiritually justified is, so to speak, a hiding of the leaven and a sort of commingling of the Word of God with our soul. The effect of this is that it chastises the flesh, destroys sin, and purges out the old leaven, so that it alone holds sway in all members and leavens the whole person.

Therefore since in the Scriptures we are called one bread and one drink, and since doctrine likewise is called bread and drink,[20] one has to become accustomed to these allegories and understand the mingling and the changing of the meal and the leaven as meaning

[19] Jerome, *Commentarius*, 430.
[20] Presumably this is a reference to 1 Cor. 10:17.

the changes of doctrines and of people in their souls. Accordingly, although the apostle is speaking in this passage of evil teaching, still, because he is employing a general statement, he must also be understood as referring to any evil lust whatever. And whenever we begin to be titillated by this, we must check it at once with this saying: "A little leaven leavens the whole lump." For if you do not resist at the beginning, it will grow strong and will contaminate your whole body and soul because you consent to it or take pleasure in it. But if that Law of Moses which had no taste of evil at all is a leaven, as the apostle thinks, what will our traditions be, which have so foul a smell and emit the stench of flesh and blood?

10. *I have confidence in you in the Lord that you will take no other view than mine.*

Paul qualifies his statement in a beautiful way, lest he be thought to have confidence in man. "I have confidence in you, yet not in you but in the Lord." And even though it means the same thing to say: "I am confident about you in the Lord," there is something or other that is more appealing to me in the hidden emphasis when he says, as if he were writing in Hebrew: "I have confidence in you in the Lord." For this, too, seems to be a kind of flattering compliment prompted by his fatherly concern, namely, that he has confidence in them, but in no other way than in the Lord. Now this statement, "you will take a view *[sapietis],*" which is so frequent in the New Testament and which sometimes means "wisdom" or "prudence," as in Rom. 8:6 — "To set the mind on the flesh is death" — should finally be familiar to us. For that which is called an effort of the mind, an attempt, an intention, a seeming, a feeling, a sentiment, an opinion, a judgment, a resolution, a design, a plan, a deliberation, a mind, etc., is all expressed with this Greek word φρόνημα or φρόνησις. Therefore Ps. 1:1 says: "Blessed is the man who does not walk in the counsel of the wicked," which in German is called *Gutdunckel,* as when we say: *Es dunckt mich so recht* ("I think it is right that way"). "No other view" cannot be referred to what immediately precedes, but it refers to the argument and substance of the whole epistle. Therefore the sense is: "You have learned the Gospel from me. I hope that you will take no new view, no other view; I hope that you will not change," as he again compliments them and makes a pious assumption, although they had already begun to take another view, or another opinion had begun to seem good to them.

And he who is troubling you will bear his judgment, whoever he is.

"He is troubling"; that is, with his teachings he is dislodging you from the true faith and is driving you from the position in which you were standing. But will pious zeal and a good intention, as they say, excuse that person? Or ignorance? Or the fact that he is a disciple of the apostles, and a great one at that? "No!" he says. No matter who and how great he is, it is no trifling sin that he has done; he will bear his judgment." This, too, is a figure of speech in Scripture: "To bear one's burden, one's judgment, one's iniquity," by which their damnation is meant. For those who are in Christ do not bear their burden; but, as Is. 53:4, 6 says, "Christ Himself has borne our griefs, and the Lord has laid on Him the sins of us all." Moreover, for every man it is impossible to bear his sin, and yet he is compelled to bear it, as Ps. 38:4 says, "For my iniquities have gone over my head; they weigh like a burden too heavy for me."

Therefore it is a horrible thing that Paul says here: "He will bear his judgment." Note, too, with what pride he takes the man's personal status from him. "Whoever he is, it does not matter to me; even if he is an apostle or a disciple of the apostles, his personal status means nothing." Such great contempt for personal status do we see in Paul, and such great evils committed under the roles and masks that men assume. Yet even so we cannot be sufficiently persuaded. Indeed, we knowingly and willingly take delight in being seduced by the claim of sanctity, authority, power, limitation, privileges, and utterly vain things of this sort. For nowadays one is not allowed to say in the church: "Whoever he is." But it is enough to say: "Thus this man thinks; thus he wants it; thus he orders it." Then the whole universal church has said this, until certain heralds of Antichrist have reached the point that they prate in the foulest manner that no one is allowed to say — especially not to the Roman pontiff — "Why are you doing this?" Furthermore, they prate that the pope has no judge on earth,[21] and that Christ would not have provided adequately for His church if He had not assigned to a human being such great power as this man has. In view of its services to Christ our age deserves to hear utterances of this kind; they are sillier than the worst kind of godlessness.

---

[21] A quotation from the bull *Unam sanctam* of Boniface VIII, reprinted in Carl Mirbt (ed.), *Quellen zur Geschichte des Papsttums und des römischen Katholizismus* (Tübingen, 1924), p. 211.

11. *But if I, brethren, still preach circumcision, why am I still persecuted?*

For, as Paul said above, in the first chapter (v. 10): "Or am I trying to please men? If I were still pleasing men, I would not be a servant of Christ." With these words he points out exactly what he points out here, namely, that for the sake of the Word of Christ by which circumcision is abolished he has suffered persecutions at the hands of the Jews, as is described in Acts and in many epistles. Therefore he is saying: "Even from this evidence you learn that circumcision is nothing and that I myself, as I write to you, am acting in such a way that I shall even suffer persecution on this account. I would not suffer this if I were in agreement with those people and were teaching circumcision."

St. Jerome thinks that those false apostles had also misused Paul's name to subvert the Galatians; for they said that even Paul had circumcised Timothy and had made a vow in Cenchreae, as was mentioned above.[22] But note that he does not say: "If I still allow circumcision." No, he says: "If I preach circumcision." It was not to be preached as necessary, although it was to be tolerated as harmless, provided that faith in Christ was the governing principle.

In that case the stumbling block of the cross has been removed.

If circumcision is preached, the Jews are appeased. Then there ceases to be a stumbling block for them. For this is the same word that Paul used above when he said: "You are severed" (Gal. 5:4). That is, the stumbling block is inactive, idle, empty; and the word signifies, of course, that the stumbling block will no longer be active among the Jews.

But what sort of logic is it when one says: "Circumcision is preached; therefore the stumbling block of the cross ceases"? Then is it not to be desired that the stumbling block of the cross did not exist? Or is it your wish, Paul, that as many as possible be offended? Who could bear this?

As to the first point one must say that Paul properly ascribes the stumbling block that is in Christ to the Jews. Thus he says in 1 Cor. 1:23-24: "We preach Christ crucified, a stumbling block to Jews and folly to Gentiles; but to us, who believe, the power and wisdom of God." And in Luke 2:34 Simeon says of the Jews: "He is set for the

[22] Jerome, *Commentarius,* 432.

fall and rising of many in Israel." And in Is. 8:13-15 we read: "The Lord of hosts, Him you shall regard as holy; let Him be your fear, and let Him be your dread. And He will become a sanctuary for you, but a stone of offense and a rock of stumbling to both houses of Israel, a trap and a snare to the inhabitants of Jerusalem." Hence it is correct to say that if Paul were pleasing the Jews by preaching circumcision and were approving their godless righteousnesses, they would not be taking offense and would not be persecuting him.

As to the second point one can say that the apostle does not want a stumbling block to exist but is citing the evident experience that the stumbling block of the cross has not been removed, in order to prove that circumcision was not being preached by him. Therefore the meaning is: "From this very fact you learn that circumcision is not being preached by me, for you see that the stumbling block of the cross does not cease. The rage of the Jews continues, and they still take offense, just as they keep on persecuting me. There would undoubtedly be a cessation of both if I were preaching circumcision. Therefore the actual experience on both sides — that I am suffering and that they are being offended — should be abundant proof for you that we are not in agreement about circumcision."

Let this be enough for the foolish Galatians. Otherwise he who is looking for a loftier answer to this question will have to treat the well-known Gospel passage (Matt. 18:7) which states: "It is necessary that stumbling blocks come." Likewise Rom. 11:8, where we read: "He gave them a spirit of stupor, etc." And Matt. 26:34 states that it had to happen this way in order that the Scriptures might be fulfilled. But here we do not mention this ocean, although I would not deny that the apostle touched lightly on that matter in this passage.

12. *I wish those who unsettle you would mutilate themselves!*

St. Jerome thinks that the apostle is cursing here but is going to a great deal of trouble to excuse or at least to extenuate it.[23] But since we have learned from what was said earlier that saints are wont to curse and formerly were also wont to do so, and since Christ also cursed the fig tree (Matt. 21:19) — or if it seems too trifling a matter that a fig tree is cursed, Elisha certainly cursed human beings, namely, the children of Bethel, in the name of the Lord (2 Kings 2:24); and

---

[23] Jerome, *Commentarius*, 432.

in 1 Cor. 5:5 Paul delivered the fornicator over to Satan and says in the last chapter of that same epistle (1 Cor. 16:22): "If anyone has no love for the Lord Jesus Christ, let him be anathema, μαράνα θά," which Burgensis says is the worst kind of curse among the Hebrews, whereas our scholars understand μαράνα θά as "the Lord is coming," though mistakenly, in my opinion [24] — therefore it is not at all strange if Paul is cursing here too, calling down evil upon the outward man, through whom, as he saw, the good of the spirit was being hindered.

Jerome takes "that they would mutilate themselves" as referring to the private parts of the body.[25] For he has in mind those who are castrated, which is so great a misfortune that if it has been inflicted on men against their will, punishment is demanded by the laws of the state; and if it is done voluntarily, disgrace is incurred. In Deut. 23:1 we read: "He whose testicles are crushed or whose male member is cut off shall not enter the assembly of the Lord." And in Deut. 25:11-12 it is commanded that without any mercy they are to cut off the hand of a woman who, when men are fighting, takes hold of the other man's private parts in order to rescue her husband. Would these not be foolish and ridiculous things even if they were written in the books of heathen? Indeed, so they would be if God did not gladly make the wisdom of the world foolishness. It was not His wish that in things so shameful — though they are shameful by our own fault — our pride should feel disgust at secrets so great. The two testicles are certainly the two testaments, for a scribe who is learned in the kingdom of heaven will bring forth from his treasure things new and old (Matt. 13:52). Does not the woman's womb signify the will and the conscience? But I pass over these things, because those who are pure will discover them for themselves, while those who are impure do not hear such matters without peril. However, the woman's hand that must be cut off because she took hold of the private parts of a strange man would seem to me to be the foolhardiness of those who, in a contest between a true teacher and a false one, set aside or even twist the Scriptures and try to win by means of their own understanding and by means of human opinions.

But what does this mean? It means that when Paul, who was

[24] The meaning of this phrase from 1 Cor. 16:22 was to trouble Luther all his life; cf. his marginal gloss on it from the year of his death (W, *Deutsche Bibel*, VII, 137).

[25] Jerome, *Commentarius*, 433.

thoroughly instructed in the Law, deals with circumcision and the teachers of circumcision, he seems to wish for them that they not only be circumcised, but that they be completely mutilated, not only with respect to the foreskin but with respect to the testicles and the male member as well. He is evidently alluding to the hidden meaning which the Greek text also indicates by adding the connective "also," as follows: "Would that they would also multilate themselves!" That is to say: "If they really want to be circumcised, I wish they would also mutilate themselves and be eunuchs, whose testicles and male members are severed," that is, who are unable to teach and to beget spiritual children, and who should be thrown out of the church. For a bishop, yes, Christ, is the husband of the church, which He makes fruitful with the seed of the Word of God through His testicles and male member in complete chastity and holiness. The members of the ungodly, however, should be cut off, because they plant a foreign seed and an adulterous word.

13. *For you were called to freedom, brethren; only do not use your freedom as an opportunity for the flesh.*

One must supply the word "use," for Paul has resorted to an aposiopesis and has omitted the verb.

But through love be servants of one another.

Others read: "Through the love of the spirit be servants of one another." It makes little difference. What Origen, as St. Jerome recounts, invents about the hidden meaning and about the flesh of the Law I neither understand nor follow.[26] To me the apostle's thought and logic seem plain. When he says: "You were called to freedom," this means: "You were called out of the slavery of the Law into the freedom of grace." It is because people so often falter on this point that I myself am so often compelled to speak of it. The Law, I say, makes slaves, since it is from fear of threats and because of a craving for promised rewards, not without an ulterior motive, that the Law is fulfilled by them. And so it is not fulfilled. But since it is not fulfilled, it makes them guilty and the slaves of sin. Faith, however, brings it about that after receiving love we keep the Law, not under compulsion or because we are attracted for a time but freely and steadfastly. To become circumcised, therefore, is a characteristic of

---

[26] Jerome, *Commentarius*, 435—436.

slavery. But to love one's neighbor is a characteristic of freedom, because the former is done under threat of the Law by those who are unwilling, while the latter is done by those who are willing out of love that flows freely and gladly.

Furthermore, this statement, "Only do not [use] your freedom as an opportunity for the flesh," is one that Paul makes to keep us from understanding this freedom according to the stupid notion whereby we wish that everyone were permitted and free to do as he pleases. In the same way he also opposes this in Rom. 6:14, when, teaching the same freedom, he says: "You are not under the Law but under grace." Here we have Paul's assertion of freedom from the Law. But immediately he raises an objection to himself: "What then? Are we to sin because we are not under the Law? By no means!" (Rom. 6:15.) This is what he is saying here, namely, that opportunity is made for the flesh if freedom is understood in this fleshly way. We are not free from the Law (as I have said above) in a human way, by which the Law is destroyed and changed, but in a divine and theological way, by which we are changed and from enemies of the Law are made friends of the Law. In line with this thought 1 Peter 2:16 also says: "As free men, yet without using your freedom as a pretext for evil, but as servants of God." Behold, here you have what is meant by "an opportunity for the flesh," namely, a pretext for evil, which causes them to think that because they are no longer bound by any Law, they are not obliged to do what is good and to live rightly, whereas, on the contrary, it is the aim of freedom that now we do what is good, not from compulsion but gladly and with no ulterior motive. But in this passage, too, the apostle himself says that this freedom is a servitude of love. "Through love be servants of one another," says Paul. For freedom consists in this, that we have no other obligation than to love our neighbor. But love teaches very easily how all things are done rightly. Without it nothing can be taught in a satisfactory manner.

See, therefore, how foolish they are if they suppose that through the freedom by which we are freed from the Law and from sin license is given for sinning. Why do they not reverse the situation and take it that through the freedom by which they are made free from righteousness license is given to do good works? For if they consider it a correct inference to say: "I am released from sin; therefore I shall commit sin," one must also draw the inference: "I am released from righteousness; therefore I shall perform righteousness." If the latter does not follow, neither does the former. This foolish figment of the imagination comes from a human opinion and the practice of self-justification, as I have said, because human justification takes place through works. For this reason freedom and exemption from righteousness are thought of as coming after the attainment of "acquired" righteousness. But the righteousness of faith is bestowed before works take place, and it itself is the origin of works. Consequently, it is the freedom to do, just as the former is the freedom to neglect. The two behave in far different ways, as Is. 55:9 says: "As the heavens are higher than the earth, so are My ways higher than your ways." Therefore such a carnal imagination as this understands the freedom of righteousness rather as hateful slavery, for it hates the Law and its works. Hence it values no other kind of freedom than that the Law be changed and abolished, while its own hatred remains. Therefore in this passage "for the flesh" is not taken allegorically; it is taken in its proper sense as meaning the vices of the flesh, or the flesh in which are found the vices by which we are prompted to seek the things that are our own and to neglect the things that are our neighbor's. But this is contrary to love; and he who uses freedom in such a way is using it as an opportunity for the flesh, in order that the flesh, now that freedom has been granted, may have opportunity to serve its own desires and to despise one's neighbor.

14. *For the whole Law is fulfilled in this one word: You shall love your neighbor as yourself.*

This we read in Lev. 19:18. Rom. 13:8-10 says the same thing: "Owe no one anything, except to love one another; for he who loves his neighbor has fulfilled the Law. For 'You shall not commit adultery, You shall not kill, You shall not steal, You shall not bear false witness, You shall not covet,' and any other commandment, are repeated in this sentence: 'You shall love your neighbor as yourself.'" The Greek has "summarized" or "summed up" instead of "renewed." In several places Jerome translates it this way.[27] Therefore in this passage, too, the word "fulfilled" must be understood as "summed up" or "comprised." I am saying this to prevent anyone from thinking that the apostle is teaching that in this way the old Law is fulfilled through

---

[27] The Latin is *instaurare*.

a new Law, on the ground that this latter represents a spiritual understanding and consists of spiritual words; for grace alone is the fulfillment of the Law, and words do not fulfill words, but reality fulfills the words, and mighty deeds confirm speech. Besides, is not this thoroughly spiritual commandment to love one's neighbor written in Lev. 19:18? Therefore the whole Law is summed up in this one sentence, but it is fulfilled by grace. Accordingly, we have been called to freedom; we perform the whole Law if in love we serve only our neighbor whenever he has need of it.

Therefore what was said before is correct, namely, that the servitude of the spirit and freedom from sin, or from the Law, are identical, just as the servitude of sin and of the Law are identical with freedom from righteousness, or from righteousness and the Spirit. A person goes from servitude to servitude, from freedom to freedom, that is, from sin to grace, from fear of punishment to love of righteousness, from the Law to fulfillment of the Law, from the word to reality, from a figure to truth, from a sign to substance, from Moses to Christ, from the flesh to the spirit, from the world to the Father. All this takes place at the same time.

But since the apostle calls this commandment the sum total of all laws, and since everything is "included" — as Jerome translates — in this one chief point of love, it is necessary to dwell on this matter for a little while.

In the first place, how many describe what must be said, what must be done, what must be endured, what must be thought! Surely there are many things men can do to one another when there are so many senses, so many members, so many charges, so many cases, so that of the making of laws and of books there is no end (Eccl. 12:12). For how many commandments the tongue alone requires! How many the eyes! How many the ears! How many the hands! How many the sense of taste! How many the sense of touch! Then, too, how many the household requires! How many one's friends! O countless reptiles! If you do not believe this, look at the exceedingly unfruitful study of rights and laws that goes on today. But with what brevity, how quickly, how effectively, this commandment takes care of everything! It lays its hand on the head, on the source, on the root of all these things — on the heart, I say, out of which, according to Prov. 4:23, proceeds either life or death, since indeed among the other works of men some are more internal, others more external, but not one is more intimate than love, than which nothing is found more deeply hidden in the human heart. When this emotion of the heart has been set on the right course, the other parts no longer need any commandments; for everything flows out of this disposition of the heart. As this is, so is everything; and without it all other things are foolish exertions. Of these Eccl. 10:15 says: "The toil of a fool wearies him." On the other hand, Prov. 14:6 says: "Knowledge is easy for a man of understanding." For this reason the prophets call the righteousnesses of men labor and sorrow. In Ps. 7:14 we read: "He has conceived sorrow and brought forth iniquity." Likewise, "Sorrow will be turned on his head" (v. 16). And in another psalm (140:9) we read: "Let the mischief of their lips overwhelm them!" And in Ps. 10:7 it is written: "Under his tongue is labor and sorrow." For thus the Hebrew word אָוֶן is sometimes translated with "sorrow" *(dolor)* and sometimes with "labor" *(labor)*, which means wickedness, or, more correctly, the ungodly righteousness of laws and of works that never gives rest to the heart of man. Therefore the word בֵּית אָוֶן (Hos. 4:15), that is, "house of an idol," is frequently used. For this is what the prophet called the house in which Jeroboam set up the golden calves and caused Israel to sin. For in these righteousnesses without love there is a great deal of toil and labor but no fruit. Hence St. Jerome, writing on this passage, deplores such people. He says: "But now, when all things are more difficult, we do even ordinary things partway. The only thing we do not do is that which is both rather easy to do and without which everything we do is useless. The body feels the harm of fasting; vigils macerate the flesh; alms are sought with strenuous effort; and no matter how fervent faith is, it is still not without pain and fear that blood is shed in martyrdom. There are people who would do all these things; but love alone is without labor." [28] What do you think [Jerome] would have said if he had seen that in our day, with its multitude of laws and superstitions, love is not only without labor but has been utterly extinguished? For in my opinion nothing can arise that is more fatal to love than an abundance of laws and traditions by which men are led astray into works and because of which they busy themselves to such an extent with human righteousnesses that they are even compelled to forget about love.

Therefore let us look now at the emphasis and force Paul's words

[28] Jerome, *Commentarius*, 437.

have. In the first place, the apostle describes the noblest virtue, namely, love. For he does not say: "Be courteous to your neighbor, give him your hand, impart benefits to him, greet him, or do any other kind of external work"; he says: "Love him," since indeed there are those "who speak peace with their neighbors, while mischief is in their hearts" (Ps. 28:3).

Secondly, Paul depicts the choicest object of love in that he sets aside all considerations of person and says "your neighbor." He does not say: "You shall love the rich, the powerful, the learned, the wise, the upright, the righteous, the handsome, the pleasant, etc." Without any qualification he says "your neighbor." By this very fact he is declaring that in the sight of men we are indeed all different in personal status and rank, but that in the sight of God we are one lump and of equal reputation. For to observe a distinction of persons annihilates this commandment completely, as do those who loathe the unlearned, the poor, the weak, the lowly, the foolish, the sinners, the troublesome. For they take into consideration, not the people themselves but their masks and appearances; and so they are deceived.

In the third place, Paul shows us the noblest pattern for both when he says "as yourself." Patterns for other laws have to be sought outside ourselves; this one is shown to us within ourselves. Furthermore, external patterns do not motivate us sufficiently, because they are not felt and are not alive. This pattern, however, is felt within; it is alive, and it teaches most effectively, not with letters, not with words, and not with thoughts but with the actual feeling of experience. For who is not vitally aware of how he loves himself, how he seeks, plans, and tries everything that is beneficial, honorable, and necessary for himself? But this whole awareness is a living indication, an inward reminder, and a proof immediately at hand of what you owe your neighbor. You owe him exactly what you owe yourself, and you owe it from the same disposition of the heart.

Why, then, do we busy ourselves with many books? Why do we look for many teachers? Why do we exert ourselves with works and righteousnesses? All laws, all books, and all works must be tested according to the norm of this inward feeling and disposition of the heart. It is in this that a Christian man must be trained by all his works throughout his life.

Accordingly, no more effective pattern for this divine doctrine could have been given, because this is not one that we look at and hear about as we do the patterns given for the other laws; but this is one that we experience and live. We can never be away from it, nor can it ever be away from us. Neither could a worthier object be given than your neighbor, that is, he who is most similar and akin to yourself. Nor could a more perfect kind of virtue be given than love, which is the source of everything that is good, just as lust is the root of everything that is evil. And certainly all that is best is contained in this very short commandment. Therefore it is most truly the sum, the head, the completion, and the end of all laws. Without it all other laws deservedly count for nothing.

Therefore you have no reason to complain about not knowing what or how much you owe your neighbor. Away with those sharp distinctions the teachers make! The Word is near you, in your heart (cf. Deut. 30:14). It is written in such fat letters that you can touch it, since you are alive and are aware of this rule. Love "as yourself," it says, no less than you love yourself. But how much you love yourself no one could tell you better than you yourself, since you are aware of this very thing which can only be guessed at for you by someone else. For this reason no one could tell you better than you yourself what should be done, said, and desired for your neighbor. For here the proverb that a man is his own worst teacher does not hold true. On the contrary, in this matter you will be your own best and least misleading teacher, while all others will be misleading. So easy and so near is the Law God has laid down that no one can be excused if he does not live rightly.

Alas! This matter is neglected in our day by the preachers as it is by their hearers, while in the meantime there are such great swarms of caterpillars and locusts, yes, bloodsuckers, which laud, invoke, multiply, and insist on indulgences, vigils, offerings, the building of churches, the establishing of altars, memorials, anniversaries, and all the other things of this kind that serve gain more than love. Brotherly love, which alone covers the multitude of sins (1 Peter 4:8), is always omitted. The result is that those theologians indeed speak correctly when they assert that no work is good without love. But of all men they are the worst teachers when they say that we do not know when we are acting in love.[29] Indeed, they compel us to imagine that love is a sort of quiet and hidden quality in the soul. What do they want to accomplish with this dream except to say that we are not aware of that which is nearest and most alive within us, namely, the very pulse

---

[29] Cf. p. 173, note 12.

of life, that is, the disposition of our hearts? Or does this Mercury want to make a sort of Plautine Sosia out of us, so that we are neither aware of nor recognize our own selves?[30] Am I unable, I ask you, to be aware whether another person pleases or displeases me? Why, then, do I find fault with someone or praise him according to whether he is obnoxious or amiable? Or am I not even aware of it when I speak ill of people, do them harm, speak well of them, or good to them?

But this, they say, can be a natural disposition of the heart; for nature is a most deceitful emulator of grace. My answer is: I admit that nature tries mightily to emulate grace, but only as far as to the cross. From the cross, however, it turns aside completely; indeed, it has the very opposite in mind and fights against grace with utter hostility. But by the "cross" I mean opposition. For nature loves, praises, does good, and speaks well as long as it has not been offended. But when you injure nature or oppose its will, then it does its own work, and its love falls away and turns to hatred, shouting, malice, etc. For its clinging was a matter of appearance, not of truth. It loved the person and the outward appearance, not the reality itself. It was a friend, not of the neighbor but of the neighbor's goods and property. Love, however, never falls away. It bears all things, believes all things, endures all things (1 Cor. 13:7). It loves an enemy as well as a friend. Neither does it change when the neighbor changes; for just as the neighbor remains a neighbor, no matter how much he changes, so love remains love, no matter how much it is injured or aided.

Therefore the cross is the means of testing and, as they say, the Lydian touchstone of love in which there is nothing that would give you the right to say that love is a hidden quality and that you can neither know nor be aware of whether you love your neighbor. If in such circumstances you are aware that you are keeping a pleasant disposition, have no doubt that you are stronger than nature and that Christ has endowed you with love. But if you become bitter, then recognize that this is nature, and search for love. Nature's love seeks to be agreeable and quiet. Indeed, as the poet says, it approves friendships on the basis of their usefulness; it seeks its own advantage and aims only at getting what is good.[31] But Christian love is a strong

[30] Plautus, *Amphitruo*, where Mercury persuades Sosia that he has lost his identity.

[31] Luther is distinguishing between *amor* as natural love and *charitas* as Christian love.

kind of love that perseveres in the midst of trouble, approves its friendships on the basis of the services it renders, seeks the advantage of others, and is ready to give, not to receive. Indeed, genuine love hands out good things and accepts evil things; but carnality accepts good things and hands out evil things or at least takes flight.

Beware, too, of those who think as follows: Prayer or any work at all that is done without any consideration of one's neighbor is done in love, provided that it proceeds from the quality that is present and hidden within. This is an exceedingly crude conception. In fact, it is pernicious to the highest degree. On the contrary, you pray in love when, prompted by a kindly attitude toward your brother, you pray for him, whether he is a friend or an enemy. You speak well in love when you oppose a defamer for no other reason than that you have embraced your brother, whether friend or enemy, in your heart and are unable to let his reputation be besmirched — not, I say, because you hope for glory or friendship but out of the pure kindness with which you wish him well. In this way you do all other things in love when in them you look for nothing but the good and advantage of your neighbor, in short, of anyone at all, friend or an enemy.

Behold, this instruction will teach you how far along you are in your Christianity. Here you will find out whom you love and whom you do not love, to what extent you are making progress or are falling short. For if you have only one person toward whom you are not kindly disposed, you are now nothing, even if you perform miracles. Finally by this rule you will learn — you yourself, without a teacher — how to distinguish between mere works and works that are good. Then you will see clearly that it is better to wish your neighbor well, to speak well of him, to do good to him, and to make your whole life be a serving of your neighbor in love, as the apostle has said a little earlier, than if you built all the churches of the whole world, had the merits of all the monasteries, and performed the miracles of every last saint without serving your neighbor in these things. Behold, this is the teaching which today they are not only ignorant of but which they completely overwhelm with their traditions as with innumerable troops. In practice they teach never to love one's neighbor except for personal considerations, while they merely engage in heated disputations in the matter of works and make distinctions with regard to outward appearances.

No less carefully must one understand that very popular distinction which is made among natural law, the written law, and the law of the Gospel. For when the apostle says here that they all come together and are summed up in one, certainly love is the end of every law, as he says in 1 Tim. 1:5. But in Matt. 7:12 Christ, too, expressly equates that natural law, as they call it — "Whatever you wish that men would do to you, do so to them" — with the Law and the prophets when He says: "For this is the Law and the prophets." Since He Himself, however, teaches the Gospel, it is clear that these three laws differ not so much in their function as in the interpretation of those who falsely understand them. Consequently, this written law, "You shall love your neighbor as yourself," says exactly what the natural law says, namely, "Whatever you wish that men would do to you [this, of course, is to love oneself], do so to them [as is clear, this certainly means to love others as oneself]." But what else does the entire Gospel teach? Therefore there is one law which runs through all ages, is known to all men, is written in the hearts of all people, and leaves no one from beginning to end with an excuse, although for the Jews ceremonies were added and the other nations had their own laws, which were not binding upon the whole world, but only this one, which the Holy Spirit dictates unceasingly in the hearts of all.

One should also note most carefully that from the words of this commandment some of the fathers drew the opinion that the love here prescribed begins with oneself, because, as they say, love of oneself is prescribed as the rule according to which you should love your neighbor.[32]

I used to think about these things in an effort to understand them, but the exertion is useless. I shall not decide in advance for anyone but shall make bold to set forth my own opinion. I understand this commandment in the following way: It commends love only of one's neighbor, not love of oneself. In the first place, because love of oneself is in everyone inherently. Secondly, because if Paul had meant this to be the sequence, he would have said: "You shall love yourself, and your neighbor as yourself." But now he says: "You shall love your neighbor as yourself," that is, just as you already love yourself, without any commandment. But in 1 Cor. 13:5 the apostle Paul, too, ascribes this quality to love that it does not look for its own advantage, since it completely renounces love of oneself. Christ

---

[32] Cf. p. 290, note 12.

commands that one deny oneself and hate one's own life (cf. Mark 8:34 f.). And Phil. 2:4 says clearly: "Let each of you look not only to his own interests but also to the interests of others." Finally, if a man had the right kind of love of himself, he would no longer be in need of the grace of God, because the same love, if it is the right kind, loves both oneself and one's neighbor; for this commandment demands the same love, not another love. But, as I have said, the commandment presupposes that a man loves himself. And when Christ says in Matt. 7:12: "Whatever you wish that men would do to you," He is certainly declaring that affection and love of self are already present in them; and, as is obvious, He is not commanding it in this passage either. Therefore, as I have said, according to the opinion I make bold to have, the commandment seems to be speaking of the perverse love because of which everyone, forgetful of his neighbor, looks only to his own interests. This, on the other hand, becomes the right kind of love when one forgets oneself and serves only one's neighbor. The members of the body also point this out, since every one of them serves the other at its own risk. For the hand fights in defense of the head and receives injuries for this; the feet sink in mud and water for the sake of saving the body. But when love observes such an arrangement — an arrangement which Christ, however, wanted to destroy utterly with this commandment — the desire for one's own interests is fostered in an exceedingly dangerous manner.

But if one must concede absolutely that love of oneself is ranked first here, I at least shall ascend to a higher level and say that love of this kind is always wrong so long as it is in itself, and that it is not good unless it is outside itself in God; that is, that with my affection for myself and my love of myself completely dead, I look for nothing but that God's completely undefiled will be done in me. Then I am ready for death, for life, and for any form my potter wants to give me. This is arduous and very difficult, and for nature it is impossible. For in this case I am loving myself, not in myself but in God, not in my own will but in God's will. And in this way I shall then also love my neighbor as myself, wishing and striving that only the will of God be done in him and that his own will be done in no way at all. But I do not think that they understood it in this way, nor does the commandment seem to be speaking of this love in particular. Therefore I want everyone to be warned to beware of heathen teachings like "You must be a neighbor to yourself" and similar ones. For these teachings are perverted. Besides, they are twisted contrary to the force of grammar; for "neighbor" is a word used only with reference to someone else. For this reason a Christian has to say: "You must be a neighbor to someone else," as this commandment also indicates.

But now the question is asked how the whole Law is comprehended in this one commandment, especially so many rites and so many ceremonies of the Old Testament. Does the man who loves his neighbor do all these things? For it is not difficult to understand that the commandments of the Decalog are comprehended in this one, as has been deduced from the apostle's Epistle to the Romans (13:9). But who in our time sacrifices cattle, receives circumcision, observes seasons and years, etc., as we honor our parents, do not kill, do not commit adultery, do not steal, etc.? St. Jerome, in his usual way, thinks that the ceremonies are fulfilled in a spiritual way.[33] But what shall we say about the laws of other nations — laws which the apostles and even Christ Himself ordered to be kept in like manner? In the end we shall be causing the apostle to be equivocal, since, while using the same word, he would be teaching that the Decalog is fullfilled in one way and that ceremonies are fulfilled in another way.

In agreement with what I stated before I say that once the spirit of love has been received by the hearing of faith, then whatever other deeds are prescribed so far as ceremonies and human actions are concerned, whether among the Jews or among the Gentiles, they are permissible. But they are to be kept, not on the ground that salvation lies in keeping them or in their works. No, they are to be kept out of love for the sake of those with whom we must live, as long as they themselves demand that these requirements be kept by us, in order that peace may not be destroyed and turned into schisms and dissensions; for love endures all things (1 Cor. 13:7). And in these matters it is not so much transgressing the laws themselves that we must fear as that those who live according to these laws may be offended, for love commands us to be subject to their wishes. Accordingly, if God had wanted the ceremonies of the Law to continue in force, or if for the sake of some necessity one should keep one or more of them, then by all means this has to be done. But now

[33] Jerome, *Commentarius*, 436—438.

that He has abrogated them, they do not bind us at all. Thus one must be subject to the laws of emperors, of popes, of towns, of states, and of provinces only, as Christ says (Matt. 17:27), to avoid giving offense to them and in order not to injure love and peace. And so it is clear that one cannot even think of a law that is not embraced by love. For without any doubt you would want to be obeyed if you had decreed something. Accordingly, you are urged by the law of nature and of love to render this obedience also to someone else, especially to God and to the powers that represent God, provided that you take care not to make salvation rest on these commandments of men but understand that you must serve others through love.

On the other hand, the lawmakers themselves are much more under obligation to love, in order that when they see that their laws are burdensome to their subjects or even harmful, they may be concerned to regard the advantage of others in every way and to abolish these laws. This applies most of all, however, to those who make laws in the church; for without a doubt they themselves would not want to be burdened by even one syllable of a law. But unless they do the same thing for others, they are not bishops; then they are pirates, who impose on their fellowmen unbearable burdens, which they themselves are unwilling to touch with even a finger.

From this, dear reader, you understand why I am in the habit of calling certain papal laws acts of tyranny. Today these laws should be abolished for very many and very valid reasons: first, because they are burdensome and hateful to the whole world — to which fact the bishops should yield; secondly, because they are merely devices for snaring money and are shamelessly offered for sale by means of indulgences; thirdly, because they serve the cause of godlessness, while in the meantime they totally destroy true righteousness, in which there is salvation, and totally destroy love. Nevertheless, for the sake of love they should be observed wherever contempt for them would cause offense.

Finally I think it is sufficiently clear again that the apostle is speaking not only of ceremonial laws but actually of all laws. For when faith has been received, love fulfills them all gladly and freely. This means that it truly fulfills them. But it does not place in them or in their works the assurance of salvation, for this is a slavish act and does not fulfill a single law.

15. *But if you bite and devour one another, take heed that you are not consumed by one another.*

When it is the apostle's purpose to exhort to love, he adds almost simultaneously in all his letters that they should have the same mind, that they should not be puffed up one against the other by the various gifts bestowed on them. For thus — in Rom. 12:4 ff. and 1 Cor. 12:12 ff. — he presents the picture of the body and its members, the way in which the members are concerned for one another, and how the one serves and does not injure the other. The apostle knows that the Galatians are human and that the more extraordinary the gifts, the more harmful they are if love is lacking. Knowledge puffs up; the exercise of power puffs up; in short, all things puff up except love, which builds up (1 Cor. 8:1). It alone uses all things rightly, because with all the gifts of God it does not try to please itself but renders service to others. Where love is not present, there one finds controversy, strife, and wrangling; and, as Paul says in Rom. 12:3, people do not think with sober judgment but think more of themselves than they should. This, I say, seems to me to be the evil that the apostle is touching on — the evil which offers the most resistance to the service of love. For as long as everyone is puffed up with pride over the gift given to him and does not think of how he may serve someone else with this gift but thinks of how he may be advanced, contention and rivalry inevitably arise, likewise mutual contempt, disparagement, condemnation, rash judgment, anger, envy, shouting, malice, etc. Paul pursues the same thought at some length in Eph. 4:31 f. and in Phil. 2:1-4, but here he passes over it briefly.

The meaning, then, is this: "I know that you are human, that you can be tempted as long as one person wishes to be looked upon as more distinguished than the other, and as long as you are unwilling to be good stewards of the manifold grace of God in you (1 Peter 4:10). But take care that you do not disparage, do not bite one another, do not give in to this kind of temptation. On the contrary, as I have said, serve one another by means of love, everyone with the gift in which he is rich — one in teaching, another in giving," as Paul says in Rom. 12:3 at greater length. But this should not be done in such a way that he who teaches becomes puffed up with pride over against him who is able to give because perchance this person has not given as much as he who teaches wishes. Nor should the one who is able to give be puffed up over against him who teaches because perchance he does not think he needs that person's teaching. And so in the case of all the other gifts. For, as I have said, this kind of conceit is very close to those who are able to do something and, as a result, pride themselves on having no need of others and thus fail to serve one another in love but are consumed with mutual contempt, hatred, arrogance, disparagement, etc.

16. *But I say, walk by the Spirit, and do not gratify the desires of the flesh.*

Paul means to say: "This statement of mine, that you should not bite and devour yourselves, means only that I want you to live by the Spirit. Then the result will be that you do not do things of this sort. I know that at times desires of this kind are aroused in you. But do not yield to them. No, walk by the Spirit, that is, make progress, and become more spiritual." Paul has the same thing in mind when he says in Rom. 8:13: "If you live according to the flesh, you will die; but if by the Spirit you put to death the deeds of the body, you will live." Here he calls putting the deeds of the flesh to death by the Spirit walking by the Spirit and resisting temptation, in order that they may not bite and die. It is impossible for us not to be prompted to bite and devour, but by the Spirit one must resist these promptings.

Now this figurative expression, "to bite and devour," is an excellent one. It occurs very often in Holy Writ. Hence we read in the psalm (57:4): "The sons of men whose teeth are spears and arrows." Ps. 3:7 states: "Thou dost break the teeth of the wicked." And in Prov. 30:14 we read: "There are those whose teeth are swords, whose teeth are knives, to devour the poor from off the earth, and the needy from among men." Then there is the word "to gulp down" in Prov. 1:12: "Like Sheol, let us gulp him down alive." And Ps. 52:4 says: "You love all words that destroy [that is, that devour, that swallow up], O deceitful tongue." But with the word "to bite" Paul seems to understand accusing, disparaging, finding fault; and with the word "to devour" the taking of revenge and the exercise of violence. With the word "to be consumed," on the other hand, he seems to understand the ruination of both parties.

Note the force of the verb. "Do not gratify," says Paul. For between "doing" and "gratifying" the desires of the flesh or of the Spirit there is, in the Pauline sense, this difference (as is found in the last chapter of the third book of St. Augustine's *Against Julian*), that "doing" one's desires means having them, being titillated and aroused by them, whether to anger or to lust; but "gratifying" them means consenting to them and fulfilling them.[34] These are the works of the flesh. But not having or not doing these desires will take place, according to the twenty-fourth chapter of the first book of St. Augustine's *Retractations*, when we shall no longer have our mortal flesh.[35] This is why he says that all the saints are still partly carnal, although, according to their inward man, they are spiritual (*Against Julian*, Book 6).[36] Thus love itself feels desire in keeping with the desire of the spirit. Consequently, it cannot feel desire according to the flesh. But it does not gratify its desire, because it cannot be without the desire of the flesh. And, to interject a word of warning, it is not only the desire of the flesh that he calls lust but the desire inherent in all works, as he will presently enumerate. Augustine's words, therefore, are these: "The desires of the flesh are not gratified if one does not consent to them; although they are stirred up by impulses, nevertheless they are not gratified by deeds." This is why Paul said to the Romans (7:18): "To will is present with me, but how to perform I find not." For to do good means not to indulge in desires, but to "perform" what is good means not to desire. Thus the desires of the flesh are not "gratified," even though they occur. Nor are our good works "achieved," even though they occur.[37]

From all this it is clear what the Christian life is, namely, a trial, warfare, and a struggle. It is also clear how those who are being tried by various shocks are to be trained, so that they do not despair if they have not yet felt that they are free from the evil prompting of any sin whatever. Thus in Rom. 13:14 Paul says: "And make no provision for the flesh, to gratify its desires." And in Rom. 6:12 he says: "Let not sin reign in your mortal bodies, to make you obey its passions." No one can avoid desire, but it is possible for us to keep from obeying the desires.

[34] Augustine, *Contra Julianum haeresis Pelagianae defensorem*, III, 26, 62, *Patrologia, Series Latina*, XLIV, 733—734.

[35] Augustine, *Retractationes*, 1, 23 (24), 2, *Corpus Scriptorum Ecclesiasticorum Latinorum*, XXXVI, 111.

[36] Augustine, *Contra Julianum haeresis Pelagianae defensorem*, III, 15, 46, *Patrologia, Series Latina*, XLIV, 848—849.

[37] This is a play on the word *fieri*, which can mean either "to be done" or "to happen."

I have presented these matters rather carefully and extensively on account of my faultfinders, who deny that every good act is at the same time still partly evil and say that the sin of desire is called a sin in an improper sense.[38] But as for you, believe the apostle and Augustine, who say that what is good occurs but is not achieved. Now for a good thing to be done is good, but for it not to be achieved is bad, because the Law of God should be achieved. Yet all the saints fall short of it and thus commit sin in every work. Nor is it sin in an improper sense; but it is sin indeed, because it is not grace in an improper sense or God in an improper sense or Christ in an improper sense or the Holy Spirit in an improper sense who remits and purges away these sins. It is indeed true that, as Augustine testifies, the guilt of sin has passed away in Baptism.[39] Nevertheless, the impulse remains. This means that God, according to Ps. 32:2, does not impute sin but heals it; for if He wanted to impute it, as He could truly and justly do, it would be altogether mortal and damnable.

17. *For the desires of the flesh are against the spirit, and the desires of the spirit are against the flesh.*

Just as "spirit" in this passage does not signify chastity alone, so it follows necessarily that "flesh" does not signify lust alone. I have had to say this because it has become an established usage almost among all to understand "desires of the flesh" only in the sense of "lust." [40] According to this usage, it would be impossible for the apostle to be understood. In his excellent treatment of this thought in Rom. 7:22 ff. he explains it at greater length and says: "For I delight in the Law of God in my inmost self, but I see in my members another law at war with the law of my mind and making me captive to the law of sin which is in my members." For Paul did not say this in the role of others, as St. Augustine, in the eleventh chapter of the sixth book of his *Against Julian*, states that he had once understood or rather misunderstood him; but that, he says, is how the Manichaeans and the Pelagians understood Paul.[41] Thus St. Peter, in

---

[38] Cf. p. 256, note 22.

[39] Augustine, *Contra Julianum haeresis Pelagianae defensorem*, VI, 18, 51—52, *Patrologia, Series Latina*, XLIV, 852—854.

[40] Cf. *Luther's Works*, 1, p. 114, note 46.

[41] Augustine, *Contra Julianum haeresis Pelagianae defensorem*, VI, 23, 70 to 73, *Patrologia, Series Latina*, XLIV, 865—868; on the Manicheans and Pelagians, ibid., chs. 18, 57, cols. 856—857.

his first epistle (2:11), says: "I beseech you as aliens and exiles to abstain from the passions of the flesh that wage war against your soul."

Here St. Jerome gets himself deeply involved in the question how to find a neutral ground and neutral works between the flesh and the spirit.[42] Following his beloved Origen, he distinguishes spirit, soul, and flesh. Accordingly, he divides spiritual man from animate and carnal man. And although this threeness seems to be established from 1 Thess. 5:23, where we read: "May your spirit and soul and body be kept, etc.," still I do not venture to agree or disagree, both because in the passage quoted Peter obviously takes spirit and soul as being the same, since he calls it the soul that the desires make war against, whereas Paul says that the desires of the flesh are against the spirit, and also because to me the apostle seems to take carnal and animate man as being the same.[43]

In my temerity I do not make a complete separation of flesh, soul, and spirit. For the flesh experiences no desire except through the soul and spirit, by virtue of which it is alive. By spirit and flesh, moreover, I understand the whole man, especially the soul itself. Briefly, to give a very crude comparison, just as I may call flesh that is injured or ill both healthy and ill (for no flesh is altogether illness), because, to the extent that it begins to be healed and is healthy, it is called health, but where injury or illness is left, it is called illness; and just as illness or injury hinders the rest of the flesh, healthy though it is, from doing perfectly that which healthy flesh would do — so the same man, the same soul, the same spirit of a man, because he is associated with and tainted by the disposition of the flesh, is spirit insofar as he savors the things that are of God (Matt. 16:23), but is flesh insofar as he is influenced by the enticements of the flesh; and if he consents to these, he is altogether flesh, as is stated in Gen. 6:3. On the other hand, if he consents entirely to the Law, he is altogether spirit; and this will take place when the body becomes spiritual. Accordingly, one must not imagine that these are two distinct human beings. But it is like a morning twilight, which is neither day nor night yet can be called either one. Nevertheless, day, as that toward which it is tending after the darkness of night, is more appropriate. By far the most beautiful illustration of both truths is that half-alive

[42] Jerome, *Commentarius*, 439—441.

[43] On dichotomy and trichotomy in Luther cf. *Luther's Works*, 21, p. 303, note 2.

man in Luke (10:30 ff.) who, on being taken up by the Samaritan, was indeed being healed but still was not fully restored to health. Thus we in the church are indeed in the process of being healed, but we are not fully healthy. For the latter reason we are called "flesh"; for the former, "spirit." It is the whole man who loves chastity, and the same whole man is titillated by the enticements of lust. There are two whole men, and there is only one whole man. Thus it comes about that a man fights against himself and is opposed to himself. He is willing, and he is unwilling. And this is the glory of the grace of God; it makes us enemies of ourselves. For this is how it overcomes sin, just as Gideon overcame Midian, namely, with a most glorious triumph, so that the enemies slaughtered themselves (Judg. 7:22). Thus the water that is poured into the wine at the altar fights at first with the wine until it is absorbed and becomes wine.[44] So it is with grace; and, as was said above, the leaven is hidden in three measures until the whole is leavened (Matt. 13:33).

For these are opposed to each other, to prevent you from doing what you would.

Look at how bold the apostle is! He has no fear at all of the fire. He denies free will. This is amazing for us to hear. He says that what we want cannot be done even though we have established the will (certainly on Aristotle's authority) as the queen and mistress of all our powers and actions.[45] And this error and exceedingly great heresy would be tolerable if he had said this about those who are outside grace. Now — in order that he may have no excuse to keep him from being burned at the stake — he affirms this of those who live by the spirit of grace. In Rom. 7:14 the same man says: "But I am carnal, sold under sin. The good that I want I do not do. The evil that I do not want, this I do." If one who is righteous and saintly complains of his sin in this way, where will the sinner and the ungodly person appear with their works among those who are good in general, and morally good at that? The grace of God has not made the will perfectly free. Will the sinner make himself free? Why are we not showing good sense?

[44] The practice of mixing water with the wine in the Eucharist goes back to the early church: cf. Irenaeus, *Adversus haereses*, V, 2, 3; Cyprian, Epistle 63, 13. It was defended and defined at the Council of Trent, Session XXII, 7, 9.

[45] See, for example, Aristotle, *Metaphysics,* IX, 5.

Enough has been said about the difference between spirit and flesh. Neither one does away with the other in this life, even though the spirit tames the flesh against its will and subjects it to itself. Consequently, no one dares boast that he has a clean heart or that he is cleansed from filth; for my flesh does nothing of which it would not be said that I myself do it. But if the heart is not clean, then no work is clean either; for as the tree, so the fruit. I am saying this again in opposition to the faultfinders who find in themselves good actions without any defect or sin that is improperly so called, and who pit their faulty opinions against so clear a text of Paul. "You do not do the things you want," he says, because of the rebelliousness of the flesh, which resists the law of your mind and the will of your spirit.

Here the apostle does not preserve the distinction that was made above between "doing" and "performing," because, as is clear, he takes "You do not do" in the sense of "you do not perform." But in Rom. 7:19 he does not observe it either when he says: "I do not do the good I want"; that is, I do not perform. But when he says: "The evil that I hate is what I do," here he is observing that distinction, because he does the evil but does not perform it. But if someone does not like this distinction made by Augustine, let him look at it in another way, provided that he does not disregard this sense, that there is in us a battle between the spirit and the flesh — a battle which prevents us from fulfilling the Law perfectly — that for this reason we are sinners as long as we are in the flesh, and that in every work we need the forgiving mercy of God and must say: "Enter not into judgment with Thy servant, O Lord; for no man living is righteous before Thee" (Ps. 143:2).

18. *But if you are led by the Spirit, you are not under the Law.*

"I have told you," says Paul, "to walk in the spirit and to follow the desires of the spirit while resisting the desires of the flesh, and not to bite and devour one another but to serve one another in love, which is the fulfilling of the Law. For if you do this, and thus are led by the spirit and obey the desires of the spirit, behold, you are not under the Law. You owe the Law nothing; instead, you are fulfilling the Law. Why, then, did you want to return again to the Law? Why are you trying to fulfill the Law in another way?"

I have said often enough above that "to be under the Law" means failing to fulfill it or fulfilling it in a slavish fashion, without a cheerful disposition. It is not the Law, however, or nature that acquires this cheerful disposition; faith in Christ Jesus acquires it. And this being led by the Spirit, this obeying the desires of the Spirit, this battle and struggle which constitutes our whole life, brings it about that God mercifully pardons us for failing to do the things we want to do. For we are not yet spirit, but we are being led by the Spirit. For John 3:6 — "That which is born of the Spirit is spirit" — shows what we ought to be. But this passage shows what we are. We ought to be spirit, but we are still in the process of being led and, so to speak, in the process of being formed by the Spirit. But those who are under the Law are also in the works of the flesh, as Paul says in Rom. 7:5: "While we were living in the flesh, our sinful passions, aroused by the Law, were at work in our members to bear fruit for death." So, too, in Rom. 8:14: "Those who are led by the Spirit of God are sons of God." For this leading and prompting is identical with the drawing of which John 6:44 says: "No one can come to Me unless the Father draws him." Similarly in John 12:32: "When I am lifted up, I will draw all men to Myself"; that is: "I will prompt them pleasantly. I will make them cheerful and willing. By the Spirit I will arouse a desire in those whom Moses and the Law with its terrors used to force or for a time used to encourage like children, with temporal promises." Thus the bride speaks in the Song of Solomon (1:4): "Draw me after You; we shall run to the fragrance of Your ointments." This means: "With the word of the Law and dire threats Moses and the prophets terrify and oppress me while I am weak and unwilling; but do Thou draw me gently, and anoint me pleasantly with the Word of grace and the memory of the mercy Thou hast shown." For the fragrance of the ointments is the Gospel of the grace of God. Here one notes the fragrance of the ointment of God's grace, that is, perceives it by faith. For this reason it is stated in Ecclus. 24:20: "On the streets I gave forth a sweet smell like cinnamon and aromatic balm. I yielded a sweet fragrance like precious myrrh." And in Ps. 45:8 we read: "Your robes are all fragrant with myrrh and aloes and cassia." Thus Paul says (2 Cor. 2:15 f.): "We are the aroma of Christ among those who are being saved, etc." The same "drawing" is also called "whistling" in Is. 7:18: "In that day the Lord will whistle for the fly which is in the farthest boundaries of Egypt"; that is, He will breathe upon them with His Holy Spirit. He will arouse their spirit, so that they feel desires that are contrary to the flesh. Thus in 1 Kings 19:11 ff. it is written that Elijah did not perceive the Lord in the mighty wind or in the earthquake or in the fire (all of which are the terrors of the Law) but in the whistling of a gentle breeze; for the Law of the Lord is fulfilled, not with gloom or out of necessity but with gladness and pleasure.

19. *Now the works of the flesh are plain: fornication, impurity, licentiousness, wantonness,*

20. *service of idols, sorcery, enmity, strife, jealousy, anger, quarrels, dissensions, party spirit,*

21. *envy, murder, drunkenness, carousing, and the like.*

Here most plainly of all it is evident that flesh is understood, not only in the sense of lustful desires but as absolutely everything that is contrary to the spirit of grace. For heresies, or party spirit and dissensions, are faults of the keenest minds and of such as shine with an exceedingly saintly outward appearance. I am saying this in order to establish what I said above: that by flesh the whole man is meant and that in like manner the whole man is meant by spirit, likewise that the inward and the outward man, or the new man and the old, are not distinguished according to the difference between soul and body but according to their dispositions. For since the fruits or works of the spirit are peace, faith, continence, etc., and since these take place in the body, who can deny that the spirit and its fruit are in the body and in the members of the flesh, as 1 Cor. 6:19 expressly states? "Do you not know," says Paul, "that your members are the temple of the Holy Spirit?" Note that not only the soul but also the members of the body are a spiritual temple. And again: "Glorify God, and bear Him in your body" (cf. 1 Cor. 6:20). He does not say "in your soul." On the contrary, since feelings of envy and of enmity are faults of the heart, who will deny that the flesh is in the soul? Therefore the whole man is a spiritual man insofar as he savors the things that are of God (Matt. 16:23), and the whole man is carnal insofar as he savors the things that are his own.

Since the apostle has no knowledge of Aristotelian philosophy, he does not call these faults conditions in the soul;[46] he calls them actual works, to all of which he ascribes one condition, namely, the

---

[46] Luther may be thinking of a passage like Aristotle, *De anima*, III, 10—11.

flesh, that is, the whole man descended from Adam. For to this very day those people are searching for the basis of vices and virtues and have not yet discovered whether these are to be located in the rational or in the irrational part of man. "Blessed is the man whom Thou dost chasten, O Lord, and whom Thou dost teach out of Thy Law" (Ps. 94:12), that he may be freed from those foolish and vain thoughts, "and that Thou mayest give him respite from those very evil days, until a pit is dug for the wicked" (v. 13). With the apostle, therefore, you should scorn the conditions and other deliriums of moral philosophy and know that you are either flesh or spirit, and that both are recognized by their fruits, which the apostle plainly enumerates here.

There is scarcely any agreement with respect to the number of the vices. St. Augustine sets the number at thirteen; St. Ambrose, at sixteen; our [Latin version], at seventeen. St. Jerome mentions fifteen. He omits licentiousness and murder, and says, "In the Latin codices adultery, licentiousness, and murder are also mentioned in this catalog of vices; but one must realize that no more than fifteen works of the flesh are named. On these we have commented." These are Jerome's words. Erasmus and Stapulensis almost agree with our translator, except that they add adultery and remove either wantonness or licentiousness.[47]

But the apostle is not opposing each fruit [of the Spirit] to each work [of the flesh]. Without any pattern he is setting one over against many and many over against many, so that he is opposing love and joy to fornication, impurity, and wantonness, which are perverted kinds of love and perverted kinds of joy; peace, patience, long-suffering, kindness, and goodness, to enmity, strife, disputes, anger, quarrels, etc.; faith, to heresies, idolatry, and sorcery; continence, to drunkenness and carousing.

In the first place, there is "fornication," which is known well enough.

In the second place, there is "impurity," in which St. Jerome includes all abnormal and unspeakable pleasures.

In the third place there is "wantonness" (for the word "licentiousness" of our text seems to have been brought into the text from the

---

[47] Jerome, *Commentarius*, 442—446; Augustine, *Epistolae ad Galatas expositio, Patrologia, Series Latina*, XXXV, 2139—2140; Ambrose (ascribed), *Commentaria in XII epistolas beati Pauli, Patrologia, Series Latina*, XVII, 389.

margin, where someone wrote it as a gloss to explain "impurity" or "wantonness," or had noted that it was so found in other manuscripts). But although St. Jerome gives it a general meaning that extends even to excess on the part of those who are married, still the Greek word ἀσέλγεια means lasciviousness or, as Ambrose says, obscenity, which can refer to morals and also to gestures and to speech.

In the fourth place, there is "service of idols," which itself is known well enough but now at least is not the gross idolatry that existed among the heathen. On the other hand, those whose God is the belly (Phil. 3:19) and those who are avaricious are, in the apostle's view, also idolaters (Eph. 5:5). Idolaters are all sycophants or swaggerers, as are all who glory in man, either in themselves or in another person. Thus not a few rulers and bishops are idols today.

In the fifth place, there is "sorcery," an evil which today is having an astonishing growth. According to Jerome, moreover, it is called the poisonous art; for the Greek word φάρμακον means poison or medicament. Hence a sorceress is called poisonous. Therefore the apostle is referring to magicians, wizards, enchanters, and any others who, by means of compacts with devils, deceive their neighbors, harm them, and steal from them. But it is clear on the authority of so great an apostle that those sorceries are not unreal but are able to work harm — something that many do not believe.

In the sixth place, "enmity" seems to mean grudges and secret hatred against one another. "Controversy," which in our text is "strife" — in Greek it is ἔρις, that is, "quarrel" — is a work of enmity. "Jealousy," or zeal, has been spoken of above. "Anger" is well known. "Quarrels" — which, as St. Jerome thinks, are more aptly expressed with the Greek word ἐριθεῖαι — take place, of course, when someone, eager for an argument, takes delight in someone else's vexation and with womanish scolding picks a fight and goads his opponent on. You could gather all this better from experience and from the example of two adversaries than you could from a description. For first they are hostile and in disagreement. Then, as soon as any opportunity whatever is given, they wrangle. While wrangling, however, they become jealous, as each one strives to be superior to the other. But when they are jealous, they get angry. In their anger, however, they look on both sides for something to say or do or omit which could bite and goad the other; that is, they quarrel. When quarreling, however, they get into dissension, and everyone is quick to defend his own position and to weaken the position of the other person. As a result of this, sects and heresies arise, as everyone draws others to his side and takes them away from the other person. From this source envy is nourished — a savage evil. Finally they plunge into killing and murder. And that is the end of this evil. As an example take two opponents in a court of law or two states at odds with each other or two sophists and theologasters contending for their own opinions. Therefore the apostle has distinguished nine grades or categories of that bitter and jaundiced desire of the flesh, so greatly does he abhor the enemies of love. Jerome adds here that everyone who understands Scripture in any other way than the meaning of the Holy Spirit demands is called a heretic, even if he has not withdrawn from the church. This is a stern judgment on the Aristotelian theologians.

Next, in the seventh place, there is "drunkenness," which is forbidden not only with regard to wine but with regard to every other kind of drink. Hence Luke 1:15 says: "He shall drink no wine nor strong drink," that is, anything intoxicating. Of course, abstinence from wine is commended in various passages of Scripture. So is sobriety. On the other hand, what drunkenness has caused is sufficiently shown by the historical accounts of the same Scripture in the cases of Noah and Lot, whose drunkenness was not their own fault yet did not occur without harm to others (Gen. 9:21 ff.; 19:30 ff.). But these stories are well known everywhere. Hence Christ says in Luke 21:34: "Take heed to yourselves lest your hearts be weighed down with dissipation and drunkenness." And it is certainly clear enough that in our lands drunkenness is a kind of plague sent upon us by divine wrath.[48] Everywhere we flee from a plague that strikes the flesh, and with all zeal we arm ourselves and exercise care not to be carried off by it; but into this plague we plunge ourselves with signal blindness, and there is no one even to warn us, let alone stop us. In fact, this plague rages so violently that there can be no hope of purging it out.

Finally there is "carousing," which in Luke 21:34 is called dissipation. Just as drunkenness weighs down the hearts too much with drinking, so dissipation weighs them down too much with eating. And this widespread evil is having an astonishing growth even among the leaders of the people and the great ones of Israel, and with such extravagance, such pomp, and such an abundance and variety of dishes

---

[48] See also *Luther's Works*, 13, p. 216.

that with the effort they put forth they seemingly want to make a mockery of the notorious feasts of the ancients. The word "carousing" *(comessatio)*, however, comes from the name Comus, who was called the god of festivity and of dissipation by the Greeks.[49] Thus just as sexual lust is named for Venus,[50] so dissipation is named for Comus. Both, of course, are very powerful and closely related deities. The latter is served by the belly; the former, by what is under the belly. Comus sustains Venus and invigorates her. Otherwise, without Ceres and Bacchus, Venus is cold.

At the end Paul adds "and the like," for who could survey the whole Lernean Swamp [51] of carnal life? For under jealousy and zeal he has adequately included arrogance and vainglory; under anger, envy, dissension, etc., he has included slander, cursing, shouting, and blasphemy; likewise deceit, fraud, treachery, lying. For he has designated a few categories in order that the Galatians may not pretend that they do not know how to resist the desires of the flesh.

I warn you, as I warned you before, that those who do such things shall not inherit the kingdom of God.

Behold, this is what it means to walk in the spirit and not to perform the lusts of the flesh, to be led by the Spirit, not to be under the Law, and to comprehend the whole Law under the one heading of love — namely, if these things are not done. Now you see how faith alone is not sufficient. Yet faith alone justifies, because if it is genuine, it obtains the spirit of love. But the spirit of love flees all these things and in this way fulfills the Law and attains the kingdom of God. Accordingly, it must all be ascribed to faith; faith, however, to the Word; the Word, however, to the mercy of God, who sends apostles and preachers of the Word, so that all our sufficiency is from God (2 Cor. 3:5), from whom every boon and every perfect gift come (James 1:17).

These are the matters that should have been treated among the people, and treated in the order in which they are presented by the apostle, namely, that those who despair of their own strength hear the Word of faith first; that those who hear, believe; that those who believe, invoke; that those who invoke, be heard; that those who have

---

[49] The word *comessatio* is actually derived from *comedere*.

[50] Cf. the English words "venery" and "venereal."

[51] A reference to the Lernean Swamp, where Hercules slew the Hydra.

been heard, receive the spirit of love; that after receiving the spirit they walk in the spirit and do not perform the desires of the flesh but crucify them; and that those who have been crucified, arise with Christ and possess the kingdom of God. We, however, burden souls with works we have chosen and decided on; we always teach and never attain a knowledge of the truth. Yes, in opposition to godliness we set up free will and our own virtues; we teach presumptuousness and flaunt merits of congruity and condignity with the utmost fruitlessness. Finally we take away the knowledge of Christ completely and multiply for men consciences that are wretched to the highest degree.

St. Augustine's comment on the words "who do such things" is this: "Such things," he says, "are done by those who consent to their carnal desires and resolve to do them even if no opportunity is given to carry it out." [52] And he adds a strange distinction. "It is one thing," he says, "not to sin and another thing not to have sin, for a man in whom sin does not reign does not sin. He is the one who does not yield obedience to his lusts. But the man in whom those lusts do not exist at all not only does not sin but does not even have sin." Even though this can be achieved in many respects in this life, still it cannot be hoped for in every respect except when the resurrection and changing of the flesh takes place. This distinction teaches exactly what was sufficiently stated above, namely, that a man is righteous and holy and does not sin insofar as he walks in the Spirit; but insofar as he is still prompted by lusts, he is a sinner and carnal. Therefore he has sin in his flesh, and his flesh sins; but he himself does not sin. This is a strange thought. The same man sins, and at the same time he does not sin. It is here that those two statements of the apostle John are brought into harmony. The first is found in 1 John 1:8: "If we say we have no sin, we deceive ourselves"; the second occurs in 1 John 3:9 and 5:18: "No one born of God commits sin." All the saints, therefore, have sin and are sinners; yet no one of them sins. They are righteous in accordance with the fact that grace has worked healing in them; they are sinners in accordance with the fact that they still must be healed.

22. *But the fruit of the spirit is love, joy, peace, patience, benevolence, goodness, long-suffering, gentleness, faith, moderation,*

[52] Augustine, *Epistolae ad Galatas expositio, Patrologia, Series Latina,* XXXV, 2139.

23. *self-control, chastity.*

There is no doubt that Paul enumerated only nine fruits, as is clear from St. Jerome, St. Augustine, and the Greek text, where they are listed as follows: "The fruit of the spirit is love, joy, peace, patience, kindness, goodness, faith, gentleness, self-control." But it is evident that the number grew to twelve as a result of the inexperienced industriousness of some men. When they had found the word "patience" in a gloss, in the margin, or in Jerome, they put it into the text in fourth place, where "long-suffering" should have been put. This they transferred to seventh place. Then they saw that according to St. Jerome "self-control" has the meaning of "moderation" and "chastity." They added these two to the text and changed the positions of "faith" and "gentleness." [53]

Consequently, the basis for their doctrine of the twelve fruits comes to nothing, not only for want of the number but also because of their method of understanding it. For they make out of these fruits qualities of their own that inhere subjectively in the soul. The apostle, however, makes of them living works of the spirit that are spread out through the whole man; for he sets them in opposition to the works of the flesh. Furthermore, "spirit" in this passage (despite Jerome's insistence to the contrary) does not mean the Holy Spirit; it means the spiritual man. Therefore the antithesis is "works of the flesh" — "fruits of the spirit." The "flesh" is the evil tree that bears thorns and thistles; the "spirit" is the good tree that bears grapes and figs, as we read in Matt. 7:16 ff. For Ambrose, too, says that the law of the spirit produces these works; and St. Jerome, getting back on the right road, interprets "spirit" as the good tree. Furthermore, Paul speaks of the works, not the fruits, of the flesh; and of the fruits, not the works, of the spirit. Why this? Surely because the works of the flesh serve no good purpose, since no one can derive enjoyment from thorns and thistles; but they are evil works that only do harm. The works of the spirit, however, are profitable, and we can derive eternal enjoyment from them. They are the figs and grapes of the Land of Promise. Therefore the name "fruit" is the proper way of commending them.

The first fruit is "love," concerning which it has been said that it is not a quality that is hidden. But, as St. Augustine says about

---

[53] Jerome, *Commentarius,* 446 ff.; Augustine, *Epistolae ad Galatas expositio, Patrologia, Series Latina,* XXXV, 2140.

faith, everyone sees it with the greatest certainty if he has it.[54] Thus everyone is also aware with certainty of having hope; and thus he also sees love with the greatest certainty, especially in time of trial, if he has it. Therefore it is that affectionate impulse toward an angry God and toward an offending neighbor. For love of God proves itself when He smites and afflicts, as was shown in the case of the martyrs and in the suffering Christ; and love for one's neighbor proves itself when the neighbor offends and seems to deserve hatred. Otherwise almost no virtue is more open to imitation; so much so that in Rom. 12:9 this is the one thing the apostle is concerned about when he says: "Let love be genuine." For God has many who love Him. Of them it is written in the psalm (48:19, Vulgate): "He will make acknowledgment to Thee when Thou hast done good to him." And in Ps. 78:36 we read: "But they flattered Him with their mouths; they lied to Him with their tongues." Therefore although it may be hidden in time of peace, yet in war people are aware of nothing more vividly than love, hope, and faith, unless they have no awareness of distrust, despair, and hatred either.

Like love, "joy," the second fruit, has to do with God and with one's neighbor. It has to do with God when we are glad because of His divine mercy and even in the midst of the world's storms praise and bless the Lord in the fiery furnace day and night. But it has to do with our neighbor when we are not envious of his goods but wish him joy in them as though they were our own and praise the gifts of God that he has. But just as the adherents of the flesh feign love in tranquil times, so it is with joy too. They praise God and the gifts of God in men, but only till they are offended. Then the works of the flesh come rushing forth. They disparage the gifts of God which they had formerly praised. They are saddened if their disparagement meets with no success and if the reputation of their neighbor is not diminished. For no one believes how deep the malice of the flesh is, so many does it send smugly to destruction until they are tried and approved.

The apostle's words seem plain and clear; but if you put them to use, you will find out how hard it is not to do the works of the flesh, which to those fools seem very far away in spite of the fact that they themselves are as full of them as they can be. For even over and above the religion, over and above the observances, over

---

[54] Cf. p. 173, note 13.

and above the good works, over and above the regulations, the statutes, the traditions, and the man-made morals of these fools the works of the flesh rush forth at full tilt. But here they also receive love of righteousness as a covering for their zeal; and in accordance with their saintly religion they smugly destroy love, peace, and joy. Today this madness has hold of nearly all the monasteries, all the churches, and, as the psalmist says, "the picked men of Israel" (78:31). For in those who are openly bad these things are easily recognized; but under the tonsures, the badges of office, and other sacred rites that Behemoth stuffs himself and reigns smugly, while they believe they render God a service if they love the flesh of their own party but persecute and denounce outsiders with undying hatred.

The third fruit is "peace"; and this, too, is twofold. When it has to do with God, it is the good conscience that relies on the mercy of Christ. But at times it surpasses all understanding (Phil. 4:7), when it is disturbed because God hides Himself and turns away His face, and the conscience is left to itself. It has to do with one's neighbor, however, when one yields to his will. For this peace can never exist among men if everyone wants to justify, protect, seek, and demand his own advantage, as today the Roman Curia and its laws have filled the church with controversies, disputes, and legal proceedings. Meanwhile they are content with a little crumb of peace in which they reach agreement with their own people and make for themselves a covering for their wickedness, so that there is nothing they are less likely to think than that they are submerged in works of the flesh. For they do not pay attention to how many they are at variance with; they consider how many they are in agreement with. And they are even ready to teach peace to others. Such people understand absolutely nothing about the peace that Paul commends in Rom. 12:18 when he says: "So far as it depends upon you, live peaceably with all." Nor do they understand Matt. 5:9, where we read: "Blessed are the peacemakers, for they shall be called sons of God."

But the jurists — with utmost learning, of course — excuse the dissolution of this peace when they teach repelling force with force and declare ostentatiously that one has to uphold what is right, as if it were not the highest right of all to relinquish one's own right and to give up one's coat to the enemy who takes it away (Matt. 5:40) and even to throw in the undergarment. In short, it is impossible to uphold the Gospel and the rights of men at the same time. Hence it is impossible for peace to exist at the same time with rights, especially in our age, where the Gospel is nothing and rights are all in all. This is the angel in the Apocalypse who was sent in God's wrath to take peace from the earth (Rev. 6:4).

The fourth fruit is "long-suffering," μακροθυμία in Greek. For this is not ὑπομονή, that is, patience, or ἀνοχή, that is, toleration, although St. Jerome wants to take patience and long-suffering as synonyms.[55]

But it seems to be one thing to tolerate the wicked and another thing to suffer the wrongs they do and even to look forward to their improvement, to wish for their well-being, and to have no thought of vengeance. This is characteristic of "long-suffering." Rom. 2:4 says: "Or do you despise the riches of His goodness and patience and long-suffering?" It is goodness by which He does good to them; it is patience by which He suffers them to abuse His benefits as they thanklessly return evil for good; and it is long-suffering by which He looks forward to their improvement.

The fifth fruit is "benevolence"; the sixth, "goodness." According to Jerome, these differ as follows: Benevolence is a mild, amiable, calm virtue, one that is well suited for the fellowship of all who are good, invites to close acquaintance, is winsome in its address and temperate in its behavior. Hence St. Ambrose translates it with "mildness."[56] This is generally and inelegantly called "amicability" (*amicabilitas*); in German we say *freuntlich* (friendly), *holdselig* (gracious), *leudselig* (affable). In Greek we have χρηστότης, which in 2 Cor. 6:6 is translated with "kindness," where it says: "in kindness, in the Holy Spirit." Hence in Rom. 16:18 Paul called "winsome words" χρηστολογίαι. And in my opinion it would have been more correct to say "kindness" (*suavitas*) than "benevolence" (*benignitas*), because malignity, the vice that is the opposite of benevolence, is too harsh to apply to those who are morose and unpleasant (*insuaves*). For of the unpleasant one says: "He is a good man, but he does not know how to accommodate himself to the ways of people" (*Er ist frum, aber gar tzu unfreuntlich und nit leudselig*). Therefore it is possible for "goodness" to be rather grim and to have a wrinkled brow because of austere ways. Still it is free to do good, does no one any harm, and is of service to all. But it lacks something in the way of good manners.

[55] Jerome, *Commentarius*, 448.

[56] Jerome, *Commentarius*, 448; Ambrose (ascribed), *Commentaria in XII epistolas beati Pauli, Patrologia, Series Latina*, XVII, 389.

The seventh fruit is "faith," which St. Jerome understands to be what is described by the apostle in Heb. 11:1 as "the substance of things hoped for." For Jerome explains "substance" as being "possession." He says: "Because we hope that what we possess by faith will come." For a long time I, too, was of this opinion, because I had observed that in Holy Writ "substance" is used almost everywhere for goods and possession, especially since for this I had the support of what Jerome says about this passage. For why should one recount what the sententiaries have compiled regarding "substance"?[57] But after my dear Philip Melanchthon — who, though young in body, is a venerable old graybeard in intellect and whom I avail myself of as my instructor in Greek[58] — did not allow me to understand it this way and showed that when "substance" means "goods," it is called in Greek, not ὑπόστασις (the word the apostle uses in Heb. 11:1) but οὐσία, βρωτόν, or ὕπαρξις, I have changed my opinion and concede that according to my understanding ὑπόστασις, or "substance," properly means "existence" and the "essence" of which anything subsists in itself, as Chrysostom understands it. Or it also means a promise, an agreement — but there is no time now to discuss this more extensively — or an expectation — meanings that the force and the peculiar nature of the word from which ὑπόστασις comes permit. But it is possible in this passage for "faith" to be taken, not without reason, as "truthfulness," "faithfulness," or "honesty," which deceives no one and is necessary to the highest degree in business affairs and in the community life of mortal men. Thus we also find that faith is of two kinds. The one kind is directed toward God, to whom we are faithful, not so much because we keep our promises as because we believe His promises; the other kind is directed toward our fellowman, to whom we are faithful when we keep, and adhere to, our agreements and promises.

The eighth fruit is "gentleness," which Jerome sets in opposition to "anger" and "quarrels." Perhaps it is hard to distinguish it from "long-suffering." But "gentleness" is known as "mildness," because it is the virtue that is not provoked to anger and does not take vengeance. "Long-suffering," however, goes beyond this and expects the improvement of the wicked who have not yet been a source of irritation.

[57] Peter Lombard, *Sententiae*, I, 23, 4, *Patrologia, Series Latina*, CXCII, 584.

[58] Philip Melanchthon had come to the University of Wittenberg in August of the previous year.

The ninth fruit is "self-control" or, more correctly, "temperance," which we must understand in reference not only to chastity but also to drink and food. Its meaning, therefore, embraces chastity and moderation. Therefore here it also bridles the licentiousness of married persons, so that they may live continently and temper the lust of the flesh with moderation.

23. *Against such there is no law.*

Mindful of the proof he has undertaken to give, Paul always dwells on the Law, which does not justify those who trust in it. Thus in 1 Tim. 1:9 he says: "The Law is not laid down for the just but for the lawless and for murderers of fathers, etc." Those who are of the former sort do not need the Law. Why, then, do the Galatians return to the Law, not only of the Decalog but also of ceremonies? For you see that the apostle is speaking not only of the Ceremonial Law but especially of the Moral Law.

Once again, however, the apostle is theologizing in his characteristic manner. Therefore one must beware of understanding him in a stupid way, as if the righteous man did not have to live a good life and do good deeds (for this is what the uninstructed understand not being under the Law to mean). But the righteous has no law, because he owes the Law nothing, since he has the love which performs and fulfills the Law. Just as three plus seven (the example is Augustine's)[59] do not have to be ten but are ten, and there is no law or rule that one must seek in order that they may become ten, so a house that has been built does not have to be built; for it is what the builder's art, as a law, was seeking. So a righteous man does not have to live a good life, but he lives a good life and needs no law to teach him to live a good life. So a virgin does not have to be a virgin; but if she were seeking to become a virgin by some law, would she not be out of her mind? The unrighteous man, however, has to live a good life, because he does not live the good life which the Law requires. Paul is stressing all this in order that they may not presume to become righteous on the basis of the Law and of works, but in order that by faith they may receive the spirit without the Law and without works and thus may render satisfaction to the Law, as has been stated abundantly enough in what has preceded.

[59] See Augustine's discussion of the spontaneity of the Christian life, *Epistolae ad Galatas expositio, Patrologia, Series Latina*, XXXV, 2139—2141.

24. *And those who belong to Christ Jesus have crucified the flesh with its passions and desires.*

Paul is replying to a hidden question with which someone, prompted by what has been said before, might ask: "If there is no law against people of this kind, and they are righteous and not debtors to the Law, then why do you tell them not to do the works of the flesh but to walk in the spirit and to do other things? Are you not demanding an obligation from them? Are you not prescribing a law? Are not your commandments against them? Why do you contradict yourself?" What other answer do you think he would give than what we have learned above, namely, that those who are perfect in these fruits are not under the Law. They completely fulfill the Law. Therefore the Law is not at all against them. But since in the flesh there is no one who attains this goal perfectly, those who belong to Christ are preserved at least in this respect that they crucify their flesh and fight against its desires, and thus fulfill the Law of God in the spirit, even though in the flesh (as Paul says in Rom. 7:25) they serve the law of sin. Consequently, the description of the fruits of the spirit, against which there is no law, is rather a goal that is set up in front — a goal toward which those who are spiritual must strive. This does not mean that Paul thinks some have reached this goal. Therefore the Law is not against them insofar as they live in the spirit, but it is against them insofar as they are prompted by the desires of the flesh.

That this is a rule for understanding all other matters in which the righteous and the saints are praised on earth is beautifully and amply proved by St. Augustine in his *On Nature and Grace*.[60] Thus Rom. 6:6 says, "Our old man was crucified with Christ." And above (Gal. 2:20) Paul said: "I have been crucified with Christ; it is no longer I who live, but Christ who lives in me." I pass over what St. Jerome recounts here from Origen, nor do I care for it very much.[61] The apostle had said that there is no law against the spirit which brings forth the fruits commanded by the Law. So they, on the other hand, do not do the works of the flesh, but they do what is good and turn away from what is evil. Why? Because they are Christ's. They belong to Christ, not to Moses, not to the Law. But if they are Christ's, they undoubtedly have a crucified flesh, not by the Law, which was

---

[60] Augustine, *On Nature and Grace*, 44—45.

[61] Jerome, *Commentarius*, 449—450.

inciting the flesh more, but through Christ. It is as if he were saying: "You cannot belong to Christ if you want to belong to the Law. If you belong to the Law, you will not crucify the flesh, and the Law will be against you." Therefore those who belong to Christ are not under the Law, and at the same time they crucify the flesh with its vices and desires.

Jerome thinks that "vices" — or "passions" in Greek — is a rather general term and is added to "lusts" because the passions are also referred to pain. What, however, if by "vices" or "passions" he should understand the violent emotions of an irascible disposition as they rage in the bitterness of the heart, and by "lusts" the feelings of concupiscence as they afford pleasure with a titillation of the flesh? But let everyone be entirely free to have his own opinion.

The form of this crucifixion is well known. For the nails are the Word of God. They penetrate by the impulse of God's grace and prevent the flesh from following its desires. Thus Eccl. 12:11 says, "The sayings of the wise are like goads, and like nails firmly fixed are the collected sayings given by one Shepherd," that is, by Christ through the apostles and prophets.

CHAPTER SIX

5:25. *If we live by the spirit, let us also walk by the spirit.*

I DO not think it matters much that our [Latin] codices start the sixth chapter at this point. Jerome and the Greek texts begin it later with "Brethren, if a man is overtaken, etc." [1]

In this epistle Paul observes the same order that he observes in the Letter to the Romans. For there, too, he teaches faith first, through eleven chapters. In the twelfth chapter he treats of love and the fruits of the spirit; and in the thirteenth and those remaining he is at pains to point out that one should take an interest in those who are weak in faith. Thus here, too, after instructing them in faith and love, he makes it his concern that, among other evidences of good moral conduct, they do not disdain those who are weak or have fallen. For this is how St. Augustine — rightly, in my opinion — thinks this is said, namely, against those who, after they have been led back from the letter to the spirit, despise the weaker ones and vainly glory in themselves.[2] For this reason, he thinks, they are admonished, if they are spiritual, not to please themselves but to bear with the infirmities of the weak, as Paul says in Rom. 14:1 and 15:1. For if they failed to do this, they would indeed have begun in the spirit but would not be walking in the spirit, having become proud despisers of their brethren.

Therefore the meaning is this: "I am certain that you have been instructed in the spirit — whether as a result of this letter or as a result of my previous teaching — but that among you there are left some who are troubled with doubts and are not yet able to distinguish between the sound judgment of faith and the works of the Law, since, because of scruples of conscience, they are not willing to desist from the works of the Law and do not trust sufficiently in the

---

[1] See p. 97, note 80.

[2] Augustine, *Epistolae ad Galatas expositio*, Patrologia, Series Latina, XXXV, 2142.

righteousness of faith alone. These, I say, one must not despise. No, one must treat them with gentle care until they are strengthened and made firm by the experience and example of the strong." For such persons, like the poor, are always left in the midst of a people in order that there may be some toward whom you can practice the duties of love. Therefore "if we live by the spirit, let us walk by the spirit"; that is, let us persevere and make progress. This will happen if we do not let the infirmity of the weak tempt us to disdain them and to be pleased with ourselves. For this would be turning aside from the spirit, pleasing ourselves, and failing to serve others in love. Thus today, too, there is a large throng of those who are weak, even among the very learned, and are miserably tormented by a conscience under pressure of human laws and do not have the courage to trust solely in faith in Christ. But the boys and effeminate men who are ruling in the church do not make any concessions at all to our weaknesses. No, with boisterous violence they put forth the solid masses of their opinions merely to fortify their tyranny as soon as you do not give the answer they want. "Therefore you are a heretic, a heathen, a schismatic," they say. But of this elsewhere.

"Let us walk." This is the same verb that Paul used above, in the fourth chapter (v. 25): "is connected with that, etc." Therefore the meaning is: "Sinai is a mountain in Arabia which is connected, that is, which extends, walks, goes, as far as Jerusalem," as was said in that passage. And below (6:16): "Whoever will follow this rule," that is, will go, will walk. For the force and proper meaning of this verb, as Erasmus has rendered it, is to advance in order, to proceed on the right way, to go forward.[3] Moreover, the apostle uses the word appropriately in this passage. He means that they should not turn aside either to the left or to the right but should advance in a straight line and in order, and walk in the spirit they have received.

For since among the people there are both those who are strong and those who are weak, a twofold offense arises — the one on the left, among the weak; the other on the right, among the strong. The apostle is striving to keep them in the middle and to prevent both offenses. There is offense on the part of the weak when those things are done which the weak do not comprehend and are unable to distinguish from the evil outward appearance. Of this Rom. 14 treats most extensively. For example, when the weak saw that others were

---

[3] The Latin word Erasmus used was *procedere*.

eating all the foods forbidden in the Law as unclean, they, under the pressure of their conscience, did not dare eat the food themselves. Nevertheless, they did not dare condemn the example of the others either. Here Paul became a Jew with the Jews and weak with the weak, in order to serve them through love until they should become strong in Christ. Hence Rom. 14:15 says: "If your brother is being injured by what you eat, you are no longer walking in love." This is how one should think about all other ceremonies, those that have to do with days, festivals, clothing, etc. The other offense is on the part of the proud, when they, in turn, are offended at the weak and are impatient with their slowness and stupidity. Thus with no consideration for the weak they made use too freely of the freedom of Christ over against the Law in that they did these things with resultant offense to the weak, whereas they should rather have observed the whole Law before offending a single person; for this is how one walks by the spirit. For what benefit is there in using the spirit of freedom against the spirit and against love? "We are free to do so," they say. Certainly. But your freedom should be esteemed less than a brother's weakness, because no harm is done to you when your freedom is impeded. On the other hand, your brother is harmed when his weakness is offended through your freedom. It is characteristic of love, however, that you regard those things that are to another's advantage and consider, not so much to what extent you have freedom for yourself as to what extent you can benefit your brother. For this is the service to which love subjects you as it sets you free from the service of the Law. But today, good God, what monstrosities of the worst sort are perpetrated! And later all these things are left for the weak to bear and to interpret in a pious way — things which the very strongest are scarcely able to bear! Lacking a shepherd, however, they are not shepherds today. Everything is different in outward appearance, different in worth and in reality.

26. *Let us have no self-conceit, no provoking of one another, no envy of one another.*

Paul is explaining at great length what he had said. "Then," he says, "you will be walking and advancing rightly by the spirit, if you who are strong do not become puffed up toward the weak, do not take satisfaction in yourselves and pride yourselves over against them because they are not like you, as the well-known Pharisee glorified God in his conceit and poured shame on the tax collector (Luke 18:11 ff.).

For if you do this, you, with your utterly fruitless glorying, will provoke and irritate the weaker ones to envy; and thus, by turns, you will be provoking, and they will be envying; and neither you nor they will be advancing in the right order of the spirit. You the devil jostles to the right, them to the left; you through conceit, them through envy. But no! In keeping with Christ's example, your strength should take their weakness upon itself until they, too, become strong. For if we live by the spirit and in love, we do not live for ourselves; then we live for our brothers. Therefore we shall do what is serviceable and necessary for them." "Owe no one anything," says Paul, "except to love one another" (Rom. 13:8); and in 1 Cor. 8:13 he says: "If food is a cause of my brother's falling, I will never eat meat." Why? Because I love my brother, and his salvation is incomparably more important to me than my freedom, by which I am free to do what he does not yet understand to be permitted. Thus if my righteousness, wisdom, capacity, or any action whatever that is entirely permissible to me causes my brother to fall, I must give it up and render service to love.

But look now at what the exemptions, the privileges, the indulgences, and the confessionals are doing. Have not the laws of the bishops become merely nets for snaring money and stumbling blocks for consciences? Is not all Germany filled with the constant complaint that butter and other milk products are allowed on fast days to those who have bought the lead and wax of the Roman Curia, while in the meantime the rest believe in their ignorance that these things are not allowed even if the supreme pontiff were to grant permission?[4] To such a degree have the laws of men become rooted in them. For they consider murder, fornication, drunkenness, envy, and all the works of the flesh far less important than eating that privileged butter. And here not one of the bishops or privileged persons has pity on this crowd, but incredible greed multiplies these privileges without end, without measure. By these privileges the weak are only provoked to defame, curse, and condemn. On the other hand, those strong and exceedingly hardy despisers of the laws, puffed up in their boldness, despise those who are weak and call them *bon christian,* that is, half-stupid.[5] That is the present-day custom and manner of

---

[4] See the documents assembled in the St. Louis edition, XV, 56—105.

[5] A reminiscence of Luther's journey to Rome; he discusses the epithet *bon christian* in his *Lectures on Genesis* (W, XLIV, 770).

fulfilling love. How much better the supreme pontiffs would do either by abolishing the laws entirely, in order that all might know the freedom they have in Christ, or by granting privileges to none — privileges with such hell for so many weak consciences! How will they render an account to Christ for so many offenses to their brothers for whom Christ died? But the frenzy of greed does not allow them to hear about this love, even from a distance.

But these are still childish and utterly trifling matters. Let us come to those in which even the most highly learned and the very strongest are offended — so great is the victory of the devil in the church.

What an uproar, pray, what talk, what a stench the Roman Curia is causing on account of the bishops' palliums and annates, which are utterly disemboweling the bishoprics and pastorates of Germany![6] What about the pillaging of all the pastorates, the consuming and devouring of the monasteries and churches — to the point that there is no altar, not even underground, that does not render total service to the greed of the Roman muleteers,[7] while in the meantime men who are learned, good, and beneficial to the people are perishing of hunger and need? Truly the Romans harvest our material things but sow for us spiritual things, that is, things full of wind, so that we live on spirit and wind. For spirit means wind, just as in Hosea (12:11) Ephraim feeds on the winds. No wonder, I say, if the very strongest are unable to bear these things; for they are beyond limit and difficult even for the perfection of an apostle to bear. But no one of the bishops cares about these things. Consequently, they seem to rejoice in the fact that we are provoked and they are hated; and they seem to offer the well-known excuse of a Caesar: "Let them hate, provided that they fear."[8] For there is no lack of inflated bladders of this kind — bladders that glory only in their power.

Furthermore, who is not most bitterly provoked by the foremost of all offenses (for those that have been mentioned are temporal)? What an abundance of decisions there is in the matter of robbery,

---

[6] The pallium was granted by the pope to archbishops and certain bishops; the annates were the income from an ecclesiastical benefice for the first year and were paid to the papal curia.

[7] The term *mulio* was an epithet already in classical Latin; Luther uses it here for the cardinals.

[8] A favorite quotation of Luther's from Suetonius; cf. *Luther's Works*, 13, p. 210, note 70.

usury, inheritances, and testaments — in fact, every kind of reimbursement, questionable as well as certain, no matter whether this is owed to minors or to paupers! They even thrust forgiveness of dreadful sins upon those who do not want it as well as upon those who want it — to say nothing of selling it to them in the most frivolous manner; and they do so under the pretext of erecting one lifeless building in honor of St. Peter or with some less important reason as an excuse.[9]

I grant that these things must be borne. One should not be spiteful; one should not bite. But who will give us bones strong enough to bear these things? Or is it not permissible to complain of our weakness? Is it not permissible to say: "They must be borne, but we are not able to do so"? Surely it is not disparagement or spitefulness if a burden impossible to bear is placed on me and I should cry out that I lack the strength. Furthermore, if, when we are dealing with Holy Writ, we censure, if we bite into, if we condemn, these and similar things, our conduct is unimpeachable and in keeping with our duty. Or why do those princes, so learned and strong, demand of us toleration of these things and not much rather demand of themselves that they do not provoke us, especially since before telling us not to be indignant they should see to it that we are not provoked? Then, since in view of their station they owe a greater debt of love, they should be far more careful not to provoke than we should be not to be indignant, in order that in this way we, who should live by the spirit, may advance by the spirit — we not provoked and they not hated.

Perhaps, dear reader, you will say that I am always assailing the Roman Curia, something that till now has been exceedingly rare. I answer: The Lord is my witness that I am not doing this because of my own inclination or pleasure, since I wish for nothing more ardently than to lie hidden in a corner; but since I am altogether obligated to deal publicly with Holy Writ, I want to render as pure a service as I can to my Lord Jesus Christ. For if Divine Scriptures are treated in such a way as to be understood only with regard to the past and not to be applied also to our own manner of life, of what benefit will they be? Then they are cold, dead, and not even divine. For you see how fittingly and vividly, yes, how necessarily, this passage applies to our age. Because others have not dared this or have not understood it — it is not surprising that the teachers of theology

---

[9] The special indulgence which had called forth Luther's ninety-five theses of 1517 was to go for the completion of the new St. Peter's basilica.

have not been hated. To me it is certain that the Word of God cannot be rightly treated without incurring hatred and danger of death, and that if it gives offense — especially to the rulers and aristocrats of the people — this is the one sign that it has been treated rightly. It is a stone of stumbling in consequence of which the judges of the peoples are devoured. In short, the church is crying out that the rulers are persecuting her and that the rulers have crucified Christ.

6:1. *Brethren, if a man is overtaken in any trespass, you who are spiritual should restore him in a spirit of gentleness. Look to yourself, lest you, too, be tempted.*

Read Erasmus on why the apostle has suddenly changed the number and has not gone on to say: "Look to yourselves, lest you, too, be tempted." [10] For what he says has greater force if it is addressed to one person individually and pertains to each one separately.

This teaching is certainly most appropriate and has also been arranged with marvelous skill by the apostle for achieving the formation of love in them. First he calls them "brethren," more with kindly encouragement, as if he were asking this of equals, than with authority, as if he were demanding it of inferiors. Then he says "if a man," not "if a brother," as if he were saying: "If out of human weakness — because we are human beings — a brother has fallen." With this word itself he shows how — namely, with pity — we should look upon others when they fall, and that we should be readier to extenuate than to exaggerate. For the latter is characteristic of the devil and slanderers; the former, of the Paraclete and those who are spiritual. And "overtaken" — in the sense of "taken unawares," "having fallen because of a lack of caution" — is a word with which he similarly teaches us to extenuate the sin of a brother, because — unless he manifestly has sinned out of hardened wickedness and with no hope of reform — it is our duty to ascribe his fall, not to wickedness but to a lack of caution or even to weakness, just as St. Bernard taught his followers that if one was unable in any way to excuse a brother's sin, at least one should say that it was a great and insuperable temptation by which he was overtaken, and that he was seized by what was more than he could bear.[11] Paul says "in any trespass," "in any fall" (for

---

[10] Cf. Erasmus, *Paraphrasis, Opera,* VII, 964—965.

[11] See, for example, Bernard of Clairvaux, *Sermones in Cantica Canticorum,* XXXV, 5—7, *Patrologia, Series Latina,* CLXXXIII, 900—902.

it is very easy to fall), not "in any wickedness." Again he uses an extenuating word. For the mildest term we can use for sin is a "slip" or a "fall." Here Paul calls it a "trespass."

"You who are spiritual" — a wonderful statement to remind them of their duty and at the same time to teach them their duty. The duty it teaches is that they should be spiritual. If they are spiritual, let them do what characterizes spiritual people. But what else does it mean to be spiritual than to be a child of the Holy Spirit and to have the Holy Spirit? But the Holy Spirit is the Paraclete, the Advocate, the Comforter. When our conscience accuses us, He protects us in the presence of God and comforts us by giving a good testimony to our conscience and to our trust in the mercy of God. He excuses, extenuates, and completely covers our sins. On the other hand, He magnifies our faith and good works. Those who imitate Him in the presence of fellowmen with regard to the sins of their fellowmen are spiritual. Satan, on the other hand, is called the devil,[12] the detractor and calumniator, because he not only accuses us and makes our evil conscience worse in the presence of God but also disparages what is good about us and vilifies our merits and the faith of our conscience. He is imitated in the presence of their fellowmen by those who, with regard to the sins or even the good works of their fellowmen, exaggerate, enlarge, and expand the sins of their fellowmen but, on the other hand, minimize, find fault with, and disapprove of their good works. Hence St. Augustine says on this passage: "Nothing so demonstrates the spiritual man as his treatment of someone else's sin, when he plans how to set him free rather than how to deride him, and how to help him rather than how to revile him. On the other hand, you will demonstrate as carnal the man who deals with someone else's sin only in order to judge and censure, as the Pharisee insulted the tax collector but had no pity on him."[13]

"Restore in a spirit of gentleness." For the statement of St. Gregory is true. "True justice has compassion," he says, "false justice is indignant."[14] Thus in Luke 9:51 ff., when John and James, in accordance with the example of Elijah, wanted to call down fire from heaven

[12] The Greek word διάβολος, from which "devil" comes, means "slanderer"; cf. *Luther's Works*, 23, pp. 196—197.

[13] Augustine, *Epistolae ad Galatas expositio, Patrologia, Series Latina*, XXXV, 2143.

[14] Gregory I, *XL homiliae in Evangelia*, II, 34, 2, *Patrologia, Series Latina*, LXXVI, 1246.

upon the Samaritans, Christ forbade them, saying: "Do you not know what spirit's children you are? The Son of Man did not come to destroy souls but to save them." So we should give thought, not to how we may destroy but to how we may save the brother who is a sinner.

Discussing this topic in Rom. 15:1, Paul says: "But we who are stronger ought to bear with the failings of the weak, and not to please ourselves." Note the modesty and restraint of the Pauline spirit. He speaks of "failings" and the "weak," whereas some arrogant and self-righeous or heresy-hunting person (quick as they are to condemn and burn [15] their fellowmen) would have called it heresy, or crimes against the Holy Roman Church; for that is how they speak when they are talking about the greatest sins. Paul, however, calls those sins failings, whatever they may be; and the sinners he calls weak, because he speaks with the tongue of the Paraclete, not of the devil. Finally he appends an example (Rom. 15:3): "For Christ did not please Himself; but, as it is written, 'The reproaches of those who reproach Thee fell on Me'" (Ps. 69:10). According to Isaiah (cf. 53:4), this means: "He bore our sins," so far was He from abandoning, accusing, and damning us with them and in them. But He dealt with us just as if He Himself had done those things which we had done. He paid for what He had not robbed. Thus in Phil. 2:5 ff. Paul adduces the same example and says: "Let this mind be in you which was also in Christ Jesus, who, being in the form of God, thought it not robbery to be equal with God, but emptied Himself, taking on the form of a servant and was made in the likeness of men; and being found in fashion as a man, etc." Behold, Christ is like men, that is, like the sinners and the weak. And He displays no other nature and no other form than that of a man and a servant, since He does not despise us, though He is in the form of God, but takes on our form and bears our sins in His own body (1 Peter 2:24). But this statement is too significant to be dealt with in a few words. In fact, the masters of theology do not have an understanding of it. Meanwhile we shall postpone it.

Accordingly, Christ governs His church in such a way that just as He predicted in the Old Testament (Deut. 15:11) that there would always be the poor among the people in order that the people might have opportunity to practice brotherly love, so in the New Testament

[15] We have adopted the reading in the Erlangen edition, *exurere*, in place of the *exuere* in the Weimar edition.

He always lets some sinners remain and allows some to fall, in order that the stronger may have reason to practice evangelical and Christian brotherliness, lest love be idle and even founder. But the hypocrites, of all men the most perverse, fail to understand this arrangement made by the will of God and seize upon it to practice their own spitefulness. To brothers who fall they give consideration only in order to accuse, to bite, and to persecute; and they are unable to act in any other way than Simon the Leper did toward Mary Magdalene (Matt. 26:6 ff.) and the Pharisee toward the tax collector (Luke 18:11-12).

Finally Paul adds: "Look to yourself, lest you, too, be tempted." Even here he speaks with restraint and does not say "lest you, too, fall," as he says elsewhere: "Let him who stands take heed lest he fall" (1 Cor. 10:12). But he says "lest you be tempted." He calls that person's fall a temptation. It is as if he were saying: "If you have fallen, I would say it was a temptation rather than a crime on your part. With the same gentleness you, too, must suppose it to have been a temptation whenever you see someone who has fallen; and you should not castigate your brother's fall with harsh names." Behold, the apostle's words serve not only as a lesson but at the same time as an example. Among the rhetoricians of the world it is a very brilliant achievement to place words in such a way that in them you see that the thing itself is observed and shown simultaneously. Paul — I should rather say the Holy Spirit — has this characteristic. Consequently, St. Gregory makes the excellent statement: "Whenever we look at sinners, we must first of all bewail ourselves in them, because we either have fallen or can fall into similar sins." "For there is not a sin a man does," says Augustine, "that another man could not do too, if God should forsake him." [16] Nor do I disdain the little verse that someone made up for himself as a reminder of this fact: "We are, have been, or can be what this man is." [17] And would that the Thomists, the Scotists, and the moderns would thus settle their question whether universals are real things or are terms predicated indifferently of real things! [18] Man is man. Flesh is flesh. Flesh has never done anything that similar flesh would not do wherever God did not make a distinction.

[16] Cf. p. 112, note 8.

[17] A medieval version of the saying "There, but for the grace of God, go I!"

[18] A reference to the scholastic debate over whether "universals," i. e., general concepts, are real or are merely names.

2. *Bear one another's burdens, and so fulfill the law of Christ.*

In a very beautiful and thoroughly golden maxim Paul sums up the two teachings he has previously mentioned. There are, he says, certain apprehensive individuals who do not distinguish between the law of faith and the law of men. One must bear with them and by all means refrain from taking offense at them. There are others who sin even against the Law of God. Nor are these to be despised out of a stupid zeal for God, but one must bear with both kinds in Christian love. The former must be instructed; the latter, restored. The former must be shown what they should know; the latter what they should do. And in this way the shaping of their faith as well as their works must be served. For the first need the teaching of faith, the second need instruction in virtuous living. Thus everywhere love finds something to bear, something to do. Moreover, love is the law of Christ. But to love means to wish from the heart what is good for the other person, or to seek the other person's advantage. Now if there were no one who errs or falls — that is, no one who needs what is good — whom are you going to love, whose good are you going to desire, whose good are you going to seek? Love is not even able to exist if there are none who err and sin, who, as the philosophers say, are the proper and adequate "object" of love or the "material" of love.[19] Carnality, however — or love that consists in lust — looks for others to wish for its benefit and to want for it what it itself desires. That is, it looks for its own advantage; and its "material" is one who is righteous, saintly, pious, good, etc. These people surely are perverting this teaching, inasmuch as they want their own burdens to be borne, to have the sole enjoyment of benefits provided by others, and to be carried along. For they are the kind who disdain having the uneducated, the useless, the hot-tempered, the foolish, the troublesome, and the surly as companions in life but look for people who are cultured, pleasant, kindly, quiet, and saintly. That is, they want to live, not on earth but in Paradise, not among sinners but among angels, not in the world but in heaven. In their case one has to fear that they are receiving their reward here and have their kingdom of heaven in this life. For they are unwilling, with the bride, to be a lily among thorns (Song of Sol. 2:2) or, with Jerusalem, to be situated in the midst of the heathen or, with Christ, to rule in the midst of enemies (Ps. 110:2). In fact, they make the cross of

---

[19] The technical terms are *obiectum charitatis* and *materia dilectionis*.

Christ of no effect (1 Cor. 1:17) in themselves, and the love they have is inactive, is snoring, and is carried on other shoulders.

Consequently, those who, in order to become good, flee the company of such people are doing nothing else but becoming the worst of all. And yet they do not believe this, because for the sake of love they are fleeing the proper duty of love, and for the sake of salvation they are fleeing what is the true epitome of salvation. For the church was always best when it was living among the worst people. For in bearing their burdens its love shone with a wonderful glow, as Ps. 67:14 says, "Her back parts are in golden sheen." That is, the forbearance of the Christian dove (which is what is meant by the "back parts") is completely and exceedingly radiant with the golden glow of love. Otherwise why did Moses not also abandon his stiff-necked people? Why did Elijah and the prophets not abandon the idolatrous kings of Israel?

As a result, the separation of the Bohemians from the Roman Church can by no kind of excuse be defended from having been an impious thing and contrary to all the laws of Christ, because it stands in opposition to love, in which all laws are summed up.[20] For this solitary allegation of theirs, that they defected because of fear of God and conscience, in order not to live among wicked priests and bishops — this is the greatest indictment of all against them. For if the bishops or priests or any persons at all are wicked, and if you were aglow with real love, you would not flee. No, even if you were at the ends of the ocean, you would come running to them and weep, warn, reprove, and do absolutely everything. And if you followed this teaching of the apostle, you would know that it is not benefits but burdens that you have to bear. Therefore it is clear that the whole glory of this Bohemian love is mere sham and the light into which an angel of Satan transforms himself (2 Cor. 11:14).

We, who are bearing the burdens and the truly intolerable abominations of the Roman Curia — are we, too, fleeing and seceding on this account? Perish the thought! Perish the thought! To be sure, we censure, we denounce, we plead, we warn; but we do not on this account split the unity of the spirit, nor do we become puffed up against it, since we know that love rises high above all things, not only above injuries suffered in bodily things but also above all the

---

[20] At the Leipzig Debate in July 1519, Luther's endorsement of certain teachings of John Hus brought upon him the charge of Hussite heresy and also brought him into contact with Hussite leaders.

abominations of sins. A love that is able to bear nothing but the benefits done by another is fictitious. Surely, just as our common people — as we see — are at the bottom in rank, so they are at the top in love; for with the utmost patience they allow themselves to be skinned and flayed to the bones by their pastors. On the other hand, those who are puffed up because of their very high rank are absolutely unable to bear the loss of even a penny, let alone endure a word or deed directed against their privileges. And Thou, O Lord, art righteous, and Thy judgment is right (Ps. 119:137). Thus the last will be first, and the first last (Matt. 20:16).

3. *For if anyone thinks he is something, when he is nothing, he deceives himself.*

Paul gives a very beautiful and a very strong reason for both doctrines. This is the reason: We are all equal, and we are all nothing. Why, then, does one man puff himself up against the other, and why do we not rather help one another? Furthermore, if there is anything in us, it is not our own; it is a gift of God. But if it is a gift of God, then it is entirely a debt one owes to love, that is, to the law of Christ. And if it is a debt owed to love, then I must serve others with it, not myself. Thus my learning is not my own; it belongs to the unlearned and is the debt I owe to them. My chastity is not my own; it belongs to those who commit sins of the flesh, and I am obligated to serve them through it by offering it to God for them, by sustaining and excusing them, and thus, with my respectability, veiling their shame before God and men, as Paul writes in 1 Cor. 12:23 that those parts of the body that are less honorable are covered by those that are more honorable. Thus my wisdom belongs to the foolish, my power to the oppressed. Thus my wealth belongs to the poor, my righteousness to the sinners. For these are the forms of God of which we must empty ourselves, in order that forms of a servant may be in us (Phil. 2:6), because it is with all these qualities that we must stand before God and intervene on behalf of those who do not have them, as though clothed with someone else's garment, not unlike the priest, when, on behalf of those standing about, he sacrifices in a ritual garb that does not belong to him. But even before men we must, with the same love, render them service against their detractors and those who are violent toward them; for this is what Christ did for us. This is that furnace of the Lord in Zion (Is. 31:9), that tender compassion of the Father, who wants to tie us together with such inestimable virtue. By this badge, by this symbol, by this mark, we Christians are distinguished from all nations, in order that we may be God's private property, a priestly race, and a royal priesthood.

St. Jerome explains this passage in two ways: (1) "who thinks he is something, when he is nothing," that is, since before God we all are nothing, as has been said; (2) "he who thinks he is something and nevertheless is nothing deceives himself"; that is, if anyone feels that he is something and in fact is superior to another, and pleases himself in this, thinking highly only of himself, considering only his own advantage and not how he may serve others thereby — he is in fact deceiving himself, because by this very feeling of haughtiness of his he causes himself to be nothing, since then the gift of God is without effect in him, and he himself is like the one who does not have it, just as a miser does not have something even when he has it, because he does not have it in the use for which riches exist to be had. Therefore just as this rich man is not rich but is poor, so that man who thinks he is something is nothing. This is the understanding that St. Jerome follows.[21] And with this understanding there is offered in a different way a reason for the teachings stated earlier, namely, that if one does not bear another's burdens but is puffed up with his own understanding, then he becomes nothing, and it is the same as if he had nothing. Indeed, he has it to his own loss. I like both explanations. Jerome, however, makes an additional comment and notes the proper meaning of the verb "deceives," which in Greek means "deceives the mind,"[22] because he is not the person he thinks he is.

4. *But let each one test his own work, and then his reason to boast will be in himself alone and not in his neighbor.*

It is the nature of vainglory to compare itself with those who are unlike itself, and from this comparison there follow contempt for one who is inferior and the sort of bladder that is inflated with one's own good qualities. For vainglory does not rejoice so much in the fact that it is or has something as in the fact that others are nothing or have nothing. Thus the well-known Pharisee did not glory so much in his own holiness as in the fact that everybody else seemed unlike himself, especially the tax collector. For he would not want the others to become better than or equal to himself. Consequently, his glory

---

[21] Jerome, *Commentarius*, 456—457.

[22] For the obvious typographical error *mentum* we have read *mentem*.

is glory in another and outside himself, namely, in one who is worse and inferior. This is malevolence, always the companion of vainglory; it is rejoicing over the badness of others and being sad over the goodness of others. This the apostle forbids, in order that no one may have this glory in another — glory that is utterly distant from love and should be distant.

"But let him test his own work"; that is, let him disregard another person's work and not look to see how bad the other person is but how good he himself is. Let him strive to be found approved in good works himself. But let him not take someone else's work as a reason for becoming smug and starting to snore, as if he had to be considered good in the sight of God because he is better than that wicked person, with the result that in this way he is more presumptuous because of the other person's wickedness than he is on the basis of his own work, apart from the wickedness of the other person. Your works do not become better because of that person's wickedness. Therefore live and act in such a way as to test your own work, to what extent you are able to glory in yourself and in your own conscience, as Paul says in 2 Cor. 1:12: "For our boast is this, the testimony of our conscience" — certainly not the appearance of someone else's work. But a person tests his work if he looks to see how diligent he is in love to bear the weaknesses of others. And certainly if a man were to observe this practice, he would easily refrain from rash judgments and disparaging remarks, since he would find out that he either loves or does not love his neighbor.

5. *For each man will have to bear his own load.*

This pertains to the preceding in the following way: "Why do you glory in another person? Why do you puff yourself up because of someone else's sin or weakness? Are you the one who will render account for him?" Or, as Paul says in Rom. 14:4 with the same thought in mind: "Who are you to pass judgment on the servant of another? It is before his own master that he stands or falls." And he goes on (v. 12): "So each of us shall give account of himself," which, by a Scriptural figure of speech, he here calls "bearing his own load," and earlier "bearing his judgment" (Gal. 5:10). For this reason I would also understand the statement "But let each one test his own work" somewhat differently, in keeping with the same thought Paul expresses in Rom. 14:22: "The faith that you have, keep between yourself and God." That is, the fact that you know that all things are permissible is your own work. But glory in this and in yourself before God, and do not use this liberty openly so as to glory in this faith of yours on the basis of your neighbor's weakness, caring nothing about the offense given to him. This general meaning, however, will not hold for all cases of offense; it will hold only for those cases that occur in connection with a law of men, such as the confessionals and other opportunities sold for cash to some but held back from others, with the result that there is offense.

6. *Let him who is taught in the Word share all good things with him who teaches.*

The apostle prescribes another and final ethical teaching. This is that they should supply the bodily things and necessities of life to the elders who teach the Word of God and sow spiritual things. "For the laborer deserves his wages," says Christ (Luke 10:7), as Paul pursues this thought at greater length in 1 Tim. 5:18 and 1 Cor. 9:9.

But one wonders why it pleased the translator to mix in words that are entirely Greek. Κατηχίζω means "I teach" and "I instruct." [23] Hence "catechumens" are those who are instructed in the religion of Christ.

Here Paul treats the philosophy of the Stoics with contempt, since he calls the things that are necessary for the body "good things," whereas the Stoics, distorters and violent manhandlers of words that they are, count among the "good things" nothing but wisdom and virtue (that is, pride based on vainglory).[24] We know that everything God made was very good and that every creature of God is good (Gen. 1:31). But evil use makes them evil. They are not evil by their own fault. An evil use makes wisdom and virtue (the "good things" of the Stoics) the worst of all evil things, since they do nothing but puff up if love is lacking (1 Cor. 8:1).

Note the weight of the words. It is to the "instructor in the Word" that a sharing in all good things is owed. But to those who do not preach or teach the Word this doctrine does not apply at all. Certainly the first and greatest work in the church is the preaching of the Word, which is what the Lord laid upon Peter three times (John

[23] The Latin translation had used *catechizatur* instead of a native Latin word like *docetur* or **instruitur**.

[24] Cf. also *Luther's Works*, 2, pp. 323—331, on physical goods as gifts from God.

21:15 ff.) and what He most persistently demands of everyone. But now nothing is farther to the rear or more despised than this. There are so many duties for jurists, for judges, for officials, so many chants and ceremonies for priests and monks; but the voice of one shouting in the wilderness is rare (Is. 40:3) — so rare that there is almost nothing more unlike the church than the church itself.

It is not superfluous that Paul adds "in the Word" or, as the Greek has it in the accusative, "the Word." There are, have been, and will be many who out of their own head tell many fables or opinions and traditions of men, as we see today to our sorrow. But the "Word" itself, which surely means the Gospel of Christ — where, I ask, does it resound? Or if, contaminated by the glosses of men, it does resound, it says: "My throat has become hoarse" (cf. Ps. 69:3), so that even when it does resound in this way, it cannot be heard. Therefore such men, too, should not expect that the sharing of all good things applies to them.

Then note that Paul says: "Let him share." For nowadays they are not content with having a share, even though they do not teach the Word; but they demand every kind of authority and the possession of all things. And now the one who is instructed is almost begging from his instructor. For the church has grown to the point that it has begun to transfer empires and to confer worldly dominions. "What indeed has this to do with the Word? Let us leave this to the brothers." This is also what my friend Sylvester says, namely, that the pope is a twofold emperor of the whole world and lord over all things.[25] Nor is this surprising, because, of course, when the apostle Paul, being ignorant of grammar, wanted to say: "Let everybody give all his goods to the Roman pontiff and make him emperor," what came into his mouth was a very stingy expression, so that he said: "But let him who is taught share in all good things with his instructor in the Word." But I believe that if he had known that someday "having a share" would have to be understood as "having dominion," that "instruction in the Word" would have to be understood as "power to dominate," and that "he who is instructed" would have to be understood as "the whole world," he would without a doubt have been silent about this doctrine.

"Are you biting again?"[26] I am not biting; but because it is nec-

[25] Cf. *Luther's Works*, 31, p. 255.
[26] A reference to the words of Prierias, calling Luther a dog.

essary to explain the Scriptures, I am pointing out the practices of our age, in order that we may see what the glory of the church has come to and which is the true church or the false church. And, to speak freely, it is impossible for the Scriptures to be explained and for other churches to be reformed unless that "real universal," the Roman Curia, is reformed as soon as possible.[27] For the Roman Curia is unable to hear and uphold the Word of God so that it is taught purely. But if God's Word is not taught, no aid can be brought to the rest of the churches.

"All good things," says Paul. What the apostle means is a big question, for here he seems to be talking like Sylvester, since he prescribes a sharing in all good things, except (as I have said) that he assigns this only to those who preach the Word. Since there are and have been an infinite number of these, and since everyone owes all things to everyone, many worlds would have to be discovered to enable any given person to get possession of all good things. But enough of this. What Paul calls "all good things" are the things a teacher has need of, that is, temporal goods, by which he stays alive, since, being busy with the Word, he cannot gain them by his own work but receives all things from him whom he instructs. At the same time this word spoken by Paul hinders a teacher from accepting "good things," to the vexation of believers, from others than those whom he is teaching. Nor should the one who is instructed allow this very thing to be necessary for the instructor; but, says Paul, "let him share with the latter in all good things" and contribute from his own goods whatever the instructor needs. If this rule is to be observed, then there will not be one donation to the pope; another to the bishops, who are in the middle; and another to the common priests — all from one and the same people. Then begging will be different from what is prescribed here. But now the times are different; for these commandments were given when the shepherds of the church were not supplied with income and resources. And perhaps this teaching of the Spirit was better than the custom that reigns now. For now we are seeing what is written in Prov. 28:2: "When a land transgresses, it has many rulers." And today this multitude is called the hierarchy and the classification of the church according to lower and higher ranks.

[27] Cf. p. 390, note 18.

7. *Do not be deceived; God is not mocked.*

Paul is mentioning greed, which is always crafty in giving excuses whenever some contribution is to be made. The apostle does not expressly say what these excuses are. Indeed, he could not name them all. St. Jerome mentions many.[28] In the Old Testament, too, it was the same concern which cautioned that the Levites, who had nothing except what they received from the people, should by no means be forgotten.

In addition, there is the fact that the preacher of the Word inevitably offends many people and is exposed to hatred. Consequently, this precept of Paul's is necessary to the highest degree on account of those who are greedy and are filled with hatred, but also on account of those who are careless. For there are also people who do not contribute because they assume that this is being done in abundance by others. Paul, however, anticipates these pitiful evasions in an excellent way and tells them not to be deceived, that God is not mocked, even though they may be able to deceive and delude their fellowman.

For whatever a man sows, that he will also reap.

Paul applies a general maxim to a specific case. This maxim — it is well known to him — he also makes use of in 2 Cor. 9:6; for it is a proverbial saying and is beautifully allegorical. He who refuses to share his good things with his teacher is sowing the work of greed. Hence he will also reap the reward of greed. So it is in all other works, good and evil; for with this general axiom Paul concludes all his injunctions pertaining to morals; with it he concludes the epistle itself.

8. *For he who sows to his own flesh will from the flesh reap corruption; but he who sows to the spirit will from the spirit reap eternal life.*

Here again flesh must not be understood as referring to lust alone; but, in keeping with the apostle's way of speaking, it must, as the text itself compels, be understood as referring to all that is not spirit, that is, to the whole man. For a false understanding of the words gave the heretic Tatian his reason for condemning sexual intercourse of man and woman on the basis of this passage. But St. Jerome learnedly

---

[28] Jerome, *Commentarius*, 458—459.

refutes him.²⁹ Accordingly, flesh and spirit are presented by the apostle in an allegorical way as two fields. The two seeds are two works. One of these is the seed of love, which Paul has described sufficiently above (Gal. 5:22) in the nine fruits; the other is the seed of the flesh, which we have seen (Gal. 5:19-21) in the works of the flesh. The two harvests are corruption and eternal life. Erasmus understands corruption to be the fruit that is corruptible and destined to perish.³⁰ After it has been corrupted, it is the same as no fruit at all.

"To his own flesh" — not "to his spirit" — seems to have been added purposely by the apostle to exclude the thought of the man's insemination in the flesh of the woman, lest he be thought to be speaking of this — although it is true that this also is a corruptible fruit, since a mortal human being is born from the seed of the male. From this, however, it does not follow that sexual intercourse is evil. But what, pray, is there that is sowed and reaped in the entire earth that is not corruptible? Consequently, the apostle's allegory must be understood explicitly by taking "sowing" to mean nothing else than "doing works," as is expressly clear from what follows.

9. *And let us not grow weary in well-doing, for in due season we shall reap, if we do not lose heart.*

Paul himself clarifies the allegory he uses. He does not say: ["And let us not grow weary] sowing to the spirit." No, he says: ["And let us not grow weary] in well-doing." Yet he adds the words "in due season we shall reap." He retains the other part of his allegory. So careful did he have to be to avoid seeming to give heretics an opportunity to spread false statements about marriage. "Sowing to the spirit," therefore, means doing good works; "sowing to the flesh" means doing evil works. This doctrine he now extends in length, and he exhorts to perseverance through the comfort of the recompense to come. For not he who begins but he who perseveres will be saved (Matt. 10:22). It is easy to begin with one work, but to finish and to persevere is hard and subject to many hindrances that press in opposition. This fact is of such a nature, says Jerome, that while sinners daily increase in evil works, we grow weary in a good work.³¹

---

²⁹ Cf. p. 127, note 27.
³⁰ Cf. Erasmus, *Paraphrasis, Opera,* VII, 966.
³¹ Jerome, *Commentarius,* 461.

10. *So then, as we have opportunity, let us do good to all men, and especially to those who are of the household of faith.*

Paul extends the doctrine in breadth, which is no less difficult than the length. "Let us do good to all men," to heathen, Jews, the thankful, the unthankful, friends, enemies, neighbors, strangers. In short, just as is said of love, no person is regarded. Behold, how great the breadth of Christian benevolence is! For it must be all-encompassing, as Christ also says in Matt. 5:46: "If you love those who love you, what reward have you? Do not even the tax collectors do this?" Nevertheless, Paul gives precedence to those who are of the household of faith, because we have been bound to them with a closer tie, inasmuch as they are from the same house, the church, and from the same household of Christ, and have one faith, one Baptism, one hope, one Lord, and everything the same. St. Jerome, however, thinks that the teachers themselves, on whose account Paul had begun this doctrine, are also meant here, in order to conclude the doctrine with reference to the same people, as if he wanted "those who are of the household of faith" to be understood as being the servants of Christ who teach faith in His house.[32]

Jerome also points out that the apostle uses the words "as we have opportunity," namely, that the present life is the time of sowing, as Christ also says (John 9:4): "Work while it is day; night comes, when no one can work." These statements seem to contend against purgatory. For though the doctors say that there is nothing in purgatory but satisfaction — or, with their newly discovered word, "completion of suffering" — still I fail to see how satisfaction or "completion of suffering" is not a good work.[33] Therefore I understand the apostle to be speaking about works of this life, and that his word says nothing about purgatory, as I have stated elsewhere.

11. *See with what kind of letters I have written to you by my own hand.*

St. Jerome understands "with what kind of letters" to mean with large letters (for the Greek word πηλίκος, taken this way, refers to size rather than to quality), since he holds that up to this point some-

---

[32] Jerome, *Commentarius*, 462.

[33] The usual Anselmic term for the work of Christ was *satisfactio;* but because the *satis* done by Christ was thought to be His suffering and death, the term *satispassio* (whence the English "satispassion") was developed.

one else wrote the epistle at Paul's dictation, presumably with smaller letters, and that from this passage to the end Paul finished it with larger letters, in order that they might clearly distinguish his handwriting and thus realize what great concern he had for them, and at the same time in order to remove the suspicion that false teachers were carrying false letters forged under his name.[34] For in other epistles too Paul usually adds the signature "Greetings from Paul, by my own hand" (cf. Col. 4:18; 1 Cor. 16:21; 2 Thess. 3:17).

But I follow Erasmus, who thinks that the whole epistle was written by the apostle with his own hand.[35] In this way Paul establishes his fervor. It is as if he were saying: "Ordinarily I never write with my own hand; but look what a big epistle I have written with my own hand for the sake of your salvation. True, I have written larger epistles, but by someone else's hand (cf. Rom. 16:22). Consequently, you, too, should regard the matter with earnestness as great as that with which I have written about it." O what an apostolic man, to have such great concern for souls!

12. *It is those who want to make a good showing in the flesh that would compel you to be circumcised, and only in order that they may not be persecuted for the cross of Christ.*

Paul is repeating briefly what he has written. For at the outset (1:10) he said: "If I were pleasing men, I would not be a servant of Christ. Or am I seeking to please men?" For to the Jews this preaching of Christian liberty was as displeasing as anything could be, since their circumcision, which they considered necessary for salvation, made them presumptuous. To ward off and soothe the fury of the Jews, the false apostles were teaching what was pleasing to these people, namely, that circumcision was necessary. It is certain, therefore, that these false apostles were from among the Christians, not from among the Jews, because they were in dread of being persecuted for the sake of the cross which they had professed. They loved their own life and peace more than they loved Christ.

"In the flesh" is said in contrast with the spirit, and the verb "to make a good showing" is taken in an absolute way, as it was earlier. Therefore the meaning is: "They wish to make a good showing in the flesh"; that is, they wish to make a good showing in a carnal, not in

---

[34] Jerome, *Commentarius*, 462—463.
[35] Cf. Erasmus, *Paraphrasis, Opera*, VII, 966.

a spiritual way, because by being pleasing in a carnal way, they please men, whereas by being pleasing in the spirit or in a spiritual way they please God.

Note also that "they would compel you to be circumcised." Circumcision per se did no harm; but to compel it and make it necessary, as though faith did not suffice for righteousness, was damnable. Thus Paul said above (2:14): "Why do you compel the Gentiles to live like Jews?"

You may ask whether the apostle is disparaging and rashly judging the false apostles on the grounds that they feared the persecution of the cross of Christ and sought their own glory in the flesh of the Galatians, as he says later (v. 13). Who told him that they were fearful and out for glory? For one cannot, without sinning, make conjectures about the faults of those who are absent, especially if they deny them. Perhaps they would have denied them and could not have been refuted. But the apostle, being instructed in the spirit, knows that a man who does not preach or understand Christ aright cannot be without fear of the cross and without vainglory. He who does not have the spirit of Christ inevitably loves his own life more than he loves Christ. Then it is just as inevitable that he is puffed up with pride over his knowledge. Thus he is bound to collapse under adversity and to become haughty in prosperity, since he is unable in either case to conduct himself as one who is upright and stable. Therefore we can, without risk, generalize and pronounce this verdict about one and all if we see that they do not know Christ, namely, that they are fearful in adversity and vainglorious in prosperity, downcast and elated alike at the wrong time. On the other hand, one who is really a Christian is uplifted in adversity, because he trusts in God; he is downcast in prosperity, because he fears God. He is not disheartened when he is suffering, nor does he become vainglorious when he is being honored. He is upright and stable everywhere.

13. *For even those who receive circumcision do not themselves keep the Law, but they desire to have you circumcised that they may glory in your flesh.*

Paul said the same thing above in chapter five (v. 3), namely, that he who has received circumcision is obligated to keep the whole Law; for even though they outwardly circumcise the flesh, they nevertheless do not fulfill either this law of circumcision or any other law, since they do everything out of fear of the Law that threatens them, not with cheerfulness of spirit. But it has been stated rather often that to fulfill the Law without a freely willing disposition is the same as not fulfilling it and, instead, is feigning the works of the Law. For what is not done willingly is, in God's sight and in truth, not done but, in the sight of men, appears to be done. Paul is again confidently asserting that all those are transgressors of the Law who receive circumcision and try to keep any law at all with their own powers. He is again refuting our theologians, who think that works done without the grace of the Spirit are morally good and fulfill the Law so far as the substance of the act is concerned, but that they are not sins or contrary to the Law.[36] But the verdict stands firm that willingness and the cheerfulness of spirit to fulfill the Law is acquired in no other way than by faith in Christ, and that all others are haters of the Law and for this reason are guilty of transgression.

"That they may glory in your flesh" — that is, glory in a carnal way with respect to you in the fact that they were your teachers, taught you good things, and are wise and religious. For it is impossible for a teacher in any profession whatever not to glory unless he is well established in Christ and knows in his heart that "it is not you who speak" (Matt. 10:20), and that you have "one Master, Christ" (Matt. 23:10). So tenacious is the lust for praise and glory, especially in spiritual things and gifts like knowledge and virtues.

14. *But far be it from me to glory except in the cross of our Lord Jesus Christ, by which the world has been crucified to me, and I to the world.*

The meaning is: Let those people glory in wisdom, in virtue, in righteousness, in works, in teaching, in the Law, or even in you and any human beings whatever. I glory in being foolish, sinful, weak, one who has suffered and has been found to be without the Law, without works, without the righteousness that comes from the Law; in short, without everything but Christ. It is my will and my joy that in the sight of the world I am foolish, evil, and guilty of all crimes, as Paul says in 2 Cor. 12:9: "I will gladly boast of my weaknesses, that the power of Christ may rest upon me." For the cross of Christ has condemned all things that the world approves, even its wisdom and righteousness, as Paul says in 1 Cor. 1:19: "I will destroy the wisdom of the wise, and the cleverness of the clever I will thwart."

---

[36] See also p. 76, note 59.

And in Matt. 5:11 Christ says: "Blessed are you when men shall curse you and bandy your name about as evil and revile you."

Behold this means not only being crucified with Christ and sharing His cross and sufferings with Him but also glorying in these things and joyfully accompanying the apostles, because we are considered worthy to suffer shame for His name (Acts 5:41). But those who strive for and obtain honors, riches, and pleasure for the name of Jesus and then shun contempt, poverty, and sufferings — are they glorying in the cross of Christ? Indeed not. They are glorying in the world while nevertheless professing the name of Christ in pretext and making a mockery of it.

Therefore "to be crucified to the world" means, as Paul said above, in chapter two (v. 20), that it is no longer he himself but Christ who lives in him, and that he has crucified the flesh together with its vices and subjected it to the spirit, which has no taste for the things that are on earth and of this world, not even its forms of righteousness and wisdom; but he glories that he lacks all these things and is not affected by them, since his assurance of salvation is based on Christ alone. That "the world is crucified to him" means that the world, not Christ, lives in men; that the world has the flesh flourishing with its vices and dominating in its sins; that with the apostle it has no taste for the things that are above but glories in having abundance in this life and in acquiring riches and putting its hope in man. Accordingly, Paul does not do, or have a taste for, the things that please the world; nor does the world do, or have a taste for, the things that please Paul. To the one the other is dead, crucified, despised, and detested.

15. *For neither circumcision counts for anything, nor uncircumcision, but a new creation.*

This was sufficiently explained in chapter five (v. 6), namely, that both are permissible, but that neither is necessary for salvation. Consequently, whether there is uncircumcision or circumcision has no relevance to the matter at all, no more than riches and scarcity.

"A new creation" — that is, the new man, who (Eph. 4:24) is "created after the likeness of God in true righteousness and holiness"; and according to Ps. 51:10: "Create in me a clean heart, O God." And note that true righteousness pertains to the spirit, true holiness to purity of the flesh, so that he who by faith is righteous in the spirit also lives purely in the flesh by chastity. For he says "true" in contrast with specious and simulated righteousness and holiness, which come from the Law and do not make a new man. It is after the likeness of man, not after the likeness of God, that everyone of this sort lives and is formed. Thus we read in James 1:18: "Of His own will He brought us forth by the Word of truth that we should be a kind of first fruits of His creatures."

16. *Peace and mercy be upon all who walk by this rule, upon the Israel of God.*

"Walk" (στοιχήσουσιν) is the same verb (στοιχῶμεν) that is used above (5:25). "Walk," that is, go, by this rule. By what rule? It is this rule, that they are new creatures in Christ, that they shine with the true righteousness and holiness which come from faith, and that they do not deceive themselves and others with the hypocritical righteousness and holiness which come from the Law. Upon the latter there will be wrath and tribulation, but upon the former will rest peace and mercy.

Paul adds the words "upon the Israel of God." He distinguishes this Israel from the Israel after the flesh, just as in 1 Cor. 10:18 he speaks of those who are the Israel of the flesh, not the Israel of God. Therefore peace is upon Gentiles and Jews, provided that they go by the rule of faith and the spirit.

17. *Henceforth let no man trouble me, for I bear on my body the marks of Jesus.*

In the Greek text we read: "Henceforth let no one cause me toil." St. Jerome understands this in two ways: (1) that Paul was concerned lest they again cause him toil by making it necessary for the Galatians to be reformed anew; (2) that he wanted to anticipate the quarrelsomeness of those who would want to contradict him.[37] It is as if he were saying: "What I have said is right and true; but if anyone more ready to quarrel than to be instructed is unwilling to agree to the truth and is looking for something to say in reply, let him know that he does not deserve an answer." Thus he writes to the Corinthians: "But if anyone seems to be quarrelsome, we have no such custom; nor does the church of God" (cf. 1 Cor. 11:16). I like this latter sense because St. Augustine also teaches that those who are quarrelsome should be abandoned; and he himself, in his books *The City of God*, makes the announcement that he is unwilling to give any further an-

---

[37] Jerome, *Commentarius*, 466.

swer to totally meaningless loquacity.³⁸ Thus the apostle, too, casts aside those who are eager for a quarrel, lest he toil in vain with them; for they yield no fruit but only cause toil. What if this meaning, too, were not unsuitable: "Let no one revive the Law for me again. This causes foolish exertions that consist in works yet are nothing but sins," as Ps. 10:7 says, "Under his tongue are toil and grief" (Vulgate)? Such people Christ calls to Himself when He says: "Come to Me, all who labor" (Matt. 11:28). These toils the Children of Israel prefigured in Egypt. But I move on.

Although "marks" — in Latin this word means signs that are stamped on — may be taken here as referring to the sufferings of Paul, nevertheless — because Paul likes to make use of military allegories and metaphors — he certainly understands them in the sense of the distinctive tokens of the Christian life, which are the crucifixion and subjection of the flesh. In addition, they are the fruits of the spirit. For just as slaves bear the distinctive tokens, the arms, and the colors of their masters, so Paul and every Christian carries in his own body the cross of his lusts and vices — not indeed in the way in which it is customary nowadays to picture on a wall or in paintings and books the distinctive tokens of Christ assembled on a shield. No, every Christian carries this cross in the body — and in my own body, not in someone else's. What good will it do if you carry even in gold and precious stone, not only the distinctive tokens but also the very nails, yes, the very wounds and blood of Christ, and never express the living image in your body? Moreover, circumcision and the works required by human laws are the marks of Moses and of popes and of Caesars. These alone are looked at now, and they are of such infinite variety that the emperor, together with all his nobles, hardly has so many kinds of distinctive marks.

18. *The grace of our Lord Jesus Christ be with your spirit, brethren. Amen.*

For among the apostles this is the way of concluding an epistle, where men say farewell.

"The grace of our Lord," says Paul — not the wrath of the Law, not the servitude of the Law, which was given through the servant Moses, but grace and truth, which came through Jesus Christ (John 1:17).

---

³⁸ Augustine, *City of God*, II, 1.

In conclusion, I am certain that those for whom it is death to get an understanding of my views will also vehemently abominate this spittle of mine, because I have treated everything too freely and have discussed this epistle far differently from the way they themselves understand it. And where I have complained about the burdens and offenses of the papal laws, they will picture me to themselves as a rebel against the church. Where I have preferred the Gospel to the decrees, they will invent the story that I have condemned the decrees. Where I have subordinated the power and prestige of the supreme pontiff to fraternal love and need, they will shout that I am a blasphemer and twice seven times a heretic. I ask these people, by Jesus Christ our common Lord, that if they are altogether unable to refrain from calling me proud, rash, arrogant, irreverent, offensive, seditious, bloody, schismatic, and by whatever name they have been pleased to honor me with up to this time — well, let it happen; and if I do not with complete goodwill forgive them all this, then may the Lord Jesus never forgive me. Indeed, if the purity of the doctrine taught by me could be outside the pale of danger, I would gladly and thankfully bear the reproach of being called a heretic. In short, cursed be the name of Martin, cursed forever be the glory of Martin, in order that only the name of our Father who is in heaven may be hallowed (Matt. 6:9). Amen.

For as a rebel who is exceedingly proud I fear that I may become puffed up over these utterly evil names and rejoice more at my own gain than grieve at the wickedness of those people. Let them at least grant me — indeed, let them grant themselves — this one thing, that little by little they set aside the utterly odious mask of Martin and look freely and solely at the apostle Paul. And then let them compare him with the appearance presented by the church, which today is most wretched. For I do not think that in their hearts they are so stupid as not to realize what the multitude of laws has done today. For how many souls are strangled and perish every day on account of this one tradition which forbids wives to all priests without any distinction! It is horrible to contemplate the offenses as well as the perils caused by this one law. Similar to this are the many others, which are simply the handmaids of sin, death, and hell, to say nothing meanwhile of the loss of sincere godliness, which has gradually died away under the tyranny of these laws. If it is considered a matter deserving of such tears that the blood of so many thousands is shed because of the will of one emperor, what do you think of this (open your eyes!), that because of the will of one man or one Roman Church so many thousands of souls are lost forever? In short, if we weigh the meaning of love, it will be easy to understand that such boldness in establishing laws is a power, not for the building but for the destruction of the whole church. The fewer the laws by which a commonwealth is administered, the more fortunate it is. But as for our ecclesiastical commonwealth, when one law of love has been established in order that this might be the most fortunate commonwealth of all, because of what great wrath of Almighty God does it endure, in place of that one extinct law, clouds, forests, and oceans of laws, so that you would scarcely be able to learn even their titles! Finally, as if this were not enough, they are at pains even now to come to our aid with no other remedy for sin than the multiplication of new laws, the heaping of sins upon sins, and, as the prophet says (Hab. 2:6), loading themselves with thick mud.

Somebody else may have abundant opinions of his own, but I consider these laws of men to be the most harmful Turks of all. And no other people than that of God's own possession had to be smitten with this plague of God's unbearable wrath, because its ingratitude, being the worst in comparison with all the peoples of the earth, also deserved by far the severest punishment in comparison with all the peoples of the earth. For there is no nation in all the world whose wretchedness could be compared with ours so far as this plague is concerned. O God, how long wilt Thou in Thy wrath hold back Thy mercies?

But I shall conclude with Isaiah, as he groans and laments: "So Thou didst lead Thy people, to make for Thyself a glorious name. Look down from heaven and see, from Thy holy and glorious habitation. Where are Thy zeal and Thy might? The yearning of Thy heart and Thy compassion are withheld from me. For Thou art our Father, though Abraham does not know us and Israel does not acknowledge us; Thou, O Lord, art our Father, our Redeemer from of old is Thy name. O Lord, why dost Thou make us err from Thy ways and harden our heart, so that we fear Thee not? Return for the sake of Thy servants, the tribes of Thy heritage. Thy holy people possessed Thy sanctuary a little while; our adversaries have trodden it down. We have become like those over whom Thou hast never ruled, like those who are not called by Thy name. O that Thou wouldst rend the heavens and come down, that the mountains might quake at Thy presence — as when fire kindles brushwood and the fire causes water to boil — to make Thy name known to Thy adversaries, and that the nations might tremble at Thy presence! When Thou didst terrible things which we looked not for, Thou camest down, the mountains quaked at Thy presence. From of old no one has heard or perceived by the ear, no eye has seen a God besides Thee, who works for those who wait for Him. Thou meetest him that joyfully works righteousness, those that remember Thee in Thy ways. Behold, Thou wast angry, and we sinned; in our sins we have been a long time, and shall we be saved? We have all become like one who is unclean, and all our righteous deeds are like a polluted garment. We all fade like a leaf, and our iniquities, like the wind, take us away. There is no one that calls upon Thy name, that bestirs himself to take hold of Thee; for Thou hast hid Thy face from us, and hast delivered us into the hand of our iniquities. Yet, O Lord, Thou art our Father; we are the clay, and Thou art our Potter; we are all the work of Thy hand. Be not exceedingly angry, O Lord, and remember not iniquity forever. Behold, consider, we are all Thy people. Thy holy cities have become a wilderness, Zion has become a wilderness, Jerusalem a desolation. Our holy and beautiful house, where our fathers praised Thee, has been burned by fire, and all our pleasant places have become ruins. Wilt Thou restrain Thyself at these things, O Lord? Wilt Thou keep silent, and afflict us sorely?" This is written in Is. 63:14-19 and 64:1-12. In this prayer Isaiah has depicted the appearance of the church today in such a way that it cannot be depicted more aptly. Would that God would pour into our hearts the spirit of this prayer, so that we might assuage His anger as soon as possible!

THE END

INDEXES

Index

By WALTER A. HANSEN

Abel 146, 147, 211
Abesse 80 fn.
Abiathar 135
Ablative 175
Ablutions 90
Abraham 35, 142, 222,
  247, 258, 260, 262,
  264, 265, 266, 267,
  268, 274, 278, 279,
  280, 282, 283, 284,
  287, 289, 291, 310,
  311, 322, 323, 324,
  330, 334, 409
  children of 251, 252,
    253, 254, 255, 263
  faith of 252, 253, 254
  flesh of 253, 254
  Seed of 18
Abscondita 84 fn.
Absolution 216
Abstinence 92
Accusative 179, 212, 397
Achilles 103
Activity 25
Actors 220
Acts 163, 179, 210, 250,
  323, 343
Acu tangere 125 fn.
Ad dialogum Silvestri
  Prieriatis de potestate papae responsio,
  by Luther 156 fn.
Adam 181, 250, 260,
  262, 288, 289, 368
  old 84
Adiaphora 161, 202
Adoption 289
Adultery 88, 188, 219,
  260, 348, 357, 368
Adversity 68, 403

Adversus haereses, by
  Irenaeus 127 fn.,
  208 fn., 364 fn.
Adversus Marcionem, by
  Tertullian 201 fn.
Advocate 388
Aeneid, by Vergil 24 fn.,
  61 fn.
Affliction(s) 12, 23, 24,
  33, 35, 133, 134,
  143, 231
Africa 60
Against Helvidius, by
  St. Jerome 196
Against Jovinian, by
  St. Jerome 82 fn.
Against Julian, by St. Augustine 361, 362 fn.
Against Latomus, by Luther 252 fn.
Against the Heavenly
  Prophets, by Luther
  105 fn.
Against the Pagans, by
  Arnobius 43 fn.
Air 149, 284
All Saints at Wittenberg
  153
Allegory 37, 127, 226,
  310, 311, 312, 315,
  316, 322, 324, 340,
  400, 407
Alms 350
Altar(s) 126, 286, 352,
  364, 385
Alveld 280 fn.
Amana, Mt. 315
Ambition 80, 132
Ambrose, St. 83, 179,
  214, 218, 245, 271,
  368, 369, 373, 376

Amicabilitas 376
Amicability 376
Ammon 321
Ammonites 321
Amon 317
Amor 353 fn.
Amorites 315
Anabaptists 34, 53, 60,
  62, 88, 147, 148,
  149
Anacletus 218 fn.
Anacoluthon 316, 318
Anagoge 312
Analogy 263, 264, 265,
  283
Anathema 177, 178, 179,
  183, 345
ἀνάθεμα 177, 178
Angel(s) 5, 35, 38, 40,
  45, 102, 108, 129,
  143, 146, 171, 178,
  180, 226, 271, 272,
  297, 300, 301, 302,
  303, 310, 311, 314,
  376, 391
  evil 227
  of Satan 392
  religion of 239
Anger 368, 369, 371,
  377, 410
Annates 237, 385
Annius of Viterbo 267 fn.
Anniversaries 352
Annotationes in Job 31,
  by St. Augustine
  175 fn.
Annotationes to the
  Greek New Testament, by Erasmus
  159 fn., 175 fn.,
  179 fn., 201,

209 fn., 212 fn., 309 fn., 326 fn.
ἀνοχή 376
Anselm 172 fn., 288 fn.
Antichrist 89, 110, 129, 342
Aorist 176
Ape 161
Apocalypse 227, 376
Apocope 263 fn.
Aposiopesis 346
Apostles' Creed 201 fn.
Apostleship 164, 168, 180, 205
Apostolici regiminis, bull 297 fn.
Aquinas, Thomas 52 fn., 113 fn., 234 fn., 267 fn.
Arabia 193, 314, 315, 316, 317, 382
   Felix 317
   Petraea 314, 317
Arabian Desert 314, 317
Arabic 315
Arabs 315
Archbishops 385 fn.
Archdeacon 153
Arcturus 245
Aristotle 23 fn., 24 fn., 29 fn., 219, 328, 364, 367 fn.
   categories of 181 fn.
   ethics of 225
Arius 62
Arnobius 43 fn.
Arsenius 14
Asceticism 88
ἀσέλγεια 369
Asia 117
Assyrians 164, 330
Astrologers 295
Athanasius 333
Attalus 280
Augsburg 154, 157
Augustine, St. x, 22 fn., 83, 84 fn., 97, 101, 112, 156, 169, 172 fn., 173, 174, 176, 179, 188, 205, 211, 212, 219, 226, 227 fn., 228, 234, 236 fn., 238, 245,

248, 256, 261, 271, 274, 275 fn., 277, 281, 285 fn., 288, 290 fn., 294, 295, 299, 310, 312, 314, 319, 321, 332, 334, 337, 361, 362, 368, 372, 373, 378, 379, 381, 388, 390, 406, 407 fn.
Augustinian 153, 281
Aulus Persius Flaccus 326 fn.
Authority 4, 9, 15, 46, 61, 64, 99, 100, 101, 129, 141, 156, 157, 164, 166, 168, 171, 178, 191, 192, 196, 197, 207, 212, 261, 272, 283, 284, 297, 304, 324, 327, 337, 342, 369, 397
Aristotle's 364
Autodidact 20
Avarice 80
Axe 29

Baal 154, 176
Babylon 169, 281
Bacchus 371
Baptism 85, 93, 148, 193, 362, 401
Barlaam and Joasaph, by John of Damascus 136 fn.
Barnabas 165, 190, 195, 200, 202, 208, 213, 214
Basilica, St. Peter's 386 fn.
Bastards 254
Bear 58
Behemoth 375
Believer(s) 8, 9, 23, 30, 32, 47, 76, 83, 89, 96, 117, 118, 119, 120, 121, 124, 129, 136, 142, 148, 162, 167, 184, 202, 241, 245, 254, 255, 280, 290, 310, 398
Belly 69, 131, 132, 296, 369, 371

Benedict, St. 83, 84
Benedictine 281
Benefice, ecclesiastical 385 fn.
Benevolence 376
Benignitas 376
Benjamin 155, 187
Bernard, St. 43, 83, 84, 85, 89, 300, 387
Bethaven 220
Bethel 262, 344
Bible x, 206; *see also* Divine Scripture(s), Holy Scripture, Holy Writ, Sacred Scripture, Scripture(s), Word of God
"Bigmouth" 59
Bishop(s) 44, 96, 97, 110, 121, 122, 129, 130, 166, 281, 296, 297, 303, 346, 358, 369, 384, 385, 392, 398
   of Cyprus 216
   of Jerusalem 216
Bishopric 166, 385
Black Cloister 122 fn.
Bladder(s), inflated 385, 394
Blasphemy 22, 69, 71, 81, 89, 102, 112, 136, 141, 158, 230, 240, 371
Blocks 81
Bloodsuckers 352
Boas, Marcus 125 fn.
Bodenstein, Andreas 153
Bohemians 392
Bon christian 384
Bondage of the Will, by Luther 36 fn.
Boniface VIII 342
Book of Acts 143
Bread 58, 69, 298, 340
   holy 55
Breeze 367
Brevia, apostolic 157
Brevia apostolica 157 fn.
Breviarium de temporibus, by Pseudo-Philo 367 fn.
Bride 93, 184, 315, 391

Bridegroom 93
Briefe, by Luther 130 fn., 177 fn.
βρωτόν 377
Bull(s), papal 237, 297, 342 fn.
Burgensis 345
Butter 384
Cabala 221
Caesar(s) 281, 385, 407
Caesarea 197
Cain 146, 147, 262
Cajetan, Cardinal 154 fn., 156, 157, 158
Calling 74, 119, 120, 140
Canaan 254, 314
Canons 153
  sacred 250
Capitalis 71 fn.
Cardialgia 244 fn.
Cardinals 122, 157, 385 fn.
Carlstadt 118 fn., 129 fn., 153
Carnality 249, 354, 391
Carousing 91, 368, 370, 371
Carpenter 29
Carthusian(s) 88, 91, 281
Catachresis 43
Catechizatur 396 fn.
Catechumens 396
Caterpillars 352
Cattle 90, 227, 245, 357
Cedar 317
Celibacy 44, 138
Cenchreae 211, 343
Cephas 214, 217
Cephe 218
Ceremonies 9, 15, 25, 31, 53, 54, 55, 59, 62, 90, 131, 138, 139, 161, 204, 219, 235, 276, 287, 294, 295, 298, 299, 355, 357, 383, 397
Ceres 371
Chaldeans 295
Chants 397
Charitas 353 fn.
Charity 46

Charms 244
Chastity 18, 68, 84, 89, 95, 329, 346, 362, 364, 373, 378, 393, 405
Cherubim 22, 231
Children of Israel 135, 267, 314, 407
χρηστολογίαι 376
χρηστότης 94, 376
Christ
  Agent of righteousness 226
  body of 103
  death of 10, 19, 26, 49, 50, 76, 82, 83, 264, 265, 401 fn.
  freedom in 10
  Head and Bridegroom of church 43
  household of 401
  insignia of 143
  invocation of 92
  is our righteousness and life 144
  kingdom of 30, 86, 94, 114
  knowledge of 17, 49, 147
  mask of 17
  religion of 396
  resurrection of 19, 82
  righteousness of 51, 251, 317
  suffering of 82, 134, 238, 401 fn.
  victory of 10, 82, 83 et passim
Christian(s) 30, 31, 32, 35, 39, 43, 44, 45, 47, 49, 50, 51, 52, 59, 61, 66, 68, 74, 81, 82, 84, 87, 91, 93, 96, 103, 113, 114, 133, 136, 147, 153, 158, 179, 182, 197, 204, 215, 216, 222, 225, 226, 227, 241, 242, 248, 250, 280, 281, 283, 289, 297, 308, 328, 332, 334, 335, 340, 357, 394, 402, 403, 407

false 92
freedom of 154
strive to avoid works of the flesh 85
Christianity 31, 186, 354
  pagan critics of 43 fn.
Christological controversies 206 fn.
Chronology, by Luther 267 fn.
Chrysostom 377
Church(es) 31, 36, 37, 42, 44, 46, 53, 56, 59, 70, 71, 81, 83, 84, 85, 89, 91, 97, 98, 99, 100, 103, 104, 106, 107, 108, 109, 110, 112, 113, 121, 122, 123, 124, 126, 127, 128, 133, 134, 139, 148, 159, 161, 164, 165, 166, 168, 169, 175, 183, 186, 187, 197, 198, 200, 206, 209, 210, 215, 216, 218, 219, 226, 227, 231, 236, 247, 248, 249, 276, 280, 281, 286, 297, 298, 304, 307, 311, 317, 318, 320, 321, 330, 338, 342, 346, 352, 354, 358, 364, 375, 382, 385, 387, 389, 392, 396, 397, 401, 406, 408, 410
  bellowing in 141
  catholic 69
  Christian 97
  false 398
  flourishes and grows under persecution 43
  heavenly 155
  of Gentiles 146
  of Rome 122 fn., 178
  papal 91
  primacy of, in Jerusalem 208 fn.
  Roman 153, 154, 155, 156, 157, 158, 159, 297, 392, 409
  true 398
  two titles for 156 fn.

Church fathers x
Cilicia 197
Cinctures 141
Circumcision 9, 10, 11, 12, 15, 16, 20, 25, 30, 42, 45, 52, 59, 62, 130, 131, 137, 138, 139, 141, 143, 200, 203, 209, 210, 251, 252, 256, 257, 280, 298, 309, 327, 329, 330, 331, 333, 334, 335, 343, 344, 346, 357, 402, 403, 404, 405, 407
City of God, by St. Augustine 101 fn., 172 fn., 219, 227 fn., 406, 407 fn.
Classics x
Claudianists 60 fn.
Claudius 210
Clement 217 fn.
Cleophas 195
Clergy 4, 68, 69, 121, 122, 204, 215
Cleric 204
Clothing 55, 62, 83, 122, 140, 257, 335, 383
"Cockeyed" 59
Colloquialism 244
Comedere 371 fn.
Comessatio 371
Comfort 3, 19, 21, 22, 25, 26, 27, 32, 33, 71, 73, 74, 75, 76, 78, 81, 84, 109, 111, 115, 126, 400
Comforter 11, 12, 34, 388 fn.
Commentaria in XII epistolas beati Pauli, ascribed to St. Ambrose 179 fn., 214 fn., 245 fn., 368 fn., 376 fn.
Commentarius in Epistolam S. Pauli ad Galatas, by St. Jerome 55 fn., 96 fn., 130 fn., 163 fn.,

166 fn., 168 fn., 169 fn., 173 fn., 176 fn., 177 fn., 179 fn., 183 fn., 186 fn., 187 fn., 190 fn., 193 fn., 194 fn., 199 fn., 201 fn., 202 fn., 205 fn., 208 fn., 210 fn., 217 fn., 219 fn., 223 fn., 226 fn., 239 fn., 241 fn., 243 fn., 244 fn., 245 fn., 247 fn., 248 fn., 253 fn., 259 fn., 261 fn., 263 fn., 268 fn., 269 fn., 283 fn., 285 fn., 287 fn., 288 fn., 290 fn., 295 fn., 298 fn., 299 fn., 300 fn., 301 fn., 304 fn., 305 fn., 307 fn., 308 fn., 309 fn., 310 fn., 312 fn., 314 fn., 317 fn., 327 fn., 331 fn., 332 fn., 333 fn., 338 fn., 339 fn., 340 fn., 343 fn., 344 fn., 345 fn., 346 fn., 348 fn., 350 fn., 357 fn., 363 fn., 368 fn., 373 fn., 376 fn., 379 fn., 394 fn., 399 fn., 400 fn., 401 fn., 402 fn., 406 fn.
Commonwealth 113, 409
Comus 371
Conceit 383, 384
Concessions 3
Concupiscence 380
Condemnation 167, 227, 260, 359
Condignity 372
Conferre 207
Confession 13, 73, 107, 130, 146, 293
Confessionals 384, 396

Confessions, by St. Augustine 101 fn., 337 fn.
Congruity 28, 249
Conscience(s) 4, 7, 13, 14, 15, 21, 27, 40, 41, 47, 48, 49, 51, 54, 75, 96, 107, 110, 115, 116, 117, 118, 119, 120, 121, 130, 164, 191, 216, 221, 237, 287, 311, 318, 321, 327, 328, 329, 334, 340, 345, 372, 382, 383, 384, 388, 392, 395
  accusing 111
  agony of 5
  bad 126
  despairing 12
  distressed 11
  erring 87
  foolish 167
  freedom of 6
  good 126, 335, 375
  guilty 220
  sad 11
  scruples of 381
  serenity of 141
  troubled 171
  weak 385
  zeal of 169
Constantine 3 fn.
Constantinople 218
Contempt 102, 103, 203, 240, 360, 405
  for Law 201
Continence 9, 367, 368
Contra duas epistolas Pelagianorum, by St. Augustine 256 fn.
Contra Julianum haeresis Pelagianae defensorem, by St. Augustine 316 fn., 362 fn.
Contrition 8, 13, 222
Controversy 369, 375
Corinth 123, 124
Corinthian(s) 51, 108, 122, 124, 260, 301, 406

INDEX   417

Corpus Christianorum,
   Series Latina
   161 fn., 177 fn.,
   191 fn., 312 fn.,
   319 fn., 332 fn.
Corpus Scriptorum
   Ecclesiasticorum
   Latinorum 227 fn.,
   361 fn.
Corruption 127, 154, 173,
   276, 400
Council(s) 156, 158,
   297
Council of Trent 364 fn.
Courage 22
Cowl(s) 31, 87, 141
Crab 13
Creation, new 138, 139,
   140, 141
Creator 38, 88, 297
Creed 42, 84, 85
Cretans 243
Crotus Rubianus 130 fn.
Cur deus homo, by Anselm 288 fn.
Curia 147, 157, 158, 159,
   179, 375, 384, 385,
   386, 392, 398
Curse(s) 12, 35, 38, 46,
   63, 232, 256, 259,
   260, 261, 262, 275,
   288, 345
   pope's 111
Custodian 16, 153, 243,
   277, 278, 279, 283
Cyprian 84, 364 fn.
Cyprus 216

Damascus 136 fn., 183,
   190, 191, 192, 193
Damnation 8, 17, 19,
   132, 214, 342
Daniel 167
Das hertzgespan 244
David 55, 73, 77, 80, 81,
   102, 112, 135, 165,
   262, 302
Day(s) 7, 52, 132, 194,
   285, 295, 296, 331,
   335, 383
De anima, by Aristotle
   367 fn.

De baptismo, by St. Augustine 84 fn.
De correctione Donatistarum, by St. Augustine 169 fn.
De perpetua virginitate
   B. Mariae adversus
   Helvidium, by St.
   Jerome 196 fn.
De viris illustribus, by
   St. Jerome 161 fn.,
   185 fn., 195 fn.
Deaf 248
Death 4, 5, 7, 8, 14, 15,
   21, 27, 32, 35, 44,
   46, 48, 50, 51, 56,
   65, 74, 77, 81, 87,
   92, 109, 117, 120,
   122, 128, 134, 135,
   136, 143, 145, 158,
   168, 202, 212, 221,
   226, 230, 232, 234,
   235, 237, 240, 256,
   268, 269, 273, 290,
   297, 302, 313, 314,
   320, 324, 341, 349,
   356, 360, 366, 387,
   408
   eternal 18, 26, 98, 104,
      124
   hour of 73 fn., 83
   of Christ 10, 15, 19,
      26, 49, 50, 76, 82,
      83, 171, 264, 265
   of sin 238
   spiritual 239
Decalog 51, 188, 219,
   223, 230, 268, 288,
   313, 357, 378
   righteousness of 265
   works of 265, 286, 327,
      335
Decretals 154 fn., 156,
   178, 218, 236
Decretum Magistri Gratiani, ed. by Emil
   Friedberg 218 fn.
Deferrari, Roy J. 297 fn.
Deity 10
Demons 44, 123, 147,
   149, 166, 172, 291,
   311
Denzinger, Henry 297 fn.

Despair 5, 22, 26, 34,
   67, 73, 78, 79, 81,
   87, 137, 275, 374
Deutsche Bibel, by Luther 345 fn.
Devil(s) 4, 5, 6, 7, 12,
   19, 21, 22, 23, 24,
   35, 37, 42, 45, 47,
   49, 56, 58, 59, 70,
   78, 87, 88, 90, 92,
   94, 109, 110, 111,
   118, 124, 125, 127,
   136, 145, 146, 170,
   244, 245, 297, 304,
   369, 384, 385, 387,
   388
   arrows of 143
   father of lies 11
   highly skilled persuader 33
   kingdom of 19, 31
   malice of 53
   martyrs of 8
   mask of 43
   slavery to 19, 51
   slaves of 50
   venom of 135
   διάβολος 388 fn.
Dialectic 23, 24, 30, 31
Dichotomy 363
Die elbe 244
Diet 88
Diet of Augsburg 297 fn.
Dignitaries 130
Dirt 13
Discipline 96, 278
Discord 91
Disobedience 132, 222
Dispensation(s) 215, 216
   of death and sin 226
Disputation Against
   Scholastic Theology,
   by Luther 292 fn.
Disputes 368
Dissension 371
Dissipation 370, 371
Disticha Catonis, ed. by
   Marcus Boas 125 fn.
Divine Majesty 297
Divine Scripture(s) 154,
   156, 308, 386; see
   also Bible, Holy
   Scripture, Holy

Writ, Sacred Scripture, Scripture(s), Word of God
Doctrine(s) 3, 9, 22, 27, 28, 40, 42, 47, 63, 71, 73, 74, 75, 81, 84, 85, 91, 100, 101, 102, 103, 105, 108, 109, 111, 112, 116, 119, 124, 135, 145, 147, 179, 225, 227, 248, 281, 285, 286, 299, 341, 373, 393, 396, 397, 400, 401, 408
Catholic 148
Christian 37, 41, 51, 106, 107
divine 180, 351
false 35, 122
heretical and seditious 43
human 180
is like a mathematical point 37
new 104
of Christ 129
of demons 44, 123
of devil 136
of faith 19, 36, 38, 39, 41, 42, 52, 53, 57, 59, 61, 62, 188, 222, 311
of human traditions and works 10
of justification 17, 19, 36, 46, 60, 87, 104, 120, 145
papal 18
pernicious 339
perverse 340
pure and divine 133
sound 33, 52, 129
true 36, 44, 79, 144
yeast of 46
Dog 116, 397 fn.
Dogmas 164, 211
Dolor 350
Dominic, St. 141
Donation of Constantine 3 fn.
Donatists 60
Doubt(s) 109, 381

Dough 339, 340
Dove 392
Dragon 11
Drunkenness 91, 368, 370, 384
Dung 187, 189, 219, 299

Earth 5, 39, 41, 46, 58, 64, 83, 122, 149, 154, 161, 174, 179, 225, 253, 262, 284, 298, 319, 342, 348, 360, 376, 379, 391, 400, 405, 409
Earthquake 367
Easter 296
Ecclesiastical History
by Eusebius 195, 217, 280 fn.
by Sozomen 216 fn.
Eclogues, by Vergil 244 fn.
Efficax et operosa quidditas 29 fn.
Egypt 226, 227 fn., 267, 268, 289, 366, 407
Egyptians 31, 126
Eighteenth Sunday After Trinity 57 fn.
Elect 27
Elector John 125 fn.
Elijah 367, 388, 392
Elisha 262, 344
Ellipsis 201, 205, 298, 300
Emmanuel 330
Enarrationes in Psalmos, by St. Augustine 312 fn., 332 fn.
Enchanters 369
Enchantments 245
Encratites 127
Enmity 368, 369
Envy 48, 66, 73, 97, 109, 141, 159, 306, 359, 367, 370, 371, 384
Epaphroditus 81
Ephraim 385
ἐπιείκεια 66
Epiphonema 20 fn., 30 fn.
Episcopacy 210

Episcopate 164
Epistle
canonical 230 fn.
catholic 230 fn.
to the Corinthians 299
to the Galatians ix, x, 87, 145
to the Hebrews 272
to the Romans 167, 177, 285, 357
to Titus 243
Epistles
by Horace 116 fn.
by St. Jerome 194 fn.
Epistolae ad Galatas expositio, by St. Augustine 174 fn., 176 fn., 179 fn., 205 fn., 226 fn., 228 fn., 234 fn., 261 fn., 277 fn., 281 fn., 285 fn., 294 fn., 295 fn., 299 fn., 334 fn., 368 fn., 372 fn., 373 fn., 378 fn., 381 fn., 388 fn.
Epitasis 246 fn.
Erasmus x, 36 fn., 159, 162, 175, 179, 201, 209, 212, 238, 239 fn., 245, 248, 307, 309, 315, 326, 336, 339, 368, 382, 387, 400, 402
ἐριθεῖαι 369
ἔρις 369
Erlangen edition 389 fn.
Error(s) 22, 23, 25, 32, 33, 37, 38, 39, 60, 64, 76, 83, 84, 86, 89, 100, 104, 105, 106, 108, 109, 112, 113, 128, 135, 140, 153, 168, 213, 217, 236, 295, 303, 337, 364
Es dunckt mich so recht 341
Esau 267
Esse aliquid 201
Ethics 225
Eucharist 107, 364 fn.

INDEX

εὐδοκία 174
Eunuchs 346
Eunuchus, by Terence 59 fn., 98 fn.
εὐπροσωπῆσαι 130
Eusebius 185, 195, 217, 280 fn.
Evangelicals 48, 125
Eve 260, 288, 289
Excommunication 110
Execration 177
Exemptions 384
Exodus 314
Expiation 65
Extravagantes 154
Eye(s) 37, 39, 134, 140, 141, 245, 304, 338, 349, 410
Ezekiel 111

Facies 206, 214
Faintheartedness 22
Faith 5, 6, 8, 9, 10, 14, 15, 20, 21, 22, 23, 24, 25, 26, 27, 29, 30, 31, 32, 34, 36, 37, 40, 42, 47, 48, 54, 56, 62, 63, 64, 71, 72, 73, 74, 75, 76, 78, 82, 83, 85, 88, 89, 90, 92, 93, 94, 95, 96, 97, 100, 103, 107, 109, 114, 118, 120, 124, 127, 129, 132, 137, 139, 140, 141, 144, 145, 146, 153, 156, 159, 161, 168, 170, 172, 173, 176, 177, 178, 179, 184, 189, 197, 198, 203, 210, 213, 214, 215, 216, 218, 219, 220, 221, 222, 223, 225, 227, 228, 231, 232, 233, 234, 236, 238, 239, 241, 246, 247, 248, 250, 251, 255, 258, 259, 260, 263, 265, 266, 270, 274, 275, 276, 278, 279, 280, 281, 283, 284, 285, 286, 289, 290, 291, 294, 298, 299, 302, 303, 304, 306, 311, 327, 328, 329, 330, 331, 332, 333, 336, 337, 338, 343, 350, 357, 358, 366, 367, 368, 371, 373, 374, 377, 378, 381, 388, 391, 395, 396, 403, 404, 406
 acquired 28, 335
 doctrine of 19, 36, 38, 39, 41, 42, 52, 53, 56, 57, 59, 60, 61, 66, 68, 77, 99, 110, 188, 222, 311
 false 169
 historical 28
 household of 401
 infused 28, 335
 kingdom of 171
 of Abraham 252, 253, 254
 pure 340
 righteousness of 7, 42, 229, 240, 242, 264, 348, 382
 true 342
 working through love 335
Faith, Hope, and Charity, by St. Augustine 22 fn.
Faithfulness 95, 119, 377
False apostles 3, 7, 8, 9, 15, 32, 33, 36, 40, 41, 42, 45, 52, 99, 100, 108, 116, 124, 129, 130, 131, 132, 133, 136, 142, 143, 161, 165, 166, 167, 168, 180, 183, 187, 192, 194, 196, 205, 207, 208, 211, 244, 245, 247, 280, 295, 304, 306, 307, 343, 402, 403
Family 56, 281
Famine 123, 126, 210
Fanatic(s) 20, 38, 46, 129
Fanatical spirits 4, 8, 33, 44, 52, 72, 103, 104, 118, 119, 121
Fast days 384
Fasting(s) 31, 69, 84, 88, 92, 96, 138, 174, 350
Fasts 55, 68, 89, 296
Favoritism 166
Female 204
Feriae 138
Festivals 383
Festus Porcius 256
Fetus 308
Fides historica 28 fn.
Fieri 361 fn.
Fifth Lateran Council 297 fn.
Figs 79, 373
Figure(s) of speech 31, 200, 280, 312, 333, 336, 342, 395
Filth 31
Fire 27, 62, 69, 276, 284, 303, 364, 388, 410
First Table 132
Fish 31
Flesh 7, 16, 21, 24, 25, 49, 54, 55, 58, 59, 64, 65, 66, 67, 69, 70, 71, 73, 74, 75, 76, 77, 78, 79, 80, 81, 82, 84, 85, 86, 87, 88, 89, 91, 92, 93, 95, 96, 97, 98, 99, 102, 103, 109, 111, 113, 127, 130, 132, 133, 134, 137, 140, 141, 142, 143, 158, 170, 173, 174, 180, 187, 190, 191, 192, 196, 225, 227, 229, 231, 232, 233, 235, 236, 237, 238, 239, 249, 250, 260, 282, 288, 290, 301, 302, 310, 311, 314, 318, 320, 321, 322, 324, 328, 329, 331, 333, 334, 340, 341, 346, 347, 348, 349, 350, 360, 361, 362, 363, 364, 365, 366, 367, 368, 370, 371, 372, 373, 374, 375, 378, 379, 380, 384,

390, 393, 399, 400, 402, 405, 406
Abraham's 253
cannot be without sin 68
freedom of 3, 4, 35, 48, 51
license and lust of 50
reason and wisdom of 138
yoke and obligation of 50
Flies 227
Flood 91, 146
Fomes 228 fn.
Food(s) 15, 31, 44, 54, 55, 81, 82, 83, 92, 126, 138, 213, 217, 257, 275, 335, 378, 383, 384
Forgiveness of sins 5, 6, 9, 10, 14, 19, 41, 61, 68, 70, 71, 74, 76, 77, 79, 80, 82, 85, 86, 96, 106, 109, 111, 112, 115, 120, 121, 132, 141, 142, 164, 386; *see also* Remission of sins
Forma substantialis 29 fn.
Fornication 88, 112, 368, 384
Fornicator 339, 345
Fortitude 23, 24, 25
Francis, St. 18, 83, 141
Rule of 141 fn.
stigmata of 142
Franciscan(s) 141
Fraud 126
Freedom 4, 17, 19, 31, 48, 49, 201, 203, 204, 213, 217, 232, 236, 284, 286, 316, 324, 329, 348, 383, 384, 385
Christian 5, 7, 11, 48, 50, 51, 72, 326
eternal 8
evangelical 202, 214
from Law 326, 347
from righteousness 325, 349
from sin 325, 349
from traditions of pope 138
in Christ 10
of Christians 154
of conscience 6
of flesh 3, 4, 8, 35, 51
of Gospel 200, 202
of grace 346
of opinion 248
political 8
theological or spiritual 4, 325
Freuntlich 376
Friars 113 fn.
mendicant 124
Friday 296
Friedberg, Emil 218 fn.
Frogs 227
Future infinitive 176

Gabriel 270
Galatia 97, 99, 124, 167, 177
Galatians ix, x, 3, 7, 9, 31, 32, 33, 36, 39, 40, 42, 52, 54, 59, 62, 79, 99, 108, 116, 129, 131, 132, 144, 148, 161, 162, 165, 168, 174, 175, 177, 179, 187, 190, 191, 194, 196, 197, 198, 208, 217, 243, 244, 245, 249, 250, 251, 254, 255, 263, 292, 298, 301, 302, 303, 304, 305, 306, 307, 308, 310, 315, 323, 331, 338, 339, 343, 344, 359, 371, 378, 403, 406
Galileans 289
Genesis 252, 253, 267, 309, 310
Genitive 175, 212, 302
Gentile(s) 42, 139, 142, 143, 165, 186, 194, 196, 197, 200, 203, 204, 208, 210, 211, 212, 213, 215, 217, 218, 219, 247, 254, 260, 263, 264, 265, 266, 281, 283, 290, 292, 295, 302, 336, 343, 357, 403, 406
church of 146
Gentleness 95, 106, 111, 112, 298, 313, 373, 377, 388, 390
oil of 301
German 130, 244 fn., 341, 376
Germans 37, 157
Germany 107, 127, 157, 158, 384, 385
Gerson 81
Gideon 330, 364
Gloss(es) 227, 369, 373, 397
Gluttony 92
God
judgment of 8, 19, 26
kingdom of 64, 79, 91, 92, 97, 98, 250, 329, 337, 371, 372
knowledge of 286, 294
mask of 43, 44
mercy of 5, 18, 44
never looks upon the persons 206, 217, 281
wrath of 4, 5, 7, 8, 19, 21, 26, 27, 50, 78, 409
et passim
Godhead 290
Godlessness 154, 199, 257, 260, 293, 303, 327, 328, 342, 358
Godliness 47, 53, 71, 99, 123, 372, 408
Godly 40, 44, 46, 49, 51, 77, 80, 82, 99, 102
Gold 51, 55, 61, 122, 171, 336, 407
Gomorrah 48
Goodness 368, 373, 376, 395
Gospel 3, 8, 9, 10, 13, 18, 33, 35, 42, 43, 44, 47, 48, 49, 50, 54, 62 fn., 82, 85, 89, 90, 92, 94, 99, 100, 101, 102, 105, 107, 108, 116, 118,

119, 122, 123, 124,
126, 130, 140, 141,
142, 153, 156, 158,
162, 165, 167, 175,
176, 177, 178, 179,
182, 183, 184, 186,
187, 188, 190, 191,
193, 194, 195, 196,
204, 207, 208, 209,
210, 211, 214, 215,
217, 230, 241, 249,
263, 298, 299, 303,
310, 317, 318, 338,
340, 341, 344, 355,
366, 375, 376, 397
  freedom of 200
Government(s) 91, 98
Grace 3, 7, 11, 14, 15,
16, 18, 19, 24, 38,
42, 48, 61, 85, 86,
88, 90, 102, 108,
117, 120, 140, 141,
142, 143, 144, 146,
149, 164, 170, 172,
175, 176, 177, 180,
184, 185, 186, 187,
188, 189, 203, 209,
212, 219, 220, 223,
224, 226, 234, 235,
238, 240, 242, 246,
249, 252, 256, 260,
261, 264, 266, 273,
274, 275, 276, 277,
279, 283, 284, 285,
287, 291, 292, 293,
294, 301, 308, 311,
312, 313, 314, 317,
318, 319, 320, 321,
322, 324, 327, 330,
331, 332, 333, 335,
347, 349, 353, 356,
359, 362, 364, 366,
367, 372, 380,
390 fn., 407
  freedom of 346
  kingdom of 171
Grain 55, 329
Grammar 202, 357, 397
Grammarian(s) 28, 178
Grapes 79, 373
Grasshoppers 325
Gratian 154 fn.
Gratitude 273

Gravamina 157 fn.
Greece 98
Greed 31, 48, 61, 67,
125, 126, 154, 257,
337, 384, 385, 399
Greek(s) 125, 163, 175,
179, 201, 212, 213,
246, 274, 290, 291,
307, 315, 319, 326,
336, 348, 369, 371,
376, 377, 380, 394,
396, 397
Gregory, St. 83, 84, 85,
89, 110, 388, 390
Gutdunckel 341

Habit, monastic 88
Hagar 310, 311, 314,
315, 322, 323
  means "journey
  abroad" 317
Hair shirt(s) 13, 84, 88
Ham 146
Hannah 322
Harlot(s) 14, 123
Hatred 31, 42, 43, 47,
53, 58, 66, 67, 69,
71, 78, 81, 102,
103, 104, 132, 137,
141, 172, 179, 181,
233, 276, 277, 284,
301, 348, 353, 360,
369, 374, 375, 387,
399
Hay 52, 55, 62
Health 363
Heartburn 244 fn.
Heathen 94, 99, 124,
146, 147, 245, 345,
369, 382, 391, 401
  virtues of 172
Heathenism 293
Heaven 5, 18, 20, 22,
27, 33, 38, 39, 40,
41, 44, 45, 46, 64,
83, 84, 86, 93, 108,
129, 158, 165, 178,
179, 225, 226, 292,
297, 298, 311, 316,
318, 319, 329, 337,
348, 388, 391, 408,
409, 410
  kingdom of 340, 345

Hebdomad 194
Hebraism 165, 208
Hebrews 32, 163, 178,
187, 191, 210, 345
Hector 103
Heir(s) 243, 264, 282,
283, 289, 291, 323,
324
Hell 4, 8, 9, 21, 33, 46,
69, 133, 158, 167,
221, 311, 385, 408
  gates of 155
  kingdom of 31
  tyranny of 154
Hellenists 197
Hercules 154 fn., 371 fn.
Heresiarch 91
Heresy 22, 23, 25, 32,
67, 72, 89, 97, 109,
364, 367, 368, 370,
389
Hussite 392 fn.
Heretic(s) 19, 43, 53,
54, 83, 84, 91, 92,
123, 124, 131, 132,
133, 134, 135, 136,
148, 153, 169, 178,
239, 303, 370, 382,
399, 400, 408
Hermit(s) 9, 68, 69, 75,
83, 85
Hermon 177, 315
Herzspann 244 fn.
Hezekiah 43
Hierarchy 398
Hildesheim edition of
Erasmus' *Opera*
159 fn.
Historia tripartita 216 fn.
Historiae adversus paganos, by Orosius
227 fn.
Historians 98
History 28, 60, 97, 98,
268
Holdselig 376
Holidays 62, 296
Holiness 68, 77, 82, 83,
86, 87, 89, 140, 141,
277, 280, 302, 346,
394, 405, 406
  presumptions of 115
  self-chosen 85

Holy Roman Church 389
Holy Scripture 35, 38, 46, 136, 200, 214; see also Bible, Divine Scripture(s), Holy Writ, Sacred Scripture, Scripture(s), Word of God
Holy Spirit 23, 28, 32, 46, 82, 110, 121, 137, 140, 141, 144, 165, 168, 172, 185, 221, 226, 234, 247, 248, 261, 263, 276, 290, 318, 326, 335, 355, 362, 366, 367, 370, 373, 376, 388, 390
 cannot be received without Christ 131
 judgment of 9 et passim
Holy Trinity 290, 340
Holy Writ 156, 200, 220, 240, 312, 317, 360, 377, 386; see also Bible, Divine Scripture(s), Sacred Scripture, Scriptures(s), Word of God
Honesty 95, 377
"Hooknose" 59
Hope 20, 21, 22, 23, 24, 25, 26, 27, 46, 64, 68, 72, 73, 97, 100, 218, 326, 328, 332, 333, 374, 401, 405
 of gain 314
Horace 116 fn.
Horse 232
Horula 73 fn.
Hosea 385
Household
 of Christ 401
 of faith 401
Householder 113, 119
Housewife 61
Humility 52, 86, 99, 216, 302
Hunger 126, 143, 385
Hus, John 392 fn.

Husband(s) 61, 68, 114, 232, 281, 320, 321, 345, 346
Hydra 371 fn.
Hyperbole 31, 304
Hypocrisy 31, 92, 131, 188, 204, 212, 213, 214, 215, 217, 274, 340
Hypocrite(s) 30, 54, 75, 79, 92, 96, 172, 174, 214, 215, 216, 220, 223, 258, 284, 321, 324, 334, 390

Idolaters 51, 90, 369
Idolatry 31, 67, 69, 87, 88, 89, 90, 91, 141, 148, 188, 293, 368, 369
Ignorance 342, 384
 affected 292
 gross 292
 invincible 292, 293
Illness 363
Illusions 245
Immorality 89
Immortality of human soul 297 fn.
Immunities 3
Impatience 22, 67, 69, 70, 71, 72, 73, 78, 80, 109
Impiety 161
Imprecation 177
Impurity 89, 368, 369
In praesumptuosas Martini Lutheri conclusiones de potestate papae dialogus, by Sylvester Prierias 157 fn.
In regione angelorum 239 fn.
In religione angelorum 239 fn.
Incarnation 268
Incest 108
Indulgence(s) 198, 328, 337, 352, 358, 384
 special 386 fn.
Indulgence traffic 124 fn., 328

Infants 244, 245, 248, 249
Ingratitude 49, 56, 72, 102, 103, 127, 128, 240, 293, 409
Innocent III 164 fn.
Insanity 147
Insemination 319, 400
Instaurare 348 fn.
Institutes, by Justinian 240 fn.
Insuaves 376
Intellect 22, 23, 24, 25
Intercourse 321, 399, 400
Intermediary 270, 271, 272
Intoxication 91, 92, 95
Invocavit Sunday x
Io. Annius ex Philone 267 fn.
Irenaeus 127 fn., 208 fn., 364 fn.
Iron 10, 13
Isaac 142, 251, 252, 253, 267, 284, 310, 311, 318, 322, 323
Isaiah 29, 35, 44, 163, 200, 245, 281, 322, 335, 389, 409, 410
Ishmael 253, 284, 310, 311, 318, 322, 323
Ishmaelites 323
Israel 16, 80, 111, 135, 142, 146, 187, 268, 323, 330, 344, 350, 370, 375, 406, 409
 kings of 392
Italy 147
Itaque lex paedagogus noster fuit in Christo 278 fn.

Jacob 267
James 38, 167, 195, 196, 200, 208, 213, 331, 388
 the Less 195
Jealousy 369, 371
Jena editors 244 fn.
Jeremiah 166, 189, 220, 234, 262 fn.
Jeroboam 350

INDEX

Jerome, St. x, 35, 36 fn., 55, 68, 69, 82, 84, 85, 92, 95, 96 fn., 101, 130, 161, 163, 166, 167, 168, 169, 173, 174, 175 fn., 176, 177, 179, 182, 183, 185, 186, 187, 190, 191, 193, 194, 195, 196, 199, 201, 202, 205, 207, 208, 209, 210, 211, 212, 213, 215, 217, 219, 222, 223 fn., 226, 228, 239, 241, 243, 244, 245, 247, 248, 250, 253, 257, 259, 261, 262, 263, 268, 269, 270, 271, 283, 285, 287, 288 fn., 290, 291, 295, 296, 298, 299, 300, 301, 302, 303, 304, 305, 307, 308, 309, 310, 312, 314, 317, 318, 321, 327, 331, 332, 333, 338, 339, 340 fn., 343, 344, 345, 346, 348, 349, 350, 357, 363, 368, 369, 370, 373, 376, 377, 379, 380, 381, 394, 399, 401, 402 fn., 406

Jerusalem 93, 155, 193, 196, 199, 200, 208 fn., 296, 311, 314, 315, 317, 318, 337, 344, 382, 391, 410
  Bishop of 208
  earthly 316
  heavenly 316
  new 319

Jew(s) 9, 16, 30, 38, 42, 55, 111, 117, 123, 130, 138, 139, 142, 143, 147, 167, 177, 180, 190, 197, 200, 202, 203, 204, 208, 210, 211, 213, 215, 217, 218, 221, 246, 247, 250, 252, 265, 274, 279, 280, 281, 284, 285, 290, 295, 296, 302, 306, 309, 320, 322, 334, 335, 343, 344, 355, 357, 383, 401, 402, 403, 406
  kingdom and priesthood of 15

Jo. Annius 267
Job 230, 231, 245, 287, 335
John 52, 65, 136, 167, 185, 195, 200, 208, 230, 372, 388
John Frederick 125 fn.
John of Damascus 136 fn.
John the Baptist 35, 235
Jonadab 229
Jordan 177
Joseph 155, 165, 195, 267
Joses 195
Judah 330
Judaism 186, 189, 213, 214, 247, 280, 293
Judas 195, 205, 206, 261
Jude 48
Judea 122, 161, 197, 198, 311, 314, 316
Judge(s) 10, 11, 22, 26, 34, 88, 120, 199, 212, 242, 287, 342, 387, 397
Judgment(s) 41, 57, 74, 77, 91, 98, 100, 108, 113, 117, 118, 120, 127, 136, 140, 155, 207, 215, 258, 263, 274, 281, 293, 300, 341, 342, 359, 365, 381, 393
  distorted 89
  of God 8, 15, 19, 26
  of Holy Spirit 9
  of men 14, 15
  rash 395
Jurists 245, 248, 275, 397
Justice 241, 388
Justification 11, 16, 28, 29, 30, 36, 64, 65, 66, 78, 106, 138, 139, 168, 203, 214, 225, 228, 238, 240, 246, 269, 270, 274, 348
  doctrine of 17, 19, 36, 46, 87, 104, 120, 145
Justinian 240 fn.

κατά 212
κατὰ πρόσωπον 212, 214
καταρτίζετε 111 fn.
κατηχίζω 396
κατηχούμενος 125
κενοδοξία 97, 98, 99, 101, 104, 116
κενόδοξος 97 fn., 99, 103, 116, 117
κεφαλή 218
Kindness 368, 373, 376
King(s) 16, 31, 102, 122, 130, 159, 210, 241, 242, 303, 335
  of Assyrians 164
  of Israel 392
Kingdom(s) 62, 98, 100, 111, 139
  of Christ 30, 86, 94, 114
  of devil 19, 31, 59
  of faith 171
  of glory 171
  of God 64, 79, 91, 92, 97, 98, 250, 329, 337, 371, 372
  of grace 171
  of heaven 340, 345
  of hell 31
  of Jews 15
  of pope 9
Knowledge 10, 22, 23, 34, 115, 177, 185, 189, 245, 269, 270, 272, 275, 292, 303, 350, 359, 372, 403, 404
  natural 53
  of Christ 17, 25, 49, 147
  of God 286, 294
  of good literature 124
  of grace and of faith 144

of sacred literature 124
of sin 184, 238, 318, 328
of true doctrine 79
of true holiness 85
Koran 90
Krauth, Charles P. 31 fn.

Labor 350
Lambs 244
Land of Promise 289, 314, 373
Lang, Johann x, 177 fn.
Lasciviousness 369
Last Day 68
Last Judgment 120, 121, 171, 277
Latin 175, 178, 179, 231 fn., 234 fn., 348 fn., 385 fn., 407
Law(s)
 canon 295
 Ceremonial 139, 161, 188, 223, 228, 230, 248, 256, 257, 265, 287, 358, 378
 contempt for 201
 freedom from 326, 347
 guardianship of 243
 Moral 18, 139, 188, 259, 378
 natural 355
 papal 215, 358, 408
 righteousness of 7, 16, 17, 189, 198, 218, 239, 246, 249, 264, 266, 267, 276, 283, 286, 291, 311, 317, 318, 319, 328
 Sinaitic 319
 slavery of 7, 217, 314, 319, 346
 works of 7, 12, 13, 75, 78, 173, 175, 202, 203, 214, 218, 222, 223, 224, 225, 228, 231, 232, 234, 238, 239, 242, 243, 245, 247, 250, 251, 252, 255, 256, 257, 258, 259, 260, 264, 266, 272, 274, 283, 284, 286, 291, 319, 321, 322, 327, 329, 331, 334, 336, 340, 381, 404
 written 355
 et passim
Layman 55, 61, 204
Lead 384
Leaders, Hussite 392 fn.
Learning 156, 172, 256, 375, 393
Leaven 339, 341, 364
 of Pharisees 340
Lebanon 315
Lectures on Galatians, by Luther 67 fn., 240 fn.
Lectures on Genesis, by Luther 384 fn.
Lefèvre d'Étaples, Jacques 315 fn.
Legacy 264, 265
Legislation dealing with ecclesiastical matters 250 fn.
Legispositio 289
Leipzig 315
Leipzig Debate 158, 392 fn.
Lent 216, 296
Leo X, pope 157 fn., 218
Lernean Swamp 371
Letter to Paulinus, by St. Jerome 194
Letter to the Romans 381
Leudselig 376
Leviathan 161
Levites 123, 399
Liber interpretationis hebraicorum nominum, by St. Jerome 161 fn., 177 fn., 191 fn., 321 fn.
Liberty 176, 203, 286, 396
 Christian 3, 198, 402
Lice 227
Licentiousness 48, 368, 378
Life 3, 5, 13, 17, 19, 25, 33, 34, 41, 44, 46, 47, 48, 58, 60, 62, 63, 73, 74, 81, 84, 85, 86, 88, 94, 98, 107, 109, 111, 112, 115, 119, 120, 121, 125, 135, 141, 144, 147, 158, 161, 168, 173, 181, 186, 206, 210, 219, 222, 223, 226, 229, 258, 259, 260, 271, 273, 293, 295, 308, 313, 316, 329, 338, 340, 349, 351, 353, 354, 356, 365, 372, 386, 391, 402, 403, 405
 ascetic 10, 83
 carnal 371
 celibate 57, 67, 68, 82
 chaste and sober 95
 Christian 30, 31, 32, 239, 303, 361, 378 fn., 407
 community 377
 eternal 6, 9, 10, 11, 14, 18, 32, 39, 61, 88, 90, 124, 127, 145, 222, 400
 frugal 92
 future 8, 302, 328
 holy 35, 91, 102
 is like a physical point 37
 monastic 140
 mortal 281
 necessities of 284, 396
 of experience 234
 physical 239
 present 8, 39, 49, 64, 65, 95, 127, 239, 401
 religious 136
 spiritual 52, 239
 to come 64, 65, 127, 128, 169, 224, 232, 233, 317
Likeness of God 140, 141, 280, 405, 406
Lily 391
Lindus 154
Lion 3, 58
Lives of the Fathers 14, 112

INDEX 425

Locusts 227, 325, 352
Log(s) 58, 81, 112
Lombard, Peter x, 222 fn., 290 fn., 333 fn., 377 fn.
Long-suffering 368, 373, 376, 377
Lord's Day 296
Lord's Prayer 42
Lord's Supper 36, 37, 41, 62 fn., 82, 107
Lot 321, 370
Love 5, 25, 28, 29, 30, 31, 37, 38, 39, 40, 41, 42, 47, 48, 49, 50, 51, 53, 54, 55, 56, 57, 58, 59, 61, 62, 63, 64, 65, 66, 67, 68, 72, 93, 95, 99, 101, 106, 108, 113, 114, 159, 169, 172, 180, 181, 182, 203, 204, 215, 216, 218, 221, 233, 234, 235, 236, 237, 241, 260, 277, 278, 279, 290, 291, 295, 298, 303, 304, 305, 306, 307, 313, 326, 329, 333, 335, 336, 337, 346, 347, 348, 349, 350, 351, 352, 354, 355, 356, 357, 358, 359, 361, 365, 368, 370, 371, 372, 373, 375, 378, 381, 382, 383, 384, 385, 386, 387, 391, 392, 393, 395, 396, 400, 401, 408, 409
  Christian 353 fn.
  natural 353 fn.
  works of 52
Luke 143, 163, 185, 193, 195, 210, 364
Lupinus, Peter 153
Lust(s) 50, 154, 173, 224, 233, 235, 236, 237, 238, 249, 257, 260, 275, 276, 277, 278, 287, 326, 341, 363, 364, 371, 378, 380, 391, 399, 407
  for praise and glory 404
  obedience to 372
Luther ix, 13 fn., 16 fn., 20 fn., 27 fn., 30 fn., 32 fn., 36 fn., 57 fn., 62 fn., 67 fn., 69 fn., 70 fn., 73 fn., 82 fn., 84 fn., 85 fn., 98 fn., 101 fn., 104 fn., 109 fn., 111 fn., 113 fn., 118 fn., 119 fn., 122 fn., 123 fn., 124 fn., 125 fn., 129 fn., 130 fn., 141 fn., 153, 154 fn., 156 fn., 157 fn., 158 fn., 159 fn., 164 fn., 176 fn., 201 fn., 206 fn., 220 fn., 230 fn., 235 fn., 236 fn., 240 fn., 244 fn., 250 fn., 252 fn., 263 fn., 267 fn., 278 fn., 280 fn., 285 fn., 289 fn., 292 fn., 295 fn., 304 fn., 317 fn., 345 fn., 353 fn., 363 fn., 367 fn., 384 fn., 385 fn., 386 fn., 392 fn., 397 fn.
Luther the Expositor, by Jaroslav Pelikan 20 fn.
Luther's Works ix, 8 fn., 13 fn., 14 fn., 15 fn., 16 fn., 20 fn., 24 fn., 27 fn., 28 fn., 32 fn., 34 fn., 37 fn., 43 fn., 45 fn., 63 fn., 67 fn., 69 fn., 73 fn., 81 fn., 85 fn., 90 fn., 94 fn., 98 fn., 105 fn., 109 fn., 110 fn., 112 fn., 125 fn., 127 fn., 138 fn., 142 fn., 147 fn., 158 fn., 164 fn., 173 fn., 176 fn., 181 fn., 187 fn., 211 fn., 220 fn., 221 fn., 228 fn., 231 fn., 235 fn., 236 fn., 240 fn., 249 fn., 252 fn., 286 fn., 292 fn., 295 fn., 317 fn., 328 fn., 335 fn., 337 fn., 362 fn., 363 fn., 370 fn., 385 fn., 388 fn., 396 fn., 397 fn.
Lydian touchstone 353
Lyra 70 fn., 245

Magicians 369
Magistra 156 fn.
Magistrate(s) 50, 61, 82, 90, 113, 119, 123, 148, 281
μακροθυμία 94, 376
Male 131, 204, 400
Malediction 177
Malevolence 395
Manet ibi locus 21 fn.
Manichaeus 288
Manicheans 60, 288 fn., 362
μαράνα θά 345
Marcion 288 fn.
Mark 161, 196
Marriage 127, 128, 138, 148, 400
Martin 408
Martyr(s) 164, 195, 280, 296, 374
  of devil 8
Martyrdom 350
Mary 81
  James's 196
  Magdalene 195, 196, 390
  mother of James and Joses 195
  sister of the Lord's mother 195
  virginity of 288
  wife of Cleophas 195
Mask(s) 31, 43, 281, 342, 351
Mass(es) 135
  anniversary 124
  Low 84, 89

Massa perditionis 275 fn.
Mater 156 fn.
Materia dilectionis 391 fn.
Mathematicians 60
Matthew 185, 196, 310
Matthias 165
Maximianists 60 fn.
μὴ ἐνέχεσθε 326
Meal 340
Meat 31, 138, 384
Mediator 11, 86, 268, 271, 272, 275
Meekness 106, 107, 109, 111
Meinhold, Peter 24 fn.
Meissen 315
Meissinger, Karl ix
Melanchthon, Philip x, 377
Memorials 352
Menius, Justus 130 fn.
Menstruation 220
Mercury 200, 353
Mercy 3, 15, 18, 44, 81, 100, 110, 113, 140, 142, 172, 174, 185, 220, 221, 222, 227, 266, 270, 274, 275, 286, 328, 345, 365, 366, 371, 374, 375, 388, 406, 409
Mercy seat 22, 64, 86, 231
Merit(s) 10, 19, 140, 174, 179, 189, 203, 221, 240, 251, 263, 266, 270, 328, 329, 388
  of condignity 372
  of congruity 28, 249, 372
Messiah 146
Metaphor(s) 127, 407
Metaphysics, by Aristotle 364 fn.
μεταστρέψαι 176
Metonymy 179
Micah 123, 335
Middle Ages 84 fn.
Midian 330, 364
Mildness 376, 377
Milk 384

Ministers 37, 41, 47, 62, 82, 100, 101, 108, 119, 122, 123, 124, 126, 127, 128, 129
Ministry 49, 51, 98, 99, 100, 102, 103, 104, 115, 116, 117, 118, 119, 120, 123, 125, 126, 192, 209, 210, 226, 249
Minorite(s) 60, 141, 142, 281
Miracle(s) 146, 209, 251, 288, 291, 303, 304, 336, 354
Mirbt, Carl 342 fn.
Mirror 34
Misfortune(s) 67, 298, 330, 345
Missa privata 84 fn.
Mizar, Mt. 177
Moab 317, 321
Moabites 321
Moderation 373, 378
Monastery 90, 136, 204, 354, 375, 385
Monasticism 84
Money 58, 128, 158, 198, 216, 236, 237, 308, 358, 384
Monk(s) 9, 13, 14, 25, 55, 60, 61, 68, 69, 71, 73, 75, 76, 81, 83, 84, 85, 88, 89, 91, 92, 101 fn., 135, 140, 141, 148, 166, 281, 329, 397
Monkey 220
Months 7, 52, 295, 296, 331
Moon 149
Morals 36, 47, 60, 109, 125, 176, 214, 256, 268, 369, 375, 399
Mores amici noveris, non oderis 94 fn.
Moses 15, 16, 18, 56, 59, 109, 130, 131, 138, 139, 178, 179, 180, 185, 187, 219, 222, 226, 235, 247, 255, 256, 257, 259, 261, 267, 269, 272, 274,

295, 296, 318, 320, 331, 334, 335, 341, 349, 366, 379, 392, 407
Mother 58, 288, 308, 310, 317, 319, 321
  of James and Joses 195
  of the churches 158
  of the sons of Zebedee 195, 196
  the Lord's 195
Mud 356, 409
Muleteers, Roman 385
Mulio 385 fn.
Murder 23, 31, 80, 89, 133, 297, 368, 370, 384

Naaman the Syrian 287, 335
Nebuchadnezzar 335
Need 125, 126, 237, 329, 385, 408
Neighbor(s) 30, 31, 50, 51, 52, 54, 55, 56, 57, 58, 62, 63, 64, 66, 67, 71, 75, 114, 203, 295, 298, 313, 347, 348, 349, 351, 352, 353, 354, 355, 356, 357, 369, 374, 375, 395, 396, 401
Neutralist(s) 239, 256
New Testament 236, 341, 389
Nicholas 218
Nicomachean Ethics, by Aristotle 23 fn., 29 fn.
Nimrods 158
Noah 146, 370
Nobles 102, 123, 124, 125, 126, 198, 407
νόμος 319, 321
Nose 134, 158
Nun 61

Oath 12, 196
Obedience 7, 14, 18, 61, 113, 120, 163
  to lusts 372
Obesse 80 fn.
Obiectum charitatis 391 fn.

INDEX

Obscenity 369
Occupatio 63 fn.
Ocean(s) 344, 392, 409
Octave 288
Oecolampadius 119 fn., 129 fn.
Offering(s) 126, 211, 335, 352
Office 117, 118, 119, 163, 164, 165, 192, 193, 209, 375
Ogdoad 194
Old Testament 55, 202, 236, 272, 357, 389, 399
On Christian Doctrine, by St. Augustine 236 fn., 312
On Illustrious Men, by St. Jerome 195
On Marriage and Concupiscence, by St. Augustine 188
On Nature and Grace, by St. Augustine 228, 379
On the Grace of Christ and on Original Sin, by St. Augustine 275 fn.
On the Spirit and the Letter, by St. Augustine 188, 219 fn., 274, 314 fn.
On the Trinity, by St. Augustine 238 fn., 288, 290 fn.
Onesimus 108
Onocentaurs 245
Opera, by Erasmus 159 fn., 239 fn., 245 fn., 248 fn., 307 fn., 315 fn., 336 fn., 339 fn., 387 fn., 400 fn., 402 fn.
Operari 209
Oppression 158
Optima conscientia 13 fn.
Orator 24
Ordinaries 153
Orient 335
Origen 169, 185, 202, 236, 250, 259, 312, 346, 363, 379
Orion 245
Orosius 227 fn.
Ostriches 245, 281
Oxen 7
οὐσία 377

Pagan(s) 91, 157, 325
παιδαγωγός 278
Palestine 340
Palliums 237, 385
Papacy 53, 60, 63, 84, 87, 91, 100, 110, 113, 121
Papist(s) 6, 8, 9, 18, 19, 68, 87, 91, 107, 118, 126, 133, 138, 148, 149
Parable(s) 310, 319
Paraclete 387, 388, 389
Paradise 145, 391
Paradox 319
  Stoic 326
Paraphrasis, by Erasmus 159 fn., 239 fn., 245 fn., 248 fn., 307 fn., 315 fn., 336 fn., 339 fn., 387 fn., 400 fn., 402 fn.
Parent(s) 56, 82, 149, 158, 215, 219, 320, 357
  our first 145
Partiality 53, 61, 103
Passion, Christ's 168, 212
Passivity 25
Passover 289
Pastor(s) 110, 112, 113, 115, 121, 122, 124, 125, 237, 297, 308, 393
Pastorates 385
Patience 20, 24, 25, 94, 106, 126, 157, 303, 368, 373, 376, 393
Patrimony of Peter 122 fn.
Patrologia, Series Latina 55 fn., 96 fn., 112 fn., 130 fn., 163 fn., 174 fn., 175 fn., 176 fn., 179 fn., 196 fn., 205 fn., 214 fn., 226 fn., 228 fn., 234 fn., 245 fn., 261 fn., 277 fn., 281 fn., 285 fn., 290 fn., 294 fn., 295 fn., 299 fn., 300 fn., 333 fn., 334 fn., 361 fn., 362 fn., 368 fn., 372 fn., 373 fn., 376 fn., 378 fn., 381 fn., 387 fn., 388 fn.
Paul passim
Paulinus 209, 308
Paulus, which means "little" 154 fn.
Peace 5, 13, 18, 23, 38, 41, 42, 43, 44, 47, 48, 59, 62, 66, 73, 91, 94, 95, 103, 108, 121, 130, 134, 135, 137, 141, 142, 144, 148, 170, 174, 184, 185, 204, 219, 224, 242, 289, 318, 357, 358, 367, 368, 373, 374, 375, 376, 402
Pearls 48
Peasants 102, 124
Pelagians 219, 314, 362
πηλίκος 401
Penances 13
Peninnah 322
Pentecost 296, 319
Perdite vixi 85 fn.
Perdition 34, 98, 110, 189, 275, 288, 292
Perfectus 71 fn.
Persecution(s) 25, 42, 43, 44, 46, 49, 101, 102, 103, 129, 130, 131, 134, 135, 145, 180, 181, 301, 302, 322, 323, 343, 403
  Roman 227 fn.
Persius 326
Persona 206

Peter, St. 3, 7, 80, 94, 156, 162, 167, 178, 185, 192, 193, 194, 195, 197, 200, 208, 210, 211, 212, 213, 214, 215, 217, 218, 238, 243, 247, 248, 297, 334, 336, 338, 362, 386, 396
  Patrimony of 122
πέτρα 218
πέτρος 218
Pharaoh(s) 16
Pharisee(s) 112, 172, 187, 219, 340, 383, 388, 390, 394
φάρμακον 369
Philippians 239
Philo 161, 267
Philosopher(s) 47, 164, 219, 240, 250, 391
  Stoic 326
Philosophy 24, 37, 285
  Aristotelian 367
  moral 29, 172, 368
φρόνημα 341
φρόνησις 341
Physician 185, 277
Piety 33, 154, 159, 160, 188
  pretense of 80
Pirates 358
Plague(s) 3, 86, 370, 409
  of Egypt 226, 227
Plautus 125 fn., 353 fn.
Play on words 80 fn., 154 fn., 361 fn.
Pleiades 245
Pope(s) 3 fn., 19, 31, 44, 45, 51, 89, 122, 124, 129, 130, 133, 135, 138, 139, 140, 147, 153, 154, 157, 177, 179, 206, 207, 215, 216, 236, 295 fn., 297, 342, 358, 385 fn., 397, 398, 407
  curses of 111
  kingdom of 9
  slavery of 49
  supreme heresiarch and head of all heretics 91
  synagog of 110
  tyranny of 48, 50
Pork 216
Porphyry 190, 191, 214
  tree of 181
Position 162, 370
Potter 60, 410
Poverty 65, 72, 122, 123, 262, 298, 329, 405
Praescriptus 245, 246
Prayer(s) 76, 92, 97, 121, 165, 216, 286, 296, 354, 410
Preacher(s) 39, 53, 54, 102, 103, 118, 121, 122, 125, 126, 127, 129, 184, 193, 248, 308, 352, 371, 399
Predestination 190, 255, 294
Prelates 130, 164, 227
Prestige 164
Presumption(s) 71, 115, 132, 323
  of saintliness 136
Presumptuousness 23, 372
Pretense(s) 141, 148
Pride 48, 67, 70, 71, 97, 113, 174, 192, 217, 270, 342, 345, 359, 403
  holy 162
Prierias 397 fn.
Priest(s) 9, 55, 123, 124, 125, 135, 142, 166, 281, 329, 392, 393, 397, 398, 408
Priesthood(s) 166, 210
  of Jews 15, 139
  royal 394
Primogeniture 322
Prince(s) 44, 45, 69, 111, 122, 125, 130, 155, 159, 210, 303, 317, 386
Prior 113 fn.
Privilege(s) 3, 384, 385, 393
Procedere 382
προεγράφη 245
Promise(s) 10, 13, 16, 21, 23, 26, 27, 112, 142, 146, 219, 224, 251, 252, 253, 254, 255, 263, 264, 265, 266, 267, 268, 270, 272, 273, 274, 275, 278, 282, 283, 310, 319, 322, 323, 324, 334, 335, 366, 377
Prophet(s) 15, 44, 93, 123, 135, 146, 158, 179, 189, 222, 235, 245, 259, 275, 289, 295, 296, 317, 318, 323, 334, 350, 355, 366, 380, 392, 409
  false 18, 166
Propitiator 11, 64, 68, 74, 75, 76, 86
Proscription 245
πρόσωπον 206
Prosperity 403
Proverbs 274
Prudence 23, 24, 25, 36
Psalms 46, 75, 81, 93
Pseudapostles 331
Pseudo-Philo 267 fn.
Pun 157 fn.
Punishment(s) 8, 12, 33, 44, 50, 86, 107, 110, 124, 170, 188, 219, 245, 278, 284, 286, 291, 311, 332, 345, 409
Pupil(s) 119, 247, 306
Purgatory 401

Quarrel(s) 368, 369, 377, 407
Quellen zur Geschichte des Papsttums und des römischen Katholizismus, by Carl Mirbt 342 fn.
Qui videbantur esse aliquid 201
Qui volet ingenio cedere, nullus erit 98 fn.
Quo maius nihil est neque habet 72 fn.
Quoad substantiam facti 260 fn.

Radheim 153
Rahner, Karl 297 fn.
Rainbow 27 fn.
Rank 162, 193, 208, 209, 210, 250, 281, 393, 398
Rashness 23
Rationalis individuaque substantia 206 fn.
Real presence 62 fn.
Reason 6, 26, 47, 53, 54, 56, 57, 85, 86, 88, 89, 181, 189, 219, 285, 293
  of flesh 138
Rebaptism 84 fn., 149
Redeemer 256, 259, 409
Redemption 34, 82, 144, 147, 241, 260, 328
Reductio 312
Reformation ix, 335
Regard for persons 206
Regula prima of "Rule of 1221" 141 fn.
Religion(s) 87, 91, 135, 136, 146, 148, 281, 337, 374, 375
  false forms of 89
  of Anabaptists 88
  of angels 239
  of Christ 396
  true 161
  wicked 141
Remission of sins 184, 185, 222, 269, 318; *see also* Forgiveness of sins
Repentance 184, 189
Reply to Faustus the Manichean, by St. Augustine 97 fn.
Resurrection 97, 296, 372
  of Christ 19, 82, 167, 168, 194
Retractations, by St. Augustine 361
Revelation(s) 9, 24, 25, 90, 101, 142, 182, 183, 190, 191, 192, 193, 196, 199, 277
  of Christ's divine nature 171

Revolution 91
Revolutionaries 133
Rhetoric 23, 24, 31
Rhetoric, by Aristotle 24 fn.
Rhetoricians 390
Rhodes 154 fn.
Riches 65, 134, 219, 250, 286, 394, 405
Right hands of fellowship 208
Righteousness
  civic 203
  false appearance of 172
  freedom from 325, 349
  godless 344
  incipient 22
  many kinds of 240 fn.
  of Christ 51, 251, 317
  of Decalog 265
  of faith 7, 42, 229, 240, 242, 264, 348, 382
  of Law 7, 16, 17, 189, 198, 218, 225, 239, 246, 249, 264, 266, 267, 276, 283, 286, 291, 311, 317, 318, 328
  of monastic order 13
  on the basis of works 11
  perfect 22
  polluted 260
  service of 325
  zeal for 111
  et passim
Rivo Torto 141 fn.
Rock 10, 338
  of stumbling 344
Rogatists 60 fn.
Roman emperor 3
Roman pontiff 3, 4, 110, 155, 156, 296, 342, 397
Romans 104, 168, 219, 255, 269, 306, 325, 361, 381, 385
Rome 108, 124, 147, 154, 155, 177, 218, 337
  Church of 122 fn., 178

Luther's journey to 157 fn., 384 fn.
Roots 81
Rotundus 71 fn.
Rosaries 87
Rudens, by Plautus 125 fn.
Rule, monastic 140, 141
Rule of Francis 141 fn.

S. Pauli Epistolae xiv. ex vulgata editione, adjecta intelligentia ex Graeco cum commentariis, by Jacques Lefèvre d'Étaples 315 fn.
Saba 317
Sabbath 55, 249, 257, 295, 296, 332
Sacrament(s) 10, 37, 41, 82, 83, 87, 91, 102, 105, 106, 117, 118, 238
Sacramentarians 37, 39, 60, 106, 111, 112
Sacred Scripture x, 22, 29, 39, 42, 126; *see also* Bible, Divine Scripture(s), Holy Scripture, Holy Writ, Scripture(s), Word of God
Sacrifice(s) 7, 25, 55, 89, 132, 145, 314, 335
Sacrilege 154
Sadness 22, 26, 51, 70, 74, 111
Sailor 29
Saint(s) 35, 42, 50, 54, 61, 64, 66, 70, 71, 73, 75, 76, 77, 79, 80, 81, 82, 83, 85, 86, 87, 96, 109, 115, 122, 136, 161, 169, 172, 192, 210, 214, 247, 262, 344, 354, 361, 362, 372, 379
Saintliness 14, 15, 136, 206, 207
Salome 195, 196

Salvation 9, 11, 19, 35, 38, 46, 47, 56, 57, 73, 74, 98, 99, 102, 103, 104, 117, 119, 120, 121, 130, 139, 143, 154, 161, 171, 172, 178, 184, 185, 189, 190, 198, 202, 204, 222, 248, 259, 269, 288, 290, 334, 357, 358, 384, 392, 402, 405
Samaritan(s) 364, 389
Samson 149 fn.
Samuel 204
Sanctification 34, 82, 241
Sanctity 14, 53, 60, 61, 91, 115, 156, 342
Sandals 141
Santiago de Compostela 337 fn.
Sapietis 341
Sarah 310, 311, 322
  means "princess" or "lady" 317
Satan 12, 19, 35, 40, 43, 48, 49, 53, 58, 84, 99, 101, 109, 110, 118, 119, 123, 124, 137, 143, 144, 145, 146, 147, 345, 388
  angel of 392
  battle against 3
  has a thousand tricks 34
Satiety 123
Satires, by Aulus Persius Flaccus 326 fn.
Satis 401 fn.
Satisfactio 401 fn.
Satispassio 401 fn.
Satum 340
Satyrs 245, 281
Saul 134, 204
Savior 12, 27, 34, 35, 93, 133, 142, 144, 257
Saw 29
Saxony 315
Saxum 218
Scandals 19, 117
Schism(s) 60, 169, 357
Schismatic 382

Scholiasts 315
Schoolmaster(s) 114, 154
Schoolmistress 156
Schools 123, 206
Schubert, Hans von ix
Scorpions 69
Scotists 390
Screech owls 281
Scribes 205
Scripture(s) 11, 15, 20, 25, 27, 34, 51, 60, 75, 77, 79, 115, 128, 157, 176, 181, 183, 191, 201, 206, 212, 220, 228, 229, 230, 233, 235, 242, 244, 245, 251, 252, 253, 254, 258, 261, 264, 268, 273, 274, 280, 317, 321, 323, 324, 329, 333, 336, 337, 340, 342, 344, 345, 370, 398; *see also* Bible, Divine Scripture(s), Holy Scripture, Holy Writ, Sacred Scripture, Word of God
  four senses of 311
Sea 18, 143, 149
Seasons 7, 15, 53, 54, 55, 132, 286, 295, 296, 331, 357
Second Commandment 119, 292
Second Epistle to the Corinthians 302
Second Table 132
Sect(s) 19, 43, 47, 60, 62, 91, 99, 101, 107, 109, 114, 117, 148, 265, 280, 370
Sectarian(s) 9, 20, 33, 34, 36, 52, 53, 91, 107
Sedition 47, 148
Seditionist 135
See, apostolic 158
Self-confidence 132
Self-control 373, 378
Self-denial 14
Self-justification 348

Self-righteous 14, 25, 53, 87, 321
Self-righteousness 17, 18, 146, 185
Senir 315
Senses of Scripture
  allegorical 311, 312
  anagogical 311, 312
  formal 312
  historical 312
  literal 311
  mystical 312
  spiritual 312
  tropological 311
Sensuality 249, 321
Sentences, by Peter Lombard, x, 222 fn., 290 fn., 333, 377 fn.
Sententiaries 377
Sententiarists 222
Sententiastri 222 fn.
Septuagint 261
Sermones de diversis, by Bernard of Clairvaux 300 fn.
Sermones in Cantica Canticorum, by Bernard of Clairvaux 387 fn.
Serpent 5, 11, 262
Service
  of righteousness 325
  of sin 325
Sex(es) 67, 69, 281, 288, 289
Sexton 103
Sexual
  desire 48, 67, 68, 69, 70, 71, 73, 74, 78, 80, 81, 87, 89, 92, 96
  intercourse 89, 321, 399, 400
  lust 132, 141, 371
Sham 141
Sheep 164, 236, 304, 308
Sheol 360
Shepherd(s) 164, 236, 304, 337, 338, 380, 383, 398
Shield 407
Shiloah 163, 330
Shiloh 163

INDEX

Shimei 262
Ship 18, 29
Shipwreck 18, 62
Sich fein wissen zu stellen 130 fn.
Sick 55
Sidon 288
Sidonians 315
Signatum 235 fn.
Signum 235 fn.
Sila 163
Silas 163
Siloam 163, 164
Silva 157 fn.
Silver 46, 51, 55, 122, 171
Simon 46, 195
  the Leper 390
Simony 237
Simul iustus, simul peccator 231 fn.
Sin(s)
  death of 238
  forgiveness of 5, 6, 9, 10, 14, 19, 41, 61, 64, 68, 70, 71, 74, 76, 77, 79, 82, 85, 86, 96, 106, 111, 112, 115, 120, 121, 132, 141, 142, 164, 386
  freedom from 325, 349
  knowledge of 184, 238, 318, 328
  mortal 28, 55, 76, 214
  original 105
  penes personam 76 fn.
  penes substantiam facti 76 fn.
  remission of 184, 185, 222, 269, 318
  service of 325
  tyranny of 26
  et passim
Sinai, Mt. 314, 315, 316, 318, 319, 382
Sinner(s) 12, 14, 26, 34, 35, 68, 69, 72, 77, 170, 176, 185, 190, 205, 218, 219, 220, 221, 222, 225, 226, 227, 230, 231, 232, 233, 236, 272, 274, 279, 288, 303, 319, 320, 324, 325, 326, 329, 351, 364, 365, 372, 389, 390, 391, 393, 400
Slander(s) 102, 103, 120
Slavery 4, 5, 6, 104, 201, 203, 204, 232, 233, 267, 268, 284, 291, 314, 315, 316, 317, 324, 325, 326, 348
  eternal 9
  of Law 7, 217, 314, 319, 346
  of pope 49
  to devil 19, 51
  yoke of 7, 8, 10
Smugness 7, 50, 59, 125
Snake 116
Snobbery 323
Sobriety 174, 370
Society 97, 114
Soliditas 218
Solomon 165, 167, 315
Son of God 5, 15, 18, 107, 136, 145, 146, 178, 185, 186, 189, 190, 191, 239, 240, 302
Son of Man 12, 389
Song of Solomon 184, 366
Song of Songs 315
Sophists 22, 28, 51, 63, 64, 65, 67, 70, 71, 75, 76, 77, 81, 82, 83, 86, 113, 339, 370
Sorcery 87, 90, 368, 369
  spiritual 85
Sorrow 32, 65, 67, 72, 81, 93, 110, 111, 118, 134, 135, 350, 397
Sosia 353
Sozomen 216 fn.
Spalatin x
Spiridon, St. 216
St. James's 337
St. Louis
  edition 384 fn.
  editors 244 fn.
Stapulensis 245, 261, 307, 314, 368
State(s) 56, 91, 115, 117, 219, 358, 370
Staupitz, Johann x, 73, 113 fn.
Steadiness 3
Stephen 195, 197, 268, 271
Stigmata 143, 144
  of Francis 142
Stoics 81, 396
στοιχήσουσιν 406
στοιχῶμεν 406
Stomach 53
Stone(s) 58, 76
  of offense 344
  of stumbling 387
  precious 407
Strife 368, 369
Stubble 52, 55, 62
Stubbornness 106, 108
Stündlin 73 fn.
Suavitas 376
Subversion 133
Suetonius 385 fn.
Suffering(s) 101, 128, 129, 133, 143, 144, 268, 401, 405
  of Christ 82, 134, 238, 401 fn.
  of Paul 407
Summa Theologica, by Thomas Aquinas 52 fn., 113 fn. 234 fn., 267 fn.
Sun 39, 57, 64, 69, 149
Sunbeam 39
Superstition(s) 31, 52, 54, 57, 58, 60, 83, 89, 161, 201, 244, 285, 292, 296, 338, 350
Supreme pontiff(s) 155, 156, 385, 408
Swaggerers 369
Swine 48, 50
Sycophancy 130 fn.
Sycophants 130, 133, 369
Syllogism 255
Sylvester Prierias 156, 157 fn., 158, 397, 398

Synagog(s) 132, 146, 190, 193, 200, 311, 317, 318, 319, 320, 321
Synecdoche 31, 139
Syria 197

Talmudic regulations 227
Tapinosis 187 fn., 286, 294
Tarsus 197
Tatian 399
Tax collector(s) 13, 14, 383, 388, 390, 394
Teacher(s) 32, 33, 36, 40, 47, 61, 99, 116, 119, 125, 129, 130, 131, 132, 148, 153, 167, 174, 182, 183, 188, 194, 197, 198, 207, 292, 299, 305, 306, 335, 340, 345, 351, 352, 354, 398, 399, 401, 404
faithful 124
false 52, 402
of theology 386
pernicious 244, 339
wicked 59
Temperance 174, 378
Temptation(s) 6, 11, 12, 23, 33, 34, 80, 81, 94, 106, 113, 167, 290, 302, 303, 359, 360, 390
Terence 59 fn., 98 fn.
Tertullian 201 fn.
Testator 264, 265, 314
Testicles 345, 346
Tetragrammaton 221
θάνατος 319
Thanklessness 154, 272
Thanksgiving 93
The Sources of Catholic Dogma, by Henry Denzinger 297 fn.
Theologasters 370
Theologian(s) 22, 91, 100, 116, 155, 177, 181, 236, 248, 249, 267, 271, 335, 336, 352, 404

Aristotelian 370
deceitful 289
lay 158
Theology 23, 25, 37, 59, 62 fn., 153, 156, 159, 160, 219, 222, 225, 230, 240, 328, 389
teachers of 386
This Is My Body, by Luther 37 fn.
Thistles 79, 373
Thola 147
Thomas, St. 101 fn.
Thomists 390
Thorns 79, 373, 391
Timothy 16, 211, 303, 334, 335, 343
Tinder 228
Titus 97, 178, 200, 201, 215
Toleration 376, 386
Tonsures 31, 87, 141, 286, 375
Torah 309
Tower of Babel 242
Toys 57
Tradition(s) 9, 14, 25, 44, 55, 110, 122, 138, 157, 165, 177, 187, 188, 219, 227, 276, 285, 298, 312, 341, 350, 354, 375, 408
human 10, 13, 18, 19, 140, 329
Transference 312
Trial(s) 27, 32, 49, 54, 71, 72, 73, 78, 79, 113, 316, 318, 361, 374
Abraham's 253
Tribulation(s) 22, 25, 27, 34, 170
Trichotomy 363
Trinitarian controversies 206 fn.
Tripartite History 216
Tropology 312
Truthfulness 377
Turk(s) 9, 89, 159, 179, 237, 335, 409
Turmoils 19

Tyranny 23, 110, 113, 147, 236, 237, 276, 286, 297, 358, 382, 408
of hell 154
of pope 48, 50
of sin 26
Tyrant(s) 5, 43, 45, 72, 110, 123, 124, 198, 237

Unam sanctam, bull 342 fn.
Unbelief 8, 67, 70, 71, 81, 109, 140, 214, 232
Unbeliever(s) 34, 76, 245, 281, 310
Uncircumcision 30, 137, 138, 139, 141, 209, 280, 330, 333, 334, 335, 405
Uncleanness 86, 260, 276
Ungodliness 173, 337
Ungodly 172, 185, 291, 329, 346
Unity 107, 215, 265, 280, 281, 392
Universals 390
Unrighteousness 71, 101
Unworthiness 205, 270
Uriah 80
Usury 386
Ut figulus figulo 60 fn.

Vainglory 80, 99, 102, 103, 104, 105, 106 fn., 115, 120, 121, 142, 371, 394, 395, 403
Valla, Lorenzo 3 fn.
Venereal 371 fn.
Venery 371 fn.
Vengeance 376, 377
Venus 371
Vergil 24 fn., 61 fn., 179, 244
Vestments 31, 53
Vicar 155
Victory 71, 87, 158
of Christ 10, 82, 83
of devil in the church 385
Vigilance 3

INDEX

Vigils 55, 68, 124, 174, 350, 352
Vincentius 310
Violence 23
Virgin Mary 195
Virginity 95, 288
Virtue(s) 58, 59, 84, 93, 94, 95, 115, 129, 130, 145, 154, 156, 169, 174, 196, 220, 240, 241, 242, 259, 289, 291, 303, 404
of heathen 172
Vita experimentalis 234 fn.
Vitae patrum 112 fn.
Vocabulary of the Philosophical Sciences, by Charles P. Krauth 31 fn.
Vocation 61, 119, 121, 167
Vow(s) 10, 18, 19, 25, 71, 73, 89, 135, 211
Vulgate x, 239 fn., 374, 407

Wantonness 92, 96, 368, 369
War 47, 70, 71, 72, 170, 239, 362, 363, 374
Warfare 361
Water(s) 26, 58, 69, 81, 82, 149, 163, 164, 220, 222, 227, 276, 284, 330, 356, 364, 410
Wax 384
Wealth 121, 130, 134, 393
Wednesday 296
Weimar
 edition ix, 111 fn., 389 fn.
 editors ix, 81 fn., 182 fn., 239 fn.
 text 19 fn., 33 fn., 49 fn., 103 fn., 187 fn., 198 fn.
Whistling 366
Wick, dimly burning 27
Wickedness 10, 31, 44, 82, 131, 132, 136, 175, 260, 350, 375, 387, 388, 395, 408
Wife 56, 67, 68, 127, 195, 204, 232, 252, 281, 320, 408
Will 22, 23, 24, 25, 69, 77, 89, 91, 165, 173, 174, 224, 235, 356, 375, 406, 409
free 172, 175, 181, 220, 278, 292, 325, 326, 328, 338, 339, 364, 372
Wind(s) 27, 100, 149, 367, 385, 410
Wine 83, 184, 290, 321, 364
 abstinence from 370
Wisdom 10, 25, 34, 39, 42, 76, 82, 89, 98, 117, 134, 139, 140, 145, 148, 153, 156, 166, 167, 169, 181, 196, 207, 209, 220, 241, 242, 275, 319, 341, 343, 384, 393, 396, 404, 405
 divine 136
 godless 244
 heavenly 24
 of flesh 138, 140
 of world 345
 presumptions of 115
Witch(es) 90, 245
Witchcraft 90, 243, 244
Wittenberg 113 fn., 123, 153, 315
 University of 377 fn.
Wizards 369
Wol geberden 130 fn.
Wolf 58, 247
Womb 345
Wood 52, 55, 62, 134
Word of God 6, 23, 26, 27, 38, 53, 56, 57, 70, 78, 82, 85, 87, 88, 101, 105, 138, 140, 159, 164, 200, 205, 209, 249, 296, 303, 305, 340, 346, 380, 387, 396, 398; *see also* Bible, Divine Scripture(s), Holy Scripture, Holy Writ, Sacred Scripture, Scripture(s)
Work(s)
 ceremonial 52, 327, 329
 doctrines of 10, 18, 52
 evil 114, 400
 good 11, 14, 17, 30, 49, 52, 53, 54, 55, 56, 62, 63, 73, 76, 77, 78, 88, 127, 128, 129, 168, 188, 221, 247, 248, 293, 313, 328, 347, 375, 388, 400, 401
 human 6, 25
 moral 189, 327
 neutral 363
 of Decalog 265, 286, 335
 of devil 136
 of Law 7, 12, 13, 75, 78, 173, 175, 202, 203, 214, 218, 222, 223, 224, 225, 228, 231, 232, 234, 238, 239, 242, 243, 245, 247, 249, 250, 251, 252, 255, 256, 257, 258, 260, 264, 266, 272, 274, 283, 284, 286, 291, 321, 322, 327, 329, 331, 334, 336, 340, 381, 404
 of legalistic righteousness 161
 of love 52, 140
 ostentatious 53
 self-chosen 31, 57, 90, 140, 141
 spectacular 83
 superstitious and unnatural 85
 et passim
Work-righteousness 167
World 5, 11, 15, 18, 19, 24, 25, 27, 31, 35, 39, 40, 43, 45, 47, 54, 56, 59, 61, 68, 69, 86, 91, 97, 100, 102, 103, 104, 105,

107, 110, 118, 122, 125, 130, 132, 133, 134, 135, 136, 137, 138, 140, 141, 142, 143, 144, 146, 148, 156, 158, 165, 170, 173, 174, 178, 210, 242, 269, 274, 277, 283, 285, 286, 287, 301, 336, 340, 354, 355, 358, 374, 390, 391, 397, 404, 405
Christian 163
regards Christians as dangerous 44
unthankful 117
wisdom of 345
Worship 9, 10, 25, 30, 44, 56, 89, 90, 91, 136, 139, 176, 204, 293, 298
angelic 89
false 141
godless forms of 135
new forms of 88
ungodly forms of 83
wicked forms of 84, 122
Worthiness 205
Wrath 18, 34, 109, 164, 184, 235, 257, 260, 266, 269, 303, 313, 324, 370, 407
of God 4, 5, 7, 8, 19, 21, 26, 27, 50, 78, 154, 170, 376, 409

XL homiliae in Evangelia, by Gregory I 388 fn.

Year(s) 7, 285, 295, 331, 357
of jubilee 296
of release 296
Yeast 36, 37, 39, 45
of doctrine 46
υἱοθεσία 289
ὕπαρξις 377
ὑπομονή 376
ὑπόστασις 377
Yoke 7, 8, 10, 13, 135, 155, 326
of flesh 50

Zacharias 185
Zarephath 288, 335
Zeal 9, 39, 49, 53, 133, 178, 187, 189, 214, 217, 240, 243, 300, 301, 305, 306, 307, 327, 342, 369, 370, 371, 375, 391, 409
for righteousness 111
of conscience 169
Zebedee 195, 196
Zelus iusticiae 111 fn.
Zion, Mt. 93, 177, 221, 318, 393, 410
Zwingli 20 fn., 62 fn., 119 fn.

INDEX TO SCRIPTURE PASSAGES

Genesis
 1:31 — 396
 3:5 — 145
 3:14 — 262
 3:15 — 5, 148
 3:17 — 262
 3:19 — 298
 4:11 — 262
 6:3 — 250, 363
 9:21 ff. — 370
 10:8, 9 — 158
 12:2 ff. — 264
 12:3 — 253, 267
 15:4 — 253
 15:13 — 268
 16:11 — 310
 17:1 ff. — 264
 17:11 — 235
 17:14 — 131
 19:30 ff. — 370
 21 — 264
 21:5 — 267
 21:10 — 322
 21:14 — 284
 22:18 — 253, 275
 25:5 f. — 284
 25:26 — 267
 42:34 — 155
 49:10 — 163
 50:26 — 267

Exodus
 3:8 — 314
 3:22 — 126
 10:21 — 31
 12:11, 12 — 289
 12:29 — 16
 12:40 — 268
 20:7 — 119
 20:13 — 235
 20:17 — 235
 23:20-22 — 222
 24:8 — 314
 25:19 — 22

Leviticus
 6:3 — 109
 18:5 — 258
 19:18 — 51, 114, 348, 349

Deuteronomy
 3:9 — 315
 6:5 — 65
 12:8 — 305
 15:11 — 389
 18:15 — 334
 21:23 — 261
 23:1 — 345
 25:11, 12 — 345
 27:16 — 255
 27:26 — 18
 30:14 — 352
 34:6 — 15

Joshua
 6:17 — 177
 7:2 — 220

Judges
 1:33 — 211
 7:16 — 330
 7:22 — 364
 15:4 — 149

1 Samuel
 1:4, 5 — 322
 2:5, 9 — 322
 2:30 — 119
 10:6, 7 — 204
 16:7 — 206
 21:6 — 55
 22:22 — 135

2 Samuel
 11 — 80
 14:17 — 102
 16:10 — 262

1 Kings
 18:28 — 154
 19:11 ff. — 367
 19:18 — 176

2 Kings
 2:24 — 262, 344

1 Chronicles
 22:14 — 165

Job
 1:8 — 231
 7:21 — 231
 9:20 — 231
 29:15 — 244
 31:27, 28 — 175
 38:31, 32 — 245

Psalms
 1:1 — 235, 244, 329, 341
 1:4 — 19
 1:4, 5 — 100
 1:6 — 280
 2:4 — 125
 2:12 — 176
 3:7 — 360
 4:2 — 54
 4:4 — 70
 7:9 — 206
 7:14 — 350
 7:16 — 350
 8:6, 7 — 171
 9:17 — 46
 10:7 — 350, 407
 11:3 — 230
 14:3 — 174, 224, 274
 15:1, 2 — 280
 18:36 — 229
 19:6 — 337
 22:22 — 221
 25:11 — 221
 28:3 — 351
 31:1 — 241
 32:2 — 362
 32:5, 6 — 76
 32:11 — 93
 34:18 — 26
 34:21 — 181
 37:6 — 120
 37:7 — 170
 38:4 — 342
 39:6 — 220
 42:1 — 275
 42:3 — 275
 42:6 — 177
 44:22 — 134
 45:2 — 184
 45:8 — 165, 366
 49:18 — 374
 51:10 — 405

51:13, 14 — 185
51:17 — 26
51:18 — 174
52:4 — 360
53 — 181
55:15 — 46
57:4 — 360
67:14 — 392
68:18 — 171
69:3 — 397
69:4 — 182
69:10 — 389
69:16 — 279
71 — 312
72:1, 7 — 241
73:3 — 170
78:5 — 187
78:31 — 375
78:36 — 374
82:6 — 181, 333
85:10 — 170
89:17 — 104
94:12, 13 — 368
96:10 — 206
96:13 — 242
102:21 — 221
104:15 — 318
105:3 — 104
107:20 — 164
109:4 — 182
109:28 — 262
110:2 — 43, 318, 391
111:1 — 281
111:3 — 270
112:3 — 270
116:10 — 25, 43
116:11 — 165, 174, 181, 220, 275
118:8 — 39
119:11 — 340
119:21 — 262
119:137 — 393
120:7 — 182
130:3 — 74
130:3, 4 — 77
131:1 — 239
133:1 — 280
133:3 — 177
140:9 — 350
141:6 — 229
143:1 — 241
143:2 — 73, 77, 225, 275, 365

145:14 — 111
147:12, 13 — 317
147:15 — 200

Proverbs

1:12 — 360
1:16 — 337
3:32 — 244
4:23 — 349
9:8 — 169
14:6 — 350
28:2 — 398
30:14 — 360
30:33 — 158
31:26 — 274

Ecclesiastes

7:20 — 259
10:15 — 350
12:11 — 380
12:12 — 349

Song of Solomon

1:2, 3 — 184
1:4 — 366
2:2 — 391
2:14 — 184
4:8 — 315

Isaiah

1:11 — 335
2:3 — 318
2:8 — 176
7:18 — 366
8:6 — 163
8:6 ff. — 330
8:7 — 164
8:13-15 — 344
9:4 — 224
9:6 — 203, 224
10:15 — 29
12:26 — 294
13:21, 22 — 245, 281
31:9 — 393
34:13 — 245
37:23 — 135
38:17 — 43
40:3 — 397
40:9 — 144
42:3 — 12, 27
48:22 — 170
49:21, 22 — 320

52:7 — 200
53:1 — 248
53:4 — 389
53:4, 6 — 342
53:12 — 44, 261
54:1 — 319
54:8 — 5
55:9 — 348
58:8 — 317
59:7 — 337
63:14-19 — 410
64:1-12 — 410
66:2 — 27
66:23 — 296

Jeremiah

2:13 — 220
2:23 — 220
8:11 — 289
9:26 — 330
17:5 — 262
19:9 — 158
23:21 — 166, 200
23:26, 27 — 18
31:33 — 234
35:14, 16 — 229
48:10 — 262
49:14 — 248

Lamentations

2:14 — 189
3:33 — 215

Ezekiel

1:6 ff. — 200
34:4 — 111

Daniel

9:7 — 275
9:24 — 270

Hosea

4:15 — 220, 350
12:11 — 385

Joel

1:9-13 — 123
2:32 — 275

Amos

6:6 — 165

INDEX

Obadiah
  1:1 — 248

Micah
  1:7 — 123
  6:6 — 235

Habakkuk
  2:4 — 258
  2:6 — 409
  3:2 — 248
  3:14 — 262

Zechariah
  2:8 — 134
  9:9 — 93

Malachi
  2:2 — 262
  3:9 — 262

Matthew
  3:7 — 4
  3:17 — 88
  5:3 — 298
  5:9 — 375
  5:11 — 262, 405
  5:11, 12 — 44, 134
  5:12 — 45
  5:18 — 37, 41, 46, 114
  5:29 — 304
  5:40 — 375
  5:46 — 401
  6:9 — 408
  6:12 — 85, 184
  6:12-15 — 66
  7:3 — 112
  7:6 — 48
  7:12 — 53, 56, 355, 356
  7:16, 17 — 79
  7:16 ff. — 373
  7:20 — 158
  7:26 — 52, 62
  8:20 — 122
  9:2 — 6, 12
  9:12 — 185
  9:13 — 12
  10:20 — 166, 192, 404
  10:22 — 400
  11:15 — 249
  11:28 — 12, 27, 407
  11:29 — 34
  11:30 — 135
  12:1 — 55
  12:43-45 — 50
  13:13 — 20, 256, 310
  13:20 — 32
  13:33 — 340, 364
  13:52 — 345
  15:8, 9 — 85
  15:14 — 20
  16:6 — 340
  16:17 — 192, 250
  16:18 — 155, 338
  16:19 — 330
  16:23 — 319, 363, 367
  17:5 — 35, 88
  17:27 — 358
  18:7 — 344
  18:9 — 244
  18:23-35 — 115
  20:6 — 155
  20:12 — 321
  20:16 — 393
  21:19 — 262, 344
  22:37-39 — 63
  22:39 — 55
  23:10 — 167, 404
  23:11, 12 — 208
  23:25-27 — 172
  23:27 — 188, 259
  23:34 — 169
  25:14 — 167
  25:26-30 — 159, 167
  25:41 — 262, 263
  26:6 ff. — 390
  26:34 — 344
  27:28-38 — 122
  27:34 — 111
  27:56 — 195
  27:69-75 — 156
  28:1 — 196
  28:20 — 156

Mark
  5:25, 26 — 220
  5:34 — 304
  6:3 — 195
  8:34 f. — 356
  10:52 — 304
  12:14 — 206
  15:40 — 195

Luke
  1:15 — 370
  1:68 — 185
  1:77, 78 — 185
  2:7 — 122
  2:11 — 108
  2:14 — 144, 174
  2:34 — 343
  2:35 — 81
  2:48 — 81
  4:18 — 35
  4:26 — 288
  6:46 — 257
  7:47 — 277
  9:51 ff. — 388
  10:7 — 126, 396
  10:20 — 93
  10:30 — 227
  10:30 ff. — 364
  10:30-37 — 58
  11:21 — 43
  11:34 — 37, 244
  11:36 — 37
  12:1 — 340
  12:48 — 103
  13:14 — 55
  13:27, 28 — 34
  14:28 ff. — 242
  14:33 — 242
  16:15 — 181
  17:21 — 337
  18:11 — 112
  18:11, 12 — 390
  18:11 ff. — 383
  18:13, 14 — 220
  19:10 — 12
  19:40 — 147
  21:15 — 166
  21:34 — 370
  22:37 — 261
  23:28 — 300
  24:46 f. — 184

John
  1:12 — 184, 221, 279
  1:17 — 15, 226, 407
  3:6 — 366
  3:18 — 19, 34
  3:27 — 292
  3:36 — 18
  4:14 — 222
  4:23 — 155

6:44 — 179, 292, 366
6:45 — 320
6:63 — 271
7:18 — 101
7:24 — 214
8:35 — 284, 317
8:36 — 6
8:44 — 11, 136, 145, 166
8:56 — 268
9:4 — 128, 401
9:7 — 163, 164
10:8 — 164, 166
12:25 — 181
12:32 — 366
13:34, 35 — 113
14:30 — 45
15:19 — 135
15:20 — 159
16:2 — 44, 165
16:11 — 24
16:33 — 12, 170
19:25 — 195
19:30 — 228
21:15 ff. — 397
21:17 — 338

Acts

1:24-26 — 165
3:6 — 122
3:23 — 334
4:32 — 210
5:41 — 133, 405
7:1 ff. — 197
7:6 — 268
7:53 — 271
8:20 — 46
9 — 193
9:4 — 134
9:4-6 — 183
9:4 ff. — 165
9:15 — 70, 145
9:19, 20 — 190
9:26 ff. — 195
9:29, 30 — 196
10 — 156
10:34 — 281
10:44 — 248
10:44 ff. — 247
11:28 — 210
13:2 — 165, 190
14:16 — 146
15:7-11 — 161

15:9 — 188, 219
15:10 — 7
15:22 — 163
15:28 — 211
16:3 — 211
17:28 — 290
18:18 — 211
20:29 — 247
21:23 ff. — 211
26:24 — 256
28:23 — 179

Romans

1:1 f. — 165
1:3, 4 — 185, 302
1:4 — 167
1:16 — 56, 290
1:16 f. — 241
1:18 ff. — 218
1:23 — 292
2:4 — 376
2:10 — 290
2:11 — 61, 103
2:13 — 257
2:14, 15 — 53
2:16 — 120
2:17 ff. — 218
2:21 — 188, 274
2:22 — 285
2:25 — 327, 330
2:27, 29 — 284
3 — 8
3:9 — 274
3:9 ff. — 224
3:10 — 174
3:10-12 — 274
3:19, 20 — 274
3:20 — 184, 318
3:21 — 266
3:23 — 104
3:25 — 64, 86
3:28 — 234
3:31 — 229
4 — 8, 263
4:1 ff. — 248
4:9 — 251
4:11 — 251
4:14 — 264, 267
4:15 — 184, 226, 266, 269
4:18 — 27
4:25 — 168, 238
5 — 269

5:3 — 133
5:3-5 — 25
5:5 — 221, 234, 326
5:10 — 171
5:12 — 240
5:19 — 222
5:20 — 269, 277
5:20, 22 — 325
6 — 234, 238
6:6 — 229, 379
6:10 — 238
6:12 — 361
6:14, 15 — 347
7 — 8, 269
7:1 — 233
7:2 ff. — 232
7:5 — 320, 366
7:7 — 313
7:9 ff. — 226
7:10 — 70, 269
7:11 — 226, 269
7:14 — 70, 227, 235, 364
7:18 — 174, 250, 361
7:19 — 365
7:22 f. — 231, 362
7:23 — 21, 70, 72, 227, 236
7:24 — 70
7:25 — 77, 81, 379
8 — 234, 238
8:1 — 227
8:2 — 227, 234
8:3 — 229
8:4 — 227
8:3, 4 — 65
8:6 — 341
8:8, 9 — 239
8:9 — 290
8:13 — 70, 360
8:14 — 366
8:15 — 290
8:16 — 172
8:17 — 291
8:17-25 — 25
8:23 — 65, 67
8:24 — 21
8:24, 25 — 20
8:28 — 327
8:32 — 100, 221
8:37 — 24
9:4, 5 — 142
9:6 ff. — 255

9:7, 8 — 251
9:8 — 282
9:16 — 174, 294
9:23 — 174
9:33 — 72
10 — 255
10:2 — 305
10:3 — 241
10:4 — 34, 96
10:5 — 258
10:10 — 241
10:13 — 275
10:14 — 248
10:15 — 164, 184
10:17 — 220
11:1 — 155
11:7 ff. — 285
11:8 — 344
11:32 — 274
12 — 381
12:3 — 359
12:4 ff. — 359
12:9 — 374
12:10 — 93, 98, 102
12:15 — 300
12:18 — 375
12:21 — 59
13 — 381
13:8 — 204, 384
13:8-10 — 348
13:9 — 357
13:10 — 63, 65, 235
13:14 — 69, 280, 361
14 — 382
14:1 — 381
14:4 — 82, 395
14:6 — 180
14:10 — 120
14:12 — 395
14:15 — 383
14:16 — 102, 104
14:22 — 395
14:23 — 76, 132, 250
15:1 — 381, 389
15:2 — 182
15:3 — 389
15:4 — 25
15:26 — 210
16:18 — 49, 376
16:22 — 402

1 Corinthians
1:17 — 42, 392
1:18 — 118
1:19 — 404
1:23, 24 — 179, 343
1:30 — 34, 82, 241, 328
1:31 — 207
2:2 — 155
2:8 — 146
2:14 — 138
2:15 — 89, 136
3:3 — 250
3:4 — 181
3:11, 12 — 51
3:12 — 52, 55, 62
3:22 f. — 158
4:1 — 62
4:2 — 119
4:7 — 102
4:9 — 143, 301
4:11-13 — 143
5:5 — 345
5:6 — 36, 339
5:6 f. — 339
5:7, 8 — 339
5:10 — 173
6:19, 20 — 367
7:9 — 69
7:18, 19 — 334
8:1 — 359, 396
8:13 — 384
9 — 123
9:9 — 396
9:11 — 124
9:13, 14 — 126
9:20 — 211
9:20, 21 — 202
9:22 — 300
9:24 — 337
10 — 123
10:12 — 112, 390
10:17 — 340
10:18 — 406
10:33 — 182
11:16 — 406
12:4 ff. — 168, 208
12:12 ff. — 359
12:23 — 59, 393
13:2 — 115, 336
13:4 — 93, 291
13:5 — 308, 355
13:7 — 41, 59, 95, 106, 114, 353, 357
13:8 — 64
13:12 — 171
13:13 — 25, 72
14:22 — 180, 310
14:40 — 139
15:9 — 155, 192
15:24 — 64
15:24-28 — 171
15:26 — 319
15:28 — 64
15:42, 43 — 4
15:50 — 250
15:56 — 226, 238, 239, 269
16:21 — 129, 402
16:22 — 345

2 Corinthians
1:5 — 134
1:12 — 117, 395
2:6-8 — 110
2:7, 8 — 108
2:14 — 302
2:15 f. — 366
3:3 — 234
3:5 — 371
3:6 — 236, 271, 284, 313
3:7 — 226
3:14 — 77
4:4, 5 — 143
4:7 — 19, 94
5:21 — 260
6:3 — 104
6:6 — 376
6:7 — 117
6:8 — 102, 118
6:10 — 27
7:5 — 81, 135
8 — 123
9 — 123
9:6 — 399
10:3 — 239
11 — 187
11:2, 3 — 306
11:5 — 192
11:13 — 166
11:14 — 35, 392
11:18 ff. — 302
11:23-26 — 143, 299
11:26 — 186
11:28 — 81
12:1 ff. — 302
12:7 — 101

12:9 — 133, 404
12:9, 10 — 137, 302
12:11 — 193

Galatians

1:6 — 339
1:8 — 45, 108, 129, 214
1:10 — 170, 343, 402
1:11, 12 — 179
1:17 — 191
1:20 — 212
2:2 — 159
2:7, 9 — 165
2:11-14 — 156
2:14 — 214, 403
2:16 — 63, 243
2:20 — 65, 168, 246, 308, 379, 405
2:21 — 246
3 — 90, 127
3:1 — 32
3:2 — 133, 291, 336
3:4 — 129
3:9 — 142
3:10 — 12, 63, 274
3:13 — 36
3:19 — 146
3:21 — 270
3:22 — 285
3:24, 25 — 16
3:28 — 204
4:1 ff. — 202
4:4, 5 — 65, 77
4:5 — 284
4:6 — 189
4:10 — 331
4:16 — 301
4:17 — 104
4:19-22 — 400
4:20 — 301
4:24-31 — 180
4:25 — 382
5:3 — 256, 403
5:4 — 343
5:6 — 25, 280, 291, 405
5:9 — 46
5:10 — 108, 395
5:12 — 108
5:13 — 65
5:16 — 96
5:20 — 67

5:21 — 97
5:24 — 237
5:25 — 406
6:1 — 80
6:2 — 66, 94
6:12 — 42, 180
6:13 — 12, 256, 307, 403
6:16 — 382

Ephesians

2:3 — 324
2:19 — 317
4:12 — 103
4:24 — 140, 141, 280, 405
4:26 — 69
4:31 f. — 359
5:5 — 64, 369
5:17 — 168
5:26 — 26
5:27 — 85
6:11-17 — 97
6:13 — 26
6:15 — 200
6:16 — 21, 22, 26, 35, 78, 84, 137, 144
6:17 — 26, 78

Philippians

1:24 — 239
2:1-4 — 359
2:3 — 97
2:4 — 356
2:5 ff. — 389
2:6 — 393
2:21 — 116
2:25-27 — 81
3 — 187
3:4-7 — 187
3:9 — 187
3:18, 19 — 131
3:19 — 100, 120, 369
3:20 — 337
4:4 — 93
4:7 — 170, 375

Colossians

1:5 — 20
1:24 — 134
2:3 — 10, 34
2:8 — 285

2:16 — 298
2:18 — 89, 239
2:20 — 285
3 — 238
3:10 — 139
4:18 — 129, 402

1 Thessalonians

2:14 f. — 180
5:21 — 155, 206, 307
5:23 — 363

2 Thessalonians

2:3 — 110
3:17 — 129, 402

1 Timothy

1:5 — 235, 335, 355
1:9 — 96, 235, 320, 378
1:15 — 35
1:19 — 62, 149
4:1 — 44, 123
5:18 — 396
6:5 — 99
6:16 — 84

2 Timothy

1:15 — 117
2:15 — 63
3:9 — 120
4:2 — 303
4:3 — 116

Titus

1:7 — 97
1:8 — 96
1:11 — 178
1:12 — 243
1:15 — 188, 204, 216, 256
2:5 — 96
2:12 — 173

Philemon

10 — 108

Hebrews

2:2 — 271
3:1 — 163
5:12 — 285

INDEX

6:6 — 246
8:6 — 272
8:10 — 234
9:10 — 250, 335
9:15 — 268
9:17 — 268
10:16 — 234
11:1 — 377
11:4 — 145
11:36 ff. — 210

James

1:17 — 371
1:18 — 406
2:10 — 38, 331
2:19 — 172, 291
4:4 — 170

1 Peter

1:25 — 144
2:11 — 363

2:16 — 49, 347
2:21 — 238
2:22 — 64
2:24 — 238, 389
3:18 — 302
4:1 — 237
4:2 — 239
4:8 — 352
4:10 — 359
4:15 — 133
5:8, 9 — 3

2 Peter

1:4 — 173
2:5 — 146

1 John

1:8 — 230, 372
3:8 — 136
3:9 — 230, 372

3:18 — 52
4:10 — 65
5:4 — 5
5:18 — 230, 372

Jude

4 — 48

Revelation

2:9 — 110
3:17 — 115
6:4 — 376
12:9, 10 — 11
16:1 ff. — 227

APOCRYPHA

Ecclesiasticus

7:24 — 215
18:7 — 169
24:20 — 366